Research Anthology on Machine Learning Techniques, Methods, and Applications

Information Resources Management Association
USA

Volume II

Published in the United States of America by
IGI Global
Engineering Science Reference (an imprint of IGI Global)
701 E. Chocolate Avenue
Hershey PA, USA 17033
Tel: 717-533-8845
Fax: 717-533-8661
E-mail: cust@igi-global.com
Web site: http://www.igi-global.com

Library of Congress Cataloging-in-Publication Data

Names: Information Resources Management Association, editor.
Title: Research anthology on machine learning techniques, methods, and applications / Information Resources Management Association, editor.
Description: Hershey, PA : Engineering Science Reference, an imprint of IGI Global, [2022] | Includes bibliographical references and index. | Summary: "This reference set provides a thorough consideration of the innovative and emerging research within the area of machine learning, discussing how the technology has been used in the past as well as potential ways it can be used in the future to ensure industries continue to develop and grow while covering a range of topics such as artificial intelligence, deep learning, cybersecurity, and robotics"-- Provided by publisher.
Identifiers: LCCN 2022015780 (print) | LCCN 2022015781 (ebook) | ISBN 9781668462911 (h/c) | ISBN 9781668462928 (ebook)
Subjects: LCSH: Machine learning--Industrial applications. | Computer security--Data processing. | Medical care--Data processing. | Data mining. | Artificial intelligence.
Classification: LCC Q325.5 .R46 2022 (print) | LCC Q325.5 (ebook) | DDC 006.3/1--dc23/eng20220628
LC record available at https://lccn.loc.gov/2022015780
LC ebook record available at https://lccn.loc.gov/2022015781

British Cataloguing in Publication Data
A Cataloguing in Publication record for this book is available from the British Library.

For electronic access to this publication, please contact: eresources@igi-global.com.

List of Contributors

Abirami, S. / *Thiagarajar College of Engineering, India* 1072
Abiramie Shree T. G. R. / *Thiagarajar College of Engineering, India* 1143
Abuassba, Adnan Omer / *University of Science and Technology Beijing (USTB), Beijing, China & Arab Open University - Palestine, Ramallah, Palestine* 568
Ahuja, Ravinder / *Jaypee Institute of Information Technology Noida, India* 776
Alberto, Damian / *Indian Institute of Technology Bombay, India* 47
Ali, Syed Shahzaib / *National University of Computer and Emerging Sciences, Pakistan* 1271
Amudha P. / *Avinashilingam Institute for Home Science and Higher Education for Women, India* 596
Anitha Elavarasi S. / *Sona College of Technology, India* 528, 1446
Anitha N. / *Kongu Engineering College, India* 1330
Arora, Anuja / *Jaypee Institute of Information Technology, India* 693
Arul Murugan R. / *Sona College of Technology, India* 1
Aswathy M. A. / *VIT University, India* 1395
Atmani, Baghdad / *Laboratoire d'Informatique d'Oran (LIO), University of Oran 1 Ahmed Ben Bella, Algeria* 1311
Awan, Mubashar Nazar / *National University of Computer and Emerging Sciences, Pakistan* 1271
Bachani, Nikita H. / *Institute of Technology Nirma University, Ahmedabad, India* 1255
Bagwe, Bhagyashree R. / *VIT University, India* 882
Baimuratov, Ildar Raisovich / *Itmo University, St. Petersburg, Russia* 909
Balogun, Jeremiah Ademola / *Obafemi Awolowo University, Nigeria* 252
Banga, Alisha / *Satyug Darshan Institute of Engineering and Technology Faridabad, India* 776
Baranwal, Astha / *VIT University, India* 882
Barsoum, Ayad / *St. Mary's University, San Antonio, USA* 870
Basheer, Shakila / *King Khalid University, Abha, Saudi Arabia* 586
Beg, Mirza O. / *National University of Computer and Emerging Sciences, Pakistan* 1271
Bekdaş, Gebrail / *Istanbul University-Cerrahpaşa, Turkey* 26, 308
Benbelkacem, Sofia / *Laboratoire d'Informatique d'Oran (LIO), University of Oran 1 Ahmed Ben Bella, Algeria* 1311
Berlanga, Antonio / *Grupo de Inteligencia Artificial Aplicada. Universidad Carlos III de Madrid, Spain* 753
Bezerra, Francisco Nivando / *Programa de Pós-Graduação em Ciências da Computação do IFCE, Fortaleza, Brazil* 274
Bhargavi, Peyakunta / *Sri Padmavati Mahila Visvavidyalayam, India* 472
Bogomolov, Timofei / *University of South Australia, Australia* 817

Bogomolova, Svetlana / *Business School, Ehrenberg-Bass Institute, University of South Australia, Australia* 817
Casañola-Martin, Gerardo M. / *North Dakota State University, Fargo, USA* 38
Chaabane, Sondès / *University Polytechnique Hauts-de-France, CNRS, UMR 8201 – LAMIH, Laboratoire d'Automatique de Mécanique et d'Informatique Industrielles et Humaines, F-59313 Valenciennes, France* 1311
Chahal, Poonam / *MRIIRS, Faridabad, India* 421
Chandna, Manika / *Jaypee Institute of Information Technology Noida, India* 776
Chaurasia, Siddharth / *University of Lucknow, Lucknow, India* 1233
Chellamuthu, Gunavathi / *VIT University, India* 1351
Chhinkaniwala, Hitesh / *Adani Institute of Infrastructure Engineering, Gujarat, India* 681
Chitra, P. / *Thiagarajar College of Engineering, India* 1072
Choudhary, Tanu / *Manav Rachna International Institute of Research and Studies, India* 621
Corrales, David Camilo / *Telematic Engineering Group, University of Cauca, Popayán, Colombia and Department of Computer Science and Engineering, Carlos III University of Madrid, Madrid, Spain* 396
Corrales, Juan Carlos / *Telematic Engineering Group, University of Cauca, Popayán, Colombia* 396
Datta, Stuti Shukla / *Amity University, India* 849
Dayananda P. / *Department of Information Science and Engineering. J.S.S. Academy of Technical Education, Bengaluru, India* 224
Devi Priya R. / *Kongu Engineering College, India* 1330
Devulapalli, Krishna / *Indian Institute of Chemical Technology, Secunderabad, India* 1023
Dey, Sowvik / *Brainware University, Kolkata, India* 327
Dhanda, Mudrika / *Royal Holloway University, UK* 849
Dhanda, Namrata / *Amity University, India* 849
Filho, Pedro P Rebouças / *Programa de Pós-Graduação em Ciências da Computação do IFCE, Fortaleza, Brazil* 274
Fong, Simon / *University of Macau, Macau SAR* 241
Frochte, Jörg / *Bochum University of Applied Sciences, Germany* 379
Gairola, Reetika / *Jaypee Institute of Information Technology, India* 693
Gamidullaeva, Leyla / *Penza State University, Russia & K. G. Razumovsky Moscow State University of Technologies and Management, Russia* 939
Gamidullaeva, Leyla Ayvarovna / *Penza State University, Russia* 137
Ganapathi, Padmavathi / *Avinashilingam Institute for Home Science and Higher Education for Women, India* 952
Gandhi, Ishit / *Institute of Technology Nirma University, Ahmedabad, India* 1255
Gandhi, Usha Devi / *VIT University, Vellore, India* 586
Garg, Sanjay / *Institute of Technology Nirma University, Ahmedabad, India* 1255
Gepp, Adrian / *Bond University, Australia* 734
Ghosh, Anupam / *Netaji Subhash Engineering College, Kolkata, India* 327
Ghosh, Monalisa / *Indian Institute of Technology Kharagpur, India* 177
Ghosh, Swarup Kr / *Brainware University, Kolkata, India* 327
Goyal, Vishal / *Punjabi University, India* 1062
Guggulothu, Thirupathi / *University of Hyderabad, Hyderabad, India* 800
Gupta, Bharat / *Jaypee Institute of Information Technology, Noida, India* 1381
Gupta, Madhuri / *Jaypeee Institute of Information Technology, Noida, India* 1381
Heryadi, Yaya / *Bina Nusantara University, Indonesia* 107

Hiremath, Neelambika Basavaraj / *Department of Computer Science and Engineering, J.S.S. Academy of Technical Education Bengaluru, India* 224
Ho, Siu Cheung / *The Hong Kong Polytechnic University, Hong Kong* 1210
Hrnjica, Bahrudin / *University of Bihac, Bosnia and Herzegovina* 486
Idowu, Peter Adebayo / *Obafemi Awolowo University, Nigeria* 252
Imran, Muhammad Ali / *University of Glasgow, UK* 1494
Iyyanki, Muralikrishna / *Independent Researcher, India* 1038
Jagadeesan D. / *Cherraan's Arts Science College, India* 1294
Jagannathan, Jayanthi / *Sona College of Technology, India* 1446
Jain, Arti / *Jaypee Institute of Information Technology, India* 693
Jain, Shikha / *Jaypee Institute of Information Technology, India* 693
Jain, Tarun / *Manipal University Jaipur, India* 930
Jayanthi J. / *Sona College of Technology, India* 528
Jayanthi, Prisilla / *Administrative Staff College of India, India* 1038
Jeyaprakash, Hemalatha / *Thiagarajar College of Engineering, India* 1002
Jyothi, Singaraju / *Sri Padmavati Mahila Visvavidyalayam, India* 472
K., Vignesh Saravanan / *Ramco Institute of Technology, Rajapalayam, India* 642
K., Vijayalakshmi / *Ramco Institute of Technology, Rajapalayam, India* 642
Kadri, Farid / *Big Data & Analytics Services, Institut d'Optique Graduate School, Talence, France* 1311
Kanarev, Sergey / *Penza State University, Russia* 137
Kannimuthu S. / *Karpagam College of Engineering, India* 1351
Karthick, G. S. / *Bharathiar University, India* 198
Kashyap, Ramgopal / *Amity University, Raipur, India* 447
Kayabekir, Aylin Ece / *Istanbul University-Cerrahpaşa, Turkey* 308
Kenekayoro, Patrick / *Mathematics / Computer Science Department, Niger Delta University, Amassoma, Nigeria* 346
Klaine, Paulo Valente / *University of Glasgow, UK* 1494
Klinger, Volkhard / *FHDW Hannover, Hanover, Germany* 548
Korolkiewicz, Malgorzata W. / *University of South Australia, Australia* 817
Kumar, Kuldeep / *Bond University, Australia* 734
Lemmen, Markus / *Bochum University of Applied Sciences, Germany* 379
Li, Hao / *University of Texas at Austin, USA* 714
Li, Tengyue / *University of Macau, Macau* 241
Liu, Zhijian / *North China Electric Power University, China* 714
Luo, Xiong / *University of Science and Technology Beijing (USTB), Beijing, China* 568
M, Vanitha / *VIT University, India* 882
M. K., KavithaDevi / *Thiagarajar College of Engineering, India* 1002
Maldonado, Mark / *St. Mary's University, San Antonio, USA* 870
Maltarollo, Vinicius Gonçalves / *Faculty of Pharmacy, Federal University of Minas Gerais, Belo Horizonte, Brazil* 292
Manickam, Valli / *Administrative Staff College of India, India* 1038
Manukumar, Shanthi Thangam / *Anna University, India* 59
Martinez, Fernando Enrique Lopez / *University of Oviedo, Spain* 1482
Mehr, Ali Danandeh / *Antalya Bilim University, Turkey* 486
Mishra, Sushruta / *KIIT University (Deemed), India* 664
Misra, Puneet / *University of Lucknow, Lucknow, India* 1233

Mkrttchian, Vardan / *HHH University, Australia* 137, 939
Mohan, Jagannath / *VIT Chennai, India* 1395
Moiz, Salman Abdul / *University of Hyderabad, Hyderabad, India* 800
Molina, José M. / *Grupo de Inteligencia Artificial Aplicada. Universidad Carlos III de Madrid, Spain* 753
Moreno-Ibarra, Marco / *Instituto Politecnico Nacional, Mexico* 1107
Muthuswamy, Vijayalakshmi / *Amity University, India* 59
Namlı, Ersin / *Istanbul University-Cerrahpasa, Turkey* 68
Narayan, Valliammal / *Avinashilingam Institute for Home Science and Higher Education for Women, India* 149
Natarajan, Jayapandian / *Christ University, India* 976
Neto, Ajalmar R Rocha / *Instituto Federal do Ceará, Fortaleza, Brazil* 274
Nigdeli, Sinan Melih / *Istanbul University-Cerrahpaşa, Turkey* 26, 308
Nikam, Kakasaheb Rangnarh / *HPT Arts & RYK Science College Nashik MH India, Nashik, India* 1415
Núñez-Valdez, Edward Rolando / *University of Oviedo, Spain* 1482
Oliveira, Saulo A. F. / *Programa de Pós-Graduação em Engenharia de Telecomunicações do IFCE, Fortaleza, Brazil* 274
Onireti, Oluwakayode / *University of Glasgow, UK* 1494
Panasenko, Svetlana / *Plekhanov Russian University of Economics, Russia* 939
Pankajavalli, P. B. / *Bharathiar University, India* 198
Parah, Shabir Ahmad / *University of Kashmir, India* 1062
Parikh, Satyen M. / *FCA, India* 1129
Parthasarathy P. / *VIT University, Vellore, India* 586
Patel, Ajay M / *AMPICS, India* 1129
Patel, Hiral R. / *Ganpat University, India* 1129
Patel, Nimesh V / *C.U Shah University, Wadhawan (Surendranagar-Gujarat), India* 681
Patricio, Miguel A. / *Universidad Carlos III de Madrid, Spain* 753
Pham-The, Hai / *Hanoi University of Pharmacy, Hanoi, Vietnam* 38
Pillai, Anuradha / *J. C. Bose University of Science and Technology YMCA, India* 621
Prayaga, Chandra / *University of West Florida, Pensacola, USA* 1023
Prayaga, Lakshmi / *University of West Florida, Pensacola, USA* 1023
Premalatha K. / *Bannari Amman Institute of Technology, India* 1351
Priyadharshini P. / *Thiagarajar College of Engineering, India* 1143
Priyan M.K. / *VIT University, Vellore, India* 586
Qin, Ying / *Beijing Foreign Studies University, Beijing, China* 362
Ramezani, Niloofar / *George Mason University, USA* 90
Rani, Manisha / *D. N. College, India* 621
Rashid, Mamoon / *Lovely Professional University, India & Punjabi University, India* 1062
Rath, Mamata / *Birla Global University, India* 664, 1193
Riascos, Alvaro J / *University of los Andes and Quantil, Bogotá, Colombia* 1427
Rodríguez, Jhonn Pablo / *University of Cauca, Popayán, Colombia* 396
Rodríguez-Pardo, Carlos / *Grupo de Inteligencia Artificial Aplicada. Universidad Carlos III de Madrid, Spain* 753
S., Geetha / *VIT University, India* 1002
S., Kavi Priya / *Mepco Schlnek Engineering College, India* 642

Saldana-Perez, Magdalena / *Instituto Politecnico Nacional, Mexico* 1107
Saranya T. / *Thiagarajar College of Engineering, India* 1143
Sathiyamoorthi V. / *Sona College of Technology, India* 1
Sathya D. / *Kumaraguru College of Technology, India* 1294
Schmidt, Marco / *Bochum University of Applied Sciences, Germany* 379
Serna, Natalia / *University of Wisconsin-Madison, Madison, USA* 1427
Shaju, Barani / *Avinashilingam Institute for Home Science and Higher Education for Women, India* 149
Siau, Keng / *City University of Hong Kong, Hong Kong SAR* 1460
Sigamani, Rama Mercy Sam / *Avinashilingam Institute for Home Science and Higher Education for Women, India* 1165
Singh, Harjeet / *Mata Gujri College, India* 1062
Singhal, Chetna / *Indian Institute of Technology Kharagpur, India* 177
Sivakumari S. / *Avinashilingam Institute for Home Science and Higher Education for Women, India* 596
Sousa, Lucas S / *Programa de Pós-Graduação em Ciências da Computação do IFCE, Fortaleza, Brazil* 274
Souza, Richard Demo / *Federal University of Santa Catarina (UFSC), Brazil* 1494
Sudha V. / *Kumaraguru College of Technology, India* 1294
Swathy Akshaya M. / *Avinashilingam Institute for Home Science and Higher Education for Women, India* 952
Tanwar, Sudeep / *Institute of Technology Nirma University, Ahmedabad, India* 1255
Thangavel M. / *Thiagarajar College of Engineering, India* 1143
Tianxing, Man / *Itmo University, St. Petersburg, Russia* 909
Torres-Ruiz, Miguel / *Instituto Politecnico Nacional, Mexico* 1107
Turkan, Yusuf Sait / *Istanbul University-Cerrahpasa, Turkey* 1086
Tyagi, Amit Kumar / *School of Computing Science and Engineering, Vellore Institute of Technology, Chennai, India* 421
Verma, Jai Prakash / *Institute of Technology Nirma University, Ahmedabad, India* 1255
Verma, Vivek K. / *Manipal University Jaipur, India* 930
Vertakova, Yulia / *Southwest State University, Russia* 939
Virmani, Charu / *Manav Rachna International Institute of Research and Studies, India* 621
Virmani, Shivani / *Jaypee Institute of Information Technology Noida, India* 776
Vivek, Vishal / *Jaypee Institute of Information Technology Noida, India* 776
Wahyono, Teguh / *Satya Wacana Christian University, Indonesia* 107
Wallis, Mark / *Bond University, Australia* 734
Wang, Weiyu / *Missouri University of Science and Technology, USA* 1460
Wong, Kin Chun / *The Hong Kong Polytechnic University, Hong Kong* 1210
Yau, Yuen Kwan / *The Hong Kong Polytechnic University, Hong Kong* 1210
Yip, Chi Kwan / *The Hong Kong Polytechnic University, Hong Kong* 1210
Yucel, Melda / *Istanbul University-Cerrahpaşa, Turkey* 26, 68, 308
Yumurtaci Aydogmus, Hacer / *Alanya Alaaddin Keykubat University, Turkey* 1086
Zhang, Dezheng / *University of Science and Technology Beijing (USTB), Beijing, China* 568
Zhukova, Natalia Alexandrovna / *St. Petersburg Institute for Informatics and Automation of Russian Academy of Sciences (SPIIRAS), St. Petersburg, Russia* 909

Table of Contents

Preface xxi

Volume I

Section 1
Fundamental Concepts and Theories

Chapter 1
Introduction to Machine Learning and Its Implementation Techniques 1
Arul Murugan R., Sona College of Technology, India
Sathiyamoorthi V., Sona College of Technology, India

Chapter 2
Review and Applications of Machine Learning and Artificial Intelligence in Engineering: Overview for Machine Learning and AI 26
Melda Yucel, Istanbul University-Cerrahpaşa, Turkey
Gebrail Bekdaş, Istanbul University-Cerrahpaşa, Turkey
Sinan Melih Nigdeli, Istanbul University-Cerrahpaşa, Turkey

Chapter 3
Machine Learning Applications in Nanomedicine and Nanotoxicology: An Overview 38
Gerardo M. Casañola-Martin, North Dakota State University, Fargo, USA
Hai Pham-The, Hanoi University of Pharmacy, Hanoi, Vietnam

Section 2
Development and Design Methodologies

Chapter 4
Classification and Machine Learning 47
Damian Alberto, Indian Institute of Technology Bombay, India

Chapter 5
A Novel Resource Management Framework for Fog Computing by Using Machine Learning Algorithm 59
Shanthi Thangam Manukumar, Anna University, India
Vijayalakshmi Muthuswamy, Amity University, India

Chapter 6
High Performance Concrete (HPC) Compressive Strength Prediction With Advanced Machine Learning Methods: Combinations of Machine Learning Algorithms With Bagging, Rotation Forest, and Additive Regression 68
Melda Yucel, Istanbul University-Cerrahpaşa, Turkey
Ersin Namlı, Istanbul University-Cerrahpasa, Turkey

Chapter 7
Modern Statistical Modeling in Machine Learning and Big Data Analytics: Statistical Models for Continuous and Categorical Variables 90
Niloofar Ramezani, George Mason University, USA

Chapter 8
Machine Learning Applications for Anomaly Detection 107
Teguh Wahyono, Satya Wacana Christian University, Indonesia
Yaya Heryadi, Bina Nusantara University, Indonesia

Chapter 9
Machine Learning With Avatar-Based Management of Sleptsov Net-Processor Platform to Improve Cyber Security 137
Vardan Mkrttchian, HHH University, Australia
Leyla Ayvarovna Gamidullaeva, Penza State University, Russia
Sergey Kanarev, Penza State University, Russia

Chapter 10
Malware and Anomaly Detection Using Machine Learning and Deep Learning Methods 149
Valliammal Narayan, Avinashilingam Institute for Home Science and Higher Education for Women, India
Barani Shaju, Avinashilingam Institute for Home Science and Higher Education for Women, India

Chapter 11
Machine Learning-Based Subjective Quality Estimation for Video Streaming Over Wireless Networks 177
Monalisa Ghosh, Indian Institute of Technology Kharagpur, India
Chetna Singhal, Indian Institute of Technology Kharagpur, India

Chapter 12
Architecting IoT based Healthcare Systems Using Machine Learning Algorithms: Cloud-Oriented Healthcare Model, Streaming Data Analytics Architecture, and Case Study 198
G. S. Karthick, Bharathiar University, India
P. B. Pankajavalli, Bharathiar University, India

Chapter 13
Machine Learning Techniques for Analysis of Human Genome Data 224
Neelambika Basavaraj Hiremath, Department of Computer Science and Engineering, J.S.S. Academy of Technical Education Bengaluru, India
Dayananda P., Department of Information Science and Engineering. J.S.S. Academy of Technical Education, Bengaluru, India

Chapter 14
A Fast Feature Selection Method Based on Coefficient of Variation for Diabetics Prediction Using Machine Learning ... 241
Tengyue Li, University of Macau, Macau
Simon Fong, University of Macau, Macau SAR

Chapter 15
Development of a Classification Model for CD4 Count of HIV Patients Using Supervised Machine Learning Algorithms: A Comparative Analysis ... 252
Peter Adebayo Idowu, Obafemi Awolowo University, Nigeria
Jeremiah Ademola Balogun, Obafemi Awolowo University, Nigeria

Chapter 16
An Improved Retinal Blood Vessel Detection System Using an Extreme Learning Machine ... 274
Lucas S Sousa, Programa de Pós-Graduação em Ciências da Computação do IFCE, Fortaleza, Brazil
Pedro P Rebouças Filho, Programa de Pós-Graduação em Ciências da Computação do IFCE, Fortaleza, Brazil
Francisco Nivando Bezerra, Programa de Pós-Graduação em Ciências da Computação do IFCE, Fortaleza, Brazil
Ajalmar R Rocha Neto, Instituto Federal do Ceará, Fortaleza, Brazil
Saulo A. F. Oliveira, Programa de Pós-Graduação em Engenharia de Telecomunicações do IFCE, Fortaleza, Brazil

Chapter 17
Classification of Staphylococcus Aureus FabI Inhibitors by Machine Learning Techniques ... 292
Vinicius Gonçalves Maltarollo, Faculty of Pharmacy, Federal University of Minas Gerais, Belo Horizonte, Brazil

Chapter 18
Optimum Design of Carbon Fiber-Reinforced Polymer (CFRP) Beams for Shear Capacity via Machine Learning Methods: Optimum Prediction Methods on Advance Ensemble Algorithms – Bagging Combinations ... 308
Melda Yucel, Istanbul University-Cerrahpaşa, Turkey
Aylin Ece Kayabekir, Istanbul University-Cerrahpaşa, Turkey
Sinan Melih Nigdeli, Istanbul University-Cerrahpaşa, Turkey
Gebrail Bekdaş, Istanbul University-Cerrahpaşa, Turkey

Chapter 19
Knowledge Generation Using Sentiment Classification Involving Machine Learning on E-Commerce ... 327
Swarup Kr Ghosh, Brainware University, Kolkata, India
Sowvik Dey, Brainware University, Kolkata, India
Anupam Ghosh, Netaji Subhash Engineering College, Kolkata, India

Chapter 20
An Exploratory Study on the Use of Machine Learning to Predict Student Academic Performance 346
Patrick Kenekayoro, Mathematics / Computer Science Department, Niger Delta University, Amassoma, Nigeria

Chapter 21
Machine Learning Based Taxonomy and Analysis of English Learners' Translation Errors 362
Ying Qin, Beijing Foreign Studies University, Beijing, China

Chapter 22
Concerning the Integration of Machine Learning Content in Mechatronics Curricula 379
Jörg Frochte, Bochum University of Applied Sciences, Germany
Markus Lemmen, Bochum University of Applied Sciences, Germany
Marco Schmidt, Bochum University of Applied Sciences, Germany

Chapter 23
A Process for Increasing the Samples of Coffee Rust Through Machine Learning Methods 396
Jhonn Pablo Rodríguez, University of Cauca, Popayán, Colombia
David Camilo Corrales, Telematic Engineering Group, University of Cauca, Popayán, Colombia and Department of Computer Science and Engineering, Carlos III University of Madrid, Madrid, Spain
Juan Carlos Corrales, Telematic Engineering Group, University of Cauca, Popayán, Colombia

Section 3
Tools and Technologies

Chapter 24
Artificial Intelligence and Machine Learning Algorithms 421
Amit Kumar Tyagi, School of Computing Science and Engineering, Vellore Institute of Technology, Chennai, India
Poonam Chahal, MRIIRS, Faridabad, India

Chapter 25
Machine Learning, Data Mining for IoT-Based Systems 447
Ramgopal Kashyap, Amity University, Raipur, India

Chapter 26
Object Detection in Fog Computing Using Machine Learning Algorithms 472
Peyakunta Bhargavi, Sri Padmavati Mahila Visvavidyalayam, India
Singaraju Jyothi, Sri Padmavati Mahila Visvavidyalayam, India

Volume II

Chapter 27
Genetic Programming as Supervised Machine Learning Algorithm 486
Bahrudin Hrnjica, University of Bihac, Bosnia and Herzegovina
Ali Danandeh Mehr, Antalya Bilim University, Turkey

Chapter 28
Programming Language Support for Implementing Machine Learning Algorithms 528
Anitha Elavarasi S., Sona College of Technology, India
Jayanthi J., Sona College of Technology, India

Chapter 29
Data Driven Symbiotic Machine Learning for the Identification of Motion-Based Action Potentials 548
Volkhard Klinger, FHDW Hannover, Hanover, Germany

Chapter 30
A Heterogeneous AdaBoost Ensemble Based Extreme Learning Machines for Imbalanced Data 568
Adnan Omer Abuassba, University of Science and Technology Beijing (USTB), Beijing, China & Arab Open University - Palestine, Ramallah, Palestine
Dezheng Zhang, University of Science and Technology Beijing (USTB), Beijing, China
Xiong Luo, University of Science and Technology Beijing (USTB), Beijing, China

Chapter 31
Network Support Data Analysis for Fault Identification Using Machine Learning 586
Shakila Basheer, King Khalid University, Abha, Saudi Arabia
Usha Devi Gandhi, VIT University, Vellore, India
Priyan M.K., VIT University, Vellore, India
Parthasarathy P., VIT University, Vellore, India

Chapter 32
Hybridization of Machine Learning Algorithm in Intrusion Detection System 596
Amudha P., Avinashilingam Institute for Home Science and Higher Education for Women, India
Sivakumari S., Avinashilingam Institute for Home Science and Higher Education for Women, India

Chapter 33
Applications of Machine Learning in Cyber Security 621
Charu Virmani, Manav Rachna International Institute of Research and Studies, India
Tanu Choudhary, Manav Rachna International Institute of Research and Studies, India
Anuradha Pillai, J. C. Bose University of Science and Technology YMCA, India
Manisha Rani, D. N. College, India

Chapter 34
Machine Learning Techniques to Mitigate Security Attacks in IoT 642
Kavi Priya S., Mepco Schlnek Engineering College, India
Vignesh Saravanan K., Ramco Institute of Technology, Rajapalayam, India
Vijayalakshmi K., Ramco Institute of Technology, Rajapalayam, India

Chapter 35
Advanced-Level Security in Network and Real-Time Applications Using Machine Learning Approaches 664
Mamata Rath, Birla Global University, India
Sushruta Mishra, KIIT University (Deemed), India

Chapter 36
Investigating Machine Learning Techniques for User Sentiment Analysis 681
Nimesh V Patel, C.U Shah University, Wadhawan (Surendranagar-Gujarat), India
Hitesh Chhinkaniwala, Adani Institute of Infrastructure Engineering, Gujarat, India

Chapter 37
Thwarting Spam on Facebook: Identifying Spam Posts Using Machine Learning Techniques......... 693
Arti Jain, Jaypee Institute of Information Technology, India
Reetika Gairola, Jaypee Institute of Information Technology, India
Shikha Jain, Jaypee Institute of Information Technology, India
Anuja Arora, Jaypee Institute of Information Technology, India

Chapter 38
Performance Prediction and Optimization of Solar Water Heater via a Knowledge-Based Machine Learning Method.. 714
Hao Li, University of Texas at Austin, USA
Zhijian Liu, North China Electric Power University, China

Chapter 39
Credit Rating Forecasting Using Machine Learning Techniques 734
Mark Wallis, Bond University, Australia
Kuldeep Kumar, Bond University, Australia
Adrian Gepp, Bond University, Australia

Chapter 40
Machine Learning for Smart Tourism and Retail 753
Carlos Rodríguez-Pardo, Grupo de Inteligencia Artificial Aplicada. Universidad Carlos III de Madrid, Spain
Miguel A. Patricio, Universidad Carlos III de Madrid, Spain
Antonio Berlanga, Grupo de Inteligencia Artificial Aplicada. Universidad Carlos III de Madrid, Spain
José M. Molina, Grupo de Inteligencia Artificial Aplicada. Universidad Carlos III de Madrid, Spain

Chapter 41
Comparative Study of Various Machine Learning Algorithms for Prediction of Insomnia 776
Ravinder Ahuja, Jaypee Institute of Information Technology Noida, India
Vishal Vivek, Jaypee Institute of Information Technology Noida, India
Manika Chandna, Jaypee Institute of Information Technology Noida, India
Shivani Virmani, Jaypee Institute of Information Technology Noida, India
Alisha Banga, Satyug Darshan Institute of Engineering and Technology Faridabad, India

Chapter 42
Detection of Shotgun Surgery and Message Chain Code Smells using Machine Learning Techniques 800
Thirupathi Guggulothu, University of Hyderabad, Hyderabad, India
Salman Abdul Moiz, University of Hyderabad, Hyderabad, India

Chapter 43
Identifying Patterns in Fresh Produce Purchases: The Application of Machine Learning Techniques 817
Timofei Bogomolov, University of South Australia, Australia
Malgorzata W. Korolkiewicz, University of South Australia, Australia
Svetlana Bogomolova, Business School, Ehrenberg-Bass Institute, University of South Australia, Australia

Section 4
Utilization and Applications

Chapter 44
Machine Learning Algorithms 849
Namrata Dhanda, Amity University, India
Stuti Shukla Datta, Amity University, India
Mudrika Dhanda, Royal Holloway University, UK

Chapter 45
Machine Learning for Web Proxy Analytics 870
Mark Maldonado, St. Mary's University, San Antonio, USA
Ayad Barsoum, St. Mary's University, San Antonio, USA

Chapter 46
Machine Learning in Python: Diabetes Prediction Using Machine Learning 882
Astha Baranwal, VIT University, India
Bhagyashree R. Bagwe, VIT University, India
Vanitha M, VIT University, India

Chapter 47
A Knowledge-Oriented Recommendation System for Machine Learning Algorithm Finding and Data Processing 909
Man Tianxing, Itmo University, St. Petersburg, Russia
Ildar Raisovich Baimuratov, Itmo University, St. Petersburg, Russia
Natalia Alexandrovna Zhukova, St. Petersburg Institute for Informatics and Automation of Russian Academy of Sciences (SPIIRAS), St. Petersburg, Russia

Chapter 48
Machine-Learning-Based Image Feature Selection 930
Vivek K. Verma, Manipal University Jaipur, India
Tarun Jain, Manipal University Jaipur, India

Chapter 49
Machine Learning Application With Avatar-Based Management Security to Reduce Cyber Threat 939
Vardan Mkrttchian, HHH University, Australia
Leyla Gamidullaeva, Penza State University, Russia & K. G. Razumovsky Moscow State University of Technologies and Management, Russia
Yulia Vertakova, Southwest State University, Russia
Svetlana Panasenko, Plekhanov Russian University of Economics, Russia

Chapter 50
A Review of Machine Learning Methods Applied for Handling Zero-Day Attacks in the Cloud Environment 952
Swathy Akshaya M., Avinashilingam Institute for Home Science and Higher Education for Women, India
Padmavathi Ganapathi, Avinashilingam Institute for Home Science and Higher Education for Women, India

Chapter 51
Cyber Secure Man-in-the-Middle Attack Intrusion Detection Using Machine Learning Algorithms 976
Jayapandian Natarajan, Christ University, India

Volume III

Chapter 52
A Comparative Review of Various Machine Learning Approaches for Improving the Performance of Stego Anomaly Detection 1002
Hemalatha Jeyaprakash, Thiagarajar College of Engineering, India
KavithaDevi M. K., Thiagarajar College of Engineering, India
Geetha S., VIT University, India

Chapter 53
Wearable Devices Data for Activity Prediction Using Machine Learning Algorithms 1023
Lakshmi Prayaga, University of West Florida, Pensacola, USA
Krishna Devulapalli, Indian Institute of Chemical Technology, Secunderabad, India
Chandra Prayaga, University of West Florida, Pensacola, USA

Chapter 54
Machine Learning for Health Data Analytics: A Few Case Studies of Application of Regression 1038
Muralikrishna Iyyanki, Independent Researcher, India
Prisilla Jayanthi, Administrative Staff College of India, India
Valli Manickam, Administrative Staff College of India, India

Chapter 55
Drug Prediction in Healthcare Using Big Data and Machine Learning 1062
Mamoon Rashid, Lovely Professional University, India & Punjabi University, India
Vishal Goyal, Punjabi University, India
Shabir Ahmad Parah, University of Kashmir, India
Harjeet Singh, Mata Gujri College, India

Chapter 56
Smart Pollution Alert System Using Machine Learning 1072
P. Chitra, Thiagarajar College of Engineering, India
S. Abirami, Thiagarajar College of Engineering, India

Chapter 57
Application of Machine Learning Methods for Passenger Demand Prediction in Transfer Stations of Istanbul's Public Transportation System 1086
Hacer Yumurtaci Aydogmus, Alanya Alaaddin Keykubat University, Turkey
Yusuf Sait Turkan, Istanbul University-Cerrahpasa, Turkey

Chapter 58
Classification of Traffic Events in Mexico City Using Machine Learning and Volunteered Geographic Information 1107
Magdalena Saldana-Perez, Instituto Politecnico Nacional, Mexico
Miguel Torres-Ruiz, Instituto Politecnico Nacional, Mexico
Marco Moreno-Ibarra, Instituto Politecnico Nacional, Mexico

Section 5
Organizational and Social Implications

Chapter 59
Challenges and Applications for Implementing Machine Learning in Computer Vision: Machine Learning Applications and Approaches 1129
Hiral R. Patel, Ganpat University, India
Ajay M Patel, AMPICS, India
Satyen M. Parikh, FCA, India

Chapter 60
Review on Machine and Deep Learning Applications for Cyber Security 1143
Thangavel M., Thiagarajar College of Engineering, India
Abiramie Shree T. G. R., Thiagarajar College of Engineering, India
Priyadharshini P., Thiagarajar College of Engineering, India
Saranya T., Thiagarajar College of Engineering, India

Chapter 61
Adoption of Machine Learning With Adaptive Approach for Securing CPS 1165
Rama Mercy Sam Sigamani, Avinashilingam Institute for Home Science and Higher Education for Women, India

Chapter 62
Machine Learning and Its Use in E-Commerce and E-Business 1193
Mamata Rath, Birla Global University, India

Chapter 63
A Machine Learning Approach for Predicting Bank Customer Behavior in the Banking Industry 1210
Siu Cheung Ho, The Hong Kong Polytechnic University, Hong Kong
Kin Chun Wong, The Hong Kong Polytechnic University, Hong Kong
Yuen Kwan Yau, The Hong Kong Polytechnic University, Hong Kong
Chi Kwan Yip, The Hong Kong Polytechnic University, Hong Kong

Chapter 64
Data-Driven Trend Forecasting in Stock Market Using Machine Learning Techniques 1233
Puneet Misra, University of Lucknow, Lucknow, India
Siddharth Chaurasia, University of Lucknow, Lucknow, India

Chapter 65
Evaluation of Pattern Based Customized Approach for Stock Market Trend Prediction With Big Data and Machine Learning Techniques 1255
Jai Prakash Verma, Institute of Technology Nirma University, Ahmedabad, India
Sudeep Tanwar, Institute of Technology Nirma University, Ahmedabad, India
Sanjay Garg, Institute of Technology Nirma University, Ahmedabad, India
Ishit Gandhi, Institute of Technology Nirma University, Ahmedabad, India
Nikita H. Bachani, Institute of Technology Nirma University, Ahmedabad, India

Chapter 66
Algorithmic Machine Learning for Prediction of Stock Prices 1271
Mirza O. Beg, National University of Computer and Emerging Sciences, Pakistan
Mubashar Nazar Awan, National University of Computer and Emerging Sciences, Pakistan
Syed Shahzaib Ali, National University of Computer and Emerging Sciences, Pakistan

Chapter 67
Application of Machine Learning Techniques in Healthcare 1294
Sathya D., Kumaraguru College of Technology, India
Sudha V., Kumaraguru College of Technology, India
Jagadeesan D., Cherraan's Arts Science College, India

Chapter 68
Machine Learning for Emergency Department Management 1311
Sofia Benbelkacem, Laboratoire d'Informatique d'Oran (LIO), University of Oran 1 Ahmed Ben Bella, Algeria
Farid Kadri, Big Data & Analytics Services, Institut d'Optique Graduate School, Talence, France
Baghdad Atmani, Laboratoire d'Informatique d'Oran (LIO), University of Oran 1 Ahmed Ben Bella, Algeria
Sondès Chaabane, University Polytechnique Hauts-de-France, CNRS, UMR 8201 – LAMIH, Laboratoire d'Automatique de Mécanique et d'Informatique Industrielles et Humaines, F-59313 Valenciennes, France

Chapter 69
Prediction of High-Risk Factors in Surgical Operations Using Machine Learning Techniques 1330
Anitha N., Kongu Engineering College, India
Devi Priya R., Kongu Engineering College, India

Chapter 70
Data Mining and Machine Learning Approaches in Breast Cancer Biomedical Research 1351
Gunavathi Chellamuthu, VIT University, India
Kannimuthu S., Karpagam College of Engineering, India
Premalatha K., Bannari Amman Institute of Technology, India

Chapter 71
Survey of Breast Cancer Detection Using Machine Learning Techniques in Big Data 1381
Madhuri Gupta, Jaypeee Institute of Information Technology, Noida, India
Bharat Gupta, Jaypee Institute of Information Technology, Noida, India

Chapter 72
Analysis of Machine Learning Algorithms for Breast Cancer Detection 1395
Aswathy M. A., VIT University, India
Jagannath Mohan, VIT Chennai, India

Chapter 73
Early Stage Diagnosis of Eye Herpes (NAGIN) by Machine Learning and Image Processing Technique: Detection and Recognition of Eye Herpes (NAGIN) by Using CAD System Analysis 1415
Kakasaheb Rangnarh Nikam, HPT Arts & RYK Science College Nashik MH India, Nashik, India

Chapter 74
Machine Learning Based Program to Prevent Hospitalizations and Reduce Costs in the Colombian Statutory Health Care System 1427
Alvaro J Riascos, University of los Andes and Quantil, Bogotá, Colombia
Natalia Serna, University of Wisconsin-Madison, Madison, USA

Section 6
Emerging Trends

Chapter 75
Current Trends: Machine Learning and AI in IoT 1446
Jayanthi Jagannathan, Sona College of Technology, India
Anitha Elavarasi S., Sona College of Technology, India

Chapter 76
Artificial Intelligence, Machine Learning, Automation, Robotics, Future of Work and Future of Humanity: A Review and Research Agenda 1460
Weiyu Wang, Missouri University of Science and Technology, USA
Keng Siau, City University of Hong Kong, Hong Kong SAR

Chapter 77
Big Data and Machine Learning: A Way to Improve Outcomes in Population Health Management 1482
Fernando Enrique Lopez Martinez, University of Oviedo, Spain
Edward Rolando Núñez-Valdez, University of Oviedo, Spain

Chapter 78
The Role and Applications of Machine Learning in Future Self-Organizing Cellular Networks 1494
Paulo Valente Klaine, University of Glasgow, UK
Oluwakayode Onireti, University of Glasgow, UK
Richard Demo Souza, Federal University of Santa Catarina (UFSC), Brazil
Muhammad Ali Imran, University of Glasgow, UK

Index xxiv

Preface

Machine learning, due to its many uses across fields and disciplines, is becoming a prevalent technology in today's modern world. From medicine to business, machine learning is changing the way things are done by providing effective new techniques for problem solving and strategies for leaders to implement. Machine learning is driving major improvements in society including the promotion of societal health, sustainable business, and learning analytics. The possibilities for this technology are endless, and it is critical to further investigate its myriad of opportunities and benefits to successfully combat any challenges and assist in its evolution.

Staying informed of the most up-to-date research trends and findings is of the utmost importance. That is why IGI Global is pleased to offer this three-volume reference collection of reprinted IGI Global book chapters and journal articles that have been handpicked by senior editorial staff. This collection will shed light on critical issues related to the trends, techniques, and uses of various applications by providing both broad and detailed perspectives on cutting-edge theories and developments. This collection is designed to act as a single reference source on conceptual, methodological, technical, and managerial issues, as well as to provide insight into emerging trends and future opportunities within the field.

The *Research Anthology on Machine Learning Techniques, Methods, and Applications* is organized into six distinct sections that provide comprehensive coverage of important topics. The sections are:

1. Fundamental Concepts and Theories;
2. Development and Design Methodologies;
3. Tools and Technologies;
4. Utilization and Applications;
5. Organizational and Social Implications; and
6. Emerging Trends.

The following paragraphs provide a summary of what to expect from this invaluable reference tool.

Section 1, "Fundamental Concepts and Theories," serves as a foundation for this extensive reference tool by addressing crucial theories essential to understanding the concepts and uses of machine learning in multidisciplinary settings. Opening this reference book is the chapter "Introduction to Machine Learning and Its Implementation Techniques" by Profs. Sathiyamoorthi V. and Arul Murugan R. from Sona College of Technology, India, which aims in giving a solid introduction to various widely adopted machine learning techniques and serves as a simplified guide for the aspiring data and machine learning enthusiasts. This first section ends with the chapter "Machine Learning Applications in Nanomedicine and Nanotoxicology: An Overview" by Prof. Gerardo M. Casañola-Martin from North Dakota State

University, USA and Prof. Hai Pham-The of Hanoi University of Pharmacy, Vietnam, which discusses the recent advances in the conjunction of machine learning with nanomedicine.

Section 2, "Development and Design Methodologies," presents in-depth coverage of the design and development of machine learning techniques for their use in different applications. This section starts with the chapter "Classification and Machine Learning" by Prof. Damian Alberto from the Indian Institute of Technology Bombay, India, which addresses the classification concept in detail and discusses how to solve different classification problems using different machine learning techniques. This section ends with "A Process for Increasing the Samples of Coffee Rust Through Machine Learning Methods" by Prof. David Camilo Corrales from the University of Cauca, Colombia & Carlos III University of Madrid, Spain and Profs. Juan Carlos Corrales and Jhonn Pablo Rodríguez from the University of Cauca, Colombia, which describes how coffee rust has become a serious concern for many coffee farmers and manufacturers and provides a process about coffee rust to select appropriate machine learning methods to increase rust samples.

Section 3, "Tools and Technologies," explores the various tools and technologies utilized in the implementation of machine learning for various uses. This section begins with "Artificial Intelligence and Machine Learning Algorithms" by Prof. Amit Kumar Tyagi from Vellore Institute of Technology, India and Prof. Poonam Chahal of MRIIRS, India, which considers how machine learning and deep learning techniques and algorithms are utilized in today's world. This section closes with the chapter "Identifying Patterns in Fresh Produce Purchases: The Application of Machine Learning Techniques" by Profs. Malgorzata W. Korolkiewicz, Timofei Bogomolov, and Svetlana Bogomolova from the University of South Australia, Australia, which applies machine learning techniques to examine consumer food choices, specifically purchasing patterns in relation to fresh fruit and vegetables.

Section 4, "Utilization and Applications," describes how machine learning is used and applied in diverse industries for various technologies and applications. The opening chapter in this section, "Machine Learning Algorithms," by Profs. Namrata Dhanda and Stuti Shukla Datta from Amity University, India and Prof. Mudrika Dhanda from Royal Holloway University, UK, introduces the concept of machine learning and the commonly employed learning algorithm for developing efficient and intelligent systems. The closing chapter in this section, "Classification of Traffic Events in Mexico City Using Machine Learning and Volunteered Geographic Information," by Profs. Magdalena Saldana-Perez, Miguel Torres-Ruiz, and Marco Moreno-Ibarra from Instituto Politecnico Nacional, Mexico, implements a traffic event classification methodology to analyze volunteered geographic information and internet information related to traffic events with a view to identify the main traffic problems in a city and to visualize the congested roads.

Section 5, "Organizational and Social Implications," includes chapters discussing the impact of machine learning on society and business. The opening chapter, "Challenges and Applications for Implementing Machine Learning in Computer Vision: Machine Learning Applications and Approaches," by Prof. Hiral R. Patel from Ganpat University, India; Prof. Ajay M. Patel of AMPICS, India; and Prof. Satyen M. Parikh from FCA, India, discusses the fundamentals of machine learning and considers why it is important. The closing chapter, "Machine Learning Based Program to Prevent Hospitalizations and Reduce Costs in the Colombian Statutory Health Care System," by Prof. Alvaro J. Riascos from the University of los Andes and Quantil, Colombia and Prof. Natalia Serna of the University of Wisconsin-Madison, USA, suggests a hospitalization prevention program in which the decision of whether to intervene on a patient depends on a simple decision model and the prediction of the patient risk of an annual length-of-stay using machine learning techniques.

Section 6, "Emerging Trends," highlights areas for future research within the machine learning field. Opening this final section is the chapter "Current Trends: Machine Learning and AI in IoT" by Profs. Jayanthi Jagannathan and Anitha Elavarasi S. from Sona College of Technology, India, which addresses the key role of machine learning and artificial intelligence for various applications of the internet of things. The final chapter in this section, "The Role and Applications of Machine Learning in Future Self-Organizing Cellular Networks," by Profs. Muhammad Ali Imran, Paulo Valente Klaine, and Oluwakayode Onireti from the University of Glasgow, UK and Prof. Richard Demo Souza of Federal University of Santa Catarina (UFSC), Brazil, provides a brief overview of the role and applications of machine learning algorithms in future wireless cellular networks, specifically in the context of self-organizing networks.

Although the primary organization of the contents in this multi-volume work is based on its six sections, offering a progression of coverage of the important concepts, methodologies, technologies, applications, social issues, and emerging trends, the reader can also identify specific contents by utilizing the extensive indexing system listed at the end of each volume. As a comprehensive collection of research on the latest findings related to machine learning, the *Research Anthology on Machine Learning Techniques, Methods, and Applications* provides computer scientists, managers, researchers, scholars, practitioners, academicians, instructors, and students with a complete understanding of the applications and impacts of machine learning techniques. Given the vast number of issues concerning usage, failure, success, strategies, and applications of machine learning, the *Research Anthology on Machine Learning Techniques, Methods, and Applications* encompasses the most pertinent research on the applications, impacts, uses, and development of machine learning.

Chapter 27
Genetic Programming as Supervised Machine Learning Algorithm

Bahrudin Hrnjica
University of Bihac, Bosnia and Herzegovina

Ali Danandeh Mehr
Antalya Bilim University, Turkey

ABSTRACT

This chapter presents the theory and procedures behind supervised machine learning and how genetic programming can be applied to be an effective machine learning algorithm. Due to simple and powerful concept of computer programs, genetic programming can solve many supervised machine learning problems, especially regression and classifications. The chapter starts with theory of supervised machine learning by describing the three main groups of modelling: regression, binary, and multiclass classification. Through those kinds of modelling, the most important performance parameters and skill scores are introduced. The chapter also describes procedures of the model evaluation and construction of confusion matrix for binary and multiclass classification. The second part describes in detail how to use genetic programming in order to build high performance GP models for regression and classifications. It also describes the procedure of generating computer programs for binary and multiclass calcification problems by introducing the concept of predefined root node.

INTRODUCTION

As an evolutionary computation technique, Genetic Programming (GP) is one of the most popular and widely used. It is inspired by biological evolution, where each individual in the population represents possible solution of the problem. Individuals in the population are breeding, by exchanging their genetic materials and producing offspring. Individuals in the population have fitness values which play a role in the process of selecting and creating the new population. The offspring and its parents are potential

DOI: 10.4018/978-1-6684-6291-1.ch027

members of the new population. Who will be the 'inhabitant' of the new population depends of the fitness value and selection method. The new population is created by selecting individuals with one of defined selection method by taking into account the fitness value of the members. Selection method takes the fitness of each individual from that population and decide if this individual is good to be the member of the new population. Different selection methods treat each individual differently. Once the new population is created, members are tested how to solve the problem. The best individual in the current population represents solution of the problem for current evolution (iteration). At the end of the evolution process the best individual, which is the best result of all previous evolutions, represents the best solution for the problem. Individuals in GP are called computer programs.

The structure of the computer program is the reason why the GP is so popular and widely used. There are several ways how to represent the computer programs in GP. The tree structure is the most popular representation, where nodes of computer programs are initialized from the function and terminal sets. They can be in different shape which allow diversity of the population and better condition of the mating and breeding.

As possible solution of machine learning problem, GP computer programs are generated on different way for each type of the problem. In case of regression problems, GP programs are usually generated from algebraic, logical and conditional functions and terminals. Due to the fact that the solution for regression problems can take any continuous numeric value, computer structure does not have any constrains in its construction except protected operations. For classification problems construction of computer programs should be carefully planned, including that the root node must be pre-defined. This chapter will cover all aspects of supervised machine learning and how each category of the ML can be applied in GP.

MACHINE LEARNING

Machine Learning (ML) is a sort of artificial intelligence (AI) that provides learning algorithms, mostly for the computers, with the ability to learn, without being explicitly programmed. The process of ML consists of searching the data to recognize the pattern in the data. The recognizing process can be defined as process of computer learning. Once the patterns are recognized, the computer can make prediction for new or unseen data based on persisted knowledge with more or less accuracy.

ML can be categorized based on the task that is going to be solved:

- Supervised,
- Unsupervised and
- Reinforcement learning.

In supervised ML, the learning process consists of finding the rule that maps inputs (features) to outputs (labels). During the learning process, available data can be divided on the two sets. The training set is used for training and collecting the knowledge from the data. The second set is called validation or testing set which the learning algorithm uses for test against overfitting.

Unsupervised learning is the process of discovering patterns in data without defined output. With unsupervised learning, the correct result cannot be determined because no output variable is defined. Algorithms are left to their capability to discover as much as possible knowledge from the data. Because there is no output variable, there is no need for splitting available data set into training and testing part, and all data is used for training and extracting the patterns and knowledge. This kind of learning can be applied in image and signal processing, computer vision, etc.

Reinforcement ML is the process where computer interacts with a dynamic system in which it must achieve goal (like driving a vehicle or playing a game). Reinforcement learning provides feedback consisting of the information how the last action was treated, was it successful or failure. Based on the feedback, computer can learn and make further decisions.

Supervised ML is based on type of the output, and it can be characterized as regression and classification. In regression problems, output variable is represented as continuous number, while in classification problems, the output variable is discrete rather than continuous, and consists of two or more classes. Furthermore, classification problems can be divided as binary and multi class classification problems. In binary, the output variable can consist of only two values. Examples of spam filter, medical disease testing, fraud detection, predictive maintenance, etc. are the representation of typical binary ML problem. Whereas multi class classification problems consist of the output where more than two values are defined. Pattern recognition, handwriting recognition, election prediction, weather forecasting (sunny, cloudy, rain, snow) etc. are the representation of typical multiclass classification problems.

Another way of categorizing ML is how to generalize its output. It can be distinguished:

- Instance-based ML,and
- Model-based ML.

In case of *instance-based learning* hypotheses are created from the training data set directly. Instances of the data set themselves represent the knowledge. The learning process is created based on examples. The simplest example of the instance-based learning is lookup table (Russell & Norvig, 2010).

Model-based ML is based on the model which is constructed from the training data set in form of mathematical expression. Model is constructed with different technics of learner's estimators. For example, regression analysis is trying to estimate regression coefficients of polynomial expression which represent the model. In case of genetic programming model is constructed using evolution of error driven induction (Koza, 1992). Once the model is determined and validated, it can be used to predict the result for unseen data, which is the main purpose of this kind of the models.

In this chapter, different kind of model-based ML problems are introduced.

REGRESSION IN MACHINE LEARNING

Regression problems in ML can be described as recognizing the pattern between input parameter(s) and output variable when the output variable is a continuous numeric value. In context of the GP, the regression can be described as the process where the goal is to find the computer program that fits the given training dataset. Assuming that the training data set is defined by Table 1 the ML task is to find the best possible mathematical function, which takes the input parameters (features) x_1, x_2 and x_3, that fit the output variable y with minimum error.

One of the basic ML algorithm which solves this kind of problem is regression analysis. Regression analysis is statistical process of determination of the relation between input parameters (x_1, x_2, x_3, ..., x_n) and one output variable y. The result of regression process is the mathematical model which can be expressed as polynomial of certain degree:

$$y = f(x_n). \tag{1}$$

The result of linear regression analysis for training data set represented by Table 1 is the regression model given with the following expression:

$$\hat{y} = f\left(x_1, x_2, x_3\right) = 12.39 + 12.47x_1 - 2.70x_2 - 1.58x_3. \tag{2}$$

Once the model is determined the model output can be computed, and the process of model evaluation can be started. Table 2 shows the result of regression analysis.

The output value of the regression model (2) is shown on the Table 2 in the column $\hat{y}$, while the last column from table indicates the residual between the observed output and the output calculated by the model.

Exactly how the regression model fits the data from the Table 1. is usually called model evaluation, and can be described by using several approaches.

Evaluation of Regression Models

Evaluation process can be defined as set of methods for measuring the performance of the model. The evaluation result may detect the weakness and the strength of the model. Based on the result of the evaluation process one may decide if the model is acceptable for production or not. In other words, before model is used in the production, it is important to evaluate it and establish certain level of confidence of its performance. The evaluation process incorporates the output values of the calculated model and the output of observed data set. Usually, observed data set is divided into two groups, one for development, and the other for testing.

Table 1. Data set of regression problem

x_1	x_2	x_3	y
0.19	2.95	2.99	2.10
1.51	0.08	2.23	26.45
2.26	0.46	0.1	39.33
1.34	0.19	0.51	28.74
2.48	1.34	1.7	36.37
0.56	1.84	1.27	12.12
1.61	2.62	0.08	24.95
1	2.66	2.99	13.01
2.52	0.77	2.12	37.65
2.94	1.61	2.82	41.41
2.4	1.71	2.85	33.23
0.23	0.26	1.91	12.05
2.96	2.74	2.07	38.78

Table 2. Data set with regression analysis result

x_1	x_2	x_3	y	$\hat{y}$	**Residual**
0.19	2.95	2.99	2.10	2.077	0.03
1.51	0.08	2.23	26.45	27.48	-1.03
2.26	0.46	0.1	39.33	39.18	0.15
1.34	0.19	0.51	28.74	27.78	0.96
2.48	1.34	1.7	36.37	37.02	-0.65
0.56	1.84	1.27	12.12	12.41	-0.29
1.61	2.62	0.08	24.95	25.28	-0.33
1	2.66	2.99	13.01	12.96	0.05
2.52	0.77	2.12	37.65	38.39	-0.74
2.94	1.61	2.82	41.41	40.25	1.16
2.4	1.71	2.85	33.23	33.20	0.03
0.23	0.26	1.91	12.05	11.54	0.51
2.96	2.74	2.07	38.78	38.64	0.14

Several model evaluations criteria can be used in order to determine how model is good, or how model fits and predicts the data. Results of the model evaluation can be classified as quantitative and qualitative performance measures (Bennett et al., 2013).

Quantitative Performance Measures

Quantitative testing tries to establish quantitative values between the model and observed data. One of the quantitative performance measures is *direct comparison method* where model output compares with observed values. The direct value comparison tries to find similarities between the calculated model and output of the observed data on whole dataset level. Standard summary statistics like mean, mode, median, range, variance etc. represent methods for direct comparison. Table 3 shows the most frequent used direct methods, where n indicates the total number of observations, y observed output, y_i- indicates ith observation, although $\overline{y}$ - indicates the average value of the output variable.

Table 3. List of the most frequently used direct comparison methods

Nr	Name	Formula/Description	Description
1	Mean	$\overline{y} = \frac{1}{n}\sum_{i=1}^{n} y_i$	
2	Mode	*Mode=freq(y_i)*	The most frequent value in a data set.
3	Median	$Median = \begin{cases} y_{\frac{n}{2}}, for\, n = 2k \\ \frac{y_{\frac{n-1}{2}} + y_{\frac{n+1}{2}}}{2}, for\ n = 2k+1 \end{cases}$	Represents the middle value in data set.
4	Range	*Range = max(y) – min(y)*	Represent the interval from minimum to maximum value.
5	Variance	$\sigma = \frac{1}{n}\sum_{i=1}^{n}\left(y_i - \overline{y}\right)^2$	Measures of the spread.
6	Scatter plot	$y = f_{scatter}(y)$	Graphical representation of dispersion and correlation of two variables.

Intention of direct value comparison is that summary statistics values computed on the observed data output y would be as close as possible to the model output $\hat{y}$. Important thing of direct value comparison is that individual output values are not compared, since the intention of the method is to evaluate properties and behaviors of the whole data set.

Scatter Plot

Scatter plot is one of the most effective and simple way of model evaluations. Usually represents graphical picture of correlation between two variables. For example, the scatter plot can be constructed from the variables from more than one data set. Usually, the scatter plot represents graphical picture of the correlation between two variables where x axes may represent observed data output, while y axes show the model output. In that case the perfect model should result with the line through the origin with 45-degree slope (i.e., 1:1 line).

Points around the line show discrepancy between two variables. The scatter plot could be analyzed by calculation of statistical measures against model and observed data outputs.

Figure 1. Example of Scatter plot between observer output and model output

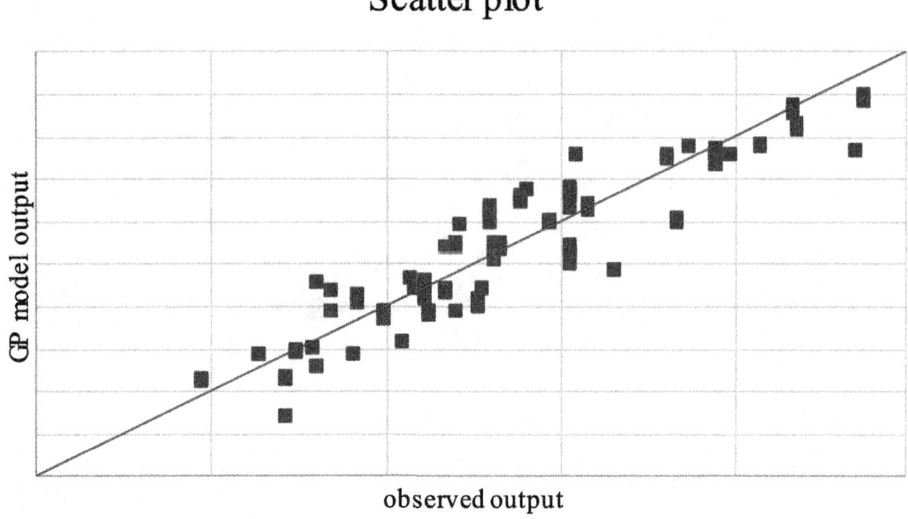

Residual and Residual Plot

One of the basic model evaluation is residual. The residual indicates difference between an observed value, and the value calculated by the model. This is simple subtraction from the two values. Residuals can be mathematically defined as follows:

$$e = y_i - \hat{y}_i, \tag{3}$$

where:

- y_i: Indicates observed value for ith sample,
- $\hat{y}_i$: Indicates the value calculated by the model (2) (or predicted value) for ith sample.

It is common to make graphical representation of residuals by making residual plot. The Figure 2 shows the example of the residual plot, where the x axes indicate the model output and the y axes represents the residual values.

As can be seen from the residual plot, the regression model (2) fits the data very accurately, because the residual plot shows uniform dispersion of residual values around the zero line. The residual of the observed and model output represents the simplest statistics measure. In combination with residual plot, it is used for quick overview of the performance model

Figure 2. Residual plot of the regression model: The zero line indicate the perfect model

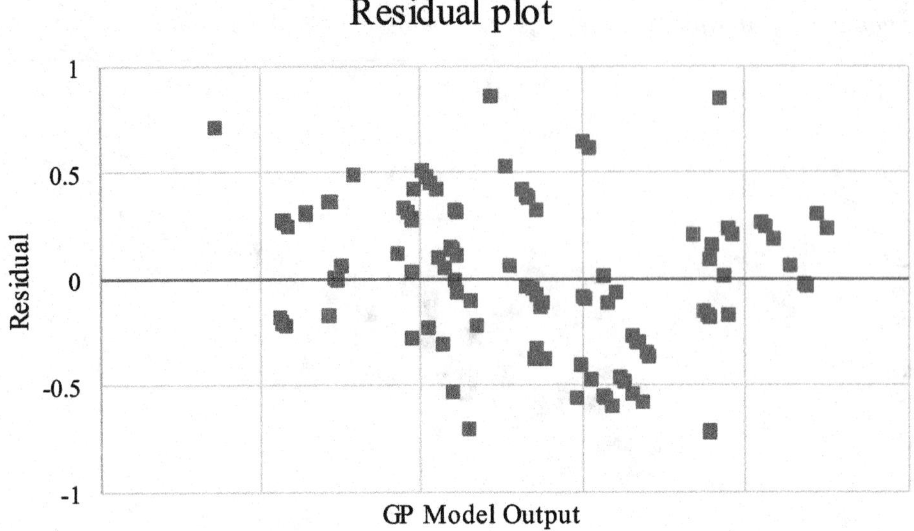

Regression Performance Statistics

For deeper look in to the model performance, the several statistics measures can be used:

- Absolute error, (AE) and mean absolute error, (MAE),
- Squared error, (SE) and mean square error, (MSE)
- Root square error, (RSE) and root mean square error, (RMSE).
- Pearson's coefficient (r) and coefficient of determination (R^2),
- Percent bias PBIAS,
- Nash–Sutcliffe Efficiency, NSE.

Let the y_i indicates ith sample of the observed data set, the $\hat{y}_i$ indicates the ith model calculated sample, and n indicated total number of the sample in the data set.

Absolute error can be defined as summation of the all observed data and predicted values. Simply, it can be defined as:

$$AE = \sum_{i=1}^{n} \left| y_i - \hat{y}_i \right|. \tag{4}$$

The mean absolute error is calculated by dividing the AE with the number of samples *n*.

$$MAE = \frac{1}{n}\sum_{i=1}^{n}\left|y_i - \hat{y}_i\right|, \tag{5}$$

where *n* indicated number of samples in the dataset.

The squared error is basic measure in every statistical model evaluation. It can be expressed summations of the square of the difference between observed samples and corresponded predicted values. It is expressed as:

$$SE = \sum_{i=1}^{n}\left(y_i - \hat{y}_i\right)^2. \tag{6}$$

Usually, squared error is divided by number of samples *n*, which produces the mean squared error. The MSE can be express as:

$$MSE = \frac{1}{n}\sum_{i=1}^{n}\left(y_i - \hat{y}_i\right), \tag{7}$$

where *n* indicates the number of samples in the dataset.

By calculating the square root from the term (6) the root square error (RSE) is calculated.

$$RSE = \sqrt{\sum_{i=1}^{n}\left(y_i - \hat{y}_i\right)^2}. \tag{8}$$

When the root square is applied to MSE, it produces *root mean square error*. RMSE is defined as the square root of the residual means square. It can also be viewed as the average discrepancy between the observed and predicted valued

$$RMSE = \sqrt{\frac{1}{n}\sum_{i=1}^{n}\left(y_i - \hat{y}_i\right)^2}, \tag{9}$$

All above statistics measures should be as low as possible. In case the above measures are zero, this means the model perfectly describe the observed dat. Since above statistics are calculated on all data set, it can be good to be fitness function in GP.

Pearson's correlation coefficient (*r*) calculates the degree of linear correlation. Value can be in range of -1 to 1. The value $r=0$ indicated the linear correlation doesn't exist between observed data and predicted value. If $r<0$ or $r>0$ indicate negative or positive linear correlation, while $r=-1$ or $r=1$ indicate perfect negative or positive correlations between observed data and predicted values. Pearson's correlation coefficient can be calculated as the covariance of the observed and predicted values divided by the product of their standard deviations. The r is expressed as:

$$r = \frac{\sum_{i=1}^{n}\left(y_i - \overline{y}\right)\left(\hat{y}_i - \overline{\hat{y}}\right)}{\sqrt{\sum_{i=1}^{n}\left(y_i - \overline{y}\right)^2}\sqrt{\sum_{i=1}^{n}\left(\hat{y}_i - \overline{\hat{y}}\right)^2}}, \tag{10}$$

where, y_i- observed data samples, $\overline{y}$ mean of the observed data, $\hat{y}_i$ – predicted values, $\overline{\hat{y}}$ – mean of the predicted value, and n is the number of the observations.

Coefficient of determination (r^2) is amount of the variance of the observed data can be described by the models predicted values. The value of r^2 ranges from 0 and 1. Similarly, 0 value of the coefficient of determination indicates no correlation between observed data and predicted values, while r^2=1 indicates the perfect correlation. Coefficient of determination can be expressed as:

$$r^2 = \frac{\sum_{i=1}^{n}\left(\hat{y}_i - \overline{\hat{y}}\right)^2}{\sum_{i=1}^{n}\left(y_i - \overline{y}\right)^2}. \tag{11}$$

It can be easily proofed that square of the Person's correlation coefficient is coefficient of determination.

Percent Bias is defined as the average tendency of the predicted data to be larger or smaller than corresponded observed data. Value lower than zero indicates GP model is overestimated, while positive value of the PBIAS indicates GP model underestimate (Gupta, Sorooshian, & Yapo, 1999). PBIAS is calculated as:

$$PBIAS = \frac{\sum_{i=1}^{n}\left(y_i - \hat{y}_i\right)100}{\sum_{i=1}^{n} y_i}, \tag{12}$$

Nash–Sutcliffe Efficiency, NSE determines the relative magnitude of the residual variance compared to the observed data variance. Value range of the parameter are from minus infinity to one. The NSE =1 indicates a perfect model.

$$NSE = 1 - \frac{\sum_{i=1}^{n}\left(y_i - \hat{y}_i\right)^2}{\sum_{i=1}^{n}\left(y_i - \overline{y}\right)^2}, \tag{13}$$

where $\overline{y}$ indicates average value of the observed data.

In case NSE is between 0 and 1, it is viewed as acceptable performance. When NSE<0 indicates the observed mean can predict better than calculated GP model. So, the closer value to 1 the model is more accurate (Nash & Sutcliffe, 1972).

BINARY CLASSIFICATION

Binary classification (BC) is one of the three main categories in supervised ML. The main idea behind the binary classification problems is identifying to which set of two values the current observation output belongs to. The categories are predefined and the output must fall in one of those two possible results. Beside the fact that there are only two possible output values, the various meanings can be produced. Binary output can take values like 0 or 1, *"yes"* or *"no"*, *True* or *False*, '+' or '-' etc. In all cases one class can be treated as positive and second class as negative. In some application, this is of crucial importance e.g. in medicine where positive value can be treated positive on some disease and negative means healthy patient.

Once the model is determined, comparison between the model results and observed output can be categorized in four categories:

- *True Positive* (*a*), when positive observation is correctly predicted,
- *False Positive* (*b*), when negative observation is incorrectly predicted,
- *False positive* (*c*), when positive observation is incorrectly predicted,
- *True Negative* (*d*), when negative observation is correctly predicted,

The four possible results could be inserted in the table defining the confusion matrix (Fawcett, 2006).

Table 4. Confusion matrix, with n - observations

n	**Predicted YES**	**Predicted NO**
Observed YES	TP (*a*)	FN (*c*)
Observed NO	FP (*b*)	TN (*d*)

Confusion matrix is constructed in a way that rows represent observed or actual values, and columns represent predicted values. The *n* in the top left corner of the table represents the number of observations. One can easily conclude that the number of correctly predicted observations is: $a + d$, and the number of incorrectly predicted is: $b + c$.

Number of *b* and *c* can be differently analyzed for different kind of problems. For example, in medicine, false negative means that diagnose is negative on patient which actually has disease, and false positive means diagnose is positive on a patient which has no disease. This kind of statistics errors are called *type I* and *type II error*. In some other cases, *false positive* can be treated as one of the correctly predicted value, or at least can make less damage. What that actually means is the fact that junk email can make less damage, than the situation when Spam filter marks very important mail as a spam. In context of spam filter, *false positive* means that some of spam messages are treated as regular email, which is less expensive than *false negative*, where some important emails are detected as spam and are lost forever. In some other cases, the *false positive* and *false negative* can be treated equally as false predicted values.

To illustrate an example of BC problem, one can start from the data set shown in Table 1. Since the output values should be binary, the transformation data from the numerical into binary has to be performed. The transformation process is based on practical experience. In case of quality control data collection, the binary value can indicate is the product ready for delivery or not, based on some numerical measurements. Let's say the good product is indicated when the y value in in Table 1 is lower than 30, otherwise the product is not good and cannot be delivered. Table 5 shows binary data transformation as the last column.

From Table 5 numerical column y, is transformed to binary column y_{BIN}. After data transformation, the new column (y_{BIN}) is defined in to the table showing output variable as binary $\{GOOD, BAD\}$. On this way, our regression problem is transformed into binary.

Table 5. Data transformation from numerical into binary

x_1	x_2	x_3	y	y_{BIN}
0.19	2.95	2.99	2.10	GOOD
1.51	0.08	2.23	26.45	GOOD
2.26	0.46	0.10	39.33	BAD
1.34	0.19	0.51	28.74	GOOD
2.48	1.34	1.70	36.37	BAD
0.56	1.84	1.27	12.12	GOOD
1.61	2.62	0.08	24.95	GOOD
1.00	2.66	2.99	13.01	GOOD
2.52	0.77	2.12	37.65	BAD
2.94	1.61	2.82	41.41	BAD
2.40	1.71	2.85	33.23	BAD
0.23	0.26	1.91	12.05	GOOD
2.96	2.74	2.07	38.78	BAD

Evaluation a Binary Classification Model

Once the binary classification model is calculated, one should provide set of statistical tools and procedures to see if the model is good and reliable, and how it predicts the result for unseen and future data. Evaluating models and predicting outcome plays very important role in many engineering fields. Forecasting for floods, tornados, rainfall, earthquake etc. can save many lives, prevent money loss and bring economic benefits. The first step in the evaluation of the binary model is calculation of the extended confusion matrix. The following table represents the extended confusion matrix of n observations.

Extended confusion matrix contains addition row and column showing total number of positive and negative observations, and predictions. Table 6 is starting point for calculation performance and skill parameters of the binary classifier.

Table 6. Confusion matrix with additional total row and column

n		Predicted		
		YES	NO	Total
Actual	YES	TP (*a*)	FN (*c*)	a + c = actual yes
	NO	FP (*b*)	TN (*d*)	b + d = actual no
	Total	*a*+*b* = pred. yes	*c*+*d*= pred. no	*a*+*b*+*c*+*d* = total

Performance Measure of the Binary Classifier

Around the confusion matrix several indicators can be calculated, which can describe performance and accuracy of the binary classifier. There are several parameters for binary classifier evaluation (Kuhn & Johnson, 2013):

- Accuracy,
- Precision,
- Recall,
- F1 Score,
- ROC curve and AUC,
- Lift curve and AUC.

Accuracy or Total Accuracy, (A), represents the ratio of correctly predicted value by total observations. Accuracy is the first parameter to be calculated in order to evaluate the classifier. Total accuracy can be expressed by:

$$A = \frac{a+d}{a+b+c+d} = \frac{a+d}{n}. \tag{14}$$

In contras of accuracy the error rate is ratio of incorrectly predicted values and total observations. Error rate can also be expressed with accuracy by:

$$Err = \frac{b+c}{a+b+c+d} = 1 - A. \tag{15}$$

In case of unbalanced data, where most observations belong to the one of two classes, Accuracy parameter cannot be very helpful. The parameter has high accuracy value indicating the strong performance, but the accuracy is related to only one class. In order to avoid this, additional parameters must be calculated.

Precision or Positive Predicted Value, (P), represents the measure of model ability to positively predicted observed data. Precision can be expressed with:

$$P = \frac{a}{a+b} = p. \tag{16}$$

Recall or True Positive Rate, (R): Parameter is the measure of model ability to predict positive observed values. In other words, the Recall measure can be expressed by:

$$R = \frac{a}{a+c} = r. \tag{17}$$

In context of these two parameters it can be concluded that for nearly balanced dataset, classifier that predicts mostly positive observations, would have a high value of *recall* parameter. However, lower value of *precision,* indicates that many of observations with negative value are incorrectly predicted. High values for both show that the classifier predicts in a closely manner.

Precision can be seen as measure of quality, whereas *Recall* is a measure of quantity. Figure 3 graphically represents the meaning of the precision and recall.

Figure 3. Precision and recall graphic representation

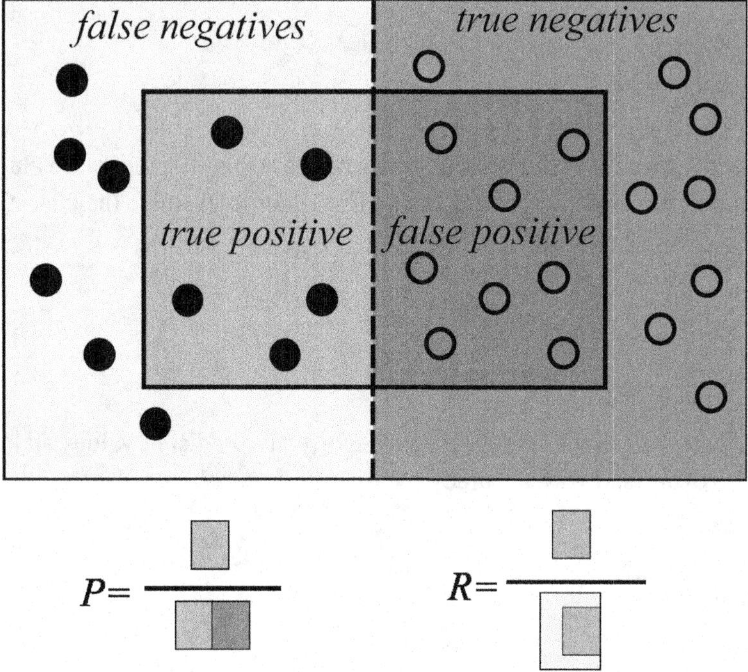

While the Precision is going to answer on question *How many selected items are relevant,* and Recall is trying to answer on the question *How many relevant items are selected.*

F1 Score: Parameter is defined by precision and recall. F1 Score represent harmonic mean of precision and recall. It can be expressed as:

$$F = 2\frac{pr}{p+r}. \tag{18}$$

The F1 Score tends to be average when these two parameters are close.

Precision and Recall could usually be depicted as graph, in the form of *Precision/Recall* curve (Figure 4).

Figure 4. Precision-Recall curve in evaluation of binary classifier

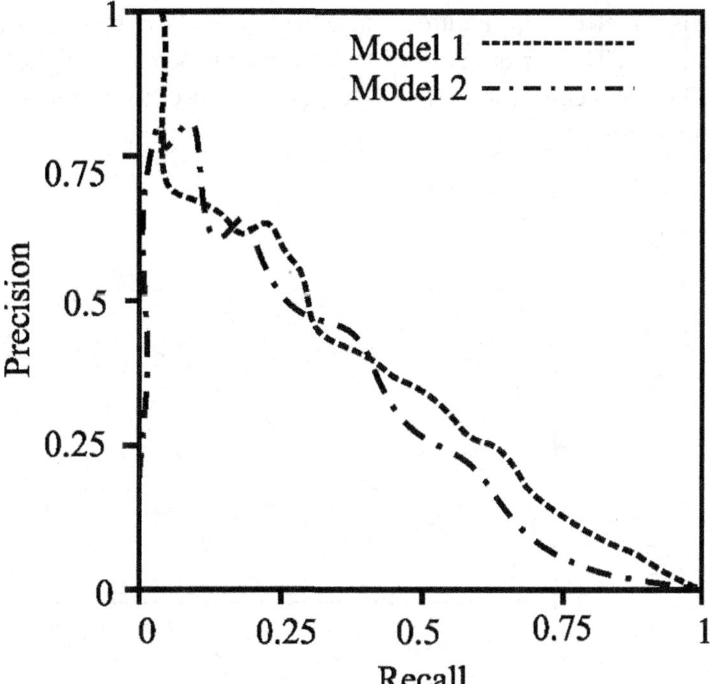

Precision and Recall are inversely related which means when the precision increases the recall decreases and vice versa. The balancing between these two parameters is very important.

The AUC score is the area under Precision/Recall curve and can be used for performance measure. The value of the AUC can be between 1 and 0, meaning that the value closer to 1 is closer to perfect classifier, while the score close to 0.5 indicates the classifiers with the random performance.

Specificity or True negative rate, (S): Parameter is the measure of model ability to predict negative observed values. In other words, the Recall measure can be expressed by:

$$S = \frac{d}{d+b}. \tag{19}$$

ROC Curve

Evaluation of *true positive rate* vs. *false positive rate* can be graphically described by Receiver Operating Characteristic (ROC) curve and the corresponding Area Under the Curve (AUC). The ROC curve represents the most important evaluation method for binary classifier. It provides handy way to visualize accuracy of prediction. ROC curve is constructed when the threshold value is varying from 0 and 1. For different value of the threshold the true positive rate and false positive rate are calculated. The ROC curve analysis usually tried to find optimal value of the threshold that best discriminates between two classes for maximize value of the two parameters (Fawcett, 2006).

Simple ROC curve is depicted on the Figure 5 where the *false positive rate* is horizontal axes, and *true positive rate* is vertical axes. The performance of the classifier is better when the ROC curve is closer to upper left corner. The worst case is when the ROC curve is closer to diagonal plot, which indicates classifier with random performance.

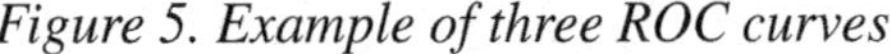

Figure 5. Example of three ROC curves

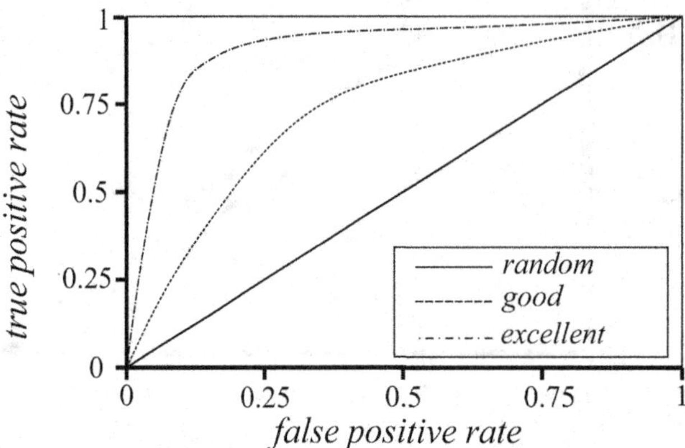

Area under curve refers to the area under ROC curve. This is the most important parameter that can be obtained from the curve. The maximum value of AUC is 1, and represents the perfect classifier (Powers, 2011). The Figure 5 shows three ROC curves. It can be calculated three AUC values, one for each ROC curve. The best classifier has the greatest AUC value. From Figure 5 the curve 3 (dot dash line) which is closest to left vertical and up horizontal line has the greatest AUC value. In order to calculate AUC parameter, one my use one of methods classical methods for integration e.g. trapezoidal rule.

In contrast to ROC curve, the Lift curve parameter indicates the degree to which classifier predicts better than randomly-generated classifier It can be expressed as ratio of percentage of correctly predicted positive values and true positive rate (Figure 6).

When positive rate and number of true positive cases are put in to graph, the lift curve is presented. Lift curve is constructed by taking different values of threshold, trying to depict what would be the optimal classifier. During the construction of the Lift curve, output probability values should be sorted, and carefully analyzed, in order to get optimal classifier.

Figure 6. Example of three different Lift curves

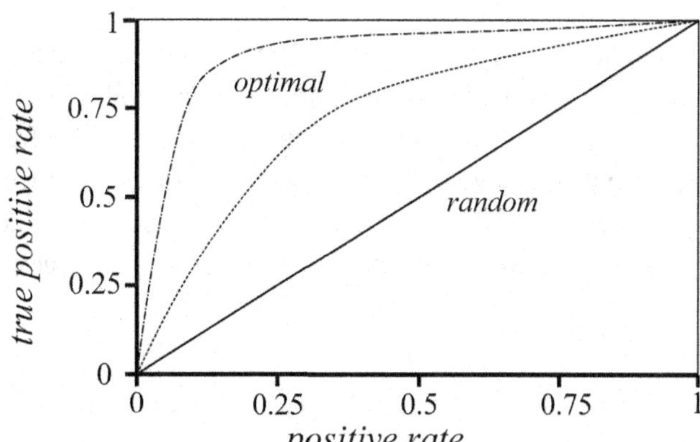

Threshold

Since binary classifier deals with only two result values, the model output result can be in form of probability value. In order to compute accuracy from the probability value, the threshold value must be defined. Threshold value is boundary by which the result turns into positive or negative result. Usually threshold value is 0.5, giving the equal chance for both events to happen. In real world, threshold value is often to be different than 0.5, because for some events, the error rates should be improved by giving different threshold value than 0.5. For example, the classifier with threshold value 0.5 predicts the positive values with 75%, and 100% for negative values. By changing the threshold value from 0.5 to 0.3 one can make this model perfect.

Figure 7 shows model evaluation with two different threshold values, making this mode perfect by changing the threshold value from 0.5 to 0.3.

Figure 7. Evaluation of binary classifier with different threshold values

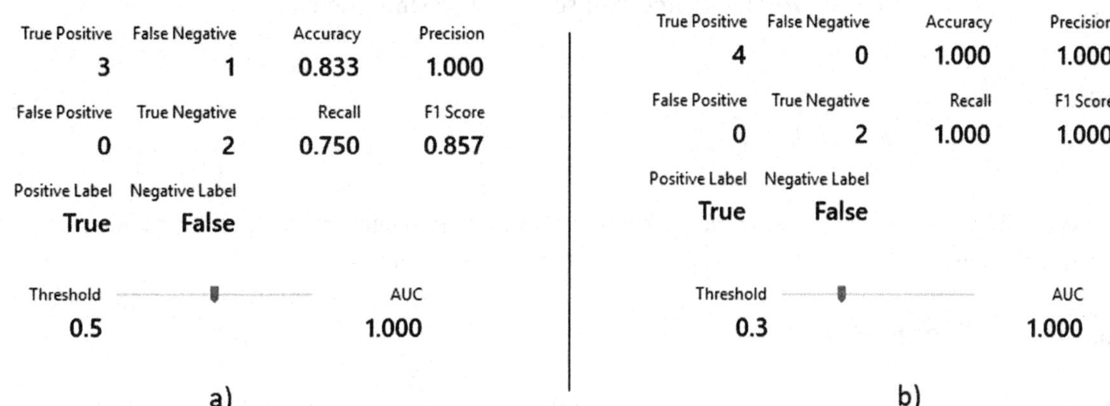

Skill Score of Binary Classifier

A large number of skill scores have been developed for binary classifiers based on the Confusion matrix. Skill scores are trying to measure the relative accuracy of the model, with respects to reference or predefined value. From different engineering fields, reference can be of different type and value.

In general, skill score represents improvements over the predefined reference value, measured in percentage. If the model predicts the observed data with particular measure of accuracy A_{cc}, and the perfect accuracy is denoted by A_{perf}, the skill score with respect to the reference accuracy A_{ref}, can be expressed as:

$$SS_{ref} = \frac{A_{cc} - A_{ref}}{A_{perf} - A_{ref}}. \tag{20}$$

As can be seen, skill score has consistent results regardless of the accuracy measure. In case $A=A_{perf}$, the skill score $SS_{ref}=1$, which makes the perfect skill value. On the other hand, if $A=A_{ref}$ then $SS_{ref}=0$, which means there is no improvement of the model. In case $A<A_{ref}$, the model is inferior due to reference value, showing the skill score as negative. Skill scores are used when two or more complex models are being compared.

Peirce Skill Score

In case the accuracy is represented as total accuracy A, and reference accuracy is the random reference, the skill score can be expressed as:

$$A_{rand} = \left(\frac{a+c}{n}\right)^2 + \left(\frac{b+d}{n}\right)^2, \tag{21}$$

Such defined skill score is called *Peirce skill score* (Wilks, 2006). The score is also called true skill statistics. Based on the terms (20), the Peirce skill score can be simplified as:

$$PSS = \frac{ad - bc}{(a+c)(b+d)}. \tag{22}$$

The score is perfect when $PSS=1$, and when the $PSS=0$, it indicates the random classifier. Negative value of PSS showing the classifier has property which is below random.

Heidke Skill Score

One of the most popular and widely used score is *Heidke Skill Score* (HSS). HSS score is based on common skill score term (20), where accuracy measure A_{cc} is replaced with total accuracy A given by following term:

$$A_{cc} = A = \frac{a+d}{n}. \tag{23}$$

In Heidke Skill score, the reference accuracy (A_{ref}) represents the random prediction. The random prediction can be expressed as:

$$A_{ref} = \frac{a+b}{n}\frac{a+c}{n} + \frac{c+d}{n}\frac{b+d}{n}. \tag{24}$$

By substituting (23) and (24) into (20), where perfect accuracy A_{pef}=1, Heidke Skill Score can be simplified as:

$$HSS = \frac{2\left(ad-bc\right)}{\left(a+c\right)\left(c+d\right)+\left(a+b\right)\left(b+d\right)}. \tag{25}$$

Similar as in general skill score formulation, HSS can take values between -¥ to 1. The value of HSS=1 indicate the perfect classifier, while 0 indicates random classifier. Negative value of HSS indicates classifier which is worse than random classifier.

Assume the binary classifier predicts the output from Table 5, and those results are shown in Table 7.

Table 7. Comparison of observed and predicted data

Features			**Observation**		**Prediction**
x_1	x_2	x_3	y	y_{BIN}	$\hat{y}$
0.19	2.95	2.99	2.10	GOOD	GOOD
1.51	0.08	2.23	26.45	GOOD	GOOD
2.26	0.46	0.10	39.33	BAD	GOOD
1.34	0.19	0.51	28.74	GOOD	GOOD
2.48	1.34	1.70	36.37	BAD	GOOD
0.56	1.84	1.27	12.12	GOOD	GOOD
1.61	2.62	0.08	24.95	GOOD	GOOD
1.00	2.66	2.99	13.01	GOOD	GOOD
2.52	0.77	2.12	37.65	BAD	GOOD
2.94	1.61	2.82	41.41	BAD	BAD
2.40	1.71	2.85	33.23	BAD	GOOD
0.23	0.26	1.91	12.05	GOOD	GOOD
2.96	2.74	2.07	38.78	BAD	BAD

Based on the Table 7, confusion matrix can be computed in a following way that the observed values represent rows, and predicted values represent the columns (Table 8).

Table 8. Confusion matrix for binary classifier

		Predicted		
Observed	n=13	GOOD	BAD	Totals
	GOOD	7	0	7
	BAD	4	2	6
	Totals	11	2	13

Once the confusion matrix is defined, the evaluation process can be started. Based on the previously defined performance parameters, Figure 8 shows the result of evaluation process.

As can be seen the Figure 8, Accuracy is nearly 70%, while Precision=0.636, and Recall =1. The reason why Recall is 1, is because the binary classifier has predicted all positive values.

Figure 8. Evaluation binary classifier with ROC curve calculated by GPdotNET

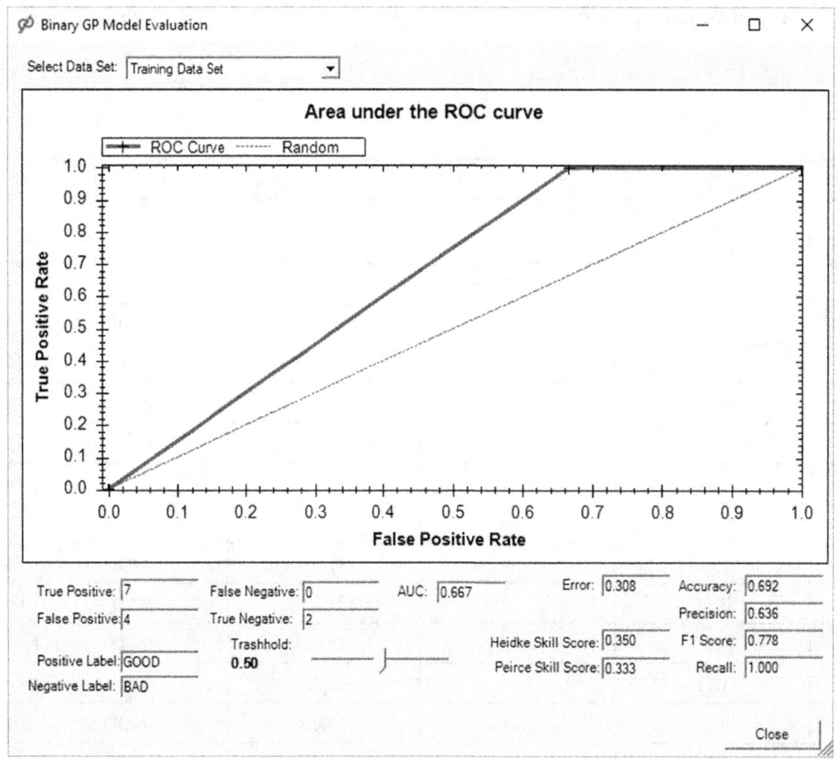

MULTICLASS CLASSIFICATION, MCC

In supervised ML, *Multi Class Classification* (MCC) is defined as problem of the output classification into one of several (more than two) values. Classification output can be any set of logical values: *colors= {red, green, blue}*, *weekdays = {Monday, Tuesday, Wednesday, Thursday, Friday, Saturday}*, *intensity= {low, medium, high}*, etc. There are plenty of examples when MCC is used. In weather forecasting the information is often given as one of three or more classes, *"cold", "normal" and "warm"*. Moreover, the weather information can be given with certain probability. For example, 70% chance for rain and 10% chance of sun, is very good reason for taking an umbrella, instead of 10% chance to rain and 80% chance for sun.

Beside class prediction, it is common to provide the probability for happening of certain class. The categorical data can also be generated in order to recognize text also known as text recognition, where the output of such data set are letters from A to Z and numbers from 0 to 9. In ML the text recognition represents the most popular example of MCC problem.

To illustrate an example of MCC problem, assume the data is collected and presented in the Table 9, where there are three input parameters x_1, x_2 and x_3, and one numerical output label y. In classification problem, at first the output variable should be transformed from numerical to discreate variable with several classes.

Transformation from numerical into categorical value should be based on practical experience. In case of temperature, weather classification can be classified differently in different climate regions. The temperature of 20°C can be normal in southern and central Europe, but in Greenland or South and North Pole this is very high and unusual temperature. Starting data set for MCC is based on the previous regression example, where the output continuous values are going to be transformed in to categorical.

Table 9. Experimental measurements and its categorization

x_1	x_2	x_3	y	y_{CAT}
0.19	2.95	2.99	2.10	C1
1.51	0.08	2.23	26.45	C2
2.26	0.46	0.10	39.33	C3
1.34	0.19	0.51	28.74	C2
2.48	1.34	1.70	36.37	C3
0.56	1.84	1.27	12.12	C1
1.61	2.62	0.08	24.95	C2
1.00	2.66	2.99	13.01	C1
2.52	0.77	2.12	37.65	C3
2.94	1.61	2.82	41.41	C3
2.40	1.71	2.85	33.23	C3
0.23	0.26	1.91	12.05	C1
2.96	2.74	2.07	38.78	C3

From Table 9 numerical output *y*, can be transformed to categorical, on the following way. Let the C_1 class be any value lower than 20, while C_2 class can be any value between 20 and 30 and the last category C_3 is any number greater than or equal to 30. After data transformation, the new column (y_{CAT}) can be added in to the table showing output variable as categorical with three classes $\{C_1,C_2,C_3\}$. On this way, our regression problem is transformed into categorical. The one of the reasons among others of such data transformation can be simplification of the prediction (forecast) process.

From the previous example, categorical problem can be defined by transforming the continuous numerical values into set of classes. On the other hand, categorical value can be directly defined by observing such experiment or perfume such measure that the output value is categorical value. For example, if the observation is defined of the recording the color, or day of the week, etc.

Evaluation of Multiclass Classifier

The most of the binary classifier evaluations can be established in case of multiclass classifier with some generalization. The first step in evaluation of multiclass classifier is to compute the confusion matrix. Since MCC has more than two classes, the confusion matrix can be large as more classes are defined by the classifier. In case of *n* classes, the confusion matrix is *nxn* format.

From Table 9, the confusion matrix can be defined as 3*x*3 matrix, since three classes C_1, C_2 and C_3 are defined. Assume the multiclass classifier predicts the output from the Table 9 and those results are shown in Table 10.

Table 10. Comparison of observed and predicted data

Features			Observation		Prediction
x_1	x_2	x_3	y	y_{CAT}	$\hat{y}$
0.19	2.95	2.99	2.10	C1	C2
1.51	0.08	2.23	26.45	C2	C3
2.26	0.46	0.10	39.33	C3	C1
1.34	0.19	0.51	28.74	C2	C2
2.48	1.34	1.70	36.37	C3	C3
0.56	1.84	1.27	12.12	C1	C1
1.61	2.62	0.08	24.95	C2	C2
1.00	2.66	2.99	13.01	C1	C1
2.52	0.77	2.12	37.65	C3	C3
2.94	1.61	2.82	41.41	C3	C2
2.40	1.71	2.85	33.23	C3	C3
0.23	0.26	1.91	12.05	C1	C1
2.96	2.74	2.07	38.78	C3	C3

Based on the Table 10 the confusion matrix can be computed in a following way that the observed values represent rows, and predicted values represent the columns. The result is shown in Table 11.

Table 11. Confusion matrix for 3 class classifier

		Predicted			**Totals**
Observed	n=13	C1	C2	C3	
	C1	3	1	0	4
	C2	0	2	1	3
	C3	1	1	4	6
Totals		4	5	4	13

From Table 11 the four outcomes between observed and predicted values for each class can be defined:

- TP: *true positive*, which indicate correctly predicted positive observed value.
- FN: *false positive*, indicate incorrectly predicted positive observed value.
- FP: *false negative*, indicates incorrectly predicted negative observed values.
- TN: *true negative*, indicate correctly predicted negative observed values.

From the Table 11 following values could be calculated for each class (Table 12).

Based on Table 12, the confusion matrix for all three classes is shown in Table 13.

Table 12. Performance values for 3 class classifiers

C_1	TP_1	C_{11}	3
	FP_1	$C_{21}+C_{31}$.	1
	FN_1	$C_{12}+C_{13}$	1
	TN_1.	$C_{22}+C_{23}+C_{32}+C_{33}$	8
C_2	TP_2	C_{22}	2
	FP_2		2
	FN_2	$C_{21}+C_{23}$	1
	TN_2	$C_{11}+C_{13}+C_{31}+C_{33}$	8
C_3	TP_3	C_{33}.	4
	FP_3	$C_{13}+C_{23}$	1
	FN_3	$C_{31}+C_{32}$	2
	TN_3	$C_{11}+C_{12}+C_{21}+C_{22}$	6

Table 13. Cumulative performance values for 3 class classifier

TP	$\sum_{i=1}^{3} TP_i$	9
FP	$\sum_{i=1}^{3} FP_i$	4
FN	$\sum_{i=1}^{3} FN_i$	4
TN	$\sum_{i=1}^{3} TN_i$	22

Once the calculation of the confusion matrix is done, one can start with the performance calculation. In multiclass classifier, usually performance parameters are given in average form to give general view of the classifier. In fact, there are two kinds of average results for each parameter: *micro-average* (μ) and *macro-average (m)*.

The main difference between micro and macro average is the intension of the analysis. If one wants to see how the classifier predicts all classes on average level, the macro-average should be used. On the other hand, if one wants to see how classifier predicts each class separately micro-average should be used. Macro-averaging trying to relativize all classes equally, whereas micro-averaging desires more frequent class (Sokolova & Lapalme, 2009).

Let the N be number of classes, tp_i, tn_i, fn_i and fp_i true positive, true negative, false negative and false positive for each class C_i, Table 14 shows most important performance parameters for multiclass classifiers, (Ferri, Hernandez-Orallo, & Modroiu, 2009).

The tp_i, tn_i, fn_i and fp_i are calculated for each class based on the Table 12 and Table 13. Macro average parameters are calculated from per class corresponded parameter values divided by the number of classes N.

Skill Scores for Multiclass Classifier

Let consider Table 15 define the confusion matrix for multiclass classifier defined with n. classes. In the Table 15, $n(O_i,F_j)$ denotes the number of observed category i that is predicted with category j. $N(O_i)$ denotes the total number of observations in category i, $n(F_j)$ denotes the total number of predicted j category, where N is total number of observations/predictions.

Table 15 is starting point for calculation multi class classifier skill scores. Beside the basic counts of predicted and observed values, it also contains totals of predicted and observed values for each class.

Peirce Skill Scores for Multiclass Classifier

Based on the Table 15 Peirce's skill score (PSS) can be calculated as follows (Wilks, 2006):

$$PSS = \frac{\sum_{i=1}^{n} n\left(O_i, F_i\right) - \frac{1}{N}\sum_{i=1}^{n} N\left(O_i\right) N\left(F_i\right)}{N - \frac{1}{N}\sum_{i=1}^{n} N\left(O_i\right)^2}. \tag{26}$$

The PSS value can be between (-¥, 1). Negative values indicate that a forecast is worse than randomly generated forecast, while 1 indicates perfect forecast. In case of confusion matrix from Table 11 PSS Skill score can be calculated on the following way:

$$PSS = \frac{9 - \frac{58}{13}}{13 - \frac{61}{13}} = 0.546. \tag{27}$$

Table 14. Micro and Macro average performance parameters

Performance Parameter	Symbol	Description
Overall Accuracy	$A = \sum_{i=1}^{N} \left[\frac{tp_i}{tp_i + fn_i + fp_i + tn_i} \right]$	Overall Accuracy is the sum of correct classifications divided by the total number of observation.
Average Accuracy	$A_{avg} = \frac{1}{N} \sum_{i=1}^{N} \left[\frac{tp_i + tn_i}{tp_i + fn_i + fp_i + tn_i} \right]$	Average Accuracy per-class, effectiveness of a classifier.
Error Rate	$E_r = \frac{1}{N} \sum_{i=1}^{N} \left[\frac{fp_i + fn_i}{tp_i + fn_i + fp_i + tn_i} \right]$	Average classification error per-class.
Micro-average precision	$P_\mu = \frac{\sum_{i=1}^{N} tp_i}{\sum_{i=1}^{N} tp_i + fp_i}$	Ratio of total true positive prediction and all positive observations for all classes.
Micro-average Recall	$R_\mu = \frac{\sum_{i=1}^{N} tp_i}{\sum_{i=1}^{N} tp_i + fn_i}$	Ration of total true positive prediction and all positive prediction for all classes.
Micro-average F1Score	$F_\mu = 2 \frac{P_\mu R_\mu}{P_\mu + R_\mu}$	Harmonic mean of corresponded precision and recall.
Macro-average precision	$P_m = \frac{1}{N} \sum_{i=1}^{N} \left[\frac{tp_i}{tp_i + fp_i} \right]$	Average per-class ratio of true positive prediction and all positive observations for all classes.
Macro-average Recall	$R_m = \frac{1}{N} \sum_{i=1}^{N} \left[\frac{tp_i}{tp_i + fn_i} \right]$	Ration of total true positive prediction and all positive prediction for all classes.
Macro-average F1Score	$F_m = 2 \frac{P_m R_m}{P_m + R_m}$	Harmonic mean of corresponded precision and recall.

Table 15. Confusion matrix for N class classifier

	Predicted					Totals
Observed	n	C_1	C_2	…	C_n	
	C_1	$n(O_1,F_1)$	$n(O_1,F_1)$	…	$n(O_1,F_n)$	$N(O_1)$
	C_2	$n(O_2,F_1)$	$n(O_2,F_1)$	…	$n(O_2,F_n)$	$N(O_2)$
	…	…	…	…	…	…
	C_n	$n(O_n,F_1)$	$n(O_n,F_1)$	…	$n(O_n,F_n)$	$N(O_n)$
Totals		$N(F_1)$	$N(F_2)$	…	$N(F_n)$	N

Heidke Skill Score for Multiclass Classifier

Similar to binary classifier, Heidke skill score (HSS) for MCC can be defined as measure of skill in forecast as (Wilks, 2006):

$$HSS = \frac{\sum_{i=1}^{n} n\left(O_i, F_i\right) - \frac{1}{N}\sum_{i=1}^{n} N\left(O_i\right)N\left(F_i\right)}{N - \frac{1}{N}\sum_{i=1}^{n} N\left(O_i\right)N\left(F_i\right)}. \tag{28}$$

The HSS value can be between (-∞, 1). Negative values indicate that a forecast is worse than randomly generated forecast, while 1 indicates perfect forecast. In case of confusion matrix from the Table 11 HSS Skill score can be calculated on the following way:

$$HSS = \frac{9 - \frac{58}{13}}{13 - \frac{58}{13}} = 0.532. \tag{29}$$

From (27) and (29) it can be seen that *PSS<HSS*, which means that the classifier has less skill to discriminate among events and non-events, rather than a skill to correctly classify number of hits that would be expected by chance. Full evaluation process of the MCC model given by Table 10 is shown in Figure 9.

Figure 9. Evaluation of MCC model calculated by GPdotNET

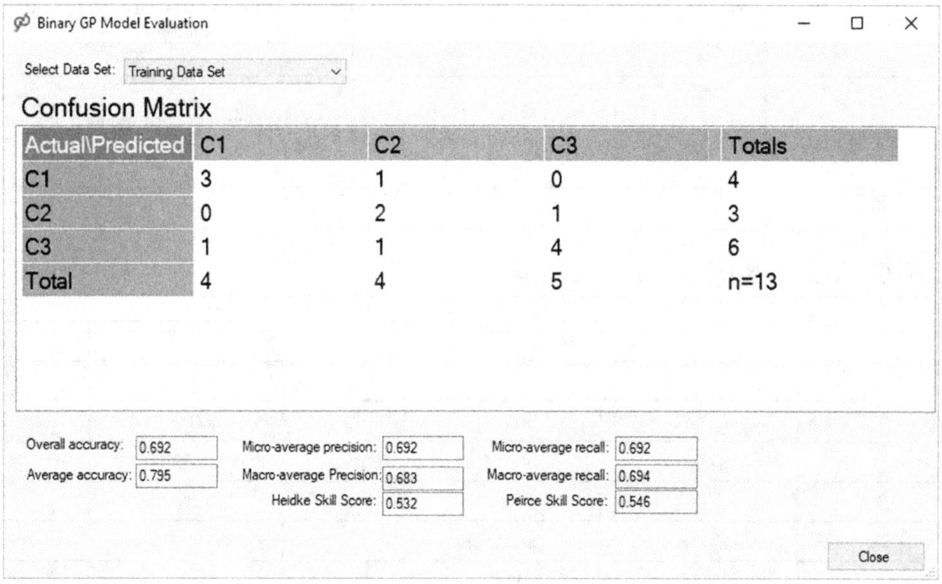

Binary GP Model Evaluation

Select Data Set: Training Data Set

Confusion Matrix

Actual\Predicted	C1	C2	C3	Totals
C1	3	1	0	4
C2	0	2	1	3
C3	1	1	4	6
Total	4	4	5	n=13

Overall accuracy: 0.692
Average accuracy: 0.795
Micro-average precision: 0.692
Macro-average Precision: 0.683
Heidke Skill Score: 0.532
Micro-average recall: 0.692
Macro-average recall: 0.694
Peirce Skill Score: 0.546

Close

As can be seen average accuracy has greater value than overall accuracy which indicates the classifier has better performance on macro level.

GENETIC PROGRAMMING AND REGRESSION

Solving regression problems with GP has been recognized as successful method since the beginning of the GP. Due to its simple and powerful concept, using GP in solving regression problems has been proved in many areas, especially in problems where other regression methods may not give expected result. Successful GP application of regression problems can be found in Hydrology, Space research, games, Weather Forecast, Mechanical Engineering, etc. The last chapter of the Book describes in detail some of the book authors GP applications.

Regression problem in GP can be solved by using program induction which include the inductive discovery from the space of possible computer programs. In regression, GP computer programs, as potential solution (models) are represented as tree expression so called Symbolic Regression (Koza, 1992).

Regression models as the result of regression analysis are described with mathematical expressions usually in polynomial form. In case of linear regression, the regression models are linear polynomial, or nonlinear polynomial of certain degree when the nonlinear regression is considered. Furthermore, regression models can also be logarithmic, or trigonometric. In all cases, classic regression analysis begins with predefined form of the mathematical expression, where the task of the regression analysis is to find the regression coefficients. In real world problems of modelling this is recognized as limitation factor. Due to this fact, the regression analysis starts with linear model, calculate the regression coefficients, then test and validate regression model. If the model doesn't satisfy set of test procedures, the model is rejected, and the regression analysis starts from the beginning with assuming the different kind of the model, usually with higher degree of polynomial. This process is looping until the suitable model is found.

Solving regression problems with GP is not limited on polynomial forms nor any mathematical functions. In GP, construction of the regression model can be included any function e.g. trigonometric, transcendent as well as Boolean, conditional and any other custom defined or automatically defined functions (Koza, 1992). Which function would be part of the GP regression model, evolution of the GP algorithm would decide based on fitness value and selection method. On the other words, the best regression model will go through the evolution process of survival.

Assume the regression problem, given by Table 1, has to be solved in GP. After applying GP algorithm, the best solution is found and it is shown in Figure 10.

The computer program has tree structure generated from function set $F=\{+, -, *, /\}$, and terminal set $T=\{x_1,x_2,x_3,c_1\}$, where x_i are predictors and c_1 random constants. Based on the best computer program, calculated output is shown in y_{GP} column of Table 16.

If the GP model shown in Figure 10 transforms in to mathematical expression and simplify, the following expression is given:

$$y_{GP} = f\left(x_1, x_2, x_3, c_1\right) = 10.73 + 12.74x_1 - 2.69x_2 - x_3. \tag{30}$$

As can be seen, terms (2) and (30) have the same polynomial degree, but different coefficients. Among dozens of the GP parameters, fitness function is most important parameter in order to get best possible solution. In the case of GP model (30) the RMSE was used.

Figure 10. Best computer program found for the regression problem given by Table 1

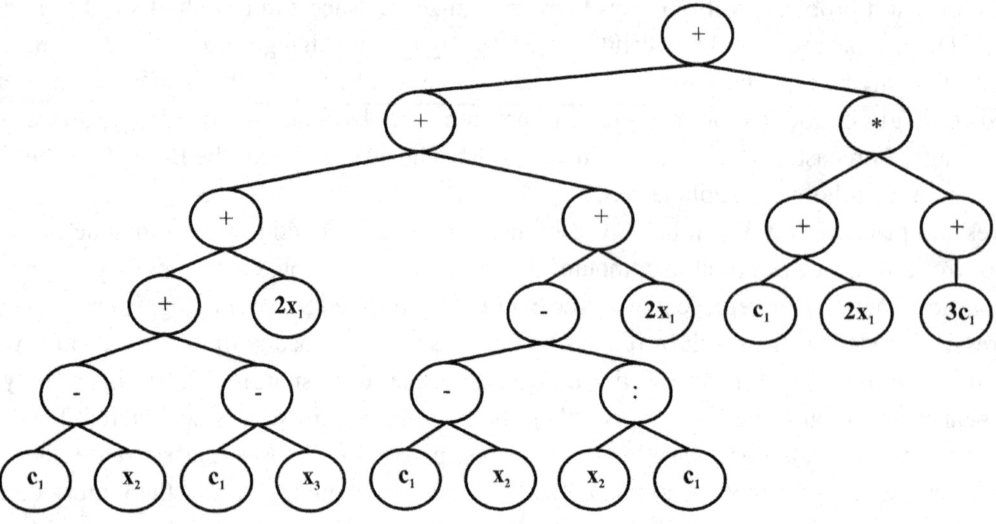

Table 16. GP model result for typical regression problem

x_1	x_2	x_3	y	y_{GP}
0.19	2.95	2.99	2.1	2.23
1.51	0.08	2.23	26.45	27.52
2.26	0.46	0.10	39.33	38.18
1.34	0.19	0.51	28.74	26.78
2.48	1.34	1.70	36.37	37.02
0.56	1.84	1.27	12.12	11.65
1.61	2.62	0.08	24.95	24.12
1.00	2.66	2.99	13.01	13.33
2.52	0.77	2.12	37.65	38.64
2.94	1.61	2.82	41.41	41.03
2.40	1.71	2.85	33.23	33.86
0.23	0.26	1.91	12.05	11.05
2.96	2.74	2.07	38.78	39.00

Fitness Function in Regression

The best measure for computer program to be solution to regression problem is the error. The small error value the better solution for the regression. This is the key concept of error-driven evolution of symbolic regression in GP (Koza, 1992). The obvious solution for fitness of computer programs is error measure. As can be seen from the previous section where "Regression and Machine learning" were introduced, the error between the model and observed data can be calculated on various ways.

Assume, the Root Mean Square Error (RMSE), given by term (9) is selected to be the fitness function for GP computer programs. As cane be seen previously, RMSE is given by:

$$RMSE = \sqrt{\Sigma \frac{1}{n}\left(y_i - \widehat{y_i}\right)^2}, \tag{31}$$

where:

- y_i: Observer output,
- $\widehat{y_i}$: Output calculated by the GP model,
- n: The number of samples.

Assume RMSE (See Equation (9)) has been selected as the fitness function for GP computer programs. Since RMSE takes only values greater than or equal to 0, and regarding the fact that the value closer to zero is better, the best computer programs is the one with the minimum fitness value in the population. On the other hand, fitness value in classification problems can be number of correctly calculated sample, which leads to the fact that the best computer program is the one with the maximum fitness value. In both cases, this kind of fitness value is called *raw fitness*. It represents the error between the observed and model output.

Since the best fitness value can be minimum or maximum depending of the type of the problem, this kind of fitness measures is not suitable for computer implementation. Due to this issue, several fitness types can be defined (Koza, 1992):

- Raw fitness, f_{raw}
- Standardized fitness, f_{std}
- Adjusted fitness, f_{adj}

Standardized fitness transforms the raw fitness so that the minimum value is always the best fitness value. The raw fitness is transform in to standardized fitness on the following way:

- In case the lower raw fitness is better, raw fitness became the standardized fitness,

$$f_{std_i} = f_{raw_i} \tag{32}$$

- In case the greater fitness value is better, standardized fitness is calculated from the raw fitness for the ith iteration on the following way:

$$f_{std_i} = max\left(f_{raw}\right) - f_{raw_i}, \tag{33}$$

With such definition, standardized fitness is always aligned in the same direction: the lesser fitness value the better solution.

The adjusted fitness is defined in the way that the greater fitness value will always produce better computer program. This fitness type is the most suitable for the computer calculation. The adjusted fitness is defined as:

$$f_{adj_i} = \frac{1}{1 + f_{raw_i}}, \tag{34}$$

where f_{adj_i} – indicates the adjusted fitness for the it h iteration, f_{raw_i} - indicates the raw fitness for the ith iteration. Adjusted fitness takes the real values from the interval (0, 1), where 0 – indicated very bad computer program, and the 1 represent computer program with correct result. In most computer implementation adjusted fitness is multiply by 1000 in order to get better fitness value range.

In the case of the GP model given by term (30), RMSE = 0.89, whereas the regression model given by term (2) has RMSE= 0.61. By calculating the adjusted fitness and multiply with 1000 for both models, the following fitness values are calculated:

$$f_{adj}\left(\hat{Y}_{GP}\right)1000 = 528.7,$$

$$f_{adj}\left(\hat{Y}\right)1000 = 622.6, \tag{35}$$

where:

- $f_{adj}\left(\hat{Y}_{GP}\right)$: Indicates adjusted fitness for GP model (30),
- $f_{adj}\left(\hat{Y}\right)$: Indicates adjusted fitness for regression model (2).

Since the perfect model has adjusted fitness value f_{adj}=1000, it can be concluded the model given by (2) has better performance in context of RMSE measure.

For regression problems, GP implementation has no specific constrains in computer programs constructions. The fitness function is selected among the various statistics measures presented in the section of "Regression in Machine Learning", and transformed in to adjusted fitness, so that the maximum fitness value represents the best solution in the population.

GENETIC PROGRAMMING AND BINARY CLASSIFICATION

Creating binary classifier in GP can be very challenging task. There are many examples of binary classification mainly in medicine testing for disease to determine if a patient is positive or not. In production, binary classification can be used in order to determine if a product "*pass or fail*" quality control, or in predictive maintenance, "*if machine will fail in certain number of hours or days*" in the future. In context of GP, binary classification problem can be defined as population of computer programs whose result is binary value, or continuous value between 0 and 1. In GP, computer programs are generated randomly, and they produce the output value which can be any real number. In context of binary classification, the first problem in GP is how to real value output transform in to binary value.

Let Figure 11 shows the possible computer programs in the population. Let the c_1 and c_2 represent the constants and x_1 and x_2 represent input parameters or features. Based on this fact the terminal set is defined as $T=\{c_1,c_2,x_1,x_2\}$. Assume, the function set is defined with the following primitive functions $F=\{+, -, *, /, \text{Log}, \text{Sin}\}$.

Figure 11. Tree representation of computer programs in GP

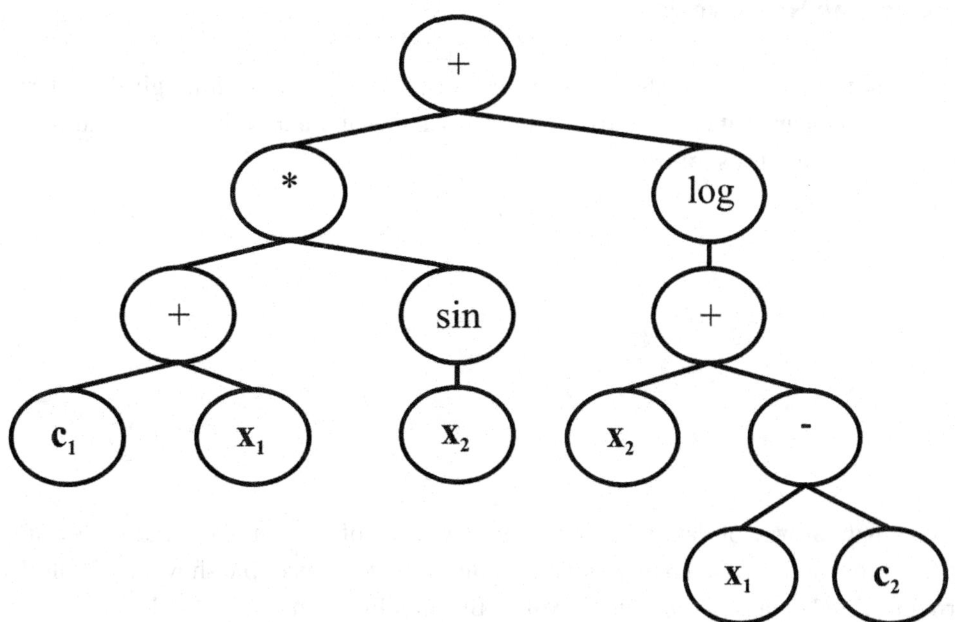

The computer program depicted in Figure 11 can be written in analytic form as:

$$y_{GP} = \left(c_1 + x_1\right) * \sin x_2 + \log\left(x_1 + x_2 - c_2\right) \tag{36}$$

Let's describe the training set by Table 17.

At the end, let the random constants represent the fowling set $C=\{c_1=2, c_2=3\}$.

Table 17. Training dataset for binary classification problem

NR	x_1	x_2	y
1	1	10	Yes
2	2	15	Yes
3	3	20	No
4	4	25	No
5	5	30	No

Table 18. Observed and predicted values of binary data set

NR	x_1	x_2	y	y_{GP}
1	1	10	Yes	0.314
2	2	15	Yes	4.798
3	3	20	No	6.963
4	4	25	No	1.771
5	5	30	No	-4.208

If the model (36) is applied to the training data set represented by Table 17 the model result is as shown in the y_{GP} column of Table 18.

As can be seen, calculated output values are continuous numbers. In order to make this computer program useful in context of binary data, it should be found suitable way to transform those values into the meaning form of "Yes" or "No" (1 or 0).

Step Function as Root Node

There are several possibilities how the output values of the computer program given by term (36) can be transformed into binary values. The first approach which can be used is that *if* condition is defined at the root of the program is as follows:

```
if(Ygp>0)
{
Ygp=1(Yes)}
else
{
Ygp=0 (No);
}
```

This is very natural way of data transformation where set of real numbers can be transformed into binary set. Such function is called *Step function*. In the case of the example shown by Table 18, in order to transform predicted data (y_{GP}) into binary value, the *Step* function can be used.

If the root of the tree structure of each computer program in the population is defined as *Step* function, all computer programs would give the binary output. The computer program from Figure 11 can be transformed in Figure 12.

From the picture above the analytic form of above figure can be written as:

$$Y_{GP} = Step\left[\left(c_1 + x_1\right)\sin x_2 + \ln\left(x_1 + x_2 - c_2\right)\right] \tag{37}$$

With assumption that the *Step* function is the root node value of the computer program given by term (37), now refer to an updated Table 18 (Table 19).

Figure 12. Computer program with fixed root node as STEP function

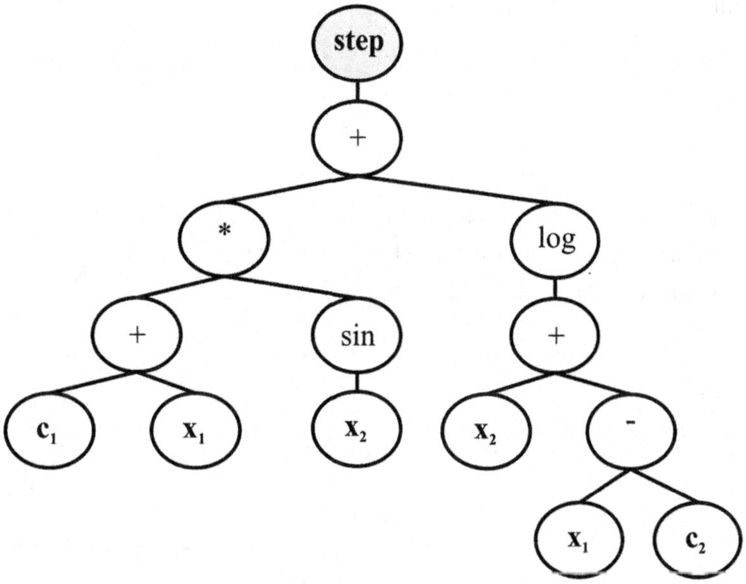

Table 19. Observed and predicted values using Step function of binary data set

NR	x_1	x_2	y	y_{GP}	$Step(y_{GP})$
1	1	10	Yes	0.314	1 (Yes)
2	2	15	Yes	4.798	1 (Yes)
3	3	20	No	6.963	1 (Yes)
4	4	25	No	1.771	1 (Yes)
5	5	30	No	-4.208	0 (No)

Once the *Step* function is defined as root node of computer program, the GP binary classification is defined.

One can conclude that GP can be applied in modelling binary problems by specifying predefined root node, PDRN, of each computer program in the population with *Step* function. Since binary data usually follows the binomial distribution of the two events which have the same probability to happen, binary genetic programming can be defined in a way that computer programs return probability of the event.

Sigmoid as Root Node

Let assume the probability of events have the same chance to happen. Probability value of such events can be expressed as:

$$p(\text{yes})=0.5,\ p(\text{no})=0.5 \tag{38}$$

The new approach can be defined to replace the *Step* function from the previous computer program with Sigmoid function. The *Sigmoid function* is defined as:

$$sigmoid\left(y\right) = \frac{1}{1+e^{-f(x)}} \tag{39}$$

As can be seen the *Sigmoid* function returns values between 0 and 1, and the value can be treated as probability of the event. The *Sigmoid* function takes any real value as an argument and returns value between 0 and 1. *Sigmoid* function graph is depicted in Figure 13.

Figure 13. Sigmoid graph

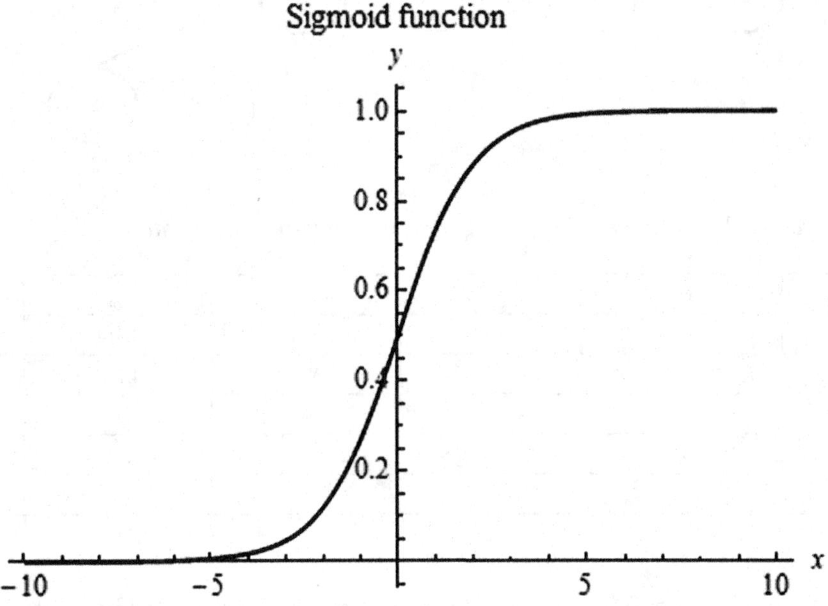

If this function is defined as the root node for the previous example, all results would be between 0 and 1, and can be treated as probability values. Now the computer program looks like on Figure 14.

With Sigmoid function as the root node, the output values are shows in the last column of the Table 20.

As can be seen values are between 0 and 1, and can be treated as probability of the event. From the first row, it can be concluded with the probability of 89% that 'Yes' event will happen. Also, the output of second row which is 0.14 shows that with 14% of confidence the 'Yes' event will happen, or 86% of confidence that the opposite event ('No') will happen. It can be easily concluded that the threshold value is 0.5, which indicates inflection point of the *Sigmoid* function.

Figure 14. Sigmoid function as the root node in GP computer program

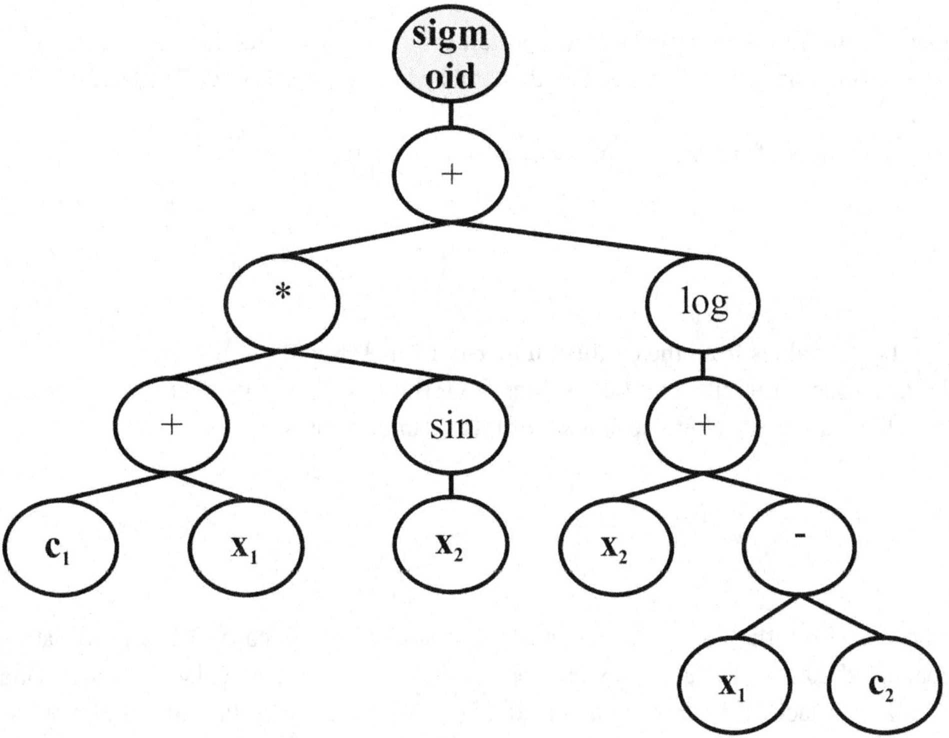

Table 20. Result data when the Sigmoid function is the root node

NR	x_1	x_2	y	y_{GP}	$Step(y_{GP})$	$Sigmoid(y_{GP})$
1	3	9	Yes	2.113	1	0.89
2	4	4	Yes	-1.800	0	0.14
3	5	1	No	4.950	1	0.99
4	1	0	No	-0.964	0	0.28
5	4	9	No	2.525	1	0.93

Fitness Function in Binary Classifier

In the previous section, it can be seen how computer program can be transformed in order to search for binary classification based problems. It has also shown that in order to predict classifier the root node must contain special function. Usually, the *Step* or *Sigmoid* function can be defined to get computer program compatible with binary classifier. Once such computer programs are defined the standard definitions of fitness function must be changed too, because standard fitness function like RMSE, or MSE are not suitable to be applied in binary classification problems.

Accuracy as Fitness Function

The first idea of the fitness function would be the percentage of correctly predicted values. In other word, the fitness function can be described by the total accuracy parameter defined in the section Binary Classification.

Thus, the raw fitness of the binary computer program can be expressed as:

$$f_{raw} = \frac{a+d}{n}, \tag{40}$$

where a, d and n are values from the confusion matrix from Table 4.

Such defined fitness function can take values from 0 to 1. It is convenient to express the previous term (40) as adjusted fitness. Now the adjusted fitness can be expressed:

$$f_{adj} = \frac{1}{1+f_{raw}}1000. \tag{41}$$

As can be seen from the previous section, the accuracy holds in case of balanced data set, but in case of unbalanced data set the accuracy cannot avoid dominance of one class. In such condition, the population suffers of lack of diversity which leads evolution to converge fast and offer results with high precision of the one class and bad prediction of second class (Urvesh, Mengjie, & Mark, 2010).

Skill Scores as Fitness Function

Using skill scores for unbalanced binary classifier, diversity in the GP population of computer programs can be increased. When the fitness function is based on skill score the dominance of the one class is relativized, which leads that computer programs with lower total accuracy have more chance to survive in the population.

Thus, the fitness function of the computer program can be expressed as:

$$f_{raw} = HSS = \frac{2(ad-bc)}{(a+c)(c+d)+(a+b)(b+d)}. \tag{42}$$

In case of using skill score for binary classifier, fitness function can take value from minus infinity to 1. In such case, adjusted fitness values can also be applied by multiplying by 1000. Now, the adjusted fitness can be expressed as:

$$f_{adj} = \frac{1}{1+f_{raw}}1000. \tag{43}$$

With skill score as fitness function each computer program indicates how to predict the observed value relative to random prediction that are statistically independent of the observations. With such fitness definition, dominance of one class can be avoided on certain level, and the population can increase the diversity which brings better chance to get better solution.

GENETIC PROGRAMMING AND MULTICLASS CLASSIFICATION

Modelling multiclass classification problems in GP can be defined in similar fashion as in the previous case. Instead of dealing with only two outcomes, more than two outcomes may appear. For this reason, multiclass classification can be defined as generalization of binary classification. From Koza's book, classification is defined as concept of decision tree creation. The classification process starts by applying an attribute test from the beginning of the decision tree. Output of the test determines which branch of the decision tree should be visited. Calculation process continues for each internal point of the tree. When the external point is visited the process terminates, and the result indicated last visited label (Koza, 1992). Illustration of the example of the GP decision tree can be described by the Figure 15. The figure shows decision tree in context of classification for Quinlan's binary classification (Quinlan, 1986).

Figure 15. GP decision tree for the classification problem of Saturday morning

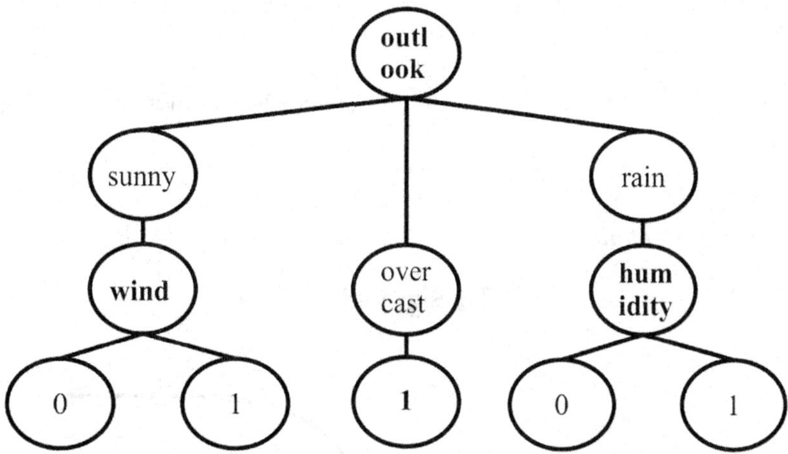

In order to solve Quinlan's Saturday mornings problem, GP is defined so that the terminal set *T*= {0,1} which represents the classes of the problem, function set represents the attribute testing functions *F*= {TEMP, NUM, OUT, WIND}, while the training data set consists of 14 training cases (Koza, 1992).

Besides the concept of the induction of decision tree, there are many other GP approaches for MCC which are successfully applied. In contrast to induction of the decision tree, Iba, Paul, and Hasegawa (2010) introduces the hybrid genetic programming approach based on GMDH technique. This approach integrates a GP-based adaptive search of tree structures, and local parameter tuning mechanism employing statistical search. Hybrid approach consists of classic tree based structural search and multiple regression analysis to establish so called STROGANOFF (i.e. STructured Representation On Genetic Algorithms for NOnlinear Function Fitting) adaptive program. The fitness evaluation is based on a Minimum Description Length (MDL) criteria, which has influence on the tree growth in GP.

In this section MCC will be based on the concept of predefined root node. In other words, initialization of the computer program will always start with generated specific function as root node, then the computer program generation would follow the standard GP procedures for evolution. In order to get classification output, the special predefined function is defined. Two predefined functions are introduced:

- **Scaled Sigmoid Function:** Can be defined as sigmoid function whose result is scaled from (0,1) to (0, n), where n is number of classes.
- **Sofmax Function:** Can be defined as generalization of logistic function which transform a n-dimensional vector of real values in to n-dimensional vector of real values between (0,1), whose sum is equal to 1.

Scaled Sigmoid as Root Node

The root node of computer program can be defined as function which can accept real value arguments and return categorical value. The candidate for such function can be *Scaled Sigmoid* function. The *Scaled Sigmoid* function is defined as follows:

$$ssig\left(y,n\right)=\frac{n}{1+e^{-f(x)}}, \tag{44}$$

where n indicates number of classes for MCC problem. The Scaled Sigmoid function can be graphically represented as follows:

Figure 16. Graphical representation of 3 x scaled Sigmoid function

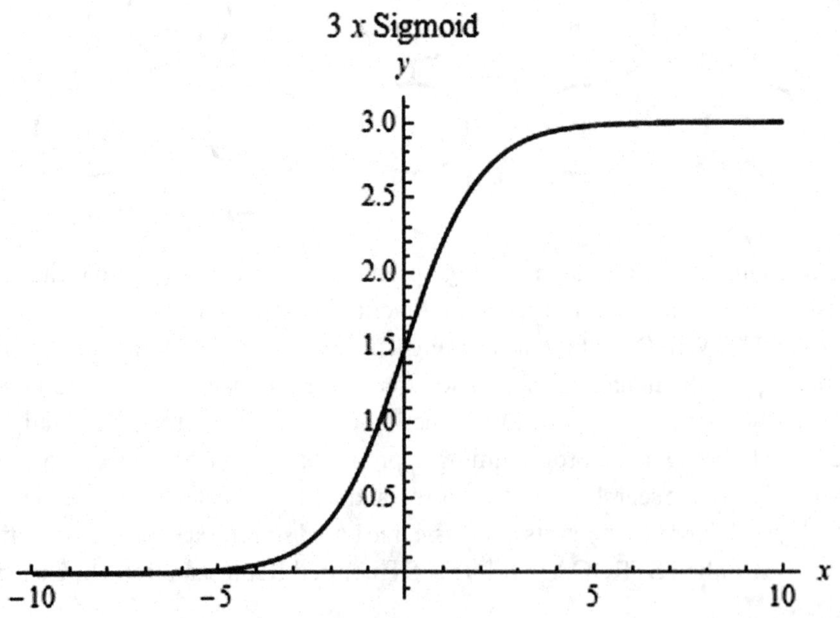

From Figure 16 it can be seen the argument of the function can be any real number, where the function returns the value between (0 –n). This function can be used as multiclass classifier or can be used as the root node of the computer program for MCC problems.

Assume the best computer program is presented on the Figure 17. As can be seen the best computer program perfectly describes the training data set from the Table 10.

Figure 17. GP computer program as solution to MCC problem

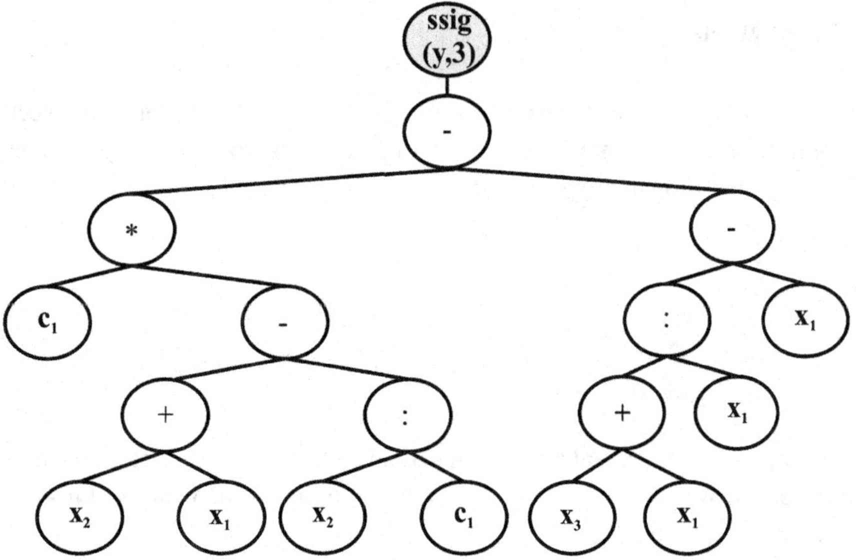

Table 21. Scaled Sigmoid function applied to categorical data

Features			Observation		Prediction	
x_1	x_2	x_3	y	y_{CAT}	*Ssig*(*y*,3)	*Trunc*(*ssig*(*y*,3))
0.19	2.95	2.99	2.10	C1	0.00	0 - C1
1.51	0.08	2.23	26.45	C2	1.39	1 – C2
2.26	0.46	0.10	39.33	C3	2.73	2 – C3
1.34	0.19	0.51	28.74	C2	1.96	1 – C2
2.48	1.34	1.70	36.37	C3	2.50	2 – C3
0.56	1.84	1.27	12.12	C1	0.12	0 - C1
1.61	2.62	0.08	24.95	C2	1.75	1 – C2
1.00	2.66	2.99	13.01	C1	0.08	0 - C1
2.52	0.77	2.12	37.65	C3	2.56	2 – C3
2.94	1.61	2.82	41.41	C3	2.62	2 – C3
2.40	1.71	2.85	33.23	C3	2.09	2 – C3
0.23	0.26	1.91	12.05	C1	0.00	0 – C1
2.96	2.74	2.07	38.78	C3	2.55	2 – C3

The computer program from Figure 17 contains Scaled sigmoid function *ssig*(*y*,3) by indicating the three class MCC problem. When Scaled Sigmoid function is applied to the result of Table 10 the result is shown in the last column of Table 21.

The calculated values of *Scaled Sigmoid* function are between 0 to 3. If class names be defined to corresponded values 0, 1 and 2, the multiclass classifier can be defined. The last column of Table 21 represents integer values by removing decimal part of *Scaled Sigmoid* function, also known as *Truncate* function. The value of the last column represents the numeric value of defined class. As can be seen the computer program perfectly described training data set.

Softmax as Root Node

Softmax function is generalization of the logistics function that takes *n*- dimensional vector of arbitrary real values and returns the *n*- dimensional vector $\sigma(z)$ of real values from the [0,1] segment. The S*oftmax* function is defined by the following expression:

$$\sigma\left(z\right)_i = \frac{e^{z_i}}{\sum_{j=1}^{n} e^{z_j}}, \tag{45}$$

where $i=1,2,\ldots,n$.

Such output can be used to represent a categorical distribution, which indicates the probability distribution over the *n* classes. We can find *Softmax* application in many MCC algorithms e.g. ANN, Naïve Bayes classifiers, etc. (Alpaydin, 2014).

Beside categorical distribution, SoftMax function has very interesting properties, which make it very powerful. One of main property is the fact that the sum of the output vector component is equal to 1, which can be treated as generalization of logistic function. Each value in the vector indicate the probability.

Assume the best computer program is presented on the Figure 18. As can be seen the best computer program contains the SoftMax function as root node, and perfectly describes the training data set from the Table 10.

The computer program from Figure 18 is defined with *Softmax* function as root node. Number of arguments of the *Softmax* function is 3 which is related to the number of classes in MCC. Evaluation of the computer programs against the training data set shown in Table 10, and GP model output is calculated in the last column of Table 21.

The computer program from the Figure 18 perfectly described the training data set.

Fitness Evaluation in GP for MCC

Fitness function is the key of success for every GP application. Same as in previous BC problems, fitness function of MCC problems is calculated based on confusion matrix describe in previous section. The classification statistics represent of counting the number of true positive, true negatives, false positive and false negative outcomes. These statistics are used to get various statistics performance measures and skill scores. The fitness function evaluation in MCC problems is the same as fitness defined in binary GP. Beside performance statistics (e.g., total accuracy), the related multiclass classification version of skill scores can be used too.

Figure 18. GP computer program as solution to MCC problem with SoftMax root node

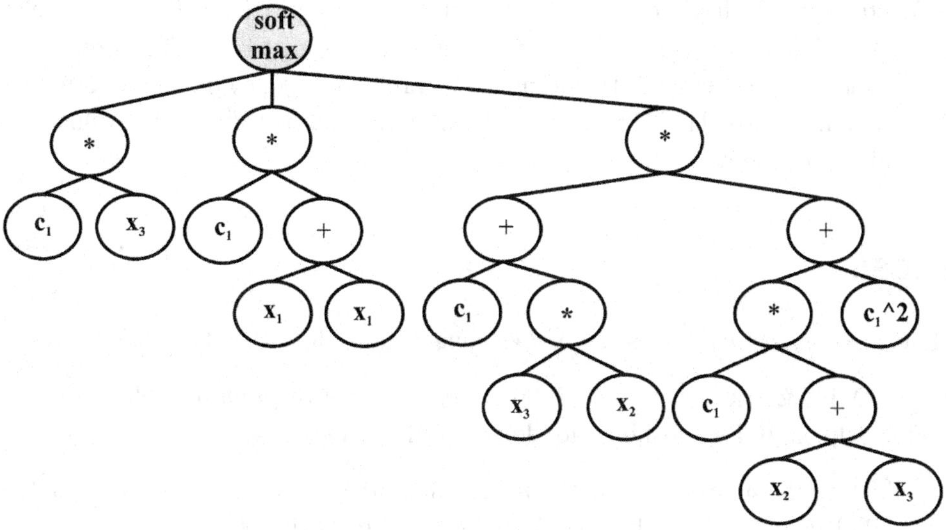

Table 22. Softmax function applied to categorical data

Features			Observation		Prediction
x_1	x_2	x_3	y	y_{CAT}	*Softmax*(*y*)
0.19	2.95	2.99	2.10	C1	0 - C1
1.51	0.08	2.23	26.45	C2	1 – C2
2.26	0.46	0.10	39.33	C3	2 – C3
1.34	0.19	0.51	28.74	C2	1 – C2
2.48	1.34	1.70	36.37	C3	2 – C3
0.56	1.84	1.27	12.12	C1	0 - C1
1.61	2.62	0.08	24.95	C2	1 – C2
1.00	2.66	2.99	13.01	C1	0 - C1
2.52	0.77	2.12	37.65	C3	2 – C3
2.94	1.61	2.82	41.41	C3	2 – C3
2.40	1.71	2.85	33.23	C3	2 – C3
0.23	0.26	1.91	12.05	C1	0 – C1
2.96	2.74	2.07	38.78	C3	2 – C3

CONCLUSION

Three kinds of supervised ML were introduced in this chapter. The basic GP structure, seen in the Chapter 1, has been modified in order to solve all three supervised ML problems. By default, GP was originally developed to solve symbolic regression problems in which numerical inputs/output are used. The chapter showed how GP structure must be modified in order to solve binary or multi-class classification problems. Application of a predefined root node was discussed here in an effective and handy way. Sigmoid and step functions were introduced for binary classification problems and scaled sigmoid or Softmax functions were introduced for multiclass classification problems. Once the tree structure is defined, fitness function and model evaluation must have been adjusted too. The introduced root node functions have more than one output, depending of the problem type, so the model evaluation can be aligned to binary or multiclass classifier. Once the classifiers are defined, the model evaluation for binary and multiclass classifier can be applied.

REFERENCES

Alpaydin, E. (2014). *Introduction to Machine Learning*. Cambridge, MA: The MIT Press.

Back, T., Fogel, D. B., & Michalewicz, Z. (2000). *Evolutionary Computation 1- Basic Algorithms and Operators*. Philadelphia: IOP Publishing Ltd. doi:10.1201/9781420034349

Back, T., Fogel, D. B., & Michalewicz, Z. (2000). *Evolutionary Computation 2- Advanced Algorithms and Operators*. Philadelphia: IOP Publishing Ltd. doi:10.1201/9781420034349

Bennett, N. D., Croke, B. F., Guillaume, J. H., Hamilton, S. H., Jakeman, A. J., Marsili-Libelli, S., . . . Guariso, G. (2013, February). *Characterising Performance of Environmental Models*. Environmental Modelling & Software.

Dean, J. (2014). *Big Data, Data Mining, and Machine Learning*. John Wiley & Sons. doi:10.1002/9781118691786

Fawcett, T. (2006). An Introduction to ROC analysis. *Pattern Recognition Letters*, *27*(8), 861–874. doi:10.1016/j.patrec.2005.10.010

Ferri, C., Hernandez-Orallo, J., & Modroiu, R. (2009). An experimental comparison of performance measures for classiðcation. *Pattern Recognition Letters*, *30*(1), 27–38. doi:10.1016/j.patrec.2008.08.010

Hsieh, W. W. (2009). Machine Learning Methods. In *The Environmental Sciences - Neural Networks and Kernels*. Cambridge, UK: Cambridge University Press.

Iba, H., Paul, T. K., & Hasegawa, Y. (2010). *Applied Genetic Programming and Machine Learning*. New York: CRC Press.

Koza, J. R. (1992). *Genetic Programming: On the Programming of Computers by Means of Natural Selection*. Cambridge, MA: MIT Press.

Kuhn, M., & Johnson, K. (2013). *Applied Predictive Modeling*. New York: Springer. doi:10.1007/978-1-4614-6849-3

Michalewicz, Z. (1996). *Genetic Algorithms + Data Structures = Evolution Programs*. New York: Springer. doi:10.1007/978-3-662-03315-9

Powers, D. M. (2011). Evaluation: From precision, recall and f-measure to roc., informedness, markedness & correlation. *Journal of Machine Learning Technologies*, *2*(1), 37–63.

Quinlan, J. R. (1986). Introduction of Decisions tree. *Machine Learning*, *1*(1), 81–106. doi:10.1007/BF00116251

Russell, S., & Norvig, P. (2010). *Artificial Intelligence: A Modern Approach* (3rd ed.). Pearson Education, Inc.

Sokolova, M., & Lapalme, G. (2009). A systematic analysis of performance measures for classiðcation tasks. *Information Processing & Management*, *45*(4), 427–437. doi:10.1016/j.ipm.2009.03.002

Urvesh, B., Mengjie, Z., & Mark, J. (2010). Genetic Programming for Classiðcation with Unbalanced Data. *13th European Conference*, 1-13.

Wilks, D. S. (2006). *Statistical Methods in the Atmospheric Sciences*. Amsterdam: Elsevier Inc.

This research was previously published in Optimized Genetic Programming Applications; pages 48-101, copyright year 2019 by Medical Information Science Reference (an imprint of IGI Global).

Chapter 28
Programming Language Support for Implementing Machine Learning Algorithms

Anitha Elavarasi S.
Sona College of Technology, India

Jayanthi J.
Sona College of Technology, India

ABSTRACT

Machine learning provides the system to automatically learn without human intervention and improve their performance with the help of previous experience. It can access the data and use it for learning by itself. Even though many algorithms are developed to solve machine learning issues, it is difficult to handle all kinds of inputs data in-order to arrive at accurate decisions. The domain knowledge of statistical science, probability, logic, mathematical optimization, reinforcement learning, and control theory plays a major role in developing machine learning based algorithms. The key consideration in selecting a suitable programming language for implementing machine learning algorithm includes performance, concurrence, application development, learning curve. This chapter deals with few of the top programming languages used for developing machine learning applications. They are Python, R, and Java. Top three programming languages preferred by data scientist are (1) Python more than 57%, (2) R more than 31%, and (3) Java used by 17% of the data scientists.

MACHINE LEARNING

Machine learning (ML) is one of the essential applications of artificial intelligence (AI) that makes the computer system to automatically learn and improve their performance from its own experience without being explicitly trained. ML refers to the set of techniques meant to deal with huge data in the most intelligent way in order to derive actionable insights. The purpose of ML is to automate the data analysis process by constructing algorithms and make appropriate prediction on the new input data that

DOI: 10.4018/978-1-6684-6291-1.ch028

arrives their by enhancing the system performance. A computer program is said to learn from experience E with respect to some class of tasks T and performance measure P, if its performance at tasks in T, as measured by P, improves with experience E (Singh, 2018). Machine learning algorithms are classified into four main types, such as:

- **Supervised Learning Algorithm**: Learning maps an input to an output based on the label value (i.e input-output pairs).
- **Unsupervised Learning Algorithm:** System learns from data which has not been labeled or categorized. Systems can infer a function to describe a hidden structure from unlabeled data.
- **Semi-supervised Learning Algorithm:** Combination of supervised and unsupervised learning. In this approach the system learns by make use of a small amount of labeled data for training from a large amount of unlabeled data in-order to maximize the learning capability.
- **Reinforcement Learning Algorithm**: System ought to take action in an *environment* so as to maximize the *reward.*

Steps Involved in Machine Learning

Machine learning is a method of data analysis that automates analytical model building. I t can learn from data identify patterns, and make decisions with minimal human interventions. The steps involved in solving the given problem are:

- Problem definition
- Data preparation
- Algorithm evaluation
- Performance analysis
- Visualizing results

LANGUAGES SUPPORT FOR MACHINE LEARNING

"Machine Learning – The Scorching Technology Fostering the Growth of several industries"

While you update technology news, you could probably see and hear machine learning everywhere from retail to space for any good reasons. Everyday a new app, product or service discloses that it is using machine learning to get smarter and useful results. It can be used at machine domains starting from on your way to work (Google Maps for suggesting Traffic Route, making an online purchase (on Amazon or Walmart), and for communicating with your friends online (Facebook). Figure 1 shows the popular machine learning languages and tools.

Figure 1. Popular Machine Learning tools

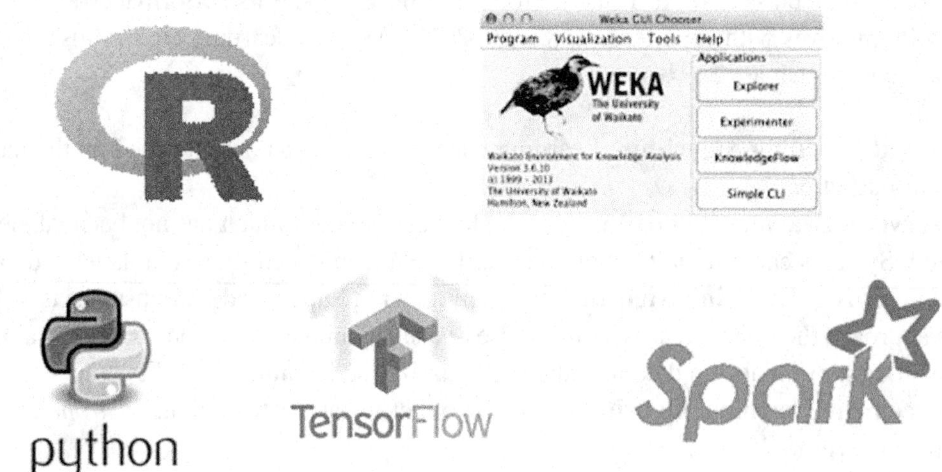

Case Study: Programming Languages and Healthcare Domain

The top healthcare applications that can influence Machine Learning in the world are

1. Medical Image Diagnosis

Computer vision has been one of the most ground-breaking inventions and has reformed the way medical diagnosis is being carried out. The medical image diagnosis has been one of the liveliest applications of machine learning in healthcare. Today, there are many companies that are functioning on using ML to diagnose diseases based on the images taken from various medical imaging instruments.

2. Drug Discovery

Drug discovery is one of the most upfront and fast-growing applications of ML in healthcare. Several new drugs are regularly being discovered to treat various medical disorders. ML speed up this process of drug discovery and reduces the time necessary to develop new medicines. This application is advantageous to pharmaceutical companies which are under a constant pressure of outpacing their competitors, as ML helps them in rapidly developing effective drugs before somebody else in the market does.

3. Robotic Surgery

Robotic surgery is one of the leading edge of ML applications in healthcare and is turning out to be one of the most trustworthy choices in this field. This technology empowers doctors to perform different types of complex surgeries with greater precision. Sometimes surgeries can get extremely complicated as there could be injuries in insignificant and tight areas, which are tough for the surgeons to work on it. Robotic surgery offers better visualization and greater access to such areas, making it easy for the surgeon involved. Although this technique is generally used for minimally invasive procedures, intermittently they are used in traditional open surgical procedures. ML is not directly used in such cases, however its applications, such as robotic and robot-assisted surgeries are proving to be highly beneficial for steadiness of the movement and motion of robotic arms, when being controlled by surgeons.

4. Personalized Medicines

Personalized medicine, also known as precision medicine, is a procedure that differentiates patients into diverse groups, where the medications and treatment plans will be custom-made to an individual patient depending on their menace of disease or foreseen response. As every human being is different, even two people suffering from same illness may require different quantities of medicines. ML can be used to personalize each person's medicine dosage, based on various factors such as medical history, genetic lineage, age, weight, diet, patient history, stress levels, etc. This application also helps patients to decide whether they should undergo certain complicated treatments, such as chemotherapy, surgery, etc., based on factors such as medical history age, etc.

5. Remote Healthcare Assistance

Machine learning is being progressively used in patient monitoring systems and in helping healthcare providers keep a track of the patient's condition in real time. The machine can identify patterns related to the patient's condition, follow-up with health status, detect improvements, and recommend treatments based on the patient's condition. Furthermore, these systems equipped with ML algorithms can call for help in case of any emergencies.

6. Promoting Superior After Care and Healthy Lifestyle

Using ML, devices can be programmed to promote elderly person after care and healthy lifestyle among patients by providing suitable direction about the measures to be followed post treatment. The device can analyse the nature of the patients and the life style followed and appropriate measures to improve their health condition need to be suggested. ML technology can be used to improve quality of life.

Widespread Languages in Practice

Python

Python is a general-purpose, open source high level programming language developed by Python Software Foundation. It was first released in 1991 by Guido van Rossum. Code readability is emphasized by python. Using python, user can create anything from desktop software to web applications and frameworks. It supports dynamic type, automatic memory management, object-oriented programming paradigms, procedural, and standard library. Python programming language runs on any platform, ranging from Windows to Linux to Macintosh, Solaris etc. Machine learning Libraries and Packages included in python are:

- **Numpy** is used for its N-dimensional array objects.
- **Pandas** is a data analysis library that includes dataframes.
- **Matplotlib** is 2D plotting library for creating graphs and plots.
- **Scikit-learn** the algorithms used for data analysis and data mining tasks.
- **Seaborn** a data visualization library based on matplotlib.

Decision Tree Implementation Using Python

Decision tree (2019) uses a tree like model to classify the sample into two or more homogeneous sets based on a criterion. Each internal node represents a test on an attribute and each branch represents an outcome of the test. It is one of the supervised learning algorithms. This can be used for classification and prediction.

Steps Involved in Decision Tree (Analytics, 2016)

Step 1: Import necessary library like panda, numpy etc
Step 2: Create tree object using DecisionTreeClassifier
Step 3: Train the model
Step 4: Predict the output

Coding:

```
#Create Tree Object
1.        model = tree.DecisionTreeClassifier(criterion='gini')
#Train the model using predictor(X) and target(Y) - training data
2.        model.fit(X, y)
3.        model.score(X, y)
#Predict Output for the test data(x_test)
4.        predicted= model.predict(x_test)
```

R Programming Language

R is an open source programming language used for statistical analysis, graphics representation and reporting. R is freely available under the GNU General Public License. It run on a various platform such as Linux, Windows and Mac. R is an interpreted language. The data manipulation, calculation and graphical display facilities included in R [https://www.r-project.org/about.html] are:

- An effective data handling and storage facility.
- A suite of operators for calculations on arrays, in particular matrices.
- A large, coherent, integrated collection of intermediate tools for data analysis.
- Graphical facilities for data analysis and display either on /off -screen.
- A well-developed, simple and effective programming language which includes conditionals, loops, user-defined recursive functions and input and output facilities.

CRAN (Comprehensive R Archive Network), approximately 8,341 packages are available today. The users can install these ML packages simply by using the syntax: install.packages . Some of the machine learning packages included in R are:

- Package e1071 offer Functions for latent class analysis,fuzzy clustering, support vector machines, naive Bayes classifier etc,
- Package C50 offers decision trees and rule based models for pattern recognition application.
- Rpart for building regression trees.
- Deep learning and neural network can be practiced through packages such as nnet,rnn,deepnet etc.
- Package kernlab supports Kernel-based machine learning methods for classification, regression, clustering, dimensionality reduction. Among other methods it includes Support Vector Machines, Spectral Clustering, Kernel PCA etc.
- Optimization using Genetic Algorithms can be practiced through rgenoud, Rmalschains.
- Package arules provides implementations of Apriori, mining frequent itemsets, maximal frequent itemsets, closed frequent itemsets and association rules.
- Package frbs implements Fuzzy Rule-based Systems for regression and classification. Package RoughSets provides implementations of the rough set theory (RST) and the fuzzy rough set theory (FRST).

Linear Regression Implementation in R

Linear regression (Prabhakaran, n.d.) establishes a linear relationship between the predictor variable and the response variable. It is used to predict the value of an outcome variable based on one or more input predictor variables. The function used for building linear models is lm() which takes in two main arguments, namely: formula and data.

lm(sales ~ youtube, data = marketing)

Scatter plots can help visualize any linear relationships between the dependent and independent variables which can be drawn using

scatter.smooth(x=Attribute_x, y=Attribute_y, main="TitleX vs Y")

Correlation suggests the level of linear dependence between two variables. It can take values between -1 to +1. This can be calculated using cor().

Steps Involved in Linear Regression Process

Step 1: Load the data.
Step 2: Create the training and test data samples from original data.
Step 3: Develop the model on the training data and use it to predict it on the test data
Step 4: Evaluate the measures.
Step 5: Compute the prediction accuracy and error rates

Coding:

```
# Use the marketing data set which contains the impact of three
# advertising medias (youtube, facebook and newspaper) on sales.
# In-order to predict future sales based on advertising budget
# spent on youtube regression model is developed.
# load and inspect 4 rows of marketing data

1.        head(marketing, 4)

# linear model using lm()

2.        model <- lm(sales ~ youtube, data = marketing)

# Add regression line to the scatter plot

3.        ggplot(marketing, aes(x = youtube, y = sales)) +
 geom_point() +
   stat_smooth()
4.        correlation_acc <-cor(youtube, sales)
```

Java Machine Learning Library

Java-ML (Java machine learning library) consists of a collection of machine learning algorithms for classification, clustering, regression, filtering, etc (Abeel, de Peer, and Saeys, 2009). It provides a common interface for various machine learning algorithms. Well documented source code and plenty of code samples and tutorials for library 0.1.7 is available in the URL: http://java-ml.sourceforge.net/api/0.1.7/

A set of machine learning library and 170 data set from the well-known repositories (UCI Machine Learning Repository) is available in the URL: https://sourceforge.net/projects/java-ml/files/. Some of the machine learning library available in Java-ML are:

- **Net.sf.javaml.classification:** Provides several classification algorithms
- **Net.sf.javaml.classification.evaluation**: Provides algorithms and measures to evaluate classification algorithms.
- **Net.sf.javaml.clustering:** Provides algorithms to cluster data.
- **Net.sf.javaml.core.kdtree:** Provides a KD-tree implementation for fast range- and nearest-neighbors-queries.
- **Net.sf.javaml.featureselection:** Provides algorithms to evaluation the worth of attributes and attribute sets.
- **Net.sf.javaml.featureselection.ranking:** Provides feature ranking algorithms.

Clustering Implementation using Java ML

Clustering is the task of grouping a set of data objects such that objects in the same group are more similar to each other than to those in other groups. In other words data elements are cluster in such a manner that the distance between elements within a group should be minimum, and data element among different cluster should be maximum. It is one of the unsupervised learning algorithms.

Steps involved in k-means Clustering process:

Step 1: Loading the input file: Java-ML supports CSV, TSV and ARFF formatted files.

Dataset data = FileHandler.loadDataset(**new** File("iris.data"), 4, ",");

The first parameter of loadDataset is the file to load the data from. The second parameter is the index of the class label (zero-based) and the final parameter is the separator used to split the attributes in the file.

Dataset data = ARFFHandler.loadARFF(**new** File("iris.arff"), 4);

the ARFFHandler only has two arguments, the first one to indicate the file that should be loaded and the second one to indicate the index of the class label.

Step 2: Clustering process using k-Means Algorithm: C*reate four number of cluster using k-means algorithm*

Clusterer km=**new** KMeans(4);

Step 3: Cluster evaluation: *Create a measure for the cluster quality*

ClusterEvaluation sse= **new** SumOfSquaredErrors();

Java-ML provides a large number of cluster evaluation measures that are provided in the package net.sf.javaml.clustering.evaluation (Java.ml, n.d.).

Coding:

```
Dataset data = FileHandler.loadDataset(new File("iris.data"), 4, ",");
Clusterer km=new KMeans(4);
Dataset[] clusters = km.cluster(data);
ClusterEvaluation sse= new SumOfSquaredErrors();
double score=sse.score(clusters);
```

Figure 2 shows the comparison of popular machine learning software between 2015 and 2017. More than 50% of the people use python and R language for their machine learning applications.

Figure 2. Comparison of machine learning software

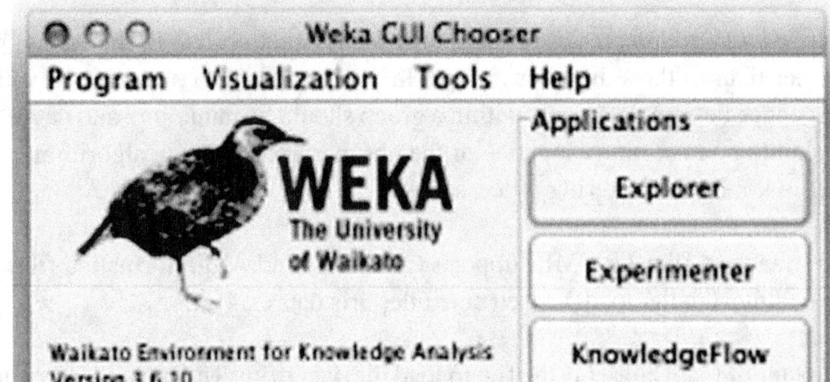

MACHINE LEARNING TOOL KIT

Weka

Weka is an open source **Java**-based workbench consist of a collection of machine learning algorithms for the purpose of data analysis, data mining and predictive modelling. It has tools for data preparation, classification, regression, clustering, association rules mining, and visualization. The algorithms can either be applied directly to a dataset or called from your own Java code. Weka can be downloaded from the URL http://www.cs.waikato.ac.nz/ml/weka/. Successful installation of weka (Aksenova, 2004) is shown in figure 2 with four different option for the user to select, such as:

- Simple CLI provides a simple command-line interface and allows direct execution of Weka commands.
- Explorer is an environment for exploring data.
- Experimenter is an environment for performing experiments and conducting statistical tests between learning schemes.
- KnowledgeFlow is a Java-Beans-based interface for setting up and running machine learning experiments.

WEKA supports decision trees and lists, instance-based classifiers, support vector machines, multilayer perceptrons, logistic regression, and bayes' nets.

Figure 3. Weka Home screen

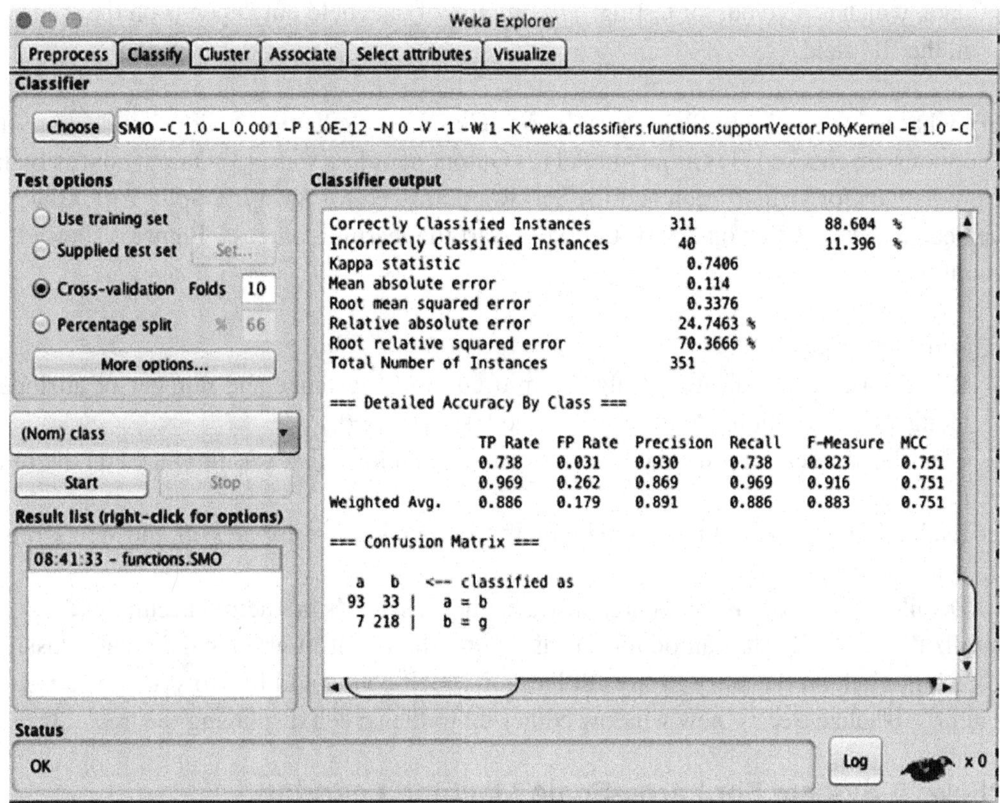

Implementation of Classification using Weka

Classification is the process of accurately predicting the data to a target class. For example to classify whether a person can be identified as low, medium, or high credit risks person. This approach uses class label in-order to categorise the person.

Steps Involved in Classification (Aksenova, 2004)

1. **Loading the Dataset:** It supports Attribute-Relation File Format (ARFF) file format.
2. **Choosing a Classifier:** Click on 'Choose' button in the 'Classifier' box just below the tabs and select the required algorithm (for example: C4.5 classifier WEKA -> Classifiers -> Trees ->J48.)
3. **Setting Test Options**: select the appropriate the test options given below
    a. Use training set. Evaluates the classifier on how well it predicts the class of the instances it was trained on.
    b. Supplied test set. Evaluates the classifier on how well it predicts the class of a set of instances loaded from a file. Clicking on the 'Set…' button brings up a dialog allowing you to choose the file to test on.
    c. Cross-validation. Evaluates the classifier by cross-validation, using the number of folds that are entered in the 'Folds' text field.

d. Percentage split. Evaluates the classifier on how well it predicts a certain percentage of the data, which is held out for testing. The amount of data held out depends on the value entered in the '%' field.

Identify what is included into the output. In the 'Classifier evaluation options' make sure that the following options are checked (1) Output model (2) Output per-class stats, (3) Output confusion matrix, (4) Store predictions for visualization and (5) Set 'Random seed for Xval / % Split' to 1. Once the options have been selected, Click on 'Start' button to start the learning process. Figure 3 shows the classification output.

4. Analyzing
    - Run Information indicate the algorithm used, no of instance and number of attribute used along with the split mode for training and test data used.
    - Classifier model is a pruned decision tree in textual form that was produced on the full training data.
    - Evaluation on test split. This part of the output gives estimates of the tree's predictive performance,
    - Detailed Accuracy By Class demonstrates the classifier's prediction accuracy.
5. **Visualization:** WEKA has an option of displaying the result in graphical format (classification tree). Right-click on the entry in 'Result list' for which you would like to visualize a tree. Select the item 'Visualize tree'; a new window comes up to the screen displaying the tree.

Tensorflow: A System For Large-Scale Machine Learning

TensorFlow is an open-source library used for machine learning applications which are large and heterogeneous in nature. It uses the notation of dataflow-based programming abstraction for various computation processes both within and across the machine. Wrapping of scripting and dataflow graph enables the user to make use of varied architecture without modifying the underlying system (Abadi et al., 2016). The dataflow graph expresses the communication between sub computations explicitly, thus making it easy to execute independent computations in parallel and to partition computations across multiple devices. Tensor Processing Units (TPUs) makes the architecture more flexible for the developer. The execution of Tensorflow application requires two phases, first phase defines the symbolic dataflow graph and the second phase executes an optimized version of the program. Performance can be improved with the help of multicore CPUs and GPUs running the deep learning algorithm and their by saving the power. TensorFlow offers various APIs to develop applications on desktop, mobile, web, and cloud. TensorFlow Keras provides API for creating and training deep learning models. Classification, regression, over fitting and under fitting models can be developed using TensorFlow model

Building simple image classifier (TensorFlow, n.d.) using Tensor Flow

Step 1: Import the TensorFlow library into your program
Step 2: Load and prepare the MNIST dataset. Convert the samples from integers to floating-point numbers
Step 3: Build the tf.keras model by stacking layers. Select an optimizer and loss function used for training
Step 4: Train and evaluate image classifier model:

Figure 4. Classification output

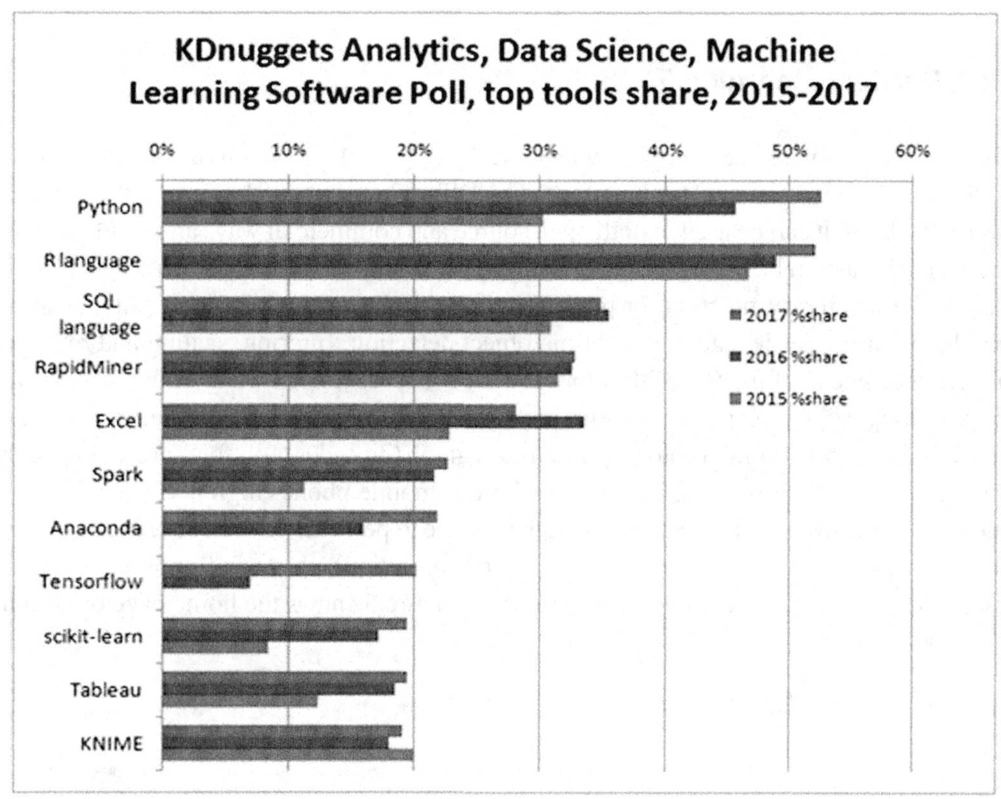

Coding:

```
import tensorflow as tf

mnist = tf.keras.datasets.mnist
(x_train, y_train),(x_test, y_test) = mnist.load_data()
x_train, x_test = x_train / 255.0, x_test / 255.0

model = tf.keras.models.Sequential([
  tf.keras.layers.Flatten(input_shape=(28, 28)),
  tf.keras.layers.Dense(512, activation=tf.nn.relu),
   tf.keras.layers.Dropout(0.2),
   tf.keras.layers.Dense(10, activation=tf.nn.softmax)
 ])

 model.compile(optimizer='adam',
              loss='sparse_categorical_crossentropy',
              metrics=['accuracy'])

```

```
model.fit(x_train, y_train, epochs=5)
model.evaluate(X_test,y_test)
```

Dlib-ml: A Machine Learning Toolkit

Dlib-ml is open source software developed by Davis E. King (2009). It contains a wide range of machine learning algorithms developed in C++ language. The Dlib-ml toolkit can be accessed from the URL - http://dlib.net/ml.html. It can be used in both open source and commercial ways and is released as Boost Software License. This can be configured and installed on Windows, Linux and Mac operating system. It provides numerous library function for performing tasks related to image processing (management and manipulation of images ie feature extraction, object detection, filtering, scaling and rotation, visualization etc.), machine learning (algorithm for classification, regression, clustering, unsupervised and semi supervised algorithm, deep learning etc), networking (to provide network service- socket API), algorithms for sorting and finding cryptographic hashes, graph (provides tools for representing undirected and directed graphs) etc. Dlib-ml can be used in robotics, mobile phones high performance computing environment. Dlib-ml also provides certain python interface to perform the task of classification (binary classifier), image processing (face detection, jitter, face recognition), clustering, support vector machine (structural SVM, SVM rank) and video object tracking. Figure 5 shows the home page of Dlib library.

Figure 5. Home page of DLib library

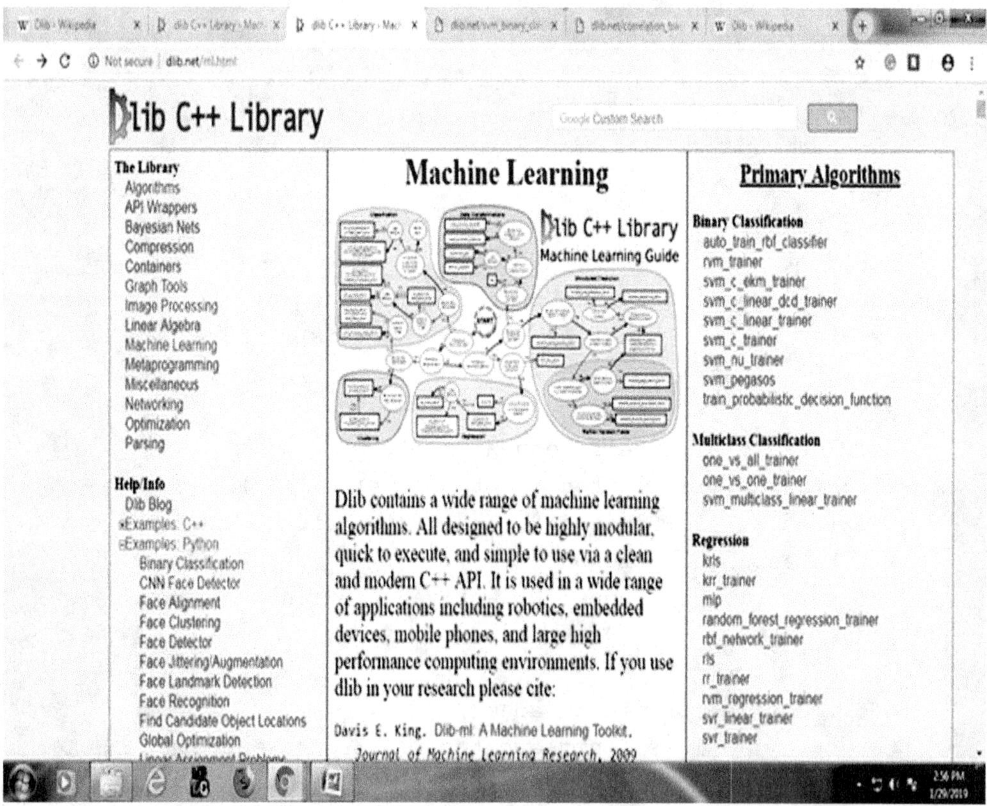

Scikit-Learn: Machine Learning in Python

Scikit-learn an easy-to-use interface integrated with the Python language (Pedregosa et al., 2011) shown in figure 6 . It provides python based machine learning algorithm for both supervised and unsupervised problems. It has been given under simplified BSD (Berkeley Software Distribution) license to promote its usage both on academic and commercial sectors. BSD licenses are a family of permissive free software licenses, imposing minimal restrictions on the use and distribution of covered software (Scikt-learn, 2019). Scikit- learn can be accessed from the URL - http://scikit-learn.sourceforge.net. The features that differentiate Scikit- learn from other python based machine learning tool kit are (1) it depends only on numpy and scipy to facilitate easy distribution (2) it focuses on imperative programming (3) it incorporates compiled code. The technologies involved on scikit-learn are (1) Numpy the base data structure to handle data and model parameters, (2)Scipy provides algorithms for linear algebra, sparse matrix representation and basic statistical functions and (3) Cython combines C and Python to reach higher performance.

Figure 6. Home page of Scikit

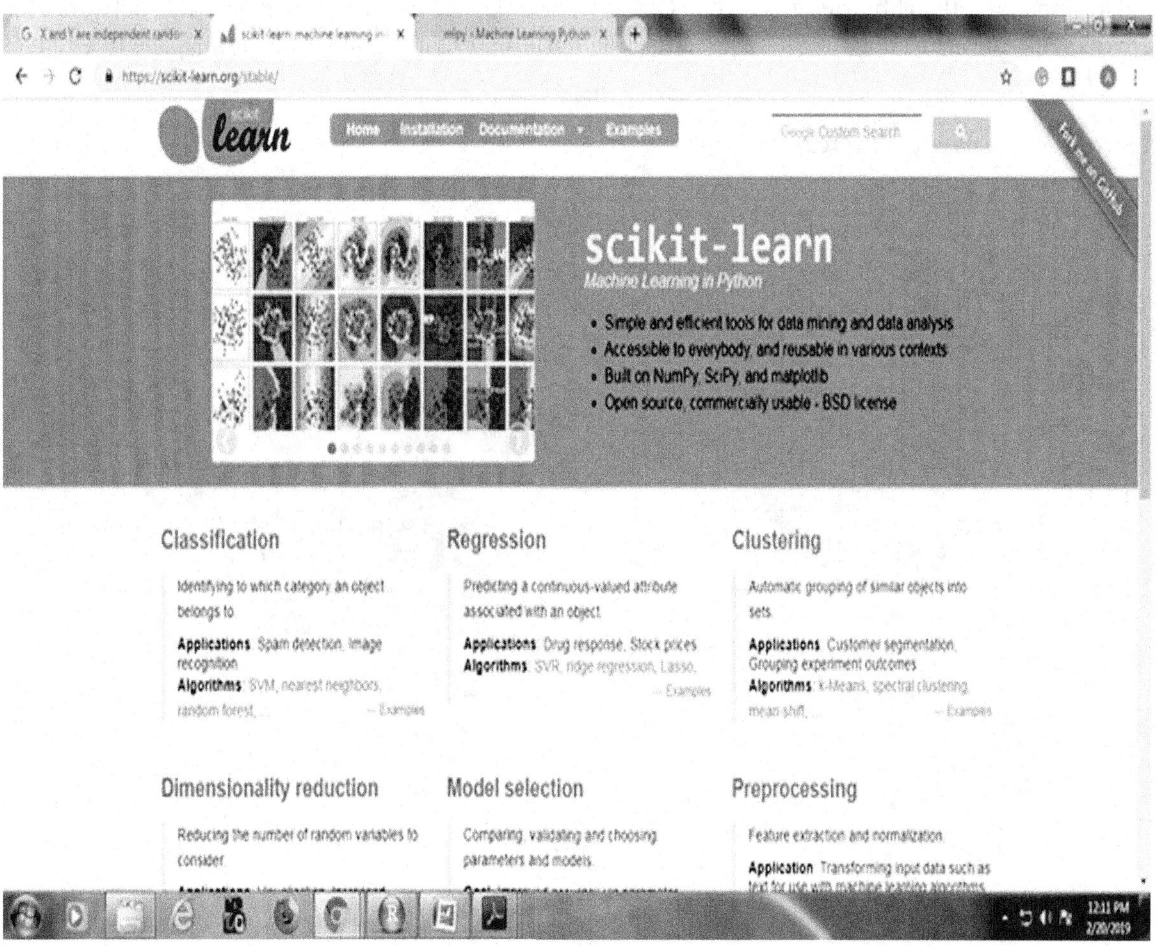

Orange: Data Mining Toolbox in Python

Orange is an open source data analysis tool kit released under General Public License (GPL) (Demsar et al., 2013). It runs on Windows, Mac OS and Linux operating system. Versions up to 3.0 include core components in C++ with wrappers in Python are available on GitHub. It provides a component-based design which is simple to use and ensure high interactivity through scripting. This can be used by any type of user such as experienced user, programmers, students etc. The features offered by orange are:

1. data management and preprocessing,
2. classification,
3. regression,
4. association,
5. ensembles,
6. clustering,
7. evaluation,
8. projections.

The popular Python libraries included in Orange are numpy for linear algebra operation, networkx for networks operation and matplotlib for visualization purpose. Figure 7 shows the home page of Orange.

Figure 7. Home page of Orange

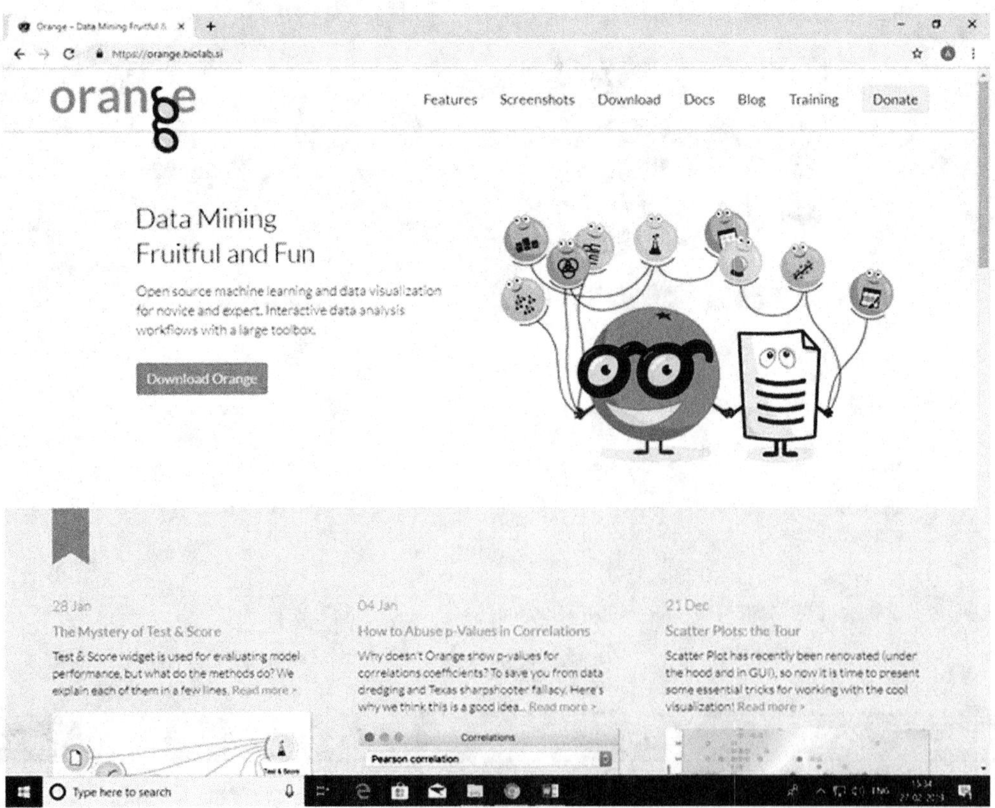

Implementation of Naive Bayes using Orange

Naïve Bayes is a classification method based on the Bayes theorem. It is based on a probabilistic approach. Download and install Orange from github. On successful installation use the python environment or command line to import orange. Orange supports discrete attributes for naïve Bayes algorithm.

Steps to build naïve bayes

Step 1: Load the required library.
Step 2: Load the data set.
Step 3: Constructs naive Bayesian learner using the class NaiveBayesLearner.()

Coding

```
# Load the lenses dataset and constructs naive Bayesian learner
# Apply classifier to the first 100 data instances
import Orange
lenses = Orange.data.Table('lenses')
nb = Orange.classification.NaiveBayesLearner()
classifier = nb(lenses)
classifier(lenses[0:100], True)
```

MLPY: Machine Learning Python

Machine Learning Python (mlpy) (Albanese et al.., 2012) is an open source python machine learning library distributed under the GNU General Public License version 3. This can be accessed using the URL: http://mlpy.sourceforge.net and its home page is shown in figure8. mlpy is built on top of the NumPy/SciPy packages. It supports methods for both supervised and unsupervised problems such as Support Vector Machines, Linear Discriminate analysis LDA, k-nearest neighbor, Hierarchical Clustering, k-means clustering, Principal Component Analysis (PCA), Wavelet Transform etc.

Table 1 shows the various popular machine learning algorithm supported by various toolkit.

Table 1. Support of machine learning algorithm by various toolkit

Algorithm	scikit-learn	mlpy	Orange	Dlib
Support Vector machine	Yes	yes	Yes	yes
k-Nearest Neighbors	Yes	Yes	Yes	No
PCA	Yes	Yes	Yes	No
k-Means	Yes	Yes	No	Yes
Hierarchical Clustering	Yes	Yes	Yes	No
Logistic Regression	Yes	Yes	Yes	No

Figure 8. Home page of mlpy

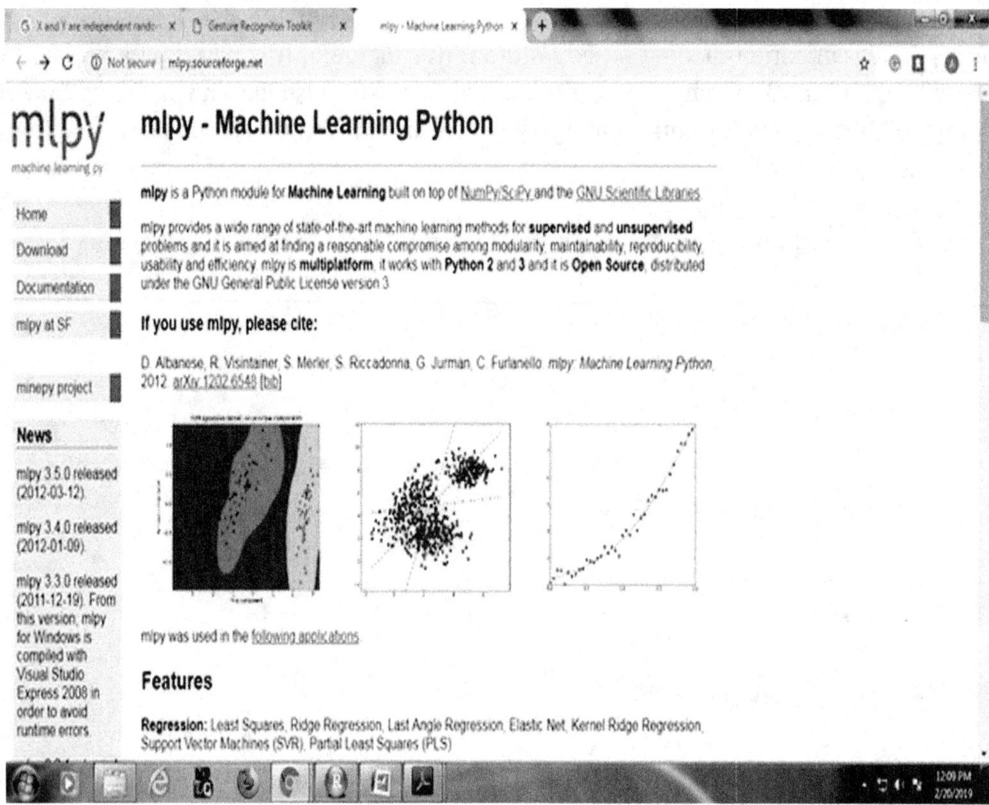

Programming Language Selection for Healthcare Domain

JAVA

The language which is useful in providing solution to a healthcare problems (Krill, 2014) using machine learning is plenty. Most widely used languages would be java, Python, R etc. If the need is on maintaining (Electronic Health Record) EHR, and if no managerial restrictions and governance for what to use, then it is better to with Java. Since it consisting of wider range of API's that supports machine learning.

Java offers the widest collection of deliver options: desktop apps, server apps, web apps, cloud apps, etc. It's the language that creates the least number of conventions about what platform you're running, providing a reliable performance across multiple devices. Since medical data are highly secured, Java provides some of the best security out there, both in terms of software quality and built-in support for encryption, which is required by HIPAA. Java is logically robust, accommodating scalable APIs better than any other language.

It supports to create Cloud based EHR's and Java remains a critical technology that fascinates powerful interest and passion always. Java is a staple of enterprise computing world to solve several sensitive issues like healthcare. Java anchors Android apps development where Apps becomes the part and part of life.

Java EE (Enterprise Edition) 8 is also in the works and is expected to focus on supporting the latest Web standards, ease of development, and cloud support. Python is well-known among the most commonly used programming languages in the world. It lets you work more effective and productive and what's more, it is also considered to be one of the safest programming languages.

PYTHON

Python is widely used to produce web-applications for medical services. Software development using Python also allows the following capabilities:

- Web and Internet Development
- Database Access
- Desktop GUIs
- Scientific & Numeric
- Education
- Network Programming

Its main performance indicators in development process comprise ability to meet deadlines, quality and volume of code. In order to achieve these indicators during the development process one of the commonly used framework is Django. This framework is based on Python was developed in July 2005. Django promises a trustworthy list of built-in modules that are very useful and can be customized. Also it is provided with built-in security provisions against the three main sorts of web app attacks.

Being secure and having open-ended opportunities of modifying Django framework, it's been opted by many developers to realize requests and meet requirements for any business idea related to telemedicine and eHealth projects. There is a framework in Python for building API called Flask. It is often used for building prototypes which is very much helpful in delivering fruitful products. It guarantees stability and security features.

Advantages of using Python in Healthcare

1. Python, Django and other frameworks are enabled with quality principles agreeable with HIPAA checklist.
2. Supports healthcare projects in the Big data project domain too.
3. It is in line with the Database back-end assistance.
4. Perform platform independence with characteristics focused on iPods, iPhones and the web.

Python healthcare applications are used by many medical start-ups. Some of them are:

1. **Roam Analytics** is a platform that uses complete contextual data and machine learning to empower biopharmaceutical and medical device companies. The predictive insights are useful making knowledgeable decisions and provide better treatments. It could achieve the best possible treatments.
2. **AiCure** is an NIH and VC-founded healthcare start up. AiCure practices artificial intelligence to visually confirm medication absorption. The clinically-validated platform works on smartphones to reduce risk and optimize patient behaviour.

3. **Drchrono** is an American company that provides a software as a service patient care platform consisting of a Web- and cloud-based app for doctors and patients that makes electronic health records available digitally. It supports practice management and medical billing services.

CONCLUSION

Machine Learning is learning from data. Machine Learning Programs are hardware intensive as they include a number of intense mathematical computations like matrix multiplications and all. With the advent of GPU's, TPU's and faster processor computations are not that time consuming. Machine Learning is a product of statistics, mathematics, and computer science. As a practice, it has grown phenomenally in the last few years. It has empowered companies to build products like recommendation engines, self-driving cars etc. Libraries tend to be relatively stable and free of bugs. If we use appropriate libraries, it reduces the amount of code that is to be written. The fewer the lines of code, the better the functionality. Therefore, in most cases, it is better to use a library than to write our own code. An open source library consists of all the minute details that are dropped out of scientific literature. This chapter covers some of the case studies using python, java, R etc would motivate and use relevant tools for the implementation of machine learning algorithms. Based on the requirement the language for implementation can be selected and it should always ensures the quality.

REFERENCES

A Complete Tutorial on Tree Based Modeling from Scratch. (n.d.). Retrieved from https://www.analyticsvidhya.com/blog/2016/04/complete-tutorial-tree-based-modeling-scratch-in-python

Abadi, M., Barham, P., Chen, J., Chen, Z., Davis, A., & Dean, J. (2016). Tensorflow: a system for large-scale machine learning. OSDI, 16, 265-283.

Abeel, T., de Peer, Y. V., & Saeys, Y. (2009). Java-ML: A Machine Learning Library. *Journal of Machine Learning Research*, *10*, 931–934.

Aksenova, S. (2004). *Machine Learning with WEKA WEKA Explorer Tutorial for WEKA Version 3.4. 3.* sabanciuniv.edu

Albanese, D., Visintainer, R., Merler, S., Riccadonna, S., Jurman, G., & Furlanello, C. (2012). *mlpy: Machine learning python.* arXiv preprint arXiv:1202.6548

Decision Tree. (2019, May 31). Retrieved from https://en.wikipedia.org/wiki/Decision_tree

Demšar, J., Curk, T., Erjavec, A., Gorup, Č., Hočevar, T., & Milutinovič, M. (2013). Orange: Data mining toolbox in Python. *Journal of Machine Learning Research*, *14*(1), 2349–2353.

King, D. E. (2009). Dlib-ml: A machine learning toolkit. *Journal of Machine Learning Research*, *10*(Jul), 1755–1758.

Krill, P. (2014, September 30). *Four reasons to stick with Java, and four reasons to dump it*. Retrieved from https://www.javaworld.com/article/2689406/four-reasons-to-stick-with-java-and-four-reasons-to-dump-it.html

Pedregosa, F., Varoquaux, G., Gramfort, A., Michel, V., Thirion, B., & Grisel, O. (2011). Scikit-learn: Machine learning in Python. *Journal of Machine Learning Research*, *12*, 2825–2830.

Prabhakaran, S. (n.d.). *Eval(ez_write_tag([[728,90],'r_statistics_co-box-3','ezslot_2',109,'0']));Linear Regression*. Retrieved from http://r-statistics.co/Linear-Regression.html

Scikit-learn. (2019, May 30). Retrieved from https://en.wikipedia.org/wiki/Scikit-learn

Singh, H. (2018, June 26). *Machine Learning- What, Why, When and How?* Retrieved from https://towardsdatascience.com/machine-learning-what-why-when-and-how-9a2f244647a4

TensorFlow. (n.d.). Retrieved from https://www.tensorflow.org/tutorials

The R Project for Statistical Computing. (n.d.). Retrieved from https://www.r-project.org/

Weka 3: Machine Learning Software in Java. (n.d.). Retrieved from http://www.cs.waikato.ac.nz/ml/weka

This research was previously published in the Handbook of Research on Applications and Implementations of Machine Learning Techniques; pages 402-421, copyright year 2020 by Engineering Science Reference (an imprint of IGI Global).

Chapter 29
Data Driven Symbiotic Machine Learning for the Identification of Motion-Based Action Potentials

Volkhard Klinger
FHDW Hannover, Hanover, Germany

ABSTRACT

Understanding and modelling technical and biological processes is one of the basic prerequisites for the management and control of such processes. With the help of identification, the interdependencies of such processes can be deciphered and thus a model can be achieved. The verification of the models enables the quality of the models to be assessed. This article focuses on the identification and verification of motion and sensory feedback-based action potentials in peripheral nerves. Based on the acquisition of action potentials, the identification process correlates physiological and motion-based parameters to match movement trajectories and the corresponding action potentials. After a brief description of a prototype of a biosignal acquisition and identification system, this article introduces a new identification method, the symbiotic cycle, based on the well-known term symbiotic simulation. As an example, this article presents a data-driven method to create a human readable model without using presampled data. The closed-loop identification method is integrated into this symbiotic cycle.

1. INTRODUCTION

Identification of technical processes for analysis, optimization and control is a major challenge. This focus also includes the use of identification methods and applications for the biotechnology sector. In this project identification in particular plays an important role in enabling an interface between the brain and the control of movement based on data from peripheral nerves.

DOI: 10.4018/978-1-6684-6291-1.ch029

So, the identification of motion- and sensory feedback-based action potentials in peripheral nerves is a great challenge in medical technology. It is the prerequisite for applications like prosthesis control or limb stimulation. Based on the acquisition of action potentials, the identification process correlates physiological and motion-based parameters to match movement trajectories and the corresponding action potentials.

The identification method used in this context is based on the continuous mode symbiotic cycle, combining a physical system, a simulation system and an agent-based machine learning system. As an example, a data-driven method to create a human readable model without using presampled data is presented. All components in the system interact in a symbiotic way. The result of each component is used as an input by the others and vice versa.

First of all, the prototype of biosignal acquisition and identification system using a multistage agent-based solution builder identification method is introduced (Klinger and Klauke, 2013) and then the closed-loop identification method, implemented using a symbiotic continuous system (Aydt, Turner, Cai and Low, 2008; Aydt, Turner, Cai and Low, 2009) is presented. The prototype is acting as the physical target system in the symbiotic cycle, presented subsequently. This paper focuses on the interaction between the identification method, based on a data driven approach and its verification. We present the closed-loop identification method, implemented using a symbiotic continuous system (Aydt, Turner, Cai and Low, 2008; Aydt, Turner, Cai and Low, 2009), consisting of a robotic based trajectory generation, the nerve simulation and an agent-based machine learning system. We introduce the model generation process and show the closed-loop verification approach of the identification method.

1.1. The Prototype for a Biosignal Acquisition and Identification System

The key challenge is the human machine interface of prosthesis and its movement control. The objective is to use biosignals for the information transfer between human being and prosthesis. So an interface is needed to interfere between the command-level and the actuator- and sensor- level. The approach discussed in this paper is based on the direct use of the action potentials of peripheral neural bundles via an electroneurogram (ENG) (Gold, Hence, and Koch, 2007; Neymotin, Lytton, Olypher, and Fenton, 2011). So, the employment of invasive intra-neural sensors (Micera, Carpaneto, and Raspopovic, 2010; Micera, Citi, Rigosa et al., 2010; Raspopovic, Capogrosso, Petrini et al., 2014) is in this project not in the focus, but the identification (Cesqui, Tropea, Micera, and Krebs, 2013) of motion-based action potentials is the proposal to realize a smart minimal-invasive solution. To record ENG-signals with a very low amplitude, which are only of the order of a few microvolts, a special frontend-hardware/software system has been designed, realized in two different Hardware- and Software-prototypes, introduced in (Klinger, 2015) and (Klinger and Klauke, 2013). In this paper, the focus is on a new combined identification and verification method, taking advantage of a continuous symbiotic system (Aydt, Turner, Cai and Low, 2008; Aydt, Turner, Cai and Low, 2009). This work continues the former work about system identification presented in (Bohlmann, Klauke, Klinger, and Szczerbicka, 2011; Bohlmann, Klinger, and Szczerbicka, 2009; Bohlmann, Klinger, and Szczerbicka, 2010).

The prototype of a Smart Modular Biosignal Acquisition, Identification and Control System (SMoBAICS), shown in Figure 1, integrates all necessary tasks (Hazan, Zugaro, and Buzsáki, 2006).

The biosignal acquisition is done by the Modular Biosignal Acquisition System (MBASY)-subsystem, the next generation of our own frontend-hardware/software-system. The MBASY is redesigned to get a better functionality and to optimize the modular concept (Klinger, 2015). The central part of the iden-

Figure 1. System overview

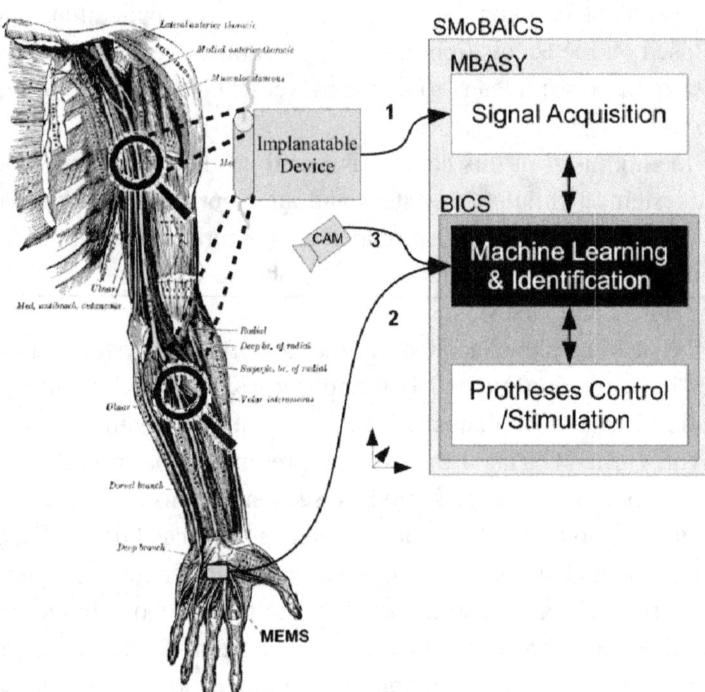

tification process is integrated in the biosignal identification and control system) (BICS). It consists of two parts: the machine learning & identification and the control/stimulation from a prosthesis. While the second part is designed by state-of-the-art technology, the new machine learning & identification method, presented in this paper, is composed of multi-agent-based (Weiss, 2015; Alkhateeb, 2011) optimization algorithm and an evolutionary correlation of different types of nerve signals and of additional information like camera positioning or micro-electro-mechanical systems (MEMS) (Klinger, 2016).

Before describing the overall function one aspect regarding the learning procedure has been taken into consideration. The objective of SMoBAICS is the action potential based control or stimulation of upper or lower limbs of handicapped human beings. SMoBAICS provides not only a base identification step (learning phase) but an ongoing supervision (operating phase). Obviously, the operating phase has to be executed on a small body mounted system but in this paper the focus is not on this system detail.

In Figure 1 a typical application is shown, the cuff-electrode is implanted in the upper arm enclosing a neural bundle. The action potentials are recorded by the MBASY and passed to the BICS (1). Two additional information streams are used by the BICS for the action potential based identification: a camera-based motion capturing, used during the learning phase (3), and a motion tracking device at the end effector (e.g. the hand), used during the operational phase (2). These data streams are important for the identification.

1.2. Identification and SMoBAICS

The new machine learning and identification method is the most complex module within SMoBAICS. To understand or control any type of complex process a process model is essential, an empirical process description does not provide a detailed functional and time related process specification. The process model, based on the combination of physical equations and a graph structure, allows the reconstruction of process behaviour, the optimization of the entire process and a forecast of process behaviour. This paper describes a new method to generate a process model from scratch, without using any type of initial model description. This method is based on machine learning and symbiotic simulation and describes a type of symbiotic cycle. The model generation is a continuous process and provides therefore an adaptation to changing process parameters, like friction or bearing clearance, boundary conditions and constraints.

2. DATA DRIVEN SYMBIOTIC MACHINE LEARNING

Based on the classification of symbiotic simulation in (Aydt, Turner, Cai and Low, 2008; Aydt, Turner, Cai and Low, 2009), the symbiotic cycle combines a, a, a and a data driven agent based online machine learning system with a real-world process (Trianni, 2014). In Table 1 the different classes of symbiotic systems are shown corresponding to (Aydt, Turner, Cai and Low, 2009).

Table 1. Overview of various classes of symbiotic simulation systems (Aydt, Turner, Cai and Low, 2009)

Class	Purpose	Loop	Meaning of	Type of
			What-if Scenarios	Symbiosis
SSCS	Control of a	Closed	Control	Mutualism/
	physical system	(Direct)	options	Parasitism
SSDSS	Support of an	Closed	Decision	Mutualism/
	external decision maker	(Indirect)	options	Parasitism
SSFS	Forecasting of a	Open	Different assumptions for	Commensalism
	physical system		environmental conditions	
SSMVS	Validation of a	Open	Alternative models or	Commensalism
	simulation system		different parameters	
SSADS	Detection of anomalies	Open	Reference model only	Commensalism
	either in the physical system			
	or in the simulation model			

The central challenge in this paper is on the one hand to create a system which can produce a human readable model without the existence of prior data, model or knowledge (Yang, Koziel, and Leifsson, 2013). And on the other hand, to be able to simulate and/or predict the behaviour of the system without a known model. Both challenges presuppose each other. First it is basically a kind of chicken or the egg dilemma. The simulation system needs a model, this is produced by the machine learning system, which needs some sort of input data, but this data is produced by the motion of the robot, finally controlled by the simulator. The basic method proposed and demonstrated in this paper is the symbiotic solution. If all steps are running in parallel the central dilemma disappears. This is what is called the symbiotic cycle, shown in Figure 2.

Figure 2. Symbiotic cycle

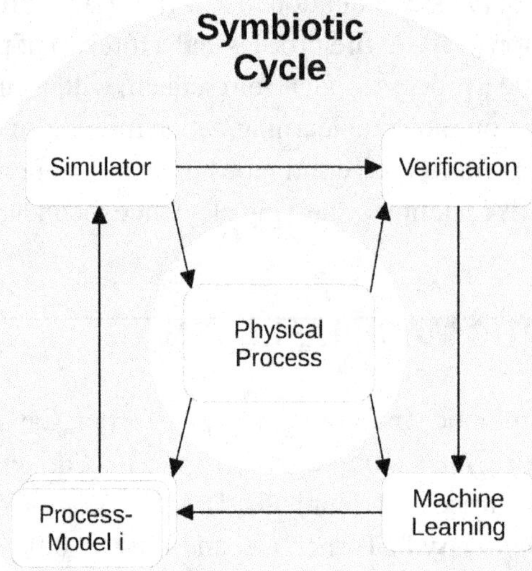

All components of the self-learning system are connected by using a streaming event-driven approach. If an event which could cause an action in a different component is happening, it is immediately streamed to the corresponding component. In fact, there is no macroscopic sequence or stepping between components. Everything is processed simultaneously in parallel. The machine learning module for example continuously outputs model candidates at a relatively unknown rate. The simulator then reacts by profiling the solution proposal. Clearly this could lead to a short-time overload of modules, if some burst input is generated. To minimize this effect, buffering and load balancing technologies are used.

In the following subsections the different components of the symbiotic cycle are introduced in more detail. Five modules form this symbiotic cycle which is application independent.

2.1. Process

The process block covers all physical relations of the considered process. Analog inputs or outputs have to be transformed using analog-to-digital- or digital-to-analog-converters. For the acquisition of biosignals, essential for the SMoBAICS approach, the specific MBSY-system is necessary providing a frontend-electronic for sub-micro voltage signals, like ENG (Klinger, 2015). The interface to the digital in-/out-signals is handled using the process data streaming protocol (PDSP) managing distributed process data flows (Bohlmann, Klinger, Szczerbicka, and Becker, 2010). This protocol is designed to be used in mixed continuous and discrete environments (Zeigler, Praehofer, and Kim, 2000) referred to as hybrid. Focusing on symbiotic simulation (Fujimoto, Lunceford, Page, and Uhrmacher, 2002), PDSP is primary designed to satisfy four modes of operation (analytic, transparent, online, prediction); here the focus is on the online mode. In this mode PDSP is used to simulate a process and transmit the results back to the process. The data is directly transmitted between the physical process and the simulator. Therefore, latency is minimized although proxy servers may be necessary for large scale simulations.

2.2. Simulator

In the simulator block two different approaches are used, dependent from the application. For general purpose it is a Java based simulation system specifically designed for high speed online and symbiotic simulations. The simulator especially has online compiling capabilities, e.g. models can be compiled during run-time in memory and then dynamically injected into the simulator. It is capable to dynamically load or receive models (basically any kind of java program) and simulate multiple isolated instances in the same memory/thread context. The simulator combines Java class loading mechanism and byte code enhancing to calculate user defined metrics while processing prior structural unknown models on the fly. In combination with an OSGI framework, PDSP can be directly embedded to running simulations.

For the specific application of ENG -based identification currently the well-established NEURON framework for empirically-based simulations of neurons and networks of neurons is used (Carnevale and Hines, 2006), (Coates, Larson-Prior, Wolpert, and Prior, 2003), (Law and Kelton, 2000). The different constraints, like myelin structures, all-or-none, two directions of information flow, frequency borders of the action potentials, etc. has been taken into account. We have configured the simulator and realized a complex neural bundle including our cuff-electrode setup to generate verification data for several information transfer scenarios. Therefore, a cross-sectional area of the nerve bundle is part of the configuration, shown in Figure 3.

This simple model, used to provide proof of verification concept, consists of 121 individual axons which run in parallel being arranged in a square grid. There are physiological parameters, like axon diameter and membrane characteristics, used with regard to the anatomical data from the selected laboratory animals (here: rats). It is obviously possible to redefine these parameters according other laboratory animals or later on human beings. The simulation environment uses the Hodgkin-Huxley model (Hodgkin and Huxley, 1952) to simulate the axon internal membrane, the ion channels and the extracellular space (Klinger and Klauke, 2013). This model, consisting of these 121 axons, is the current mock-up for modelling, e.g. an arm movement, based on the muscles, controlled by specific axons, like forearm agonist/antagonist and the corresponding sensor information based on proprioceptors (ppc). The axon arrangement of this abstract model simplifies the verification process; real nerve bundles of human beings consists of ten thousand of axons and have inter- and intraindividual characteristics. With regard to the evaluation of identification performance and resource requirements more complex models are in the focus.

The action potentials used for the NEURON-simulator are derived by human arm modelling via Matlab Robotics Toolbox (Corke, 2011) or using a real robot arm or prosthesis. With this model for verification it is possible to concentrate on specific muscle groups and their reactuatory answer and therefore verification pattern can be generated. The simulation environment uses the Hodgkin-Huxley model (Hodgkin and Huxley, 1952) to simulate the axon internal membrane, the ion-channels and the extra-cellular space. So, the propagation of action potentials along the axons is modelled using these equations. Furthermore, the mechanisms concerning the passive membrane channels are included.

Figure 3. Nerv Bundle: Axon Model

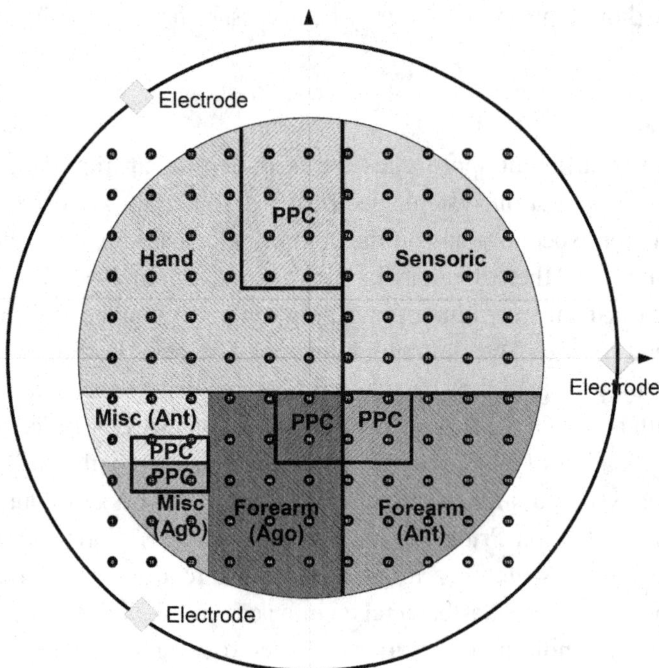

2.3. Machine Learning

The machine learning is based on evolutionary algorithms – a generic population-based metaheuristic optimization algorithm inspired by biological evolution – embedded in a multi-stage and multi-agent implementation, shown in Figure 4.

The planet structure models the environment for the populations inside the evolutionary algorithm. Every planet provides a data field, the software agents can operate on. The number of planets is scalable, the current predetermined size is $n = 9^4 = 6561$. Using a multiprocessor system, the number of planets have to be multiplied by the number of cores. Data acquired from the process connection are preprocessed, equal to the filling of the planet structure. The preprocessing consists of several steps to guarantee a high average information content of the data, so called data entropy. One step is an appropriate data preprocessing.

All real data recorded from the cuff-electrode have to be preprocessed to improve the data conditioning. The verification data generated from the NEURON-simulator can be used directly:

- **Filtering:** The recorded action potentials are disturbed by intrinsic noise. In addition, these are overlaid by a substantial extrinsic noise, originated for example by electromyogram (EMG) from surrounding muscles. Therefore, the recorded data has to be filtered with integrated analogue filter and additional digital filter;
- **Re-sampling:** The recorded data has two main weaknesses: The samples are asynchronous and aperiodic. In order to get a time series of data samples the following steps are performed:

Figure 4. The architecture of the machine learning

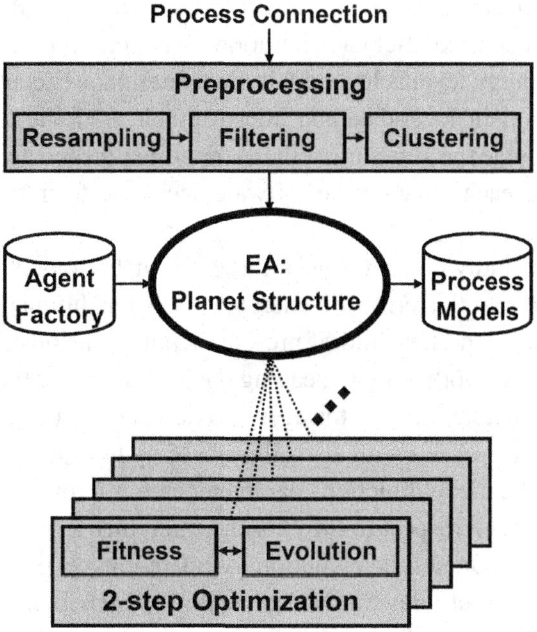

- **Interpolation and FIR Filter (finite impulse response):** For each sequence the given values are interpolated and smooth the result with a convolution;
- **Error Correction:** The interpolated data is equalized with the original samples gained from the Data Factory;
- **Down-sampling:** We pick Euclidean equidistant samples from each sequence and combine them to data samples with a time-stamp.

During the machine process the data samples will not stay in their chronological ordering. To be able to perform time derivation, it is necessary to save the chronological neighbors for each sample. The resulting time series of equidistant data samples p consists of a time-stamp p_{time}, a vector $p_{data} = [p_{out}, p_{in}]$, with $p_{out} \in R$ and $p_{in} \in R^m$, containing the output and input data and its chronological neighbors and . With P we denote the set of all such data samples. Furthermore, we define the delta value $p_{in}^{\Delta} \in R$ with:

$$\left(P_{in}^{\Delta}\right) := \frac{1}{2}\left(\frac{\left(P_{in}\right)-\left(P_{in}^{pre}\right)}{P_{time}-P_{time}^{pre}}+\frac{\left(P_{in}\right)-\left(P_{in}^{post}\right)}{P_{time}-P_{time}^{post}}\right) \tag{1}$$

$$\left(P_{out}^{\Delta}\right) := \frac{1}{2}\left(\frac{\left(P_{in}\right)-\left(P_{in}^{pre}\right)}{P_{time}-P_{time}^{pre}}+\frac{\left(P_{in}\right)-\left(P_{in}^{post}\right)}{P_{time}-P_{time}^{post}}\right) \tag{2}$$

In the central part of Figure 4, the agent factory, the model library and the 2-step optimization, dedicated to every planet, is shown. The agents have 4 essential features: an age, an energy level, an area and their model function, approximating the corresponding process function. Moreover a replication mechanism is implemented, meaning the agents are able to produce a child and put it on an area. The age and the energy level are increased after each iteration. All operations an agent can perform, have an energy effort, by which the energy level is lowered, if the operation is executed. Furthermore the agents have the ability to learn from their local data and improve their model function by executing different evolutionary operations to change the structure of the model function and a local optimization algorithm to calibrate the parameters. In each iteration the software agents perform the following operations:

- **Calculate Fitness:** The individual evaluates the error of his model function with respect to a chosen metric. According to this error the energy level is recalibrated. If it is negative, the agent is removed from the planet and his child, if present, is put on his position;
- **Move:** The agent moves to another area, meaning the local test data he uses is modified, so that he can use new data in the next iteration. If the agent carries a child, it is set to the former area. Agents in a multi planet system cantrave l with a small probability to different planets;
- **Local Optimization:** The model functions parameters are improved by trying to reduce the error of the current local data with respect to the chosen search metric;
- **Evolutionary Operation:** One of the evolutionary operations, explained below, is performed;
- **Nomination:** The agents elect a few individuals with the highest fitness values and age on each planet. Next the global fitness value of these agents is calculated. The 25 best agents form the so-called Elite Population, containing the best dissimilar agents. The model-function of the elite agents are evaluated on the whole data set. If any of these functions has an error below a certain error bound, the algorithm terminates and this function is returned. Copies of these agents are then spread across all planets to distribute their information to other agents.

The Evolutionary Operation consists of:

- **Mutation:** The agents model function gets changed randomly: Either a sub-tree of the model function is exchanged or new operations are inserted;
- **Crossover:** When an agent moves it may happen that the chosen area is already occupied with another individual. In this case, a sub-tree of the individuals model function is replaced by a randomly chosen, suitable sub-tree of the other agents model function;
- **Replication:** The agent duplicates himself;
- **Global Optimization:** The agents, which own enough energy or are not adult yet, optimize the parameters of their model function in the Memetic Coprocessor, explained below.

One further step is the data filling. This last step of the data preprocessing arranges the data samples on a 2D surface of a so-called planet. The surface of the planets is built in a recursive pattern of squares containing nine elements, filled meander like. This method leads to the planet size 9^4. This arrangement has the advantage that the data set used for the local optimization consists of data samples, which may be spread more widely across the input sequences.

The global optimization is realized on memetic coprocessors, running on an extra processor core, executing more sophisticated algorithms for a global optimization. In the current configuration a downhill-simplex algorithm (Nelder and Mead, 1965) is used. The algorithm chosen for this local parameter optimization is resource-saving, because it is executed for all agents in every iteration.

The machine learning provides the capability of running the evolutionary algorithm described above on several planets at the same time. If this is the case, some of the areas on each planet get marked as so-called beam areas. After each iteration copies of all individuals placed on such an area are send to a randomly chosen area on a randomly chosen planet, provided the chosen area is not yet occupied by an agent. In the experiments 100 of the 6561 areas on every planet were marked as beam areas. Our implementation associates each planet to one processor core, on an additional processor core a universe supervisor is executed. This supervisor manages the elite population using the data from all planets and controls the termination condition. The information exchange between the cores is implemented via a non-blocking Message Passing Interface.

2.4. Process Model

The area provides data samples to learn from and calculate the error of the model function ($R^m \rightarrow R$) is stored in a tree representation. This function is composed of elementary operations (Schmidt and Lipson, 2007), like +, –, *, /, *sin*, *sqrt* the variables $x_1, x_2, \ldots, x_m$ a set of parameters within their model function. We are currently convinced that a mathematical model has many advantages over a typical description of a neural network. With a mathematical model, dependency within the model, changes in the model, for example due to aging, friction, etc., and a partitioning of the model into sub-modules can be handled more easily. However, there are a lot of questions, for example the performance and efficiency in identifying such mathematic models. In Figure 5 an exemplary model of low complexity is shown.

Figure 5. Mathematical model

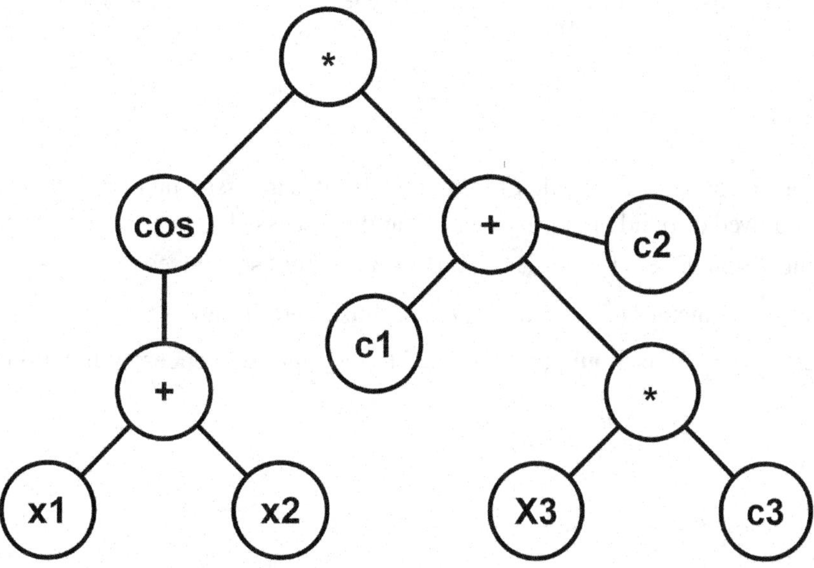

According the multi-agent capability, there are several models existing (Weiss, 2013). The number of currently active agents and their inner candidate function is regulated by a software PID control. It is programmed to use the available processing power in nearly optimal conditions. The best models are picked according their ability to survive multiple times longer than the mean agent population. This metric corresponds to the selection of the fittest agents. The complexity of the process models is problem-related dynamic. It depends on the number of input variables, constants and operations. The complexity is defined by counting the number of nodes in the tree representations. The differences between both verification methods are illustrated in Figure 7.

The open-loop method allows a verification of the potential-level (electrode-data) against the command-level (Stim-Pattern). It is not able to generate new adequate verification patterns to improve the quality of the model behavior according to specific system states. The new method including the symbiotic cycle integrates the verification in a complex and interactive exchange of data between physical process, process model, machine learning and the simulator. The closed-loop verification provides detailed check between the trajectory level and the command-level, including the potential-level. The identification block controls the generation of trajectory-related Stim-Pattern. One major advantage of this method is the fact that no initial model is necessary; the continuous symbiotic system generates it from scratch.

Regarding the use of the prosthesis two alternatives are shown in Figure 7 in the actuator level: The real robot, a physical system, or a serial robot, simulated by Matlab. Both alternatives are working as the cause and effect element, closing the gap between command and trajectory level. While the serial robot provides joint torques related to a simulated trajectory, the real robot provides the trajectory information via a camera system or an integrated device (see Figure 1).

To create a symbiotic online learning environment all data from the physical process is streamed via PDSP to and from central routing software. Machine learning and the massive parallel simulation are running outside the real-time domain. The control simulation, which is using the currently best-known model, is running inside an embedded system in real time. Communication between the two domains basically consists of a model transmission and a movement direction proposal directed into the real time domain. Data transmission directed to the machine learning, verification and simulation is a set of streamed time series data.

2.5. Verification

The verification block confirms the quality of the model and is an essential part, it helps to evaluate the model which is improved or build up during identification process. The verification strategy is based on a set of process input sequences ($\left(x_1\right)_t,\cdots,\left(x_m\right)_t$, $t \in N$) and output sequences ($\left(y_1\right)_t,\cdots,\left(y_j\right)_t$, $t \in N$) and of the simulation output sequences ($\left(z_1\right)_t,\cdots,\left(z_j\right)_t$, $t \in N$), illustrated in Figure 6:

The output sequences of the simulator are related to the input sequences by functional relationships f: $R^m \rightarrow R$:

$$f_1\left(\left(x_1\right)_t,\ldots,\left(x_m\right)_t\right)=\left(y_1\right)_t, t\in \mathrm{N}$$
$$f_j\left(\left(x_1\right)_t,\ldots,\left(x_m\right)_t\right)=\left(y_j\right)_t, t\in \mathrm{N}$$

In principle, the verification method can be executed with synthetic data (generated by a model of the evaluated system) or live data (acquired from the physical process). Using the synthetic data verification, no physical process is necessary; the verification can be used related to, for example, an regression analysis, based on a well-known mathematical equation. For applications based on a physical model, PDSP is used to establish an interface to the physical process.

The Curve Fitting, presented in (Klinger and Klauke, 2013), provides an open loop verification, which is not able to start the verification process without an initial model. Furthermore, this open loop verification is not able to control the verification process to increase the quality of the model. Precisely for this reason, a closed-loop verification process has been designed, based on the symbiotic cycle, shown in Figure 2 in section 2.

3. APPLICATIONS AND VERIFICATION MOCK-UP

This section focuses on evaluating the identification method. The application of a prosthesis control based on nerve signals is complex and challenging. The use of different methods makes it possible to evaluate them; here the closed-loop approach is in focus, which has some advantages over the open-loop approach. The closed-loop approach makes it possible to have a model verified by a physical system without having a certain idea of what the model actually looks like. In Figure 6 the relationship between movement and identification is shown abstractly:

Movement Model (forces, links, joints) Data Identification Block Verification

Figure 6. Mapping from movement to verification

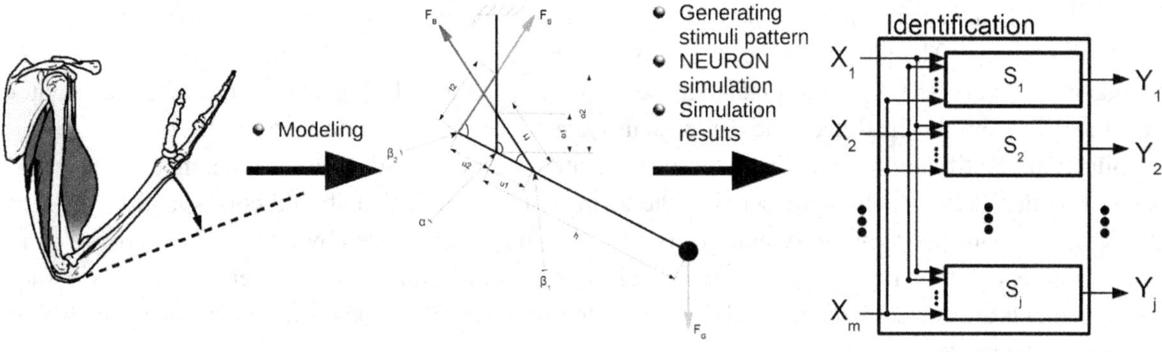

Figure 7 shows the complete verification process including all parts of the symbiotic cycle related to the biotechnology application.

Here the physical process, the human being, is replaced by Matlab (movement modeling) and NEURON (physiological modeling), providing an verification set-up for prototyping and optimization. We use this set-up for evaluation if the identification procedure with regard to quality, performance, repeatability and reproducibility.

The use of Matlab and Neuron allows a verification of specific Axon configurations that is completely detached from the kilogram application (human). These specific Axon configurations are used, for example, to check the function of the identification algorithm using special applications. This includes for example:

Figure 7. Open- and closed-loop verification

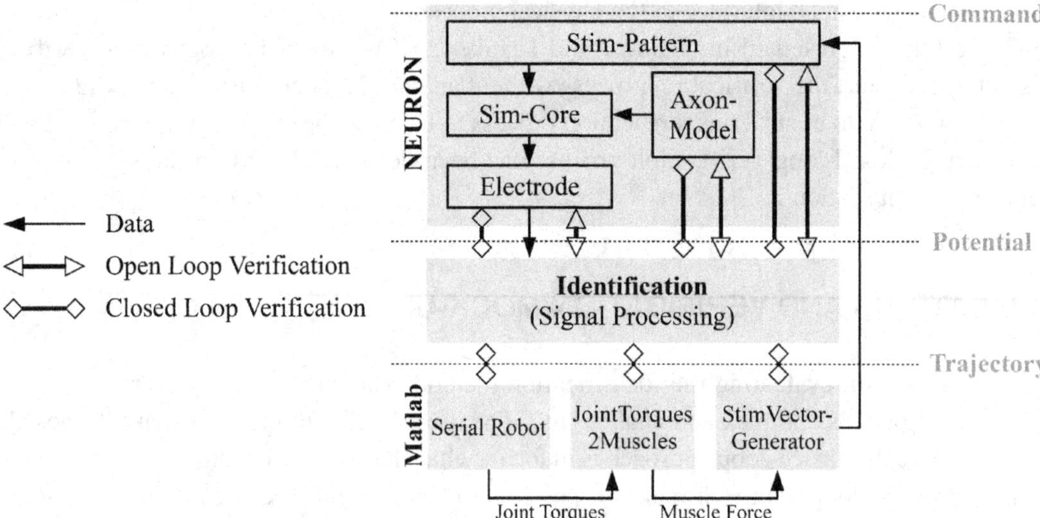

- Checking the localization function of individual axons;
- Checking the superposition of the sum of action potentials;
- Checking the superposition of reciprocating action potentials, moving back and forward, related to the motor and sensory axons, etc.

Another planned verification scenario, which can also be integrated into the symbiotic cycle, is shown in Figure 8. The physical process is now represented by a human being. The action potentials are taken by the cuff-electrode, implanted as described in section 1. Using an external device as a gateway, the data from the cuff-electrode can be sent via a wireless communication stream to the machine learning and identification server. This server generates the model and simulates this model to present the verification data, which is presented in the form of a trajectory that should correspond to the arm movement. The influence of the symbiotic simulation, which is expressed by a recommendation for the next movement, can be represented as additional information. In this way, the user can check whether the movements are correctly recognized and he is integrated in the context of the symbiotic cycle during creation of the model.

This specific verification scenario, shown in Figure 8, is currently in preparation, some hardware- and software components are in the design phase.

In an additional approach, the physical model is first of all simplified; here, only the robot arm is in the foreground in order to obtain an evaluation of the efficiency, quality and repeatability of the identification method. Experiments with the entire biological system are currently under way but there is still a need to narrow down the number of parameters of the identification method.

In this paper this key aspect of the proposed closed-loop identification method is shown. We are using the identification method to generate the model from a real robot using camera information. Against to the SMoBAICS approach the inputs/outputs are digital signals which make it possible to focus the problem on the identification and verification method. After the model set-up from the real robot system, this closed-loop verification can be used according Figure 7. The real robot, used in this set-up, is shown in Figure 9.

Figure 8. Online presentation of the verification results

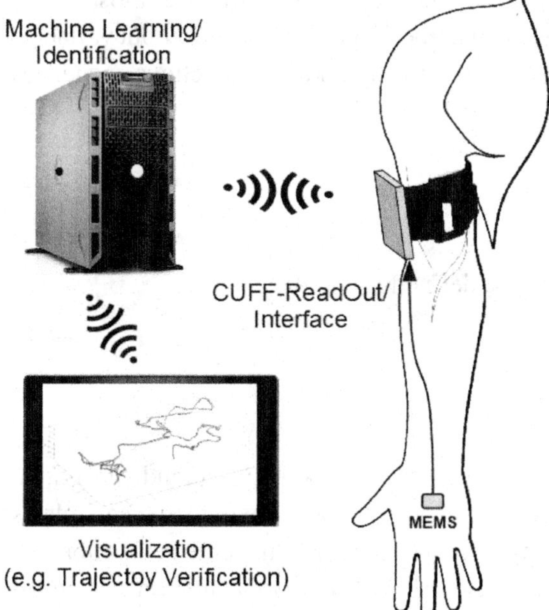

Figure 9. Real Robot: Demonstrator system

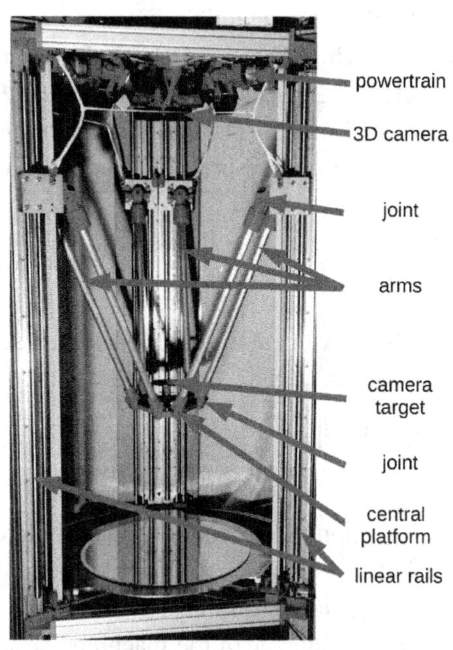

To integrate a robot as a prosthesis prototype this demonstrator system, a parallel delta robot has been used. It basically consists of 6 vertical linear rails grouped into 3 pairs. These are placed around the working area in 120° spacings. Each linear axis is connected to a joint, which is connected to an arm and again to a joint. These joints are all linked to a central platform. As common to all parallel kinematic chains a move in one actuator influences the position of the central platform in all possible degrees of freedom (DOF). This 6 linear actuators are the output stage of the simulation. To be able to detect the concrete position of the system a depth camera combined with a standard 2D camera is mounted above the working area inside the robot. The depth camera used is an infrared structured light sensor. In the experiment the camera follows a round target placed in the center of the platform. Camera output (after some processing) is the position of the platform. This is a 6 channel output: 3 spatial directions and 3 rotation angles. These 6 channels are the sensor output of the robot and the input for the simulation system. All 6 sensors and 6 actuators combined add up to the input for the machine learning part. This has been referenced in the previous chapter as p_{data}. The position of all actuators influences the position of all axis, so the complete information set is required to be able to calculate an accurate prediction model. To create a symbiotic online learning environment the delta robots internal real time network is connected to an external computer. All data produced by the robotic system is streamed via PDSP to and from a central routing software. Machine learning and the massive parallel simulation are running outside the real time domain. The control simulation, which is using the currently best known model, is running inside an embedded system in real time. Communication between the two domains basically consists of a model transmission and a movement direction proposal directed into the real time domain.

To realize the symbiotic machine learning system described in this paper, one central question is: Where should the symbiotic robot acquire new data? The basic idea is to collect new experimental data at a location where the possible solutions generated by the machine learning system differ most.

We define $x_i \in R$ as the input variables, $p_j \in R$ as the constant parameter and $y_j \in R$ as the output variables of a suggested model. The machine learning system produces a list of candidate functions sequences $f_{e,j}(x_0 \ldots x_n, p_0 \ldots p_m) = y_i$. e is defined as the solutions index (typically $c < 30 = c_{max}$):

$$D_j = \left\{ f_{g,i} - f_{g,j} \mid i \neq j \,\text{and}\, g,h = 0,\cdots,e_{max} \right\} \tag{3}$$

Now the movement direction s for data acquisition can be defined as:

$$s = \underset{d \in D_j, j=|0..6}{argmax} \left\| \nabla d \right\|_1 \tag{4}$$

This direction s is calculated by the simulator on the fly while processing new input data and transmitted to the robotic system. The simple idea behind this is to acquire new input data where model candidates tend to have different results. This leads to a continuous hypothesis filtering in the elite generation.

The basic challenge of the machine learning system can also interpreted a global non linear optimization problem. The concept behind the above formulated feedback metric is to continuously adapt the target function, while machine learning is running. The adaption process described is on the other hand based on the output of the candidate functions $f_{e,j}(x_0 \ldots x_n, p_0 \ldots p_m) = y_i$ evaluated by the online simulation system. This is again what is defined as the symbiotic cycle. If the global target is the deepest valley on the multidimensional target function, then the symbiotic circle will force secondary minima to increase their value by sampling new contradictory data from the physical system. The only valleys not affected are the global optima formed by different possible formulations of a globally valid and correct process model. Data transmission directed to the machine learning, verification and simulation is a set of streamed time series data. All calculations outside the real time domain are processed on two quad Intel Xeon E7-8860v3 computer systems (128 logical cores) with 1TB of DDR4 RAM each. The real time control System located in the head box of the physical system consists of 14 Arm Cortex M4 Microcontrollers and three 8 Core Arm Cortex-A7 Processors. Local compute power is therefore relatively small compared with the cloud connected machine learning modules.

4. RESULTS

To demonstrate the emergent effects arising from the combination of all modules of the symbiotic cycle the same machine learning system has been used as in (Bohlmann, Klinger, Szczerbicka, and Becker, 2010).

There are some characteristics of this identification method, what makes the application of this method seem promising. First of all, it takes some time at the beginning to acquire enough input data to generate a start-up model from scratch. It is remarkable that this identification method finds a solution even without a start model, which makes it suitable for general use.

In Figure 10 and Figure 11 error values and the complexity of the solutions are shown. We picked this two axis because the solution to be found is quite different. Actuator A (in the back of the robotic system) has a much simpler equation than the actuators in the front. Although this behavior is not intuitive for a symmetric robot, this is correct. It arises from the fact that these actuators are aligned to the Y-Axis of the camera. Therefore, the resulting equation does not include any coordinate transformations. The solution for this actuator is found in about 150s and has a complexity (sum of nodes in function tree, exemplary shown in Figure 5) of 21 including 4 parameters.

Figure 10. Error values and complexity (Axis A)

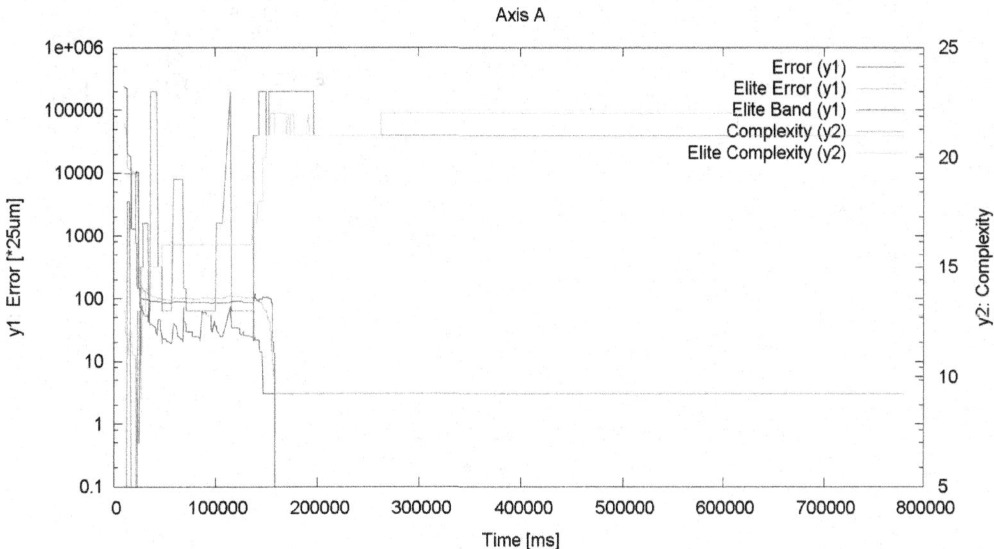

For actuator B the task is a little more challenging. Here the system requires about 800s to get to a 33 node solution including 5 parameters.

The first conclusion is in all cases: As predicted, it takes some time at the beginning to acquire enough input data to construct a complex solution. Secondly, the error does not progressively decrease as often found in offline machine learning. This is caused by the closed-loop feedback metric sampling new data of some model candidate. It is a direct result from new online data injected to the machine learning progress. These spikes for the three actuators are depicted in Figure 12, presenting the decreasing error band for the 3 actuators A, B and C. The interesting aspect here is, that the peaks sometimes but in most cases not correspond to others. We found that this is a direct result from the argmax operator in Formula 4 in section 3. It is mainly caused by the selection of one pair out of all actuators to determine the robotic movement direction until a different pair has a higher rating.

By far, the most amazing aspect is the comparison of the offline performance (Bohlmann, Klauke, Klinger, and Szczerbicka, 2011) of the system and the online system interacting with the physical robot. While the offline machine learning system is only capable to identify models with a tree complexity of around 19 nodes with non-good success rate, the online system identifies a model with complexity of 33 nodes. Furthermore, as described in (Bohlmann, Klinger, Szczerbicka, and Becker, 2010), the machine learning modules offline performance decreases dramatically if additional noise is present in the input data. Obviously, experiments described in this paper additionally and inherently contain measuring noise through the use of a real physical system. The direct and automated online interaction of online simulation, verification, machine learning and physical process produce far better performance than each component alone could produce.

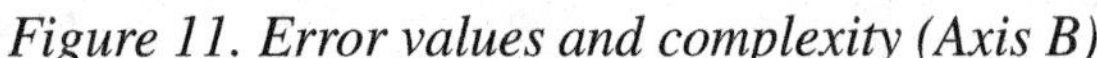

Figure 11. Error values and complexity (Axis B)

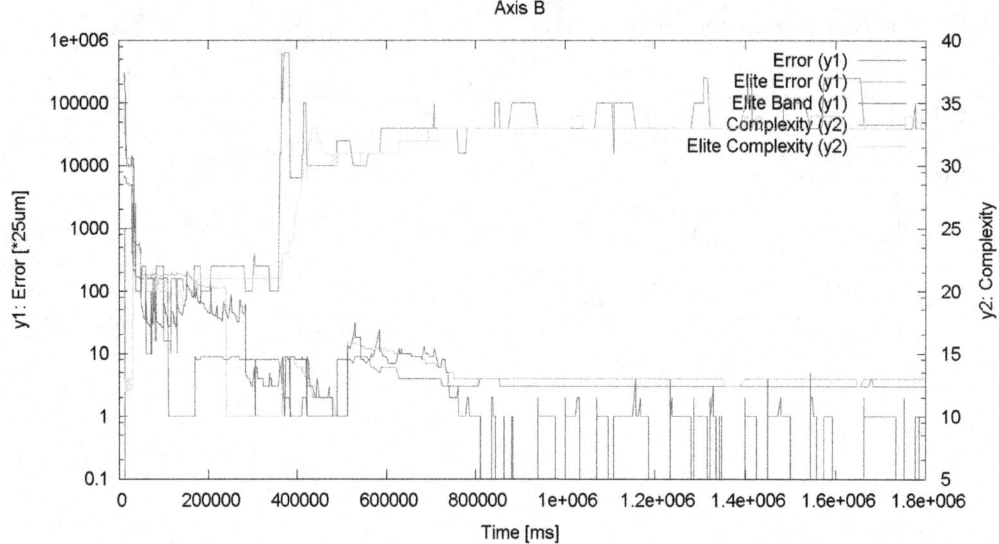

Figure 12. Error band for actuators A, B, C

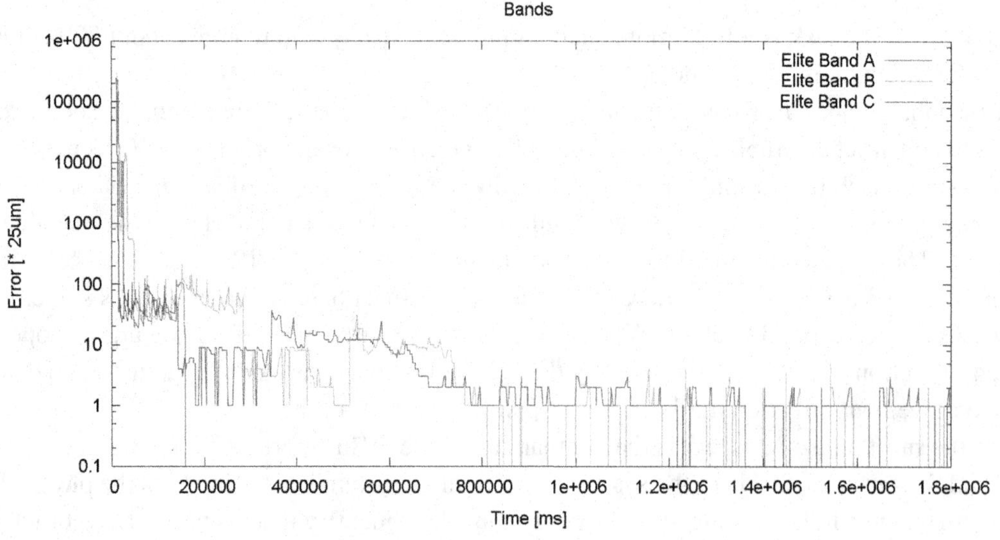

5. SUMMARY AND FURTHER WORK

The acquisition and identification system of motion-based action potentials in neural bundles for exo-prostheses control or for handicapped limb stimulation provides an integrated solution from action potential recording up to the identification procedure. This paper focuses on a new method based on a continuous symbiotic cycle, providing a closed-loop approach for an integrated identification and verification. While an open-loop approach helps to identify well-known processes, e.g. for improving the overall model quality, the closed-loop approach, using the symbiotic cycle, helps to generate a physical process model from scratch and forms an adaptable and scalable identification environment. The symbiotic cycle provides a closed-loop approach for verification on different levels of abstraction. This closed-loop approach shows the verification results at the adequate level and therefore improves the applicability.

In this paper the performance of the integrated identification and model generation is shown on a real robot. As it is continuously present, the robotic controller can react to changes in the system. The most valuable result in fact is that model complexity which could be learned from a real-world process is clearly higher using a continuously interacting system. This continuous symbiotic system, introduced as the symbiotic cycle, where different components, like machine learning, simulator and process models are interacting with a physical or technical process, improves the identification progress and opens the symbiotic simulation approach also for the field of biotechnology applications.

The further work has the following key aspects:

- Evaluation of the whole identification process and integrating of the missing elements using the continuous symbiotic cycle;
- Evaluation of the overall identification with regard to quality and performance and therefore the applicability;
- Completion and commissioning of all components of the online verification, shown in Figure 8;
- Adapting the symbiotic cycle to a clinical environment, to replace the Matlab-based part and to integrate the identification into a learning environment and the concerning applications.

REFERENCES

Alkhateeb, F. (2011). *Multi-Agent Systems - Modeling*. Control, Programming, Simulations and Applications.

Aydt, H., Turner, S. J., Cai, W., & Low, M. Y. H. (2008a). Symbiotic simulation systems: An extended definition motivated by symbiosis in biology. In *Proceedings of the 22nd Workshop on Principles of Advanced and Distributed Simulation, PADS '08* (pp. 109–116). IEEE Computer Society 10.1109/PADS.2008.17

Aydt, H., Turner, S. J., Cai, W., & Low, M. Y. H. (2009). Research issues in symbiotic simulation. In *Proceedings of the 2009 Winter Simulation Conference*. 10.1109/WSC.2009.5429419

Bohlmann, S., Klauke, A., Klinger, V., & Szczerbicka, H. (2011). Model synthesis using a multi-agent learning strategy. In *The 23rd European Modeling & Simulation Symposium (Simulation in Industry)*, Rome, Italy.

Bohlmann, S., Klinger, V., & Szczerbicka, H. (2009). HPNS - a Hybrid Process Net Simulation Environment Executing Online Dynamic Models of Industrial Manufacturing Systems. In *Proceedings of the 2009 Winter Simulation Conference*.

Bohlmann, S., Klinger, V., & Szczerbicka, H. (2010a). System Identification with Multi-Agent-based Evolutionary Computation Using a Local Optimization Kernel. In *The Ninth International Conference on Machine Learning and Applications* (pp. 840–845). 10.1109/ICMLA.2010.130

Bohlmann, S., Klinger, V., Szczerbicka, H., & Becker, M. (2010b). A data management framework providing online-connectivity in symbiotic simulation. In *24th EUROPEAN Conference on Modelling and Simulation, Simulation meets Global Challenges*, Kuala Lumpur, Malaysia. 10.7148/2010-0302-0308

Carnevale, N. T., & Hines, M. L. (2006). *The NEURON Book*. New York, NY: Cambridge Univ. Press. doi:10.1017/CBO9780511541612

Cesqui, B., Tropea, P., Micera, S., & Krebs, H. (2013). Emg-based pattern recognition approach in post stroke robot-aided rehabilitation: A feasibility study. *Journal of Neuroengineering and Rehabilitation*, *10*(1), 75. doi:10.1186/1743-0003-10-75 PMID:23855907

Coates, T.D., J., Larson-Prior, L., Wolpert, S., and Prior, F. (2003). Classification of simple stimuli based on detected nerve activity. *IEEE engineering in medicine and biology magazine*, *22*(1), 64–76.

Corke, P. (2011). Robotics, Vision and Control - Fundamental Algorithms in MATLAB (2nd ed.). Springer.

De Jong, K. A. (2006). *Evolutionary Computation: A Unified Approach*. MIT press.

Fujimoto, R., Lunceford, D., Page, E., & Uhrmacher, A. (2002). Technical report of the dagstuhl-seminar grand challenges for modelling and simulation. Schloss Dagstuhl, Leibniz-Zentrum für Informatik, Wadern, Germany.

Gold, C., Henze, D. A., & Koch, C. (2007). Using extracellular action potential recordings to constrain compartmental models. *Journal of Computational Neuroscience*, *23*(1), 39–58. doi:10.100710827-006-0018-2 PMID:17273940

Hazan, L., Zugaro, M., & Buzsáki, G. (2006). Klusters, NeuroScope, NDManager: A free software suite for neurophysiological data processing and visualization. *Journal of Neuroscience Methods*, *155*(2), 207–216. doi:10.1016/j.jneumeth.2006.01.017 PMID:16580733

Hodgkin, A., & Huxley, A. (1952). A quantitative description of membrane current and its application to conduction and excitation in nerve. *The Journal of Physiology*, *117*(4), 500–544. doi:10.1113/jphysiol.1952.sp004764 PMID:12991237

Klinger, V. (2015). Biosignal acquisition system for prosthesis control and rehabilitation monitoring. In A. Bruzzone, M. Frascio, & V. Novak et al. (Eds.), *4nd International Workshop on Innovative Simulation for Health Care (IWISH 2015)*.

Klinger, V. (2016). Rehabilitation monitoring and biosignal identification using IoT-modules. In A. Bruzzone, M. Frascio, & V. Novak et al. (Eds.), *5nd International Workshop on Innovative Simulation for Health Care (IWISH 2016).*

Klinger, V., & Klauke, A. (2013). Identification of motion-based action potentials in neural bundles using an algorithm with multiagent technology. In W. Backfrieder, M. Frascio, & V. Novak et al. (Eds.), *2nd International Workshop on Innovative Simulation for Health Care (IWISH 2013).*

Law, A. M., & Kelton, W. D. (2000). *Simulation Modeling and Analysis*. McGraw-Hill.

Micera, S., Carpaneto, J., & Raspopovic, S. (2010a). Control of hand prostheses using peripheral information. *IEEE Reviews in Biomedical Engineering*, *3*, 48–68. doi:10.1109/RBME.2010.2085429 PMID:22275201

Micera, S., Citi, L., Rigosa, J., Carpaneto, J., Raspopovic, S., Pino, G. D., ... Rossini, P. M. (2010b). Decoding information from neural signals recorded using intraneural electrodes: Toward the development of a neurocontrolled hand prosthesis. *Proceedings of the IEEE*, *98*(3), 407–417. doi:10.1109/JPROC.2009.2038726

Nelder, R., & Mead, J. (1965). A simplex method for function minimization. *The Computer Journal*, *7*(4), 308–313. doi:10.1093/comjnl/7.4.308

Neymotin, S., Lytton, W., Olypher, A., & Fenton, A. (2011). Measuring the quality of neuronal identification in ensemble recordings. *The Journal of Neuroscience*, *31*(45), 16398–16409. doi:10.1523/JNEUROSCI.4053-11.2011 PMID:22072690

Raspopovic, S., Capogrosso, M., Petrini, F. M., Bonizzato, M., Rigosa, J., Di Pino, G., ... Micera, S. (2014). Restoring Natural Sensory Feedback in Real-Time Bidirectional Hand Prostheses. *Science Translational Medicine*, *6*(222), 222ra19. doi:10.1126citranslmed.3006820 PMID:24500407

Schmidt, M., & Lipson, H. (2007). Comparison of tree and graph encodings as function of problem complexity. In *GECCO '07: Proceedings of the 9th annual conference on Genetic and evolutionary computation* (pp. 1674–1679). New York, NY: ACM. 10.1145/1276958.1277288

Trianni, V. (2014). Evolutionary robotics: Model or design? *Frontiers in Robotics and AI*, *1*, 13. doi:10.3389/frobt.2014.00013

Weiss, G. (2013). *Multiagent Systems. EBSCO ebook academic collection*. MIT Press.

Yang, X.-S., Koziel, S., & Leifsson, L. (2013). Computational optimization, modelling and simulation: Recent trends and challenges. *Procedia Computer Science*, *18*, 855–860. doi:10.1016/j.procs.2013.05.250

Zeigler, B. P., Praehofer, H., & Kim, T. G. (2000). Theory of Modeling and Simulation: Integrating Discrete Event and Continuous Complex Dynamic Systems (2nd ed.). San Diego, CA: Academic Press.

This research was previously published in the International Journal of Privacy and Health Information Management (IJPHIM), 71); pages 61-79, copyright year 2019 by IGI Publishing (an imprint of IGI Global).

Chapter 30
A Heterogeneous AdaBoost Ensemble Based Extreme Learning Machines for Imbalanced Data

Adnan Omer Abuassba
University of Science and Technology Beijing (USTB), Beijing, China & Arab Open University - Palestine, Ramallah, Palestine

Dezheng Zhang
University of Science and Technology Beijing (USTB), Beijing, China

Xiong Luo
University of Science and Technology Beijing (USTB), Beijing, China

ABSTRACT

Extreme learning machine (ELM) is an effective learning algorithm for the single hidden layer feed-forward neural network (SLFN). It is diversified in the form of kernels or feature mapping functions, while achieving a good learning performance. It is agile in learning and often has good performance, including kernel ELM and Regularized ELM. Dealing with imbalanced data has been a long-term focus for the learning algorithms to achieve satisfactory analytical results. It is obvious that the unbalanced class distribution imposes very challenging obstacles to implement learning tasks in real-world applications, including online visual tracking and image quality assessment. This article addresses this issue through advanced diverse AdaBoost based ELM ensemble (AELME) for imbalanced binary and multiclass data classification. This article aims to improve classification accuracy of the imbalanced data. In the proposed method, the ensemble is developed while splitting the trained data into corresponding subsets. And different algorithms of enhanced ELM, including regularized ELM and kernel ELM, are used as base learners, so that an active learner is constructed from a group of relatively weak base learners. Furthermore, AELME is implemented by training a randomly selected ELM classifier on a subset, chosen by random re-sampling. Then, the labels of unseen data could be predicted using the weighting approach. AELME is validated through classification on real-world benchmark datasets.

DOI: 10.4018/978-1-6684-6291-1.ch030

1. INTRODUCTION

Among the popular machine learning methods (Adnan,Abuassba et al.,2017a, Bezdek, 2016; Chen, Li et al., 2018; Luo, Sun et al., 2018; Luo, Jiang et al., 2019; Luo, Xu et al., 2018,Adnan,Abuassba et al.,2017b), extreme learning machine (ELM) is well-known for solving classification and regression problems in real world applications. It is designed for a single hidden layer feed-forward network (SLFN). It is proved theoretically and practically (Huang, Zhu et al., 2006; Huang, Wang et al., 2010; Huang, Zhou et al., 2012; Huang, 2014) that ELM is efficient and fast in both classification and regression (Liu, He et al., 2008; Huang, Ding et al., 2010). It eludes parameter tuning on the contrary of traditional gradient based algorithms. Imbalanced data issue appears when negative or majority class dominates another class (positive or minority); which means the number of majority class examples excessive the number of minority class examples. Many real-world applications suffer from imbalanced data, including text classification (Song, Huang et al., 2016), credit card fraud detection (Hirose, Ozawa et al., 2016), fault diagnosis (Duan, Xie et al., 2016), medical diagnosis (Mazurowski, Habas et al., 2008), and others.

As the distribution of classes is unbalanced; learning with the existence of imbalanced data is not a trivial process for standard machine learning algorithms as they tend to be biased by the negative classes and ignore the positive ones. The prediction of a concrete class is more significant than the negative one. Therefore, imbalance class learning draws more and more attention in recent years. The previously proposed research addresses this issue at data level (FernÁndez, Garcá et al., 2008), at algorithm level and cost-sensitive methods (Sun, Kamel et al., 2007; Tapkan, Özbakir et al., 2016) which combine both.

On the data level, a preprocessing technique is used to balance the original data such as under-sampling, oversampling and the hybrid of the two. Under-sampling approach eliminates a number of majority class examples; however, it wipes out some notable examples. Likewise, over-sampling approach upturns the number of minority class examples; however, it may over-fit the training data. To deal with these issues, hybrid methods are proposed. Synthetic Minority Oversampling Techniques (SMOTE) creates new synthetic examples depending on the similarity between existing ones (Rani, Ramadevi et al., 2016). It increases overlapping between classes when used for over-sampling. On the other hand, the algorithmic level is designed in a way that it is suitable for imbalanced data learning. Cost sensitive one of these algorithms, in which a penalty cost is employed for the misclassified examples, i.e. assigning the misclassified cases for majority class more cost than the minority ones (Tapkan, Özbakir, et al., 2016). Most academic researchers (Jiang, Shen et al., 2015; Zhang, Liu et al., 2016; Ren, Cao et al., 2017) proposed ELM ensemble technique to address the imbalanced classification problem. ELM ensemble methodology assigns weights to train examples that care of the misclassified samples by the previous classifier.

Weighted ELM (Li, Kong et al., 2014) and AdaBoost algorithm is combined in a unified structure. The weighted ELM provides different weights for each training example in a way that alleviate the impact of the concrete class, by conveying an extra weight for the minority class. Those weights were decided by the user which accordingly affected its performance. Nevertheless, how to determine the sample weights still an unsolved issue. A multiclass approach-based ELM ensemble which combine ELM and AdaBoost is proposed (Jiang, Shen et al., 2015). It directly applied to ELM group in face recognition application. A fuzzy activation function of ELM (Wang and Li, 2010) as base learner is proposed in vigorous AdaBoost ensemble of ELM.

Up to now, the proposed AdaBoost based ELM ensemble uses one base classifier algorithm for the training classifiers. Those models could be considered as homogenous ensemble models (Li, Kong et al., 2014; Zhang, Liu et al., 2016). This paper proposes ensemble learning which combines both data level and algorithm level using advanced AdaBoost ensemble model bases ELM. At the algorithm level multiclass AdaBoost of two types of fitted ELM algorithms namely, kernel ELM (Huang, Ding et al., 2010) and Regularized ELM (Huang, Zhou et al., 2012) are used as weak learners. These base classifiers are chosen on the basis of their better generalization and flexibility to outliers in training data, specifically, the kernel algorithm which operates on general types of the data and detects very broad types of relations. On the other hand, at data level, a random resembling strategy to split training data into equal subsets is used. To almost preserve the original data distribution; each subset keeps the same imbalanced ratio as original data. Each weak classifier is learned on a randomly chosen data subset through a randomly selected base ELM algorithm. The proposed ensemble algorithm evolves by monitoring the error of the weak classifier of the updated ensemble during training in a way that increase (decrease) weight of incorrect (correct) classified examples. A weighting sum is used to predict new patterns. We compare our model with multiclass AdaBoost ELM (MELM) algorithm (Jiang, Shen et al., 2015), Basic ELM (Huang, Zhu et al., 2004), RELM (Huang, Zhou et al., 2012) and KELM (Huang, Ding et al., 2010).This research shows that data resampling and ensemble approach using different types of ELM can improve both diversity and accuracy of imbalanced data, specifically with AdaBoost model. The remainder of the paper is arranged into four sections. Section 2 presents background of the related research. Section 3 discusses the implementation, architecture and testing phase of the proposed model. Section 4 shows the simulation setting and results. Finally, section 5 is the concluding and future work part.

2. BACKGROUND

2.1. ELM Theory

According to the ELM theorem, it is implemented with random hidden nodes. Let $\left(X_j, t_j\right)_{j=1}^{N}$ be the input for training, where, X_j represents training data vector, t_j represents training data target, and N represents the number of input data. ELM aims at minimizing the output weights β and the mean square error (MSE) simultaneously as follows (Huang, Wang et al. 2010; Huang 2014):

$$f_{ELM} = \| \beta \|_p^{\sigma 1} + \lambda \| H\beta - T \|_q^{\sigma 2} \tag{1}$$

where σ1, σ2 > 0, λ > 0, p, q = (1/2), 1, 2, …, +∞ and the hidden layer output matrix (H) is defined by:

$$\mathrm{H} = \begin{bmatrix} h(x_1) \\ \vdots \\ h(x_N) \end{bmatrix} = \begin{bmatrix} h_1(x_1) & \cdots & h_M(x_1) \\ \vdots & \ddots & \vdots \\ h_1(x_N) & \cdots & h_M(x_N) \end{bmatrix} \tag{2}$$

where M denotes the number of hidden nodes for input vector. H_j, $h_i(x_j) = \left[h_i(x_j)\right]_{i=1}^{M}$ represents the output vector in the hidden layer and T is the desired result of the input data, it is defined as follows:

$$T = \begin{bmatrix} t_1^T \\ \vdots \\ t_N^T \end{bmatrix} \tag{3}$$

ELM training algorithm is summarized by three steps (Huang, Zhu et al., 2004):

1. Set the biases bj and the input weights aj in a random manner;
2. Compute the matrix H;
3. Compute β.

Here β is obtained by:

$$\beta = H^{\dagger}T \tag{4}$$

where $H^{\dagger}$ represents Moore-Penrose (MP) inverse. MP inverse is computed by applying the orthogonal projection: $H^{\dagger}=(H^T)^{-1}H^T$, given that (H^TH) is nonsingular; or $H^{\dagger}=H^T(HH^T)^{-1}$ given that (HH^T) is nonsingular. In accordance with ridge regression theory, a positive matrix $\left(\frac{I}{\lambda}\right)$ is added to the HTH or HHT. Then, we have a solution which is equivalent to the optimized ELM with σ1 = σ2 = 2 (Huang, Zhu et al., 2004; Huang, Ding et al., 2010). So, we can have:

$$\beta = \left(\frac{I}{\lambda} + HH^T\right)^{-1} T \tag{5}$$

$$f_{RELM} = h(x)\beta = h(x)H^T\left(\frac{I}{\lambda} + HH^T\right)^{-1} T \tag{6}$$

Kernel ELM can be defined as follows:

$$\kappa(x_i, x_j) = HH^T \tag{7}$$

$$f_{KELM} = \kappa(x_i, x_j)\left(\frac{I}{\lambda} + \kappa(x_i, x_j)\right)^{-1} T \tag{8}$$

2.2. The Base Classifiers

Two types of ELM classifiers namely KELM and RELM are used as base classifiers to build AELME ensemble. Here we will briefly introduce the strengths of the selected base ELM classifiers. KELM (Huang, Ding et al., 2010) is an optimization method based extreme learning machine. It links the ELM minimal weight norm property to Support Vector Machine (SVM) maximal margin for classification. It is presented that through standard optimization for ELM, a so-called support vector network with better generalization property can be obtained by kernel ELM. However, in comparison with standard SVM, the Kernel ELM is less sensitive to the specified parameters and has fewer constraints. RELM (Huang, Zhou et al., 2012) is a constrained and optimized algorithm-based ELM for regression and multiclass classification. For better generalization of RELM, a tradeoff between the structural (weighted norm) and empirical risk (least square error) is used by regulating a proportion of them during optimization. To achieve above-described tradeoff, the observed risk in the objective function is weighted by a regulating factor gamma.

2.3. AdaBoost

Boosting is a machine learning ensemble which combines many relatively weak and inaccurate algorithms to construct an accurate dynamic one. The AdaBoost algorithm (Freund and Schapire, 1995) was the first functional boosting approach and many researchers studied it. It implemented for wide variety of applications. Techniques that describe the infrequent classes have to be highly specialized in dealing with an imbalanced dataset because of rare occurring of minority class samples. We define a function g(z) as:

$$g(z) = \begin{cases} 1, & if \ z = true \\ 0, & if \ z = false \end{cases} \tag{9}$$

The original AdaBoost algorithm (Friedman, Hastie et al., 2000) takes training data as input, initializes weights for all input samples, trains weak learners and outputs the final learner which is a collection of all the base learners in the group.

3. HETEROGENEOUS ADABOOST ENSEMBLE BASED EXTREME LEARNING MACHINES

Ensemble learning is supposed to be better than one classifier as it consists of a group of classifiers that cooperate. Each member has different bias error from another and there is slight chance for over fitting on the trained data. Machine learning techniques built on the base of maximizing accuracy and rely on the training data scattering. Consequently, they perform badly on the minority class due to the introduced bias error (Cao, Kwong et al., 2015). AdaBoost is an approach that tries to diminish the intolerance error as it pays more attention to the misclassified samples (Freund and Schapire, 1996) than true classified ones.

3.1. Architecture

In this work, data splitting, two types of ELM algorithm in one ensemble and weighting method for final classes in test phase is used. Specifically, the proposed ensemble with different types of ELM algorithm (RELM and KELM), each one is independent of the other, while achieving the diversity within the ensemble. By using different training parameters for each base classifier, it allows each classifier to generate different decision boundaries. Various errors are made by each base classifier while reducing the total error.

Training data spreading has a substantial effect on the generalization performance of the learning classifier. Therefore, the training dataset is divided into different parts with the same imbalanced ration in each part; almost to preserve the original data distribution. The data is divided by random re-sampling on the dataset. Classifiers are achieved with vast diversity and different errors. As a result, the final ensemble is diverse and accurate. For example, if we divide training data D to 3 parts D = {D1, D2, D3} then we have three training subsets: {D2, D3}, {D1, D3} and {D1, D2}. Figure 1 shows the general scheme of the proposed model.

Figure 1. General schematic diagram of the proposed approach

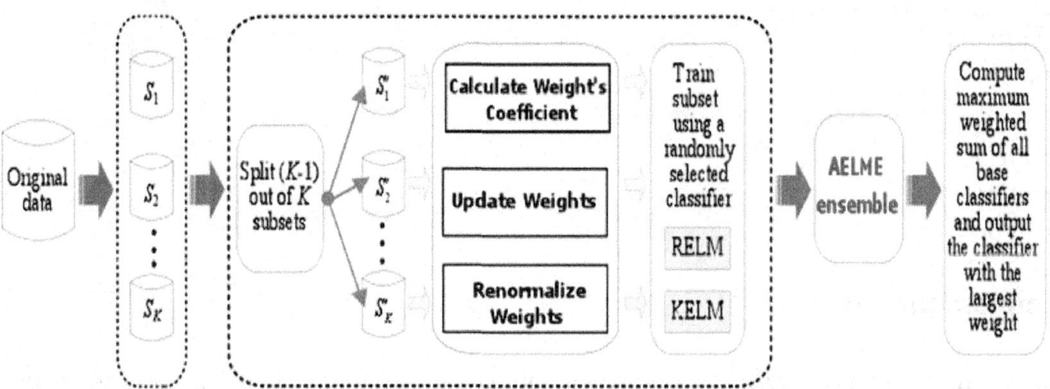

Algorithm 1. AELME

Training phase ()

Input: original training dataset

$$S = \{(x_1, y_1), (x_2, y_2), \dots, (x_N, y_N)\},$$

L: number of hidden nodes,

T: number of iterations,

C: number of classes

K: number of parts.

Output: ensemble classifier model E.

1. Split the original training dataset S:
2. $S=\{S_1,S_2,S_k\}$;
3. Setup the weights = $1/N$, $i = 1, 2, \dots, N$.
4. For m=1 to T
5. For j=1 to K
6. Set $S_{sub}=S-S_j$, reconstruct training dataset S_{tra} by resampling on S_{sub} .
7. Select a member of ELM (E_j) type from the two types (KELM, RELM).
8. Train a member of ELM E_j on S_{tra}
9. Calculate weighted error of weak classifier E_j:

10. $err_m = \frac{\sum_{n=1}^{N} w_i I\left(C_i \neq ELM_m\left(X_i\right)\right)}{\sum_{n=1}^{N} w_i}$

11. If $err_m < (1\text{-}1/C)$ and $err_m \neq 0$ then

12. Calculate the weight coefficient of weak classifier

13. E_i: $\alpha_m = \log \frac{1 - err_m}{err_m} + \log\left(C - 1\right)$

14. Update sample weights for next iteration

15. $w_i = w_i \cdot e^{\left(g\left(C_i \neq ELM_m\left(X_i\right)\right)\right)}$

16. Renormalize the weights.

17. Add Ej to E

18. Else

19. j = j - 1

20. End If

21. End For

22. End For

3.2. Implementation

Before start training phase, we split training data into k equal parts with imbalanced factor as original data by random re-sampling. Then initialize the weights for training subset to be a distribution. We select new training dataset through resampling on k-1 out of k subsets. Random selection of one weak learner out of two (KELM, RELM). Train the weighted subset via the selected weak learner. Calculate the generalization error (err_m) and the weighted error of the weak learner (αm_j which depends on err value. If err is equal to zero then it reveals that weak learner may over fit on the training data. Then it should be excluded. Update the weights such that the misclassified samples will gain weight while the correct ones will lose weight. So that next learner will focus on the misclassified ones. Finally renormalize weights and repeat above explained process, so that the final result will be a strong classifier. The implementation procedure for the ensemble construction and training stage is described as a flowchart in Figure2.

3.3. Testing Phase

Given a testing instance (X,t), an ensemble of $(T \times K)$ predictors are created. In decision making on the ensemble, for pattern X, we use weighting method to make the final decision.

Suppose there is C-classes problem, then we calculate the weighted sum for learners in the ensemble for every class. The class that receives the maximum weighted sum from all predictors is considered as the predicted label (see Tables 1 and 2).

Figure 2. Flowchart for ensemble construction

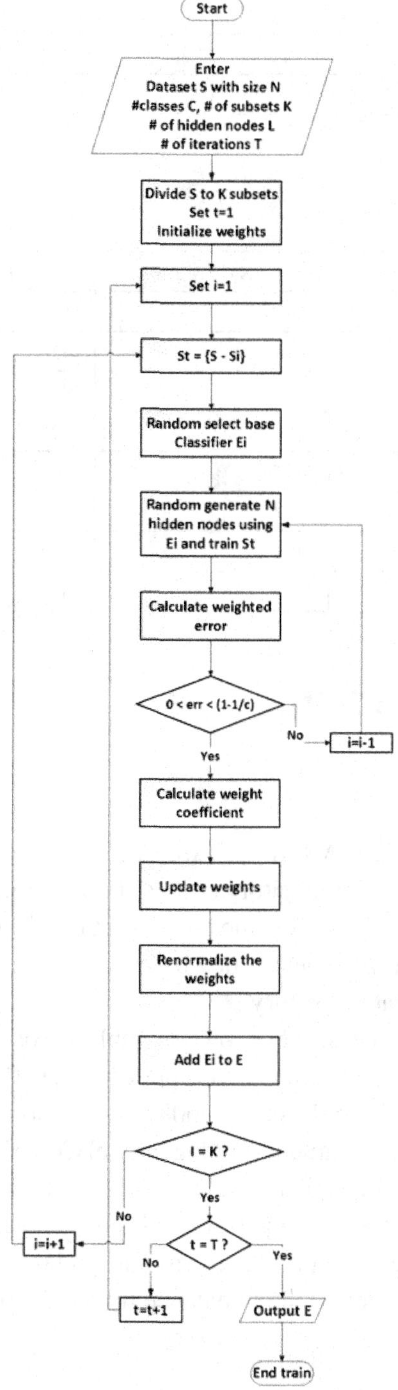

Table 1. Characteristics of the two-class datasets

Data	No. Features	No. Classes	No. Train	No. Test	IR
Dermatoloy	33	6	286	72	5.55
Shuttle	9	7	1740	436	853

Table 2. Characteristics of multiclass datasets

Data	No. Features	No. Train	No. Test	IR
new-thyroid1	5	860	215	5.14
segment0	19	1846	462	6.01
Yeast1	8	1448	297	2.46
Vehicle2	18	846	170	2.88
page-blocks0	10	5472	1095	8.79
shuttle-c0-vs-c4	9	1829	366	13.87
Yeast5	8	1484	297	32.78
shuttle−2vs5	9	3316	664	66.67

4. SIMULATION AND DISCUSSION

4.1. Simulation Settings

To evaluate the performance of the AELME model, we carried out the experiments on datasets of wide types. All of them are from Keel dataset repository (Alcalã-Fdez, Fernãndez et al., 2011): a large variety repository for imbalanced datasets. It provides imbalanced datasets from several different domains with a lot of different characteristics. For more details of what characterizes the problem areas of the datasets can be found on the web page of that repository.

We did the simulation on binary datasets as shown in Table 1. Also, we test our model on multiclass data sets as shown in Table 2 because there are some applications suffer from imbalanced data problem such as protein fold classification (Zhao, Li et al., 2008). Simulations of all algorithms on all datasets are carried out in MATLAB 8.1.0 environment running in Intel Core i5, 2.4 GHZ CPU with 4 GB RAM. To get better classification results, we repeat simulation several times and compute the average of all iterations. We split training data into (2-10) equal size subsets (according to the number of instances in the dataset) via random resampling. We consider the minority class and majority class as positive and negative, respectively. Then we can define the imbalance ratio (IR) for binary datasets as:

$$IR = \frac{\#\left(-1\right)}{\#\left(+1\right)} \tag{11}$$

Table 3. Parameters used of all models in all datasets (L: number of hidden nodes)

Dataset	AELME (C, λ, L)	MELM (C, L)	ELM L	RELM (C, L)	KELM λ
new-thyroid1	(2^{38}, 0.6, 500)	(2^{34}, 500)	490	(2^{34}, 550)	0.6
segment0	(2^{38}, 0.6, 500)	(2^{34}, 500)	520	(2^{34}, 100)	0.6
Yeast1	(2^{38}, 1.7, 95)	(2^{30}, 700)	50	(2^{30}, 800)	3.5
Vehicle2	(2^{22}, 0.9, 900)	(2^{30}, 500)	830	(2^{30}, 700)	0.1
page-blocks0	(2^{40}, 0.3, 900)	(2^{30}, 900)	300	(2^{48}, 950)	0.7
shuttle-c0-vs-c4	(2^{16}, 0.2, 300)	(2^{24}, 600)	30	(2^{20}, 250)	0.1
Yeast5	(2^{48}, 0.1, 400)	(2^{48}, 400)	370	(2^{34}, 330)	0.2
shuttle-2_vs_5	(2^{20}, 1.2, 200)	(2^{20}, 200)	30	(2^{16}, 130)	1.3
Dermatology	(2^{8}, 0.8, 450)	(2^{10}, 100)	350	(2^{8}, 150)	0.9
Shuttle	(2^{20}, 1.2, 700)	(2^{20}, 700)	570	(2^{28}, 850)	1.1

The imbalance ratio for multiclass is defined as:

$$IR = \frac{\# Max\left(t_j\right)}{\# Min\left(t_j\right)}, \text{j} = 1, \ldots, \text{C}$$

where C represents the number of classes, t_j represents the samples belonging to class tj, j = 1, …, C.

4.2. Parameter Settings

Let (λ), (L) and (C) represent the values of the kernel parameter, the number of hidden nodes and the cost parameter, respectively. Those parameters need to be chosen probably for better results. In the simulations, we have tested a set of values for all parameters. For all datasets, we have used different range of values. The range of (λ) is (0.1, 0.2, …, 10), the range of L is (10, 15, 20, …, 2000) and the range of C is (2^2, 2^4, …, 2^{50}). The optimum case of the selected parameters is illustrated in Table 3.

4.3. Evaluation Metrics

As accuracy is the most frequently used metric, we adopt it in the current study. However, to measure the achievement of the algorithms trained on unbalanced data; accuracy is not sufficient. Due to its sensitivity to the data distribution (He and Garcia, 2009). Suppose we have a binary classification problem which consists of 98% of the negative class and 2% of a positive class. Random guess gets 98% correctness by labeling all examples as negative. Even if the final accuracy is 98% but the accuracy for the positive class is zero. One more accurate measure is G-mean (Fawcett, 2004). Sensitivity (Sn) measures the true positive rate, can be defined as:

$$Sn = \frac{TP}{TP + FN} \tag{12}$$

Specificity (Sp) measures the true negative rate, can be defined as:

$$Sp = \frac{TN}{TN + FP} \tag{13}$$

G-mean could be defined in term of sensitivity and specificity which measure the overall learning algorithm performance:

$$G - mean = \sqrt{Sn \times Sp} \tag{14}$$

Another measure is receiver operating characteristics (ROC) graph (Fawcett, 2004, 2006), which is two-dimensional graph. The true positive rate plotted on the Y-axis and false negative rate plotted on the X-axis. It depicts the relative tradeoff between true positives and false positives. The result of classification is cognizable with a single point of a single classifier for concrete class and negative class rating. Figure 3 shows a ROC plot with four learners A, B, C and D. The point (0, 1) represents the case when the actual rate of minority class is one (100% accuracy). The point (0.3, 0.6) achieves 60% precision for minority class and 70% accuracy for majority class. Point (0.2, 0.2) represent the random classifier (any point on the diagonal), which predicts labels by random guess. All points in the upper triangle are better than those in lower triangle (all points close to perfect classifier point (0, 1). Therefore, if point in the graph is near to the point (0, 1), it is better than a point far away from the perfect point.

Figure 3. ROC graph with four classifiers

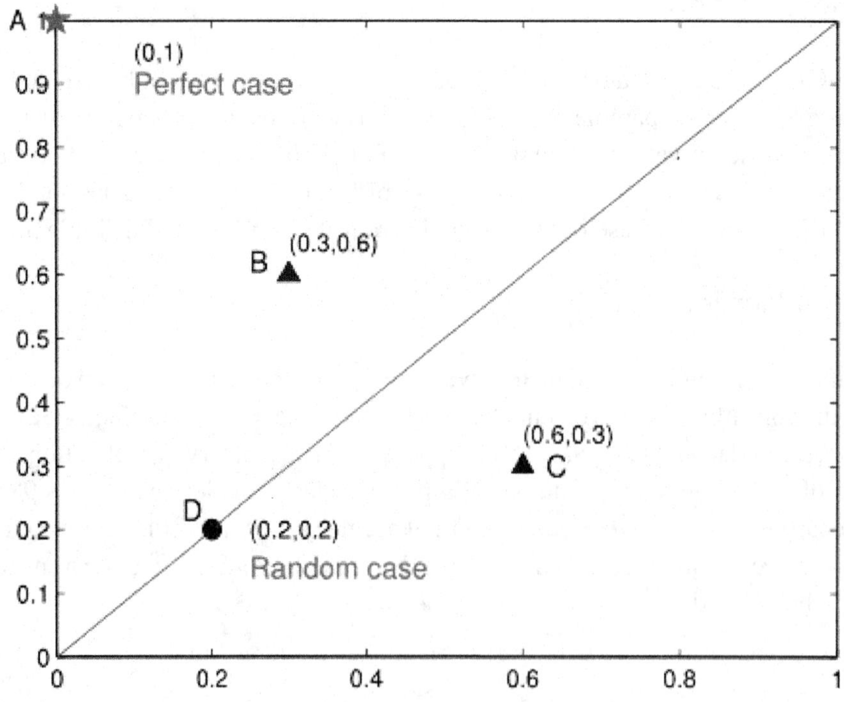

4.4. Performance Analysis and Discussion

The classification experiments on the datasets are performed using AELME and compare with multiclass AdaBoost ELM (MELM) algorithm (Jiang, Shen et al., 2015), Basic ELM (Huang, Zhu et al., 2004), RELM (Huang, Zhou et al., 2012) and KELM (Huang, Ding et al., 2010).The average classification of accuracy rates for the experiments on the binary and multiclass data sets are shown in Table 4. Accuracy rates on the tested datasets demonstrate the generalization performance of the model, as we can see from the results that AELME model achieves the highest accuracy rate in most cases. AELME accuracy is greater than other models in almost all datasets. The average mean absolute error for AELME is 0.0243 while it is 0.0326, 0.0623, 0.0345 and 0.0544 for MELM, ELM, RELM and KELM respectively on all datasets. On the average, there is 79.54%, 387%, 172% and 251.4% reduction in the error relative to AELME on all datasets, compared to MELM, ELM, RELM and KELM, respectively.

The average mean absolute error for AELME is 0.0241 while it is 0.0276, 0.0576, 0.0323 and 0.0497 for MELM, ELM, RELM and KELM respectively on multiclass datasets. On the average, there is 52.87%, 350.3%, 162.4% and 224.1% reduction in the error relative to AELME on multiclass datasets, compared to MELM, ELM, RELM and KELM, respectively.

Table 6 shows the G-mean values of all learning algorithms on binary and multiclass datasets. The average G-mean of AELME model is higher than all models on all data sets. According to the results and discussions, we can claim that AELME is better or comparable to other models in this study.

Moreover, Figure4 and Figure5 show the ROC graph for AELME and other models on two datasets with two imbalanced ratios. The point in the chart indicates the accuracy of the classes which related to one classifier. Those figures show that true positive rate and the true negative rate of AELME are increased. Figure 4 depicts huge imbalance dataset. We observe that both true majority class rate and true minority class rate are increased after applying AELME. We also used the box plot to show the experimental results in Figure 6. The box plot is none parametric tool and it is most important in data reporting because it allows the visual representation of the algorithm performance. It shows statistical characteristics: the median, maximum and minimum values and the quartiles. From Figure 6 on average AELME is better than all other models as its median is the best. The box of AELME is shorter than the boxes generated by almost all other models. It is an indication that the dispersion degree of AELME ensemble is relatively small and more consistent.

4.5. Statistical Test Result

A pair wise t-test is used for more comparisons between AELME and other models in this study. We used significance level 95% (threshold is equal 0.05). This test checks whether the mean difference in the algorithm performance over the datasets is statically significant (different from zero). Small values of P (p-value) cast doubt on the verity of the null hypothesis. A small p-value verifies that one approach is more significant than the other. The results in Table 5 show that AELME has low values compared with almost all other models. Therefore, it is evidence that the performance of AELME is better or compared with other algorithms.

Figure 4. Classification results represented by ROC graph using Yeast1 dataset with imbalance ratio equals: 2.46

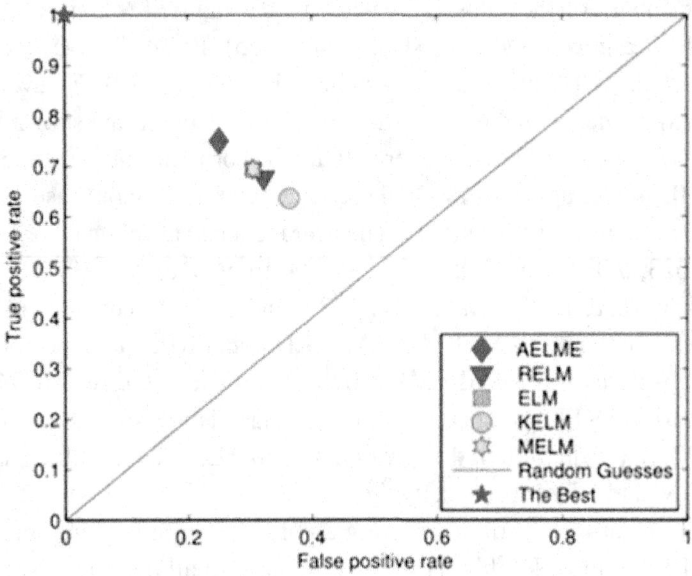

Figure 5. Classification results represented by ROC graph using Yeast5 dataset with imbalance ratio equals: 32.78

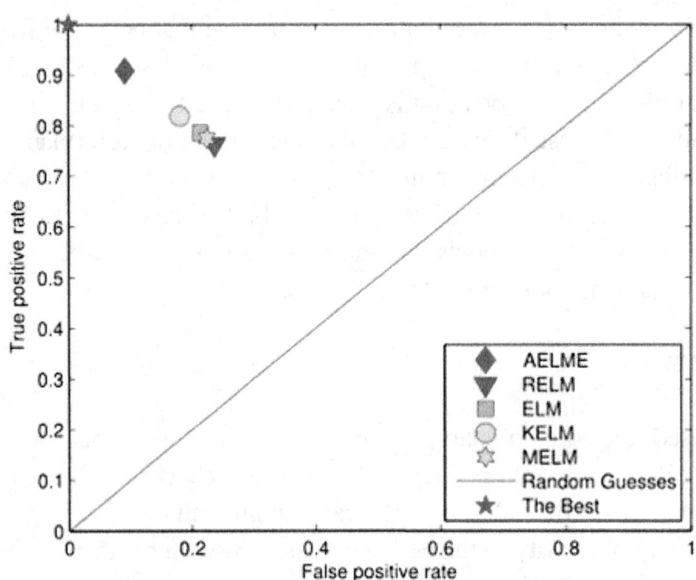

Figure 6. The box plots of experimental results over datasets

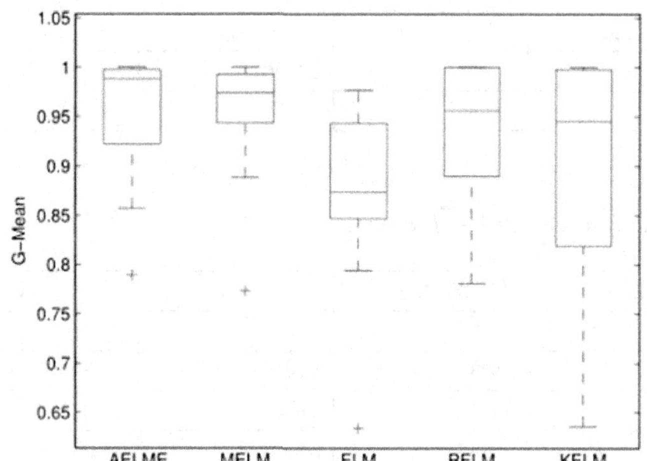

5. CONCLUSION

ELM attained considerable generalization performance; however, it is sensitive to imbalanced data. The research shows that ensemble approach is more suitable for imbalanced data. Inspired by the good achievement of ELM and AdaBoost ensemble, the research proposed a unique advanced AdaBoost ensemble based extreme learning machine (AELME) for imbalanced data classification. The proposed ensemble constructed by using regularized ELM and kernel ELM. Each one is independent of the other to achieve diversity within the proposed ELM ensemble. Using different types of ELM algorithms in the band and using different training datasets for each classifier; allows the base classifiers to generate different decision boundaries as well as altered errors. While, reducing the total error and then a combination of all classifiers would achieve more accurate results. Likewise, generalization performance of the ensemble would also be increased. Experimental results showed that the proposed ELM model is precise in term of G-mean and performance metrics. As a future work, this algorithm could be expanded to cost sensitive learning algorithm.

Table 4. Performance results of binary and multiclass problems

Dataset	AELME	MELM	ELM	RELM	KELM
new-thyroid1	1	1	0.981	1	1
segment0	0.999	0.996	0.989	0.996	0.997
Yeast1	0.836	0.824	0.764	0.855	0.765
Vehcile2	0.994	0.988	0.912	0.965	0.924
page-blocks0	0.995	0.995	0.96	0.952	0.957
shuttle-c0-vs-c4	1	0.999	0.994	1	0.997
Yeast5	0.986	0.983	0.945	0.973	0.962
shuttle-2_vs_5	0.997	0.994	0.994	1	1
Dermatology	0.968	0.952	0.863	0.925	0.861
Shuttle	0.982	0.943	0.975	0.989	0.993

Table 5. T-test results of binary and multiclass problems

	AELME	MELM	ELM	RELM	KELM
AELME		0.4658	2.1996e-4	0.0803	0.0437
MELM	0.5341		3.5706E-4	0.1880	0.0586

Table 6. G-mean results of binary and multiclass problems

Dataset	AELME	MELM	ELM	RELM	KELM
new-thyroid1	1	1	0.943	1	1
segment0	0.998	0.993	0.971	0.985	0.998
Yeast1	0.789	0.773	0.634	0.781	0.636
Vehcile2	0.992	0.984	0.881	0.954	0.912
page-blocks0	0.984	0.966	0.847	0.89	0.808
shuttle-c0-vs-c4	1	0.999	0.977	1	0.979
Yeast5	0.857	0.943	0.794	0.81	0.819
shuttle-2_vs_5	0.995	0.982	0.864	1	1
Dermatology	0.96	0.96	0.905	0.948	0.909
Shuttle	0.922	0.888	0.867	0.958	0.987

ACKNOWLEDGMENT

This research is funded by the National Natural Science Foundation of China under Grants U1836106 and U1736117, the National Key Research and Development Program of China under Grant 2016YFC0600510, the University of Science and Technology Beijing - National Taipei University of Technology Joint Research Program under Grant TW201705, and the Key Laboratory of Geological Information Technology, Ministry of Natural Resources of the People's Republic of China under Grant 2017320.

REFERENCES

Adnan, O. M Abuassba, Yao Zhang, Luo Xiong, Dezheng Zhang, Aziguli Wulamu(2017a). A Heterogeneous Ensemble of Extreme Learning Machines With Correntropy and Negative Correlation. *Tsinghua Science and Technology*. doi:10.23919/TST.2017.8195351

Adnan, O. M. (2017b). *Abuassba, Zhang Dezheng, Zahid Mahmoud*. Semi-supervised Multi-kernel Extreme Learning Machin. Elsevier Procedia Computer Science.

Alcalá-Fdez, J., Fernández, A., Luengo, J., Derrac, J., García, S., Sánchez, L., & Herrera, F. (2011). Keel data-mining software tool: data set repository, integration of algorithms and experimental analysis framework. *Journal of Multiple-Valued Logic & Soft Computing, 17*.

Bezdek, J. C. (2016). (Computational) intelligence. *IEEE Systems, Man, and Cybernetics Magazine*, *2*(2), 4–14. doi:10.1109/MSMC.2016.2558778

Cao, J., Kwong, S., Wang, R., Li, X., Li, K., & Kong, X. (2015). Class-specific soft voting based multiple extreme learning machines ensemble. *Neurocomputing*, *149*, 275–284. doi:10.1016/j.neucom.2014.02.072

Chen, M., Li, Y., Luo, X., Wang, W., Wang, L., & Zhao, W. (2018). A novel human activity recognition scheme for smart health using multilayer extreme learning machine. *IEEE Internet of Things Journal*. doi:10.1109/JIOT.2018.2856241

Duan, L., Xie, M., Bai, T., & Wang, J. (2016). A new support vector data description method for machinery fault diagnosis with unbalanced datasets. *Expert Systems with Applications*, *64*, 239–246. doi:10.1016/j.eswa.2016.07.039

Fernández, A., García, S., del Jesus, M. J., & Herrera, F. (2008). A study of the behaviour of linguistic fuzzy rule based classification systems in the framework of imbalanced data-sets. *Fuzzy Sets and Systems*, *159*(18), 2378–2398. doi:10.1016/j.fss.2007.12.023

Huang, G. B., Zhou, H., Ding, X., & Zhang, R. (2012). Extreme learning machine for regression and multiclass classification. *IEEE Transactions on Systems, Man, and Cybernetics. Part B, Cybernetics*, *42*(2), 513–529. doi:10.1109/TSMCB.2011.2168604 PMID:21984515

Liu, Q., He, Q., & Shi, Z. (2008). Extreme support vector machine classifier. In Pacific-Asia conference on knowledge discovery and data mining. Springer.

Fawcett, T. (2004). ROC graphs: Notes and practical considerations for researchers. *Machine Learning*, *31*(1), 1–38.

Fawcett, T. (2006). An introduction to ROC analysis. *Pattern Recognition Letters*, *27*(8), 861–874. doi:10.1016/j.patrec.2005.10.010

Freund, Y., & Schapire, R. E. (1995). A decision-theoretic generalization of on-line learning and an application to boosting. In *European conference on computational learning theory*. Springer. 10.1007/3-540-59119-2_166

Freund, Y. and R. E. Schapire (1996). Experiments with a new boosting algorithm.

Friedman, J., Hastie, T., & Tibshirani, R. (2000). Additive logistic regression: A statistical view of boosting (with discussion and a rejoinder by the authors). *Annals of Statistics*, *28*(2), 337–407. doi:10.1214/aos/1016218223

He, H., & Garcia, E. A. (2009). Learning from imbalanced data. *IEEE Transactions on Knowledge and Data Engineering*, *21*(9), 1263–1284. doi:10.1109/TKDE.2008.239

Huang, G.-B. (2014). An insight into extreme learning machines: Random neurons, random features and kernels. *Cognitive Computation*, *6*(3), 376–390. doi:10.100712559-014-9255-2

Huang, G.-B., Ding, X., & Zhou, H. (2010). Optimization method based extreme learning machine for classification. *Neurocomputing*, *74*(1), 155–163. doi:10.1016/j.neucom.2010.02.019

Huang, G.-B., Wang, D. H., & Lan, Y. (2010). Extreme learning machines: A survey. *International Journal of Machine Learning and Cybernetics*, *2*(2), 107–122. doi:10.100713042-011-0019-y

Huang, G.-B., Zhu, Q.-Y., & Siew, C.-K. (2006). Extreme learning machine: Theory and applications. *Neurocomputing*, *70*(1), 489–501. doi:10.1016/j.neucom.2005.12.126

Huang, G. B., Zhu, Q. Y., & Siew, C. K. (2004). Extreme learning machine: a new learning scheme of feedforward neural networks. In *2004 IEEE International Joint Conference on Neural Networks, 2004. Proceedings*. IEEE.

Li, K., Kong, X., Lu, Z., Wenyin, L., & Yin, J. (2014). Boosting weighted ELM for imbalanced learning. *Neurocomputing*, *128*, 15–21. doi:10.1016/j.neucom.2013.05.051

Luo, X., Jiang, C., Wang, W., Xu, Y., Wang, J.-H., & Zhao, W. (2019). User behavior prediction in social networks using weighted extreme learning machine with distribution optimization. *Future Generation Computer Systems*, *93*, 1023–1035. doi:10.1016/j.future.2018.04.085

Luo, X., Sun, J., Wang, L., Wang, W., Zhao, W., Wu, J., ... Zhang, Z. (2018). Short-term wind speed forecasting via stacked extreme learning machine with generalized correntropy. *IEEE Transactions on Industrial Informatics*, *14*(11), 4963–4971. doi:10.1109/TII.2018.2854549

Luo, X., Xu, Y., Wang, W., Yuan, M., Ban, X., Zhu, Y., & Zhao, W. (2018). Towards enhancing stacked extreme learning machine with sparse autoencoder by correntropy. *Journal of the Franklin Institute*, *355*(4), 1945–1966. doi:10.1016/j.jfranklin.2017.08.014

Mazurowski, M. A., Habas, P. A., Zurada, J. M., Lo, J. Y., Baker, J. A., & Tourassi, G. D. (2008). Training neural network classifiers for medical decision making: The effects of imbalanced datasets on classification performance. *Neural Networks*, *21*(2), 427–436. doi:10.1016/j.neunet.2007.12.031 PMID:18272329

Jiang, Y., Shen, Y., Liu, Y., & Liu, W. (2015). Multiclass AdaBoost ELM and its application in LBP based face recognition. *Mathematical Problems in Engineering*.

Hirose A., Ozawa S., Doya, K., Ikeda K., Lee M., Liu D. (Eds). (2016). Neural Information Processing. Springer.

Rani, K. U., Ramadevi, G. N., & Lavanya, D. (2016). Performance of synthetic minority oversampling technique on imbalanced breast cancer data. In *2016 3rd International Conference on Computing for Sustainable Global Development (INDIACom)*. IEEE.

Ren, F., Cao, P., Li, W., Zhao, D., & Zaiane, O. (2017). Ensemble based adaptive over-sampling method for imbalanced data learning in computer aided detection of microaneurysm. *Computerized Medical Imaging and Graphics*, *55*, 54–67. doi:10.1016/j.compmedimag.2016.07.011 PMID:27507324

Song, J., Huang, X., Qin, S., & Song, Q. (2016). A bi-directional sampling based on K-means method for imbalance text classification. In *2016 IEEE/ACIS 15th International Conference on Computer and Information Science (ICIS)*. IEEE.

Sun, Y., Kamel, M. S., Wong, A. K. C., & Wang, Y. (2007). Cost-sensitive boosting for classification of imbalanced data. *Pattern Recognition*, *40*(12), 3358–3378. doi:10.1016/j.patcog.2007.04.009

Tapkan, P., Özbakir, L., Kulluk, S., & Baykasoğlu, A. (2016). A cost-sensitive classification algorithm: BEE-Miner. *Knowledge-Based Systems*, *95*, 99–113. doi:10.1016/j.knosys.2015.12.010

Wang, G., & Li, P. (2010). Dynamic Adaboost ensemble extreme learning machine. *2010 3rd International Conference on Advanced Computer Theory and Engineering (ICACTE)*. IEEE.

Zhang, Y., Liu, B., Cai, J., & Zhang, S. (2017). Ensemble weighted extreme learning machine for imbalanced data classification based on differential evolution. Neural Computing and Applications, 28(1), 259-267.

Zhao, X. M., Li, X., Chen, L., & Aihara, K. (2008). Protein classification with imbalanced data. *Proteins*, *70*(4), 1125–1132. doi:10.1002/prot.21870 PMID:18076026

This research was previously published in the International Journal of Cognitive Informatics and Natural Intelligence (IJCINI), 13(3); pages 19-35, copyright year 2019 by IGI Publishing (an imprint of IGI Global).

Chapter 31
Network Support Data Analysis for Fault Identification Using Machine Learning

Shakila Basheer
King Khalid University, Abha, Saudi Arabia

Usha Devi Gandhi
VIT University, Vellore, India

Priyan M.K.
VIT University, Vellore, India

Parthasarathy P.
VIT University, Vellore, India

ABSTRACT

Machine learning has gained immense popularity in a variety of fields as it has the ability to change the conventional workflow of a process. The abundance of data available serves as the motivation for this. This data can be exploited for a good deal of knowledge. In this article, we focus on operational data of networking devices that are deployed in different locations. This data can be used to predict faults in the devices. Usually, after the deployment of networking devices in customer site, troubleshooting these devices is difficult. Operational data of these devices is needed for this process. Manually analysing the machined produced operational data is tedious and complex due to enormity of data. Using machine learning techniques will be of greater help here as this will help automate the troubleshooting process, avoid human errors and save time for the technical solutions engineers.

DOI: 10.4018/978-1-6684-6291-1.ch031

1. INTRODUCTION

Text Mining is widely used nowadays to mine useful patterns from text. Text mining has a found its use in business, medicine, education, drug discovery, etc. As an effect of this, there is a lot of research going on to analyse natural language (i.e. human produced data). But, nowadays machines also produce enormous amount of operational data which are semi-structured (e.g. system logs, usage logs, error logs etc.). The data produced by machines is the main source of identifying faults in machines. So, it is crucial to analyse machine produced data.

The machine produced data that we are considering for our course of research is 'Show Tech Support'. These are referred as Network Support data files. These files contain operational data of networking devices that are deployed at different sites. The Network Support data are the source of many useful information about the device. It contains information about the software and features that are configured in the device. The contents of support data files vary from time to time as it is a device's operational data. When there is a malfunction or fault in a device, support data files are of use. They are used to trouble shoot the faults in the networking devices. These files are unique to their make and device configuration set up. Support data files are difficult to analyse manually because of the complex nature and enormity data. Also, manual analysis is always prone to errors. So, the need for a more systematic and automated analysis arises.

This paper has outlined ongoing research work in Machine Learning and its relevance to our problem in section 2. In section 3, we have discussed about the methodology used. In section 4, a comprehensive comparison between ID3 algorithm and Rule Based induction is done.

2. LITERATURE SURVEY

2.1. Introduction to Machine Learning

In an attempt to analyse the industrial data/machine produced data research fraternity has done a significant contribution. For industrial data analysis, a strong subject expertise is needed. But, the huge result sets and internal relationships between the workflow is sometimes beyond our subjective knowledge. To overcome this, a more generic framework for processing industrial data is needed. Mr. Mariusz Kamola, in his work (2015) has comes up with a defined set of rules for choosing the most required features for predictive analysis on industrial data. Clearly, the processing framework will differ depending on the use case and type of analysis. So, choice of a suitable Machine Learning algorithm is necessary.

Surya, Nithin, Prasanna, and Venkatesan (2016), gives a brief introduction to machine learning and discusses about various machine learning techniques and pre-processing techniques. The paper discuses about three main topics. They are:

- Types of machine learning
- Machine learning techniques
- Linguistic pre-processing

Types of Machine Learning:

- **Supervised Learning:** In this technique, knowledge is referred from training datasets. Example: classification and regression;
- **Unsupervised Learning:** In unsupervised learning, there is no training datasets. In this technique, knowledge is inferred from input data that are not tagged. Example: clustering and dimensional Reduction;
- **Reinforcement Learning:** A software agent is trained to make suitable decisions to be taken which will be based on the previous experience;
- **Machine Learning:** Techniques discussed are, N-Gram and Markov Models, Neural Networks and Decision Tree classifiers;
- **Linguistic Pre-Processing:** This step is a preparatory step which prepares the process to take place. This will ensure that the text will be in a form that would be understood by the machine. Here the context of a word is understood.

2.2. Applications of Machine Learning

As discussed in section 1, Machine Learning finds it application in a variety of fields. Machine Learning is widely used in Natural Language Computing. Khan and Khan (2016) has done a comprehensive work on using Machine Learning to learn the semantics of natural language. The algorithms used in Machine Learning understand and process numerical data. In their research work, they have addressed a crucial demand of understanding the context of text data. Use of SEBLA based NLU for semantic computation has been explored in their work.

Predictive Analytics is another field of Machine Learning which has gained immense popularity. Radhika R Halde (2016), has done a thorough study of predictive analytics and algorithms that are used in it. The main focus of Halde (2016) is using predictive analytics in Education. The author has used SVM, Neural Networks, Logistic Regression, Linear Regression, Decision trees and Naïve Bayes classifier to build the prediction model and concluded that SVM and Neural Networks predicted the numeric data student more accurately. Whereas, Decision trees are more accurate when it comes to classification.

Having talked about using Machine Learning in understanding natural language. Another interesting application of Machine Learning is to make the machines recognize and analyse facial expression. Nugrahaeni and Mutijarsa (2016), discusses about using Machine Learning for recognizing facial expression and compares the performance KNN, SVM and Random Forest algorithms for classifying facial expression. The author has used facial measures as an input to the classification model. The model will classify facial expression to determine the following: happy, sad, angry, disgust, fear, neutral and surprise.

Another important application of machine learning is malware detection and fault Identification. Mr. Matthew Leeds (2016), has done a significant work in using machine learning for malware detection in Android phones. He has used classification algorithms to detect malwares in Android phones. In Nagaraja and Sadashivappa (2016), Mr. Nagaraaja and Sadashivappa have done a survey on fault diagnosis using Machine Learning algorithms. They have explored the use of Artificial Neural Networks, Fuzzy logic and SVM for fault diagnosis.

2.3. Algorithms Used in Machine Learning

In section 2.2, we have discussed about applications of Machine Learning. It is necessary to know the algorithms that are used in those applications. From the previous section it is clear that for a classification problem, Decision trees are accurate for larger datasets. In this section we have done a study on Decision trees and Rule Induction.

In Vlahovic (2016), the author has given a brief survey of decision trees and has proposed an evaluation framework for decision trees. Decision tree belongs to class of supervised learning algorithms. They have a variety of applications ranging from managerial sciences to knowledge engineering. Decision trees are classified as follows:

- Decision Analysis trees;
- Knowledge representation trees;
- Classification and regression trees; and
- Decision forests.

Decision trees were initially used to represent rules that form knowledge/expert systems. Algorithms that are used in decision trees are forward chaining and backward chaining.

The main focus of our work would be to find rules to classify the bugs that might occur in a device. Rule based Induction can be of use here. In Das, Acharjya, and Patra (2014), the authors have proposed a framework for producing decision rules using rule Induction. Rule Induction is a methodology of deriving rules from statistical information based on probabilities. Examples of such rule induction are CN2 (Clark & Niblett, 1989), RIPPER (Cohen, 1995) and C4.5 (Quinlan, 1993).

3. PROPOSED METHODOLOGY

In this section, we discuss about how we would analyse the support data files. Figure 1. shows the module description of the tool. Figure 2. describes the algorithm approached.

3.1. Module Description

3.1.1. Input

Network support data files contain information about the networking devices that have been deployed at customer sites. These files serve as a means by which one could analyse the running configurations of the networking devices and trouble shoot if a problem arises. These files are the input to our system.

3.1.2. Pre-Processing

Pre-processing is an important task that has to be carried out before Analysis. Here, we have cleansed the data to eliminated null values and extreme values. Outlier analysis was done and subject expertise was applied to decide what should be included in the dataset and what should be ignored.

3.1.3 Extract Features

In this step, subset of the features that are suitable for building the learning model are extracted from the files that are inputted in step1. In this case, Device configuration (platform and software version running on a device) and software features that are enabled or configured on a device are extracted.

3.1.4. ID3 Model and Rule Based Induction Model

The Machine Learning model that is built here is a supervised learning model. A classified dataset of bugs based on platform and software version coupled with specifics of the bug is the excellent source for identifying a bug. One way to identify the nature of a bug is to start by knowing the cause for a bug. The attribute selection step depends on strong domain knowledge and use case. A dataset containing Bug Id, Hardware Platform, software version and Features causing the bug is used to build ID3 model and Rule Based Induction model. Bug Id is the label or class that will be predicted at the end of analysis. Software version, Hardware platform and features causing the bug are the classifying attributes in our case.

Rules are constructed based on the results of Rule Based Induction and ID3 Decision trees. Features extracted in step 3 is given as an input to the rules and based on the input we will be directed through the decision tree to predict the bug ID.

Figure 1. System architecture

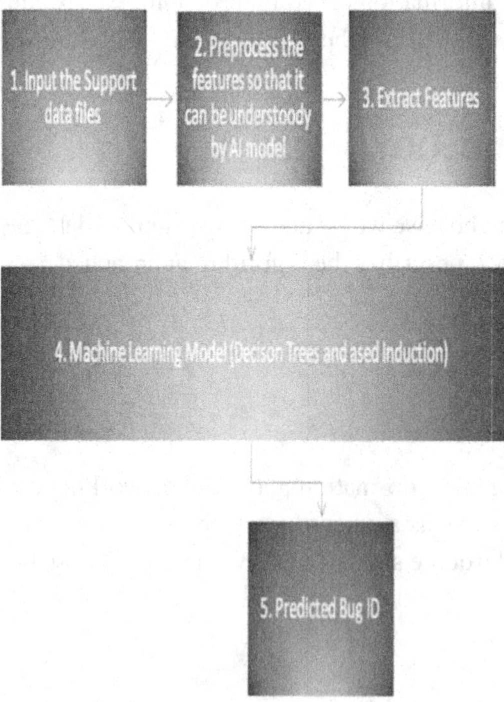

3.1.5. Output

Output of this process will be predicted bug Id. This prediction is based on a device's configuration.

3.2. Software Requirements

The system is built using python 2.7. The language has many programming constructs that help in building both large scale and small-scale software. The language is designed to support many programming styles e.g. Object oriented, functional programming and imperative programming. It has a broad range of standard library which can be used for a variety of purpose. Scikit library is used for developing the Machine Learning model.

Figure 2. Flow chart

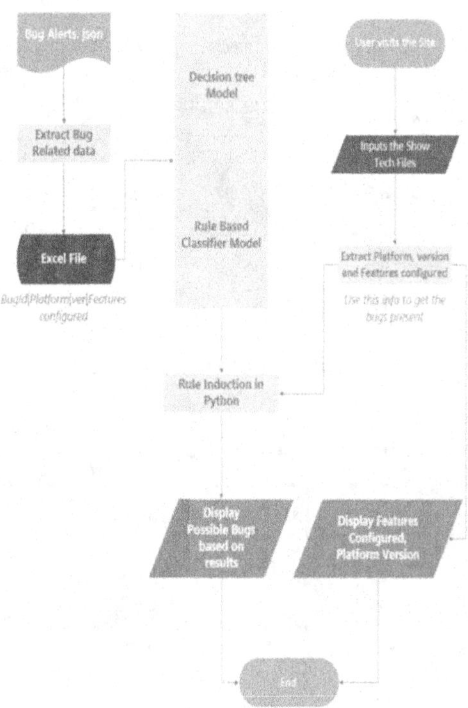

4. RESULTS AND DISCUSSIONS

The experimental setup for comparing ID3 and rule-based induction algorithms was mimicked using Rapid Miner Studio 7.4. The experiment was carried out in three segments:

1. A training dataset of size 100 was used which contained 5 class variables. The results indicate that Rule Based Induction was approximately 2% more accurate than ID3 algorithm. This is shown in Figure 3 and Figure 4 as a confusion matrix;

2. A training dataset Of size 200 with 5 class variables showed that ID3 algorithm is approximately 14% accurate than Rule based Induction. The results are shown in Figure 4 and Figure 5 as a confusion matrix;
3. A training dataset of size 347 with 5 class variables showed that ID3 algorithm outperforms Rule Based Induction by 5%. This is shown in Figure 6 and Figure 7 as a confusion matrix.

In this Confusion Matrices given below, the column headers are true values for the class variable and the row headers are the predicted class variables. For e.g. let us consider class variable 87719. From the matrix, it is clear that it has occurred three times and in all the trials it is predicted correctly. The class variable 102923 is predicted correctly 6 times but predicted as class 87719, 109929, 112650 and 117804 for four, four, three, twelve times.

Figure 3. Confusion matrix for rule-based induction (data size:100) accuracy: 33.33%

accuracy: 33.33%

	true 87719	true 102923	true 109929	true 112650	true 117804	class precision
pred. 87719	3	0	0	0	0	100.00%
pred. 102923	4	6	4	3	12	20.69%
pred. 109929	0	0	5	3	4	41.67%
pred. 112650	0	0	0	0	0	0.00%
pred. 117804	0	0	0	0	1	100.00%
class recall	42.86%	100.00%	55.56%	0.00%	5.88%	

Figure 4. Confusion matrix for ID3 algorithm (data size:100) accuracy: 31.11%

accuracy: 31.11%

	true 87719	true 102923	true 109929	true 112650	true 117804	class precision
pred. 87719	7	0	0	0	8	46.67%
pred. 102923	0	6	9	6	5	23.08%
pred. 109929	0	0	0	0	3	0.00%
pred. 112650	0	0	0	0	0	0.00%
pred. 117804	0	0	0	0	1	100.00%
class recall	100.00%	100.00%	0.00%	0.00%	5.88%	

Figure 5. Confusion matrix for rule-based induction (data size:200) accuracy: 48.89%

accuracy: 48.89%

	true 87719	true 102923	true 109929	true 112650	true 117804	class precision
pred. 87719	0	0	0	0	0	0.00%
pred. 102923	7	6	9	6	1	20.69%
pred. 109929	0	0	0	0	0	0.00%
pred. 112650	0	0	0	0	0	0.00%
pred. 117804	0	0	0	0	16	100.00%
class recall	0.00%	100.00%	0.00%	0.00%	94.12%	

Figure 6. Confusion matrix for ID3 algorithm (data size:200) accuracy: 62.22%

accuracy: 62.22%

	true 87719	true 102923	true 109929	true 112650	true 117804	class precision
pred. 87719	7	0	0	0	0	100.00%
pred. 102923	0	6	6	0	8	30.00%
pred. 109929	0	0	0	0	0	0.00%
pred. 112650	0	0	3	6	0	66.67%
pred. 117804	0	0	0	0	9	100.00%
class recall	100.00%	100.00%	0.00%	100.00%	52.94%	

Figure 7. Confusion matrix for rule-based induction (data size:347) accuracy: 75.56%

accuracy: 75.56%

	true 87719	true 102923	true 109929	true 112650	true 117804	class precision
pred. 87719	7	0	0	0	0	100.00%
pred. 102923	0	6	9	0	0	40.00%
pred. 109929	0	0	0	0	0	0.00%
pred. 112650	0	0	0	4	0	100.00%
pred. 117804	0	0	0	2	17	89.47%
class recall	100.00%	100.00%	0.00%	66.67%	100.00%	

Figure 8. Confusion matrix for ID3 algorithm (data size:347) accuracy: 80.00%

accuracy: 80.00%

	true 87719	true 102923	true 109929	true 112650	true 117804	class precision
pred. 87719	7	0	0	0	0	100.00%
pred. 102923	0	6	9	0	0	40.00%
pred. 109929	0	0	0	0	0	0.00%
pred. 112650	0	0	0	6	0	100.00%
pred. 117804	0	0	0	0	17	100.00%
class recall	100.00%	100.00%	0.00%	100.00%	100.00%	

The accuracy comparison graph for ID3 and Rule Based Induction is shown in Figure 9.

5. CONCLUSION AND FUTURE WORK

A prediction model for identifying faults in devices deployed at remote sites is built. The accuracy of the model is largely affected by the feature selection and the data size. ID3 model is proved to be more accurate for larger datasets as the classification variables are selected based on the Information entropy and Gini index whereas in Rule Based Induction vague probabilities are used to define rules. As a future scope for this paper, use of Support Vector Machines and Artificial Neural Networks for Operational/ Machine Produced data will be explored.

Figure 9. Comparison of accuracy between ID3 algorithm and rule-based induction

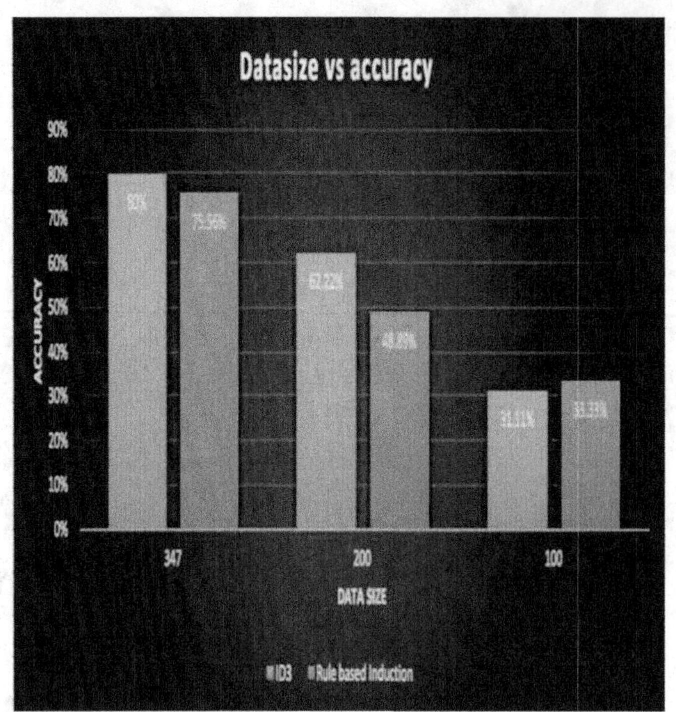

REFERENCES

Clark, P., & Niblett, T. (1989). The CN2 induction algorithm. *Machine Learning*, *3*(4), 261–283. doi:10.1007/BF00116835

Cohen, W. (1995). Fast effective rule induction. In *Proceedings of the twelfth international conference on machine learning* (pp. 115 -123).

Das, T. K., Acharjya, D. P., & Patra, M. R. (2014). Business Intelligence from online product review-a rough set based rule induction approach. In Contemporary Computing and Informatics. doi:10.1109/IC3I.2014.7019662

Kamola, M. (2015). Analytics of industrial operational data inspired by natural language processing. In *IEEE International Congress on Big Data* (pp. 681-684). 10.1109/BigDataCongress.2015.108

Khan, E. (2016). Machine Learning Algorithms for Natural Language Semantics and Cognitive Computing. In *International Conference of Computational Science and Computational Intelligence* (pp. 1146-1151).

Leeds, M. (2016). Preliminary Results of Applying Machine Learning Algorithms to Android Malware Detection. In *International Conference of Computational Science and Computational Intelligence* (pp. 1070-1073). 10.1109/CSCI.2016.0204

Nagaraja, P., & Sadashivappa, G. (2016). Fault Diagnosis of Circuits Using Statistical Parameters and Implementation using Classifiers- A Survey. In *International Conference on Communication and Signal Processing* (pp. 2162-2166).

Nugrahaeni, R. A., & Mutijarsa, K. (2016, August). Comparative analysis of machine learning KNN, SVM, and random forests algorithm for facial expression classification. In *International Seminar on Application for Technology of Information and Communication (ISemantic)* (pp. 163-168). IEEE.

Quinlan, J. R. (1993). C4.5: programs for machine learning.

Radhika, R. (2016). Application of Machine Learning Algorithms for Betterment in Education System. In *International Conference on Automatic Control and Dynamic Optimization Techniques* (pp. 1110-1114).

Surya, K., Nithin, R., Prasanna, S., & Venkatesan, R. (2016). A Comprehensive Study on Machine Learning Concepts for Text Mining. In *International Conference on Circuit, Power and Computing Technologies*. 10.1109/ICCPCT.2016.7530259

Vlahovic, N. (2016, May). An evaluation framework and a brief survey of decision tree tools. In 2016 39th International Convention on Information and Communication Technology, Electronics and Micro-electronics (MIPRO) (pp. 1299-1304). IEEE.

This research was previously published in the International Journal of Software Innovation (IJSI), 72); pages 41-49, copyright year 2019 by IGI Publishing (an imprint of IGI Global).

Chapter 32
Hybridization of Machine Learning Algorithm in Intrusion Detection System

Amudha P.
Avinashilingam Institute for Home Science and Higher Education for Women, India

Sivakumari S.
Avinashilingam Institute for Home Science and Higher Education for Women, India

ABSTRACT

In recent years, the field of machine learning grows very fast both on the development of techniques and its application in intrusion detection. The computational complexity of the machine learning algorithms increases rapidly as the number of features in the datasets increases. By choosing the significant features, the number of features in the dataset can be reduced, which is critical to progress the classification accuracy and speed of algorithms. Also, achieving high accuracy and detection rate and lowering false alarm rates are the major challenges in designing an intrusion detection system. The major motivation of this work is to address these issues by hybridizing machine learning and swarm intelligence algorithms for enhancing the performance of intrusion detection system. It also emphasizes applying principal component analysis as feature selection technique on intrusion detection dataset for identifying the most suitable feature subsets which may provide high-quality results in a fast and efficient manner.

INTRODUCTION

Network security has become a vital aspect of computer technology as there is great improvement in usage of internet. There is a tremendous growth in the field of information technology due to which, network security is also facing significant challenges. As traditional intrusion prevention techniques have failed to protect the computer systems from various attacks and intruders, the concept of Intrusion Detection System (IDS) proposed by Denning (1987) has become an essential component of security infrastructure for the networks connected to the internet and is useful to detect, identify and track the intruders.

DOI: 10.4018/978-1-6684-6291-1.ch032

Intrusion Detection System

An Intrusion Detection System (IDS) is a software application that continuously perceives computer network looking for malicious actions or strategy defilements and generates reports. According to recent studies, an average of twenty to forty new vulnerabilities in commonly used networking and computer products are discovered every month. These wide-ranging vulnerabilities in software enlarge or increase today's insecure computing/networking environment. Hence, such insecure environment has paved way to the ever evolving field of intrusion detection and prevention. The cyberspace's equivalent to the burglar alarm, intrusion detection systems complement the beleaguered firewall.

Intrusion Detection System is a security mechanism which has been acknowledged by the researchers from all over the world because of their capability to keep track of the network behaviour, so that abnormal behaviour can be detected quickly. The traditional IDS is unable to handle the recent attacks and malwares. Hence, IDS which is a vital element of the network needs to be safeguarded.

Steps of IDS are

- Monitoring and analysing traffic.
- Identifying abnormal activities.
- Assessing severity and raising alarm.

Figure 1 shows the basic architecture of intrusion detection system.

The Major Components of IDS Include

- Knowledge Base which encompasses pre-processed information provided by network experts and collected by the sensors.
- Configuration Device which provides data related to the present state of the IDS.
- Detector – ID Engine which identifies intrusive actions based on the data collected from sensors and sends an alarm to response component if intrusion occurs.
- Response Component which initiates response if an intrusion is detected.
- Data Gathering Device which is responsible for collecting data from monitored system.

The packets that are received are transmitted over the computer network and captured. Data are collected and pre-processed to remove the noise and irrelevant attributes. Then the pre-processed data are analysed and classified based on their severity actions. If the record is found normal, then it does not need any change in the action, otherwise, it is sent for report generation. Depending on the state of the data, alarms are raised to alert the administrator to handle the state in advance. The attack is modelled in order to facilitate the classification of network data.

Intrusion Detection Methods

In IDS, detection method is categorized into misuse detection and anomaly detection (Endler 1998) which are also known as knowledge based and behaviour based intrusion detection (Debar 2000) respectively. Patterns of well-known attacks are used to identify intrusions in misuse detection, whereas, anomaly

Figure 1. Basic architecture of intrusion detection system

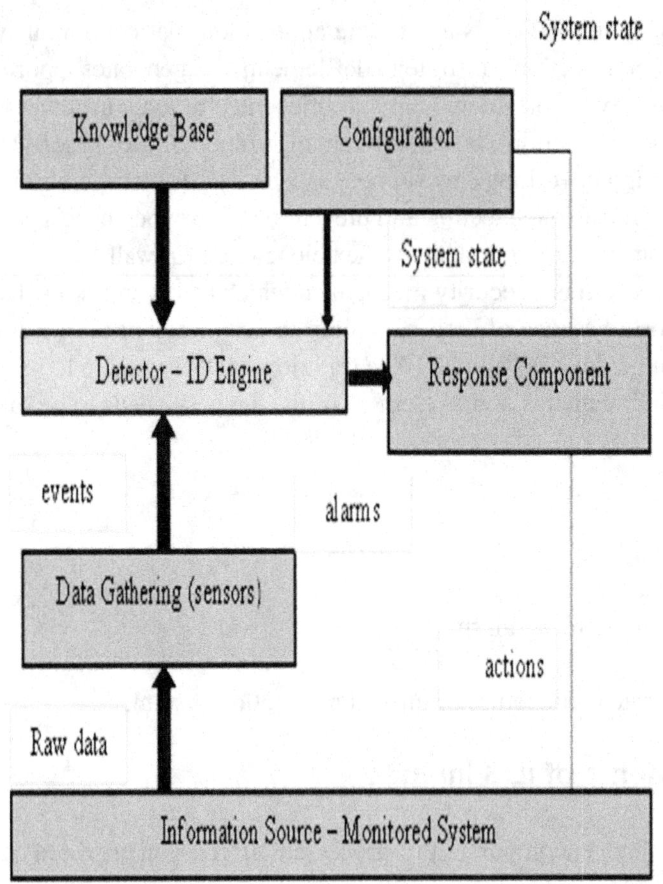

detection determines the deviation from the normal usage patterns which can be flagged as intrusions. Some IDSs combine the capabilities of both the methods by hybridization of techniques.

Misuse detection technique is also known as Signature-based detection and a database is usually used to store the signatures of known attacks which may be constantly updated. The limitation of this type of detection technique is that, if any new type of threat comes, which is not already known to the IDS, the system becomes vulnerable to that attack. Anomaly detection is also known as Profile detection, which monitors network traffic and compares it against an established baseline for normal use bandwidth, protocols, ports and devices generally connecting to each other. The administrator is given 'alerts' when the traffic is sensed as anomalous, or if the attack types are unknown. In the case of detecting a data target, intrusion detecting system can be classified as host-based and network-based (Debar 2000).

1. **Host-based Intrusion Detection System (HIDS):** It consists of a representative of a host that detects interventions by examining system calls, application logs, file-system modifications and other host activities.

2. **Network-based Intrusion Detection System (NIDS):** It detects intrusions by monitoring network traffic and observing multiple hosts. Also NIDS can obtain the means to access network traffic by linking to a network hub, network switch configured for port mirroring, or network taps.

The characteristics of intrusion detection system are shown in Figure 2.

Figure 2. Characteristics of Intrusion Detection System

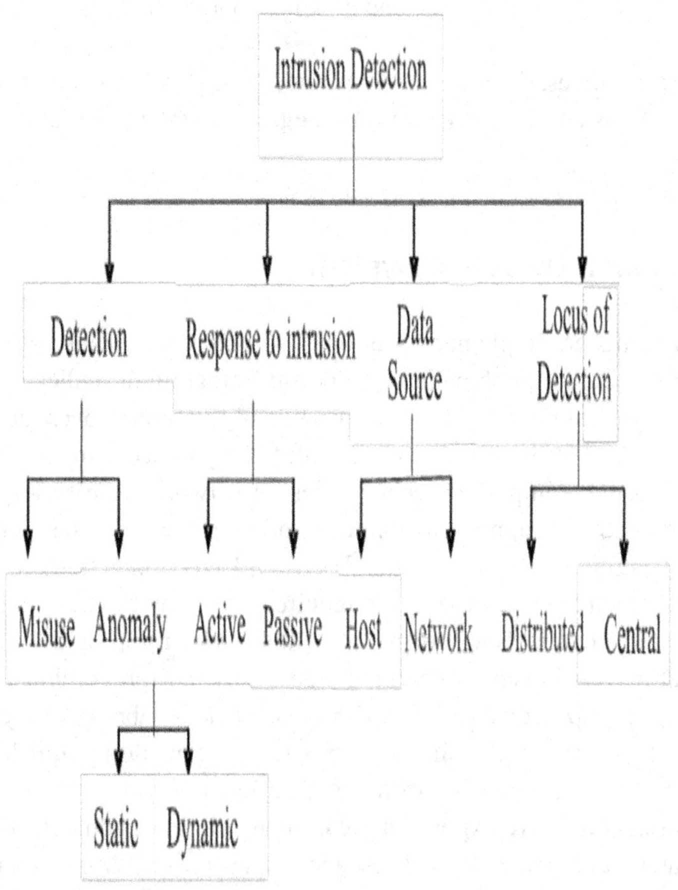

Features of Intrusion Detection System

The features of intrusion detection system are:

- The IDS must be able to detect any modifications forced by an attacker.
- Impose minimal overhead on the system.
- Be easy to deploy.
- Detects different types of attacks.

- The IDS must be able to recover from system crashes, either accidental or caused by malicious activity.

Goals of Intrusion Detection System

- Identify varied type of intrusions
    - Known and unknown attacks.
    - Detect intrusions in a timely manner.
    - Analysis to be presented in simple and understandable format.
- Be accurate
    - Reduce false positives, false negatives where, false positive is an event, incorrectly identified by the IDS as an intrusion, and false negative is an event that the IDS fails to identify an intrusion.
    - Minimize the time spent on verifying attacks.

Importance of Intrusion Detection System

Intrusion Detection Systems are implemented in order to detect malicious activities and it functions behind the firewall, observing for patterns in network traffic that might indicate malicious action. The extreme development of the internet, the high occurrence of the threats over the internet has been the cause in recognizing the need for both IDS and firewall to help in securing a network. Thus, the IDSs along with the firewall form the important technologies for network security. Joshi & Pimprale (2013) discussed that with the rapid development in communication technology, the security of computer network is one of the challenging issues and so as an Intrusion Detection system.

IDS methodologies which are currently in use require human intervention to generate attack signatures or to determine effective models for normal behavior. In order to provide a potential alternative to expensive human input, we are in need of learning algorithms. The predominant task of such learning algorithm is to discover appropriate behavior of IDS as normal and abnormal (system is under attack). The algorithm should be accurate and it should process the information in quick successions which is one of the major drawbacks in IDS because of the large amount of features.

Recently several researchers have exposed a great interest in intrusion detection based on machine learning and swarm intelligence techniques. These techniques provide improved performance in intrusion detection process with good detection rate (Dokas et al 2002). Also, to improve the performance of classifiers, currently researchers focus more on combining the techniques to exploit the advantages of individual techniques. Hence, this work focuses on hybrid swarm based intrusion detection system in which the performance of swarm intelligence algorithms and machine learning algorithms are analysed with the feature subsets formed and to classify the data and detect intrusions.

Applications of Intrusion Detection System

The application of IDS in various fields is described:

IDS in Mobile Adhoc Network

IDS are used in MANET to find the intruder when transmitting the series of packets to the destination through mobile network.

IDS in Cloud Computing

Cloud computing is the most vulnerable targets for intruder due to their distributed environment. Hence, IDS are used in the cloud to detect malicious action and improve the security measures (Shelke et al 2012).

IDS in Machine Learning

To deal with the new arising attacks in networks, machine learning can help improve intrusion detection by distinguishing attack from common traffic on the network.

MACHINE LEARNING IN INTRUSION DETECTION SYSTEM

Intrusion detection using machine learning has gained prominence among the research community in recent years. Applying machine learning techniques on network traffic data is a promising solution that helps to develop better intrusion detection systems.

Machine Learning explores algorithms that can,

- learn from data / build a model from data
- use the model for prediction, decision making or solving some tasks

The broad types of machine learning are shown in Figure 3.

Supervised Learning

The training data based on observation, measurement are accompanied by the labels indicating the class of the observation. New data is classified based on the training. In this method user has to provide training examples.

Unsupervised Learning

Unsupervised learning refers to the process of finding the hidden structure in unlabelled data. Unsupervised learning also encompasses many other techniques that seek to summarize and explain key attributes of the data.

Need of Machine Learning in Intrusion Detection

The use of machine learning techniques is important in an intrusion detection system due to the following:

Figure 3. Types of machine learning

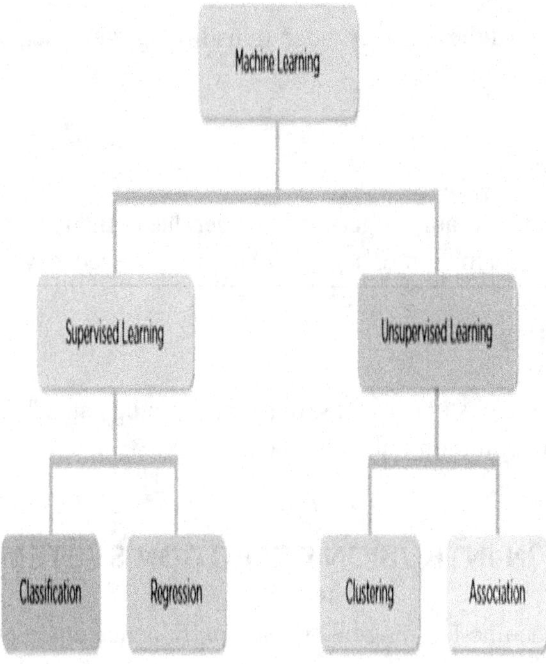

- Analyze large volumes of network data.
- Perform data summarization and visualization.
- Manage firewall rules for anomaly detection.
- Differentiate data that can be used for deviation analysis.

When machine learning is introduced into intrusion detection, it focuses on two main problems: 1) to establish the adaptive feature dataset; 2) to improve the detection rate.

Feature Selection

In machine learning and statistics, feature selection (Kira & Rendell 1992) is the method of choosing a subset of significant features for constructing robust learning models. It is also known as variable selection, feature reduction, attribute selection or variable subset selection. Feature selection also helps to acquire a better understanding about the significant features and how they are associated with each other.

In general, the feature selection process consists of three steps:

- Selects a subset of original features and evaluates each feature's worth in the subset.
- Using this evaluation, some features in the subset may be eliminated or enumerated to the existing subset.
- It checks whether the final subset is good enough using certain evaluation criterion.

The main aim is to reduce the great burden of inspecting huge volumes of audit data and realizing performance optimization of detection rules. One of the major challenges in this area is the poor detection rate, due to the large amount of features in the data set. In IDS, the amount of data is huge that contains traffic data with various features such as the length of the connection, the protocol type, and other information. Certain features may be irrelevant with very low prediction capability to the target patterns, and certain other features may be redundant due to that they are highly inter-correlated with one or more of the other features.

Due to the presence of irrelevant and redundant features in the analysis, the detection speed becomes slow and also the detection accuracy possibly decreases. Hence, irrelevant and redundant features must be eliminated from the original feature set to attain a better overall detection performance. Therefore, selecting significant set of features from the network traffic data becomes a vital task in the intrusion detection process.

As the volume of data to be processed is reduced using feature selection method, the performance of detector may be improved. Feature selection contributes to improve the overall accuracy, reduces the number of false alarms and improves the detection of instances in the training data. As there are number of feature selection approaches, it is a challenging problem to know which method perform the best, especially under what classification techniques for intrusion detection.

Classification Techniques

Classification or supervised learning models are the most widely used of all machine learning approaches, which arranges the data into predefined groups. A classification task begins with training data for which the target values are known where the classification algorithm can construct a predictive model to classify the data. Intrusion detection can also be considered as a classification problem where, each record can be classified under the category, normal or intrusion. As it is very challenging to detect new attacks, constructing a classifier model is also a challenge for an efficient intrusion detection system. The main disadvantages of using single classifier are:

- If the classifier produces wrong output, then the final result may be incorrect.
- The classifier may not be proficient to tackle the problem.

Hence, Hybrid classifiers which combine number of trained classifiers overcome the defects of single classifiers and can lead to a better performance than any single classifier. Hence, in this work, to improve the accuracy of an individual classifier, the classifiers are combined which is the prevalent approach and analyzed the performance of algorithms to detect intrusions with the feature subsets formed.

SWARM INTELLIGENCE

Evolutionary computation and swarm intelligence techniques are great examples of nature which has been a continuous source of inspiration. A swarm can be considered as a group of cooperating agents to achieve some purposeful behaviour and task. It links to artificial life, in general, there are several collective behaviours like birds flocking, ant colonies, social insects and swarm theory, which have inspired swarm intelligence researchers to devise new optimization algorithms.

The term Swarm Intelligence (SI) introduced by Beni & Wang (1993) has received extensive attention in the research community, mostly as Particle Swarm Optimization (PSO), Ant Colony Optimization (ACO), Bee Colony Optimization (BCO) and Cuckoo Search algorithm. Swarm intelligence is an artificial intelligence technique involving the study of collective behaviour in decentralized systems. Such systems are made up by a population of simple individual, interacting locally one another and with their environment. The local interaction among the individual cause a global pattern to emerge.

Researchers in the field of computer science have constructed swarm-based systems based on the efficiency of swarms to solve difficult problems. The swarm intelligence algorithms, inspired by animal behaviour in nature have been successfully applied to optimization, robotics and military applications (Grosan et al 2006).

Swarm Intelligence in Intrusion Detection System

In the last decade, there have been successful applications of nature inspired computing techniques in engineering applications and various optimization problems, such as travelling salesman problem, scheduling, robotics, network security and data mining. Swarm Intelligence (SI) approaches intend to solve complicated problems by multiple simple agents without centralized control or the provision of a global model. Use of Swarm intelligence techniques in intrusion detection problem would decompose into several simpler ones, making IDSs autonomous and cost efficient. The capability of swarm intelligence makes it as a suitable aspirant for IDS to differentiate normal and abnormal connections from huge volume of data. The unique features of SI make it perfect for intrusion detection and hence this work uses swarm intelligence algorithms in the intrusion detection for classification purpose.

RELATED STUDIES

Over the years, many researchers have done some substantial work on the development of intrusion detection system. Shrivastava presented Pulse Coupled Neural Networks (PCNN) to identify important input features and Gaussian kernel of support vector machine was integrated for classification which detected known attack types with high accuracy and low false positive rate (less than 1%). Modified Mutual Information-based Feature Selection algorithm (MMIFS) was proposed by Song et al for intrusion detection in which C4.5 classification method was used which improved most of the performance indicators. Eesa et al applied bee algorithm to select the optimal subset of features and ID3 algorithm as a classifier which obtained higher accuracy and detection rate with a lower false alarming rate for IDS.

In literature, several researchers have benchmarked a range of machine learning algorithms such as Naïve Bayes (NB), Support Vector Machine (SVM), Decision tree, Neural Networks (NN) as a single classifier to address the problem of intrusion detection, investigating that different algorithms perform better at detecting different classes of intrusions (Sabhnani and Serpen). Panda and Patra found that NB was effective in identifying network intrusion and generated detection rate of 95% whereas, false positive was high. SVM has been applied increasingly to misuse detection and anomaly detection in the last decade. The research on single classifier has been slowly replaced by the hybrid classifier which offers much promising results. Hence, combining a number of trained classifiers lead to a better performance than any single classifier.

Li and Wang established a hybrid classifier algorithm (HCA) which is composed of Kernel Principal Component Analysis (KPCA), Core Vector Machine (CVM) and Particle Swarm Optimization (PSO). The system based on HCA had better performance in reducing the classifier errors, producing low false positive rate, but the false negative rate was high. Gan et al combined CVM and Partial Least Square (PLS) algorithms to increase the ability of identifying abnormality intrusions. Chandrashekhar and Raghuveer presented K-Means clustering algorithm which were trained with neural network and classified by support vector machine. The results indicated that there was an improvement in the accuracy rate of 97.5%, 98.7%, 98.8% and 98.8% for DoS, Probe, R2L and U2R attacks respectively. Laftah Al-Yaseen et al presented Hybrid modified K-Means with C4.5 algorithm which improved the the detection accuracy with highest accuracy (90.67%) and detection rate (84.80%) in a Multi Agent System (MAS-IDS).

Mohammad Almseidin et al demonstrated that the decision table classifier achieved the lowest value of false negative while the random forest classifier achieved the highest average accuracy rate. Suad Mohammed Othman et al compared the performance of Chi-SVM classifier and Chi-Logistic Regression classifier using intrusion detection data and showed that SparkChi-SVM model produced high performance with reduced the training time. Peng et al proposed a clustering method for IDS based on Mini Batch K-means with principal component analysis (PCA). Tchakoucht TA and Ezziyyani M proposed a lightweight intrusion detection system, for probe and DoS attacks detection, used Information Gain (IG), and Correlation-based Feature (CFS) selection filters for feature selection, and employed four machine learning methods, namely C4.5, NB, Random Forest (RF) and REPTree and achieved good detection and false positive rates, of around 99.6%, and 0.3% for DoS attacks, and 99.8% and 2.7% for Probe attacks.

Kanaka Vardhini and Sitamahalakshmi proposed ACO with new heuristic function enhanced the accuracy in finding the patterns which are useful for intruder detection. The usage of performance metrics as heuristic function increased the accuracy with less time complexity. Pengyuan Pei proposed a model of fish swarm optimization algorithm based on neural network for IDS, and the detection effect of fish swarm optimization algorithm model based on neural network was stronger, detection efficiency was higher, with supreme application value. Chie-Hong et al applied the equality constrained-optimization-based extreme learning machine to network intrusion detection and the experimental results showed that the approach was effective in building models with good attack detection rates and fast learning speed. Saroj Kr. Biswas used CFS, IGR, PCA, for feature selection and k-NN, DT, NN, SVM and NB classifiers for intrusion detection and highest accuracy was obtained in all the combinations for IGR feature selection with k-NN. Bahram Hajimirzaei and Nima Jafari Navimipour proposed a new intrusion detection system (IDS) based on a combination of a multilayer perceptron (MLP) network, and artificial bee colony (ABC) and fuzzy clustering algorithms and the proposed method outperformed other IDSs with respect to the evaluation criteria in terms of MAE and RMSE.

DATASET DESCRIPTION AND VALIDATION

This section provides the description of dataset considered in this study and pre-processing of data which is carried out for data cleaning and data selection. The validation method and the performance metrics that are used for validating IDS in this work are elaborated.

Data Source

The benchmark datasets commonly used by the researchers in both misuse and anomaly detection are: DARPA 1998 TCPDump Files (DARPA98), DARPA 1999 TCPDump Files (DARPA99), KDDCup'99 dataset (KDDCUP99), 10% KDDCup'99 dataset (KDDCUP99-10), UNIX User dataset (UNIXDS), University of New Mexico dataset (UNM). In this work, as an experimental study for evaluating the performance of classification algorithms, the benchmark KDDCup'99 intrusion detection dataset is used.

The dataset description of KDDCup'99 which is derived from UCI Machine Learning Repository (Lichman 2013) is provided. In 1998, DARPA intrusion detection, evaluation program, to perform a comparison of various intrusion detection methods, a simulated environment was setup by the Massachusetts Institute of Technology (MIT) Lincoln Laboratory to obtain raw TCP/IP dump data for a Local Area Network (LAN). The functioning of the environment was like a real one which included both background network traffic and wide variety of attacks. A version of 1998 DARPA dataset, KDDCup'99, is now widely accepted as a standard benchmark dataset and received much attention in the research community of intrusion detection. This dataset is publicly available and labelled; hence, most of the researchers make use of it as network intrusion dataset. As it is a time-consuming process for generating accurate labels for custom datasets, this dataset is still used, despite its age.

Dataset Description

The KDDCup'99 dataset is a collection of simulated raw TCP/IP dump data over a period of nine weeks of simulating a U.S. Air Force Local Area Network. The seven weeks of network traffic of about four gigabytes of compressed training data were processed into five million connection records. Similarly, two weeks of test data yielded about two million connection records. There are 4,898,430 labelled and 311,029 unlabelled connection records in the dataset. The labelled connection records consist of 41 attributes.

Feature Information

The complete listing of the set of features in the dataset is given in Table 1.

In KDDCup'99 dataset, each example represents attribute values of a class in the network data flow, and each class is labelled either normal or attack. The dataset consists of one type of normal data and 22 different attack types categorized into 4 classes, namely: Denial of Service (DoS), Probe, User-to-Root (U2R) and Remote-to-Login (R2L).

- Normal connections are generated by simulated daily user behaviour such as downloading files and visiting web pages.
- Denial of Service (DoS): Attacker tries to prevent legitimate users from using a service, e.g., syn flood.
- Probe: Attacker tries to gain information about the target host, e.g., port scanning.
- User-to-Root (U2R): Attacker has local access to the victim machine and tries to gain super user privileges, e.g., various ``buffer overflow'' attacks.
- Remote-to-Login (R2L): Attackers try to gain access to the victim machine that does not have an account, e.g., guessing passwords.

Table 1. Set of features of KDDCup'99 dataset

Feature No.	Name of the feature	Feature No.	Name of the feature
1	duration	22	is_guest_login
2	protocol_type	23	count
3	service	24	srv_count
4	flag	25	serror_rate
5	src_bytes	26	srv_serror_rate
6	dst_bytes	27	rerror_rate
7	land	28	srv_rerror_rate
8	wrong_fragment	29	same_srv_rate
9	urgent	30	diff_srv_rate
10	hot	31	srv_diff_host_rate
11	num_failed_logins	32	dst_host_count
12	logged_in	33	dst_host_srv_count
13	num_compromised	34	dst_host_same_srv_rate
14	root_shell	35	dst_host_diff_srv-rate
15	su_attempted	36	dst_host_same_srv_port_ rate
16	num_root	37	dst_host_srv_diff_host_rate
17	num_file_creations	38	dst_host_serror_rate
18	num_shells	39	dst_host_srv_serror_rate
19	num_access_files	40	dst_host_rerror_rate
20	num_outbound_cmd	41	dst_host_srv_rerror_rate
21	is_host_login		

Details of 10% KDDCup'99 Dataset

The KDDCup'99 dataset consists of three components, namely: 10% KDD, Corrected KDD, Whole KDD as shown in Table 2.

In this work, 10% KDDCup'99 dataset which is a more concise version of the Whole KDD dataset is used for experimentation.

Table 2. Number of attacks in training KDDCup'99 dataset

Dataset	Normal	DoS	U2R	R2L	Probe
10% KDD	97277	391458	52	1126	4107
Corrected KDD	60593	229853	70	11347	4106
Whole KDD	972780	3883370	50	1126	41102

DATA PRE-PROCESSING

Data pre-processing is an essential task in network-based intrusion detection, which tries to classify network traffic as normal or abnormal. It is a time-consuming task which transforms the network data into proper form for further analysis as per the requirement of the intrusion detection system model. Pre-processing converts network traffic into a series of observations, where each observation is represented as a feature vector and are labelled with its class, such as "normal" or "attack". The main deficiency in KDDCup'99 dataset is the large number of duplicate/redundant instances. This large amount of redundant instances will make learning algorithms, to be partial towards the frequently occurring instances, and inhibiting it from learning infrequent instances which are generally more unsafe to networks. Also, the existence of these redundant instances will cause the evaluation results to be biased by the methods which have better detection rates on the frequently occurring instances. Eliminating redundant instances helps in reducing false positive rates for intrusion detection. Moreover, irrelevant attributes of dataset may lead to complex intrusion detection model which will reduce the detection accuracy. Hence, redundant instances are removed, so the classifiers will not be partial towards more frequently occurring instances.

The numbers of instances after removing duplicates in each attack are detailed in Table 3. It is noted that there are no duplicate instances in R2L class but DoS class contains large number of duplicates in Neptune and Smurf attack (55381 and 280149 respectively).

Table 3. Number of instances after removing duplicates

Category of attack	Attack Name (no. of instances after removing duplicates)	After removing duplicates	No. of duplicates
Normal	Normal (87832)	87832	9445
DoS	Neptune (51820), Smurf (641), Pod (206), Teardrop (918), Land (19), Back (968)	54572	336886
Probe	Portsweep (416),IPsweep (651), Nmap (158), Satan(906)	2131	1976
U2R	Bufferoverflow (30), LoadModule (9), Perl (3), Rootkit (10)	52	0
R2L	Guesspassword (53), Ftpwrite (8), Imap (12), Phf(4), Multihop(7), Warezmaster(20), Warezclient (893)	999	127
Total Examples		145586	348434

EXPERIMENTAL SETUP

After pre-processing, random sample of 10% normal data and 10% Neptune attack in DoS class are selected and they include 8783 normal instances, 7935 DoS instances, 2131 Probe instances, 52 U2R instances and 999 R2L instances. Four new sets of data are generated with the normal class and four categories of attack: DoS+10%normal, Probe+10%normal, R2L+10%normal and U2R+10%normal. In each data set, instances with the same attack category and 10% normal instances are included, where each dataset has its own distribution of categories of instances. The composition of dataset generated is given in Table 4.

Table 4. Composition of dataset generated

Dataset	Number of Instances
DoS+10%normal	16718
Probe+10%normal	10914
U2R+10%normal	8835
R2L+10%normal	10782

VALIDATION METHOD

Cross-validation (Diamantidis et al 2000) is a technique for assessing how the results of a statistical analysis will generalize to an independent dataset. It is the standard way of measuring the accuracy of a learning scheme and it is used to estimate how accurately a predictive model will perform in practice. In this work, 10-fold cross-validation method (Refaeilzadeh et al 2009) is used for improving the classifier reliability. In 10-fold cross-validation, the original data is divided randomly into 10 parts. During each run, one of the partitions is chosen for testing, while the remaining nine-tenths are used for training. This process is repeated 10 times so that each partition is used for training exactly once. The average results from the 10-fold gives the test accuracy of the algorithm.

Validation Parameters

A confusion matrix (Freitas 2003) contains information about the number of instances predicted correctly and incorrectly by a classification model and is given in Table 5. It is used to evaluate the performance of a classifier.

Table 5. Confusion matrix

Confusion Matrix		Predicted Class	
		Class = Normal	Class = Attack
Actual Class	Class = Normal	TP	FN
	Class = Attack	FP	TN

When referring to the performance of IDSs, the following terms from the confusion matrix are often used with respect to their capabilities:

- **True Positive (TP):** The number of attacks that are correctly identified.
- **False Positive (FP):** The number of normal records incorrectly classified.
- **False Negative (FN):** The number of attacks incorrectly classified.
- **True Negative (TN):** The number of normal records that are correctly classified.

The Performance metrics calculated from the above terms are: Classification Accuracy, Detection Rate (DR), False Alarm Rate (FAR) and Specificity.

The classification accuracy is the percentage of the overall number of connections correctly classified and is calculated using Equation (1).

$$Classification\,accuracy = \frac{\left(TP + TN\right)}{\left(TP + FP + TN + FN\right)} \tag{1}$$

Detection Rate (True Positive Rate) is the percentage of the number of attack connections correctly classified and is calculated using Equation (2). The term is synonymous with sensitivity and recall.

$$Detection\,Rate\left(DR\right) = \frac{TP}{\left(TP + FN\right)} \tag{2}$$

False Alarm Rate (False Positive Rate) is the percentage of the number of normal connections incorrectly classified and is calculated using Equation (3).

$$False\,Alarm\,Rate\left(FAR\right) = \frac{FP}{\left(TN + FP\right)} \tag{3}$$

METHODOLOGY

In addition to the popular and well-accepted algorithms such as genetic algorithms, ant colony optimization, and particle swarm optimization, the algorithms which appeared in the last five years include bat algorithm, cuckoo search and others. Different algorithms have different sources of inspiration, and they can also perform differently. However, some efficient approaches can be based on the combination of different algorithms. This section presents a hybrid approach which combines Cuckoo Search Algorithm (CSA) with Core Vector Machine (CVM) using principal component analysis to select the most informative features to obtain more quality results.

Cuckoo Search Algorithm

Cuckoo Search Algorithm (CSA), which is proposed by Yang & Deb (2009), is an optimization technique which imitates the breeding strategy of the cuckoos and has been employed in diverse domains. The Cuckoo search was inspired by the obligate brood parasitism of some cuckoo species which lay their eggs in the nest of host bird. Some host birds will have direct conflict with intruding cuckoos. In this case, if host birds find that the eggs are not their own, they will either throw them away or simply destroy their nests and build new ones in a different place. Parasitic cuckoos often choose a nest where the host bird just laid its own eggs. It is assumed that, each nest has one egg and it represents a solution, and a cuckoo egg represents a new solution. The objective is to employ the new and better solutions (cuckoos) to replace the existing solutions in the nests. The Cuckoo search is based on three idealized rules:

1. Each cuckoo lays one egg in a random manner by selecting the host nest at a time, where the egg represents the possible solution to the problem under study;
2. the CSA follows the survival of the fittest principle. Only the fittest among all the host nests with high quality eggs will be passed on to the next generation;
3. the number of host nests in the CSA is fixed beforehand. The host bird spots the intruder egg with a probability $pa \in [0, 1]$. In that case, the host bird will either evict the parasitic egg or abandon the nest totally and seek for a new site to rebuild the nest.

The algorithm for cuckoo search (Deb & Yang 2009) is as follows:

Algorithm: Cuckoo Search

```
begin
Generate initial population of q host nest xi, i = 1, 2, . . ., q
for all xi do
Evaluate the fitness function Fi = (xi)
end for
while (iter < MaxGeneration) or (stopping criterion)
Generate a cuckoo egg xj from random host nest by using Levy flight
Calculate the fitness function Fj = (xj)
Get a random nest i among q host nest
if (Fj > Fi) then
Replace xi with xj
Replace Fi with Fj
end if
Abandon a fraction pa of the worst nests
Build new nests randomly to replace nests lost
Evaluate the fitness of new nests
end while
```

Core Vector Machine

Core Vector Machine (CVM) (Tsang et al 2005) algorithm is an optimization technique which applies kernel methods for data intensive applications involving large data sets. The classification problem using SVM is formulated as Quadratic Programming (QP) problem. In CVM, the quadratic optimization problem involved in SVM is formulated as an equivalent Minimum Enclosing Ball (MEB) problem. It is much faster and can handle very larger data sets than existing SVM algorithms. It produces fewer support vectors on very large data sets. Core vector Machine (CVM) is suitable for efficient large-scale pattern classification. CVM has proven to produce a very good experimental result in performing classification task. The training time of CVM is independent of the sample size and obtains similar accuracies compared to the other SVM approaches (Tsang et al 2005).

It can improve the algorithm complexity defects of SVM algorithm and it also significantly reduces the space and time complexities compared to SVM. The time complexity of CVM is O(n) and space complexity does not depend on n, where n is the size of samples set. But whereas, in SVM, the time complexity is O(n3) and space complexity is O(n2).

CVM divides the da'abase between useless and useful points. The useful points are designated as the core set and correspond to all the points that are candidates to be support vectors. As there is no removing step involved, this set can only grow. Among the points of the core set, all are not vectors in the end. Figure 4 illustrates the inner circle of MEB. The inner circle of MEB contains the set of squares and the outer circle, which covers all the points, which is $(1 + \epsilon)$ expansion of the inner circle, where ϵ is the stopping tolerance (user defined parameter) and R is the radius. The set of squares is a core set.

Figure 4. Minimum enclosing ball

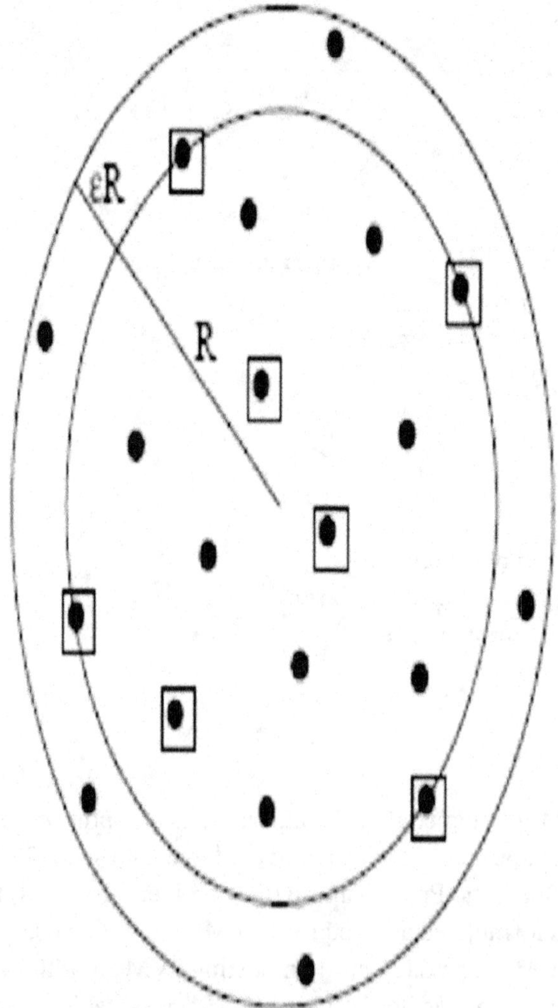

The steps in CVM algorithm are:

Algorithm: Core Vector Machine

1 Initialize the first center of the ball, the first radius in the core set
2 If no point in the remaining points falls outside the ϵ-ball then
3 Stop
4 End If
5 Take the furthest point from the center of the current ball, add it to the Core set
7 Solve the QP problem on the points contained in the core set
8 Update the ball (center and radius)
9 Go to 2nd step.

Principal Component Analysis

Principal Components Analysis (PCA) is a statistical method for analysing the data to identify patterns and to reduce the dimensions of the dataset with minimal loss of information (Han & Kamber 2006). The preferred outcome of the PCA is to form a dataset consisting of n x d-dimensional samples onto a smaller subspace that represents the data "well". A promising application is pattern classification, to reduce the computational costs and reducing the number of dimensions of the dataset by extracting a subspace that describes the data "best". The method generates a set of variables called Principal Components (PC), which are calculated using the Eigen value decomposition of the data covariance matrix or correlation matrix.

Algorithm: Principal Component Analysis

Input: Dataset consisting of n x d-dimensional samples

Output: Dataset with reduced features

1. Compute the d-dimensional mean vector
2. Calculate the covariance/correlation matrix of the data set
3. Calculate eigenvectors and corresponding eigenvalues
4. Arrange the eigenvectors by decreasing eigenvalues
5. Choose k eigenvectors with the largest eigenvalues to form a d x k eigenvector matrix

Tables 6 show the list of reduced features and the number of features selected using principal component analysis.

Table 6. Reduced features using principal component analysis

Data sets	Reduced features	# of features
DoS+10%normal	1,2,3,4,7,8,9,10,13,14,32,33	12
Probe+10%normal	1,3,4,8,9,12,13,14,15,17,18,19,24,26, 28,31,32,33,36,37	20
R2l+10%normal	1,2,3,4,6,7,18,22,23,25,26	11
U2R+10%normal	1,2,3,4,5,6,7,12,21,23	10

Hybrid CVM-CSA Model

CVM procedure is simple, and does not require sophisticated heuristics as in other decomposition methods and CSA is able to converge faster in less iteration. Thus, by combining these two recent and effective methods, it is possible to achieve better performance by combining advantages of both the methods. The CVM performs the training based on different training data sets and it finds the coreset between the entire training data points. In this model, data points from each class are chosen randomly. CVM classifier is built which locates support vectors among the chosen points. The clustering technique is needed for data selection process in CVM. Hence, the optimal cluster centroids are achieved through the cuckoo search algorithm. The points in the clusters are added to the training set and using the updated training set, CVM is trained again. The pseudocode of the hybrid approach is given below:

Algorithm: Hybrid CVM-CSA approach
Given a training data set as input;

```
 Let acc be set as 0 initially
 Begin
     Let acc be the accuracy rate during execution initially 0;
     While acc < ACC do                    //ACC is the accuracy rate thresh-
old
                 For k = 1 . . ., n do           // n is the number of itera-
tions
                Perform training using CVM classifier
                Perform clustering using Cuckoo Search algorithm
      End
   Construct classifiers;
    Update acc
End While
End
```

Moreover, in this hybrid approach, two profiles for normal data are obtained by CVM and CSA. Hence, to reduce the number of false negatives, the data item is confirmed as normal, only when both the classifiers, classify it as normal. If both classifiers confirm that the data is abnormal, then category of the intrusion is determined by the CSA classifier. If the classified results are not consistent by the classifiers, then it is considered as a new type of intrusion in the network traffic which helps IDS to enhance the performance.

ANALYSIS ON CVM-CSA APPROACH

The experimental results of the proposed hybrid classification algorithm using PCA are depicted in Figures 5 to 8. The accuracy rate obtained by the hybrid approach using PCA technique is 99.01% and a highest accuracy (99.12%) is obtained for U2R dataset. It also indicated that CVM and CSA illustrate a competitive performance by obtaining accuracy of 98.51% and 98.26% respectively.

Figure 5. Comparison on accuracy rate of CVM-CSA

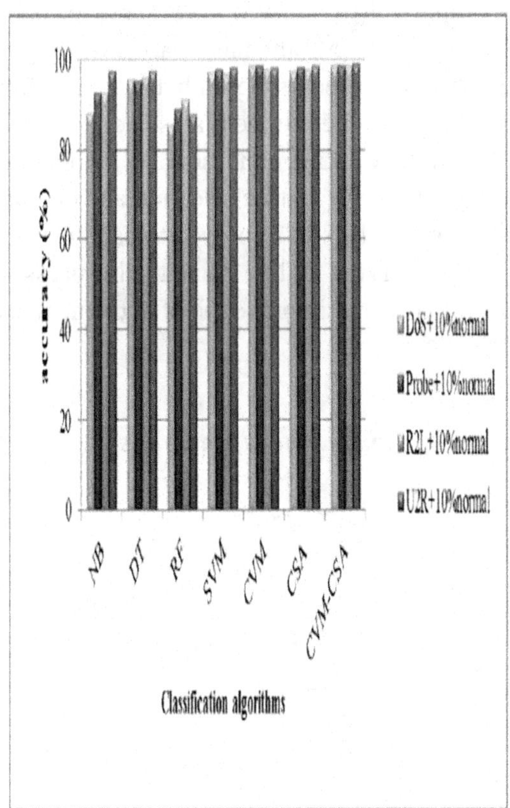

Figure 6. Comparison on detection rate of CVM-CSA

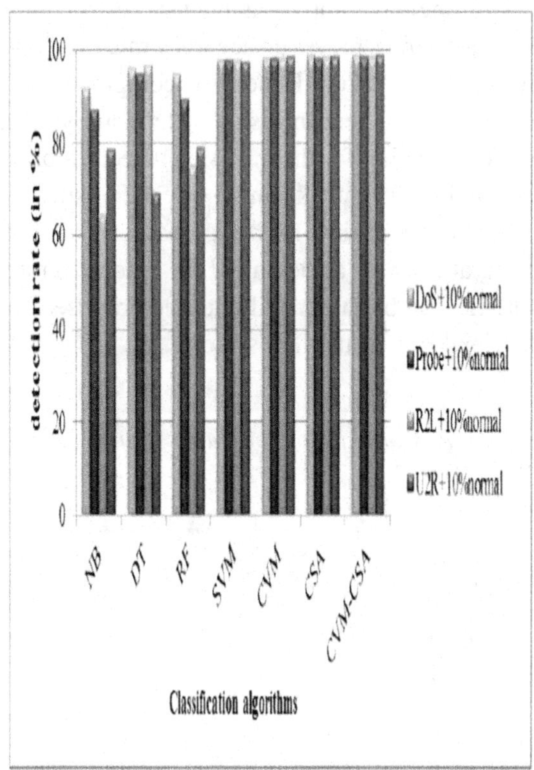

The hybrid approach, CVM-CSA using PCA obtains a detection rate of 98.76% which is comparatively higher than other methods and it is specified in Figure 6. Also the classifiers, CVM and CSA show an equivalent result (98.2% and 98.44% respectively).

The false alarm rate of the classifiers: CVM, CSA and hybrid CVM-CSA is very low and it shows a competitive performance in Figure 7. Comparatively, the false alarm rate of naïve bayes and random forest is high. It is noted from Figure 7 that, false alarm rate of the classification algorithms, CVM, CSA and CVM-CSA is very low, ranging from 0.001 to 0.003. The computation time of various classifiers is compared and is shown in Figure 8 and it indicates that the time required by CVM, CSA and hybrid CVM-CSA classifier is relatively lesser than other methods.

CONCLUSION

The major objective of this work is to provide a promising solution to address the intrusion detection problem and it focuses on classification algorithms and feature selection methods to improve the detection performance and to reduce the time required to carry out the computations for intrusion detection systems. To improve the accuracy rate of the detection system, this work refers predominantly on a hybrid approach using core vector machine and cuckoo search algorithm (CVM-CSA) and its performance is investigated on benchmark intrusion detection dataset, KDDCup'99 using a subset of features chosen using principal component analysis (PCA) algorithm. The proposed hybrid CVM-CSA approach using bat algorithm achieves an accuracy rate of 99.44%, detection rate of 99.85% and false alarm rate ranging from 0.001 to 0.002. Hence, the comparison of the metrics shows that the proposed hybrid algorithms provide an efficient Intrusion Detection System. Moreover, the results determine that, selecting appropriate algorithm for the intrusion detection problem depends on the working condition and the features involved. Future work can be extended using bio-inspired algorithms for feature selection and classification with real-time network datasets. The effectiveness of IDS can be still improved to handle newly rising attacks for achieving 100% detection rate. The privacy preserving Online Analytical Processing (OLAP) can be integrated with the proposed framework to enhance and improve the effectiveness and the flexibility of the IDS system.

Figure 7. Comparison on false alarm rate of CVM-CSA

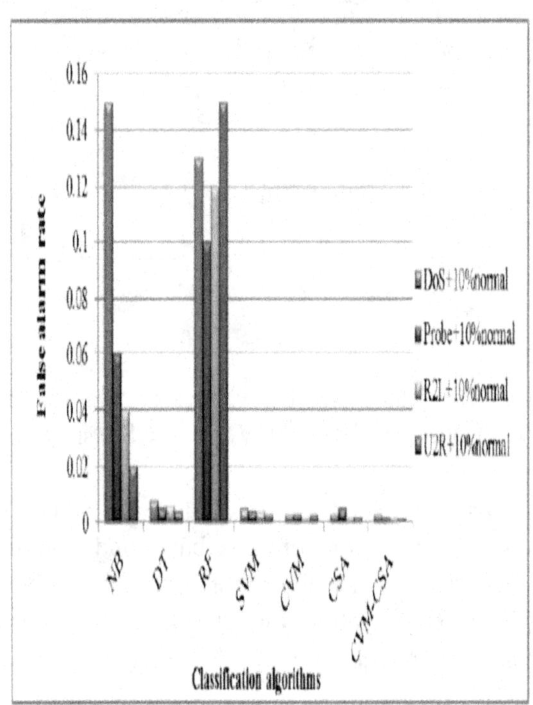

Figure 8. Training time of classifiers

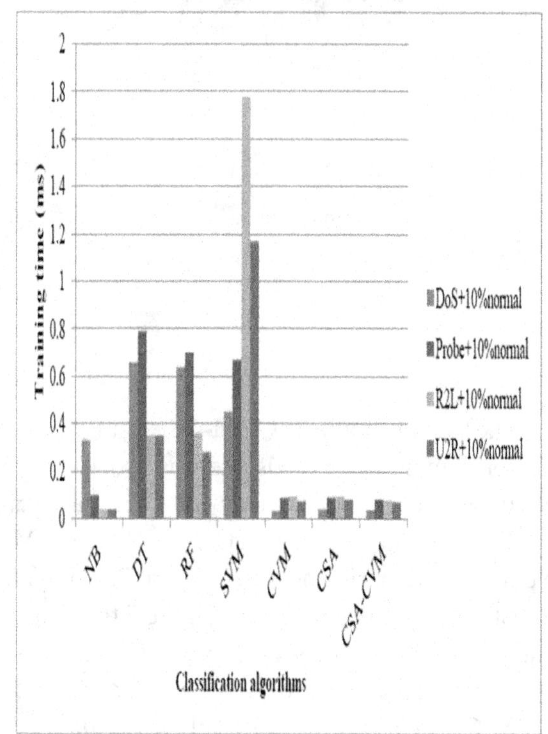

REFERENCES

Almseidin, M., Alzubi, M., Kovacs, S., & Alkasassbeh, M. (2018). Evaluation of Machine Learning Algorithms for Intrusion Detection System. In *IEEE 15th International Symposium on Intelligent Systems and Informatics* (pp.1-12). IEEE.

Amor, N. B., Benferhat, S., & Elouedi, Z. (2004). Naive bayes vs decision trees in intrusion detection systems. In *Proceedings of the 2004 ACM symposium on Applied computing* (pp. 420-424). ACM. 10.1145/967900.967989

Amudha, P., Karthik, S., & Sivakumari, S. (2015). A hybrid swarm intelligence algorithm for intrusion detection using significant features. *The Scientific World Journal*, 2015. PMID:26221625

Araújo, N., de Oliveira, R., Shinoda, A. A., & Bhargava, B. (2010). Identifying important characteristics in the KDD99 intrusion detection dataset by feature selection using a hybrid approach. In *2010 IEEE 17th International Conference on Telecommunications (ICT),* (pp. 552-558). IEEE. 10.1109/ICTEL.2010.5478852

Bache, K., & Lichman, M. (2013). *UCI Machine Learning Repository*. Irvine, CA: University of California, School of Information and Computer Science. Retrieved from http://archive. ics. uci. edu/ml

Beni, G., & Wang, J. (1993). Swarm intelligence in cellular robotic systems. In *Robots and Biological Systems: Towards a New Bionics?* (pp. 703–712). Berlin, Germany: Springer. doi:10.1007/978-3-642-58069-7_38

Bouzida, Y., & Cuppens, F. (2006, September). Neural networks vs. decision trees for intrusion detection. In *IEEE/IST Workshop on Monitoring, Attack Detection and Mitigation (MonAM)* (pp. 81-88). IEEE.

Cortes, C., & Vapnik, V. (1995). Support-vector networks. *Machine Learning*, *20*(3), 273–297. doi:10.1007/BF00994018

Data Mining with Open Source Machine Learning. (n.d.). Available from www.cs.waikato.ac.nz/ml/weka/

Debar, H. (2000). An introduction to intrusion-detection systems. *Proceedings of Connect, 2000.*

Denning, D. E. (1987). An intrusion-detection model. *IEEE Transactions on Software Engineering*, *SE-13*(2), 222–232. doi:10.1109/TSE.1987.232894

Diamantidis, N. A., Karlis, D., & Giakoumakis, E. A. (2000). Unsupervised stratification of cross-validation for accuracy estimation. *Artificial Intelligence*, *116*(1-2), 1–16. doi:10.1016/S0004-3702(99)00094-6

Dokas, P., Ertoz, L., Kumar, V., Lazarevic, A., Srivastava, J., & Tan, P. N. (2002, November). Data mining for network intrusion detection. In *Proc. NSF Workshop on Next Generation Data Mining* (pp. 21-30). Academic Press.

Eesa, A. S., Orman, Z., & Brifcani, A. M. A. (2015). A new feature selection model based on ID3 and Bees algorithm for intrusion detection system. *Turkish Journal of Electrical Engineering and Computer Sciences*, *23*(2), 615–622. doi:10.3906/elk-1302-53

Endler, D. (1998, December). Intrusion detection. Applying machine learning to Solaris audit data. In *Proceedings of the 14th Annual Computer Security Applications Conference, 1998* (pp. 268-279). IEEE.

Freitas, A. A. (2003). A survey of evolutionary algorithms for data mining and knowledge discovery. In *Advances in evolutionary computing* (pp. 819–845). Berlin, Germany: Springer. doi:10.1007/978-3-642-18965-4_33

Gan, X. S., Duanmu, J. S., Wang, J. F., & Cong, W. (2013). Anomaly intrusion detection based on PLS feature extraction and core vector machine. *Knowledge-Based Systems, 40*, 1–6. doi:10.1016/j.knosys.2012.09.004

Gandomi, A. H., Yang, X. S., & Alavi, A. H. (2013). Cuckoo search algorithm: A metaheuristic approach to solve structural optimization problems. *Engineering with Computers, 29*(1), 17–35. doi:10.100700366-011-0241-y

Gholipour Goodarzi, B., Jazayeri, H., & Fateri, S. (2014). Intrusion detection system in computer network using hybrid algorithms (SVM and ABC). *Journal of Advances in Computer Research, 5*(4), 43–52.

Grosan, C., Abraham, A., & Chis, M. (2006). Swarm intelligence in data mining. In *Swarm Intelligence in Data Mining* (pp. 1–20). Berlin, Germany: Springer. doi:10.1007/978-3-540-34956-3_1

Hajimirzaei, B., & Navimipour, N. J. (2019). Intrusion detection for cloud computing using neural networks and artificial bee colony optimization algorithm. *ICT Express, 5*(1), 56–59. doi:10.1016/j.icte.2018.01.014

Han, J., Pei, J., & Kamber, M. (2012). Data mining: concepts and techniques. Amsterdam, The Netherlands: Elsevier.

Biswas, S. K. (2018). Intrusion Detection Using Machine Learning: A Comparison Study. *International Journal of Pure and Applied Mathematics, 118*(19), 101–114.

Joshi, S. A., & Pimprale, V. S. (2013). Network Intrusion Detection System (NIDS) based on data mining. *International Journal of Engineering Science and Innovative Technology, 2*(1), 95–98.

Kantardzic, M. (2011). *Data mining: concepts, models, methods, and algorithms*. Hoboken, NJ: John Wiley & Sons. doi:10.1002/9781118029145

Kira, K., & Rendell, L. A. (1992, July). The feature selection problem: Traditional methods and a new algorithm. In AAA (vol. 2, pp. 129-134). Academic Press.

Kohavi, R., & Quinlan, J. R. (2002, January). Data mining tasks and methods: Classification: decision-tree discovery. In Handbook of data mining and knowledge discovery (pp. 267-276). Oxford, UK: Oxford University Press.

Laftah Al-Yaseen, W., Ali Othman, Z., & Ahmad Nazri, M. Z. (2015). Hybrid Modified-Means with C4. 5 for Intrusion Detection Systems in Multiagent Systems. *The Scientific World Journal, 2015*, 1–14. doi:10.1155/2015/294761 PMID:26161437

Lee, C.-H., Su, Y.-Y., Lin, Y.-C., & Lee, S.-J. (2017). Machine learning based network intrusion detection. *2nd IEEE International Conference on Computational Intelligence and Applications*. doi:10.1109/CIAPP.2017.8167184

Li, X., & Yin, M. (2015). Modified cuckoo search algorithm with self-adaptive parameter method. *Information Sciences, 298*, 80–97. doi:10.1016/j.ins.2014.11.042

Li, Y., & Wang, Y. (2012). A misuse intrusion detection model based on hybrid classifier algorithm. *International Journal of Digital Content Technology and its Applications, 6*(5).

Lichman, M. (2013). *UCI Machine Learning Repository*. Irvine, CA: University of California, School of Information and Computer Science.

Nguyen, H. A., & Choi, D. (2008, October). Application of data mining to network intrusion detection: classifier selection model. In *Asia-Pacific Network Operations and Management Symposium* (pp. 399-408). Berlin, Germany: Springer. 10.1007/978-3-540-88623-5_41

Ong, P. (2014). Adaptive cuckoo search algorithm for unconstrained optimization. *The Scientific World Journal*, 2014. PMID:25298971

Othman, S. M., Fadl, M. B. A., Alsohybe, N. T., & Al Hashida, A. Y. (2018). Intrusion detection model using machine learning algorithm on Big Data environment. *Journal of Big Data*, *5*(34).

Pengyuan, P. (2017). Studies on the Network Anomaly Intrusion Detection of a Fish Swarm Optimization Algorithm Based on Neural Network. *Revista de la Facultad de Ingeniería U.C.V., 32*(13), 585-589.

Panda, M., & Patra, M. R. (2007). Network intrusion detection using naive Bayes. *International Journal of Computer Science and Network Security*, *7*(12), 258-263.

Peng, K., Leung, V. C., & Huang, Q. (2018). Clustering approach based on mini batch K-means for intrusion detection system over Big Data. *IEEE Access: Practical Innovations, Open Solutions*.

Refaeilzadeh, P., Tang, L., & Liu, H. (2009). Cross-validation. In *Encyclopedia of database systems* (pp. 532–538). Boston, MA: Springer.

Sabhnani, M., & Serpen, G. (2003). *Application of Machine Learning Algorithms to KDD Intrusion Detection Dataset within Misuse Detection Context*. MLMTA.

Shelke, M. P. K., Sontakke, M. S., & Gawande, A. D. (2012). Intrusion detection system for cloud computing. *International Journal of Scientific & Technology Research*, *1*(4), 67–71.

Shen, X. J., Wang, L., & Han, D. J. (2016). Application of artificial bee colony optimized BP neural network in intrusion detection. *Computer Engineering*, *42*(2), 190–194.

Shrivastava, A., Baghel, M., & Gupta, H. (2013). A Novel Hybrid Feature Selection and Intrusion Detection Based on PCNN and Support Vector Machine. *International Journal of Computer Technology and Applications.*, *4*(6), 922–927.

Tchakoucht, T. A., & Ezziyyani, M. (2018). Building a fast intrusion detection system for high-speed-networks: Probe and DoS attacks detection. *Procedia Computer Science*, *127*, 521–530. doi:10.1016/j.procs.2018.01.151

Tsang, I. W., Kwok, J. T., & Cheung, P. M. (2005). Core vector machines: Fast SVM training on very large data sets. *Journal of Machine Learning Research*, *6*(Apr), 363–392.

UCI Machine Learning Archive. (2009). Available from http://www.kdd.ics.uci.edu/databases/kddcup99/task.html

Vardhini, K., & Sitamahalakshmi, T. (2017). Enhanced Intrusion Detection System Using Data Reduction: An Ant Colony Optimization Approach. International. *Journal of Applied Engineering Research*, *12*(9), 1844–1847.

Witten, I. H., Frank, E., Hall, M. A., & Pal, C. J. (2016). *Data Mining: Practical machine learning tools and techniques*. Burlington, MA: Morgan Kaufmann.

Yang, X. S., & Deb, S. (2009, December). Cuckoo search via Lévy flights. In *World Congress on Nature & Biologically Inspired Computing, 2009. NaBIC 2009* (pp. 210-214). IEEE.

Zhu, X. H. (2017). Application of artificial neural network based on artificial fish swarm algorithm in network intrusion detection. *Modern Electronic Technology, 40*(1), 80-82.

This research was previously published in the Handbook of Research on Machine and Deep Learning Applications for Cyber Security; pages 150-175, copyright year 2020 by Information Science Reference (an imprint of IGI Global).

Chapter 33
Applications of Machine Learning in Cyber Security

Charu Virmani
Manav Rachna International Institute of Research and Studies, India

Tanu Choudhary
Manav Rachna International Institute of Research and Studies, India

Anuradha Pillai
J. C. Bose University of Science and Technology YMCA, India

Manisha Rani
D. N. College, India

ABSTRACT

With the exponential rise in technological awareness in the recent decades, technology has taken over our lives for good, but with the application of computer-aided technological systems in various domains of our day-to-day lives, the potential risks and threats have also come to the fore, aiming at the various security features that include confidentiality, integrity, authentication, authorization, and so on. Computer scientists the world over have tried to come up, time and again, with solutions to these impending problems. With time, attackers have played out complicated attacks on systems that are hard to comprehend and even harder to mitigate. The very fact that a huge amount of data is processed each second in organizations gave birth to the concept of Big Data, thereby making the systems more adept and intelligent in dealing with unprecedented attacks on a real-time basis. This chapter presents a study about applications of machine learning algorithms in cyber security.

DOI: 10.4018/978-1-6684-6291-1.ch033

INTRODUCTION

With the exponential rise in technological awareness in the recent decades, technology has taken over our lives for good but with the application of computer aided technological systems in various domains of our day to day lives, the potential risks and threats have also come to the fore aiming at the various security features that include confidentiality, integrity, authentication, authorization and so on. Computer scientists, the world over have tried to come up, time and again with solutions to these impending problems. With time, attackers have played out complicated attacks on systems that are hard to comprehend and even harder to mitigate. Even upon recognition, responding in real time remained a problem. The capability of the system was hence extended using artificial intelligence and machine learning techniques. The very fact that a huge of data is processed each second in organizations gave birth to the concept of Big Data, thereby making the systems more and adept and intelligent in dealing with unprecedented attacks on a real time basis. Various authors having worked on the problem, devised a host of algorithms that may be used for purposes such as image processing, speech recognition, biomedical area, and of course cyber security domain.

The chapter primarily presents a survey about the role of machine learning when applied in the domain of cyber security. The chapter aims at introducing the reader to the basics of machine learning along with its various components and tasks associated with it. The chapter presents in detail a set of approaches to classify the various Machine Learning algorithms and goes on to recount the application of Machine Learning in our day-to-day lives. Having introduced the reader to the basics, a detailed description of the cyber security tasks in machine learning aided with examples are narrated in the later sections.

WHAT IS MACHINE LEARNING?

As the scientists focused more on solving the issues related with the computer systems including the security aspect, they drove themselves closer to a technology that acted like humans. This was the beginning of AI (Artificial Intelligence) applications that surpassed their detection as computer systems by users. Initially generated, AI applications aimed at clearing the Turing Test which is a test of a machine's ability to showcase intelligent behavior that is tantamount to or indiscernible from that of a human intelligence. But since AI was initiated with the very purpose of specific application domains such as face recognition, object recognition, it was soon realized that creating an AI that worked in terms of the human brain completely was an arduous task. Hence, the concept of Machine Learning was evolved.

Machine Learning is essentially an approach to Artificial intelligence that makes use of any system that is adept in learning like humans, i.e., from experience (Al-Jarrah et al., 2015; Buczak & Guven eta l, 2016). Just like a human brain, it aims at recognizing the patterns and upgrades itself to apply them in the future decisions. Thus, it defies the old traditions of feeding data into the systems through programming and learns by examples. The decisions in Machine Learning are driven by data rather than algorithms and also change its behavior, upon accommodating new information, that sets' it apart from the lot of technologies aiming to achieve cyber security (Michalski, 2013). Simply put, Machine Learning is a type of Artificial intelligence that allows the system to learn without being explicitly programmed wherein computer programs are developed in such a way that they change whenever exposed to new data (Cavelty, 2010).

The ultimate aim of Machine Learning techniques can be thought of as enabling software's to be able to make decisions much like humans do in cases of cyber attacks that have been previously encountered by the system and also those not encountered before. The breach of data in big organizations has incurred a huge loss, with the average cost being over $3 million. Since cyber crimes have become rhetoric in the current scenario, it is the most researched field today and the scientists have been struggling to devise techniques that could reduce the cost factor while dealing with the attacks.

Though the buzz around Machine Learning technology has just gained momentum, but the concept is as old as the computer history itself. Data produced from computer systems and sensors were processed and were derived some meaning from since the first computers were in use. The discussion has caught up pace today because of the huge amount of data available to us today, thus giving it a name, Big Data.

Big data is being created day in and day out by everything that surrounds us. Each and every digital process and information across online social media networks produces data. The various Systems, sensors and mobile devices play a role in transmitting the data. Big data is generally characterized by the 3Vs: the volume of data, the variety of data types and the velocity at which the data must be processed (Chapelle et al., 2009). Although there isn't any specific volume of data defined, the term is referred to describe terabytes, petabytes and even exabytes of data captured over time across different platforms. The data available for processing would continue to be on the rise in the future as well due to the widespread use of IoT technology. Thus, the opportunity to develop some intelligence systems using machine learning to analyze big data more easily has grown because it is technically impossible for humans to analyze the data at this big scale (Kim et al., 2007). Big Data and Machine Learning can be thought of as two components which are complementary to each other. Marrying the two concepts comes naturally to develop an intelligent system using Machine Learning that uses a lot of data. Also, to analyze Big Data, Machine learning is the only viable option. The Machine Learning technique may be thought of as an intersection of various entities that are illustrated in figure 1.

Figure 1. Components of machine learning

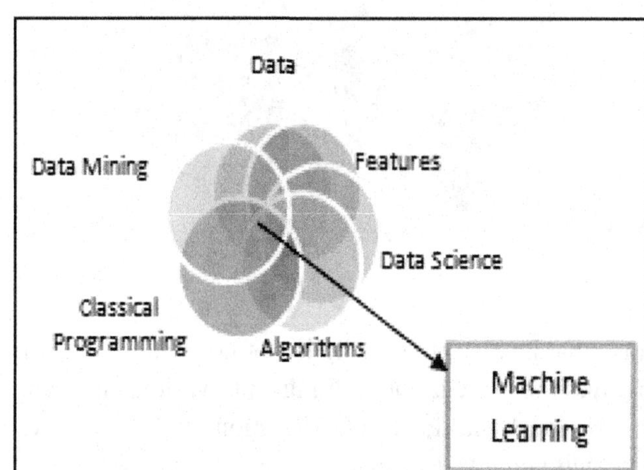

- **Data:** These are the various facts and statistics collected together, which may or may not make sense and can be used for future reference or analysis.

- **Features:** A pattern recognition or feature is an important metrics in defining the characteristics of Machine Learning.
- **Data Science:** It is a field that makes use of scientific methods, processes, algorithms and systems to get an insight from structured and unstructured data in various forms.
- **Algorithms:** A set of protocols that need to be followed in any calculations or other problem solving operations especially in computer related fields.
- **Classical Programming:** Involves the use of various programming languages that have been ousted from Machine Learning and replaced with data to recognize and evaluate patterns.
- **Data Mining:** When a huge amount of information in database repositories is analyzed with the aim of creating new information using it, this constitutes the practice of data mining.

Machine Learning is an approach of many similar ones to AI that utilizes a system which learns from experience and not meant to focus on AI goals such as copying human behavior. On the same hand, it efficiently reduces times and effectively utilizes efforts in both simple and complex scenarios such as stock prediction. A system will said to be Machine Learning when it changes its behavior while making its decision from its own learning using data rather than algorithms (Dua et al., 2016). The technique involves solving certain tasks with the use of data available at hand and also the tasks are not human-related. Some of the tasks are shown in figure 2.

Figure 2. Tasks in machine learning

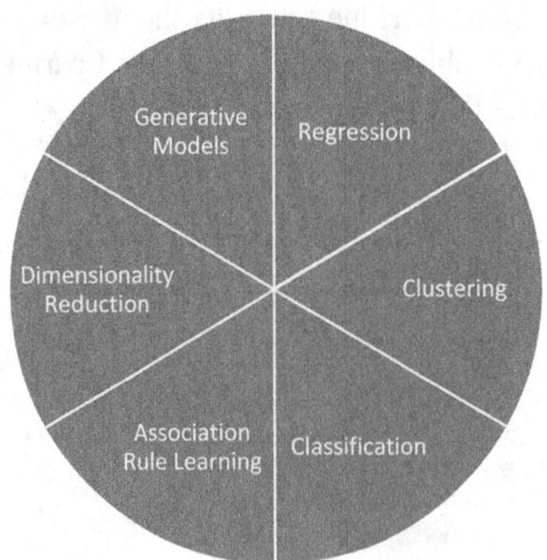

- **Regression:** It is a task that involves the prediction of next value based upon the previous values.
- **Classification:** It involves the segregation of things into various different categories.
- **Clustering:** This task is much similar to classification but here, the classes are unknown and things are grouped on their perceived similarity.
- **Association Rule Learning:** It is involved in recommendation task. Based upon previous experiences, a thing is recommended in the future.
- **Dimensionality Reduction:** Also known as generalization, it involves the task of searching common and most important features in multiple examples.

- **Generative Models:** This task deals with the creation of something new based on the previous knowledge of distribution.

With the above listed tasks in machine learning, there are different approaches to implement the tasks in machine learning which can be classified on different variations as discussed in next section.

APPROACHES TO CLASSIFY MACHINE LEARNING ALGORITHMS

Machine learning Algorithms can be classified on varying views and classification models depending upon variety of paradigms for weak boundaries and cross relationships. The detailed study of literature among the myriad of algorithms which is applied to cyber detection is represented in figure 3. It is broadly classified into shallow learning and deep learning algorithms (Huang & Stokes, 2016; Kasun et al., 2013; Kotsiants et al., 2007; LeCun et al., 2015). A domain expert who can identify the relevant data attribute before the execution of the algorithm is the primary requirement of shallow learning whereas autonomous identification of feature selection using multi-layered representation of the input data is the beauty of Deep Learning.

Figure 3. Classification of machine learning

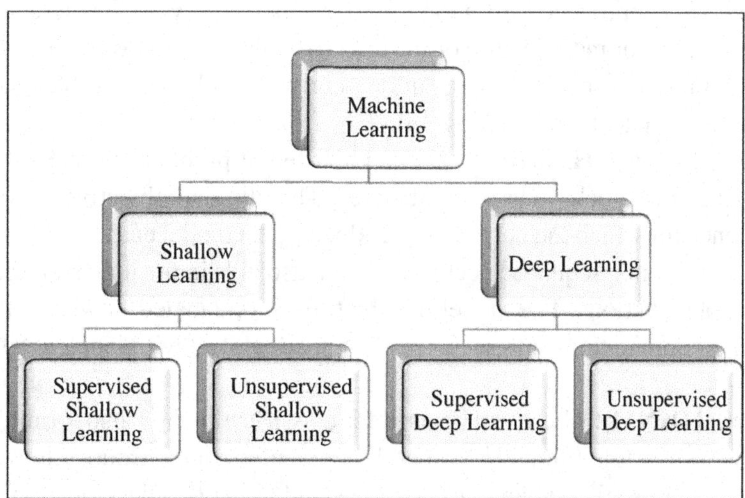

Shallow Learning and Deep Learning may be further categorized under Supervised and Unsupervised Algorithms. The former techniques are dependent on a large set of data that is pre-requisite of a training process while the latter function without a required pre-labeled training dataset (LeCun et al., 2015). This section mainly deals with the discussions of the various categorizations of ML algorithms.

SHALLOW LEARNING

1. Supervised SL algorithms

The various algorithms that fall under this sub-category have been discussed briefly:

a. **Naive Bayes Algorithm (NB):** Based upon a prior assumption that the input dataset features are independent of one another, they are generally probabilistic classifiers which are scalable and not dependent on huge training datasets to create appreciable outputs (Linda et la, 2011).
b. **Logistic Regression (LR):** These algorithms make use of a discriminative model as unlike Naïve Bayes, these are categorical classifiers. Similar to the above algorithm, this also includes a prior assumption considering the input dataset features as independent. The size of the training data has a huge role to play in assessing its performance (Marsland, 2011).
c. **Support Vector Machine (SVM):** These are the non-probabilistic classifiers used for the purpose of mapping data samples in a feature space with the aim of optimizing the distance between each available category of samples (Wang, 2005). It does not involve any assumption on the input data and perform miserably in case of multi-class classification. Long processing time may be a down-point due to their restricted scalability (Nasrabadi, 2007).
d. **Random Forest (RF):** It can be reckoned as a set of decision trees, wherein the output of each tree is taken into consideration before proposing a final response. Each of the trees has to be a conditional classifier. The tree is approached from the top to each and every node where a given condition is juxtaposed against one or more feature of the data so analyzed. Random forest algorithms fir right for large datasets and are much efficient in dealing with multiclass problems. However, greater depth of the tree may lead to over-fitting.
e. **Hidden Markov Models (HMM):** Outputs with different probabilities are achieved in this case, as the system is made to behave as a set of states. The ultimate objective thus lies in identifying the states sequence for which the output was produced. The model enables us to calculate the probable chances of an event's sequence occurrence and also aids in the understanding of the temporal behavior of the observations. The model may be trained on labeled as well as unlabeled datasets, generally for their applications into security; they are deployed with labeled datasets only (Dua et al., 2016).
f. **K-Nearest model (KNM):** These can be used for classification and also for multi-class problems. The training as well as the training part can be computationally arduous however as it involves the comparisons against all available test samples and along the classification of each of the test sample (Uma & Padmavathi, 2013).
g. **Shallow Neural Networks (SNN):** It involves a corpus of processing entities known as neurons that are organized in two or more communication networks. Though based upon neural networks, it has a very constrained amount of neurons and layers involved. The SNN is deployed in the domain of cyber-security mostly for the task of classification (Xin et al., 2018).

2. Unsupervised SL Algorithms

There are basically two categorizations under this topic which are as mentioned below:

a. **Clustering:** These are clustered group of data points that depict similar features. There are two famous classifications under clustering, known as K-means and Hierarchical Clustering. They have a very restricted scalability but offer a pliable solution that are generally deployed in the prefatory phase before selecting a supervised algorithm or moving on to the anomaly detection procedure.
b. **Association:** Its task is to identify the unknown patterns amongst available data in order to make them viable for the task of prediction. The only downpoint is the excess of data produced which does not necessarily comply with the given rules, thus making it impertinent to combine the procedure with expert and accurate human inspections .

DEEP LEARNING

Deep Neural Networks (DNN) is the very foundation upon which all Deep Learning Algorithms are based (Zhang et al., 2018) The neural networks are organized in different layers wherein each layer is proficient in autonomous representation learning.

1. Supervised DL Algorithms
   a. **Fully-Connected Feedforward Deep Neural Networks (FNN):** These are the derivates of DNN wherein each neuron is connected to the neurons in the prior layers. There are no assumptions involved regarding the input data and stands as an epitome of economically viable and flexible general-purpose solutions for the task of classification.
   b. **Convolutional Feedforward Deep Neural Networks (CNN):** This variant of DNN involves neurons that receive inputs from the subsets of neurons of the previous layers. It is much effective in analysis of spatial data but the performance seems to go downhill with the very application of algorithm to non-spatial data. The computational cost is also much less as compared with FNN.
   c. **Recurrent Deep Neural Networks (RNN):** The architectural design of RNN makes its training a hard task as it involves the neurons sending their outputs to the previous layers as well. They are excellent sequence- generators especially the long short-term memory.
2. Unsupervised DL Algorithms
   a. **Deep Belief Networks (DBN):** A composition of Restricted Boltzmann Machines is involves its modeling which is a class of neural networks that consist of no outer layers. It can be effectively deployed for the pre-training tasks they are standout in the function extraction feature. Though a training phase is required, it involves unlabeled datasets for that purpose.
   b. **Stack Autoencoders (SAE):** They are a composition of multiple Autoencoders which are neural networks having the same number of input and output neurons. Much like DBN, they are excellent at the pre-training tasks but the results are far more better when deployed for small datasets.

The next section throws light on the applications of machine learning in cyber security.

APPLICATIONS OF MACHINE LAERNING

Machine Learning techniques are deployed for an enormous range of application area across the globe. To permit users to use countless intelligent systems which are created with the aid of machine learning techniques, umpteen numbers of times in the span of a single day. While making use of mobile phones, surfing the internet or doing online shopping across commercial sites on the internet we are faced with a whole lot of intelligent systems. Organizations that develop technologies have spent huge amount of money for creating more intelligent systems (Domingos,2012). Since intelligent systems make lives easier for people, almost all machines will be intelligent in the future and there is huge demand in the market for any such technology that easies life of people. Following are the applications of Machine Learning in day-to-day life as illustrated in figure 4.

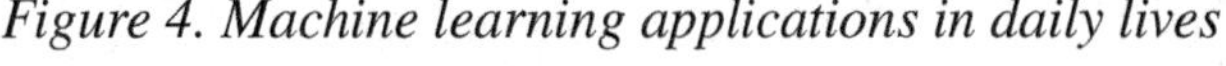

Figure 4. Machine learning applications in daily lives

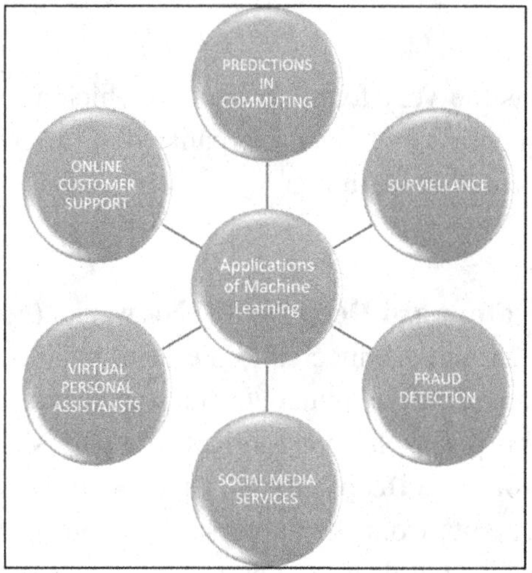

- **Virtual Personal Assistant:** Some common examples such as Siri, Alexa help the user in accessing/finding information with the use of voice. To respond to the commands, information is collected from related queries and from other resources such as phones. Based upon past involvements, the information is collected and refined and accordingly utilized to respond to the users' requests.
- **Predictions While Travelling:** The technology could be deployed for estimating congested areas based on the daily experiences. Though, GPS system may be used for navigation purposes but not all cars come equipped with it.
- **Online Customer Support:** It is a common scenario today that websites offer customers with an option to chat with a representative from the organization but they are not always live executives. To respond to user queries on a real-time basis, a bot is used. This bot tends to understand the user queries and serve them with the best possible response which is only a result of machine learning techniques.
- **Social Media Services:** While navigating across social networking sites, many of these web based sites notify about the people that "we may know" based on frequent profile visits, places and

things of interest via a continuous and comprehensive analysis of user data. There is also an added feature of face recognition that recognizes the person whenever or wherever his/her picture is posted.

- **Surveillance:** Rids a single person loaded with the work of monitoring a number of video cameras which is also subject to human error. In case of Machine Learning, the crimes may be detected even before they occur by analyzing the unusual behavior of employees and giving them an alert in order to prevent any mishap.
- **Fraud Detection:** In order to make cyberspaces more secure for information exchanges, monetary transfers organizations have started to deploy Machine Learning solutions to discern between legitimate and illegitimate transactions between two parties across a network.

MACHINE LEARNING TASKS AND CYBER-SECURITY

Here are some examples of different techniques that can be deployed to solve machine learning tasks and how they are connected with cyber-security tasks.

Regression

Regression (or prediction) is the simplest task of all. The knowledge regarding the existing data is used in such a manner to have an idea about the new data. Houses is an example of price prediction of various entities. In terms of cyber-security application, it could be extremely effective in fraud detection. The various features such as the total amount of suspicious transaction, location, etc. can be helpful in determining a probability and possibility of fraudulent actions occurrence (Zhang et al., 2019). Figure 5 depicts methods of machine learning that can be used for regression tasks.

Figure 5. Machine learning techniques for regression tasks

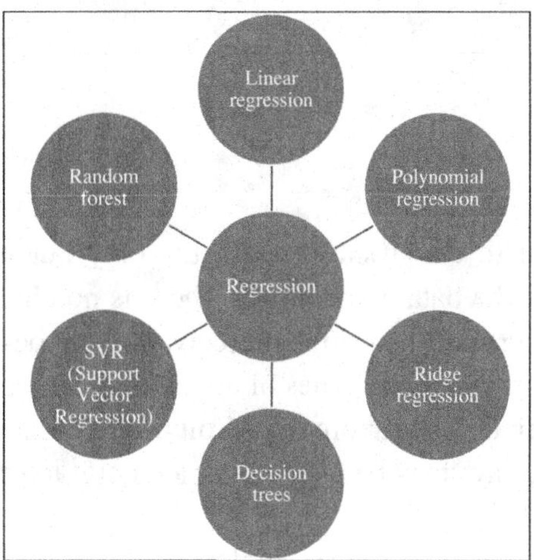

Classification

Classification is also a very straightforward task. It deals with categorization of entities or things, for instance two stacks of pictures classified by their respective types. In terms of cyber-security, a spam filter separating spams from other messages can be an efficient example. Spam filters are probably the first Machine Learning approach applied to Cyber-security tasks. The supervised learning approach mentioned above is commonly applied for classification where instances of certain groups are known. All classes need to be defined in the beginning (Uma & Padmavathi, 2013). Figure 6 depicts machine learning algorithms for classification.

It is reckoned that methods like SVM and random forests work the best. Keeping in mind the fact that there are no one-size-fits-all rules, and they probably won't operate properly for all tasks.

Figure 6. Machine learning techniques for classification

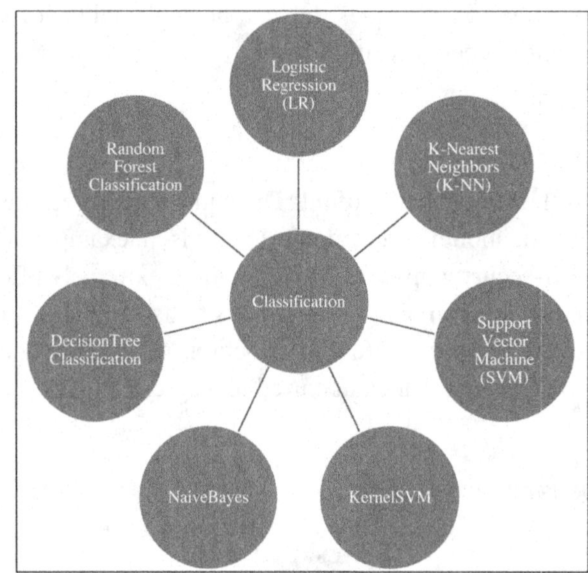

Clustering

Clustering is very much similar to classification with the only but major difference being that the information about the classes of the data is unknown. There is no clue as to whether this data can be classified. This is called "unsupervised learning". Perceivably, the best task for clustering is analysis in forensics. The reasons, of course, and outcomes of an incident are obsolete. It is very much required to classify all the activities to find some anomalies. Solutions to malware analysis such as malware protection and secure email gateways may be used to implement it to separate the legitimate files from outliers (Yousefi-Azar et al., 2017).

Another intriguing area where clustering can be deployed is "user behavior analytics". In this instance, application users are clustered together so that it is possible to comprehend if they should belong to a particular group or not. Usually clustering is not applied to solving a particular task in cyber-security as it is more like one of the subtasks in a pipeline such as grouping users into separate groups to adjust the risk values. Figure 7 depicts machine learning algorithms for clustering.

Figure 7. Machine learning techniques for clustering

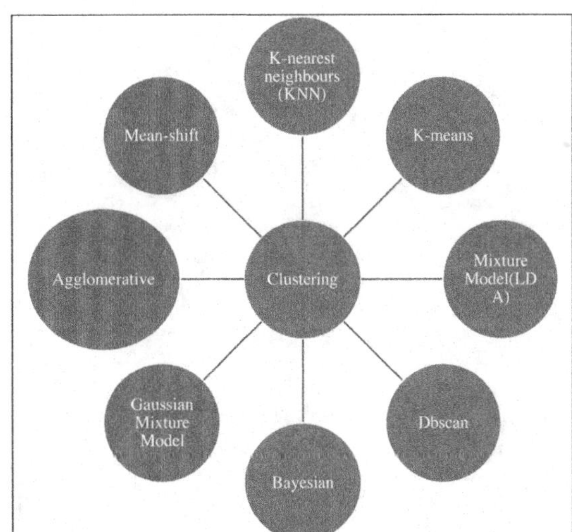

Association Rule Learning (Recommendation Systems)

There are certain applications such as Netflix and SoundCloud that are able to understand user preferences in movies and films respectively and recommend them accordingly. In cyber-security, this principle can be used primarily for incident response purposes. If a company is faced with a tide of incidents and offers various types of responses, a system learns a type of response for a particular incident such as mark it as a false positive, change a risk value and then run the investigation. Risk management solutions can also have an upper hand if they automatically assign risk values for new vulnerabilities or mis-configuration built on their descriptions. Following is the list of machine learning algorithms for solving recommendation tasks:

- Apriori
- Euclat
- FP-Growth.

Dimensionality Reduction

Dimensionality reduction or generalization is not as much popular as the task of classification, but very much necessary if you deal with complex systems with unlabeled data and many other potential features. clustering cannot be just applied because typical methods restrict the number of features or they simply do not work. Dimensionality reduction can help us in handling it and cutting out unnecessary features.Just like clustering, dimensionality reduction is also usually one of the tasks in a more complex model. As for the cyber-security tasks, dimensionality reduction is common for face detection solutions—similar to the ones that is used in Iphone. Figure 8 depicts machine learning algorithms for dimensionality reduction.

Figure 8. Machine learning techniques for dimension reality

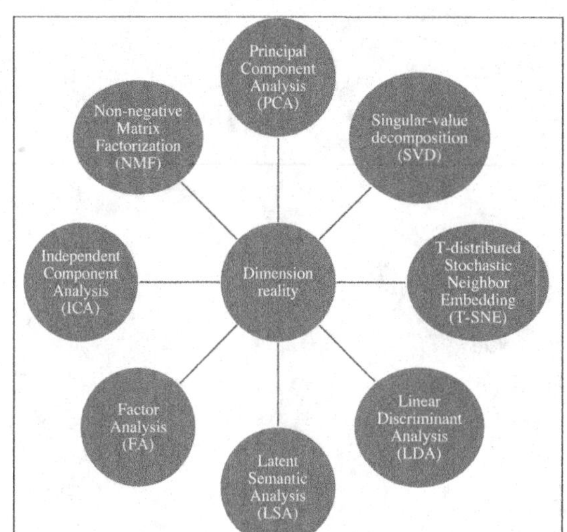

Generative Models

The task of the generative models differs much from the above-mentioned tasks. While the above tasks deal with the existing information and associated decisions, generative models are basically designed to simulate the actual data and not the decisions based upon the previous evaluated decisions. The easy task of offensive cyber-security is to generate a list of input metrics or parameters so as to test a particular application for the various Injection vulnerabilities.

An alternative to this, vulnerability scanning tool is also an option for a host of web applications. One of its modules is testing files for any unauthorized access. These tests are able to copy the existing file names to identify the new ones. For an instance, if a crawler is detected a file called "login.php", it is always recommended to check the existence of any backup or test its copies by trying different names such login_1.php, login_backup.php, login.php.2017. Generative models are very adept in doing this. Machine learning generative models are:

- Markov Chains
- Genetic algorithms

PROPOSED CYBER-SECURITY TASKS AND MACHINE LEARNING

Instead of looking at the various ML tasks mentioned above and trying to apply them to cybersecurity, let us try and have a view at the common cyber-security tasks and machine learning opportunities. There are three dimensions as to Why, What, and How. The first dimension defines the very goal, or a task like detecting threats, predicting the cyber-attacks, etc. Also, according to the Gartner's PPDRM model, all security tasks can be divided into five categories:

- Prediction
- Prevention
- Detection
- Response and
- MONITORING.

The second dimension is a technical layer and an answer to the question "What" .For example, it deals with the level at which to monitor the cyber-security issues. Following is the list of layers for this dimension:

- Network (network traffic analysis and intrusion detection);
- Endpoint (anti-malware);
- Application (WAF or database firewalls);
- User (UBA);and
- Process (anti-fraud).

Each layer also has its different subcategories. For example, network security can be Wired, Wireless or Cloud. It is to be assured of the fact that one simply cannot apply the same algorithms with the same hyper parameters to both areas, at least in the near future. The reason is the scarcity of data and algorithms to search for better dependencies of the three areas so that it becomes possible to change one algorithm to different ones. The third dimension is a question of "How" .For instance,how to check security of a specific area or region:

- In transit in real time;
- At rest;
- Historically; and so on.

For instance, if endpoint protection is a point of concern, looking for the intrusions, monitoring processes of an executable file, static binary analysis, analyzing the history of actions in this endpoint among others can be an option. There are certain tasks that need be solved in three dimensions only. At times,there are no values in some dimensions for certain tasks. Approaches may be the same in one dimension under consideration. Nonetheless, each particular point of this three-dimensional space of cybersecurity tasks has its intricacies. It is an arduous task to detail them all hence let's shift our focus on the most imperative dimension—thetechnology layers that are detailed in Table 1.

Machine Learning for Network Protection

Network protection is not merely a single area but it encompasses a whole set of different solutions that focus on various protocols such as Ethernet, wireless, SCADA, or even virtual networks like SDNs.

Table 1. Examples of cyber security tasks achieved via machine learning

Cyber-security tasks in Machine Learning	Regression	Classification	Clustering
1. Network Protection	To predict the network packet parameters	To identify different classes of network attacks	For forensic analysis
2. Endpoint Security	To predict the next system call for executable process	To demarcate the programs under various category heads such as malware, spyware and ransom ware	For malware protection on secure email gateways
3. Application Security	To detect anomalies in HTTP requests	Detect known types of attacks like injections	To detect DDOS attacks and mass exploitation
4. User Behavior	To detect anomalies in User actions	To group different users for peer-group analysis	To separate groups of users and detect outliers
5. Process Behavior	To predict the next user action and detect outliers	To detect known types of fraud	To compare business processes and detect outliers

Mostly the theme of network protection deals with Intrusion Detection System (IDS) solutions (Zhang et al., 2018). A whole lot of them used a kind of Machine Learning technique years ago and mostly dealt with signature-based approaches of security.Machine Learning in the networks security presses on the new solutions commonly referred to as "Network Traffic Analytics" (NTA) which is generally aimed at in-depth analysis of all the traffic at each layer and also to detect the attacks and anomalies. Following are the examples of machine learning that can help in achieving network protection.

1. Regression to predict the network packet parameters and compare them with the normal ones;
2. Classification to identify different classes of network attacks such as scanning and spoofing; and
3. Clustering for forensic analysis.

There could also be an evaluation of various machine learning algorithms to derive solutions for Intrusion Detection Systems. Big Data may also be involved in the approaches for Intrusion Detection System Solutions.

Machine Learning for Endpoint Protection

The new generation of anti-viruses being rolled out is dependent much on Endpoint Detection and Responses. It always comes in handy to learn the various features in executable files or in the process behavior. However, need to reckon the fact that while dealing with machine learning at endpoint layer, our solution may differ depending upon the type of endpoint (Dua et al., 2016). For example: workstation, server, and container, cloud instance, mobile, PLC, IoT device and so on. Every endpoint has its own set of specific characteristics but the tasks are almost common that includes:

1. Regression to predict the next system call for executable process and compare it with the real ones;
2. To classify the programs under various category heads such as malware, spyware and ransomware;
3. Clustering for malware protection on secure email gateways.For example:, to separate legal file attachments from outliers.

Academic papers about endpoint protection and malware specifically are gaining popularity. A wide range of them dealing with the elimination of experimental biasing in the the classification of malwares across different parameters of time and space.

Machine Learning for Application Security

Application security is an intriguing area, with much scope for protection especially by means of ERP Security.Machine Learning in application security may be applied to —WAFs or Code analysis, both static and dynamic. It should always be reckoned that Application security can differ. There are web applications, databases, ERP systems, SaaS applications, micro services, and so on to talk about variation in Application Security. It is nearly impossible to build a universal Machine Learning model to deal with all threats effectively and efficiently in the near future. However, one can try and aim at solving some of tasks. Following are instances of what one can do with machine learning for application security:

1. Regression to detect anomalies in HTTP requests (for example, XXE and SSRF attacks and auth bypass);
2. Classification to detect known types of attacks like injections (SQLi, XSS, RCE, etc.);and
3. Clustering user activity to detect DDOS attacks and mass exploitation.

The techniques may involve the detection of malicious queries while dealing with Web based attacks, the classification of the malicious scripts may also be included along with the malicious URL detection.

Machine Learning for User Behavior

The whole concept of User Behaviour started with the "Security Information and Event Management" (SIEM). Security Information And Event Management was capable of solving a number of tasks if they are configured properly including user behavior search and Machine Learning. Then the UEBA solutions declared that SIEM could not handle effectively new, more advanced types of attacks and constant behavior change.The market has come to terms with the fact that a special solution is required if the threats are regarded from the user level.However, even the UEBA tools do not necessarily cover all things connected or associated with different user behaviors. There are domain users, application users, SaaS users, social networks, messengers, and other accounts that need to be monitored.

Unlike conventional malware detection techniques that focus mainly on common attacks and the possibility to train a classifier, user behavior is one of the complex layers and unsupervised learning problem. As a rule, there is no labeled dataset as well as any idea of what to search for. Therefore, the task of generation of a universal algorithm for all types of users is tricky in the user behavior area. Below are some of the tasks that organizations try and solve with the help of Machine Learning:

1. Regression to detect anomalies in User actions (e.g., login in unusual time);
2. Classification to group different users for peer-group analysis;
3. Clustering to separate groups of users and detect outliers.

The other tasks may also include the detection of Anomalous user behaviour with the help of specifically devised algorithms and also to deal with threat detection in Cyber-security data streams among many others.

Machine Learning for Process Behavior

The process area is the last but definitely not the least. While dealing with it, it is important to know a business process in order to fulfill the purpose of finding something anomalous. Business processes can differ significantly. For instance, one can look for frauds in banking and retail systems or a plant floor in manufacturing. The two are completely unrelated, and they demand a lot of domain knowledge. In machine learning feature engineering (the way you represent data to your algorithm) is essential to achieve results. Similarly, features are different in all processes. Following are the examples of tasks in the process area:

1. Regression to predict the next user action and detect outliers such as credit card fraud.
2. Classification to detect known types of fraud.
3. Clustering to compare business processes and detect outliers.

With the rapid exponential evolution in the Artificial Intelligence and Machine Learning technologies and also the wide spectrum of cyber-security threats haunting the cyber world, Machine Learning can be of imperative importance in the coming decades to tackle the problems at hand regarding security.

Adversarial Machine Learning

It's a technique employed with the aid of malicious inputs to fool the models. The adversarial is a burgeoning menace in the field of cyber security as it can cause malfunctioning in the standard models of machine learning (Zhu et al., 2017). A sample of input data is modified in the slightest sense to make the machine learning classifiers misclassify it. The severity of it lies in the fact that the adversarial can launch attacks without even having access to the underlying model. Researches across the globe in eminent institutions hint at machine learning systems being vulnerable to the adversarial. By surreptitiously manipulating the input data, sometimes the changes are so subtle that they bypass the human eye; the malicious adversary is able to exploit a set of vulnerabilities of the machine learning algorithms and hence compromising the security. A few examples such as attacks in spam filtering, confounding of the malware code inside the network packets, fake biometric traits to masquerade a legitimate individual etc.

FRONTIERS OF CYBER SECURITY

Over the decades, cyber security threats have evolved essentially in three important ways:

Intent: Over the past years, viruses were deployed on systems by inquisitive programmers to explore the dimensions of computer systems.Today the attacks have changed humungously as cyberattacks these daya are a result of well executed plan by trained comrades in lieu of cyber warfare.

Momentum: The potential rate at which the attack spreads has also improved significantly and can affect computer systems connected via a network all over the globe in a matter of seconds.

Impact: The potential impact has increased manifold due to the immense penetration of internet across the globe and having surpassed the boundaries of traditional computer systems to have a role in our day-to-day lives.

It is a perceived notion that it is next to impossible to keep up with the momentum and rate of cyber attacks. Thus, this explanation renders Machine Learning as more of a necessity rather than a mere choice available before us.Computers are experts at redundancy unlike the human nature and can go on repeating the same task million times over without much hassle.This can prove to a demerit if the wrong action is being repaeted at such a rate.Though, it is pertinent to underscore that it is good to increase the use of ML/AI, but due diligence should also be given to bad entities that these algorithms have at their disposal. Researchers have been able to address six different facets of intersection of Machine Learning techniques with cybersecurity.

Legal and Policy Issues

AI and Machine learning is a buzz word today with its implementations found in almost every field. The results has been promising leading to a belief that Machine Learning application would invariably lead to success.While there is no denying of the fact that Machine Learning promises to improve some of the aspects of defence techniques through automation, a great amount of caution is required for the deployment of such systems. A small glitch or error may invariably jeopardize the national security and the whole national social structure. Mirai botnet in the year 2016 set the trend of botnet attacks. It involved multiple distributed denial-of-service attacks (DDoS attacks) that targeted the systems operated by Domain Name System (DNS) provider Dyn. This led the major Internet platforms and services to be unavailable to large groups of users in Europe and North America. and one can only imagine the disaster that could be impended via the use of high level and sophisticated Machine Learning programs across the world.

The other demerit that can be thought of is that if a developer loses control of his Artificial Intelligence program and causes people's faith in the application of Artificial Intelligence and Machine Learning would be gone, once and for all. Therefore, the use of Machine Learning for cyber safety should have some legal binding and adequate care should be taken in its the creation, deployment, and use by some global authority as well as local authorities entrusted with the task at national levels.

Human Factors

History has it that Stanislav Petrov, a Soviet officer, with his agile mind and experience had been able to averte a nuclear war in 1983. Petrov had been assigned to the Serpukhov-15 secret command centre outside Moscow. It was then that the attack detection algorithms warned that the United States had launched five intercontinental ballistic missiles at the Soviet Union. A normal tendency for any body in that situation would be to panic and report the situation to superior. Petrov did just the opposite. Petrov had years of experience and he knew exactly about the loopholes of the system. Hence, he could not trust the system completely which proved correct eventually. The predictive algorithms miscalculated and the alarm had been falsely triggered by sun's reflection from clouds, a data input the system's programmers had apparently not adequately anticipated (Khanna & Singh,2017).

This incident clearly highlights the future of security through Machine Learning will not only require Technical trust but Human trust as well. Even the most sophisticated computer systems can fail. But the question is whether they will 'fail well' i.e with minimum damage.Indeed, it will be these human trust factors in the operationalization of Machine Learning systems that will dictate their adoption rates.

Data: New Information Frontiers

Data is a indeed a very critical feature. Security of Machine Learning algorithms will actually help us in reckoning their true potential when trained on large, diverse training data sets. Here not only the quantity matters but quality also is a key player. Even though large volumes of data are available today which is doubling every second, most of the data lack in completeness. This is because:

1. Most of the devices which are used were not primarily designed with instrumentation and measurement as an integral feature; data available from them is not able to capture critical points.
2. Most of the times individuals and companies do not disclose data pertaining to cybersecurity events either due to reputational concerns(as this reduces stakeholder's confidence)or legal and privacy concerns.

Others concerns associated with data are Integrity and relevance. It is easy to generate simulated data sets but they do not imbibe the reality. Also regular updating of data in terms of all recent attacks should be done regularly. Data collection techniques, by their very nature, often include unintended human and technical biases. Understanding, documenting, and sharing those biases are important to ensure AI/ML effectiveness and operation. Data integrity also affects human confidence in AI/ML. If the AI/ML training data set is incomplete, includes questionable biases, or is, in general, not fully understood, then confidence in the entire system is diminished. Preprocessing of the data prior to use for training can also alter data integrity and reduce confidence.

Hardware for AI/ML and Cybersecurity

Today, a network implies human users connected by smart devices all over the globe. Network is not merely defined by electronic equipment in a room or building. Due to such vastness, it becomes an easy target for cyberattacks aided by AI bots. Many leading CISOs admit that cyberattacks is no more viewed as question that whether they will be hacked but when .Hardware holds the key in more than one way.

By incorporating security into hardware designs

- By creating hardware network architectures that can intelligently monitor the network's security state
- Creating hardware that allows AI/ML systems to solve more complex problems by eliminating existing compute barriers

AI requires a great deal of computer hardware for training purposes. This prevents the real time threat assessment and response required by cybersecurity for new threats. The only solution to this problem is by allowing computer hardware engineers to change their approach towards the concept of computing. Emphasis should be given on how data flows through a processor rather than how computations are done. Academia, funded by government agencies and industry, can lead the way by experimenting with new and novel outside-the-box architectures. Innovative approaches are the only way to shake up a field that hasn't effectively changed in the last 50 years. Without a new architecture, AI/ML will be unable to solve large-scale problems such as those in the cybersecurity application.AI/Ml can also be utilized to design and implement better hardware. AI can be incorporated into current design tools. Even if one is able to plug few of the hardware bugs, this will go a long way in making the network secure because hardware faults and design errors are among the most reliable targets for exploits. .

Software and Algorithms for AI/ML and Cyber Security

As the typical cyber security data sets are extremely large, networks for data delivery and the processing of Machine Learning models must be capable of efficiently handling staggering amounts of diverse data. The scarcity of such networks today is a major hindrance to progress in the field. Achieving such networks for real-time analytics requires even more careful software design and algorithms. Natural language processing (NLP) makes it possible to derive actionable insights from previously inaccessible data. Analyzing unstructured text with NLP enables the extraction of key actors from past cyber incidents, news stories, analysis reports, and many other similar text sources.

Cyber-security is highly dynamic due to rapid evolution in the underlying technologies and the because the offense and defense are locked in a threat–response–threat co-evolution. This dynamic and constantly evolving landscape requires constant vigilance and upgradation to threat classification, identification, and response. The adversarial characteristic nature of the cyber domain presents a modeling challenge that can be perceived as an opportunity. Cyber competitions, in which teams act and react to others, are valuable laboratories to explore interactions. The goal of these experiments is to imitate processes by which an adversary learns of defensive measures and then preempts evasive measures. Understanding an adversary's strategy, then, helps refine the models.

CONCLUSION

This chapter details the applications of machine learning in cyber security. The world has finite resources that it can dedicate to improve upon the Cyber-security issues, a fact that will inevitably lead to issues of resource allocation. A properly developed and deployed Machine Learning would be highly desirable to give the good intended crowd an overwhelming advantage over the bad intended ones. But every possibility holds an opportunity. Through hardware and Software improvements, over the time, the organisations will be better able to integrate the Machine Learning systems in their Cyber-security framework, which was next to impossible even few years ago. Machine Learning will also help in creating the integrated meaning from hundreds and thousands of disparate data streams; support automated, real-time prevention platforms; and augment humans' decision- making ability.

Repairing or mitigating vulnerabilities will remain a challenge. Most users either do not know or do not have a way to report discovered vulnerabilities. Current use cases, such as fraud detection in the banking industry and diagnosis in the health-care industry, serve as enablers for the future operationalization of AI/ML in the cybersecurity domain. Although not all use cases and current AI/ML algorithms are designed to be employed in real-time environments, they serve as foundations for real-time detect–defend or defend–attack situations in cybersecurity. For certain domains, the ability to consciously disable AI/ML actions or disregard recommendations is an enabler of AI/ML operationalization for cybersecurity.

In such cases, it is important to have the ability to disable or alter specific system aspects without necessarily turning everything off while, at the same time, comprehending any repercussions.

The chapter emphasizes on Various approaches that uses machine learning to enhance the traditional security mechanisms.

REFERENCES

Al-Jarrah, O. Y., Yoo, P. D., Muhaidat, S., Karagiannidis, G. K., & Taha, K. (2015). Efficient machine learning for big data: A review. *Big Data Research*, *2*(3), 87–93. doi:10.1016/j.bdr.2015.04.001

Buczak, A. L., & Guven, E. (2016). A survey of data mining and machine learning methods for cyber security intrusion detection. *IEEE Communications Surveys and Tutorials*, *18*(2), 1153–1176. doi:10.1109/COMST.2015.2494502

Cavelty, M. D. (2010). Cyber-security. *The Routledge Handbook of New Security Studies*, 154-162. Retrieved from https://www.researchgate.net/profile/Myriam_Dunn_Cavelty/publication/281631032_Cyber-security/links/55f1426408ae199d47c243b1/Cyber-security.pdf

Chapelle, O., Scholkopf, B., & Zien, A. (2009). Semi-supervised learning (O. Chapelle et al., Eds.; 2006) [book review]. IEEE Transactions on Neural Networks, 20(3), 542-542.

Do Hoon Kim, T. L., Jung, S. O. D., In, H. P., & Lee, H. J. (2007, August). Cyber threat trend analysis model using HMM. In *Proceedings of the Third International Symposium on Information Assurance and Security* (pp. 177-182). Academic Press.

Domingos, P. M. (2012). A few useful things to know about machine learning. *Communications of the ACM*, *55*(10), 78–87.

Dua, S., & Du, X. (2016). *Data mining and machine learning in cybersecurity*. Auerbach Publications. doi:10.1201/b10867

Dua, S., & Du, X. (2016). *Data mining and machine learning in cybersecurity*. Auerbach Publications. doi:10.1201/b10867

Huang, W., & Stokes, J. W. (2016, July). MtNet: a multi-task neural network for dynamic malware classification. In *International Conference on Detection of Intrusions and Malware, and Vulnerability Assessment* (pp. 399-418). Cham, Switzerland: Springer. 10.1007/978-3-319-40667-1_20

Kasun, L. L. C., Zhou, H., Huang, G. B., & Vong, C. M. (2013). Representational learning with extreme learning machine for big data. *IEEE Intelligent Systems*, *28*(6), 31–34.

Khanna, U., & Singh, P. (2017). *Hybrid Approach of KNN+ Euclidean Distance to Detect Intrusion within Cloud Based Systems*. Retrieved from http://www.irjaes.com/pdf/V2N3Y17-IRJAES/IRJAES-V2N2P325Y17.pdf

Kotsiantis, S. B., Zaharakis, I., & Pintelas, P. (2007). Supervised machine learning: A review of classification techniques. *Emerging Artificial Intelligence Applications in Computer Engineering, 160*, 3-24.

LeCun, Y., Bengio, Y., & Hinton, G. (2015). Deep learning. *Nature, 521*(7553), 436.

Linda, O., Manic, M., Vollmer, T., & Wright, J. (2011, April). Fuzzy logic based anomaly detection for embedded network security cyber sensor. In *2011 IEEE Symposium on Computational Intelligence in Cyber Security (CICS),* (pp. 202-209). IEEE. 10.1109/CICYBS.2011.5949392

Marsland, S. (2011). *Machine learning: an algorithmic perspective*. Chapman and Hall. Retrieved from http://dspace.fue.edu.eg/xmlui/bitstream/handle/123456789/3667/10501.pdf?sequence=1

Michalski, R. S., Carbonell, J. G., & Mitchell, T. M. (Eds.). (2013). *Machine learning: An artificial intelligence approach*. Springer Science & Business Media.

Nasrabadi, N. M. (2007). Pattern recognition and machine learning. *Journal of Electronic Imaging*, *16*(4), 049901. doi:10.1117/1.2819119

Uma, M., & Padmavathi, G. (2013). A Survey on Various Cyber Attacks and their Classification. *IJ Network Security, 15*(5), 390-396.

Wang, L. (Ed.). (2005). *Support vector machines: theory and applications* (Vol. 177). Springer Science & Business Media.

Woon, I., Tan, G. W., & Low, R. (2005). A protection motivation theory approach to home wireless security. *ICIS 2005 Proceedings*, 31.

Xin, Y., Kong, L., Liu, Z., Chen, Y., Li, Y., Zhu, H., & Wang, C. (2018). Machine learning and deep learning methods for cybersecurity. *IEEE Access: Practical Innovations, Open Solutions*, *6*, 35365–35381. doi:10.1109/ACCESS.2018.2836950

Yavanoglu, O., & Aydos, M. (2017, December). A review on cyber security datasets for machine learning algorithms. In *2017 IEEE International Conference on Big Data (Big Data)* (pp. 2186-2193). IEEE. 10.1109/BigData.2017.8258167

Yousefi-Azar, M., Varadharajan, V., Hamey, L., & Tupakula, U. (2017, May). Autoencoder-based feature learning for cyber security applications. In *2017 International joint conference on neural networks (IJCNN)* (pp. 3854-3861). IEEE. 10.1109/IJCNN.2017.7966342

Zhang, C., Patras, P., & Haddadi, H. (2019). Deep learning in mobile and wireless networking: A survey. *IEEE Communications Surveys and Tutorials*, 1. doi:10.1109/COMST.2019.2904897

Zhang, T., & Zhu, Q. (2018). Distributed privacy-preserving collaborative intrusion detection systems for VANETs. IEEE Transactions on Signal and Information Processing over. *Networks*, *4*(1), 148–161.

Zhu, J. Y., Park, T., Isola, P., & Efros, A. A. (2017). Unpaired image-to-image translation using cycle-consistent adversarial networks. In *Proceedings of the IEEE international conference on computer vision* (pp. 2223-2232). IEEE. 10.1109/ICCV.2017.244

This research was previously published in the Handbook of Research on Machine and Deep Learning Applications for Cyber Security; pages 83-103, copyright year 2020 by Information Science Reference (an imprint of IGI Global).

Chapter 34
Machine Learning Techniques to Mitigate Security Attacks in IoT

Kavi Priya S.
https://orcid.org/0000-0002-1292-9728
Mepco Schlnek Engineering College, India

Vignesh Saravanan K.
Ramco Institute of Technology, Rajapalayam, India

Vijayalakshmi K.
Ramco Institute of Technology, Rajapalayam, India

ABSTRACT

Evolving technologies involve numerous IoT-enabled smart devices that are connected 24-7 to the internet. Existing surveys propose there are 6 billion devices on the internet and it will increase to 20 billion devices within a few years. Energy conservation, capacity, and computational speed plays an essential part in these smart devices, and they are vulnerable to a wide range of security attack challenges. Major concerns still lurk around the IoT ecosystem due to security threats. Major IoT security concerns are Denial of service(DoS), Sensitive Data Exposure, Unauthorized Device Access, etc. The main motivation of this chapter is to brief all the security issues existing in the internet of things (IoT) along with an analysis of the privacy issues. The chapter mainly focuses on the security loopholes arising from the information exchange technologies used in internet of things and discusses IoT security solutions based on machine learning techniques including supervised learning, unsupervised learning, and reinforcement learning.

DOI: 10.4018/978-1-6684-6291-1.ch034

INTRODUCTION

Today's Internet becomes the connectivity of many smart devices and computers. Any real world object can be attached with a sensor and connected to the network. It paves way for many applications that benefits the users. Some common applications are automation in industry, smart home, patient's effective health monitoring applications etc. Some years back, the devices are connected in a network, which is now getting evolved smarter by the connection of any real-world objects. Clearly it states that Internet of Things(IoT) is a fast-evolving technology. Some statistics on IoT predicts that there will be more than 5 billion IoT devices connected at present. IoT can be any physical device equipped with sensors are connected with a communication channel. Through the connected network the devices can interact with the environment, i.e. collect data from surroundings and send that data for processing. Such devices that interacts with the environment to collect data is called as source node. The data is collected by source node and communicated to the base station or the sink node for processing or storage.

Consequently, an algorithm is the responsible for the data collection or data gathering and routing the data to the base station. All these devices are interconnected to share and exchange the data, that makes the IoT and wireless sensor network open to many challenges in security violations and privacy exploration for the users.

MAIN FOCUS OF THE CHAPTER

In this chapter, provides an idea about the wireless sensor network and IoT, which is an interconnection of the devices controlled through the Human machine interface (HMI). The essential features and use of connected devices or the embedded devices with the network provide a number of uses in many applications. This attractive feature also enables IoT devices connected with the network more prone to security threats and attacks. Depending on the data being communicated over the network, it inhibits an interest over the attackers with a wide range of privacy exploration. Hence providing a secured connected network has to ensure it provides solutions for the various concerns like Privacy of data, data reliability, correct responses from the connected devices, trust-worthy devices and autonomous recovery of the device when compromised. Considering these factors, the IoT requires effective solutions to achieve the above terms.

TECHNOLOGIES CONNECTING VARIOUS IOT DEVICES

The main objective of the Internet of Things is to provide an environment in which the connected devices are able to transfer information without any manual interference. Thus, the exchange of information between two devices is possible under some well-established communication technologies, which are discussed below.

Wireless Sensor Networks (WSN)

Wireless Sensor Networks are comprised of set of independent nodes with limited bandwidth and frequency through which it can communication wirelessly with other nearby devices. In traditional wireless sensor network environment, the sensor node consists of the following parts:

1. Sensor
2. Microcontroller
3. Memory
4. Radio Transceiver
5. Battery

The sensor nodes in the wireless sensor network has very limited communication range (short range communication). Hence the communication becomes multi-hop relay of information between the source and the base station. The required data is collected by the wireless sensors through collaboration amongst the various nodes, which is then sent to the sink node through a suitable routing strategy. The communication network formed dynamically by the use of wireless radio transceivers and it facilitates data transmission between nodes. Multi-hop transmission of data demands different nodes to take diverse traffic loads.

Radio Frequency Identification (RFID)

In context to the Internet of Things (IoT), RFID technology is mainly used in information tags interacting with each other automatically. For exchanging information between one another and interaction between them the radio frequency waves are used. There are some components being used in this RFID technology. The major two components are:

RFID Tags

RFID tag is a small device in which a small chip is embedded with an antenna. It serves as a unique identifier with a help of a code known as Electronic Product Code (EPC) which is also stored in the memory unit of the RFID tag. EPC provides a feature to recognize the particular tag universally with some numerical form of data associated with it. A tag reader is allied with the RFID tag to operate on the universal tag code The tags are of two main types as:

1. **Passive Tag:** These tags are activated only by a transceiver from a specified range of distance which relays on the information of the EPC.
2. **Active Tag:** The distinct EPC interacts with all its contiguous EPCs available distantly at some limited range. Active tag has an internal battery associated with it to facilitate this behavior.

RFID Readers

The RFID reader functions as the identification detector of each tag by its interaction with the EPC of the tag under its scan.

SECURITY AND PRIVACY CATEGORIES AND PROBLEMS

IoT is the network of devices embedded in motor vehicles, streets, apartments or buildings and other electronic appliances that enables the devices to collect and exchange the information. This valuable information or the service provided can be breached and compromised by attackers or illegitimate users in the motivation of financial gain or damage the reputation of the competitor. Some of the common attacks are:

1. **Device Cloning:** In device cloning security issue, any foreign/alien device can be connected to the network as an authenticated device, but it is not. It is even harder to find which are the clones and which are authenticated devices. The foreign device will quickly overload the server with bad data, causing massive breakdown leading to time delay and heavy financial loss to fix it.
2. **Exposure of Sensitive Data:** Information provided across the network needs to be encrypted. When the sensitive information is not properly protected by the application through standardized protocol or encryption technique then Sensitive Data Exposure occurs. A simple example can be transferring the data as clear text which is rendered as ASCII and can be read by text editor.
3. **Denial of Service:** In simple terms this is denying or slowing down the service. The attack on the network causing the network to slow down or even completely pull the network down by simulating the network with unwanted useless data creating a heavy traffic in the data flow. Variations of DoS threats are directly targeting the server infrastructure while others exploit the vulnerabilities in applications.
4. **Unauthorized Device Access:** There are concerns about applications that are too private which does not digest third party to control the devices. A malicious user may gain control of the devices over the network.

IoT extends it applications in almost all aspects of modern life. Therefore, security is a very crucial factor. Furthermore, the limitation of the capacity and energy of the device complicates this problem.

Security in IoT is a problem that cannot be easily solved. One major factor is that the IoT devices are battery operated and with limited resources. This also makes the IoT device very inexpensive. The security techniques consuming more energy and memory resources are not a feasible solution. Another factor is the IoT devices are adapted to dynamic changes, so it is not suitable to apply a centralized security algorithm. Machine learning techniques can be one effective solution.

This chapter elaborates the different security threats that are imposed on IoT possible machine learning techniques that can be developed to encounter these security threats.

Classification of Security Attacks in IoT

The most critical attacks in IoT can be classified as different security attacks such as Attacks on the layers, attacks based on the targets and attacks based on the performer.

- **Attacks on the Layers:** These attacks are focused on the different layers such as Application layer, Transport layer, Physical layer, Network layer and Data-link layer. Each of these layers is open to different types of attacks. For instance, flooding of the data packets in the data link layer in which nodes will suffer from high collision of data. Another instance, where the malicious nodes sends more requests to transmit the data and so deplete the energy in the batteries of other nodes causing exhaustion attacks leads to failure of the network.

- **Attacks Based on Targets:** These types of attacks focused on the targets are performed to threaten the target with data confidentiality. In these attacks, the unauthorized or malicious attackers are exposed with the information of high confidentiality such as the keys without the knowledge of the authorized users. The attackers then decrypt the keys that are weak and gain the information needed. Traffic analysis and eavesdropping are some examples of passive attacks. Meanwhile, active attackers may obtain confidential information through monitoring the network and may even change this information. Some examples of active Attacks are hole attacks, spoofing, Sybil attacks etc.,
- **Attacks Based on the Performer:** Based on the attacker's location in the communication network, we can classify as outside attacks (outside the network) and inside attacks (from inside the network). In case of the attacks performed from inside the network, one of the legitimate or authorized nodes will be the attacker. Hence, these authorized nodes can access any information required and it cannot be easily identified. These attacks can lead to data modification and eavesdropping of the data. In case of outside attacks, the attackers may send unwanted data again and again and can increase the network traffic with unwanted data. When the network is over jammed with data, the resources may lose all the energy and becomes exhausted.

Though the IoT is widely implemented in various applications, the entire communication network and substructure and setup of the IoT is deviated from the standards creating a flaw on the network. The IoT network is always suspected with confidentiality loss for the users of the IoT applications. The overall development of IoT system is affected by some predominant security threats varies over the network since this technology is built over the communication of the information relay on one or more devices. Some of the most prominent security issues arising out from the communication technology are the following:

SECURITY ATTACKS ON SENSOR NETWORKS AND IOT DEVICES

Security attacks in sensor networks can be broadly classified into two broad classes: passive and active attacks. In passive attacks the attackers focus mainly against data confidentiality, But in case of active attacks, malicious attacks are performed against data confidentiality and also against data integrity. Active attacks can also aim for the resource utilization or the disturbance of any communication and unauthorized access. An active attack can be detected, but passive attacks are a bit hard to detect.

Figure 1. Major types of passive attacks

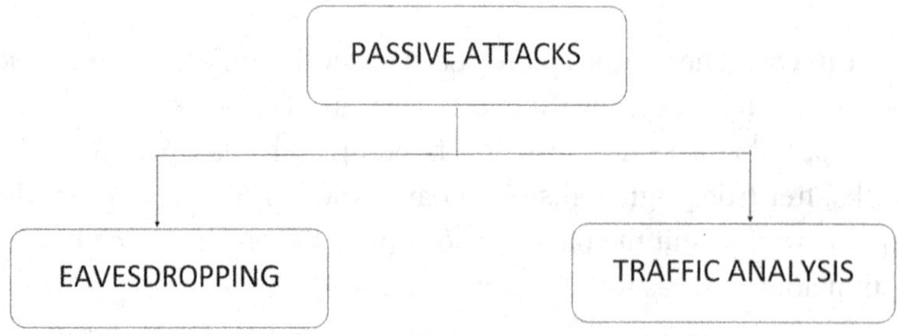

PASSIVE ATTACKS

In passive attacks the malicious nodes are not known and remain hidden to tap the communication channels to collect data. It can be defined as the monitoring and listening of the data flow channel by unauthorized intruders. The passive attacks are classified into traffic analysis types, packet-tracing, eavesdropping and camouflaged adversaries. The categorization of passive attacks is shown in Figure 1. Some other types of passive attacks include camouflage and Packet-tracing.

Monitoring and Eavesdropping

The data classified in the communication network can be monitored by tapping over the communication channel known as eavesdropping. Compared to the wired, wireless links are easier to tap. Hence, the wireless communication networks are more susceptible to passive attacks. In particular, when known security standards are used and plain data, i.e. not encrypted, are sent wirelessly, any compromised intermediate node can easily receive and read the data and listen to or watch audio–visual transmissions. For example, an adversary can easily eavesdrop credit card numbers and passwords when they are transmitted without any encryption standards over unsecured wireless sensor networks.

Camouflaged Adversaries

In this type of passive attack, the intruder can hide the number of nodes available in the wireless sensor network. So such nodes will show themselves as the legitimate nodes and intimate the other nodes to send the data packets. On receiving the packets, these nodes will misroute the packets or can perform a detail analysis on the data being private. The term camouflage is used because in this attack the sensor node compromises the other nodes in network and it also makes a false advertisement about the routing information such that all the data packets flows through this camouflaged node. Once the packets are received the data is forwarded and analysis is done on the private data being forwarded.

Packet-Tracing

In this packet tracing attack, the malicious intruder may themselves notify the position of this node and immediate sender of the other packets originating. The malicious node is capable and equipped in finding and tracking hop by hop neighbors thus leading to the actual source node from which the data is originated. Thus, the main source of the data is revealed to the malicious node causing the exploration of the privacy of the data.

Traffic Analysis

The traffic pattern of the flow of data packets in the communicating network has equal importance as the data present in the packets, and provides valuable information for the intruders. For example, by analyzing traffic patterns of the communicating network, the topology of the network can be explored. In case of wireless sensor networks, the nodes deployed at random places transmits data to the neighbor node that are very close to the base station. This node nearer to the base station is called sink node.

Ultimately, the sink node makes more data transmissions compared to the other nodes, because the sink node closer to base station is responsible for many data transmissions.

Similarly, in ad hoc networks, to ensure the scalability factor clustering is an important factor. In each cluster there will be a cluster head which will always be responsible for the data transfer from other nodes in the communicating network. It is very useful for the attackers if the cluster head is compromised or the base station itself is detected to perform a denial-of-service attack with the cluster head denying the traffic flow or eavesdropping the data packets in the network to get valuable information by analyzing the traffic. Traffic analysis can also be useful for the intruders and helps them to safeguard the network from anonymity attacks. The adversaries may also aim at identifying and spotting the origin (source nodes) of the data packets as a target. Once this information is revealed, the intruder can detect the abilities, flaws, scene of events of the possessors of the nodes.

Figure 2. Hierarchical classification of security issues

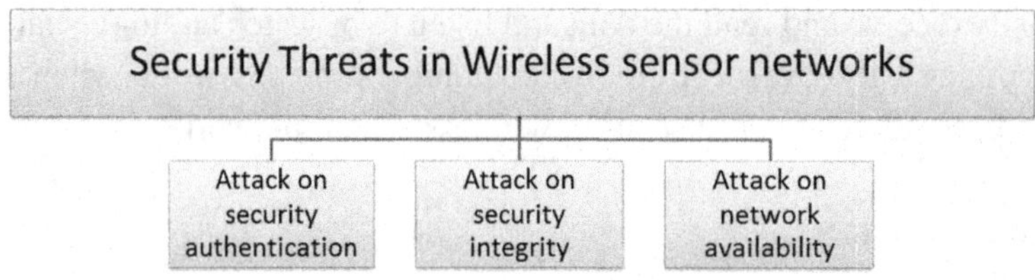

The classification on the security threats and issues faced in WSN is shown in Figure 2. In addition, there can be many other security attacks are possible in a wireless sensor network falls under three distinct classification listed below:

1. Security violation on authorization.
2. Breakdown of the integrity in privacy through silent outbreaks.
3. Security breach on the network availability.

ACTIVE ATTACKS

In active attacks the main intention of the malicious node or attackers is to affect the data flow in the data communication network. With the sign of this objective there is a possibility that the attacker and can be detected. For example, there may be degradation overall data flow and network traffic flow because of these attacks. In most cases the intruders will try to stay hidden and aims to gain unauthorized access to the network. The adversaries can also perform this attack to disturb integrity of the network and also can be a threat against confidentiality. The active attacks are classified into four groups. Figure 3 depicts the classification.

Figure 3. Types of active attacks

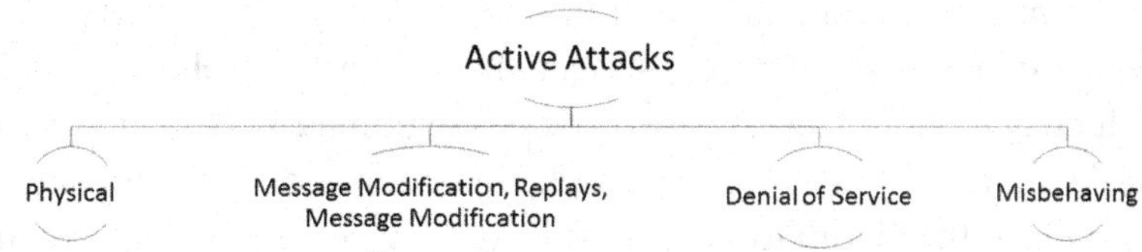

Physical Attacks

Another possible attack is the physical damage of the hardware by the intruder or system to terminate the nodes from the network and can even terminate the communication network by damaging half of the nodes available in the network. The physical attack is also considered to be responsible for affecting the fault tolerance of the network, i.e. the capability to withstand the node failures and provide all the functionalities of the network. Mostly in wireless sensor networks, the deployment of the sensor nodes is random and installed in unattended regions, which can be accessible by the intruders. Hence, they can be physically damaged by the attackers or easily defected and push out of the network. When nodes are deployed and unattended it can also be reached physically and the node can be tampered with techniques like micro-probing, laser damage on the nodes, glitch attacks and power analysis. The act of tampering the nodes can as well lead to the DoS attacks and masquerading attacks.

Therefore, the node should be resilience to tampering attacks and thus it is an open area that sensor network and its promising applications should seriously consider.

The node-tampering schemes can be grouped into invasive tampering and non-invasive tampering. Gaining unlimited access to a node is called Invasive tampering i.e. this is intentionally done to access the node. In contrast gaining such a boundless entrée to the node is not the aim of non-invasive attacks. Instead, the intruder performs this attack to analyze the properties of a node, such as the memory capability, battery energy consumption, or the time complexity and space complexity of the algorithms implemented.

Message Modification Through Masquerading Attacks

An unauthorized acting as another legitimate node is termed as masquerading. Messages or data transferred in the network can be known to these masquerading nodes and it can be captured and replayed. Finally, the intruder will modify the content of the captured messages before being replayed. There are various threats and vulnerabilities that can be developed based on these approaches. The location of the nodes in the network may dynamically change due to its movement in mobile ad hoc networks. So, there is no fixed location for the sensor nodes. The nodes inhibit autonomous mechanisms like auto-forming and auto-healing to adjust to the fluctuations in the network topology. Since the topology cannot be preserved and the routing mechanism prefers reactive techniques, the node's consistency in correspondence with the network may be difficult to trace. But the problem here is it is impossible to detect whether the node has any other access point in the existing network. The sensor networks do not use the global identifications that makes the network even easier to masquerade the network.

The data integrity of messages or the service being provided in the network can be attack through any type of attacks and may lead to modification of data violating the integrity. The act of message modification and replay of messages through masquerading attacks is also a security threat against data confidentiality. It creates an illusion that the node is a legitimate node and make the nearby nodes to show the trustworthy data to itself or another wicked node to access the private data. An intruder deceives someone and make the victim to give confidential information voluntarily through phishing. An unauthorized node that pretends as if it is an authorized node. It requests passwords, encrypted keys and other information from any other node. One such approach is the act of Masquerading that attacks and access the system illegally.

DOS ATTACK ON THE PHYSICAL LAYER

In a wireless sensor network, the physical layer is responsible for modulation and demodulation, encryption and decryption process. Since this layer provides the much needed functionality, it is highly prone to more security attacks. This security attacks that can be performed on this are mentioned below:

1. **Network Jam:** The communication network of the sensor nodes is compromised and jammed. This network causes the sensor nodes unable to communicate with other sensor nodes.
2. **Node Tampering:** The motive of this attack is to physically tamper the particular sensor node in order to extract some sensitive or confidential information.

DOS ATTACK ON THE LINK LAYER

The data streams generated in the network, detection of the data frames are processed in the link layer of wireless sensor networks. The MAC and error control mechanism is also responsibly processed by the link layer. Moreover, the reliability of the data from one point to another point or between multiple points are ensured by the link layer. The various attacks competing in this layer are:

1. **Collision of Data:** When two or more nodes transmits the data packets simultaneously on the communication channel, there will be a delay in the processing which leads to this type of attack. Due to the collision of data packets there may be minor changes in the packets. When the data packets are received at the other end, due to the minor changes inhibited it is identified as a packet mismatch.
2. **Unfairness of Data:** It is a vigorous form of the repeated data collision attack, which in turn creates a major change to the data packets making it unfair at receiving end.
3. **Exhaustion of Battery Life:** This attack causes unusual loss of the energy in the nodes due to unusual high traffic in a channel, depleting all the energy of the sensor nodes. The traffic of the channel may be increase due to producing large number of requests (Request to Send) and increased number of responses over the channel.

DOS ATTACK ON THE NETWORK LAYER

The network layer is responsible for the routing of the data traffic in communicating network. Hence the network layer is open to many attacks to compromise the routing strategy. The DoS attack is the more predominant attack in this layer. The specific attacks are:

- **Hello Flood Attack:** A single malicious node sends a useless message (Hello message), which flooded to all the nearest neighbor nodes. These neighbor nodes will then forward and replay the messages to other nodes creating a high traffic and congestion in the communicating channels. At one point the complete network is flooded with these unwanted packets and congested.
- **Homing:** This kind of attack is like focusing on the root of the processing. In homing attack, the capability of the network is compromised by searching and targeting the cluster heads in the network. Using these host nodes, the entire network can be shut down.
- **Selective Forwarding:** Normally the data is forwarded to the nodes that needs the packets. In this selective forwarding attack, the data is transmitted to a selective number of nodes by the compromised node. The compromised node may select the nodes to which they should forward the data, based on the requirement and objective of the malicious attack.
- **Sybil Attack:** A single node in the network is presented as multiple number of identities. So many nodes forward the data to this node.
- **Spoofing:** A special kind of attack which plays on replaying and misdirection of traffic.
- **Wormhole Attack:** The data packets are relocated from its original position.
- **Sinkhole:** It is a special kind of attack in which the nodes are convinced to forward the packets through the malicious node. The unauthorized node pretends as the sink node and gets all the data packets or the malicious node convinces the surrounding nodes that it is nearer to the sink and attracts the data packets. When this malicious node pretends to be the sink node, it becomes the centre and receives all data packets from the neighbors. This also paves way for many other attacks like wormhole attacks, and tamper the data by selective forwarding attack.
- **Black Hole Attack:** The illegitimate node pretends to be the neighboring node of the sink node. The power transmission of these nodes will be higher and all other nodes carry data to this node making the network vulnerable. All the data packets received will not be forwarded but dropped off by this malicious node. At some point of time the entire network traffic flow will be stopped creating a black hole region.
- **Acknowledgement Flooding:** In routing algorithms to ensure the data being received acknowledgements are used. In this flooding attack, the neighboring nodes are spoofed with a false information and forwards the acknowledgments to the destined node.

DOS ATTACK ON THE TRANSPORT LAYER

The transport layer of the wireless sensor network architecture makes available the functionality and consistency of the data communication. The DoS attacks in this layer are:

- **Flooding:** It refers to deliberate congestion of communication channels through relay of unnecessary messages and high traffic.

- **De-Synchronization:** In de-synchronization attack, fake messages are created at one node or at both endpoints nodes requesting retransmissions and corrections of non-existing error. This results in loss of energy in one or both the end-points in carrying out the retransmissions.

DOS ATTACK ON THE APPLICATION LAYER

The application layer of the wireless sensor network conveys out the accountability of traffic organization. These applications bring out the transformation of data into an understandable form or supports in gathering of information by sending enquiries. In this layer, a path-based DoS attack is introduced by stimulating the sensor nodes to generate an enormous traffic flow in the path headed for the base station. Some additional DoS attacks are as follows:

1. Greedy Attack
2. Interrogation
3. Black Holes
4. Node Subversion
5. Malfunction of node
6. Passive Information Gathering
7. False Node
8. Message Corruption

SECURITY CONCERNS AND THREATS IN RFID TECHNOLOGY

In the area of IoT applications, RFID technology plays a major role as the RFID tags are used for autonomous information exchange without any human intervention. The use of RFID tags paves way for more risks and open to security threats since it is open to outside attacks due to less security feature in the RFID technology. There are many security attacks and issues, out of which most common types are listed below:

1. Unauthorized authenticity: The RFID tags losses its capacity temporarily or permanently because of the DoS attacks. The RFID tag will start to malfunction and misbehave in scanning the tag reader when it is being compromised or attacked.
2. The attacker can perform these DoS attacks remotely, allowing them to manipulate the RFID's behavior.
3. Unauthorized cloning: The RFID tags can be manipulated through which the confidential information can be captured falls in this category. The cloning or replication of the tag is possible, once the tag is compromised thereby introducing new vulnerabilities.
4. Unauthorized tracking: An adversary traces the RFID tag's behavior which can result in providing privacy or confidential data like a person's phone number etc.
5. Unauthorized Replay: The signal used for communication between the tag and the reader is intercepted and known. This message or signal can be replayed at a later point of time by modifying the message, thus providing a fake availability of the RFID tag.

6. In addition to these threats some additional security issues in RFID technologies are:
   - Middle man attack
   - Tracking
   - Reverse Engineering
   - Viruses
   - Eavesdropping
   - Killing Tag Approach

It is also very important to take into consider on social engineering (i.e.) the human responsible for the IoT security framework also plays an important role for the management of the confidential data and are responsible for the rules to be ensured for maintaining the security. Some of the security management and security rules are:

- New security constraints, instructions and interactions are introduced.
- The efficiency of the rules is examined.
- The rules are set into operational mode and practiced.

In interconnected networks where two or more systems are connected, there can be many deviations in the security standards. These deviations will lead us into the real-world security problems. The security concerns also need to be extended to protect the individual data such as financial exchanges, person's health data, etc. In critical real-world applications that function with control systems, such as automatic control of vehicles(cars) and nuclear reactor, will lead to more serious damage of human life when compromised with attackers. Some of the major problems highlighted below:

- Protecting unauthorized interference of data.
- Preventing the endpoint devices from the unauthorized control.
- The increase in the development of the network evolves the threat on Cyber security.
- Updating security capabilities of IoT devices post installment.

MACHINE LEARNING SECURITY IN IOT

Machine learning (ML) techniques plays a quite wide role in security attacks and IoT devices should be able to choose a good defense policy against these smart attacks. The heterogeneity and dynamic behavior of the network makes the security protocols vulnerable and yet the key parameters should be determined. This becomes a more challenging task since the IoT device is equipped with very limited resources, which makes the device difficult to estimate the accuracy and providing efficient counter attack in the communicating network.

For example, the required information like authentication performance and sensitive test threshold values used in the hypothesis test for the applications with outdoor sensor deployment leads to a higher false alarm rate. To overcome such problems and to improve the efficient performance of the IoT system, one possible solution is to couple the system with machine learning techniques for improving security considerations. To develop the network safety such as detection of malwares, unauthorized access, anti-jamming offloading and illegal access control, we can apply machine learning techniques like supervised learning, unsupervised learning, and reinforcement learning.

Supervised Learning: The learning is termed as supervised, if the inputs are clearly known with their desired outputs. The dataset is provided with each input associated with an output. This training dataset is provided as the input to the machine. The machine can identify the inputs and its corresponding outputs. The algorithms under supervised learning are: neural networks, deep neural network (DNN), K-nearest Neighbor(k-NN) and random forest algorithm. These algorithms are applied in the IoT devices to build the required classification model to label the network traffic. In addition, we can also couple the security enhancement with Support Vector Machine (SVM).

Some instances where these learning algorithms applied in IoT devices are:

- Naive Bayes and SVM may be developed by IoT devices in network invasion discovery and network spoofing.
- DNN can be applied in IoT devices with sufficient memory resources and computation to detect spoofing attacks.
- To spot the network invasion we can use K-NN and random forest classifier for malware discoveries.
- Employ neural network to sense DoS attacks.

Unsupervised Learning: In contrast to the supervised learning technique, the unsupervised learning is provided with the input data only. Considering these inputs, the model will classify the data into different groups called clusters. Unlike the supervised learning that require labeled data, unsupervised learning takes only the input and finds the similarity between the input data. Using the similarity measures, unsupervised learning clusters them into different groups. Multivariate correlation analysis is done by the IoT device and can apply unsupervised learning to ensure the privacy of the network.

Reinforcement Learning: This type of learning is based on the reward scheme. No proper inputs are provided into the system. The learning is based on the previous positive outputs. Examples are playing cricket, playing a chess game, in which based on the previous move, we need to decide the next move. If the performance is good, for instance, if the opponent player's chess coin is eliminated, then the move is effective and it is rewarded and if not, no reward is given. Such type of learning is called Reinforcement learning. The learning also depends on the surrounding environment. One such example of reinforcement learning is Q-learning. IoT device can be enabled with some RL techniques such as Q-learning with different parameters to defend against various attacks by choosing the safety practices. Such type of learning ensures the privacy authentication and to detect malware and helps in anti-jamming transmissions.

In this chapters, the major considerations are malware detections in IoT, unauthorized access control and ML-based authentication to provide secure offloading.

SECURITY CONCERNED SOLUTIONS THROUGH MACHINE LEARNING

In real time IoT device implementation, there are many challenges and security considerations that are to be estimated properly, since they may lead us to security threats and issues.

1. Authentication of IoT Devices is more important and the device should authenticate itself. Only after proper authentication it should starts its transmission of data and receiving data.

2. Firewalling to ensure and allows the secured and trusted use of the packets. The devices will communicate with one another after implementing the algorithm through this firewall that provides secured communication.
3. Access control, to limit the control and privileges to the device components.
4. End-To-End Encryption, which is equipping the devices with security encryptions by implementing the software on all derives. Also preventing the interference of the unauthorized access so as to reduce security threats.

LEARNING-BASED AUTHENTICATION

With inadequate computational, memory and energy possessions it is not always applicable for IoT devices to incorporate traditional authentication schemes to distinguish identity-based attacks. In Physical (PHY)-layer verification technique, the MAC address provides security for the privacy information with a light-weight security fortification for the IoT devices. The parameters of the transmitters and radio receivers such as received signal strength (RSS) and he received signal strength indicators (RSSIs) are taken into consideration. This technique also considers the feature exploited by the PHY-layer such as channel state information (CSI) and provides security with less computation and message overheads. Nevertheless, it is thought-provoking for an IoT device working in a diverse environment with unstructured communication network, to indicate a suitable trial threshold of the endorsement and the mysterious spoofing or attacking model. The simple solution is the IoT devices can relate any Machine Learning(ML) techniques. Some ML technique-based authentication can be enabled in the IoT devices to maximize the accuracy of the authentication and to improve the utility by achieving the optimal test threshold. This technique is very similar as a Markov verdict procedure (MVP), in which the key is to determine the authentication parameters and can be made as an IoT authentication game without the conscious of the networking prototype.

The IoT system can adopt the incremental aggregated gradient (IAG) and the Frank-Wolfe (dFW) technique to improve the spoofing resistance. Such supervised learning techniques can improve the spoofing detection accuracy and also reduces the overall communication overhead. For instance, the IoT device is implemented with the authentication scheme with dFW and IAG technique to prevent spoofing attacks.

An unsupervised learning is used to authenticate the IoT devices. A non-parametric Bayesian method under unsupervised learning is used for the authentication scheme for the identification of the IoT devices. To evaluate the arrival time of the data packets, RSSIs and to monitor the intervals of the radio signals, the IGMM proximity scheme is applied in the IoT device to authentication the device. The information about the location of the devices is not revealed easily in this scheme. Through evaluating these parameters to detect malicious intruders and attackers outside the proximity range. This scheme will request the IoT device to send the ambient signals and packet arrival time internal during a specific time duration. The legal legitimate receiver in-turn will receive the data signals from the IoT device. After such authentication messages are received, the receiver applies a suitable machine learning algorithm to detect and compare the signals reported. The authenticated information is provided to the IoT resources by the IoT devices. Finally, the IoT devices are applied with the deep learning techniques such as DNN with the available computation to improve the authentication accuracy.

LEARNING-BASED ACCESS CONTROL

Many different kinds of nodes are made available in heterogeneous networks and source of data will be diverse that leads to a challenging design to access control. Machine learning techniques such as neural networks, K-NN, SVM, can be used to detect the malicious intrusion. For instance, multivariate correlation analysis (Liang Xiao, 2018) can be used to detect the DoS attack. By this scheme the network traffic features and their correlations are extracted. The accuracy of this scheme in detection increases by 2.95% to 94.8% related with the nearest neighbor-based methodology through triangle area-based approach. The IoT devices such as outdoor sensor normally has limited resource and computation constraints, that makes the device with degraded performance in intrusion detection techniques. Machine learning techniques help the IoT devices to build an effective access control protocols by ensuring extended network lifetime and conserved energy. The outlier detection scheme (Xiaoyue Wan & Xiaozhen Lu, 2018) is developed to improve the flexibility with reduced energy consumption and also to address the outlier detection in WSNs by applying the K-NN learning technique. The traditional centralized scheme when compared with the above learning technique provides an increase of the energy conservation by 61.4%. K-NN is a modest machine learning technique in which the inputs are classified with the K nearest neighbors. Euclidean distance measurement can be used to find the distance measurements between the IoT devices.

The technique proposed on detection of the unauthorized access control (Yanyong Zhang & Di Wu, 2018), utilizes a multilayer perceptron (MLP) with a hidden layer that consists of two neurons. The neural network is trained with the input connection weights and the identifying factor is introduced. Thus the MLP is trained to identify if there is a possibility of DoS attack on the device. The backpropagation (BP) that forwards the calculated results and back propagates the error rate that should be implemented. An evolutionary computation technique like particle swarm optimization can also be implemented that uses the particles to modify the associated connection weights of the perceptron. The IoT device implemented and tested in such scheme proves that the network lifetime is extended by improving the conservation of the device's energy, if the MLP exceeds a desired threshold.

LEARNING-BASED IOT MALWARE DETECTION

To detect the malware, the IoT device can evaluate the runtime behaviors of network by applying the supervised learning techniques. In the malware detection scheme, random forest classifiers and K-NN can be used by the IoT device to develop the malware detection model. The TCP packets are filtered in the IoT device. Further on considering the selection of the feature, this scheme includes the various network features like the length of the frame and frame number. These features are labeled and then selected. In the K-NN based malware discovery the data movement in the network is assigned with many sensor nodes or devices among the K closest neighbor nodes. To distinguish malwares, the network traffic labeled with the decision trees is built with random forest classifier. The analysis on the experimental results shows that the random forest based experimental results and K-NN based malware results are almost very close with true positive rates around 99.7% and 99.9%, respectively on the MalGenome dataset.

K Nearest Neighbor algorithm

A modest machine learning algorithm is classifying the inputs based on the adjacent neighbors. The network is comprised of number of nodes and each node has a set of neighboring nodes. This is the K-NN algorithm which is a lazy learning method with a set of testing phase only, and no training phase is available. So the typical K-NN algorithm has to dependent only on the test instances. The K-NN algorithm is provided with the entire dataset and stored. The algorithm looks up for the matching pattern, so it does not require any extra training phase. The erroneous data are removed from the database so as to maintain consistency. When a new instance arrives, predictions are made by recognizing the most alike neighbor and defines the output class label. The estimation of the similarity measures can be calculated with any distance-based measures. Euclidean distance, Manhattan distance are some of the distance measures that can be used.

Random Forest

In the training phase huge quantity of decision trees is built using the Random forest techniques and it is used to find the class label. Decision tree comprise of a tree like graph to sort conclusions. The nodes at the leaves in the decision tree are used to represent the attributes. Also, the nodes and edges can be used to represent the conditional attribute values. The path from the root to the leaf node expresses the grouping rubrics. A sample decision tree with binary classification is picturized in figure 4.

The nodes A1 and A2 signify the characteristics, and the conditional values are referred in the edges for finding the class labels. If the value of the attribute A1 is ≥ 0.5, then it is classified as class1. If it is less than the desired value, then it flows to the next lower level value and checks the value of the attribute A2. This explains the working of the decision tree. This enhances the performance of the random forest model. The set of input class labels and the associated set of output class labels is given as input to the algorithm. This is training phase, where the algorithm is trained with a set of inputs associated with its corresponding outputs. Once the training phase is done, the results obtained from the input classification are considered for the testing the new input data. This training process with many classified input data is repeated so as to improve efficiency of the algorithm to classify new data. Finally, any new input dataset is provided and predictions are done with the trained algorithm. The IoT devices should be capable of detecting the malwares traces in the security servers provided in the cloud or the edge devices. Further the security services should be more powerful with high computation speed and should store bulk amount of data with larger malware database.

Without the aware of the model, the IoT device is applied with the Reinforcement Learning (RL) techniques to achieve the optimal offload. To increase the malware detection rate, the offloading rate can be improved by applying the Q-Learning in the IoT device. This scheme enables the IoT device to estimate with increased accuracy gain and better detection ratio.

Table 1 provides the summary of various approaches in machine learning for secured IoT and WSNs. Though different approaches yield high accuracy, the implementation of the support vector machine is more complex than supervised learning techniques. There are quiet many encounters in acquiring the security of IoT and WSNs since machine learning should compromise between a dense layer of security and a low computational complication to be appropriate for the limited resources.

Figure 4. Sample decision tree classification

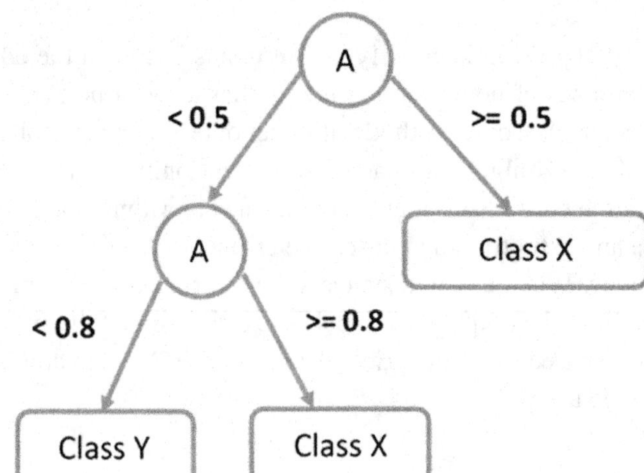

Table 1. Summarizes the various ML techniques to ensure the security

Reference papers	Type of attacks	ML techniques	Complexity
Enhancement of Security (Kaplantzis, Shilton, Mani, & Sekercioglu, 2007)	Denial of Service	Support vector machine	Simple
		DNN	Average
Distributed attack detection (Alajmi & Elleithy, 2015)	Denial of Service	DNN	High
Data forwarding attacks (Ferdowsi & Saad, 2017)[	Selective Forwarding	Support vector machine	Average
Machine Learning to secure IoT (Miettinen et al., 2017)	Middle man attack	Supervised	High
Dynamic Watermarking (Meiden, et al., 2017a)	Middle man attack	RNN	High
IoT machines (Rathore, Badarla, Jha, & Gupta, 2014)	Traffic Monitoring	DNN	Average
Compromised Devices (Outchakoucht, Hamza & Leroy, 2017)	Traffic Monitoring	Supervised	Average
Bio-Inspiration (Rathore, Badarla, Jha, & Gupta, 2014)	Unauthorized node	Support vector machine	Average

EXPERIMENTAL ANALYSIS ON INTRUSION DETECTION

This section deals with the different experimental analysis results of various techniques. Different experimental analysis is done to estimate the performance measures and accuracy rate.

The dataset selected for analysis is the standard KDDCUP99 dataset for intrusion detection. This dataset has many redundant records. This redundancy of data possibly will lead to biased results. So the NSL-KDD dataset that is an advanced version of the KDDCUP99 dataset is selected and the supervised learning algorithms are tested on that dataset. It has a total number of 42 features and the four diverse categories of simulated assaults to experiment the invasion detection system.

- **Denial of Service (DoS) Attack:** Non-availability of the system resources and heavy usage of the bandwidth leads to the DoS attacks.
- **User to Root (U2R) Attack:** At initial point the invader has access to the normal user account, then slowly gains admittance to the root system by abusing the resistances of the system.
- **Probe Attack:** Before performing or introducing any attack having an access to the entire network.
- **Root to Local (R2L) Attack:** By ill-using some of the liabilities of the network attacker achieves access to local devices by transferring packets on a remote device.

The data collected is initially preprocessed and divided into testing phase data and training phase data. The data available in textual format are completely converted into numerical data. After conversion of these data into numerical form, then the models to work on that data are built using any of the learning algorithm such as Support Vector Machine, Logistic Regression, and Random Forest classifiers. The test data provided are predicted by any of these learning algorithms implemented. The labels predicted by the models are compared with the actual labels. The methodology and experimental analysis are built with the following steps:

1. The cleansing of the dataset – preprocessing step.
2. The separation of the training dataset and testing data.
3. The implementation and build of the classifier models for the training data.
4. Predicting the new testing datasets.
5. Testing the algorithm with the training and testing dataset.
6. Comparisons of the accuracy rate of all models.

Table 2 summarizes the performance measure like Precision value, Recall value, and Accuracy rate of the supervised machine learning classifiers in pinpointing the intrusion. The values tabulated are the experimental results from the methodology implemented.

Table 2. Performance measures of different classification models

Classifying Models	Precision value	Recall value	Accuracy rate
LR	0.825	0.848	0.843
GNB	0.786	0.809	0.791
SVM	0.764	0.789	0.746
RFC	0.988	0.991	0.987

Figure 5 shows the pictorial bar chart to depict the performance analysis of the different machine learning models. Based on the outcomes it can be identified that Random Forest classifier with the peak accuracy, outstrips the other methods. While SVM has the lowermost accuracy, Logistic Regression algorithm has the good accuracy than Gaussian Naive Bayes and Support Vector Machine.

Figure 5. Performance measures graph

CONCLUSION AND FUTURE WORK

In this chapter, the different IoT and WSN attacks are identified. The promising challenges faced by the IoT device security in terms of detection of the malware, illegitimate access control, authentication of the IoT devices are discussed. In the consideration of the practical IoT applications numerous challenges should be addressed to implement the learning-based security techniques. In addition, when we implement machine learning techniques the IoT network should withstand the ruthless schemes at the start of the learning (training) process. Generally, it has difficulty in identifying the state of the attack precisely and should evade any security catastrophe at the beginning of the learning process. The protection of the IoT systems also depend on the backup mechanisms. To achieve the optimal strategy, more methods on the Reinforcement learning has to be explored and identify the cause of the network disaster at the learning stage. Some failures on the learning process such as bas feature extraction, oversampling and insufficient training data can be eradicated through supervised and unsupervised learning techniques. Therefore, to offer consistent and protected IoT services, the security solutions have to be incorporated with the machine learning based security schemes. Yet, many surviving Machine learning based security schemes have rigorous calculation and message delivery overheads, and need more training on data classification. And so, new ML methods using little computation and communication overhead are required to enrich security for IoT systems.

ACKNOWLEDGMENT

First of all, the authors thank the management and the principal of Ramco Institute of Technology and Mepco Schlenk Engineering College for encouraging us to perform such fruitful work and provided us with all the resources we needed. The authors would also like to extend thanks to their family members, colleagues, working partners and beloved friends for their supportive and heartening words in every single phase of this effort. Writers also soulfully be grateful to God, for his elegance and support to make this episode an achievement.

REFERENCES

Alajmi, N. M., & Elleithy, K. M. (2015). Comparative analysis of selective forwarding attacks over Wireless Sensor Networks. *International Journal of Computers and Applications*, *111*(14).

Ferdowsi, A. & Saad, W. (2017). Deep learning-based dynamic watermarking for secure signal authentication in the internet of things.

Kaplantzis, S., Shilton, A., Mani, N., & Sekercioglu, Y. A. (2007). Detecting selective forwarding attacks in wireless sensor networks using support vector machines. *Proceedings of International Conference on Intelligent Sensors, Sensor Networking and Information*. 10.1109/ISSNIP.2007.4496866

Meidan, Y., Bohadana, M., Shabtai, A., Ochoa, M., Tippenhauer, N. O., Guarnizo, J. D., & Elovici, Y. (2017a). Detection of unauthorized IoT devices using machine learning techniques. Retrieved from https://arxiv.org/abs/1709.04647

Meidan, Y., Bohadana, M., Shabtai, A., Ochoa, M., Tippenhauer, N. O., Guarnizo, J. D., & Elovici, Y. (2017b). ProfilIoT: A machine learning approach for IoT device identification based on network traffic analysis. *Proceedings of the Symposium on Applied Computing*. 10.1145/3019612.3019878

Miettinen, M., Marchal, S., Hafeez, I., Asokan, N., Sadeghi, A. R., & Tarkoma, S. (2017) IoT Sentinel: Automated device-type identification for security enforcement in IoT. *Proceedings of IEEE International Conference on Distributed Computing Systems*, 283.

Outchakoucht, A., Hamza, E. S., & Leroy, J. P. (2017). Dynamic access control policy based on blockchain and machine learning for the internet of things. *International Journal of Advanced Computer Science and Applications*, *8*(7), 417–424. doi:10.14569/IJACSA.2017.080757

Rathore, H., Badarla, V., Jha, S., & Gupta, A. (2014). Novel approach for security in wireless sensor network using bio-inspirations. *Proceedings of International Conference on Communication Systems and Networking*. 10.1109/COMSNETS.2014.6734875

Xiao, L., Wan, X., Dai, C., Du, X., Chen, X., & Guizani, M. (2018). Security in mobile edge caching with reinforcement learning.

ADDITIONAL READING

Abomhara, M. & Køien, G. M. (2014, May). Security and privacy in the Internet of Things: Current status and open issues. In *2014 International Conference on Privacy and Security in Mobile Systems (PRISMS)* (pp. 1-8). IEEE.

Alsheikh, M. A., Lin, S., Niyato, D., & Tan, H. P. (2014). Machine learning in wireless sensor networks: Algorithms, strategies, and applications. *IEEE Communications Surveys and Tutorials*, *16*(4), 1996–2018. doi:10.1109/COMST.2014.2320099

Alsheikh, M. A., Lin, S., Niyato, D., & Tan, H. P. (2018). Machine learning in wireless sensor networks: Algorithms, strategies, and applications. *IEEE Communications Surveys and Tutorials*, *16*(4), 1996–2018. doi:10.1109/COMST.2014.2320099

Alsumayt, A. John Haggerty., & Ahmad Lot. (2016). Detect DoS attack using MrDR method in merging two MANETs. IEEE.

Arsalan Mohsen Nia., & Niraj K. Jha. (2016). A Comprehensive Study of Security of Internet-of-Things. *IEEE Transactions on Emerging Topics in Computing*, 99.

Bharadwaj, A. Subramanyam, G., Dr., Vinay Aasthi, Dr., & Hanumat Sastry, Dr., (2016). Solutions for DDos attacks on cloud. IEEE.

Butun, I., Morgera, S. D., & Sankar, R. (2014). A survey of intrusion detection systems in wireless sensor networks. *IEEE Communications Surveys and Tutorials*, *16*(1), 266–282. doi:10.1109/SURV.2013.050113.00191

Butun, I., Morgera, S. D., & Sankar, R. (2014). A survey of intrusion detection systems in wireless sensor networks. *IEEE Communications Surveys and Tutorials*, *16*(1), 266–282. doi:10.1109/SURV.2013.050113.00191

Cañedo, J., & Skjellum, A. (2016). Using machine learning to secure IoT systems. *Proceedings of 14th Annual Conference on Privacy, Security and Trust (PST)*. 10.1109/PST.2016.7906930

Chelli, K. (2015). Security issues in wireless sensor networks: attacks and countermeasures. Proceedings. of World Congress on Engineering.

Chen, F., Deng, P., Wan, J., Zhang, D., Vasilakos, A., & Rong, X. (2015). Data mining for the internet of things: Literature review and challenges. *International Journal of Distributed Sensor Networks*, *11*(8), 431047. doi:10.1155/2015/431047

Curran, J. (2015). IoT Development Poses Security, Privacy Problems. NY-US. Retrieved April 20, 2015, from http://search.proquest.com/docview/1675863933?accountid=36155

Diro, A., & Chilamkurti, N. (2017). *Distributed attack detection scheme using deep learning approach for Internet of Things*. Future Generations Computing Systems.

Diro, A. A., & Chilamkurti, N. (2017). Distributed attack detection scheme using deep learning approach for Internet of Things. *Future Generation Computer Systems*.

Gartner Press Release. Retrieved November, 2014, from http://www.gartner.com/ newsroom/id/2905717

Gubbi, J., Buyya, R., & Marusic, S. (n.d.). [Security in Wireless Sensor Networks: Issues and Challenges.]. *Marimuthu Palaniswami*.

Husamuddin, Md. & Mohammed Qayyum. (2017). Internet of things: A study on security and privacy threats. International Conference on Anti-Cyber Crimes (ICACC). 10.1109/Anti-Cybercrime.2017.7905270

Internet of Things Global Standards Initiative. ITU. Retrieved June 26, 2015, from http://www.itu.int/en/ITU-T/gsi/iot/Pages/default.aspx

Kasinathan, P., Pastrone, C., Spirito., M. A., & Vinkovits, M. (2013). Denial-of-service detection in 6LoWPAN based Internet of Things. Piscataway, NJ: IEEE.

Kim, H.-J., Chang, H.-S., & Suh, J.-J. (2016). A study on device security in IoT convergence. Piscataway, NJ: IEEE.

Mukhopadhyay, D. (2015). *PUFs as Promising Tools for Security in Internet of Things*. IEEE.

Narayanan, A. (2014). Impact of Internet of Things on the Retail Industry. PC Quest, Cyber Media Ltd.; Retrieved May 20, 2014.

Raj, A. B., Ramesh, M. V., Kulkarni, R. V., & Hemalatha, T. (2012). Security enhancement in wireless sensor networks using machine learning. *International Conference on High Performance Computing and Communications and IEEE International Conference on Embedded Software and Systems*, 1264-1269. 10.1109/HPCC.2012.186

Riahi, C. Y., Natalizio, E., Chturou, Z., Bouab, A. (2013). A Systematic Approach of IoT Security. Retrieved 2013, from https://hal.inria.fr/hal-00868362/document

Shabana, K., Fida, N., Khan, F., Jan, S., & Rehman, M. (2016). Security issues and attacks in Wireless Sensor Networks. *International Journal of Advanced Research in Computer Science and Electronics Engineering*, *5*(7), 81–87.

Singh, V., Puthran, S., & Tiwari, A. (2017). Intrusion detection using data mining with correlation. *Proceedings of International Conference for Convergence in Technology*. 10.1109/I2CT.2017.8226204

Wind River Company. (2015). Security in Internet of Things. Retrieved January, 2015, from http://www.winddriver.com

Zeitouni, S., Oren, Y., & Wachsmann, C. (2016). Remanence decay SideChannel: The PUF Case. Piscataway, NJ: IEEE.

KEY TERMS AND DEFINITIONS

DoS: Denial of Service.

Flooding: The deliberate congestion of communication channels through relay of unnecessary messages and high traffic.

IoT: Internet of Things.

Jamming: The communication channel between the nodes is compromised and occupied and jammed, thus preventing them the sensor nodes from communicating with each other.

K-NN: K-nearest Neighbor.

Machine Learning: A field of information technology that has the ability to learn data insights by using statistical techniques.

Masquerade: A malicious node may act as another legitimate node to capture the message in the network.

RFID: Radio Frequency Identification.

SVM: Support Vector Machine.

WSN: Wireless Sensor Networks.

This research was previously published in Security and Privacy Issues in Sensor Networks and IoT; pages 65-93, copyright year 2020 by Information Science Reference (an imprint of IGI Global).

Chapter 35
Advanced-Level Security in Network and Real-Time Applications Using Machine Learning Approaches

Mamata Rath
https://orcid.org/0000-0002-2277-1012
Birla Global University, India

Sushruta Mishra
KIIT University (Deemed), India

ABSTRACT

Machine learning is a field that is developed out of artificial intelligence (AI). Applying AI, we needed to manufacture better and keen machines. Be that as it may, aside from a couple of simple errands, for example, finding the briefest way between two points, it isn't to program more mind boggling and continually developing difficulties. There was an acknowledgment that the best way to have the capacity to accomplish this undertaking was to give machines a chance to gain from itself. This sounds like a youngster learning from itself. So, machine learning was produced as another capacity for computers. Also, machine learning is available in such huge numbers of sections of technology that we don't understand it while utilizing it. This chapter explores advanced-level security in network and real-time applications using machine learning.

INTRODUCTION

Machine Learning is a recent development in the area of science and technology which is based on the foundation of Artificial Intelligence(AI). By applying AI, we needed to manufacture better and improved machines. Be that as it may, aside from couple of simple errands, for example, finding the briefest way between two points, it isn't to program more mind boggling and continually developing difficulties. There

DOI: 10.4018/978-1-6684-6291-1.ch035

was an acknowledgment that the best way to have the capacity to accomplish this undertaking was to give machine a chance to gain from itself. This sounds like a technically similar learning from its self. So machine learning was produced as another capacity for computers. Also, now machine learning is available in such huge numbers of sections of technology, that we don't understand it while utilizing it.

Machine learning (ML) is also concerned about the structure and advancement of network security and strategies that enables systems to learn and train. The significant focal point of machine learning explore is to extricate data from information consequently, by computational and measurable techniques. It is subsequently firmly identified with information mining and insights. The intensity of neural networks originates from their portrayal ability. From one viewpoint, feed forward networks are demonstrated to offer the ability of general capacity guess. Then again, intermittent networks utilizing the sigmoidal initiation work are Turing proportionate and recreates a general Turing machine; Thus, repetitive networks can figure whatever work any advanced computer can register.

Discovering designs in information on planet earth is conceivable just for human minds. The information being extremely gigantic, the time taken to register is expanded, and this is the place Machine Learning comes enthusiastically, to assist individuals with vast information in least time. On the off chance that enormous information and distributed computing are gaining significance for their commitments, machine learning as technology breaks down those huge lumps of information, facilitating the errand of information researchers in a computerized procedure and gaining square with significance and acknowledgment. The methods we use for information digging have been around for a long time, however they were not viable as they didn't have the focused capacity to run the calculations. In the event that we run profound learning with access to better information, the yield we get will prompt emotional leaps forward which is machine learning.

This chapter has been organised as follows. Section 1 depicts the Introduction part. Section 2 illustrates Security in Network and Solution in Machine Learning, section 3 focuses on Cyber attacks in IoT and Cloud Based machine learning, section 4 highlights Security and Vulnerability in Wireless Network due to various attack, section 5 details about Assortment of Machine Learning Practice for Security & Analysis, section 6 describes Risk Assessment in IoT Network and at last section 7 concludes the chapter.

SECURITY IN NETWORK AND SOLUTION IN MACHINE LEARNING

Malware investigation and categorization Systems utilize static and dynamic methods, related to machine learning calculations, to computerize the assignment of ID and grouping of malevolent codes. The two procedures have shortcomings that permit the utilization of analysis avoidance systems, hampering the ID of malwares. R. J. Mangialardo et.al,(2015) propose the unification of static and dynamic analysis, as a strategy for gathering information from malware that reductions the possibility of achievement for such avoidance strategies. From the information gathered in the analysis stage, we utilize the C5.0 and Random Forest machine learning calculations, actualized inside the FAMA structure, to play out the distinguishing proof and order of malwares into two classes and various classifications. The examinations and results demonstrated that the exactness of the bound together analysis accomplished a precision of 95.75% for the double arrangement issue and an exactness estimation of 93.02% for the different order issue. In all examinations, the brought together analysis created preferred outcomes over those acquired by static and dynamic breaks down detached.

Safeguard for Mobile Communication

A novel way to deal with ensuring cell phones has been arranged (N. Islam et.al, 2017) from malware that may release private data or adventure vulnerabilities. The methodology, which can likewise shield gadgets from interfacing with pernicious passageways, utilizes learning strategies to statically investigate applications, examine the conduct of applications at runtime, and screen the manner in which gadgets connect with Wi-Fi passageways.

Intrusion Detection System Using Machine Learning Approach

Intrusion detection is an essential section of security system such as versatile security apparatuses, intrusion detection frameworks, intrusion counteractive action frameworks, and firewalls. Different intrusion detection strategies are utilized, yet their execution is an issue. Intrusion detection execution relies upon precision, which needs to enhance to diminish false alerts and to expand the detection rate. To determine worries on execution, multilayer perceptron, bolster vector machine (SVM), and different procedures have been utilized in recent work. Such methods show impediments and are not productive for use in substantial informational collections, for example, framework and system information. The intrusion detection framework is utilized in dissecting gigantic activity information; along these lines, a productive arrangement system is important to beat the issue. This issue is considered by I.Ahmed et.al (2018) utilizing understood machine learning procedures, in particular, SVM, irregular woods, and outrageous learning machine (ELM) are connected. These systems are notable due to their capacity in grouping. The NSL-learning disclosure and information mining informational collection is utilized, or, in other words benchmark in the assessment of intrusion detection components. The outcomes demonstrate that ELM outflanks different methodologies.

Detection of Cyber Attacks

Attack detection issues in the radiant framework are acted like factual learning issues for various attack situations in which the estimations are seen in clump or online settings. In this methodology, machine learning calculations are utilized (M.Ozay et.al, 2016) to characterize estimations as being either secure or attacked. An attack detection system is given to abuse any accessible earlier information about the framework and surmount imperatives emerging from the meagre structure of the issue in the proposed methodology. Surely understood clump and web based learning calculations (directed and semisupervised) are utilized with choice and highlight level combination to model the attack detection issue. The connections among measurable and geometric properties of attack vectors utilized in the attack situations and learning calculations are broke down to recognize imperceptible attacks utilizing factual learning techniques. The proposed calculations by (M.Ozay et.al, 2016)are analyzed on different IEEE test frameworks. Trial examinations demonstrate that machine learning calculations can identify attacks with exhibitions higher than attack detection calculations that utilize state vector estimation strategies in the proposed attack detection structure.

CYBER ATTACKS IN IOT AND MACHINE LEARNING STRATEGY

The development and advancement of cyber-attacks require strong and developing cyber security plans. As a developing innovation, the Internet of Things (IoT) acquires cyber-attacks and dangers from the IT condition in spite of the presence of a layered guarded security instrument. The augmentation of the computerized world to the physical condition of IoT brings inconspicuous attacks that require a novel lightweight and conveyed attack detection system because of their engineering and asset limitations. Compositionally, Fog computing based mobile stations can be utilized to offload security capacities from IoT and the cloud to moderate the asset restriction issues of IoT and versatility bottlenecks of the cloud. Traditional machine learning calculations have been widely utilized for intrusion detection, despite the fact that versatility, highlight designing endeavors, and precision have prevented their infiltration into the security advertise. These inadequacies could be alleviated utilizing the profound learning approach as it has been fruitful in huge information fields. Aside from disposing of the need to create includes physically, profound learning is strong against transforming attacks with high detection exactness. A. Diro et.al, (2018) proposed a LSTM arrange for circulated cyber-attack detection in mist to-things communication. Critical attacks have been investigated and dangers focusing on IoT gadgets were distinguished particularly attacks abusing vulnerabilities of remote correspondences. The directed investigations on two situations show the adequacy and productivity of more profound models over conventional machine learning models.

Non-Reliable Data Source Identification Using Machine Learning Algorithm

Recent advances in machine learning have prompted imaginative applications and administrations that utilization computational structures to reason about complex marvel. In the course of recent years, the security and machine-learning networks have created novel methods for developing ill-disposed examples - malicious data sources made to deceive and in this manner degenerate the trustworthiness of frameworks based on computationally learned models. The hidden reasons for antagonistic examples and the future countermeasures has been broke down (P.McDaniel et.al, 2016) that may relieve them.

Deep Learning and Machine Learning for Interruption in Network

With the improvement of the Internet, cyber-attacks are changing quickly and the cyber security circumstance isn't idealistic. Overview report by Y.Xin et.al (2018) clarifies the key writing studies on machine learning (ML) and deep learning (DL) techniques for system enquiry of interruption identification and gives a concise instructional exercise portrayal of every ML/DL strategy. Distinctive security approaches were ordered and outlined dependent on their transient or warm connections. Since information are so essential in ML/DL strategies, it portrays a portion of the generally utilized system datasets utilized in ML/DL, talk about the difficulties of utilizing ML/DL for cyber security and give recommendations to inquire about bearings.

Security Guarded Procedures Using Machine Learning

Machine learning is a standout amongst the most overall procedures in software engineering, and it has been generally connected in picture preparing, regular dialect handling, design acknowledgment, cyber security, and different fields. Notwithstanding fruitful utilizations of machine learning calculations in numerous situations, e.g., facial acknowledgment, malware location, programmed driving, and interruption discovery, these calculations and comparing preparing information are helpless against an assortment of security dangers, initiating a critical execution diminish. Consequently, it is indispensable to call for further consideration with respect to security dangers and comparing guarded procedures of machine learning, which persuades a complete review (Q.Liu et.al, 2018). Up to this point, specialists from the scholarly community and industry have discovered numerous security dangers against an assortment of learning calculations, including credulous Bayes, strategic relapse, choice tree, bolster vector machine (SVM), rule part examination, bunching, and winning profound neural systems.

There are many implementations of machine learning approach that utilizes supervisory learning. In supervised learning, the framework attempts to gain from the past precedents that are given. (Then again, in unsupervised learning, the framework endeavors to discover the examples straightforwardly from the model given.) Speaking scientifically, regulated learning is the place you have both info factors (x) and yield variables(Y) and can utilize a calculation to get the mapping capacity from the contribution to the yield. Regulated learning issues can be additionally partitioned into two sections, in particular characterization, and relapse.

A classification issue is the dilemma at which the yield variable is a classification or a gathering, for example, "dark" or "white" or "spam" and "no spam". Regression: A regression issue is the point at which the yield variable is a genuine esteem, for example, "Rupees" or "stature." Unsupervised Learning - In unsupervised learning, the calculations are left to themselves to find fascinating structures in the information. Scientifically, unsupervised learning is the point at which you just have input information (X) and no relating yield factors. This is called unsupervised learning in light of the fact that not at all like directed learning above, there are no given right answers and the machine itself finds the appropriate responses. Unsupervised learning issues can be additionally separated into association and grouping issues. Association: An association rule learning issue is the place you need to find decides that depict substantial parts of your information, for example, "individuals that purchase X additionally will in general purchase Y". A clustering issue is the place you need to find the innate groupings in the information, for example, gathering clients by buying conduct.

- **Reinforcement Learning:** A computer program will communicate with a dynamic situation in which it must play out a specific objective, (for example, playing a diversion with a rival or driving a vehicle). The program is given criticism regarding prizes and disciplines as it explores its concern space. Utilizing this algorithm, the machine is prepared to settle on explicit choices. It works along these lines: the machine is presented to a situation where it consistently prepares itself utilizing experimentation technique.

Machine Learning supposition is a field that meets factual, probabilistic, computer science and algorithmic angles emerging from learning drearily from information which can be utilized to assemble savvy applications. The preeminent inquiry when attempting to comprehend a field, for example, Machine Learning is the measure of maths important and the unpredictability of maths required to comprehend these frameworks. The response to this inquiry is multidimensional and relies upon the dimension and enthusiasm of the person. Here is the base dimension of science that is required for Machine Learning Engineers/Data Scientists.Machine learning approaches are basically used in mathematical fields such as linera algebra including matrix operations, projections, factorisation, symmetric matrix and orthogonalisation. In Probability and statistics it includes rules and axioms, bayes'theorem, random variables, variance, expectation, conditional and joint distributions. In calculus, differential and integral calculus and partial derivatives are implemented in machine learning approachs.Further Design of Algorithm and complex optimisations includes binary tree, hashing, heap and stack operations.

Figure 1. Reinforcement in Machine Learning

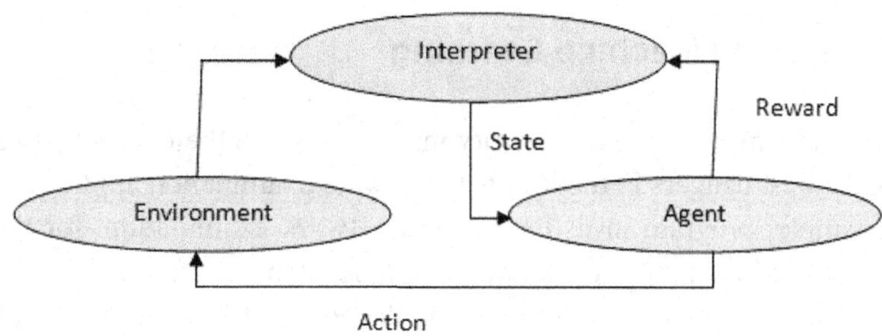

Methods in Neural Networks

It is obvious the learning speediness of feed forward neural networks is all in all far slower than required and it has been a noteworthy bottleneck in their applications for past decades. Two key purposes for might be: (1) the moderate gradient based learning calculations are broadly used to prepare neural networks, and (2) every one of the parameters of the networks are tuned ordinarily by utilizing such learning calculations. FFNN (Feed forward Neural Networks) are most widely utilized in numerous fields because of their capability such as (1) to estimated complex nonlinear mappings straightforwardly from the information tests; and (2) to give models to a substantial class of characteristic and counterfeit wonders that are hard to deal with utilizing traditional parametric methods. Then again, there need quicker learning calculations for neural networks. The conventional learning calculations are more often than not far slower than required. It isn't astonishing to see that it might take a few hours, a few days, and significantly more opportunity to prepare neural networks by utilizing customary techniques.

From a numerical perspective, look into on the estimation capacities of feedforward neural networks has concentrated on two angles: all inclusive guess on conservative information sets and estimation in a limited arrangement of preparing tests. Numerous analysts have investigated the all inclusive guess capacities of standard multilayer Feed Forward neural networks.It was demonstrated that in the event that the enactment work is nonstop, limited and nonconstant, ceaseless mappings can be approximated in measure by neural networks over minimized information sets. It was again demonstrated that feedforward networks with a nonpolynomial enactment capacity can inexact (in measure) constant capacities. In genuine applications, the neural networks are prepared in limited preparing set. For capacity estimation in a limited preparing set, a novel approach shows that a Solitary concealed Layer Feed forward Neural network (SLFN) with at most N shrouded nodes and with any nonlinear actuation capacity can precisely learn N unmistakable perceptions. It ought to be noticed that the information weights (connecting the information layer to the main concealed layer) and shrouded layer predispositions should be balanced in all these past hypothetical research functions and in addition in all handy learning calculations of feedforward neural networks.

Normally, every one of the parameters of the feedforward networks should be tuned and in this manner there exists the reliance between various layers of parameters (weights and predispositions). For past decades, inclination drop based techniques have principally been utilized in different learning calculation of feed forward neural networks. Be that as it may, unmistakably slope plunge based learning techniques are commonly ease back because of inappropriate learning steps or may effectively combine to nearby minima. Also, numerous iterative learning steps might be required by such learning calculations with the end goal to acquire better learning execution.

Malware Detection Using Machine Learning

In spite of the huge enhancement of digital security instruments and their ceaseless advancement, malware are still among the best dangers in the internet. Malware examination applies methods from a few distinct fields, for example, program investigation and network examination, for the investigation of pernicious examples to build up a more profound comprehension on a few viewpoints, including their conduct and how they advance after some time. Inside the constant weapons contest between malware designers and experts, each development in security technology is normally speedily pursued by a relating avoidance. Some portion of the viability of novel cautious measures relies upon what properties they use on. For instance, a recognition rule dependent on the MD5 hash of a known malware can be effortlessly evaded by applying standard systems like jumbling, or further developed methodologies, for example, polymorphism or changeability. For a complete survey of these procedures.. These techniques change the double of the malware, and hence its hash, yet leave its conduct unmodified. On the opposite side, creating identification decides that catch the semantics of a noxious example is considerably more hard to evade, in light of the fact that malware engineers ought to apply more mind boggling changes(Rath et.al, 2018). A noteworthy objective of malware investigation is to catch extra properties to be utilized to enhance safety efforts and make avoidance as hard as would be prudent. Machine learning is a characteristic decision to help such a procedure of information extraction. In fact, numerous works in writing have taken this bearing, with an assortment of methodologies, goals and results.

SECURITY AND VULNERABILITY IN WIRELESS NETWORK DUE TO VARIOUS ATTACK

In wireless network, associated devices such as laptops, PCs, cellular phones, appliances with communication capability are linked together to create a network. MANET is a self-arranging system of versatile switches related hosts associated by remote connections. The routers (mobile gadgets) move haphazardly and compose themselves self-assertively; along these lines, the systems remote topology may change quickly and capriciously (Rath et.al, 2018) . In MANETs each node acts as router and because of dynamic changing topology the accessibility of hubs is not generally ensured. It likewise does not ensure that the way between any two hubs would be free of pernicious hubs. The remote connection between hubs is exceptionally vulnerable to connection assaults such as passive eavesdropping, active interfering, etc.Stringent asset limitations in MANET may likewise influence the nature of security when excessive computations are required to perform some encryption(Rath et.al, 2018) . These vulnerabilities and characteristics make a case to build a security solution which provides security services like authentication, confidentiality, integrity, non-repudiation and availability. In order to achieve this goal we need a mechanism that provides security in each layer of the protocol.Various attacks on Routing Protocols in wireless networks are as follows.

1. Black Hole Attack
2. Wormhole Attack
3. Rushing Attack
4. **Passive Attacks:** The attacker just spies around the network without distracting the network operation. This attack compromises the privacy of the data and says which nodes are working in immoral way.
5. **Active Attacks:** It is a type of attack in which the attacker disturbs the normal operation of the network by fabricating messages, dropping or changing packets, by repeating or channelling them to other part of the network (Rath et.al, 2018). Basically, the content of the message is changed. It is of two types:
6. **External Attacks:** Here the attacker causes network jamming and this is done by the propagation of fake routing information. The attack disrupts the nodes to gain services.
7. **Internal Attacks:** Here the attacker wants to gain access to network and wants to get involved in network activities. Attacker does this by some malicious imitation to get access to the network as a new node or by directly through a current node and using it as a basis to conduct the attack.

Black Hole Attack

Figure 2. Black hole attack in mobile wireless network

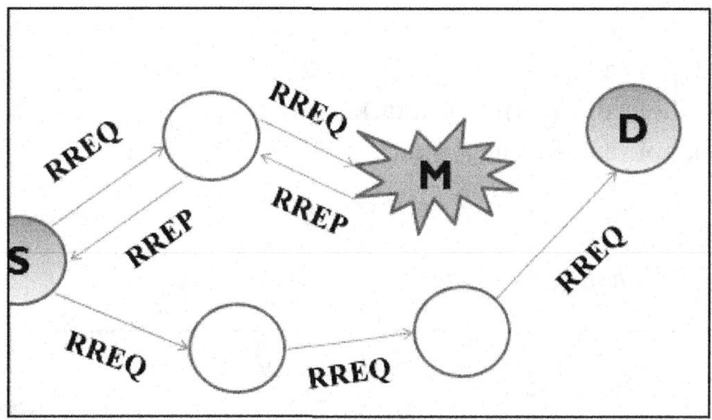

Worm hole attack-Malicious nodes eavesdrops the packets, tunnel them to another location in the network and retransmit them at the other end. Fig.2 black hole attack in mobile wireless network and Fig.3. shows Worm hole attack in wireless network.

Rushing Attack

Figure 3. Worm hole attack in wireless network

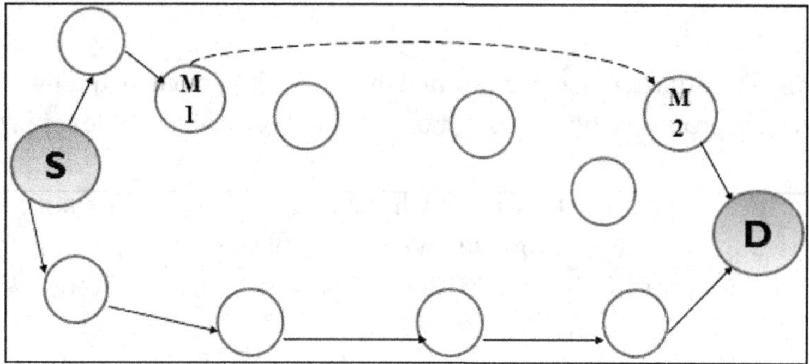

Forward ROUTE Requests more quickly than legitimate nodes can do so, increase the probability that routes that include the attacker will be discovered, attack against all currently proposed on-demand ad hoc network routing protocols.

Collaborative Attacks

Collaborative attacks (CA) occur when more than one attacker synchronize their actions to disturb a target network. Different Models of Collaborative Attack

- Collaborative Black hole attack
- Collaborative Black hole and Wormhole attack
- Collaborative Black hole and Rushing Attack

Figure 4. Collaborative black hole attack type 1

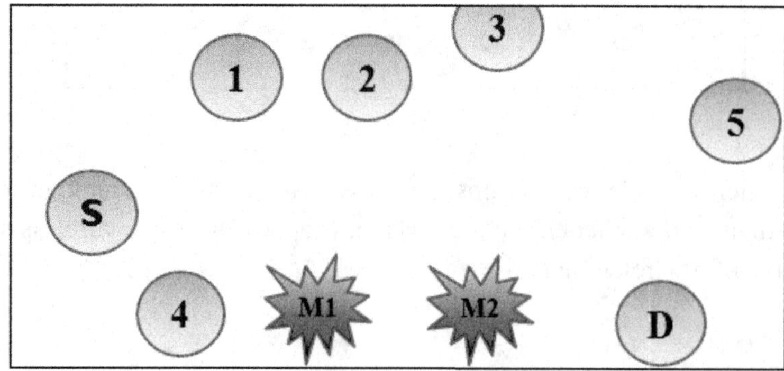

Figure 5. Collaborative black hole attack type 2

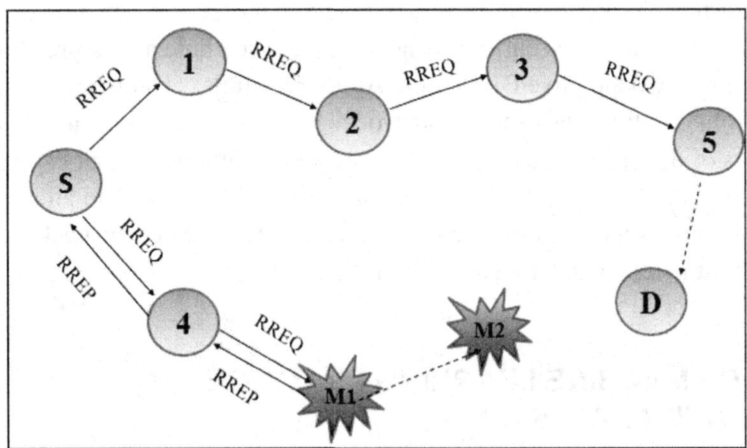

Figure 6. Collaborative black hole attack type 3

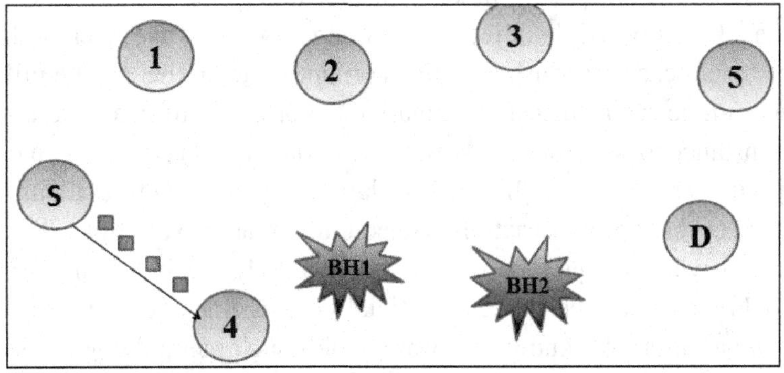

Figure 7. Collaborative black hole and worm hole attack

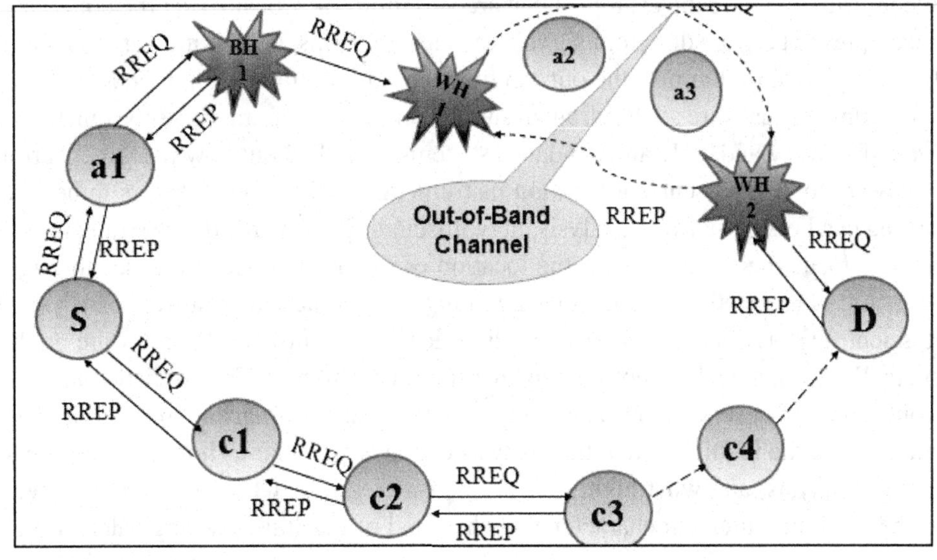

Fig.4., Fig 5 and Fig.6. show different Collaborative black hole attacks. Collaborative black hole and worm hole attack- Current Proposed Solutions to handle collaborative black hole attack are (a). Collacorative Monitoring: Collaborative security architecture for black hole attack prevention (b).Recursive Validation - Prevention of Cooperative Black Hole Attack in wireless Networks.

Fig.6 presents Collaborative black hole and worm hole attack. Monitoring is done during data transmission and loss of data packets take place. The current solutions does not specify if and how the lost data is re-transmitted. Two important overhead in Monitoring even if no attack is present, and in isolating the malicious nodes recursively. The solution is to get a count of the packets received from the destination. If the count is less than a threshold then monitor.

ASSORTMENT OF MACHINE LEARNING PRACTICE FOR SECURITY AND ANALYSIS

The most widely recognized goal with regards to malware analysis is distinguishing whether a given example is malevolent. This goal is additionally the most essential since knowing ahead of time that an example is perilous permits to square it before it winds up unsafe. Without a doubt, the greater part of surveyed works has this as principle objective. Contingent upon what machine learning strategy is utilized, the produced yield can be furnished with a certainty esteem that can be utilized by examiners to comprehend if an example needs further examination. Another significant goal is spotting similitude among malware, for instance to see how novel examples contrast from past, known ones. It was discovered four marginally unique renditions of this goal: variations location, families identification, likenesses recognition and contrasts discovery. Variations Detection. Creating variations is a standout amongst the best and least expensive techniques for an aggressor to dodge recognition systems, while reusing however much as could reasonably be expected officially accessible codes and assets. Perceiving that an example is really a variation of a known malware avoids such methodology to succeed, and makes ready to see how malware advance after some time through the improvement of new variations. Additionally this goal has been profoundly contemplated in writing, and a few evaluated papers focus on the recognition of variations. Given a noxious example m, variations location comprises in choosing from the accessible information base the examples that are variations of. Considering the colossal number of malevolent examples got day by day from significant security firms, perceiving variations of definitely known malware is pivotal to diminish the outstanding burden for human examiners.

Machine learning for malware analysis, again supplementing their commitments. quickly study writing on malware discovery and malware avoidance systems, to talk about how machine learning can be utilized by malware to sidestep current location instruments. Main review centers rather around how machine learning can bolster malware analysis, notwithstanding when avoidance strategies are utilized. Many researchers focus their overview on the location of order and control focuses through machine learning. Scientific classification of Machine Learning Techniques for Malware Analysis This area presents the scientific classification on how machine learning is utilized for malware analysis in the assessed papers. We recognize three noteworthy measurements along which studied works can be helpfully sorted out. The first describes the last target of the analysis, e.g. malware recognition. The second measurement portrays the highlights that the analysis depends on as far as how they are separated, e.g. through dynamic analysis, and what highlights are considered, e.g. CPU registers (Rath et.al, 2019). At long last, the third measurement characterizes what kind of machine learning calculation is utilized for the analysis, e.g. regulated learning. Malware Analysis Objectives Malware analysis, by and large, requests for solid recognition capacities to discover matches with the learning created by exploring past examples. Anyway, the last objective of looking for those matches contrasts. For instance, a malware expert might be explicitly keen on deciding if new suspicious examples are malevolent or not, while another might be somewhat assessing new malware searching for what family they likely have a place with. This subsection points of interest the analysis objectives of the studied papers, sorted out in three fundamental targets.

Given a deleterious example, families location comprises in choosing from the accessible information base the families that m likely has a place with. Along these lines, it is conceivable to relate obscure examples to definitely known families and, by result, give an additional esteem data to additionally examinations. Likenesses Detection. Examiners can be keen on recognizing the explicit similitudes and contrasts of the doubles to dissect as for those officially broke down. Likenesses location comprises in finding what parts and parts of an example are like something that has been as of now analyzed before. It empowers to concentrate on what is extremely new, and consequently to dispose of the rest as it doesn't merit further examination. Contrasts Detection. As a supplement, additionally distinguishing what is not the same as everything else effectively saw in the past outcomes advantageous. Actually, contrasts can direct towards finding novel viewpoints that ought to be broke down additional inside and out. Malware can be arranged by their conspicuous practices and goals. They can be keen on keeping an eye on clients' exercises and taking their touchy data (i.e., spyware), scrambling archives and requesting a payment (i.e., ransomware), or gaining remote control of a tainted machine (i.e., remote access toolboxs). Utilizing these classifications is a coarse-grained yet huge method for portraying noxious examples Although digital security firms have not as yet settled upon an institutionalized scientific categorization of malware classifications, adequately perceiving the classifications of an example can include profitable data for the analysis. The data extraction process is performed through either static or dynamic analysis, or a mix of both, while examination and relationship are completed by utilizing machine learning procedures. Methodologies dependent on static analysis take a gander at the substance of tests without requiring their execution, while dynamic analysis works by running examples to look at their conduct. A few procedures can be utilized for dynamic malware analysis. Debuggers are utilized for guidance level analysis. Test systems model and demonstrate a conduct like the earth expected by the malware, while emulators reproduce the conduct of a framework with higher precision however require more assets. Sandboxes are virtualised working frameworks giving a disconnected and solid condition where to explode malware. More nitty gritty depiction of these system are usually used to extricate highlights when dynamic analysis is utilized.

RISK ASSESSMENT IN IOT NETWORK

In light of digital ruptures, framework, vulnerabilities, assault recurrence and aggressors profile. Security risk is broke down dependent on gadget classifications and zones. Risk Mitigation is Game hypothesis based procedures that are utilized to demonstrate the risk structure. Relevant data, for example, Assessing current security levels.

There are various research oriented domains of network security in context of IoT and Machine Learning.Security Objectives/Requirements in IoT are as follows.

- System Modeling
- Identify Threats (operators and conceivable assaults)
- Identify Vulnerabilities (exploitable)
- Examining the Threat History (Likelihood)
- Counter Measures
- Risk Estimation

There are numerous functional regions of Internet of Things (IoTs) in our everyday life in which there is a high need of security and protection measures of those applications. In those applications, an assortment of IoT gadgets are utilized, for example, IoT gadgets for home and machines, lighting and warming, wellbeing checking gadgets, for example, camcorders and sensors and so forth. In wellbeing observing frameworks, gadgets for wellness, for example, wearables like FitBit Pulse, circulatory strain and glucose checking hardware and so forth. In transportation, keen answers for better transportation utilizing IoT gadgets have been created with utilization of activity flags and shrewd stopping office. In Industrial area, diverse exercises are checked utilizing IoT gadgets, for example, controlling the stream of materials, checking of oil and gas stream interferences and power use control by observing gadgets. Be that as it may, in every one of these applications security and protection have measure up to significance and are the testing issues for IoT frameworks.

As the sensor nodes in remote systems deliver high volume of information, in this way, stockpiling and their security additionally plays a major testing undertaking with Big Data related issues with in such IoT based gadgets. According to ebb and flow inquire about on Application Programming Interface, around 200 exabytes in 2014 and an estimation of 1.6 zettabytes in 2020 should be handled, 90% of these information are as of now prepared locally and the handling rate builds step by step. In a similar time the danger of basic information burglary, information and gadget control, adulteration of delicate information and also IP robbery, control and glitch of server and systems likewise can not be stayed away from. There is an extraordinary effect of information solidification and information investigation in organize setup i.e. CISCO, HPE and others. Next, in application stage regions in light of mists and firewalls at the system limits are more inclined from outer assaults.

Proactively reacting to the changing parameters of system Artificial Immune System for anchoring data frameworks dependent on human resistant framework.Fig.1. shows IoT security from research perspective. IoT needs extraordinary danger models. There is a need of conventional risk assessment structure, which can suit different danger models on equivalent terms. Most of the risk assessment philosophies are for universally useful programming frameworks and subsequently they need all encompassing methodology for evaluating risks in IoT framework because of its diversity. Also none of these location carries out risk proliferation deliberately.

CONCLUSION

Network security sphere is one of the most significant research area worked on. The Centre for Strategic and International Studies in 2014 estimated annual costs to the global economy caused by cybercrimes was between $375 billion and $575 billion. Researchers have developed some intelligent systems for network security domain with the purpose of reducing the development cost as well as to make the business network more and more secured. In this chapter newer strategies of machine learning approaches have been discussed specially ML applications of those types which can not be detected as computer programs by malware softwares/ users Artificial Intelligence based applications in view of researchers is not so easy to create an AI framework which works similar to human brain completely. Because of this, AI was started to use more specific application domain such as face recognition, object recognition etc. There is no directly contribution from human in machine learning approach . These sources of info are processing by machine learning techniques. Google isn't just self-sufficient car producer in sector. Huge numbers of the enormous companies in the vehicle business are doing research on driverless cars. For illustrative purposes, these issues were focussed that improves the network security and vulnerability.

REFERENCES

Ahmad, I., Basheri, M., Iqbal, M. J., & Rahim, A. (2018). Performance Comparison of Support Vector Machine, Random Forest, and Extreme Learning Machine for Intrusion Detection. *IEEE Access: Practical Innovations, Open Solutions*, *6*, 33789–33795. doi:10.1109/ACCESS.2018.2841987

Buczak, A. L., & Guven, E. (2016). A Survey of Data Mining and Machine Learning Methods for Cyber Security Intrusion Detection. *IEEE Communications Surveys and Tutorials*, *18*(2), 1153–1176. doi:10.1109/COMST.2015.2494502

Burmester, M., & de Medeiros, B. (2008). On the Security of Route Discovery in MANETs. *IEEE Transactions on Mobile Computing*, *8*(9), 1180–1188.

Carvalho. (2009). Security in Mobile Ad Hoc Networks. IEEE Security and Privacy, 6(2), 72–75.

Chang, J., Tsou, P., Woungang, I., Chao, H., & Lai, C. (2015). Defending Against Collaborative Attacks by Malicious Nodes in MANETs: A Cooperative Bait Detection Approach. *IEEE Systems Journal*, *9*(1), 65–75. doi:10.1109/JSYST.2013.2296197

Chaturvedi, S., Mishra, V., & Mishra, N. (2017). Sentiment analysis using machine learning for business intelligence. *IEEE International Conference on Power, Control, Signals and Instrumentation Engineering (ICPCSI)*, 2162-2166. 10.1109/ICPCSI.2017.8392100

Chen, X., Weng, J., Lu, W., Xu, J., & Weng, J. (2018). Deep Manifold Learning Combined With Convolutional Neural Networks for Action Recognition. *IEEE Transactions on Neural Networks and Learning Systems*, *29*(9), 3938–3952. doi:10.1109/TNNLS.2017.2740318 PMID:28922128

Dhurandher, Obaidat, & Verma, Gupta, & Dhurandher. (2016). FACES: Friend-Based Ad Hoc Routing Using Challenges to Establish Security in MANETs Systems. *IEEE Systems Journal*, *5*(2), 176–188.

Diro, A., & Chilamkurti, N. (2018). Leveraging LSTM Networks for Attack Detection in Fog-to-Things Communications. IEEE Communications Magazine, 56(9), 124-130. doi:10.1109/MCOM.2018.1701270

Feng, C., Wu, S., & Liu, N. (2017). A user-centric machine learning framework for cyber security operations center. *IEEE International Conference on Intelligence and Security Informatics (ISI)*, 173-175. 10.1109/ISI.2017.8004902

Ghosh & Datta. (2014). A Secure Addressing Scheme for Large-Scale Managed MANETs. *IEEE eTransactions on Network and Service Management*, *12*(3), 483–495.

He, D., Liu, C., Quek, T. Q. S., & Wang, H. (2018). Transmit Antenna Selection in MIMO Wiretap Channels: A Machine Learning Approach. *IEEE Wireless Communications Letters*, *7*(4), 634–637. doi:10.1109/LWC.2018.2805902

Islam, N., Das, S., & Chen, Y. (2017). On-Device Mobile Phone Security Exploits Machine Learning. *IEEE Pervasive Computing*, *16*(2), 92–96. doi:10.1109/MPRV.2017.26

Liu, Q., Li, P., Zhao, W., Cai, W., Yu, S., & Leung, V. C. M. (2018). A Survey on Security Threats and Defensive Techniques of Machine Learning: A Data Driven View. *IEEE Access: Practical Innovations, Open Solutions*, *6*, 12103–12117. doi:10.1109/ACCESS.2018.2805680

Mangialardo & Duarte. (2015). Integrating Static and Dynamic Malware Analysis Using Machine Learning. *IEEE Latin America Transactions, 13*(9), 3080-3087.

McDaniel, P., Papernot, N., & Celik, Z. B. (2016). Machine Learning in Adversarial Settings. *IEEE Security and Privacy*, *14*(3), 68–72. doi:10.1109/MSP.2016.51

Mozaffari-Kermani, M., Sur-Kolay, S., Raghunathan, A., & Jha, N. K. (2015). Systematic Poisoning Attacks on and Defenses for Machine Learning in Healthcare. *IEEE Journal of Biomedical and Health Informatics*, *19*(6), 1893–1905. doi:10.1109/JBHI.2014.2344095 PMID:25095272

Nguyen, D. Q., Toulgoat, M., & Lamont, L. (2011). Impact of trust-based security association and mobility on the delay metric in MANET. *Journal of Communications and Networks (Seoul)*, *18*(1), 105–111.

Ozay, M., Esnaola, I., Yarman Vural, F. T., Kulkarni, S. R., & Poor, H. V. (2016). Machine Learning Methods for Attack Detection in the Smart Grid. *IEEE Transactions on Neural Networks and Learning Systems*, *27*(8), 1773–1786. doi:10.1109/TNNLS.2015.2404803 PMID:25807571

Rath & Oreku. (2018). Security Issues in Mobile Devices and Mobile Adhoc Networks. In Mobile Technologies and Socio-Economic Development in Emerging Nations. IGI Global. doi:10.4018/978-1-5225-4029-8.ch009

Rath & Swain. (2018). IoT Security: A Challenge in Wireless Technology. *International Journal of Emerging Technology and Advanced Engineering, 8*(4), 43-46.

Rath & Pattanayak. (2019). Security Protocol with IDS Framework Using Mobile Agent in Robotic MANET. *International Journal of Information Security and Privacy, 13*(1), 46-58. Doi:10.4018/IJISP.2019010104

Rath, M. (2017). Resource provision and QoS support with added security for client side applications in cloud computing. *International Journal of Information Technology*, *9*(3), 1–8.

Rath, M. (2018). An Analytical Study of Security and Challenging Issues in Social Networking as an Emerging Connected Technology. *Proceedings of 3rd International Conference on Internet of Things and Connected Technologies (ICIoTCT).*

Rath, M., & Panda, M. R. (2017). MAQ system development in mobile ad-hoc networks using mobile agents. *IEEE 2nd International Conference on Contemporary Computing and Informatics (IC3I),* 794-798.

Rath, M., & Pati, B. (2017). *Load balanced routing scheme for MANETs with power and delay optimisation. International Journal of Communication Network and Distributed Systems* , 19.

Rath, M., & Pati, B. (2018). Security Assertion of IoT Devices Using Cloud of Things Perception. International Journal of Interdisciplinary Telecommunications and Networking, 11(2).

Rath, M., Pati, B., Panigrahi, C. R., & Sarkar, J. L. (2019). QTM: A QoS Task Monitoring System for Mobile Ad hoc Networks. In P. Sa, S. Bakshi, I. Hatzilygeroudis, & M. Sahoo (Eds.), *Recent Findings in Intelligent Computing Techniques. Advances in Intelligent Systems and Computing* (Vol. 707). Singapore: Springer. doi:10.1007/978-981-10-8639-7_57

Rath, M., Pati, B., & Pattanayak, B. (2019). Manifold Surveillance Issues in Wireless Network and the Secured Protocol. *International Journal of Information Security and Privacy, 13*(3).

Rath, M., Pati, B., & Pattanayak, B. K. (2017). Cross layer based QoS platform for multimedia transmission in MANET. *11th International Conference on Intelligent Systems and Control (ISCO)*, 402-407. 10.1109/ISCO.2017.7856026

Rath, M., & Pattanayak, B. (2017). MAQ:A Mobile Agent Based QoS Platform for MANETs. *International Journal of Business Data Communications and Networking, IGI Global, 13*(1), 1–8. doi:10.4018/IJBDCN.2017010101

Rath, M., & Pattanayak, B. (2018). Technological improvement in modern health care applications using Internet of Things (IoT) and proposal of novel health care approach. *International Journal of Human Rights in Healthcare*. doi:10.1108/IJHRH-01-2018-0007

Rath, M., & Pattanayak, B. K. (2018). Monitoring of QoS in MANET Based Real Time Applications. In Information and Communication Technology for Intelligent Systems Volume 2. ICTIS. Smart Innovation, Systems and Technologies (vol. 84, pp. 579-586). Springer. doi:10.1007/978-3-319-63645-0_64

Rath, M., & Pattanayak, B. K. (2018). SCICS: A Soft Computing Based Intelligent Communication System in VANET. Smart Secure Systems – IoT and Analytics Perspective. *Communications in Computer and Information Science, 808*, 255–261. doi:10.1007/978-981-10-7635-0_19

Rath, M., Pattanayak, B. K., & Pati, B. (2017). *Energetic Routing Protocol Design for Real-time Transmission in Mobile Ad hoc Network. In Computing and Network Sustainability, Lecture Notes in Networks and Systems* (Vol. 12). Singapore: Springer.

Rath, M., Swain, J., Pati, B., & Pattanayak, B. K. (2018). *Attacks and Control in MANET. In Handbook of Research on Network Forensics and Analysis Techniques* (pp. 19–37). IGI Global.

Rong, B., Chen, H., Qian, Y., Lu, K., Hu, R. Q., & Guizani, S. (2009). A Pyramidal Security Model for Large-Scale Group-Oriented Computing in Mobile Ad Hoc Networks: The Key Management Study. *IEEE Transactions on Vehicular Technology, 58*(1), 398–408. doi:10.1109/TVT.2008.923666

Rtah, M. (2018). Big Data and IoT-Allied Challenges Associated With Healthcare Applications in Smart and Automated Systems. *International Journal of Strategic Information Technology and Applications, 9*(2). doi:10.4018/IJSITA.201804010

Saxena, N., Tsudik, G., & Yi, J. H. (2015). Efficient Node Admission and Certificateless Secure Communication in Short-Lived MANETs. *IEEE Transactions on Parallel and Distributed Systems*, *20*(2), 158–170.

Surendran & Prakash. (2014). An ACO look-ahead approach to QOS enabled fault- tolerant routing in MANETs. *China Communications*, *12*(8), 93–110.

Wang, J., & Tao, Q. (2008). Machine Learning: The State of the Art. *IEEE Intelligent Systems*, *23*(6), 49–55. doi:10.1109/MIS.2008.107

Wang, Yu, Tang, & Huang. (2009). A Mean Field Game Theoretic Approach for Security Enhancements in Mobile Ad hoc Networks. *IEEE Transactions on Wireless Communications*, *13*(3), 1616–1627.

Wei, Z., Tang, H., Yu, F. R., Wang, M., & Mason, P. (2015). Security Enhancements for Mobile Ad Hoc Networks With Trust Management Using Uncertain Reasoning. *IEEE Transactions on Vehicular Technology*, *63*(9), 4647–4658.

Xin, Y., Kong, L., Liu, Z., Chen, Y., Li, Y., Zhu, H., ... Wang, C. (2018). Machine Learning and Deep Learning Methods for Cybersecurity. *IEEE Access: Practical Innovations, Open Solutions*, *6*, 35365–35381. doi:10.1109/ACCESS.2018.2836950

This research was previously published in Machine Learning and Cognitive Science Applications in Cyber Security; pages 84-104, copyright year 2019 by Information Science Reference (an imprint of IGI Global).

Chapter 36
Investigating Machine Learning Techniques for User Sentiment Analysis

Nimesh V Patel
C.U Shah University, Wadhawan (Surendranagar-Gujarat), India

Hitesh Chhinkaniwala
Adani Institute of Infrastructure Engineering, Gujarat, India

ABSTRACT

Sentiment analysis identifies users in the textual reviews available in social networking sites, tweets, blog posts, forums, status updates to share their emotions or reviews and these reviews are to be used by market researchers to do know the product reviews and current trends in the market. The sentiment analysis is performed by two methods. Machine learning approaches and lexicon methods which are also known as the knowledge base approach. These. In this article, the authors evaluate the performance of some machine learning techniques: Maximum Entropy, Naïve Bayes and Support Vector Machines on two benchmark datasets: the positive-negative dataset and a Movie Review dataset by measuring parameters like accuracy, precision, recall and F-score. In this article, the authors present the performance of various sentiment analysis and classification methods by classifying the reviews in binary classes as positive, negative opinion about reviews on different domains of dataset. It is also justified that sentiment analysis using the Support Vector Machine outperforms other machine learning techniques.

INTRODUCTION

Sentiment Analysis finds outs the tests of the user from their reviews provided on social networking sites, forums, blogs, e-commerce company websites. This sentiment analysis on product or item reviews can be wrapped with other web recommender systems. Like search engines, recommenders take into account the personality characteristics, past behavior of each user, a product's feature-based reviews and

DOI: 10.4018/978-1-6684-6291-1.ch036

sentiment analysis about the product for certain aspects about the product, other geographical information, and market conditions.

Sentiment analysis and classification can be performed by basically two methods: (1) Machine learning based and (2) Lexicon based techniques. The machine learning techniques can be further divided into two types (i) supervised and (ii) unsupervised learning. There are certain differences between these techniques. Supervised learning technique requires more domain knowledge and information seeds can be provided from outside to train model, but it can be applied on the multi-aspect dataset so that can reflect more user needs for specific aspects of a product. Whereas unsupervised learning does not require domain Knowledge, no rating calculations to be performed to find out sentiment scores and word ordering is not required do process sentiment analysis. Unsupervised learning diagrams and trigrams also polarized with more number of granularity levels. It can be applied to multiple domains. Another type of sentiment analysis methods is lexicon based sentiment analysis. Lexicon based technique is further divided into various categories. (i) The Dictionary Based and (ii) Corpus-based methods. The dictionary-based methods require large domain-specific knowledge, it provides aspect-sentiments extraction and Evaluation, capable of treating of negation words like NOT, also able to analyze Semantic relationships like the synonym, antonym, adjective. Whereas Corpus-Based Methods are able to deal with detection of spam and fake opinion, Segment wise score calculation, but requires deep knowledge of explicit-implicit, regular-irregular, syntactical-semantic rules. (Nimesh et al., 2015) provided more details regarding issues, challenges, working characteristics, and behaviour of sentiment analysis methods.

The work presented in this article contains five parts. The first part gives the primary sense about the significance of sentiment analysis, recommending process using sentiment analysis and the introduction of some well-known methods to perform sentiment analysis. The second part includes the related work carried out in an area by various researchers. The third part explains the process steps performed in sentiment analysis using machine learning techniques along with pre-processing tasks and other subsequent tasks to be carried out to evaluate the performance of machine learning based sentiment analysis. Next part includes discussion about the various evaluation criteria. The fifth section includes information about the used datasets, experimental setup, and the results achieved by execution. The final part includes the justification of the proposed targeted work.

RELATED WORK

In movie review domain where the application of sentiment analysis has the greatest potential to generate value, it is an interesting and challenging testing ground for different sentiment classification approaches. It was hypothesized that this was due to the tendency of reviewers to rate the individual elements of items differently from the item as a whole within the same review. (Bo Pang et al., 2002) suggest, the machine learning methods and features used when classifying movie reviews do not have to be specific to that domain but its benefits may easily transfer to other areas where sentiment classification can be applied. For binary (positive and negative) sentiment classification, (Turney et al., 2002) proposed the positive and negative terms can be counted and expressions in a review used to determine its polarity. (Kennedy et al., 2006) who had considered negation words, intensifiers, and diminishes taken into account and managed for improving the accuracy of the system. In this article Support Vector Machines (SVMs) method was proposed, and it was inferred that this machine learning algorithm performs significantly better than the term-counting method by considering negation words. (Pang et al., 2002) and (Pang et al., 2004) have compared the performance of various classification algorithms when determining the sentiment of a document, and also proved that SVMs were generally the best approach. Unigrams, bi-grams, part-of-speech (POS) tags and term positions were considered as features, and using unigrams gives the best results. When using very simple features with multi-aspect sentiment analysis the SVM classification algorithm can be effective for performing sentiment analysis.

Arjun Mukherjee, Bing Liu, 2012) done aspect extraction by providing some seed words then the model will extract and clusters aspect terms into categories simultaneously. It needs to be considered that many discovered aspects can be meaningless/non-useful and totally unsupervised methods(Suin Kim, et al. 2013; Yulan et al., 2009) can't fulfill all user aspects. This model reflects more user's needs to be discovered for specific aspects. A hierarchical technique suggested by (Suin Kim et al., 2013) by two-level tree formation for aspect-sentiments. Seeded as the model to discover aspect based sentiments for given seeded word. In this model Aspect or Sentiment polarity is modelled as a distribution of words and infer aspect-sentiment tree from review text by including the likelihood- how the review corpus is generated, prior-how the tree is generated in prior, the posterior- review observation for analysis. This model is more accurate and flexibility to discover aspect with more than two sentiments. The similar algorithm for content-based recommender system based on sentiment analysis was suggested by (Keshav R, Arvind Swaminathan et al., 2014). It extracts opinion and classifies the reviews and calculates opinion scores and prepare recommendation list. This technique has higher accuracy of prediction to prepare recommendation list. The proposed work calibrated for multiple domains (i.e. different product) add customization opinions for users, and various factors can be added like sarcasm, detection of fake opinions, etc. The Rule-based approach suggested by (Soujanya Poria et al., 2014) detects implicit aspect by assigning Implicit Aspect Clue (IAC) and map them to the corresponding aspect. This model leverages common sense knowledge and on the dependency structure of sentences. (Pravesh Kumar Singh et al., 2014) has used process flow to perform sentiment analysis using Used Naïve Bayes, Support Vector Machine (SVM) (Vidisha et al., 2016), Multilayer Perception-MLP (Neural n/w Based), Clustering, classifier algorithms and inferred that the accuracy of SVM is better than all other machine learning method when N-gram features were used.

PROPOSED APPROACH

We have implemented sentiment analysis techniques for two benchmark datasets using machine learning based supervised algorithms. The proposed framework for sentiment analysis is shown in the below diagram. The proposed approach contains the various steps of sentiment analysis using classification based on machine learning techniques. It contains the steps: (1) loading the dataset; (2) pre-processing; (3) feature–sentiment identification; (4) semantic transformation; (5) semantic score calculation; (6); classification based on calculated semantics scores (7) evaluation of sentiment analysis and classification (8) displaying comparison of approach on various datasets (Figure 1).

Figure 1. Sentiment analysis with supervised (machine learning) techniques

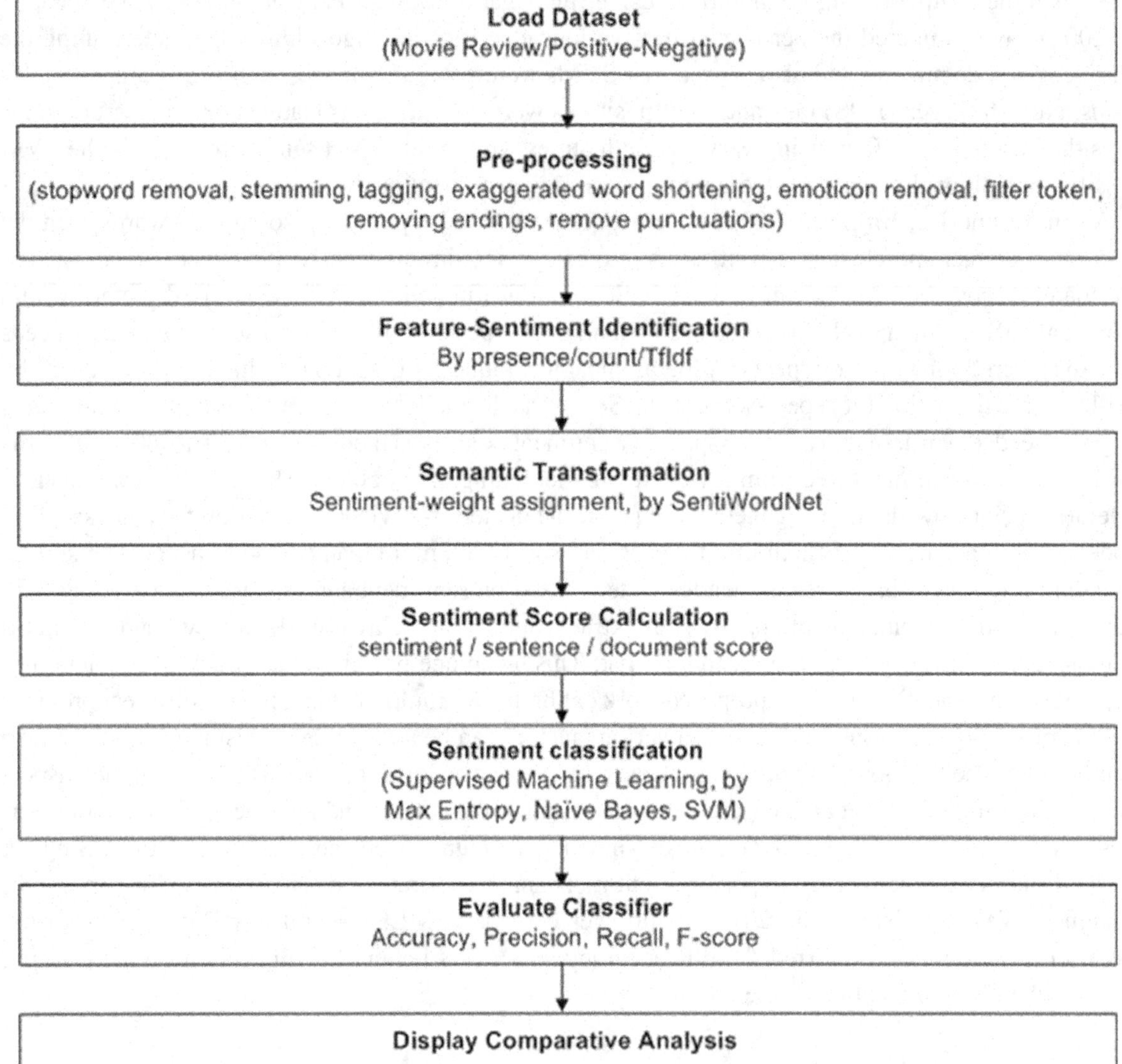

Loading the Dataset

Using two benchmark datasets (Movie review and positive-negative datasets), containing positive and negative reviews in separate directories for both the datasets. These datasets contain the textual review of customers spread all over the globe. Then we are distributing the total reviews in training and testing records datasets and passes, it into the model for sentiment analysis and classification.

Pre-Processing and Sentiment Detection

Following operations have performed on the datasets as a part of pre-processing steps to do,

- Finding sentiment words, Negation, Blind negation, split words, stop words
- Tokenization, POS tagging (Elgamal et al., 2016)
- Stemming
- Word shortening
- Emoticon detection and removal
- Hash tag and special character detection and removal

Feature-sentiment Extraction/Identification

From the review corpuses the features of the product and the sentiment words in the reviews are identified by the methods like presence/count/TfIdf (Term Frequency and Inverse Document frequency). Here presence could be identified by in terms of boolean, count as integers, and TfIdf as float value for feature-sentiment pair.

Semantic Transformation

Semantic scores to be assigned to every feature which are relevant for said user present in reviews. Every word has positive and negative score already defined in the dictionary, it would be determined from the semantic libraries like SentiWordNet. So with help of these scores, weighted score is calculated and assigned to tagged word to calculate its sentiment score.

Sentiment Score Calculation

As rating inference techniques suggested by (Qiming et al., 2014), in our proposed work we are calculating scores for word, sentence, or document, then cumulated score can be calculated by aggregating all previously calculated scores, and this score would be used to infer recommendation list based on a descending sequence of scores in product recommender system.

Sentiment Classification

The different machine learning techniques used for proposed sentiment analysis process are as under:

Maximum Entropy

When we are uniformly distributing the things, or in other words when they have the most randomness in distribution then Maximum entropy is achieved. Maximum entropy classifier is related to maximum entropy. It is a classifier which prefers the uniformity or maximum entropy if no data is observed. As it sees train data, it has to move away from the maximum entropy by explaining data. After it has explained (trained set) the data, it again tries to maximize the entropy on whatever remaining (testing set) is not seen

Naïve Bayes Classifier

The classification using Naïve Bayesian is done as follows - First, all the tweets and labels are passed to the classifier. In the next step, feature extraction is done. Now, both these extracted features and tweets are passed to the Naïve Bayesian classifier. Then train the classifier with this training data. Then the classifier dump file opened in write-back mode and feature words are stored in it along with a classifier. After that, the file is closed.

Support Vector Machine

For SVM, we have basically used 2 labels that are 0, and 1. Here the 0 represents positive, 1 represents a negative and 2 as neutral. Each word in a tweet is represented as either 0 or 1. If it is a feature word, then represent it with 1 otherwise 0. So, we get a sequence of 0s and 1s. Now this feature vector and class labels are given to an SVM classifier to classify tweets as positive, Negative, Neutral.

EVALUATION CRITERIA

For a set of items in the dataset we are evaluating the proposed approach for two different datasets, (1) Movie Review dataset, and (2) Positive-negative dataset. Here for said datasets, the methods are evaluated by verifying the results under the different evaluation measures (1) Accuracy (2) Precision (3) Recall (4) F-score. We will evaluate the performance of all three machine learning algorithms in terms of above-stated parameters for single fold and 5-fold of the dataset.

DATASET AND RESULTS

Dataset

We are applying our proposed method on two off-line benchmark datasets. Here we are testing the proposed method on two datasets, so we can verify and compare the performance of the proposed method on different domains of the dataset. Following are two datasets on which we are applying the sentiment classification and also evaluated the performance.

1. Movie Review Dataset: polarity dataset v2.0 (3.0Mb) which has 1000 positive and 1000 negative pre-processed Movie opinion reviews. Introduced in Pang/Lee ACL 2004, Released June 2004. Also provided by nltk.corpus library.
2. Positive-Negative Dataset: contains 500 positive and 500 negative pre-processed opinion reviews

These two datasets contain the good mix of positive and negative textual user reviews in both the domain, so we can have the justifiable results, and that is only attraction to choose the domain and dataset.

Results and Evaluation

Machine learning techniques for sentiment analysis and classification are applied on two separate datasets and evaluated. The individual performance between machine learning based sentiment analysis techniques is measured using the evaluation parameters: Accuracy, Precision, Recall, F-score.

The performance of the algorithms on the different dataset is as under: Movie Review Dataset: Contains 1000 Positive and 1000 Negative Pre-processed Movie Opinion Reviews (Table 1 and Figure 2).

Table 1. Evaluation of machine learning algorithms on movie review dataset

	Maximum Entropy	Naïve Bayes	SVM
Accuracy	0.7220	0.7280	0.8640
Precision	0.8060	0.8056	0.8651
Recall	0.7220	0.7280	0.8640
F-Score	0.7015	0.7096	0.8639

Figure 2. Machine Learning algorithms on the movie review dataset

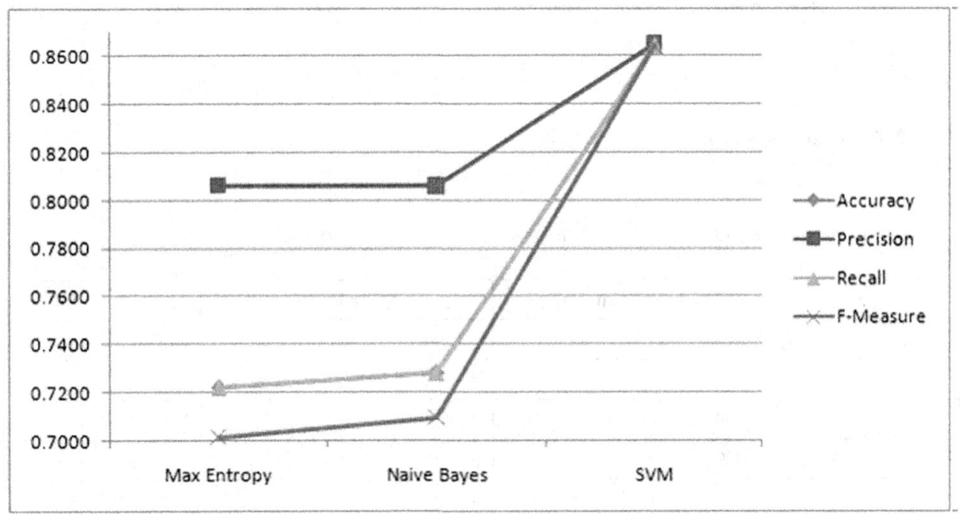

Positive-Negative Dataset: Contains 500 Positive and 500 Negative Pre-Processed Opinions Reviews (Tables 2-3 and Figures 3-4).

- The evaluation measures with their results observed by performing Training on 750 instances, Testing on 250 instances on Positive-Negative Review (Single fold)
  - Word features and without stopword removed

Table 2. Positive-negative dataset (Single fold) without stopword Removed

	Maximum Entropy	Naïve Bayes	SVM
Accuracy	0.6960	0.7120	0.8840
Precision	0.8018	0.8088	0.8842
Recall	0.6960	0.7120	0.8840
F-Score	0.6668	0.6875	0.8839

Figure 3. Positive-negative dataset (Single fold) without stopwords removed

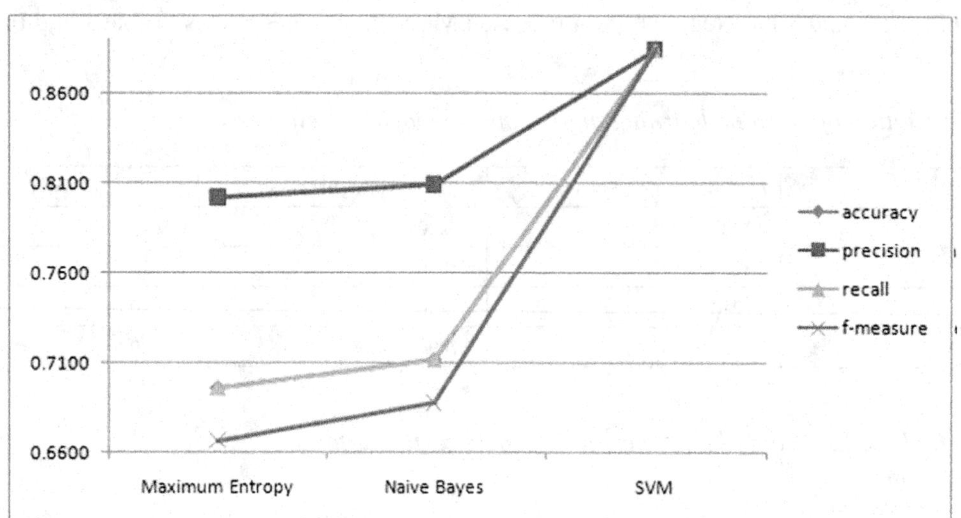

- Word features and with stopwords removed

Table 3. Positive-negative dataset (single fold) with stopwords removed

	Maximum Entropy	Naïve Bayes	SVM
Accuracy	0.7520	0.7800	0.8760
Precision	0.8153	0.8414	0.8766
Recall	0.7520	0.7800	0.8760
F-Score	0.7389	0.7696	0.8760

Figure 4. Positive-negative dataset (single fold) with stopwords removed

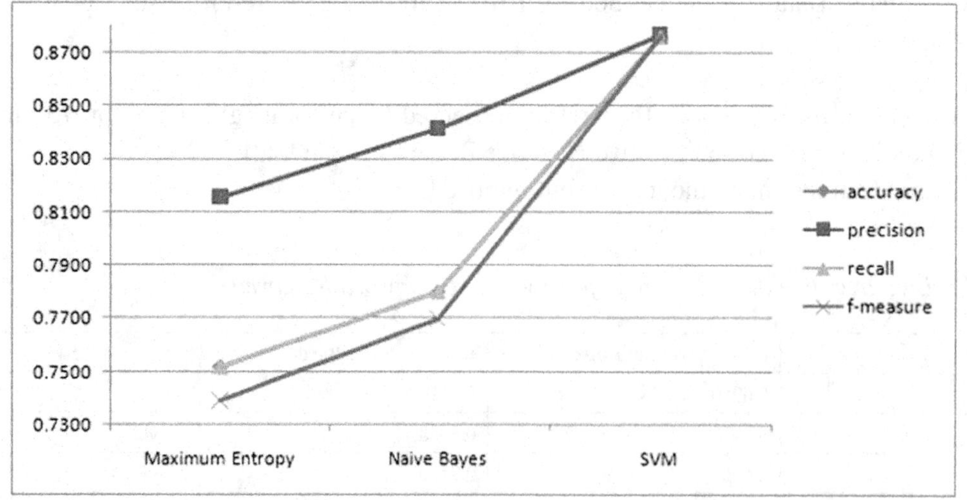

- The evaluation measures with their results observed by performing Training on 750 instances, Testing on 250 instances on Positive-Negative Review (5- fold) (Tables 4-5 and Figures 5-6)
- Word features and without stopwords removed

Table 4. Positive-negative dataset (5-fold) without stopword removed

Algorithm	Parameter	FOLD-1	FOLD-2	FOLD-3	FOLD-4	FOLD-5
Maximum Entropy	Accuracy	0.1440	0.2970	0.4250	0.5620	0.7290
	Precision	0.1611	0.3261	0.4780	0.6381	0.8155
	Recall	0.1466	0.2996	0.4295	0.5695	0.7316
	F-Score	0.1412	0.2919	0.4122	0.5445	0.7083
Naïve Bayes	Accuracy	0.1530	0.3140	0.4490	0.5930	0.7440
	Precision	0.1655	0.3350	0.4925	0.6536	0.8234
	Recall	0.1551	0.3161	0.4530	0.5995	0.7432
	F-Score	0.1515	0.3113	0.4405	0.5817	0.7247
SVM	Accuracy	0.1810	0.3560	0.5210	0.6870	0.8490
	Precision	0.1814	0.3560	0.5209	0.6865	0.8485
	Recall	0.1809	0.3562	0.5212	0.6873	0.8492
	F-Score	0.1810	0.3557	0.5207	0.6865	0.8484

Figure 5. Positive-negative dataset (5-Fold) without stopwords removed

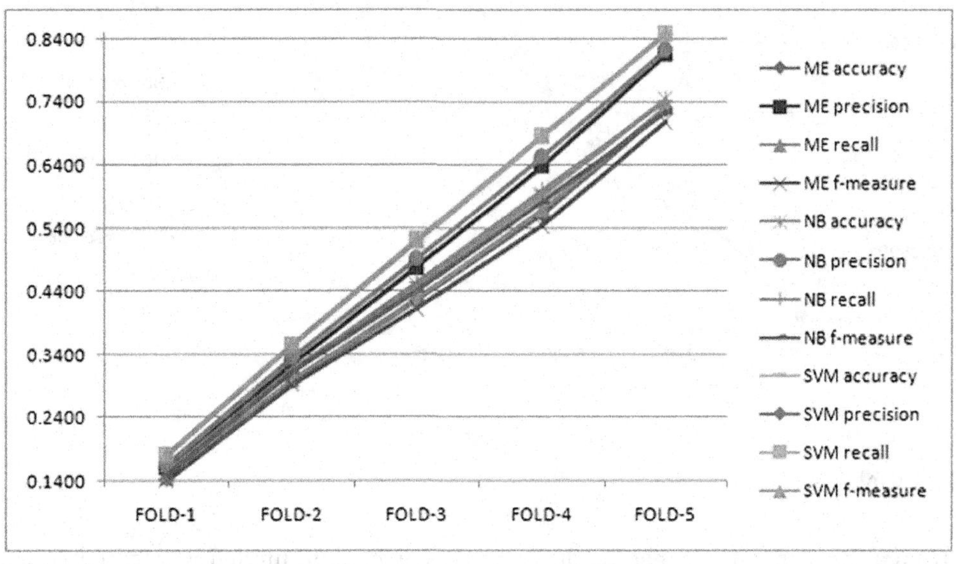

- Word features and with stopwords removed

Table 5. Positive-negative dataset (5-fold) with stopwords removed

Algorithm	Parameter	FOLD-1	FOLD-2	FOLD-3	FOLD-4	FOLD-5
Maximum Entropy	Accuracy	0.1717	0.3440	0.5056	0.6797	0.8459
	Precision	0.1674	0.3271	0.4768	0.6438	0.7995
	Recall	0.1657	0.3253	0.4735	0.6397	0.7921
	F-Score	0.1640	0.3190	0.4690	0.6430	0.7980
Naïve Bayes	Accuracy	0.1696	0.3366	0.5004	0.6790	0.8444
	Precision	0.1654	0.3178	0.4664	0.6404	0.7969
	Recall	0.1636	0.3152	0.4616	0.6352	0.7890
	F-Score	0.1660	0.3330	0.5030	0.6740	0.8500
SVM	Accuracy	0.1663	0.3329	0.5020	0.6729	0.8492
	Precision	0.1665	0.3342	0.5041	0.6753	0.8511
	Recall	0.1660	0.3327	0.5022	0.6731	0.8491
	F-Score	0.1717	0.3440	0.5056	0.6797	0.8459

Figure 6. Positive-negative dataset (5-fold) with stopwords removed

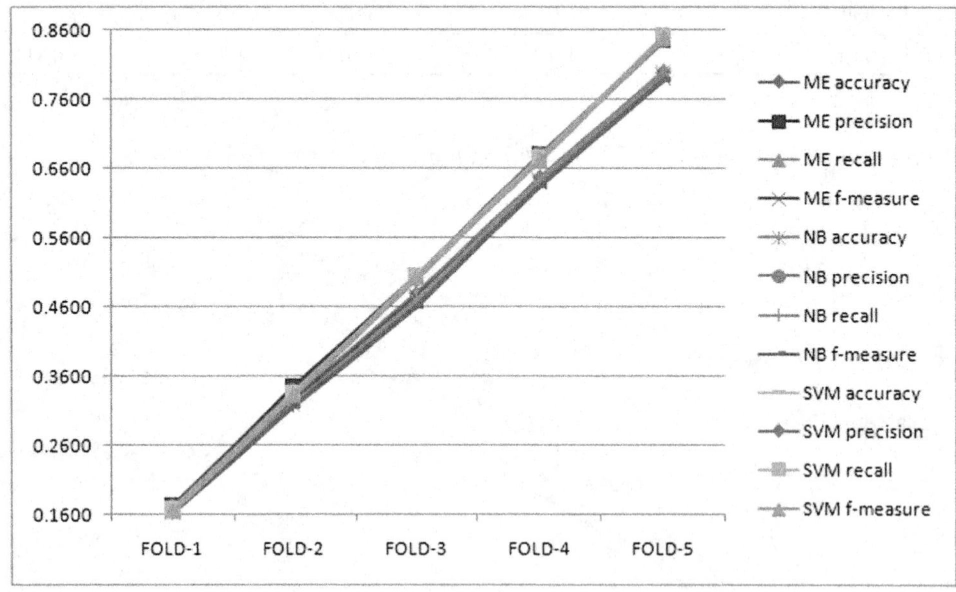

CONCLUSION

It is clear from a literature survey that the dictionaries may contain limited words, sentences, and vocabulary. The performance of lexicon-based methods totally depends upon the dictionaries and corpus created for the targeted domain. So the Machine Learning techniques of sentiment analysis perform better than the lexicon based techniques in different domains because of no requirement of such domain specific dictionaries and corpus.

The experiment performed on two different datasets (1) Movie review dataset and (2) Positive-negative Dataset, proves that the sentiment classification using Support Vector Machine outperforms the probability based other two algorithms (Naïve Bayes and Maximum Entropy) in term of Accuracy and precision.

FUTURE ENHANCEMENT

By considering the result concluded in this article it is proved that the SVM classifier works more accurately on suggested datasets. In future, we can evaluate the performance on some other domain's benchmark dataset with the calculation of new sentiment score by analyzing the textual reviews for specific aspects and by considering the ratings provided by the customers. Then based on this newly calculated score the sentiment can be classified. We can also add this proposed sentiment classification method with the product like recommender which is used to provide recommendations for a specific product which may be according to the user's taste and needful.

REFERENCES

Amolik, A., Jivane, N., Bhandari, M., & Venkatesan, M. (2016). Twitter sentiment analysis of movie reviews using machine learning techniques. *IACSIT International Journal of Engineering and Technology*, *7*(6), 1–7.

Arjun Mukherjee and B. L. (2012). Aspect Extraction through Semi-Supervise Modeling. In *50th Annual Meeting of the Association for Computational Linguistics (ACL'12)*, Jeju, Korea (pp. 339-348)

Elgamal, M. (2016). Sentiment Analysis Methodology of Twitter Data with an application on Hajj season. *International Journal of Engineering Research & Science*, *2*(1), 82–87.

Kennedy, A., & Inkpen, D. (2006, May). Sentiment Classification Of Movie Reviews Using Contextual Valence Shifters. International Journal Computational Intelligence, 22(2), 110–125. doi:10.1111/j.1467-8640.2006.00277.x

Keshav, R., Swaminathan, S. A., Goutham, R., & Naren, J. (2014). Content based Recommender System on Customer Reviews using Sentiment Classification Algorithms. *International Journal of Computer Science and Information Technology*, *5*(3), 4782–4787.

Nimesh, V. P., & Hitesh, R. C. (2015). Investigating Issues and Challenges of Sentiment Analysis Based Recommender System. *International Journal of Data Mining and Emerging Technologies*, *5*(2), 85–97.

Pang, B., & Lee, L. (2002). Thumbs up? Sentiment Classification using Machine Learning Techniques. In *EMNLP '02 Proceedings of the ACL-02 conference on Empirical methods in natural language processing (Vol. 10*, pp. 79-86). doi:10.3115/1118693.1118704

Pang, B., & Lee, L. (2004). A sentimental education: sentiment analysis using subjectivity summarization based on minimum cuts. *ACL'04 Proceedings of the 42nd Annual Meeting on Association for Computational Linguistics, Article No. 271, Spain July 21 - 26,2004.*

Peter, D. Turney, Thumbs up or thumbs down? (2002). Semantic Orientation Applied to Unsupervised Classification of Reviews. In *ACL '02 Proceedings of the 40th Annual Meeting on Association for Computational Linguistics, July 7-12* (pp. 417-424).

Poria, S., Cambria, E., Ku, L. W., Gui, C., & Gelbukh, A. (2014). A Rule-Based Approach to Aspect Extraction from Product Reviews. In *The Second Workshop on Natural Language Processing for Social Media (SocialNLP)*, Dublin, Ireland (pp. 28-37).

Pradhan, V. M., Vala, J., & Balani, P. (2016). A survey on Sentiment Analysis Algorithms for opinion mining. *International Journal of Computers and Applications, 133*(9), 7–11.

Qiming, D., Minghui, Q., Chao-Yuan, W. J. S. A., Jing, J., & Chong, A. W. (2014). Jointly Modeling Aspects, Ratings and Sentiments for Movie Recommendation. In *The 20th ACM SIGKDD Conference on Knowledge Discovery and Data Mining (KDD'14)* (pp. 193-202).

Singh, P. K., & Husain, M. S. (2014). Methodological study of opinion mining and sentiment analysis techniques. *International Journal on Soft Computing, 5*(1), 11–21.

Suin Kim and J. Z. (2013). A Hierarchical Aspect-Sentiment Model for Online Reviews. In *The Twenty-Seventh AAAI Conference on Artificial Intelligence* (pp. 526-533). AAAI.

Yulan and L. C. (2009). Joint Sentiment/Topic Model for Sentiment Analysis. In *18th ACM conference on Information and knowledge management* (pp. 375-384). New York: CIKM.

This research was previously published in the International Journal of Decision Support System Technology (IJDSST), 11(3); pages 1-12, copyright year 2019 by IGI Publishing (an imprint of IGI Global).

Chapter 37
Thwarting Spam on Facebook:
Identifying Spam Posts Using Machine Learning Techniques

Arti Jain
https://orcid.org/0000-0002-3764-8834
Jaypee Institute of Information Technology, India

Reetika Gairola
Jaypee Institute of Information Technology, India

Shikha Jain
Jaypee Institute of Information Technology, India

Anuja Arora
https://orcid.org/0000-0001-5215-1300
Jaypee Institute of Information Technology, India

ABSTRACT

Spam on the online social networks (OSNs) is evolving as a prominent problem for the users of these networks. Spammers often use certain techniques to deceive the OSN users for their own benefit. Facebook, one of the leading OSNs, is experiencing such crucial problems at an alarming rate. This chapter presents a methodology to segregate spam from legitimate posts using machine learning techniques: naïve Bayes (NB), support vector machine (SVM), and random forest (RF). The textual, image, and video features are used together, which wasn't considered by the earlier researchers. Then, 1.5 million posts and comments are extracted from archival and real-time Facebook data, which is then pre-processed using RStudio. A total of 30 features are identified, out of which 10 are the best informative for identification of spam vs. ham posts. The entire dataset is shuffled and divided into three ratios, out of which 80:20 ratio of training and testing dataset provides the best result. Also, RF classifier outperforms NB and SVM by achieving overall F-measure 89.4% on the combined feature set.

DOI: 10.4018/978-1-6684-6291-1.ch037

INTRODUCTION

In the today's world the change in the Internet technology has led us to the usage of different Online Social Networks (OSNs)[1] (Andreassen et al., 2016; Brown et al., 2008; Egele et al., 2017; Panicker & Devadas, 2015), also known as the changing web. The out bursting popularity of these OSNs have attracted huge number of users to use their platform which results into the sharing and storing of users' personal information on these networking sites. These networks help the users to interact, exchange and collaborate with their social-circle. These OSNs are also helping its users to communicate with their social community and keep their users updated with different domains such as news, active learning, job searching and web application development etc. Such vital information has aroused the interest of spammers[2] to take the advantage of the trust among users to deceive them for spammers (Adewole et al., 2017) own benefits. Facebook OSN is currently among one of the leading OSN present across the world and having over 2.05 billion[3] monthly active users. Facebook is around five times greater than its next greatest partner Twitter. A survey report[4] shows that out of 5,173 adults suggested that 30% of people get their news from Facebook, while only 8% receive news from Twitter and 4% from Google Plus. The users of Facebook not only uses Facebook for communicating with their friends but also for keeping regular updates about what is happening around the globe.

Spammers at present are discovering different ways to reach out to the users of the OSNs for spreading spam messages (Bhat & Abulaish, 2013; Prieto et al., 2013) and thereby, making the OSNs as vulnerable and exposed targets. Mostly, these spam messages are sent in high volume so that they can influence large amount of users in a short span of time. Moreover, these messages reduce the memory of the inboxes. These messages are targeted to specific audience or can be used to perform tricks such as phishing, identity theft (Gao et al., 2012). Apparently, spam which was earlier in the form of text containing irrelevant information for the users is now currently it is being noticed as it being spread using images and videos too. To do so, spammer evades the programmed filters using different techniques such as obfuscating keywords, wrapping long urls, and using image or video instead of textual content.

In this chapter, a methodology to segregate spam vs. ham post[5] from Facebook OSN is provided by combining the textual, image and video features using three supervised Machine Learning (Shalev-Shwartz & Ben-David, 2014) techniques, namely- Naïve Bayes (NB) (Lee et al., 2010), Support Vector Machine (SVM) (Shalev-Shwartz & Ben-David, 2014) and Random Forest (RF) (Breiman, 2001) using RStudio®[6]. Our methodology comprises of various stages. Firstly, data extraction is done from the Facebook posts which contain text, image and video posts followed by the data pre-processing (DP) stage. DP stage consists of stop words removal, stemming, lemmatization, photo pre-processing and url link blacklisting. The next stage consists of relevant features extraction for the identification of whether a post is spam or not. In this stage, a total of 30 features mare extracted from Facebook which includes *"status type"*, *"created time"*, *"updated time"*, *"name of the photo"* etc. Then the data is shuffled and split into different training and test data ratios i.e. 60:40, 70:30 and 80:20 respectively. Then ML techniques are applied to train the three classifiers (NB, SVM and RF). Further, using RStudio these classifiers are used in the testing phase to predict whether a given post is spam or ham. Finally, the classifiers are evaluated on the basis of standard metrics- precision, recall and F-measure.

BACKGROUND

Spam and ham posts classification of Facebook users' posts is a noticeable and prominent research issue which has been addressed by various researchers in their work. It is observed that these researchers have spam campaigns using individual features- textual features (Meligy et al., 2015), image features (Gao et al., 2012) and video features (Benevenuto et al., 2009). On one end, researchers primarily have worked on the textual posts. On the other end, few researchers have tried to classify based on image or video features. Rarely, video features have been used. Still an integrated research work is needed based on the combination of the three media types- Image, Text and Video features altogether. Research efforts in this work have been made to improve the accuracy and efficiency of the spam detection on Facebook OSN for all the three kinds of posts (text, image and video). Our proposed methodology shows the combination of these three features together to identify spam posts on Facebook, and separate those from the legitimate ham posts using the three classifiers (NB, SVM and RF).

Further, this section discusses about literature survey relevant to spammers identification on varying OSNs and Machine Learning techniques that have been used to classify spam posts. In comparison, our focus in on detection of spam messages, so that OSNs can be secured from spams that are generated by spamming bots or legitimate accounts or any other such phenomenon.

OSNs Spammer Identification

Research in spam message detection in OSNs has received growing interests in the past few years. So far, researchers' prime focus is on spam message detection using the textual information as posted by spammer using ML techniques (Chan et al., 2015; Martinez-Romo & Araujo, 2013). Spam detection is considered as a continuous fight among spammers and spam filters. Certain existing studies for spam detection in OSNs focus on identifying spam message as quite challenging. Spammer at present are finding different ways such wrapping long URLs, shuffling keywords etc. to propagate spam rigorously (DeBarr & Wechsler, 2010; Panicker & Devadas, 2015; Prieto et al., 2013; Rajalaxmi & Ramesh, 2014; Swami & Khade, 2014). These spammers may change the syntax (Gao et al., 2012) and use the techniques (Meligy et al., 2015) that can deceive the OSN users to wide extent. Hence, a lot of work needs to be done in this area to wipe out these scrap messages from the internet. Regardless of Facebook having an immune system of its own, users still experience a huge number of spam and noxious substance on general premises. Many existing ways to deal with the identification of spam in other OSN like Twitter can't be used on Facebook because of various issues (Chu et al., 2012) such as missing data e.g. account holder age, limit on post length, network details etc. Certain studies in this field looks into content based analysis and then researchers treat textual contents as collection of documents where individual messages are pre-processed and are represented using Vector Space Model (VSM) (Zhang & Wang, 2009) for text representation. Each document can also be represented using boolean occurrence of words in the document or by counting the frequency of occurrence of each word. Authors (Zhang & Wang, 2009) have proposed Bayesian model for SMS spam classification using content analysis techniques. Authors (Jin et al., 2011) introduce both image, text content features and social network features to indicate spam activities. Authors (Jeong et al., 2016) have dealt with spam in Twitter using three schemes- TSP-Filtering, SS-Filtering and Cascaded-Filtering (combine TSP and SS). These schemes are scalable and inspect user-centered two hop social networks and have better performance in terms of true positives and false positives. Authors (Gao et al., 2012) drop spam messages before they reach the intended recipients, and protect users from various kinds of fraud. They evaluate the system using 187 million wall posts from Facebook, and 17 million tweets from Twitter and observed that the true positive rate reaches 80.9% while the false positive rate reaches 0.19% in the best case. They also reveal large-scale spam campaigns in OSNs through offline studies. Although offline analysis tools are designed but none of them are usable for online spam detection. Authors (Stein et al., 2011) present framework of adversarial learning system which performs real-time read and action in Facebook. However, they lack consideration of valuable features and their performance prevents us from any further comparison. Authors (Thomas et al., 2011) filter malicious urls in real-time OSNs to identify malicious messages. Although their approach performs deep analysis of urls but our approach uses alternative information i.e. message content for the investigation. Authors (Song et al., 2011) propose sender-receiver relationship for Twitter messages. Authors (Adewole et al., 2017) consider datasets from SMS spam detection domain and Twitter microblog; and have used 18 features from content, behavioural or graph based features for spammer detection in Twitter. It is noted that the mention behaviour of spammers based on such features differs from that of the legitimate users. Authors (Yoon et al., 2010) have provided hybrid model which combines content analysis and challenge-response for mobile spam detection. Content based spam filter classifies messages as spam, legitimate or unknown. Unknown message is further authenticated using challenge-response protocol which determines whether the message is sent by human or automated program. Authors (El-Alfy & Al-Hasan, 2016) have introduced DCA algorithm for improving the performance of anti-spam filters within email and SMS data. Authors (He et al., 2014) have discussed Self-Monitoring (SM) skills for textual posts on Facebook. Popularity of the Social Networking Site- Facebook has grown unprecedented during the past few years. They have investigated the research question- whether posts on FB can also be applicable for the prediction of user psychological traits such as self-monitoring skill which are linked with the user expression behaviour within the online scenario. They also present a model to evaluate the relationship between the SM skills and the posts; evaluate the quality of responses to the Snyder Self-Monitoring Questionnaire via Internet; and explore the textual features of the posts in different SM-level groups.

ML Techniques

Researchers in the past have used various machine learning models (Cresci et al., 2017; Soman & Murugappan, 2014; Stringhini et al., 2010; Swami & Khade, 2014; Xu et al., 2016; Zhu et al., 2016) to detect spam on the social networking sites as they give promising results. Authors (Lee et al., 2010; (Stringhini et al., 2010; Yang et al., 2011) have used ML techniques to detect spamming bots in OSNs. These are the accounts that are created by spammers and are used exclusively for spamming purposes. Authors (Yardi et al., 2009) have made use of ad-hoc criteria for Twitter to identify spamming bots. Additionally, (Benevenuto et al., 2009; Chu et al., 2012) have applied supervised ML techniques to detect spammers in Youtube, Social bookmarking sites. Such websites don't focus on communication among users but their functionality is video and bookmark sharing respectively. Hence, they ignore textual and image features sets. Authors (Chan et al., 2015) have investigated the capabilities of existing spam filters for defending against certain adversarial attacks. They have proposed reweight method with rescaling function to prevent an adversarial attack using SVM based ML classifier. Although security level of spam filter in this model is increased, however, its classification accuracy over untainted samples is dropped significantly. Authors (Ezpeleta et al., 2016) have discussed a new perspective of the spam detection by focusing on spam similarities in different OSNs but dataset was not real-time extraction of data at all. They have worked on various features of spam messages using linear regression and SVM classifiers.

Authors (Gao et al., 2012) have described spam campaigns, instead of individual spam messages, for spam classification. Their system can be deployed at the OSN server side to provide online spam filtering but their system is restricted to only the textual content. Although SVM provides them 98.4% accuracy on the text message features but no image and video features are considered. Authors (McCord & Chuah, 2011) have compared the performance of RF, SVM, NB and K-Nearest Neighbor classifiers. Another, authors (Tayal et al., 2015) had discussed about relevant ML algorithms such as K-means, KNN but they focus only on crime related activities in India which are not related to spam detection. Authors (Ahmed & Abulaish, 2013) have identified features that are common to both Facebook and Twitter OSNs. They have used three different classification algorithms- NB, Jrip and J48, and observed false positive value of 0.089 and 0.075 on Facebook and Twitter dataset respectively.

SUPERVISED CLASSIFIERS

Machine learning (Breiman, 2001; Shalev-Shwartz & Ben-David, 2014) is a field of artificial intelligence which gives the computer an ability to learn itself without human intervention. The process involves searching and analyzing the data to identify a common pattern and design the possible set of actions. Machine learning algorithms are broadly categorized as supervised and unsupervised. Supervised learning (Galán-García et al., 2016) require a dataset containing both input and desired output, in addition to furnishing feedback about the accuracy of predictions during training. First step is to train the machine using the given dataset. Once training is over, the algorithm is used to predict the output for the new data. Formally, it can be defined as an input factor *(x)*, yield variable *(y)* and some calculations done in order to take the mapping capacity from the contribution to the yield as $y = f(x)$.The objective of the algorithm is to approximate the input to the output mapping function so adequately that the output variable *(y)* can be predicted correctly given the new input data *(x)*. Supervised algorithms are further grouped into two types of problems: regression and classification. A classification problem means when the input variable maps to a target category as output, such as "happy" or "notHappy" or "spam" and "notSpam". Regression problem basically estimates the relationship between variables and generates a continuous value as output. For example: predict the house price when size of the house is given. Unsupervised algorithms do not require any training using dataset with desired outcome data. Instead, they use an iterative approach to identify the common features of the data and then group the similar data together. Whenever new data arrives, it extracts the features and establishes the similarity with the existing data and concludes the output. In other words, unsupervised learning algorithm takes only the input data *(x)*. The objective of this kind of learning algorithms is to model the underlying structure or distribution in the data in order to learn more about the data. Unsupervised learning problems can be further grouped into two types of problems: clustering and association. Clustering problem means the distribution od data is analyzed to form the cluster of similar data. For example, cluster of people who like coffee. An association rule learning problem is when the relation between the data is identified. For example: people who buy bread also tend to buy milk. Since the problem of identifying the spam post is a classification problem, three supervised classifiers namely: Naïve Bayes (NB), Support Vector Machine (SVM) and Random Forest (RF) are applied. These classifiers are explained in detail in the following sub-sections.

Naïve Bayes

Naive Bayes Classifier (McCord & Chuah, 2011) technique is based on the so-called Bayesian theorem and is particularly suited when the dimensionality of the inputs is high. It is a classification algorithm for binary (two-class) and multi-class classification problems. Despite its simplicity, Naive Bayes can often outperform more sophisticated classification methods. They are probabilistic, which means that they calculate the probability of each category for a given sample, and then output the category with the highest one. The way they get these probabilities is by using Bayes' Theorem, which describes the probability of a feature, based on prior knowledge of conditions that might be related to that feature. NB (McCord & Chuah, 2011) acknowledges that the effect of the estimation of an indicator *(x)* on a given class *(c)* is free of the estimations of the different indicators. Hence NB classification can be given as in equation *(1)*:

$$P(c|x) = (P(x|c).P(c)) / P(x) \qquad (1)$$

Here, $P(c|x)$ is the back likelihood of target class given indicator. This is called the posterior probability, $P(c)$ is the probability of target class c being true (regardless of data). This is called the prior probability of class, $P(x|c)$ is the probability which is the likelihood of indicator x given class c, $P(x)$ is the earlier likelihood of indicator x (regardless of the class).

After calculating the posterior probability $P(c|x)$ for a number of different classes, the class with the highest probability is selected. This is the maximum probable class and can formally be called the Maximum a Posteriori (MAP) class.

Support Vector Machines

Support Vector Machines (Shalev-Shwartz & Ben-David, 2014) are perhaps one of the most popular and talked about machine learning algorithms. It is one of the high-performing algorithm with little tuning. Support Vector Machines are based on the concept of decision planes that define decision boundaries. A decision plane is one that separates between a set of objects having different class memberships. SVM (Shalev-Shwartz & Ben-David, 2014) is an arrangement of regulated learning strategies utilized for characterization, relapse and exceptions recognition. Binary classification is performed by using a real-valued function $f\colon x \subseteq N$ in the following way:

Input $x = (x_1,\ldots,x_n)$, assign to the positive class, if $f(x) \geq 0$, and otherwise to the negative class.

The case where $f(x)$ is a linear function of $x \in X$ with a and b as linear variables is considered, so that it can be written as in equation *(2)*:

$$f(x) = (w.x) + b \qquad (2)$$

Here, $w = \sum_{i=1}^{N} a_i y_i x_i$

Now, substitute for w in equation *(2)* which results in equation *(3)*, and on rearranging the variables equation *(4)* is generated:

$$f(x) = (\sum_{i=1}^{N} a_i y_i x_i)x + b \tag{3}$$

$$f(x) = (\sum_{i=1}^{N} a_i y_i)x_i x + b \tag{4}$$

Figure 1 shows the SVM linear classification of two different classes *A* and *B*. The distance between the line and the closest data points is referred to as the margin. The best or optimal line that can separate the two classes is the line that as the largest margin. The margin is calculated as the perpendicular distance from the line to only the closest points. Only these points are relevant in defining the line and in the construction of the classifier. The margin points are the supporting data points, also known as the supporting vectors which help in segregating the two different classes *A* and *B*. They support or define the hyperplane. The hyperplane is learned from training data using an optimization procedure (like gradient descent) that maximizes the margin.

Figure 1. SVM Classification

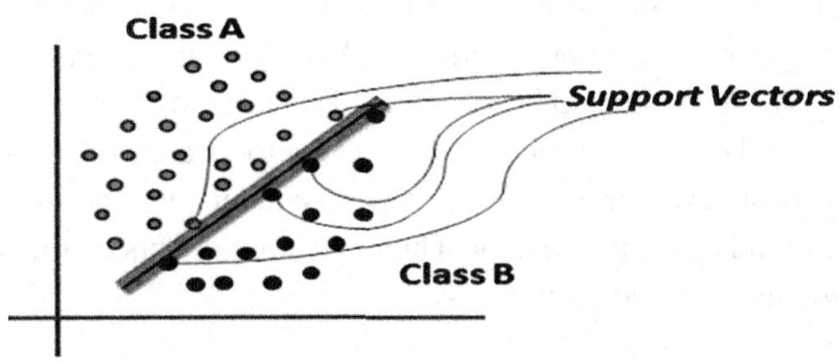

Random Forest

Random Forest (Breiman, 2001) is one most powerful machine learning algorithms. It is a type of ensemble machine learning algorithm called Bootstrap Aggregation or bagging. It can be used for the problems of classification and regression both. RF is a sort of group learning process where a group of prescient models intercept the given expectation undertaking. RF utilizes both the bagging and the random subspace methodology for including randomization within group. It is important to know that every prescient model for utilizing a group is simply being squandering the calculation time. Then choice trees make a decent decision for the group learning, as a result different outfit with changing speculations with regards to the hidden relationships is needed. Figure 2 shows how a feature *f* can be used for obtaining an output *Y*. In this process, firstly different choice trees are created named as *T1, T2* upto *Tn*. Further, these sub trees are exploited and then decision is made by the information present in the nodes. Now this different sub trees information are sacked and are presented in the form of the output *Y*. Bagging choice trees admirably and get strong prescient power. It takes the differing qualities, one additional level by fusing the arbitrary subspace technique. RF utilizes sacking and random subspaces to make group with solid assorted qualities, diminish inclination, and prescient power tends to increment definitely.

Figure 2. Random Forest Bagging Strategy

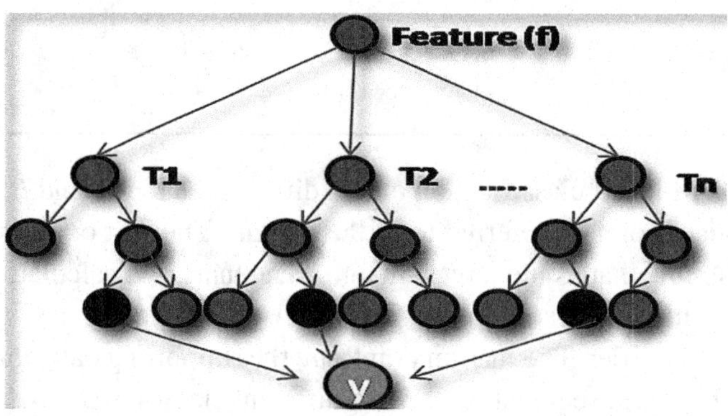

OSN DATASET COLLECTION

In this research work, Facebook dataset is used that is extracted from both the archival and the real-time extraction of posts during October 2016 to April 2017 from the Facebook Graph API[7]. Graph API Explorer is used for testing purposes, authentication of API calls, and to extract data out of Facebook platform. Facebook Graph API explorer and Facepager tool are used to extract the different kinds of posts and finally posts are organized on row per record basis. These tools are low-level HTTP-based API that can be used to file query, post new stories, manage advertisements, uploading photos and a variety of other tasks that an application is programmed for. The main components on this Facebook social graph are composed of the following three components:-

- **Node:** Node represents distinct users, photos, Facebook pages, or comments on particular posts.
- **Edge:** Edge represents connections between Facebook pages, photos, or comments on photos.
- **Field:** Field represents different sets of information that can be gathered about users e.g. birthday, current location, gender and many more.

Table 1 shows the topics that are covered from the various fields for which the posts and comments are extracted using the Graph API Explorer. The dataset contains 1.5 million posts and comments in total.

PROPOSED METHODOLOGY

The proposed methodology describes various stages that are considered for the separation of spam vs. ham post from Facebook OSN using combined features, namely- textual, image and video features and applying three ML techniques (NB, SVM and RF) as shown in Figure 3.

Table 1. Topics Coverage of Various Fields

Fields	Topics
Entertainment	Coldplay, Bahubali2, Dangal, Logan, Oscar, Lion, Thor:Ragnarok, Grammy Awards
Life Style	International Women's Day, End of Season Sale, Christmas, Iphone7, Galaxy 8
Politics	Narendra Modi, UP Elections, Yogi Adityanath, Nitesh Kumar, Jaya Lalita, Barack Obama, Hilary Clinton
Sports	India Vs. Australia, ODI, UEFA Championship league, Messi, Virat Kohli, Ms Dhoni, WWE, Ronaldo
News	Jammu & Kashmir, Syria, Russia, H1V1 Visa
# of posts and Comments	1,500,000

Once raw data is collected from the Facebook posts (both archival and real-time), Data Preprocessing (DP) stage comes into picture using RStudio®. DP consists of stop-words removal, stemming, lemmatization, photo pre-processing and url link blacklisting. Next stage consists of relevant features extraction, total of 30 features are extracted from Facebook. The entire data is then shuffled and split in varying training and test data to predict spam vs. ham posts using three supervised classifiers.

Figure 3. Proposed Architecture

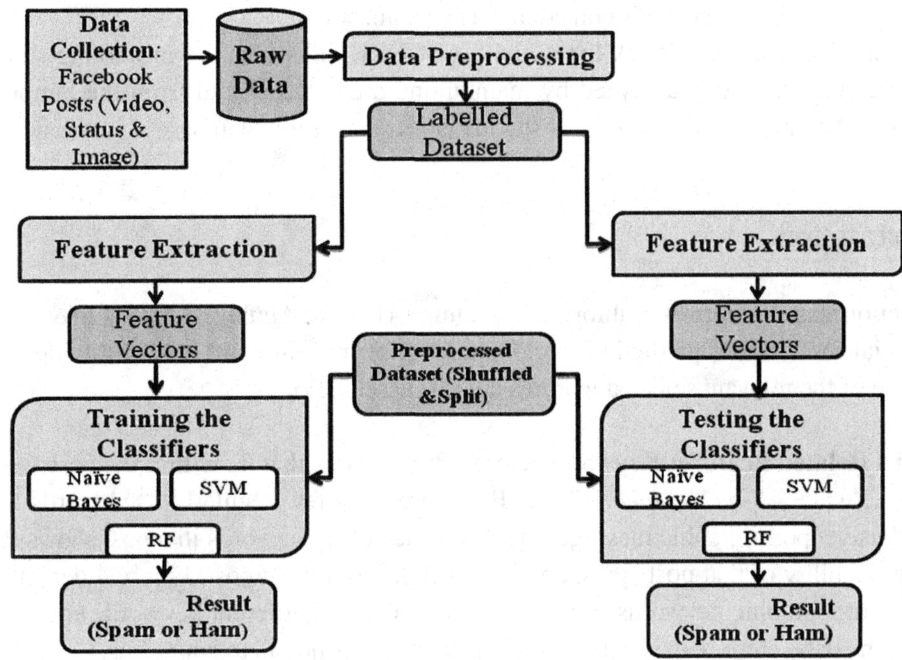

Data Preprocessing

The input for this section is raw extracted as well as repository provided dataset, which is pre-processed to make use of it while classifying to ham and spam post. Various pre-processing steps are involved during this process as detailed below-

- **Removing Stop-Words:** Stop-words (Lo et al., 2005) are the words that are commonly used but have no relevance in a language. English has some words for example: *"a", "the", "is", "was", "be", "in", "to"*. Removal of these words is necessary because by removing such words important words can be focused that are present within the sentences and which are critical for the spam detection.
- **Stemming:** Stemming is a heuristic process which groups different words with the same root together. On applying stemming derivate affixes are being chopped off from the word. For example: *"working", "worked", "works"* can be grouped to root word as *"work"*.
- **Lemmatization:** Lemmatization is the process to return the base of the word by applying morphological analysis and vocabulary search. Therefore it is termed as the lemma. For example: when on word *"toughest"* lemmatization is applied it returns *"tough"* or *"tougher"* on the basis that the used token is grammatically occurring or morphologically fit to our requirement.
- **Photo Pre-Processing:** The photo is compared by using the color value of every single expected pixel and actual pixel present in that image. If certain expected pixels differ from the actual pixels then the check fails and hence is considered as a spam.
- **URL Links Blacklisting:** Black list is the list of URL links who are promoting spam on daily basis. Such urls are being analyzed by maintaining a database build from the famous antivirus websites and comparing the results. If the url is present in this database it is considered to be a spam url.

Feature Extraction

Feature extraction stage comprises of informative features (Bhat & Abulaish, 2013; Lin & Huang, 2013) that are essential for a higher prediction rate. Features play an important role in the identification of spam and some of the relevant selected features are discussed below.

- **Keyword Related Feature:** Keywords refer to those words that lie within the posts/reviews such as *"buy", "vote", "free", "iphone"* etc. But there exist few regularly used words as a part of spam/ abusive/ pornographic messages. The presence of these words in a post shows that there is a high probability of that post is a spam/ abusive/ pornographic post. Figure 4 depicts frequency count of pornographic keywords from a scale of 0-1000 of different keywords encountered after cleaning the data. Here, x-axis contains words, and y-axis points to count hits.
- **Profile Related Feature:** Profile demographic related feature is important information that can be used for detecting spam posts which includes the *"name of account", "length of the username", "average time between posts"*. For example, Facebook page with popular football club name *"FC Barcelona"* has comparatively more pages created than the less popular club name *"Dempo Sports Club"*. Using this information, the profiles which accounts support spam content on their Facebook pages can be identified. Figure 5 shows the importance of profile related features (such

as "username", "age", "birthday", "gender", "length of username") with respect to the individual percentage of information (such as "username" occurs with 60%, "gender" occurs with 75%) in overall Facebook posts.

Figure 4. Pornographic/ Spam Keyword Frequency Hits Depending on the Most Occurring Keywords in a Post

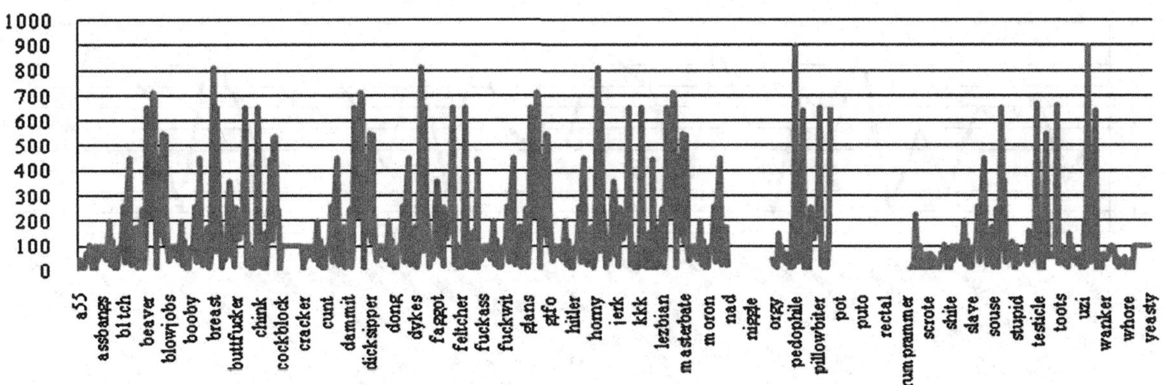

Figure 5. Percentage of Information Extracted Using Profile Related Features

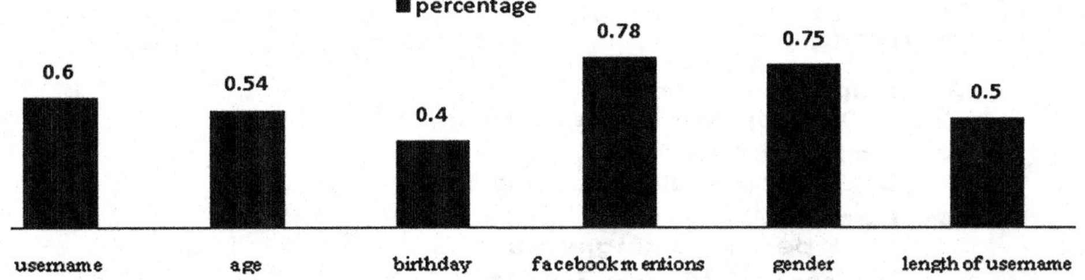

- **Content Related Feature:** Content related features includes text attributes (*"text post length"* etc.), photo attributes (*"name of photo", "caption attached" etc.*), videos attributes (*"video length", "source" etc.*). For example, consider post- *Buy new iphone 7 exclusively for 50k*, click on- "https://fastfilez.com/9L4U" which is analyzed to know whether post is spam or not.
- **URL Related Feature:** URL mentioned in the posts contains many number of characters, length of the link, number of links. For example, if a user mentions http://www.freecharge.com in his post the number url components are analysed in this process. Some of the links are already marked as bad or malicious urls in many antivirus databases and are used to find spam posts. Figure 6 shows occurrence of urls in a spam post. The x-axis represents bad urls and y-axis represents the times the url is present in spam post from a scale of 1 to 10. URLs with high peaks reflect more usage in a spam posts frequently as compared to others.
- **Trending Topics Related Feature:** Trending topics are the most recent mentioned terms on Facebook at a given time instance. Such instance can be moment, week, or month etc. The users can use the hashtag, if there are many posts containing the same term that helps the term to

become a trending topic. The endpoint search is done in the Graph API Explorer e.g. *"query = mannkibaat"* and *"related type = pages"* or *"type = groups"*, then concurrent pages and groups are displayed with their respective ids. Figure 7 shows some of the trending topics on which different users are posting their opinions.

Figure 6. Bad Urls vs. Occurrence in Spam Posts

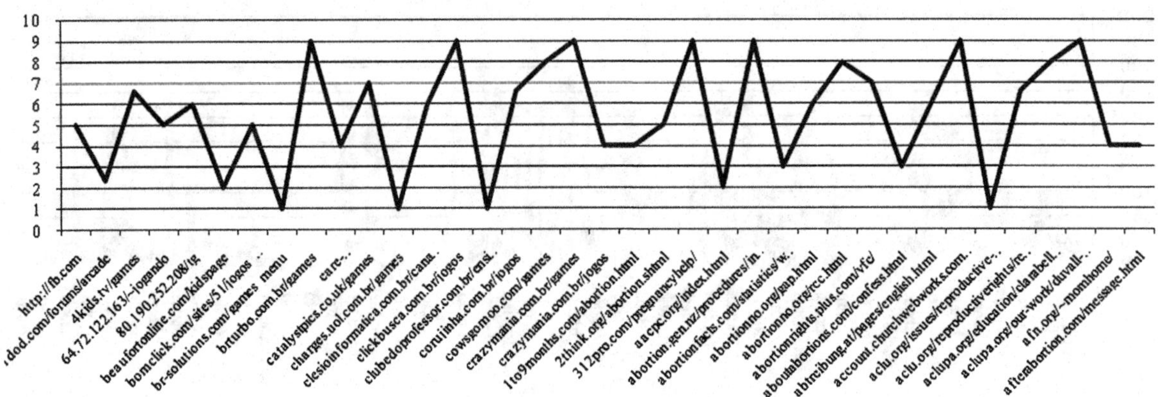

Figure 7. Trending Topics on Facebook

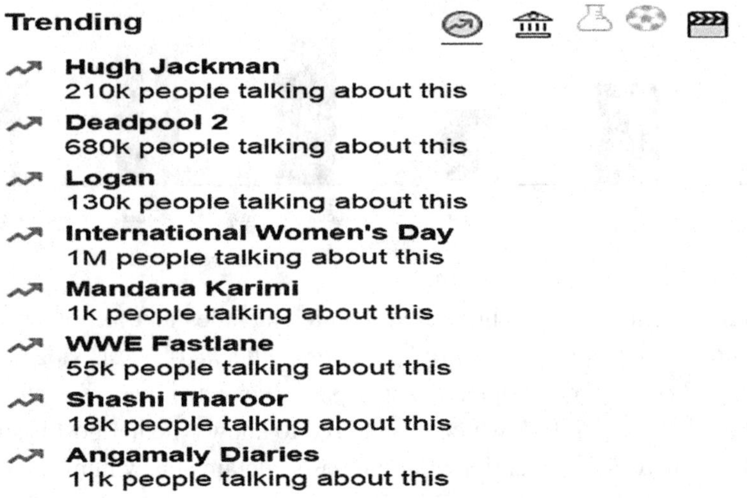

Training and Testing Using Supervised Classifiers

The entire Facebook OSN dataset is shuffled and split in varying training and test data to predict spam vs. ham posts using three supervised classifiers (NB, SVM and RF). The training and test ratio is considered as 60:40, 70:30 and 80:20 respectively. Among all, 80:20 training and test ratio gives the best result on collaborated textual, image and video features, as seen in the next section. Figure 8 shows that

ML techniques are applied to train the dataset and then three classifiers predict whether a given post is spam or ham on the test dataset.

Figure 8. Classifiers Applied to Classify Post as Spam vs. Ham

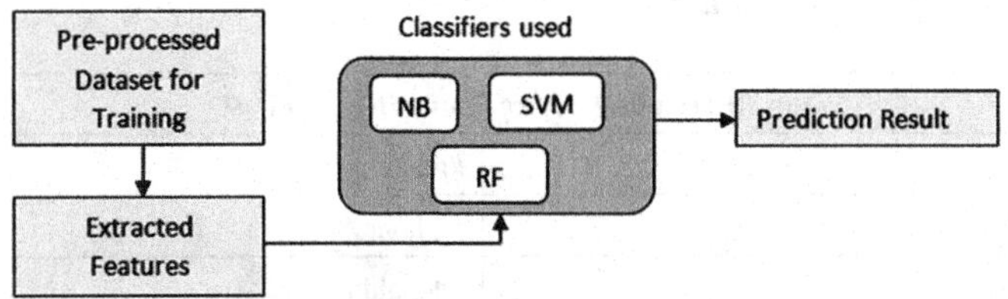

EXPERIMENTATION AND RESULTS

This section illustrates various experiments that are conducted and their corresponding results using RStudio®. Although experiments are performed on the split ratio of the dataset taken as 60:40, 70:30, 80:20 for training and test data respectively. But here the results are drawn from the 80:20 ratios as it gives the best outcomes. The following are the findings of our experimentation.

Top Frequent Keywords in Spam Posts

During the extraction of keywords as features it is observed that most spammers use common words to draw the attention of the users of the platform. It is being experimented that some words such as *"click-here"*, *"free"*, *"hurry"* are usually found in a spam post to trick the users of Facebook. Table 2 shows the top 20 most occurring keywords that are found in spam posts.

Table 2. Top 20 Most Occurring Keywords in Spam Posts

Top 20 Most Occurring Keywords in a Spam Post			
Guarantee	Free	Offer	Save
Winner	Sex	Call	Unlimited
Hurry	Gift	Apply	Viagra
Clickhere	Try	invest	Doorstep
Congratulation	Porn	Alert	iphone7

Top Trending Topics in Spam Posts

The most recent topics which are gathering big attention of the users of the Facebook are termed in the trending topics. These topics may usually last for a day, week or a month. The users can use the hashtag symbol *"#"*, to address a trending topic. These topics are used to extract similar posts on the Facebook and are used as raw data. It is being noted that with the release of iphone7 there is a tremendous growth in the page creation, posts about the release, it features and specifications. Many such topics are centre of attraction and a way to propagate more spam posts on the network. Table 3 shows some of these trending topics that are found in spam posts.

Table 3. Top 10 Trending Topics in Spam Posts

Top 10 Trending Topics Found in Spam Post	
#stocknews	#mannkibaat
#upelections	#iphone7
#uefachampionsleague	#donaldtrump
#narendramodi	#jammuandkashmir
#coldplay	#bahubali2

Percentage of URL Links for Spam Content

Post containing url links have high possibility of containing spam content than a normal post with no url. According to the 17,112 urls that are found in the total data, 11,652 are supporting spam content and 5,460 are the ones with the non-spam content. Figure 9 shows percentage of URL links supporting spam content.

Figure 9. Percentage of URL Links Supporting Spam Content

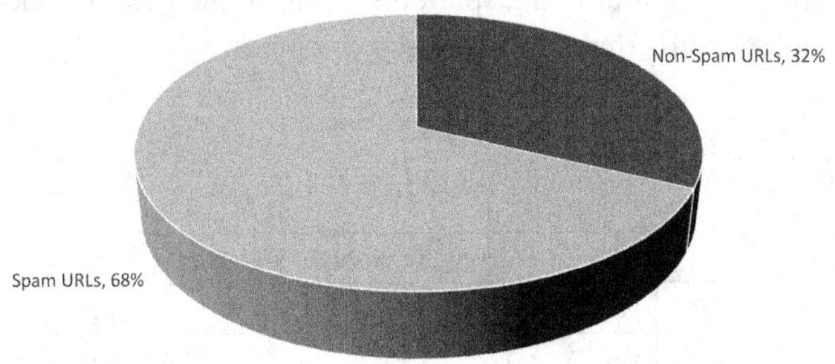

Overall Features for Spam Posts

The feature extraction phase contains total of 30 features to determine whether a post is spam or not. Table 4 lists all of these 30 features.

Top Informative Features for Spam Posts

Among all the 30 features, top 10 features are listed that are extracted as most informative features for spam detection. Table 5 lists these top 10 most informative features for spam content.

Table 4. Overall 30 Features Extracted

List of Features Used	
Textual	text length, tag person name, time, location, comments, via field, post length, links mentioned, facebook mentions, shared_stories
Image	name of the photo, caption attached, tagged person name, links references, location date, time posted, comments on the photos, URL link, length of link
Video	name of the video, video length, caption, location, date mentioned, source, live (real-time streaming videos), characters in URL, URL link, length of link, tags, time posted,

Table 5. TOP 10 Most Informative Features

Most Informative 10 Features
Shared_stories
name of the account
number of urls
Comments
length of url name of photo
video length
status tag
Caption
Real-time streaming video

Combination of all three features (Text, Image and Video)

Standard metrics (Precision, Recall and F-measure) are used for measuring the usefulness of our detection scheme on the combined features- textual, image and video features. Table 6 shows the confusion matrix for our spam detection system.

Table 6. Confusion Matrix Table

	Prediction	
	Spam	*Non Spam*
Spam	*TP*	*TN*
Non spam	*FP*	*FN*

Here,

- **TP:** TP represents true positive i.e. number of spam messages that are correctly classified as spam messages

- **TN:** TN represents true negative i.e. number of spam messages that are falsely classified as non-spam messages
- **FP:** FP represents false positive i.e. number of non-spam messages that are falsely classified as spam messages
- **FN:** FN represents false negative i.e. number of non-spam messages that are correctly classified as non-spam.

Hence, standard metrics are defined as:

- **Precision:** Model precision is defined as number of successful classification divided by number of classification, as seen in equation *(5)*

$$\text{Precision} = \text{TP} / (\text{TP} + \text{FP}) \tag{5}$$

- **Recall:** Model recall is defined as number of positive predictions that are successfully retrieved, as seen in equation *(6)*

$$\text{Recall} = \text{TP} / (\text{TP} + \text{FN}) \tag{6}$$

- **F-Measure:** Model F-measure is defined as weighted average of precision and recall, as seen in equation *(7)*

$$F\text{-}measure = 2.\frac{\Pr ecision.\operatorname{Re} call}{\Pr ecision + \operatorname{Re} call} \tag{7}$$

Table 7 shows the overall precision, recall and F-score values that are obtained for classifiers (NB, SVM and RF) while considering combined features- textual, image and video features.

Table 7. Classification Results using Combined Features

Classifier Used	Precision	Recall	F-Measure
NB	0.69	0.56	0.64
SVM	0.78	0.76	0.81
RF	0.88	0.86	**0.89**

In addition, classification results using F-score are also achieved for individual and combined features on all three classifiers. Figure 10 shows RF has outperformed SVM and NB when applied on the different features set. Image feature and video feature clearly shows that NB is not so effective in finding the spam posts. Although using textual features, SVM shows good results, but when combined features are considered then RF is the best classifier among all with F-score of 89.4%.

Figure 10. F-score vs. Features Category Graph on Three Classifiers

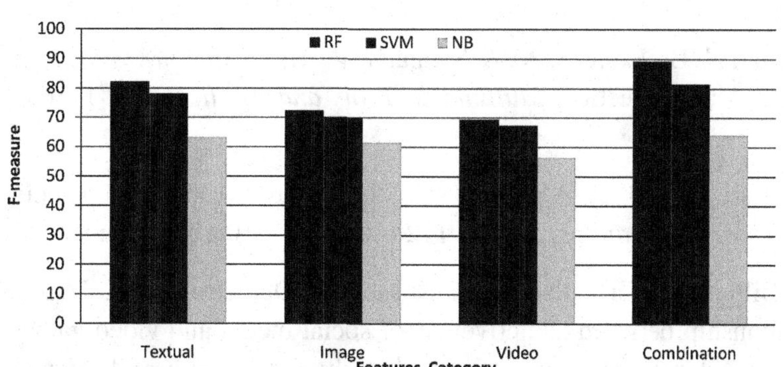

CONCLUSION

With the wide-spread popularity of Online Social Network (OSN), huge interest among spammers within OSN is also raising at an alarming rate. Particularly, Facebook has been experiencing wide spam threats from the past decade. This research work shows how spam posts on Facebook OSN can be detected using supervised machine learning techniques- (NB, SVM and RF) while combining textual, image and video features altogether using RStudio®. For this purpose, raw data of 1.5 million posts & comments is collected (both archival and real-time) from the Facebook Graph API. The Data Pre-processing stage comprises of stop-words removal, stemming, lemmatization, photo pre-processing and url link blacklisting. Feature extraction includes- keywords feature, profile related feature, content related feature, URL related feature and trending topics related feature. The entire data is then shuffled and split in varying training and test data. Among all, 80:20 training and test ratio gives the best result on collaborated textual, image and video features. Out of total 30 features, 10 features are considered as the best informative features for identification of spam vs. legitimate posts. The top 20 most occurring keywords and top 10 trending topics that are found in spam posts are also filtered out. F-score on individual and combined features are computed for all the three classifiers. RF has outperformed SVM and NB when applied on the different features set. Image feature and video feature clearly shows that NB is not so effective in finding the spam posts. Although using textual features, SVM shows good results, but when combined features are considered then RF is the best classifier among all with F-score of 89.4%. In future, researchers may explore with the combined (textual, image and video) features for spam detection over Facebook, Twitter or any other OSN using semi-supervised and unsupervised techniques.

FUTURE DIRECTIONS

In future, researchers may explore with the combined (textual, image and video) features for spam detection not only on Facebook OSN but also on other OSNs. These OSNs include Twitter, Google Plus, Linkedln, YouTube, Instagram, Tumblr, Pinterest. Researchers may apply certain other supervised techniques (such as discriminant analysis, nearest neighbours), semi-supervised techniques (such as bootstrapping), and/or unsupervised techniques (such as clustering, mixture models, generative adversarial networks, expectation maximization algorithm).

REFERENCES

Adewole, K. S., Anuar, N. B., Kamsin, A., & Sangaiah, A. K. (2017). SMSAD: A framework for spam message and spam account detection. *Multimedia Tools and Applications*, 1–36. doi:10.100711042-017-5018-x

Ahmed, F., & Abulaish, M. (2013). A generic statistical approach for spam detection in online social networks. *Computer Communications*, *36*(10), 1120–1129. doi:10.1016/j.comcom.2013.04.004

Andreassen, C. S., Billieux, J., Griffiths, M. D., Kuss, D. J., Demetrovics, Z., Mazzoni, E., & Pallesen, S. (2016). The relationship between addictive use of social media and video games and symptoms of psychiatric disorders: A large-scale cross-sectional study. *Psychology of Addictive Behaviors*, *30*(2), 252–262. doi:10.1037/adb0000160 PMID:26999354

Benevenuto, F., Rodrigues, T., Almeida, V., Almeida, J., & Gonçalves, M. (2009). Detecting spammers and content promoters in online video social networks. In *Proceedings of the 32nd International ACM SIGIR Conference on Research and Development in Information Retrieval*. New York: ACM.

Bhat, S. Y., & Abulaish, M. (2013). Community-based features for identifying spammers in online social networks. In *Proceedings of the International Conference on Advances in Social Networks Analysis and Mining*. IEEE. 10.1145/2492517.2492567

Breiman, L. (2001). Random forests. *Machine Learning*, *45*(1), 5–32. doi:10.1023/A:1010933404324

Brown, G., Howe, T., Ihbe, M., Prakash, A., & Borders, K. (2008). Social networks and context-aware spam. In *Proceedings of the ACM conference on Computer Supported Cooperative Work*. ACM.

Chan, P. P., Yang, C., Yeung, D. S., & Ng, W. W. (2015). Spam filtering for short messages in adversarial environment. *Neurocomputing*, *155*, 167–176. doi:10.1016/j.neucom.2014.12.034

Chu, Z., Widjaja, I., & Wang, H. (2012). Detecting social spam campaigns on twitter. In *Proceedings of International Conference on Applied Cryptography and Network Security*. Singapore: Springer. 10.1007/978-3-642-31284-7_27

Cresci, S., Di Pietro, R., Petrocchi, M., Spognardi, A., & Tesconi, M. (2017). The paradigm-shift of social spambots: Evidence, theories, and tools for the arms race. In *Proceedings of the 26th International Conference on World Wide Web Companion*. ACM.

DeBarr, D., & Wechsler, H. (2010). Using social network analysis for spam detection. *Advances in Social Computing*, 62–69.

Egele, M., Stringhini, G., Kruegel, C., & Vigna, G. (2017). Towards detecting compromised accounts on social networks. *IEEE Transactions on Dependable and Secure Computing*, *14*(4), 447–460. doi:10.1109/TDSC.2015.2479616

El-Alfy, E. S. M., & Al-Hasan, A. A. (2016). Spam filtering framework for multimodal mobile communication based on dendritic cell algorithm. *Future Generation Computer Systems*, *64*, 98–107. doi:10.1016/j.future.2016.02.018

Ezpeleta, E., Zurutuza, U., & Hidalg, J. M. G. (2016). A study of the personalization of spam content using facebook public information. *Logic Journal of the IGPL*, *25*(1), 30–41. doi:10.1093/jigpal/jzw040

Galán-García, P., Puerta, J. G. D. L., Gómez, C. L., Santos, I., & Bringas, P. G. (2016). Supervised machine learning for the detection of troll profiles in twitter social network: Application to a real case of cyberbullying. *Logic Journal of the IGPL*, *24*(1), 42–53.

Gao, H., Chen, Y., Lee, K., Palsetia, D., & Choudhary, A. (2012). Towards online spam filtering in social networks. In *Proceedings of the Network & Distributed System Security Symposium (NDSS)*. ACM.

He, Q., Glas, C. A., Kosinski, M., Stillwell, D. J., & Veldkamp, B. P. (2014). Predicting self-monitoring skills using textual posts on Facebook. *Computers in Human Behavior*, *33*, 69–78. doi:10.1016/j.chb.2013.12.026

Jeong, S., Noh, G., Oh, H., & Kim, C. K. (2016). Follow spam detection based on cascaded social information. *Information Sciences*, *369*, 481–499. doi:10.1016/j.ins.2016.07.033

Jin, X., Lin, C., Luo, J., & Han, J. (2011). A data mining-based spam detection system for social media networks. In *Proceedings of the VLDB Endowment*. ACM.

Lee, K., Caverlee, J., & Webb, S. (2010). Uncovering social spammers: social honeypots+ machine learning. In *Proceedings of the 33rd International ACM SIGIR Conference on Research and Development in Information Retrieval*. ACM. 10.1145/1835449.1835522

Lin, P. C., & Huang, P. M. (2013). A study of effective features for detecting long-surviving twitter spam accounts. In *Proceedings of the 15thInternational Conference on Advanced Communication Technology (ICACT)*. IEEE.

Lo, R. T. W., He, B., & Ounis, L. (2005). Automatically building a stopword list for an information retrieval system. *Journal on Digital Information Management*, *5*, 17-24.

Martinez-Romo, J., & Araujo, L. (2013). Detecting malicious tweets in trending topics using a statistical analysis of language. *Expert Systems with Applications*, *40*(8), 2992–3000. doi:10.1016/j.eswa.2012.12.015

McCord, M., & Chuah, M. (2011). Spam detection on twitter using traditional classifiers. In *Proceedings of the International Conference on Autonomic and Trusted Computing*. Springer. 10.1007/978-3-642-23496-5_13

Meligy, A. M., Ibrahim, H. M., & Torky, M. F. (2015). A framework for detecting cloning attacks in OSN based on a novel social graph topology. *International Journal of Intelligent Systems and Applications*, *7*(3), 13–20. doi:10.5815/ijisa.2015.03.02

Panicker, N. J., & Devadas, L. (2015). Filtering the walls in online social networks. *International Journal of Advanced Research in Computer Science and Software Engineering*, *5*(5), 45–52.

Prieto, M. V., Alvarez, M., & Cacheda, F. (2013). Detecting linkedin spammers and its spam nets. *International Journal of Advanced Computer Science and Applications*, *4*(9), 189–199.

Rajalaxmi, R. R., & Ramesh, A. (2014). Binary bat approach for effective spam classification in online social networks. *Australian Journal of Basic and Applied Sciences*, *8*(18), 383–388.

Shalev-Shwartz, S., & Ben-David, S. (2014). *Understanding machine learning: From theory to algorithms*. New York: Cambridge University Press. doi:10.1017/CBO9781107298019

Soman, S. J., & Murugappan, S. (2014). A study of spam detection algorithm on social media networks. *Journal of Computational Science, 10*(10), 2135–2140. doi:10.3844/jcssp.2014.2135.2140

Song, J., Lee, S., & Kim, J. (2011). Spam filtering in twitter using sender-receiver relationship. In Recent advances in intrusion detection (pp. 301-317). Springer Berlin/Heidelberg. doi:10.1007/978-3-642-23644-0_16

Stein, T., Chen, E., & Mangla, K. (2011). Facebook immune system. In *Proceedings of the 4th Workshop on Social Network Systems* (pp. 8). ACM.

Stringhini, G., Kruegel, C., & Vigna, G. (2010). Detecting spammers on social networks. In *Proceedings of the 26th Annual Computer Security Applications Conference (ACSAC)*. Austin, TX: ACM.

Swami, A. D., & Khade, B. S. (2014). A text based filtering system for OSN user walls. *International Journal of Advanced Research in Computer Science and Software Engineering, 4*(2).

Tayal, D. K., Jain, A., Arora, S., Agarwal, S., Gupta, T., & Tyagi, N. (2015). Crime detection and criminal identification in India using data mining techniques. *AI & Society, 30*(1), 117–127. doi:10.100700146-014-0539-6

Thomas, K., Grier, C., Ma, J., Paxson, V., & Song, D. (2011). Design and evaluation of a real-time url spam filtering service. In *Security and Privacy (SP), 2011 IEEE Symposium on*. IEEE. 10.1109/SP.2011.25

Xu, H., Sun, W., & Javaid, A. (2016). Efficient spam detection across online social networks. In *Proceedings of the International Conference on Big Data Analysis (ICBDA)*. IEEE. 10.1109/ICBDA.2016.7509829

Yang, C., Harkreader, R., & Gu, G. (2011). Die free or live hard? empirical evaluation and new design for fighting evolving twitter spammers. In Recent Advances in Intrusion Detection (pp. 318-337). Springer Berlin/Heidelberg.

Yardi, S., Romero, D., Schoenebeck, G., & Boyd, D. (2009). Detecting spam in a twitter network. *First Monday, 15*(1). doi:10.5210/fm.v15i1.2793

Yoon, J. W., Kim, H., & Huh, J. H. (2010). Hybrid spam filtering for mobile communication. *Computers & Security, 29*(4), 446-459.

Zhang, H. Y., & Wang, W. (2009). Application of Bayesian method to spam SMS filtering. In *Information Engineering and Computer Science, 2009. ICIECS 2009. International Conference on*. IEEE. 10.1109/ICIECS.2009.5365176

Zhu, T., Gao, H., Yang, Y., Bu, K., Chen, Y., Downey, D., ... Choudhary, A. N. (2016). Beating the artificial chaos: Fighting OSN spam using its own templates. *IEEE/ACM Transactions on Networking, 24*(6), 3856–3869. doi:10.1109/TNET.2016.2557849

ADDITIONAL READING

Chapelle, O., Schölkopf, B., & Zien, A. (2006). Semi-supervised learning. *Adaptive Computation and Machine Learning series*.

Hinton, G. E., & Sejnowski, T. J. (Eds.). (1999). *Unsupervised learning: foundations of neural computation*. MIT Press.

ENDNOTES

1 http://socialnetworking.lovetoknow.com/about-social-networking/definition-online-social-networking
2 https://www.technologyreview.com/s/403272/who-are-the-spammers/
3 https://www.statista.com/statistics/272014/global-social-networks-ranked-by-number-of-users/
4 http://www.journalism.org/2013/10/24/the-role-of-news-on-facebook/
5 ham- legitimate message which doesn't contain malicious text, image or video content
6 https://www.rstudio.com/
7 https://developers.facebook.com/tools-and-support/

This research was previously published in Social Network Analytics for Contemporary Business Organizations; pages 51-70, copyright year 2018 by Business Science Reference (an imprint of IGI Global).

Chapter 38
Performance Prediction and Optimization of Solar Water Heater via a Knowledge-Based Machine Learning Method

Hao Li
University of Texas at Austin, USA

Zhijian Liu
North China Electric Power University, China

ABSTRACT

Measuring the performance of solar energy and heat transfer systems requires a lot of time, economic cost, and manpower. Meanwhile, directly predicting their performance is challenging due to the complicated internal structures. Fortunately, a knowledge-based machine learning method can provide a promising prediction and optimization strategy for the performance of energy systems. In this chapter, the authors show how they utilize the machine learning models trained from a large experimental database to perform precise prediction and optimization on a solar water heater (SWH) system. A new energy system optimization strategy based on a high-throughput screening (HTS) process is proposed. This chapter consists of: 1) comparative studies on varieties of machine learning models (artificial neural networks [ANNs], support vector machine [SVM], and extreme learning machine [ELM]) to predict the performances of SWHs; 2) development of an ANN-based software to assist the quick prediction; and 3) introduction of a computational HTS method to design a high-performance SWH system.

INTRODUCTION

Predicting the thermal performance of solar energy systems is of huge challenge due to the complexity of the internal structures. In fact, the measurement of thermal performances of a typical solar energy system (*e.g.*, solar water heater (SWH)) requires a lot of time, economic costs and labors. Due to the

DOI: 10.4018/978-1-6684-6291-1.ch038

complicated structures, conventional physical and mathematical models usually fail to estimate their thermal performances. These problems not only dramatically hinder the acquisition of the thermal performances of solar energy systems, but also block the possibility of optimizing their thermal performance.

In the past decades, scientists have come up with a powerful prediction method to address these problems. People found that a knowledge-based machine learning model can help precisely predict the performances of some energy systems utilizing some simple independent variables as the computational inputs. With a proper machine learning algorithm, people only need to acquire a sufficient experimental database as well as perform the model training and testing, and then a predictive model can be acquired. During the training process, machine learning can "learn" the non-linear relationship between the independent and dependent variables via a "black box" fitting, and subsequently perform the predictions. The research group of Prof. S. Kalogirou, from Cyprus University of Technology, has conducted a majority of the pioneer application research on the prediction of thermal performances for energy systems (Kalogirou, 1999), leading to huge positive engineering impacts during the last two decades. Subsequently, relevant studies have become increasingly popular all over the world. Meanwhile, there are more and more new or revised machine learning algorithms developed. Among various machine learning approaches, there are some most widely used algorithms, such as artificial neural network (ANN) (Kalogirou, 1999), support vector machine (SVM) (Suykens & Vandewalle, 1999) and extreme learning machine (ELM) (Huang et al., 2006). ANN is the most prevalent algorithm due to its long history and powerful predictive capacity. The general schematic structure of an ANN model is presented in Figure 1.

Figure 1. General schematic structure of a typical ANN model. The empty circles represent the neurons. All the neurons interconnect with other neurons in the adjacent layer(s). Each neuron in the input layer represents an independent variable. The neuron in the output layer represents the dependent variable.
Reproduced with permission from Reference (Li, Liu, Liu, & Zhang, 2017).

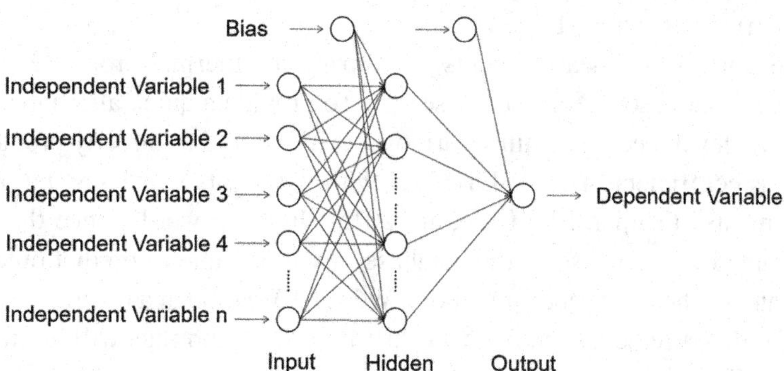

So far, despite the great progress of machine learning, engineering and industrial requirements have been rising in recent years: how to cost-effectively design and optimize a solar energy system by utilizing machine learning? Now, machine learning is a proven powerful tool for varieties of numerical predictions, and people are trying to make full use of its predictive power, as well as provide a good optimization strategy in order to acquire higher performances. Nevertheless, to the best of the authors' knowledge, very few research reports have mainly focused on the relevant studies (Peng & Ling, 2008). Recently, the authors have found that with a sufficiently large experimental database, the machine learning models are not only able to give excellent predictive performance for SWHs, but also assist an efficient and promising optimization of the thermal performances of SWHs, with the usage of a high-throughput screening (HTS) process (Zhijian Liu, Li, Liu, Yu, & Cheng, 2017). This is, so far, the first study of HTS on the optimization of energy system.

SWH is one of the most popular techniques where the solar collectors and concentrators are employed to gather, store, and utilize solar radiation to heat air or water (Mekhilef, Saidur, & Safari, 2011). Among several different types of stationary collectors, the evacuated tube solar collectors are featured by the edges of lowering the heat loss coefficient and lower economic cost than other conventional flat plate collectors. In lots of countries, the all-glass evacuated tubular solar water heaters are particularly popular due to the good thermal performance, easy installation, and good transportability. The annual production of evacuated solar tubes kept growing in lots of developing countries (*e.g.*, China) and the market share of them kept increasing at rapid speed during the past decades (Tang, Li, Zhong, & Lan, 2006).

In this Chapter, all the studies will focus on a typical SWH, the water-in-glass evacuated tube solar water heater (WGET-SWH, Figure 2). The reasons why WGET-SWH was selected as a case study are as below: i) WGET-SWH is one of the most common SWHs in developing countries; ii) experimental measurements of WGET-SWH's thermal performances is time-consuming and tedious; and iii) several most significant thermal properties (*e.g.*, heat collection rate and heat loss coefficient) of WGET-SWH have not been well-studied. In the authors' previous studies, the properties of 915 WGET-SWHs were experimentally measured according to a National Standard of China (GB/T 19141)(Zhijian Liu, Li, Zhang, Jin, & Cheng, 2015). The measured properties include heat collection rates (daily heat collection per square meter of a solar water system, MJ/m^2), heat loss coefficients (the average heat loss per unit, $W/(m^3K)$), tube length (mm), number of tubes, tube center distance (mm), tank volume (maximum mass of water in tank, kg), collector area (m^2), tilting angle (°) and final temperature (°C). Except the heat collection rate and heat loss coefficient, all other properties were measured by the "portable test instruments" (Table 1). Descriptive statistics of the measured data (maximum, minimum, range, average and standard deviation) are shown in Table 2.

According to the standard of measurements, measuring the thermal properties of a WGET-SWH requires around 15 days and a series of tedious setups. To provide a quick alternative for the measurement, the authors have developed a machine learning-based method to directly predict the heat collection rate and heat loss coefficient of a WGET-SWH with the inputs which can be measured from the "portable test instruments" (Zhijian Liu, Li, et al., 2015). In other words, once the machine learning model is properly trained with the use of the database, it will be able to predict quickly and precisely the heat collection rate and heat loss coefficient of a WGET-SWH. Such a novel measurement will help effectively reduce the measurement time from weeks to seconds, and thus will dramatically accelerate the measurements of SWHs in both industrial and commercial applications. More details will be introduced in the following Sections.

As a part of the handbook, here, the authors aim to present the predictive power of machine learning in the prediction and optimization of the thermal performances of SWHs, as well as pick the research of WGET-SWH as a case study. The content of this Chapter consists of three parts: i) Comparative studies on varieties of machine learning models (ANNs, SVM and ELM) to predict the thermal performances of SWHs; ii) Development of an ANN-based software to assist the quick and accurate prediction and iii) Introduction of a computational HTS strategy to design and optimize a high-performance SWH system.

Figure 2. Schematic picture of a representative WGET-SWH
Reproduced with permission from Reference (Zhijian Liu, Li, Liu, et al., 2017).

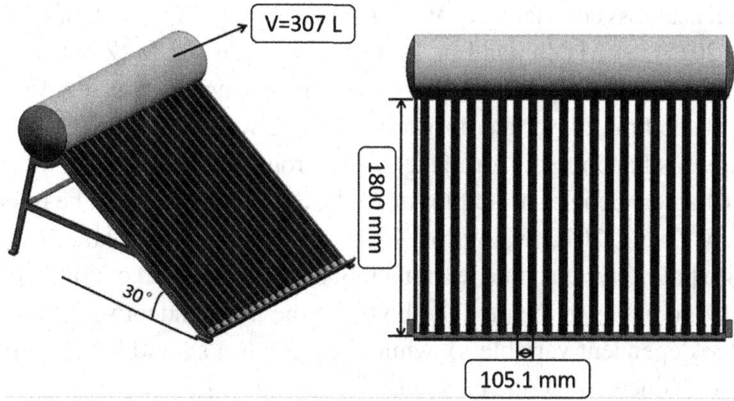

Table 1. "Portable test instruments" for measuring the properties of WGET-SWHs

Parameters	Portable Test Instruments	Accuracy
Final temperate of water	Digital thermoelectric thermometer	±0.5%
Tank Volume	Electric platform scale	±1.0%
Diameter, tube center distance, tube length, collector area	Taper ZSH-3	±0.5%

Reproduced with permission from Reference (Zhijian Liu, Li, et al., 2015).

Table 2. Descriptive statistics of the variables for 915 samples of WGET-SWHs

Items	Tube Length (mm)	Number of Tubes	TCD (mm)	Tank Volume (kg)	Collector Area (m^2)	Angle (°)	Final Temp. (°C)	HCR (MJ/m^2)	HLC (W/ (m^3K))
Maximum	2200	64	151	403	8.24	85	62	11.3	13
Minimum	1600	5	60	70	1.27	30	46	6.7	8
Range	600	59	91	333	6.97	55	16	4.6	5
Average	1811	21	76.2	172	2.69	46	53	8.9	10
Standard deviation	87.8	5.8	5.11	47.0	0.73	3.89	2.0	0.48	0.77

Reproduced with permission from Reference (Zhijian Liu, Li, et al., 2015).

Abbreviations: TCD: tube center distance, final temp.: final temperature, HCR: heat collection rate, MJ/m^2, HLC: heat loss coefficient ($W/(m^3K)$). Tank volume was defined as the maximum mass of water in tank (kg).

BACKGROUND

Machine Learning Models

Machine learning is a powerful technique for numerical prediction, classification and pattern recognition, which has been widely used in chemical (Li et al., 2016; Li, Chen, Cheng, Zhao, & Yang, 2015), medical (Wernick, Yang, Brankov, Yourganov, & Strother, 2010), biological (Sommer & Gerlich, 2013), environmental (Zhijian Liu, Li, & Cao, 2017) and energy areas (Jordan & Mitchell, 2015; Sun, He, & Chang, 2015). In the authors' recent studies, various machine learning models were used to predict the heat collection rate and heat loss coefficient of WGET-SWH, such as ANN (Zhijian Liu, Liu, et al., 2015; Zhijian Liu, Li, et al., 2015), SVM (Zhijian Liu, Li, et al., 2015) and ELM (Z. Liu et al., 2016). In terms of ANN, several typical network algorithms were used, including general regression neural network (GRNN) (Specht, 1991) and multilayer feedforward neural network (MLFN) (Hornik, Stinchcombe, & White, 1989). Because this handbook is for readers with broad interests, details of their algorithms are not discussed in this Chapter. General principles of ANN, SVM and ELM can be referred to References (Huang, Zhou, Ding, & Zhang, 2012; Kalogirou, 1999; Suykens & Vandewalle, 1999).

Before developing a predictive machine learning model, the inputs and output(s) of the model should be rationally selected. The inputs of the models should be the independent variables that are related (or partially related) to the dependent variable(s), while the output(s) should be the dependent variable(s) that should be predicted. Since one of the basic missions of machine learning is to help people acquire the knowledge that are hard to be measured or observed, it is strongly recommended that the dependent variable(s) should be the properties that are experimentally hard to be detected (if the expected dependent variable(s) can be easily acquired from experiments or can be precisely predicted by multiple linear regression or any physical models, bring in machine learning again would be a waste of time).

Development of a machine learning model for numerical prediction consists of the training and testing of datasets. The training process is essentially the process of a non-linear fitting (also called a "black-box" fitting). A good training of the dataset means that the training is neither under- nor over-fitting. Usually, if the dataset for training is not sufficiently large, there will be a huge risk of over-fitting. To ensure a good training result, a high percentage of training set is usually necessary. The testing process is a process to validate if the trained model is good, utilizing the dataset that is not previously involved in the training process. By comparing the data in the testing set (also called the "actual values") with the data predicted by the training set (also called the "predicted values"), people can calculate the root mean square errors (RMS errors), prediction accuracies (with a given tolerance) and residual values. The RMS error, prediction accuracy and residual value can be calculated by Equations (1), (2) and (3), respectively:

$$RMS\ error = \sqrt{\frac{\Sigma_{i=1}^{n}\left(Z_i - O_i\right)^2}{n_{tot}}} \tag{1}$$

$$Prediction\ accuracy = \frac{n_{good}}{n_{tot}} \times 100\% \tag{2}$$

$$Residual\ value = Z_i - O_i \tag{3}$$

where Z_i and O_i are the predicted and actual values, respectively; n_{tot} is the number of tested samples; n_{good} is the number of tested samples with good predicted results under a given tolerance. Empirically, the tolerance is usually set as $\pm 30\%$.

A well-trained model is usually accompanied by the testing result with low RMS error, high prediction accuracy and low absolute values of residual. To ensure a good target model, comparing the performances of models with different training and testing percentages is necessary. On one hand, if the percentage of training set is too high, the results given by the testing set would not be reliable. On the other hand, if the percentage of training set is too low, there is a risk of over-fitting. To further show the availability of the model, a cross-validation and/or sensitivity test should be performed (Browne, 2000). However, cross-validation usually requires extremely high computational cost. If the database is very large, a regular personal computer (PC) will no longer be effective. Fortunately, it is found that if both the training and testing datasets are sufficiently large, with a robust and stable ANN algorithm (*e.g.*, GRNN), a cross-validation process can be rationally skipped after a simplified sensitivity test.

To sum up, Table 3 shows a suggested model development process. Good training and testing processes guarantee that the machine learning model can be used for practical applications. For practical applications, people only need to acquire and input the independent variables into the model, and then the dependent variable(s) will be predicted and outputted automatically.

Table 3. A recommended machine learning development process for numerical prediction

	Steps	Notes
Step 1	Preparation of experimental database	The database should be sufficiently large.
Step 2	Selection of independent and dependent variables	Independent variables should be easily-accessible.
Step 3	Model training using the training set	Different percentages of training and testing sets should be tried.
Step 4	Model testing using the testing set	
Step 5	Calculation of RMS error, prediction accuracy and residual values	If the testing results are not acceptable, the training should be performed again with different settings.
Step 6	Cross-validation and/or sensitivity test (if necessary)	NA
Step 7	Practical applications of the well-trained model	NA

High-Throughput Screening (HTS)

HTS is generally defined as a method for experimentation previously used in medical and biological sciences (Hertzberg & Pope, 2000). With some state-of-the-art devices, algorithms and/or machines, an HTS process can help us quickly screen thousands or even millions of candidates (*e.g.*, chemical compounds (Hautier, Fischer, Jain, Mueller, & Ceder, 2010), materials (Greeley, Jaramillo, Bonde, Chorkendorff, & Nørskov, 2006), genes (Colbert, 2001) and biological designs (An & Tolliday, 2010; Wahler & Reymond, 2001)) with specific target performances for practical or scientific use. At first, the HTS was just used for drug discovery. But now it has been widely used in various areas, such as computer-assisted design of materials. The rough concept of a computational HTS process is pretty simple: the calculations of all possible candidates in a short timescale (using fast algorithms) and the screening of candidates with acceptable target performances (Li et al., 2017). Previously, Greeley and his colleagues used density functional theory (DFT) calculations to screen and design thousands of bimetallic catalysts for chemical reactions via an HTS process (Greeley et al., 2006). The predicted performances of their target design were in excellent agreement with experimental validations. Ceder and his colleagues combined DFT calculations, machine learning and an HTS method to screen all the possible ternary oxide compounds in the periodic table (Hautier et al., 2010). A large database of the nature's missing ternary oxide compounds was then developed. This study indicated that a machine learning-assisted HTS process can potentially be a good method to discover human's unknown knowledge. However, though these studies successfully used the concept of HTS for new knowledge searching, in the following years, there are very few relevant studies in the engineering area, especially the field of energy system design and optimization.

In the previous Sections of this Chapter, it is shown that machine learning can potentially be a good method for thermal performance optimization of SWH. Meanwhile, it is known that the design and optimization of a high-performance SWH is particularly difficult due to its complicated internal structure. Thus, we can come up with a "bold" idea: can we use a machine learning-based HTS process to predict "infinite" possible designs of SWHs and screen the good candidates for practical use? The answer to this question will be given in the following Sections.

THERMAL PERFORMANCE PREDICTION AND OPTIMIZATION

Prediction of Thermal Performance

To find out a good machine learning model for predicting the thermal performances of WGET-SWHs, the authors have developed a series of models with the algorithms of GRNN, MLFN, SVM and ELM, respectively. The average RMSE errors and average prediction accuracies calculated from the testing results (after multiple training and testing processes) are shown in Table 4. The prediction accuracies were calculated with the tolerance of ±30%. It should be noted that all the data used for model training and testing are in the same database, as shown in Table 2. In terms of the MLFN and ELM, only the results of the best network configurations (optimal numbers of hidden layer and hidden neuron) are shown here. Surprisingly, with the tolerance of ±30%, all the four models have shown extremely good predictive performances for both heat collection rate and heat loss coefficient, with all the average prediction accuracies reach 100% (Table 4).

Table 4. Predictive performances and modeling information of GRNN, MLFN, SVM and ELM for the predictions of the heat collection rate and heat loss coefficient for WGET-SWHs

Model	Average RMS Errors (for Heat Collection Rate)	Average RMS Errors (for Heat Loss Coefficient)	Percentages of Training and Testing Sets	Average Prediction Accuracy for Heat Collection Rate	Average Prediction Accuracy for Heat Loss Coefficient
GRNN	0.33	0.71	Training set: 85%; Testing set: 15%;	100%	100%
MLFN	0.14	0.73	Training set: 85%; Testing set: 15%;	100%	100%
SVM	0.29	0.73	Training set: 85%; Testing set: 15%;	100%	100%
ELM	0.30	0.67	Training set: 85%; Testing set: 15%;	100%	100%

Data source: References from (Z. Liu et al., 2016; Zhijian Liu, Li, et al., 2015).

To show the training and testing results of the machine learning model, here, the authors pick one of the typical modeling results of an MLFN model, for the prediction of heat collection rate of WGET-SWHs (Figures 3 and 4, respectively). It can be clearly seen that, with a good ANN training process (Figure 3), the model can precisely predict the heat collection rates of the 137 data samples in a testing set (Figure 4), with relatively low absolute residual values. It should be noted that in the testing results, there are always some data points, which, more or less, deviate from the diagonal (Figure 4a). This is certainly acceptable—as gold cannot be pure and men cannot be perfect!

Figure 3. Training results of 778 samples using an MLFN model for the prediction of heat collection rate for WGET-SWHs. (a) Predicted values vs actual values; (b) residual values vs actual values; (c) residual values vs predicted values

Reproduced with permission from Reference (Zhijian Liu, Li, et al., 2015).

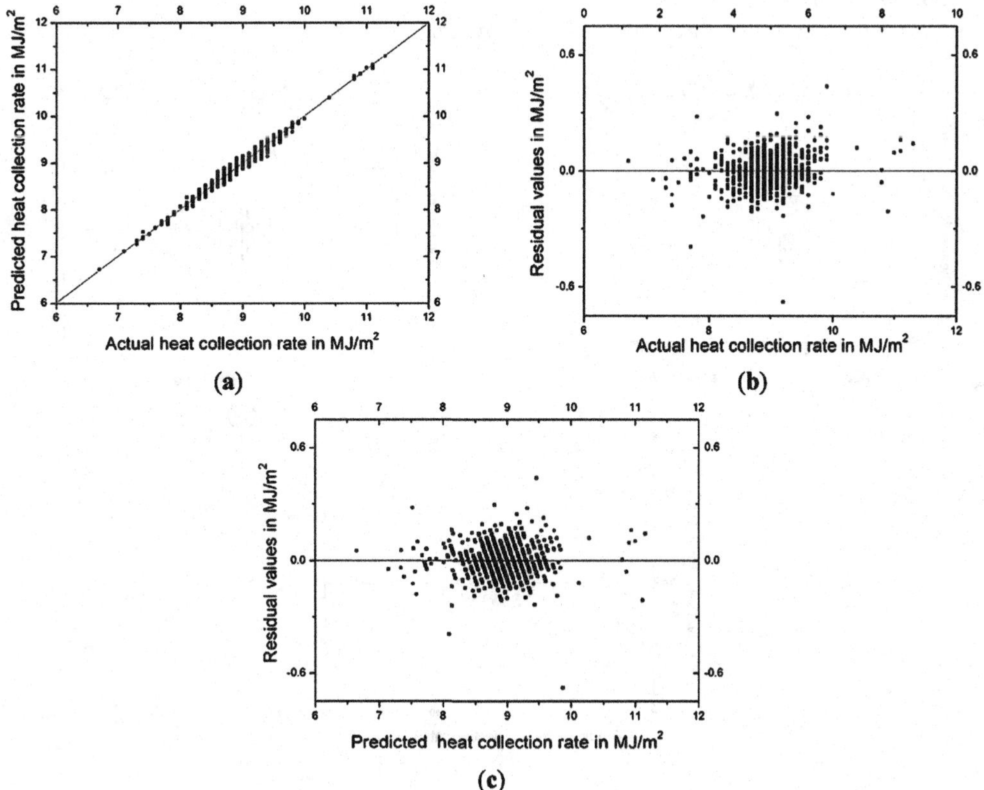

Although the performances of all the four models look quite similar (as shown in Table 4), there are still several criterions that can help us distinguish which model is the most practical one. First is the training time. As we may know, compared to GRNN and SVM, MLFN and ELM have the structures that are closer to a conventional ANN, containing undefined numbers of hidden layer and/or hidden neurons. This means that people have to compare different network configurations (*e.g.*, different number of hidden layer and/or hidden neurons) in order to get the best algorithmic structure for prediction. Compared to GRNN and SVM (which only require the training once and for all), MLFN and ELM are clearly not the best options for this case study. In terms of the comparison between GRNN and SVM, both of them have the advantage of quick training and precise prediction. It is relatively hard to decide which one is the best since they have rather similar predictive performance in this study.

So far, the conclusion here is clear: machine learning is an effective method to predict the thermal performances of WGET-SWHs. Though it is very powerful, it is still far away from real applications: officers/workers in a company or industry usually don't want to spend a lot of money to learn and purchase a machine learning or Mathlab software— either a user-friendly machine learning package or Mathlab is rather expensive. So here is a new question: how to really use this method for practical application? In the next Section, a recently-developed ANN-based software will be introduced.

Figure 4. Testing results of 137 samples using an MLFN model for the prediction of heat collection rate for WGET-SWHs. (a) Predicted values vs actual values; (b) residual values vs actual values; (c) residual values vs predicted values
Reproduced with permission from Reference (Zhijian Liu, Li, et al., 2015).

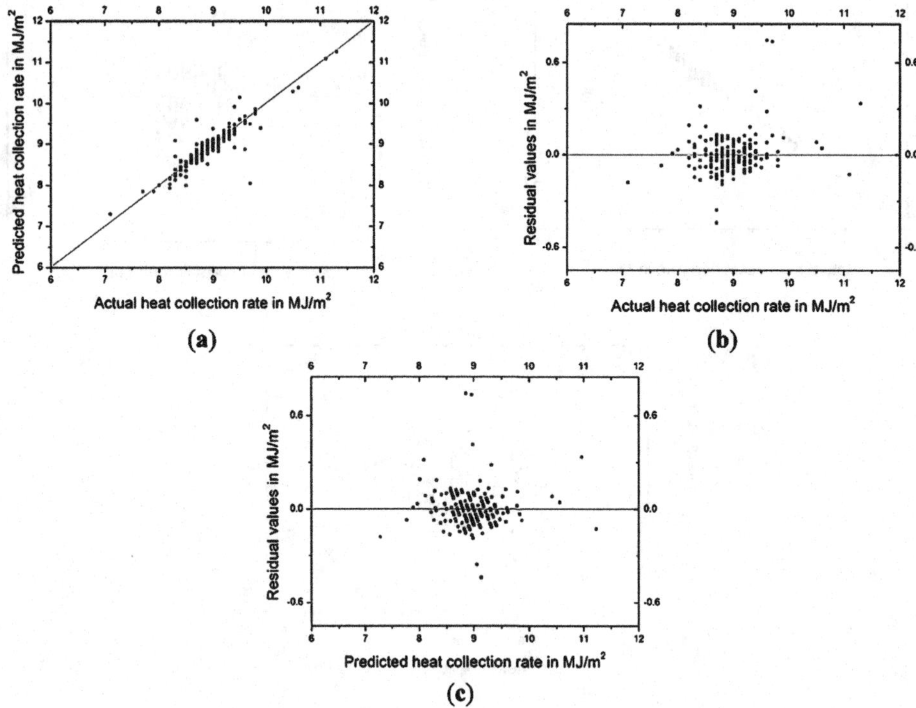

Developing an ANN-Based Software

To provide an effective support for practical applications, the authors developed an user-friendly package, *WaterHeater*, in both PC and Android platforms (Zhijian Liu, Liu, et al., 2015). The primary motivation of this study was to provide a software that could help people quickly acquire the ANN-predicted heat collection rate and heat loss coefficient of WGET-SWHs, with the simple inputs measured by the "portable test instruments" (Table 1). The reason why the authors also developed an Android-based version was that a mobile system is sometimes more user-friendly and applicable for industrial measurement (people do not always have their computers aside). Though in different platforms, there is no difference between the models inside the packages of the PC and the Android versions. With this software, people only need to use a computer or even a mobile phone to perform quick thermal measurements utilizing the "portable test instruments". The inner core of the package is a well-trained MLFN with a back-propagation algorithm and a Sigma function as the activation function. The inputs are the same as the machine learning models described in previous sections. The predictive performance of the packages was validated by the residual values calculated from the testing set (Figure 5). It should be noted that though this model has some slight deviations for predicting the heat loss coefficients when their actual values are very high or very low (Figure 5b), the general predictive performance of the network work is still acceptable for the prediction of heat loss coefficient (because most of the heat loss coefficient in the industry are around 10 W/(m^{3}K), which is neither too high nor too low). In this Section, the application of this software will be introduced. The details of software developments can be found in Reference (Zhijian Liu, Liu, et al., 2015).

Figure 5. Residual values vs. actual values in predicting (a) heat collection rates (in MJ/m^2) and (b) heat loss coefficient (in W/(m^{3}K)). All the actual values came from a testing set.
Reproduced with permission from Reference (Zhijian Liu, Liu, et al., 2015).

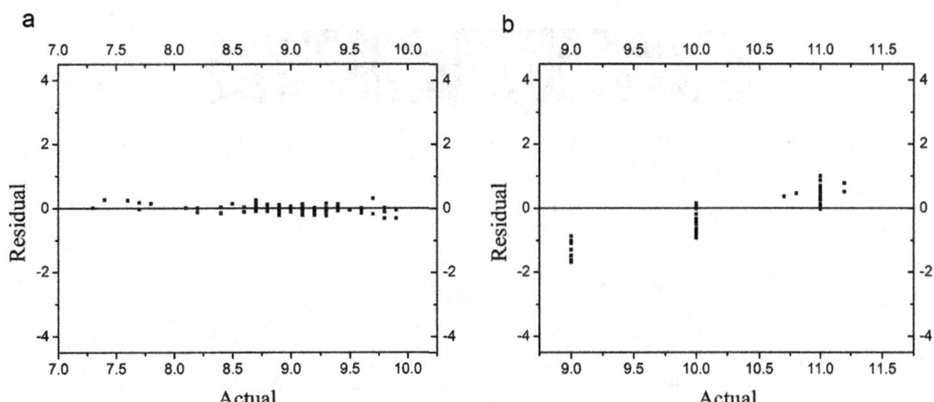

Figures 6 and 7 show the main panels of the software in PC and Android platforms, respectively. Both these two platforms consist of three parts: i) input panels, ii) output panels and iii) buttons. As their name imply, the input panel is the place for inputting independent variables, while the output panel is the place to display the dependent variables. The buttons consist of the "Reset Parameters" button and the "Start to Predict" button. By clicking the "Start to Predict" button with the values inputted in the input panel, the predicted heat collection rate and heat loss coefficient will be instantly shown in the output panel. By simply clicking the "Reset Parameters" button, all the input and output data will be erased.

Figure 6. Overview panel of "WaterHeater" in a PC platform
Reproduced with permission from Reference (Zhijian Liu, Liu, et al., 2015).

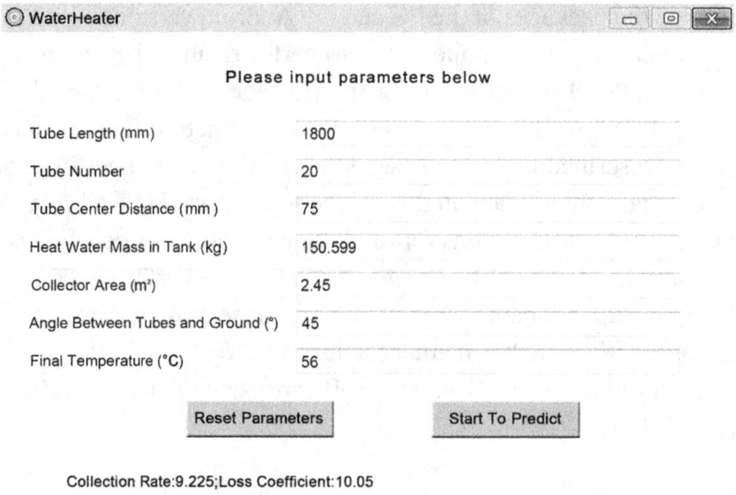

Figure 7. Overview panel of "WaterHeater" in an Android platform
Reproduced with permission from Reference (Zhijian Liu, Liu, et al., 2015).

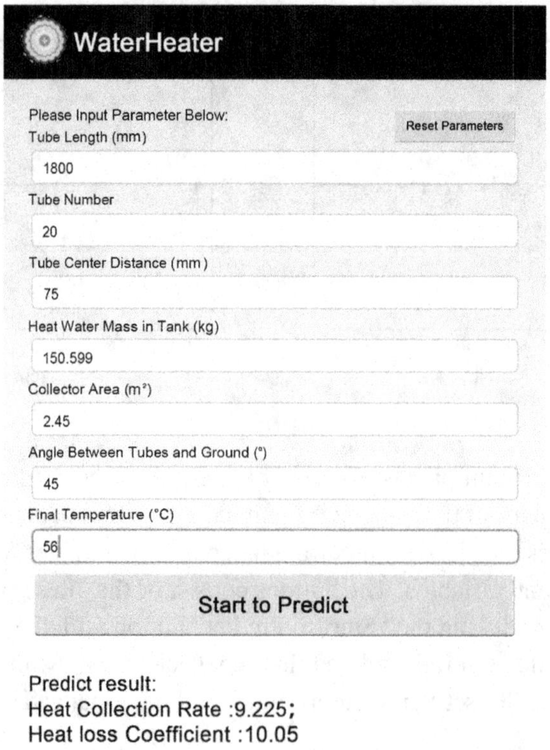

This software can provide a perfect solution for quick thermal performance estimation of WGET-SWHs. Here, a quick measurement flow chart is proposed, as shown in Figure 8. With simple measurements of independent variables using the "portable test instruments" (Table 1), fast prediction of the thermal performance of a WGET-SWH can be achieved by the software. By measuring the tube length, tube center distance, tank volume, final temperature and titling angle (between tubes and ground), the heat collection rate and heat loss efficient can be quickly predicted when all these variables are inputted into the software panel. It should be mentioned that this ANN-based method does not aim to replace the conventional measurements. Instead, it provides a quick choice to predict the thermal values for the industrial and commercial uses that require rapid estimations of thermal performances. It should be noted that, to more precisely assess the thermal performance of a WGET-SWH, standard measurements should be used (though sometimes they are very time-consuming). This software is available at http://t.cn/RLPKF08 and for the latest version, reader can contact the corresponding author of this Chapter.

Figure 8. Flow chart of the novel method using the "portable test instruments" combined with the software "WaterHeater" for the predictions of heat collection rate and heat loss coefficient
Reproduced with permission from Reference (Zhijian Liu, Liu, et al., 2015).

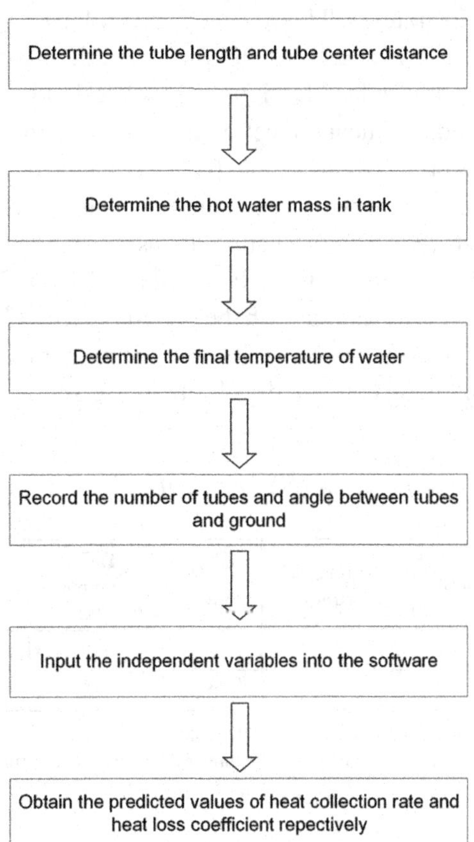

Optimizing the Thermal Performance via an HTS Strategy

It has been shown that machine learning can be such a powerful tool to predict the thermal performance of WGET-SWHs, here comes a new question: can people use this technique to predict the thermal performance of a newly designed WGET-SWH without direct experiments? The answer is yes. And it can be done in an even crazier way: screening thousands or millions of design candidates by using a well-trained machine learning model, and then selecting the candidates with good target performances. This screening strategy, as mentioned in the previous sections, is called the HTS process.

Using the optimization of heat collection rates of WGET-SWHs as a case study, the authors recently found that an HTS process with a proper ANN can be used for this mission. Usually, a high-performance WGET-SWH should have the heat collection rate as high as possible. For the screening process, the first step was to generate a large number of independent variable combinations (around 3.5×10^8 possible design combinations) as the inputs of the previously-trained ANN. Since the final temperature is not a part of the SWH installation, all the integers of final temperature between 52 and 62 °C were selected as the input. With all these independent variables (except the final temperature), people can easily construct a completed WGET-SWH in industry. The heat collection rates of the WGET-SWHs with all these possible combinations were then numerically predicted and outputted. The designed WGET-SWHs with high predicted heat collection rates will be screened and collected. For validation, the authors also experimentally installed two selected candidates and measured their thermal performances. Here, the two selected designs are respectively called "Design A" and "Design B", with the design and predicted details shown in Table 5. The predicted heat collection rates of these two designs are relatively high, no matter with which final temperature between 52 and 62 °C. As a result, both Designs A and B showed high average heat collection rates after standard measurements, as shown in Table 6. It should be noted that the environmental conditions (*e.g.*, solar radiation intensity, ambient temperature, season and location) for measuring these two designs are very similar to all the WGET-SWHs in the authors' database. That is to say, these two designs are comparable with the previous 915 WGET-SWHs. Surprisingly, it was found that the two designs had the average heat collection rate higher than all the 915 WGET-SWHs in the previous database. In the following content, details about this screening process will be introduced.

Table 5. Predicted variables of two designed WGET-SWHs

	Tube Length (mm)	Number of Tubes	TCD (mm)	Tank Volume (kg)	Collector Area (m^2)	Angle (°)	Final Temp. (°C)
Design A	1800	18	105.5	163	1.27	30	52-62
Design B	1800	20	105.5	307	1.27	30	52-62

Reproduced with permission from Reference (Zhijian Liu, Li, Liu, et al., 2017).

Abbreviations: TCD: tube center distance, final temp.: final temperature. Tank volume was defined as the maximum mass of water in tank (kg).

Table 6. Measured heat collection rates (MJ/m^2) of the two new designs

	Day 1	Day 2	Day 3	Day 4	Average	Predicted	Error Rate
Design A	11.38	11.26	11.34	11.29	11.32	11.47	1.35%
Design B	11.47	11.43	11.42	11.45	11.44	11.66	1.90%

Reproduced with permission from Reference (Zhijian Liu, Li, Liu, et al., 2017).

Being similar to a previous computational HTS concept proposed by Aspuru-Guzik and his colleagues (Pyzer-Knapp, Suh, Gómez-Bombarelli, Aguilera-Iparraguirre, & Aspuru-Guzik, 2015), a modified HTS process for the optimization in this case has been proposed, as shown in Figure 9. Details about modeling and experimental contents can be found in Reference (Zhijian Liu, Li, Liu, et al., 2017). It can be clearly seen that though a large number of new designs are generated, they will be screened with the target criterions. Only a relatively small number of designs with the predicted results fulfill the criterions will be recorded in the database. Of course, sometimes it is hard to experimentally validate all these candidates after screening. It is recommended that picking at least two cases for experimental validation can ensure that the screening results are reliable.

Figure 9. An HTS process for solar energy system optimization. Each orange circle represents a possible design. The inset shows the schematic inter-connected structure of a general ANN algorithm.
Reproduced with permission from Reference (Li et al., 2017).

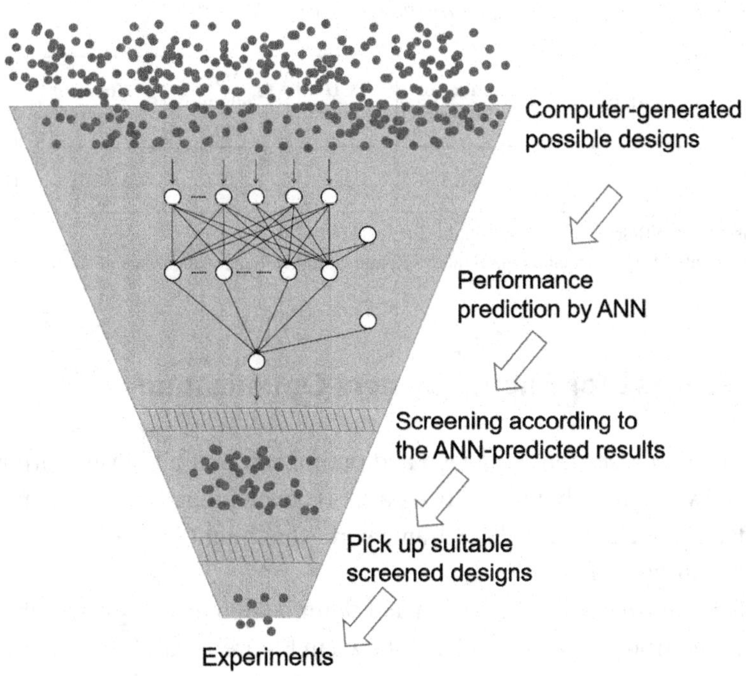

A key step of this HTS process is the generation of inputs for the new designs. Without a rational criterion for input generation, there will be infinite possible combinations of inputs, which will lead to infinite computations. For an ANN model, an interesting way is to generate the inputs according to the final weights of the network: the independent variables with larger weight contributions will be assigned more possible input values. The basic assumption here is simple: the independent variables with higher weight will lead to more significant changes to the dependent variables. It should be noted that the numerical weights do not contain any physical meaning, and the weights are usually different under different repeated training of a given ANN structure, since the initial weights of the ANN are usually selected randomly by the weight optimization algorithm. Fortunately, if each repeated ANN is well-trained, the weight values would be relatively stable in multiple trainings. This method provides a quick decision of input generations, which does not require people to know the exact physical meanings of the variables. However, sometimes people have to artificially assign more values to some independent variables. Taking the final temperature in this case as an example, it is not a part of the WGET-SWH installation, but it highly correlates with the heat collection rate. Thus, the temperature effect should not be ignored. More final temperature should be assigned than it is expected from its weight contributions. The number of each selected value for generation is shown in Table 7. All these values randomly combine with each other, constructing around 3.5×10^8 possible design combinations as the inputs of the ANN. Also, if people want to use other machine learning algorithms that do not require weight calculations (*e.g.*, SVM), the variables' physical meanings should be considered: the independent variables with more significant physical influences to the dependent variable should be assigned more selected values.

Table 7. Number of selected values of different independent variables

	Tube Length (mm)	**Number of Tubes**	**TCD (mm)**	**Tank Volume (kg)**	**Collector Area (m^2)**	**Angle (°)**	**Final Temp. (°C)**
Number of Selected Values	5	30	5	111	50	5	17

Reproduced with permission from Reference (Zhijian Liu, Li, Liu, et al., 2017).

Abbreviations: TCD: tube center distance, final temp.: final temperature. Tank volume was defined as the maximum mass of water in tank (kg).

A General HTS Process for Energy System Optimization

So far, all the essential processes for the design and optimization of a high-performance WGET-SWH have been introduced, which mainly include two parts: i) developing a predictive model and ii) screening possible candidates. Here a general HTS framework (that might be used for other energy systems) will be introduced and discussed.

The proposed HTS framework for the design and optimization of energy system is shown in Figure 10. When all the preconditions of the "cylinders" shown in Figure 10 are fulfilled, a completed machine learning-assisted HTS process can be achieved. Since the final target of this HTS process is to discover new designed candidates with optimized performance, there should be a database that record all the independent and dependent variables of the new candidates for future use. It should be noted that these predicted candidates will have the independent variables different (or partially different) from the experimental database. Also, the results from the validation experiments should be added to the previous experimental database. By combining the validation experiment results with the previous measurement database, people can reconstruct a new experimental database for future applications. People can refer to either the predicted candidate database or the new experimental data for industrial or commercial use. This framework can be achieved by a machine learning code combined with some additional simple coding. Here, the authors expect that this framework not only works for optimizing WGET-SWH, but also works for the optimization cases of other energy systems.

Figure 10. A proposed framework of machine learning-assisted HTS process for target performance optimization. "int" is the independent variable. "dep" is the dependent variable. $\{A_{in}\}$ is the original experimental database. $\{B_{in}\}$ is the generated independent variables as the inputs. $\{B_{in}(new)\}$ is the generated independent variables and their predicted dependent variables. $\{C_{in}\}$ is the new experimental database combining the original experimental database and the experimental validation results of the screened candidates.

Reproduced with permission from Reference (Li et al., 2017).

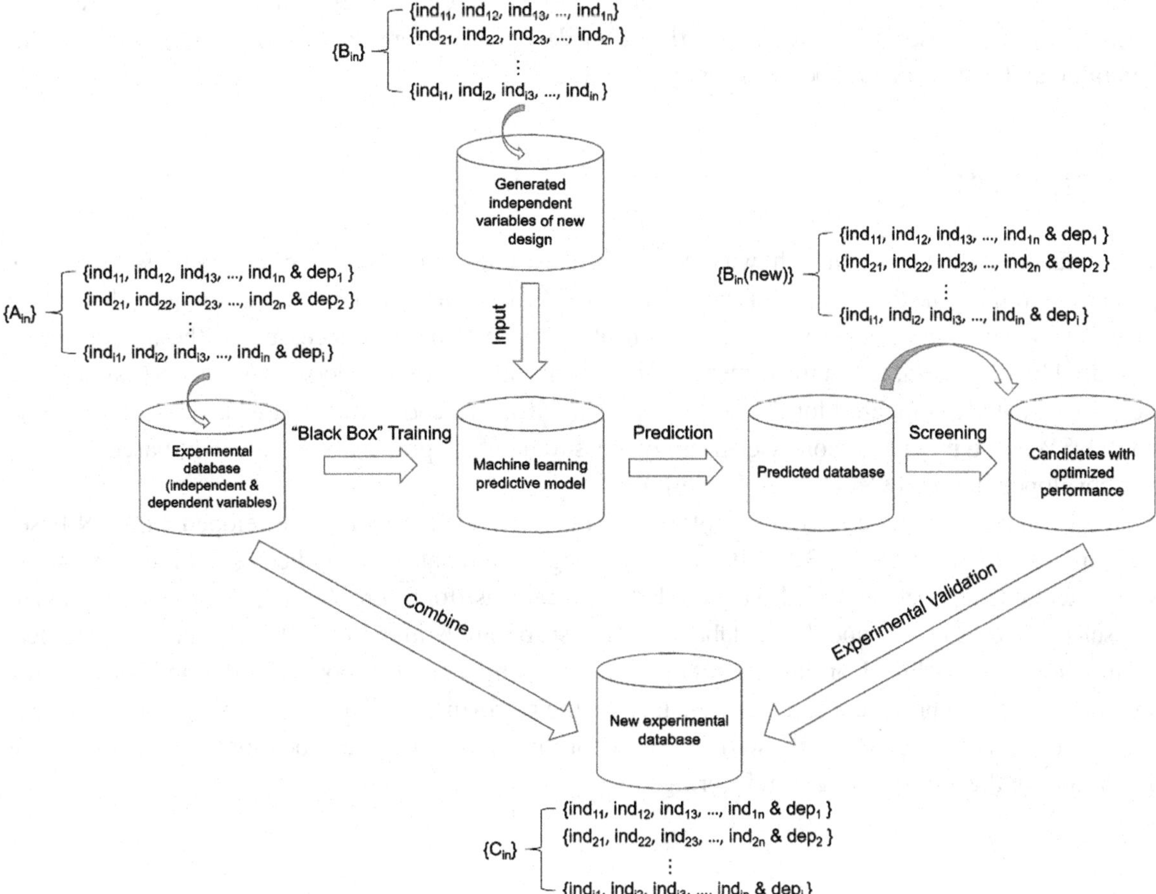

FUTURE RESEARCH DIRECTIONS

Though there is a great success on the prediction and optimization of SWHs using machine learning methods, there still remain some vital questions that should be addressed in the future: how to modify the HTS process for adopting different energy systems? Can people further simplify the HTS process and/or the generation rules of design inputs? Can people develop a user-friendly platform for the database of the designed candidates? Addressing these questions would be of great importance to make the HTS-based energy system optimization more applicable.

It should be noted that to achieve a successful HTS-assisted optimization of energy systems, both predictive model training and HTS process are necessary. Both of them require (more or less) some coding works, which meanwhile require some programming knowledge. If the thermal performance of an energy system can be easily optimized by the empirical knowledge, HTS process will no longer be recommended. Thus, the proposed HTS optimization process is only effective for the design of those energy systems with more complicated internal structures. This is the same as the basic mission of a machine learning model: to deal with those problems that are too complicated to be addressed by conventional methods. If things are simple, machine learning will no longer be cost-effective.

In the near future, it is expected to see that more commercial energy systems are optimized by a machine learning-based HTS process. With higher designed performances, it is expected that higher economic and environmental benefits can be achieved.

CONCLUSION

In this Chapter, the authors have shown that machine learning techniques are powerful tools for predicting and optimizing the thermal performance of SWHs. Picking WGET-SWH as a case study, the authors have developed a knowledge-based measurement of thermal performances using the simple inputs measured by the "portable test instruments". Various machine learning models (ANN, SVM and ELM) were subsequently compared for the prediction of the heat collection rate and heat loss coefficient of WGET-SWH. To provide a more user-friendly measurement for practical use, an ANN-based software was developed in both PC and Android platforms.

To optimize the heat collection rate of a WGET-SWH, the authors have developed an ANN-based HTS process to screen around 3.5×10^8 possible design combinations. Candidates with high predicted heat collection rates were screened and recorded into a database for future use. Validation experiments on two selected cases in the candidate database showed surprisingly high thermal performances. All these results show that machine learning not only provides a strong predictive power for thermal performance prediction, but also provide a brand new insight for the performance optimization of an energy system. The authors also expect that this new HTS-based optimization strategy can be more widely used in the near future in the area of energy engineering.

ACKNOWLEDGMENT

We are grateful to all the colleagues who involved in the data collection, programming and research discussions. This work was supported by the Major Basic Research Development and Transformation Program of Qinghai province (no. 2016-NN-141) and Natural Science Foundation of Hebei (no. E2017502051).

REFERENCES

An, W. F., & Tolliday, N. (2010). Cell-based assays for high-throughput screening. *Molecular Biotechnology, 45*(2), 180–186. doi:10.100712033-010-9251-z PMID:20151227

Browne, M. W. (2000). Cross-Validation Methods. *Journal of Mathematical Psychology, 44*(1), 108–132. doi:10.1006/jmps.1999.1279 PMID:10733860

Colbert, T. (2001). High-Throughput Screening for Induced Point Mutations. *Plant Physiology, 126*(2), 480–484. doi:10.1104/pp.126.2.480 PMID:11402178

Greeley, J., Jaramillo, T. F., Bonde, J., Chorkendorff, I. B., & Nørskov, J. K. (2006). Computational high-throughput screening of electrocatalytic materials for hydrogen evolution. *Nature Materials, 5*(11), 909–913. doi:10.1038/nmat1752 PMID:17041585

Hautier, G., Fischer, C. C., Jain, A., Mueller, T., & Ceder, G. (2010). Finding natures missing ternary oxide compounds using machine learning and density functional theory. *Chemistry of Materials, 22*(12), 3762–3767. doi:10.1021/cm100795d

Hertzberg, R. P., & Pope, A. J. (2000). High-throughput screening: New technology for the 21st century. *Current Opinion in Chemical Biology, 4*(4), 445–451. doi:10.1016/S1367-5931(00)00110-1 PMID:10959774

Hornik, K., Stinchcombe, M., & White, H. (1989). Multilayer feedforward networks are universal approximators. *Neural Networks, 2*(5), 359–366. doi:10.1016/0893-6080(89)90020-8

Huang, G.-B., Zhou, H., Ding, X., & Zhang, R. (2012). Extreme learning machine for regression and multiclass classification. *IEEE Transactions on Systems, Man, and Cybernetics. Part B, Cybernetics, 42*(2), 513–529. doi:10.1109/TSMCB.2011.2168604 PMID:21984515

Huang, G.-B., Zhu, Q., & Siew, C. (2006). Extreme learning machine: Theory and applications. *Neurocomputing, 70*(1-3), 489–501. doi:10.1016/j.neucom.2005.12.126

Jordan, M. I., & Mitchell, T. M. (2015). Machine learning: Trends, perspectives, and prospects. *Science, 349*(6245), 255–260. doi:10.1126cience.aaa8415 PMID:26185243

Kalogirou, S. (1999). Applications of artificial neural networks in energy systems. *Energy Conversion and Management, 40*(10), 1073–1087. doi:10.1016/S0196-8904(99)00012-6

Li, H., Chen, F., Cheng, K., Zhao, Z., & Yang, D. (2015). Prediction of Zeta Potential of Decomposed Peat via Machine Learning. *Comparative Study of Support Vector Machine and Artificial Neural Networks, 10*, 6044–6056.

Li, H., Liu, Z., Liu, K., & Zhang, Z. (2017). Predictive Power of Machine Learning for Optimizing Solar Water Heater Performance: The Potential Application of High-Throughput Screening. *International Journal of Photoenergy*, *2017*, 1–10. doi:10.1155/2017/4194251

Li, H., Tang, X., Wang, R., Lin, F., Liu, Z., & Cheng, K. (2016). Comparative Study on Theoretical and Machine Learning Methods for Acquiring Compressed Liquid Densities of 1,1,1,2,3,3,3-Heptafluoropropane (R227ea) via Song and Mason Equation, Support Vector Machine, and Artificial Neural Networks. *Applied Sciences*, *6*(1), 25. doi:10.3390/app6010025

Liu, Z., Li, H., & Cao, G. (2017). Quick Estimation Model for the Concentration of Indoor Airborne Culturable Bacteria: An Application of Machine Learning. *International Journal of Environmental Research and Public Health*, *14*(8), 857. doi:10.3390/ijerph14080857 PMID:28758941

Liu, Z., Li, H., Liu, K., Yu, H., & Cheng, K. (2017). Design of high-performance water-in-glass evacuated tube solar water heaters by a high-throughput screening based on machine learning: A combined modeling and experimental study. *Solar Energy*, *142*, 61–67. doi:10.1016/j.solener.2016.12.015

Liu, Z., Li, H., Tang, X., Zhang, X., Lin, F., & Cheng, K. (2016). Extreme learning machine: A new alternative for measuring heat collection rate and heat loss coefficient of water-in-glass evacuated tube solar water heaters. *SpringerPlus*. doi:10.118640064-016-2242-1 PMID:27330892

Liu, Z., Li, H., Zhang, X., Jin, G., & Cheng, K. (2015). Novel method for measuring the heat collection rate and heat loss coefficient of water-in-glass evacuated tube solar water heaters based on artificial neural networks and support vector machine. *Energies*, *8*(8), 8814–8834. doi:10.3390/en8088814

Liu, Z., Liu, K., Li, H., Zhang, X., Jin, G., & Cheng, K. (2015). Artificial Neural Networks-Based Software for Measuring Heat Collection Rate and Heat Loss Coefficient of Water-in-Glass Evacuated Tube Solar Water Heaters. *PLoS One*. doi:10.1371/journal.pone.0143624 PMID:26624613

Mekhilef, S., Saidur, R., & Safari, A. (2011). A review on solar energy use in industries. *Renewable & Sustainable Energy Reviews*, *15*(4), 1777–1790. doi:10.1016/j.rser.2010.12.018

Peng, H., & Ling, X. (2008). Optimal design approach for the plate-fin heat exchangers using neural networks cooperated with genetic algorithms. *Applied Thermal Engineering*, *28*(5-6), 642–650. doi:10.1016/j.applthermaleng.2007.03.032

Pyzer-Knapp, E. O., Suh, C., Gómez-Bombarelli, R., Aguilera-Iparraguirre, J., & Aspuru-Guzik, A. (2015). What Is High-Throughput Virtual Screening? A Perspective from Organic Materials Discovery. *Annual Review of Materials Research*, *45*(1), 195–216. doi:10.1146/annurev-matsci-070214-020823

Sommer, C., & Gerlich, D. W. (2013). Machine learning in cell biology – teaching computers to recognize phenotypes. *Journal of Cell Science*, *126*(24), 5529–5539. doi:10.1242/jcs.123604 PMID:24259662

Specht, D. F. (1991). A general regression neural network. *Neural Networks. IEEE Transactions on*, *2*, 568–576. PMID:18282872

Sun, W., He, Y., & Chang, H. (2015). Forecasting fossil fuel energy consumption for power generation using QHSA-based LSSVM model. *Energies*, *8*(2), 939–959. doi:10.3390/en8020939

Suykens, J. A., & Vandewalle, J. (1999). Least Squares Support Vector Machine Classifiers. *Neural Processing Letters*, *9*(3), 293–300. doi:10.1023/A:1018628609742

Tang, R., Li, Z., Zhong, H., & Lan, Q. (2006). Assessment of uncertainty in mean heat loss coefficient of all glass evacuated solar collector tube testing. *Energy Conversion and Management*, *47*(1), 60–67. doi:10.1016/j.enconman.2005.03.013

Wahler, D., & Reymond, J. L. (2001). High-throughput screening for biocatalysts. *Current Opinion in Biotechnology*, *12*(6), 535–544. doi:10.1016/S0958-1669(01)00260-9 PMID:11849935

Wernick, M., Yang, Y., Brankov, J., Yourganov, G., & Strother, S. (2010). Machine learning in medical imaging. *IEEE Signal Processing Magazine*, *27*(4), 25–38. doi:10.1109/MSP.2010.936730 PMID:25382956

KEY TERMS AND DEFINITIONS

Artificial Neural Network (ANN): A machine learning algorithm that performs "black box" non-linear fitting, similarly to the inter-connected neurons in human brain.

Heat Collection Rate (HCR): Daily heat collection per square meter of a solar water system, MJ/m^2.

Heat Loss Coefficient (HLC): The average heat loss per unit, W/(m^{3}K).

High-Throughput Screening (HTS): The screening of thousands or millions of target candidates using state-of-the-art experimental or computational techniques.

Solar Water Heater (SWH): The heater that transfers solar energy (in the form of heat) to water.

This research was previously published in the Handbook of Research on Power and Energy System Optimization; pages 55-74, copyright year 2018 by Engineering Science Reference (an imprint of IGI Global).

Chapter 39
Credit Rating Forecasting Using Machine Learning Techniques

Mark Wallis
Bond University, Australia

Kuldeep Kumar
Bond University, Australia

Adrian Gepp
Bond University, Australia

ABSTRACT

Credit ratings are an important metric for business managers and a contributor to economic growth. Forecasting such ratings might be a suitable application of big data analytics. As machine learning is one of the foundations of intelligent big data analytics, this chapter presents a comparative analysis of traditional statistical models and popular machine learning models for the prediction of Moody's long-term corporate debt ratings. Machine learning techniques such as artificial neural networks, support vector machines, and random forests generally outperformed their traditional counterparts in terms of both overall accuracy and the Kappa statistic. The parametric models may be hindered by missing variables and restrictive assumptions about the underlying distributions in the data. This chapter reveals the relative effectiveness of non-parametric big data analytics to model a complex process that frequently arises in business, specifically determining credit ratings.

INTRODUCTION

The notion of credit rating has been present in financial markets since 1860, where H.V. Poor began publishing financial statistics about railroad companies to attract public investments (Standard & Poor's, 2016). After this development, in 1909 J. Moody, founder of Moody's Investors Service, expanded on this idea by classifying these statistics into categories represented by letters of the alphabet. This methodology was mostly used on railway bonds. After the Great Depression in the late 1930's, the bond rating

DOI: 10.4018/978-1-6684-6291-1.ch039

system became institutionalized in the United States. The repetitive nature of strong markets followed by crashes increased the need for a measure of risk and uncertainty for investors. Nowadays, 100 percent of all commercial papers and 99 percent of corporate bonds have been rated by at least one credit rating agency in the United States. These credit rating agencies have expanded across the globe to aid the needs of investors and corporate borrowers.

Credit ratings for companies have evolved to become an integral source of information for the financial sector. This information has a range of financial and economic benefits to society. These benefits can be categorized into three groups: benefits to investors, the company and the economy. The investors benefit from this information because it is a convenient and cost-effective source of information that allows for calculated risk. Furthermore, it encourages market confidence and entices retail investors to invest their savings into corporate securities and receive higher returns. For companies, credit ratings allow them to enter the market more confidently and raise funds at a lower cost. Companies may also use credit ratings as a means for brand repair or improvement. Lastly, with regard to the overall economy, consistent and accurate credit ratings fuel public investment in the corporate sector, which in-turn stimulates economic growth. These credit rating systems can facilitate the formation of public policy guidelines on institutional investors. They also play a vital role in investor protection by encouraging ethical behavior among corporate borrowers without putting a larger burden on the government.

Although they are not perfect, it is clear that credit ratings offer a plethora of benefits to society and are necessary to sustain strong economic growth and prosperity. These ratings are formed by incorporating a range of quantitative and qualitative variables that are gathered through public information and on-site research. However, these ratings take a substantial amount of labor and time to develop, making it a very costly process. This means it is difficult for management at many companies to afford regular credit rating updates. As a result, credit rating modelling has become a large area of research due to the economic and financial benefits associated with making credit ratings more efficient and cost-effective. With the expansion of machine learning and big data analytics over the past decade, there has been an influx of credit rating models in academic literature. As machine learning is one of the foundations of intelligent big data analytics, this chapter presents a comparative analysis of both traditional statistical models and popular machine learning models for the prediction of Moody's long term corporate debt ratings for top companies in the United States.

Moody's Rating System

Moody's, alongside Standard & Poor's and Fitch Group, is one of the three largest credit rating agencies in the world. The agencies all provide international finance research on bonds that are issued by both government and commercial entities. Moody's focuses on rating a borrower's creditworthiness based on a range of factors and rating scales that are designed to estimate the expected loss suffered by an investor in the event of a default and the probability of that event occurring. These rating systems are universally comparable, meaning they can be compared across different currencies, industries and countries. Moody's provide eight main categories of credit ratings (Moody's Investor service, 2017):

1. Moody's Long-Term Ratings
2. Moody's Short-Term Ratings
3. Moody's Bank Deposit Ratings
4. Moody's Bank Financial Strength Ratings

5. Moody's Mutual Fund Ratings
6. Moody's Insurance financial strength Ratings
7. Moody's issuer Ratings
8. Moody's management quality ratings for US affordable housing provider and National Scale Ratings

For the purpose of this chapter, the main focus will be placed on Moody's Long-Term Ratings. Moody's Long-Term Ratings are assigned to a range of fixed income instruments including bonds, debentures and preferred stocks. This rating system is a reflection of two major areas of the company. First, it reflects the credit risk of the company and how likely an issuer of debt is to meet its obligation. Secondly, it reflects the indenture protection, which represents the level of legal protection of the security. Some factors that may be included in the determination of this rating may include the seniority of the bond, negative pledge clauses and guarantees.

The following ratings are possible with Moody's Long-Term Ratings:

1. **Investment-Grade:** Aaa, Aa1, Aa2, Aa3, A1, A2, A3, Baa1, Baa2, Baa3, and
2. **Speculative-Grade:** Ba1, Ba2, Ba3, B1, B2, B3, Caa1, Caa2, Caa3, Ca and C.

In this chapter, these ratings are grouped into six categories as shown in Table 1, which is consistent with the earlier work of Kumar and Bhattacharya (2006). This categorization was used to ensure that a broad range of companies and credit ratings would be analyzed.

Table 1. Categories of Moody's ratings used in this chapter

Codes	Categories	Moody's Ratings
X1	High Grade	Aaa, Aa1, Aa2, Aa3
X2	Investment Grade	A1, A2, A3
X3	Upper Medium Grade	Baa1, Baa2, Baa3
X4	Medium Grade	Ba1, Ba2, Ba3
X5	Lower Medium Grade	B1, B2, B3
X6	Speculative Grade	Caa1, Caa2, Caa3, Ca and C

BACKGROUND

This section presents a brief review of reviewing the academic literature on credit rating forecasting with a focus on modelling techniques used to predict long-term credit ratings of corporate debt.

Studies about modelling credit rating have increased substantially over the past decade, likely because of the Global Financial Crisis and the realized importance of credit rating agencies in financial markets. Prior research identifies two main benefits gained from modelling credit ratings. First, it is very costly to employ a credit rating agency to provide long-term debt ratings more frequently than once a year, particularly for smaller companies who wish to improve their financial image in the market. Companies with good credit ratings enter the market with higher confidence and can raise funds at a cheaper rate

(Kumar & Bhattacharya, 2006). On the other hand, for lending institutions and investors who create debt portfolios, it is important to have a regular indication of the riskiness of that portfolio. This also encourages economic growth through investment in the corporate sector. As a result, credit rating forecasting has become a popular area of study.

The credit rating forecasting literature is split into research using traditional statistical methods, machine learning techniques and ensemble techniques. The traditional statistical techniques used include logistic regression (Stepanova & Thomas, 2001; Steenackers & Goovaerts, 1989), linear discriminant analysis (Kumar & Bhattacharya, 2006; Khemakhem & Boujelbene, 2015) and Bayesian networks (Hajek, Olej, & Prochazka, 2016). These techniques were found to produce an average accuracy range of only 60 to 70% using financial statements ratios and other financial statement data. There was a consensus that accuracy could not be meaningfully increased further without gathering qualitative information such as that used by Moody's. As an extension to this hypothesis, Hajek, Olej & Prochazka (2016) explored the effect that news sentiment has on credit ratings. It was found that positive sentiment in the company's reports and negative words in news articles were statistically significant in predicting credit ratings.

Consistent with other areas of business modelling, there has been increased popularity in the application of non-parametric approaches to credit rating forecasting. The idea is to capture the non-linear relationships between variables and increase the predictive accuracy of the models without incorporating the qualitative variables used by Moody's. The most common techniques used include decision trees (e.g. Yobas & Crook, 2000) and k-nearest neighbors (KNN) (e.g. Henley & Hand, 1997). The performance of decision trees was found to outperform KNN when evaluated on imbalanced datasets with either a majority of low credit ratings or majority high credit ratings (Abdou & Pointon, 2011). However, there are often discrepancies in conclusions about the relative performance of these techniques when data sets of varying degrees of imbalance (skewness) (Abdou & Pointon, 2011; Henley & Hand, 1997). Overall, it is recognized that non-parametric approaches perform better than traditional statistical approaches (Abdou & Pointon, 2011).

Kernel classifiers and other modern machine learning techniques have also been applied to credit rating forecasting, encouraged by the success of other non-parametric approaches. A broad range of techniques applied and the most successful include Artificial Neural Networks (ANNs) (Kumar & Haynes,2003; Kumar & Bhattacharya, 2006), Support Vector Machines (SVM) (Cristianini & Scholkopf, 2002) and a Gaussian Process Classifier (GPC) (Shian-Chang, 2011). Overall, SVMs have had the most success. SVMs are a popular model in this field because it is believed that the formulation of the SVM embodies the structural risk minimization principle. This means that the SVM produces an optimal trade-off between complexity and the empirical accuracy (Sewell, 2008). Despite these attractive features, many practitioners believe that SVMs ability to handle sparse data has potentially been overstated. For example, it has been shown that SVMs are not always able to construct parsimonious models in system identification and financial forecasting (Huang, Chuang, Wu, & Lai, 2010). It is also argued that SVM's underperform in their predictions because of the big data nature of the financial data used in credit rating forecasting – the curse of dimensionality (Huang et al., 2010).

This weakness in SVMs has sparked the use of many probability kernel classifiers such as the Gaussian process based classifiers (Girolami & Rogers, 2006). This technique has been prominent in statistics for decades and has outperformed ANNs on smaller datasets (Lilley & Frean, 2005). Huang (2011) explored the use of Gaussian processes in predicting credit ratings compared to using SVMs for prediction. GPCs were found to outperform conventional SVMs, even when enhanced by true selection and dimensionality reduction schemes, as tested on the Taiwanese banking sector (Shian-Chang, 2011). This is due to

GPCs robustness when dealing with the high dimensionality of data using a fast-variational Bayesian algorithm proposed by Girolami & Rogers (2006) to reduce the computational loading of predictions.

Other modern research about modelling credit ratings uses ensemble techniques such as Random Forest (Wu & Wu, 2016) and Gradient Boosted Machines (GBM) (Abdou & Pointon, 2011). The resulting models are more difficult to interpret and some deem them to be similar to *black box* models. Nevertheless, they have produced high predictive performance and have a robust variable importance feature that partially explains the relationships between credit rating output and the input predictor variables (Imad, 2017).

Overall, the literature consists of a range of modelling techniques used to forecast long-term credit ratings. These techniques all have their own strengths and limitations and have all been tested on different data with diverse economic characteristics and distributions of credit ratings. There have been a range of papers claiming to produce the most accurate modelling technique; however, there has been a lack of comparisons between traditional statistical, non-parametric, ensembles and machine learning techniques on the same data set. Without such a comparison there is no solid evidence to suggest what technique results in the highest accuracy. The remainder of this chapter presents the findings from such a comparison.

DATA AND MODELLING TECHNIQUES

Data

Moody's Investor Service typically model credit ratings based on certain financial ratios. Financial ratios are often deemed to be good indicators of the company's financial health and security of the company (Ganeshalingam & Kumar, 2001). However, Moody's deems that the variables used to formulate these ratings are part of the company's intellectual property and so do not disclose these inputs (Moody's Investor service, 2017). As a result of this, financial ratios and other variables that are important in predicting the profitability, liquidity, and capital gearing of the company were gathered. The following 27 variables were considered when creating and formulating the credit rating models:

1. Operating Margin,
2. Pre-tax Margin,
3. Return on Invested Capital,
4. Return on Assets,
5. Current Ratio,
6. Quick Ratio,
7. Current Asset to Total Assets,
8. Operating Income to Net Sales,
9. Retained Earnings to Total Assets,
10. Accounts Receivable to Sales,
11. Inventory to Sales,
12. Sales to Total Assets,
13. Net Fixed Assets to Total Assets,
14. Long-Term Debt to Total Assets,

15. Total Liabilities to Total Liabilities and Equity,
16. Number of Employees,
17. Disposal of Fixed Assets,
18. Best Sales,
19. Total Assets,
20. Inventory to Current Assets,
21. Total Debt to Total Equity,
22. Total Debt to Total Capital Expenditure,
23. Cash Ratio,
24. Cash to Total Assets,
25. Asset Turnover,
26. Equity to Total Capital, and
27. Equity to Total Asset.

The above data were collected for 308 companies of the United States S&P 500 from Bloomberg with an examined time-period of January 2016 to November 2017. The companies were chosen such that Moody's Long-term Debt Ratings were available within the past five years, which resulted in useful data set for modelling. This data set also spans a range of industries and sectors, making it adequate to conduct a broad comparative evaluation.

Parametric Modelling Techniques

As mentioned in the literature review, credit rating modelling was initially conducted using parametric models such as multinomial logistic regression and linear discriminant analysis. These models are the best possible modelling techniques if the assumptions of the underlying data are satisfied. This section discusses the parametric models evaluated in this chapter.

Multinomial Logistic Regression

There are three main assumptions behind Multinomial Logistic Regression (MLR): observations are independent of one another, outcomes follow a categorical distribution derived from the covariates via a link function and there is a linear relationship between the covariates and the link-function-transformed outcome (Miyamoto, 2014). MLR is an extension from logistic regression in the sense that it produces a probability that an outcome belongs to a particular category. The link function used remains as logit, which is the logarithm of the odds – this correctly restricts the probability between 0 and 1. Other link functions are possible. For example, the probit model uses the inverse normal distribution function.

Linear and Regularized Discriminant Analysis

Observations are still assumed to be independent of one another by Linear Discriminant Analysis (LDA). In addition, data categories are assumed to be normally distributed (or at least symmetric), the covariance matrix is assumed to be the same for all categories and model accuracy is multicollinearity problems. LDA looks for linear combinations of variables that explain the data, where it focuses on attempting to model the differences between the categories of data and makes use of Bayes Theorem to estimate the probability of the output category given each input. Quadratic Discriminant Analysis (QDA) relaxes the assumption of a common covariance matrix. An extension to these modelling techniques is Regularized Discriminant Analysis (RDA) (Guo, Hastie, & Tibshirani, 2007), which is a weighted average of LDA and QDA. It introduces regularization in the modelling process to empirically determine a balance between a common covariance structure (LDA) and different covariance structures for each category (QDA). That is, RDA will automatically become more weighted towards QDA if the covariance matrix is not common to all categories. This model is the most statistically powerful and efficient technique if the data is a multivariate normal and homoscedasticity is present. In this chapter, both LDA and RDA will be evaluated.

Non-Parametric and Machine Learning Modelling Techniques

It is often argued that, particularly in smaller companies, there are not enough companies seeking financing to gain a full understanding of the population distribution of credit rating data. Therefore, it is not conclusive that the credit rating data meets the assumptions of parametric models (Guotai & Zhipeng, 2017). In fact, after a comprehensive review of such parametric assumptions, Elliot & Kennedy (1988) found that these assumptions often do not hold true for financial data. As a result, the following non-parametric modelling techniques are used in this chapter.

Artificial Neural Networks

As mentioned, Artificial Neural Networks (ANNs) have frequently been used to model credit rating. ANNs are soft computing techniques that are based on the neural structure of human brains. ANNs are able to model complexities that traditional quantitative methods used in finance and economics cannot due to the complexity in translating the system into precise functions. ANNs consist of three main layers: input, hidden and output, whereby more hidden layers are used to model more complex relationships in the data. Initially the neural connections within and between layers are set with random weights and then the model adjusts the weights during the learning process. If the prediction is correct, the ANN adjusts the weights in a positive way, whereas they are adjusted in a negative way if the outcome is negative. This modelling technique is useful when the underlying model structure is unknown, as the model has the ability to learn a wide variety of patterns from the data. ANNs have been shown to be effective at classification of groups and short-term predictions. They are also robust in the sense that they deal well with missing data and correlations between input variables (multicollinearity). However, ANNs are seen to be a *black box* technique because it is difficult to understand why the model makes the predictions it does. ANNs have also been known to over-fit the data used for training, which results in low accuracy for future predictions, particularly long-term predictions. Chapter 6 of Negnevitsky (2011) provides a more detailed introduction into ANNs.

Support Vector-Machines

Support Vector Machines (SVMs) are another type of supervised machine learning technique. They have increased in popularity in the literature in recent years (see Provost and Fawcett (2013, p. 89-94) for a brief introduction to SVMs). The SVM produces hyperplanes that divide data into the different categories. The hyperplanes are chosen such that they maximize the distance (margin) between the nearest data points of different categories. If data cannot be linearly separated, a kernel can be added to transform the data to assist separation by the SVM. This method often works effectively when there is a large number of variables (high dimensionality) and with low sample data. However, SVMs take a large amount of time to train and do not deal well with noisy data, which is data with inaccuracies.

Gaussian Process Classifier

Another non-parametric method that has been applied to credit rating forecasting is the Gaussian Process Classifier (GPC). This process is founded upon a Bayesian methodology. It assumes a prior distribution on the probability densities using the underlying mean and covariance of each variable (Shian-Chang, 2011). It assumes that each variable is drawn from a Gaussian distribution with the respective mean and variance and observing new elements creates a posterior distribution. The data is transformed using a squared-exponential kernel and parametrized using two parameters- sigma and L. Sigma (or L) dictates the height (or length) of the distribution that a point can be drawn from without being classified as an outlier. Predictions are formed by drawing from these collective underlying distributions and categorized into its appropriate category (Girolami & Rogers, 2006).

Random Forest (Ensemble)

Random Forest (Breiman, 2001) is an ensemble technique that has been applied to credit rating data with success in recent years. Random Forest utilizes multiple decision trees and bootstrapping to estimate an outcome. These decision trees are formed by recursively splitting data in two. The aim is that each one of the resulting number of groups identifies with a single category; it is common for multiple groups to be assigned the same category. One of the features of Random Forests is that only a random subset of variables is considered at each split. The other main feature is that each tree is grown to its maximum size, which means individually they are overly-complex, over-fit and will be poor future predictors. However, the accuracy is usually greatly improves then the individual predictions are combined. The way the combination is done is that each individual tree makes a separate prediction and then the category with the most votes (predictions) is assigned. This modelling technique is robust in large datasets with a large number of variables (high dimensionality), deals well with missing data and noise being present in the data, and has methods for adjusting to imbalanced data.

Gradient Boosted Machines (Ensemble)

Boosted machines combine multiple weak models together to form an accurate model. In the case of decision trees, a Gradient Boosted Machine (GBM) (Friedman, 2001; Friedman, 2002) first estimates an overly-simple decision tree (with shallow depth). The GBM then slightly improves the model based on the its prediction error. This process of gradual improvement is then repeated a large number of times to ideally achieve a substantially higher accuracy. This ensemble technique has been less popular than ANNs, but it has often produced higher accuracy (Imad, 2017).

PROCEDURE AND RESULTS

This section outlines the process behind selecting the parameters for the different models and an analysis of the predictive accuracy of each model. It also outlines the most important variables for each model.

The two measures for evaluating accuracy are the overall accuracy (percentage of correct classifications) and Cohen's Kappa statistic (Kappa). Kappa is an accuracy measure that considers both the observed accuracy of the model and the expected accuracy. It is calculated as

$$\frac{Observed\,Accuracy - Expected\,Accuracy}{1 - Observed\,Accuracy}.$$

The inclusion of the expected accuracy allows the statistic to adjust to imbalanced data sets that do not have an equal number of data points in each category. This is particularly important given that credit rating forecasting often involves imbalanced data, as mentioned earlier in the Background. A more detailed explanation of Kappa is provided in the Appendix.

In the literature, the predictive performance of models is commonly compared using hold-out or test data. This process involves training models on a random subset of the data (typically 70%) and then measuring its predictive performance on a hold-out testing set (30%); thus, obtaining a real-world estimate of model performance using new data unseen by the model. However, the resulting single estimate of accuracy can be greatly influenced by precise data split that occurred. Although very big data sets mitigate this problem, it is possible that very different results could be obtained if a different split were randomly chosen. To avoid this issue, the analysis presented in this chapter uses repeated 10-fold cross-validation, where the number 10 is a standard through modelling literature. 10-fold cross validation involves randomly splitting the data into 10 approximately equal partitions, then training the model on 9 of the data subsets and evaluating the model on the final subset. This train-evaluate process is repeated for all 10 possibilities for the subset that is used for evaluation. Further, this whole 10-fold process is then repeated 5 times, each time with a different randomly chosen 10 subsets. This results in a total of 50 accuracy measures per model. These 50 figures can be averaged to obtain a more stable estimate of model performance. Moreover, the 50 different estimates allows for the variability in model performance to be assessed and confidence intervals for both to be estimated for both overall accuracy and the Kappa statistic. It is widely understood that compared to single point estimates, confidence intervals can greatly enhance the interpretability from a managerial perspective.

Importantly, the repeated cross-validation process is common to all models. That means that the data splits are identical for all models, which enables comparison between models to be fair and valid.

Multinomial Logistic Regression

The top 20 most important variables are shown in Figure 1. This ranking was determined by determining the Area Under the receiver operating characteristic Curve (AUC) for each category pair (i.e. High Grade vs Investment Grade, Investment Grade vs Upper Medium Grade and so on). For a specific category, the maximum AUC for all the relevant pairs is used as the variable importance measure (Abdou & Pointon, 2011). The top three most important variables are long-term debt, retained earnings to assets and return on assets.

Figure 1. Variable importance ranking according to multinomial logistic regression

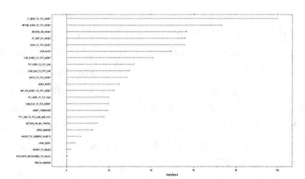

Linear and Regularized Discriminant Analysis (LDA and RDA)

The choice of model parameters can have a large influence on model accuracy; consequently, the main parameters for each model are empirically optimized using cross-validation. As with MLR, LDA does not require any parameters to be set. However, as RDA is a weighted average of LDA and QDA, the relative weights for each are determined by maximizing accuracy using cross-validation. Interestingly, the resulting RDA model weighted LDA at 100% and QDA at 0%, indicating that the same covariance structure is common to all rating categories.

In this case, LDA and RDA have the same variable importance. Similar to most machine learning techniques, discriminant analysis considers variable importance for each rating category separately. Figure 2 shows these rankings. Return on Assets is the most important predictor for all ratings except for X3 and X4, where the most important predictor is Total Assets. It is interesting to note that discriminant analysis ranks pre-tax margin as the second most important variable out of all the variables, whereas MLR ranked it last. The most important variable in multinomial logistic regression was Long-term debt to total assets and this was the 8th most important variable in LDA and RDA.

Figure 2. Variable importance ranking according to discriminant analysis

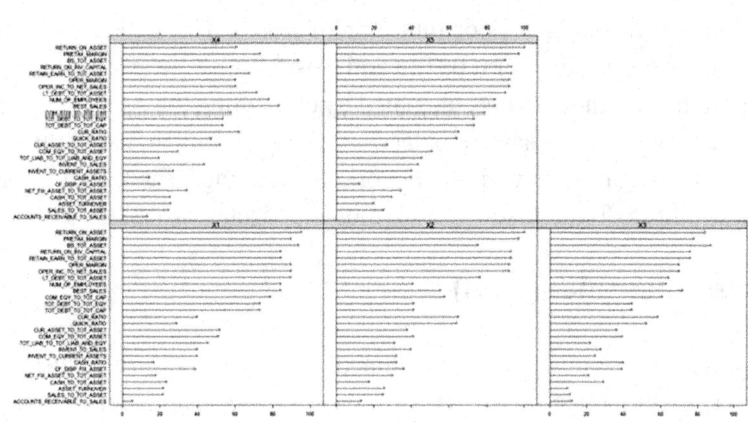

Artificial Neural Network (ANN)

The main parameters set for the ANN include the number of hidden layers and the weight decay. Weight decay is a weight update rule that causes the hidden layer weights to exponentially decay to zero if no other update is issued. Up to three hidden layers were trialed and again cross-validation was used to determine the optimum. The training tolerance was also set to 0.01 to ensure a balance between accuracy and over-fitting. The optimal model was found to be an ANN with 2 hidden layers and a weight decay of 0.1.

As shown in Figure 3, the variable importance rankings appear to be similar to RDA across all rating categories except for Debt to Assets, Number of Employees and Best Sales. The importance across the categories shift in order compared to RDA.

Figure 3. Variable importance ranking according to artificial neural network

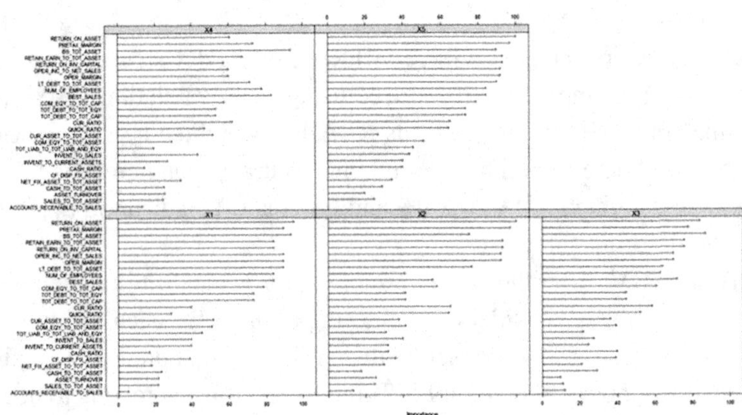

Support Vector Machine (SVM)

SVMs can be tuned using two variables in the freely available R programming language. These variables are Sigma and Cost and together they control the trade-off between the accuracy on the training data and the risk of over-fitting (resulting in poor future predictions). The settings that yielded the highest cross-validated accuracy were a Sigma of 0.03125 and Cost of 5.

The variable importance for the SVM is calculated by computing the AUC. As shown by 8, the variable importance rankings of the SVM have remained relatively similar to that of the ANN. There is only one material changes that occur in the variable importance rankings. First, Return on Invested Capital overtook Retained Earnings to Total Assets for 4th most important variable.

Gaussian Process Classifier (GPC)

The GPC in the R programming language can be tuned using one parameter when modelled using the popular Radial Basis kernel function-sigma. This sigma is a hyper-parameter for the kernel; it indicates the width of the Radial Basis of the kernel function and the Laplacian kernel (Shian-Chang, 2011). In essence, it represents how far away a data point needs to be before it is deemed an outlier. A higher sigma may lead to a more accurate model, but it also makes the model susceptible to over-fitting. This is essentially the same trade-off between accuracy and over-fitting. The optimal model was found to have a sigma of 0.135, chosen based on cross-validated accuracy.

The variable importance for a GPC is generated according to the technique specified by Linkletter, Bingham, Hengartner, Higdon, & Ye (2006). This methodology uses a Bayesian approach whereby it analyses the effects on the posterior distribution. As shown in Figure 5, the variable importance is essentially the same as for the SVM.

Figure 4. Variable importance ranking according to support vector machine

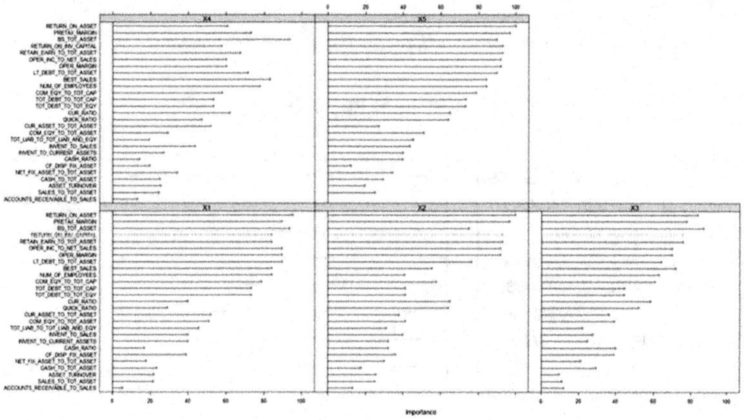

Figure 5. Variable importance ranking according to a Gaussian process classifier

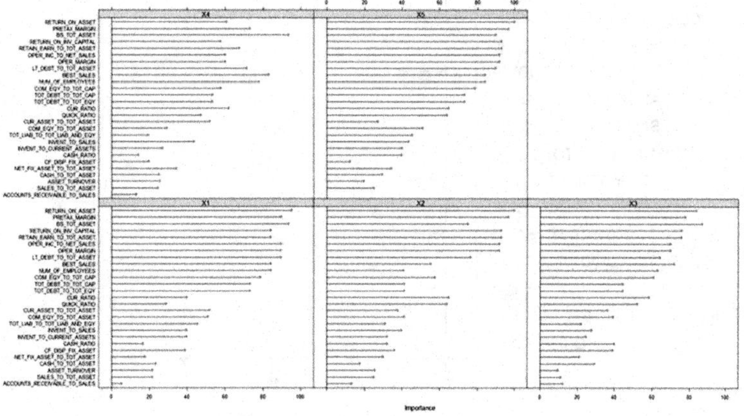

Random Forest (RF)

RF is controlled by two main parameters: the number of trees in the ensemble and the number variables to be randomly selected at each split point for each tree. 500 trees were grown based on the size of the data set. The number of variables to randomly choose is often chosen as the square root of the number of variables ($\sqrt{27} \approx 5$). However, it is prudent to empirically verify the optimum setting using cross-validation. This resulted in a setting of four, similar to the square root heuristic that suggested five.

The variable importance of the RF model is ranked using the standard metric: mean decrease in node impurity. This allows an overall ranking to be calculated, rather than a different ranking for each category. As shown in Figure 6, the variable importance is notably different to all other models. The most important variable is Best Sales, which is typically ranked around 4th in SVM and GPC and did not even make it into the top 20 most important variables for MLR. This difference is likely because unlike the other models, Random Forest is an ensemble of multiple models and so its predictions can arguably be considered more stable.

Figure 6. Variable importance ranking according to Random Forest

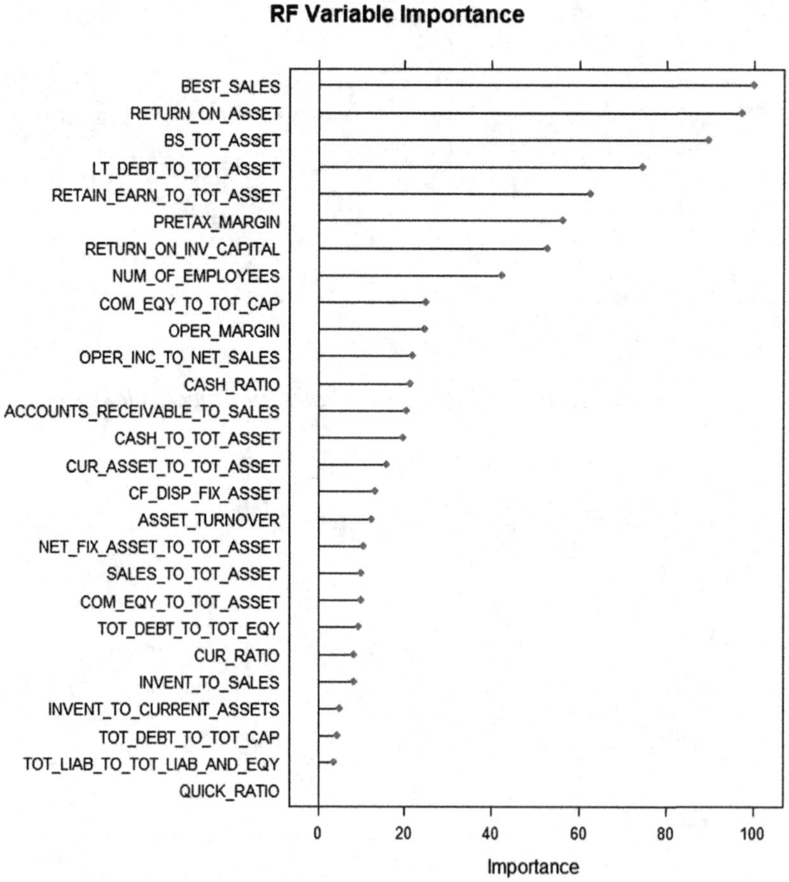

Gradient Boosted Machines (GBMs)

GBMs can be parametrized using three main variables: the number of trees, the shrinkage (or learning) factor and the size of each individual tree. The number of trees represents the amount of weak learning predictors that will be grown in the simulation and the shrinkage factor represents the learning rate of the algorithm. The learning rate determines the rate at which it shrinks the impact of incorrect predictors. Using cross-validation, the optimal settings are 1000 trees, shrinkage of 0.005 and a minimum of 30 nodes per tree.

The variable importance method used is similar to the method used for Random Forest. The importance is measured based on the mean decrease in impurity. As shown in Figure 7, the most important variable is Return on Assets followed by Best Sales. This is similar to Random Forest, the other ensemble model, but different to all the other models.

Figure 7. Variable importance ranking according to Gradient Boosted Machine

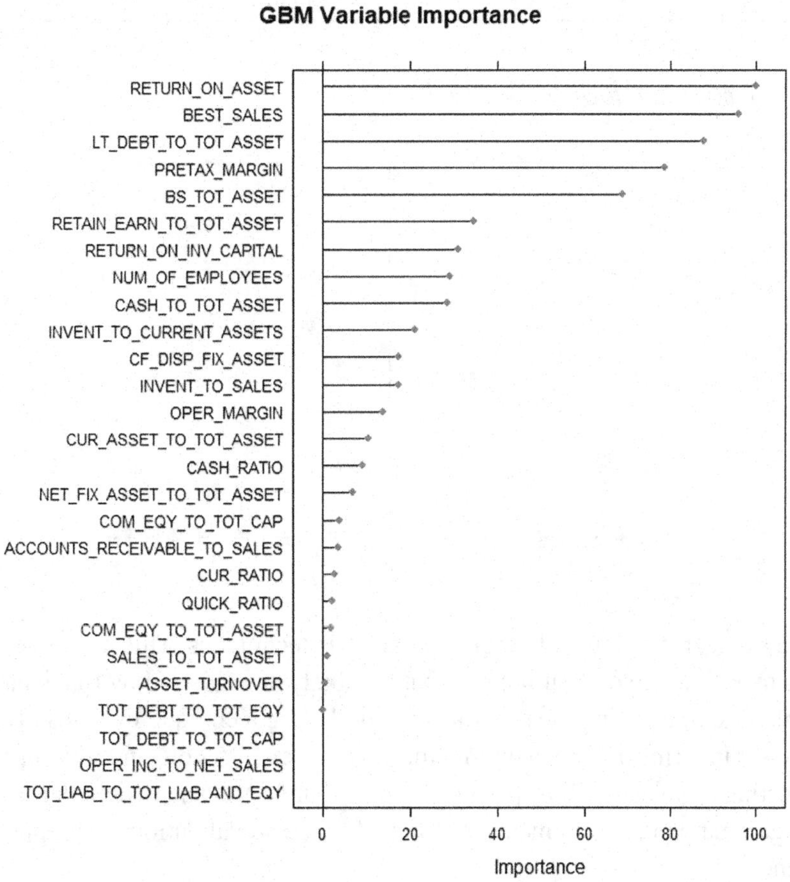

Comparison

Table 2 shows the average results for all models, while Figure 8 shows the distribution of overall accuracy and Kappa statistic results. Based on Figure 8, an overall ranking is obtained and is shown in Table 2. All modelling techniques appeared to produce relatively similar mean average accuracy, but the top three techniques produced the largest improvement above guessing (Kappa statistic). The focus of this chapter is the comparison between models.

Table 2. Comparison of model accuracy

Method	Overall Ranking	Average Accuracy	Average Kappa
RF	1	64.6%	31.3%
SVM	2	63.6%	30.6%
ANN	3	60.8%	31.5%
GBM	4	62.3%	27.4%
LDA	5	61.7%	28.8%
RDA	6	60.4%	25.3%
MLR	7	59.6%	22.6%
GPC	8	61.6%	20.6%

Figure 8. Box plot of model performance

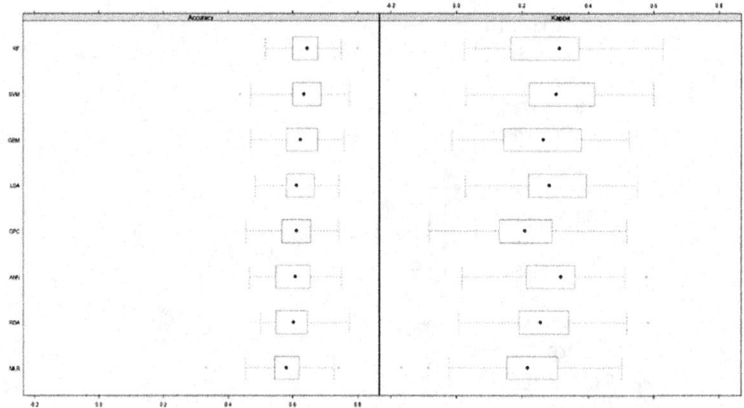

In general, the lowest ranked models are the parametric techniques. This makes sense as these modelling techniques make a range of assumptions that are likely not satisfied by financial data. The multinomial logistic regression is the poorest performing modelling technique in terms of average accuracy and the second worst in terms of Kappa, with a mean accuracy of 59.6% and a mean Kappa statistic of 22.6%. It is interesting to note that RDA performs worse than LDA. The two models are similar, but the RDA includes a gamma penalty parameter (optimized by cross-validation) that appears to reduce the accuracy of the model.

The ANN performed the best in terms of the Kappa statistic, suggesting it had the largest improvement compared to guessing the credit rating by chance. However, the overall accuracy was only the 6th best. The GPC performed relatively poorly compared to what was reported in Shian-Chang (2011), performing the worst in terms of Kappa and 5th in overall accuracy. The best overall performer was Random Forest, producing the highest overall accuracy and second highest Kappa statistic. This was followed closely by SVM, which produced the second highest overall accuracy and the third highest Kappa.

CONCLUSION

This chapter presented a comparative study of some of the most popular modelling techniques used to model credit ratings. These models were evaluated on 308 of the S&P 500 companies to predict the Moody's long-term credit rating. It was found that non-parametric techniques usually outperformed parametric techniques, likely because the underlying assumptions were not met by financial data. The top three performing modelling techniques were Random Forest, Artificial Neural Networks and Support Vector Machines. They produced models with an average accuracy of 64.6%, 63.6% and 60.1% respectively.

Credit rating forecasting is an example of an important business process that is better modelled by flexible machine learning models that, unlike traditional parametric techniques, do not make restrictive assumptions about the data. The machine learning techniques are also better able to handle collinearity between variables in the model that can cause serious problems in traditional models. Overall, as machine learning is a key component of big data analytics, credit rating forecasting is a clear example of the value and importance of big data analytics in the future business world.

An advantage of big data analytics is its adaptability to non-traditional data sources. One such example is automated sentiment analysis that determines whether there is positive or negative sentiment in text, such as annual reports or business news. Future research could incorporate the sentiment score output from big data analytics into the credit ratings models presented in this chapter. This has the potential to substantially increase accuracy given that Hajek et al. (2016) found credit ratings were affected by positive words in the relevant company's reports and negative words in associated news articles.

REFERENCES

Abdou, H., & Pointon, J. (2011). Credit scoring, statistical techniques and evaluation criteria: A review of the literature. *Intelligent Systems in Accounting, Finance & Management, 18*(2-3), 59–88. doi:10.1002/isaf.325

Breiman, L. (2001). Random Forests. *Machine Learning, 45*(1), 5–32. doi:10.1023/A:1010933404324

Cristianini, N., & Scholkopf, B. (2002). Support Vector Machines and Kernel Methods: The New Generation of Learning Machines. *AI Magazine, 23*(3), 31–41.

Elliot, J. A., & Kennedy, D. B. (1988). Estimation and prediction of categorical models in accounting research. *Journal of Accounting Literature, 7*, 202–242.

Friedman, J. H. (2001). Greedy function approximation: A gradient boosting machine. *Annals of Statistics, 29*(5), 1189–1232. doi:10.1214/aos/1013203451

Friedman, J. H. (2002). Stochastic gradient boosting. *Computational Statistics & Data Analysis, 38*(4), 367–378. doi:10.1016/S0167-9473(01)00065-2

Ganeshalingam, S., & Kumar, K. (2001). Detection and prediction of financial distress. *Managerial Finance, 27*(4), 45–55. doi:10.1108/03074350110767132

Girolami, M., & Rogers, S. (2006). Variational Bayesian multinomial probit regression with Gaussian process priors. *Neural Computation, 18*(8), 1790–1817. doi:10.1162/neco.2006.18.8.1790

Guo, Y., Hastie, T., & Tibshirani, R. (2007). Regularized linear discriminant analysis and its application in microarrays. *Biostatistics (Oxford, England)*, *8*(1), 86–100. doi:10.1093/biostatistics/kxj035 PMID:16603682

Guotai, C., & Zhipeng, Z. (2017). Multi Criteria Credit Rating Model for Small Enterprise Using a Nonparametric Method. *Sustainability*, *9*(10), 1834. doi:10.3390u9101834

Hajek, P., Olej, V., & Prochazka, O. (2016). Predicting Corporate Credit Ratings Using Content Analysis of Annual Reports – A Naïve Bayesian Network Approach. In S. Feuerriegel & D. Neumann (Eds.), Enterprise Applications, Markets and Services in the Finance Industry (pp 47-61). Springer.

Henley, W. E., & Hand, D. J. (1997). Construction of a k-nearest neighbour credit-scoring system. *IMA Journal of Management Mathematics*, *8*(4), 305–321. doi:10.1093/imaman/8.4.305

Huang, S.-C. (2011). Using Gaussian process based kernel classifiers for credit rating forecasting. *Expert Systems with Applications*, *38*(7), 8607–8611. doi:10.1016/j.eswa.2011.01.064

Huang, S.-C., Chuang, P. J., Wu, C. F., & Lai, H. J. (2010). Chaos-based support vector regressions for exchange rate forecasting. *Expert Systems with Applications*, *37*(12), 8590–8598. doi:10.1016/j.eswa.2010.06.001

Imad, B.-H. (2017). Bayesian credit ratings: A random forest alternative approach. *Communications in Statistics. Theory and Methods*, *46*(15), 7289–7300. doi:10.1080/03610926.2016.1148730

Khemakhem, S., & Boujelbene, Y. (2015). Credit Risk Prediction: A comparative study between discriminant analysis and the neural network approach. *Accounting and Management Information Systems*, *14*(1), 60–78.

Kumar, K., & Bhattacharya, S. (2006). Artificial neural network vs linear discriminant analysis in credit ratings forecast. *Review of Accounting and Finance*, *5*(3), 216–227. doi:10.1108/14757700610686426

Kumar, K., & Haynes, J. D. (2003). Forecasting credit ratings using an ANN and statistical techniques. *International Journal of Business Studies, 11*(1), 91-108.

Lilley, M., & Frean, M. (2005) Neural Networks: A Replacement for Gaussian Processes? In Intelligent Data Engineering and Automated Learning - IDEAL 2005 (pp. 195-212). Springer. doi:10.1007/11508069_26

Linkletter, C., Bingham, D., Hengartner, N., Higdon, D., & Ye, K. Q. (2006). Variable selection for Gaussian process models in computer experiments. *Technometrics*, *48*(4), 478–490. doi:10.1198/004017006000000228

Miyamoto, M. (2014). Credit risk assessment for a small bank by using a multinomial logistic regression model. *International Journal of Finance and Accounting*, *3*(5), 327–334.

Moody's Investor service. (2017). *Moody's rating system in brief.* Retrieved from https://www.moodys.com/sites/products/ProductAttachments/Moody's%20Rating%20System.pdf

Negnevitsky, M. (2011). *Artificial intelligence: a guide to intelligent systems*. Harlow, UK: Addison Wesley/Pearson.

Provost, F., & Fawcett, T. (2013). *Data science for business*. Sebastopol, CA: O'Reilly Media.

Sewell, M. (2008). *Structural Risk Minimization*. Technical Report: Department of Computer Science, University College London. Retrieved from http://www.svms.org/srm/

Shian-Chang, H. (2011). Using Gaussian process based kernel classifiers for credit rating forecasting. *Expert Systems with Applications*, *38*(7), 8607–8611. doi:10.1016/j.eswa.2011.01.064

Standard & Poor's. (2016, October 12). *Standard & Poor's History*. Retrieved from https://www.isin.net/standard-poors/

Steenackers, A., & Goovaerts, M. J. (1989). A credit scoring model for personal loans. *Insurance, Mathematics & Economics*, *8*(1), 31–34. doi:10.1016/0167-6687(89)90044-9

Stepanova, M., & Thomas, L. C. (2001). PHAB scores: Proportional hazards analysis. *The Journal of the Operational Research Society*, *52*(9), 1007–1016. doi:10.1057/palgrave.jors.2601189

Wu, H.-C., & Wu, Y.-T. (2016). Evaluating credit rating prediction by using the KMV model and random forest. *Kybernetes*, *45*(10), 1637–1651. doi:10.1108/K-12-2014-0285

Yobas, M. B., & Crook, J. N. (2000). Credit scoring using neural and evolutionary techniques. *IMA Journal of Management Mathematics*, *11*(2), 111–125. doi:10.1093/imaman/11.2.111

This research was previously published in Managerial Perspectives on Intelligent Big Data Analytics; pages 180-198, copyright year 2019 by Engineering Science Reference (an imprint of IGI Global).

APPENDIX

Cohen's Kappa statistic is best explained using an example. The following example is related to 50 events, each which is either *Yes* or *No*. The goal of the model is to predict the *Yes/No* result of each event. The accuracy of the result is derived from the underlying truth of the variable. As shown by Table 3, out of the 50 events, 20 were correctly predicted *yes* and 15 were correctly predicted *no*. That means the observed accuracy is (20+15)/50=0.70 or 70%.

Table 3. Visits to public libraries

		Truth	
		Yes	**No**
Model Prediction	**Yes**	20	5
	No	10	15

This accuracy however does not consider the expected accuracy based on the fact that, in truth, there are more *Yes* events than *No* events. Using the following equation, the Kappa statistic considers the expected chance of agreement between the truth and the model.

$$K = (P_o - P_e) / (1 - P_e),$$

where P_o represents the observed agreement and P_e represents the expected agreement.
The observed agreement is the accuracy calculated in the example above; in this case, 70%. The expected accuracy is calculated by summing the probability that the truth and the model agree on yes and agree on no:

- The model predicted *Yes* 25 (20+5) times and *No* 25 (10+15) times, which means the model predicts *Yes* 50% of the time;
- In truth, *Yes* occurs 30 (20+10) times, which represents 60% (30/50);
- Therefore, the probability that, at random, the model correctly predicts *Yes* is 0.5×0.6=0.3. The same calculation for *No* events is (1–0.5)×(1–0.6)=0.2. This process is then continued if there are more than two categories. Finally, the sum of these two figures is calculated as the expected accuracy, which is in this case 0.3+0.2=0.5.

The Kappa can then be calculated, as

$$K = \frac{0.7 - 0.5}{1 - 0.5} = 0.4$$

Chapter 40
Machine Learning for Smart Tourism and Retail

Carlos Rodríguez-Pardo
Grupo de Inteligencia Artificial Aplicada. Universidad Carlos III de Madrid, Spain

Miguel A. Patricio
Universidad Carlos III de Madrid, Spain

Antonio Berlanga
Grupo de Inteligencia Artificial Aplicada. Universidad Carlos III de Madrid, Spain

José M. Molina
Grupo de Inteligencia Artificial Aplicada. Universidad Carlos III de Madrid, Spain

ABSTRACT

The unprecedented growth in the amount and variety of data we can store about the behaviour of customers has been parallel to the popularization and development of machine learning algorithms. This confluence of factors has created the opportunity of understanding customer behaviour and preferences in ways that were undreamt of in the past. In this chapter, the authors study the possibilities of different state-of-the-art machine learning algorithms for retail and smart tourism applications, which are domains that share common characteristics, such as contextual dependence and the kind of data that can be used to understand customers. They explore how supervised, unsupervised, and recommender systems can be used to profile, segment, and create value for customers.

INTRODUCTION

The growth in the amount and diversity of data that can be obtained from people's behaviour has seen an unprecedented growth in recent years. This growth is parallel to the popularization and development of machine learning algorithms that can detect patterns in vast amounts of data. Personal electronic devices, such as smartphones, tablets or wearables are becoming ubiquitous, and the amount and variety

DOI: 10.4018/978-1-6684-6291-1.ch040

of sensors that those devices possess are raising quickly. The combination of those factors creates the opportunity of finding patterns that explain consumers' behaviours, preferences or tastes.

In this chapter, we will explore the possibility of applying artificial intelligence algorithms into smart retail and tourism problems. We will explain what are the main challenges that we need to face when creating solutions for those two fields that can learn from the past preferences and behaviours of users, as well as what are the possibilities that machine learning methods can provide for companies, both in increasing customer value and improving decision-making.

First, we will explore the use of supervised learning methods for those tasks. The use of different learning algorithms (deep neural networks, random forest, decision trees, boosting, etc.) will be motivated and compared, so that we can have a better idea on what algorithms are more suited for each task that is involved in the process of creating smart tourism applications. We will study problems such as class imbalances, overfitting, missing values or dimensionality reduction, and different ways of tackling those problems correctly. Machine learning frameworks for different programming languages will also be compared.

The use of unsupervised learning methods is of interest for this problem. Most notably, automatically detecting groups of users that behave similarly can be of great value for retail and smart tourism companies, as, from those groups, they will be able to understand better their own customers. Clustering algorithms, including Self-organised maps (SOM), Expectation-maximization (E-M), K-means or density-based methods like DBSCAN, will be compared and reviewed, as in the supervised learning part of the chapter.

The ultimate goal of using machine learning for smart retail and tourism solutions is to offer customers products and services that maximize their value. A way to do so is through recommender systems, which learn from the characteristics of products that each user has liked in the past, as well as from preferences from similar users, in order to provide a recommendation that maximizes the chance of that users buying that particular product or service. Smartphones and wearables are equipped with several sensors that can provide information about what the user is doing (is it moving, driving, running, etc.) and what are its surroundings (weather, geolocalization, etc.). This is known as contextual information, and it can provide valuable information to recommender systems. Context-aware recommender systems are algorithms that learn from past preferences of users over product taking into account the context in which they interacted with the application (e.g., e-commerce) in the past. The way in which this contextual information should be integrated into recommender systems is, nevertheless, not obvious, and there is no clear consensus in the scientific literature on to which method is preferable. In this final part of our chapter, we will analyse and compare different context-aware recommender systems, as well as different ways of representing contextual information.

In sum, the main goal of this chapters is to explore the use of three different areas of machine learning in the setting of retail and smart tourism applications: Unsupervised and supervised learning, and recommender systems. Those three areas provide algorithms that are indubitably useful for retail and touristic companies and their customers, as they can provide insights that were undreamt of in the past. Different methods will be reviewed and compared with a critical point of view and with the final goal of helping whoever is interested in creating data-driven retail and smart tourism solutions.

MACHINE LEARNING FOR RETAIL AND SMART TOURISM APPLICATIONS

Supervised Learning for User Profiling

Supervised learning is the field in machine learning concerned with learning a function that transforms an input to an output given exemplar tuples input-output. A significant part of the popularization of machine learning in many domains is due to advancements and developments in supervised learning models and the creation of vast annotated datasets. Supervised learning is typically divided in two groups, depending on the nature of the output of the function that is being learned. As such, in *regression*, the output is a natural number, whereas in *classification*, the output is the probability of the input being a member of a specific class or group. Most supervised learning algorithms that can be used for classification can also be used for regression, and vice versa. In this chapter, we will focus on classification, but the techniques can also be transferred to regression tasks.

Classification algorithms create the opportunity of inferring or estimating information about customers by means of using raw data that does not provide us with valuable information about them as an input to models that can infer valuable information. User profiling is the process of categorizing users into predefined classes, given information about them. In the retail and smart tourism domains, those classes are typically related to categories that are useful for creating value for customers. For instance, given the age of one person and the street they reside in, a classification model could be able to classify them into different groups according to their purchasing power, which is a decisive factor when purchasing products. This toy example can be extended to more descriptive classes, such as "person who likes going to concerts", etc. Supervised learning is huge topic, and we will briefly mention the techniques we believe are most useful for user profiling in the domain of retail and smart tourism. We will assume that our input data is tabular (not images, text or audio, which require a completely different set of learning algorithms) and our output is the profile of the user.

The way in which classification algorithms are trained is common for most learning algorithms. We first need a raw dataset, which is comprised of a large set of examples {input, class}. The input data can be multivariate or univariate, and the variables can be numeric, classes, etc. This dataset is preprocessed so that learning algorithms can make the most out of it, by transforming the variables into what classification algorithms expect to receive. For example, numeric variables must be normalized so that their scale does not affect the final result; missing values must be replaced, outliers must be detected and replaced (Chauvenet criteria, Dixon's Q test, Grubb's test, Mahalanobis distance), classes must be balanced (via oversampling, undersampling or generating synthetic data)(Aksoy & Haralick, 2001; Chawla, 2005; Chawla, Bowyer, Hall, & Kegelmeyer, 2002; Dougherty, Kohavi, & Mehran, 1995; Grubbs, 1950; He & Ma, 2013; Kotsiantis & Kanellopoulos, 2006; Liu, Zhang, Zhang, & Liu, 2016; Minh Phoung, Lin, & Altman, 2005; Orlov, 2011; R. B. & W. J., 1951; Rohrer, 2015), etc. In domains in which there are too many variables compared with the number of examples, this number of variables is reduced by choosing the most important ones (wrapper methods, mutual information tests, etc.) or transforming the input space into one that represents the best trade-off of number of variables and their relative variance (principal component analysis, singular value decomposition or linear discriminant analysis are common ways of doing this) (MK, 2016; University, 2016).

This dataset is then divided into a training dataset, which is used to train the classification algorithm, and a test dataset, which is used to evaluate the algorithm. The training set usually has many more samples than the test set, so that the model can learn more patterns. Optionally, it is possible to create another dataset, typically called *validation dataset*, which is used to compare different models and to find a suitable set of training hyperparameters. To evaluate the algorithms fairly, this division is done many times and the algorithm is trained and tested on different random divisions of the dataset, in a process known as cross-validation.

Many machine learning algorithms can perfectly learn the patterns in the training set, but those patterns may not be present in the test dataset. This problem is known as overfitting, which happens when the model is over-parametrized: The model has too much flexibility and has fitted noise that is present in the training dataset but is not present on new samples. To avoid this phenomenon, the most common approaches are to simplify the model, reduce the number of variables, or gather more data.

Most learning algorithms work by minimizing a scoring function, that signals the algorithm on how different the predicted output is to the real output. This scoring function is known as the loss function, and there are many different loss functions available. In classification, the most typical loss function is the cross-entropy error, which is differentiable with respect to the model parameters, but there are other widely-used functions, such as the Kullback–Leibler divergence or the mutual information. Nevertheless, the way of evaluating classification algorithms rarely uses those functions directly. Instead, other metrics are used, which are either easier to understand or more related to the problem (or both). In classification, usually the confusion matrix is reported, which shows how much each class is wrongly classified as any of the other classes, and metrics such as Positive predictive value, True Positive Rate and F1-Score are also widely used. In many problems, being able to correctly classify in one particular class is more desirable than in some other classes. For example, in the medical domain, it may be very costly to incorrectly predict that one patient is healthy than it is to incorrectly predict that they are unhealthy. Both the loss function and the metric used for reporting the results should take into consider those factors. Once the error metric has been defined, it is now possible to train different learning algorithms and compare them. The best algorithm will be the one that showed the smallest error on the test dataset.

Supervised Learning: Algorithms

In this section, several classification algorithms will be mentioned, and their capabilities will be compared so as to provide an overview onto which of them is more suitable for each problem. We will not dive into implementation or mathematical details as it is not the goal of this chapter, please use the references for details on each of those algorithms.

Linear Models

A classifier is said to be linear if it makes its classification decision by computing a linear combination of the input variables, which should be represented using a vector of scalar numbers. Linear models are usually fast in test time, they converge to a solution easily, their results are highly interpretable and, when the dimensionality of the input data is high, their results are usually comparable to those of more complex methods. Nevertheless, most problems do not show a linear behaviour, so linear models are typically used as a baseline upon which to build more complex, non-linear, models. Four sets of algorithms that belong to this class can be highlighted.

A *Naïve Bayes* classifier is a probabilistic classifier that is based on the Bayes' rule (Barber, 2010). It owes its name to its main assumption: the input variables are conditionally independent given the class. That is, if we know the output class, the input variables are all independent of each other: if we know the value of one of them, we cannot infer anything about the value of the others. This assumption usually does not hold in most domains in the real world, but it simplifies the algorithm greatly, and it is its greatest disadvantage: the conditional independence assumption makes it less accurate than other linear models. However, they provide probabilistic results, which is important in domains in which we want to know how certain we are about our predictions, and they scale well, as there are not that many parameters to estimate.

A *perceptron* classifier is a linear classifier that estimates if its input belongs to a class or to another class. It is the basis of artificial neural networks, which stack multiple perceptrons together, as well as adding non-linearities. The perceptron is usually trained in an iterative fashion, using gradient descent as the optimization algorithm. It is a simple algorithm that is easy to train and converges to the exact solution if the problem is convex and linearly separable, but as in any other linear model, its accuracy is easily surpassed by other algorithms. Additionally, it is only useful in binary classification problems. If we want to classify the input into more than 2 classes, this method is not suitable. Finally, unlike other linear methods, it does not provide a probabilistic output.

The *logistic regression* model, also known as *logit*, works similarly to the perceptron: The output is a linear combination of the input variables. Nevertheless, it extends it by adding a probabilistic interpretation to the output and support for multiple output classes. They do this by, instead of estimating if the input belongs to one class, it estimates the probability that the input belongs to each class. Therefore, its results are more interpretable, typically as accurate as the perceptron and they are easy to train. Logistic regression is typically the baseline used to compare other algorithms with.

Support Vector Machines (Nefedov, 2016) are a set of classification algorithms that find the optimal linear separation between classes. They work by transforming the input space into a higher dimensional space, in which the input data can be separated maximally. That is, they not only find a separation between classes, they find the best separation. This characteristic makes them generalize better than logistic regression models to unseen data. Using a technique known as the *kernel trick*, they can be extended to non-linear problems, and they can also be used for regression or probabilistic classification. In many classification problems, support vector machines were the state-of-the-art models until deep learning surpassed them. Nevertheless, they are extremely powerful models and are relatively fast to test and train. Despite those advantages, they are hard to interpret, and finding the optimal set of hyperparameters and configuration can be problematic.

Decision Tree Learning

Decision trees are widely used decision mechanisms that represent decision-making in a tree or graph fashion, in which nodes are connected in a hierarchical fashion (Quinlan, 1983; Russell & Norving, 2014). To make a decision on whether the input belongs to a class, the input is fed to the first node in the tree, which checks the value of one of its attributes. Depending on the value of the attribute, a different path is taken. This process is done until a terminal node is reached, which will make the decision of the class that the input example belongs to. Decision tree learning is the process of learning the structure of this tree from data. Typically, the way this is done is by choosing the attribute that best separates the classes in the dataset according to a loss function, usually entropy. Then, the dataset is divided and each of the *child* nodes in the tree performs this operation again, until the classes can be perfectly separated. To avoid over-fitting, many times, the number of nodes is limited, in a process known as *pruning*. Several algorithms can be framed in the decision tree learning field, like ID3, CART, C5.0, SEE5.0. Decision trees are one of the most easily interpretable classification models, which is an advantage in domains such as medicine. They are fast to train and test, they can provide probabilistic results, and they can be combined easily with other methods. However, they tend to overfit and its results are usually surpassed by more complex methods.

Random forests (Ho, 1998) are one of the most powerful classification algorithms in terms of their accuracy. They work by combining the predictions of several (typically thousands) decision trees that were only trained on a random subset of variables in the dataset. They can detect interactions between variables, work well on big datasets and in high-dimensional domains and provide state-of-the-art results in many domains. However, they lack the interpretability of decision trees, they are harder to train than other methods and testing is slower than in many other algorithms (as many decision trees must be checked to make a decision). Additionally, they work better when the input variables are uncorrelated.

Artificial Neural Networks

Artificial neural networks are complex machine learning models that work by stacking several perceptrons (Clevert, Unterthiner, & Hochreiter, 2015; Cuadros & Domínguez, 2014; Glorot & Bengio, 2010; Hegenbart, 2015; Jaderberg et al., 2017; Nielsen, 2017), followed by a non-linearity operation, into several layers, known as *hidden layers*. Artificial neural networks also receive the name of *deep learning* when they have at least one hidden layer. They are trained using the *back-propagation* algorithm, which allows the model to have as many hidden layers as it is wanted. They are the state-of-the-art models in many machine learning problems, including computer vision, natural language processing, protein-to-protein interaction, etc. They provide the best results in many tasks because of the non-linearity operations and because they do not saturate when they are provided with more data: they can learn indefinitely if more data is provided and if the model has enough *neurons*. They are robust to contradictory data, they have high tolerance to noise and are easy to implement thanks to the availability of high-level APIs that provide support for them. Additionally, they can be trained on any differentiable loss function, which makes them suitable for many different tasks. However, they tend to overfit, training takes a long time, their results are not interpretable, are sensitive to *adversarial noise*, and are very data-hungry, which makes them unsuitable for domains in which little data is available.

Other Models

Bayesian Networks (Barber, 2010; Friston, Mattout, Trujillo-Barreto, Ashburner, & Penny, 2007; Penny, 2012)are probabilistic classifiers that model conditional dependencies of variables and the output classes using a graph structure. Unlike *Naïve Bayes*, they do not assume conditional independencies of variables, which makes them more accurate. Given a fixed graph, finding the model parameters is usually easy, but learning the graph structure is usually hard, and done using algorithms such as Expectation-Maximization, which do not necessarily converge to an optimal solution. They are highly interpretable, accurate and can handle missing values with easy. Moreover, they can be used to estimate those missing values. However, estimation in Bayesian Networks is not trivial, and techniques like D-separation or Markov blankets are needed for this process.

Boosting (Freund & Schapire, 1997; Friedman, 1999) algorithms are a set of machine learning algorithms that work by training *weak classifiers*, such as decision tree, and iteratively train algorithms on the data points in which the decision tree cannot correctly predict the class of the input. *Gradient boosting machines* are one of the most powerful boosting models, and it uses gradient descent for helping the boosting task. This set of algorithms is similar to random forests in their advantages and disadvantages: They are powerful, but they tend to overfit, are slow in inference time, and their results are not interpretable.

K-nearest neighbours is a classification (and regression) method that, given a new data point, predicts its class by finding the K closest points to that point, and finding their most common class. There is no learning phase, which can be beneficial in domains in which datasets change a lot over time, but they are very slow (you need to compare the input point to all the other points in the dataset) in inference time, they are not interpretable, finding the optimal K is usually hard, and its accuracy is usually worse to most other models.

Wrap-Up

Supervised learning provides retail and smart tourism companies with the capability of inferring information about their customers with an unprecedented level of detail and precision. In order to do so, machine learning and data science practitioners need to be careful in the way they obtain, process and use their data, so as to make the most value out of it. Several algorithms have been compared, most of which are the basis of many machine learning projects. Nevertheless, this is an active line of research, so it is likely that more models, training algorithms and datasets will be available in the future.

Unsupervised Learning for User Segmentation

Unsupervised learning is the field in machine learning which is concerned on the discovery of patterns from unlabelled data. Unlike in supervised learning, the goal is not to learn a function that maps from one known domain to another known domain, instead it is to find internal structures in the data that allows to represent the data more densely or more compactly. Among the typical algorithms that are belong in unsupervised learning, autoencoders, clustering algorithms and dimensionality reduction methods stand out as the most widely used.

User segmentation is a process which has the goal of building groups or segments of users that are similar to each other and different to the users which belong to the other groups or segments, according to some similarity criteria. A typical use of user segmentation is to create customer segments, which allows the definition of specific marketing campaigns for each segment, thus providing them with more value and a more personalised experience. Even if the best way to create value for each customer would be to personalize campaigns individually for each user, this can be costly and difficult to automate. Customer segmentation provides a middle ground between treating the whole customer population homogenously and assuming the cost of extremely individualised marketing campaigns. This process was traditionally hand-crafted, with experts manually defining both the customer segments and the marketing campaigns that those segments were going to receive. This is a risky endeavour, as it is possible that experts in retail companies do not fully understand their customers or they introduce their own biases into the segmentation process.

A family of unsupervised learning algorithms, known as clustering algorithms, can be used for the automatic discovery of such segments, by analysing the past behaviour of the customers. This has several advantages over hand-crafting the definition of the segments. Besides the fact that machine learning methods are unbiased (the biases they reflect are contained on the data or they were manually introduced by the machine learning practitioners, but not on the methods themselves), those algorithms typically find more complex patterns than what a typical customer segmentation would use. This allows the discovery of fine-grained groups of customers with very specific behaviours. Clustering algorithms provide the opportunity of automating this task, but the variety of available methods can make it hard to choose an optimal method for solving this task.

In this section of the chapter, we will briefly introduce the clustering algorithms that we find to be the most suitable for customer segmentation in the retail and smart tourism fields. The decision between which of those algorithms are most suitable for a task depends on the goal of the task, the amount and characteristics of the data that is available and other requirements, like visualization capabilities or interpretability. An important decision to make when using a clustering algorithm is the distance metric, which is equivalent to the loss function in supervised learning: It is used to measure how much one customer behaves like another customer. Amongst those metrics, we find the Euclidean distances (L norms) and non-euclidean distances (Hamming, Gaussian, cosine similarty, Jaccard, edit distance, etc.) (Commons, 2016). Please use the references for details on those distances. It is worth noting that most of the data pre-processing methods that were mentioned in the supervised learning part of this chapter should also be used before applying any clustering algorithm. We will assume that each customer will only be placed in one group of customers (clusters are separate of each other).

Clustering Algorithms

The *expectation-maximization* algorithm (E-M) is a optimization algorithm which is used to find maximum-a-posteriori parameter estimators in machine learning models which depend on unobservable latent variables. The algorithm alternates two phases: One *expectation* step, which computes the likelihood of the data given the estimated parameters, and a *maximization*, which re-estimates the parameters given the computed likelihood. If those two steps are computed interatively enough times, the algorithm typically converges to a local minimum, as there are typically many possible solutions to this task. In clustering, this algorithm is used to find the centers of clusters (groups of points) and the size of the cluster (typically measured in standard deviations). E-M is used for many tasks, including parameter estimation in Hidden Markov Models, but they can be used for clustering by using E-M to fit a Gaussian Mixture Model, which is a cluster analysis method that assumes that each cluster can be represented using a multivariate Gaussian (A.Bilmes, 1998; Choung B Do, 2008; Lab, 2015). The advantages of this method over other clustering algorithm include that the assignation of individuals to one cluster is probabilistic, so it provides an uncertainty measurement which is useful in many domains; and it generalizes to many different clustering requirements: It is possible to assume different characteristics for the clusters (e.g. gaussian or non-gaussian shape) and the algorithm will work. Nevertheless, E-M rarely converges to the global minimum, it is highly dependent on the parameter initialization and can be slow to train. Besides, it is necessary to indicate the number of clusters (or customer segments) that the algorithm needs to find.

K-means is a clustering algorithm which implicitly uses E-M as its optimization procedure. It groups the data into K clusters, based on some similarity criteria. Given an initialization of the cluster center, the algorithm assigns to each cluster those points that are closer to that cluster than to any other cluster. Then, the center of each cluster is re-computed so that it becomes the center of the data points that were assigned to it in the previous step. Those two steps are computed until a convergence criteria is met. K-means is a widely used algorithm due to its simplicity and because it typically converges faster than other clustering methods, but it has several disadvantages. Most notably, you need to specify the value of K (which in some sense introduces biases to the algorithm), the result highly depends on the initialization of the cluster centers, and it is not possible to provide a probabilistic assignment of customer over clusters. Nevertheless, several improvements have been proposed to alleviate some of those issues ((MathWorks), 2008; Arthur, 2007; Bin Mohamad & Usman, 2013; Towers, 2013). We believe that K-means is a good baseline upon which to build more sophisticated customer segmentations. Its results can be visualized using Voronoi diagrams (Riddhiman, 2016).

Self-organising maps (SOM) are a set of unsupervised learning algorithms loosely based on artificial neural networks(Burguillo, 2013; MathWorks, n.d.; Rey-López, Barragáns-Martínez, Peleteiro, Mikic-Fonte, & Burguillo, 2011). They were designed for finding a denser representation of the input data, in a similar way to what auto-encoders typically do. They can be used for finding customer segments, as they can be used seamlessly for clustering. Unlike in many other clustering methods, the resulting clusters have a neighbourhood property (there is a pre-defined notion of distance between clusters), and the clusters are organized automatically in a map of clusters, hence the name. Thus, despite the fact that it is necessary that we pre-define the number of clusters, those clusters can be further grouped together if we find the results to be too fine-grained. We believe that this family of algorithm provide an advantageous balance of cluster quality, interpretability and other desirable properties for customer segmentation. Their results can be visualized easily by means of the Unified Distance Matrix (Binwu Wang Danfeng Sun, 2014; Rodriguez-Pardo, Patricio, Berlanga, & Molina, 2017) However, they are typically slow to train, and they typically get stuck in a local minimum, as is usual in algorithms that are trained using gradient descent.

Density-based spatial clustering of applications with noise (DBSCAN) is a clustering algorithm which bases its similarity criteria in a density estimation. More precisely, it finds an indefinite number of clusters by grouping together points that are close to each other. This allows the discovery of clusters with complex shapes, which is a significant advantage over simpler clustering methods such as K-means, which can only find circular-shaped clusters. They can also be used for the discovery of outlier points. However, they can be slow and are very sensitive to hyperparameter specification (Martin Ester Jörg Sander, Xiaowei Xu, 1996).

Ordering points to identify the clustering structure (OPTICS) is another density-based algorithm that solves one of the main problems of DBSCAN, as it can find clusters with different densities. It uses hierarchical clustering for grouping points together. Despite this improvement, they suffer from most of the other disadvantages of DBSCAN, most notably the sensitivity to hyperparameter specification. Its results can be visualized using a reachability plot (Ankerst, Breunig, Kriegel, & Sander, 1999; Boe-Hansen, Berg, Amigo, & Babamoradi, 2015).

Hierarchical clustering is a clustering methods that groups points together into a hierarchy of clusters. This can be done in two ways: a divisive clustering, which starts with only one clusters and separates the clusters in a binary fashion, or agglomerative clustering (the most typical), which groups the two most similar points or clusters together until all points have been assigned to a cluster. The main advantages of this family of clustering algorithms is that there is no need for pre-defining the number of clusters, and their results are highly interpretable as they can be visualized using a *dendrogram*. However, they are very slow to train and do not scale well when the number of data points increase. (Dzobo, Alvehag, Gaunt, & Herman, 2014; Galili, 2015; Y.-S. Lee & Cho, 2011; Mathworks, n.d.; Schonlau, 2002; Vandekerckhove, Tuerlinckx, & Lee, 2011). This method can be extended in many ways, including Ward's method (Minnesota, n.d.; Mojena, 2004; Mojena, Mojena, & Richard, 2006).

It can be burdensome to evaluate the quality of the clustering performed by the aforementioned algorithms. Unlike in supervised learning, where there are objective quality metrics that can be used to compare the results of the algorithms, in unsupervised learning those metrics do not exist to the same extent. However, there are some ways to empirically measure some desireable properties of the clusters, including the average and minimal distance between clusters, their densities, similarities, entropy, etc. (Hennig, 2013). Those results can also be analysed by domain experts (eg: What is the average age in this customer segment? What is the behaviour of this segment? Is it different to the other segments in a meaningful way?).

Wrap-Up

Unsupervised learning provides retail and smart tourism companies with the capability of automating segmenting their customers in meaningful ways. In this section we have summarised some of the state of the art algorithms that we find most suitable for this task, and briefly discussed ways of comparing the results of those algorithms.

Context-Aware Recommender Systems

Recommender Systems: Main Approaches and Their Capabilities

Recommender systems (RS) are filtering systems that are used to provide users with recommendations about items or products they have not seen, rated, or purchased yet. They gained popularity in the scientific literature in the 1990s (Schafer, Konstan, & Riedi, 1999), due to the growth of online stores, which led to an exponential increment in the amount of information that can be obtained about the preferences of users. Those circumstances created the necessary conditions for the boom in recommender systems. RS typically work by estimating how each user will rate (e.g., how much they will like) a specific item or product by analysing how they have rated similar products, using some similarity metric.

Accordingly, one of the most important decisions to make when designing a recommender system is how to represent how much a user liked an item(Bobadilla, Ortega, Hernando, & Gutiérrez, 2013; Ricci, Rokach, & Shapira, 2011). Traditionally, this is done by assigning a numeric value to those preferences. This is advantageous because numeric values are easy to work with by computers, users can easily and rapidly provide them, and they simple to store in structured databases, as opposed to more complex representations, such as user-written reviews, which require the use of complex natural language processing algorithms. Those numeric values that represent preferences of users can be obtained implicitly (eg., a user has watched a movie, listened to a song, bought a product), or explicitly (by asking the users to provide a numeric value to the product or item). Both methods have their advantages. Implicit methods are less invasive and require less user interaction, which is important for some user experiences, whereas explicit methods are more descriptive, and the users are provided with more control on the products they are recommender with. Regardless on the method, by using a numeric representation on those preferences, it is possible to predict the rating that users will give to products they do not know, by analysing how they rated similar products (the notion of similarity in recommender systems is one of their defining factors).

Recommender systems are typically classified into three groups in the scientific literature, depending on the information they use to model user preferences (Bobadilla et al., 2013; Isinkaye, Folajimi, & Ojokoh, 2015; Ricci et al., 2011). The way in which that information is beyond the introductory nature of this chapter, but many useful resources can be found in the references provided. Context-aware recommender systems are an extension of baseline recommender systems. Therefore, a brief overview of recommender systems is provided so that context-awareness can be easily understood in the context of providing users with recommendations.

Collaborative Filtering

Collaborative filtering recommender systems model user preferences over unseen products by assuming that, if one user has rated a set of items in a certain way, it is likely that they will rate unseen products similarly to how other users, who rated the first set of items in the same way, rated that product. This type of recommender system assumes that users that behaved similarly in the past will also behave similarly in the future (Ekstrand, Riedl, & Konstan, 2011; Isinkaye et al., 2015; Li, Lu, & Xuefeng, 2005; Schafer, Frankowski, Herlocker, & Sen, 2007; Schafer et al., 1999; C. Wang & Blei, 2011). Therefore, they do not use characteristics of the products themselves. Collaborative filtering has several advantages over other approaches. Most notably, they can provide more precise recommendations, over a greater variety of products, because it can find patterns that are more complex and meaningful than what other methods can handle, given enough data. They do not rely on descriptions of products, which could be used for finding characteristics that explain user preferences but can be hard to analyse robustly, and, most importantly, they do not assume that users are independent of each other. Most of those reasons explain why collaborative filtering is the basis of some of the most successful recommender systems. Nevertheless, they come with some problems. Most notably, they suffer from a problem known as cold start, which happens when not enough data has been gathered on the preferences of users, so recommendations that the system provides the users with are not accurate. Collaborative filtering works best when there are many users in the systems, which are actively rating products.

There are three common ways of implementing collaborative filtering in recommender systems. Traditionally, memory-based collaborative filtering (Baltrunas & Ricci, 2014; Kim, Lee, & Chung, 2014; J. Lee, Sun, & Lebanon, 2012; Su & Khoshgoftaar, 2009) has been the most used method. This method stores a matrix of (users, products, ratings), and then compute a similarity metric that finds, for a given user, the most similar users to them in the database (in the way they rated products in the past) and recommends products by weighting the preferences of users by that similarity metric, most typically the cosine similarity or statistical correlation. This approach has been substituted lately by model-based collaborative filtering (Breese, Heckerman, & Kadie, 1998; Chen, Liu, Huang, & Sun, 2010; Goldberg, Roeder, Gupta, & Perkins, 2001; Karatzoglou, Amatriain, Baltrunas, & Oliver, 2010; Koren & Yehuda, 2008; Lam, Vu, Le, & Duong, 2008; Rendle, n.d.; Roffo & Ing-Inf05, 2017; Schafer et al., 2007; Su & Khoshgoftaar, 2009; H. Wang, Wang, & Yeung, 2015; Yao et al., 2015), which uses complex machine learning algorithms for learning user preferences. Instead of using the raw aforementioned matrix, they learn a model from that matrix, with the goal of learning a denser representation of the preferences of users. This can be done in an unsupervised way (by using dimensionality reduction algorithms, such as singular value decomposition) or in a supervised way (most typically using Factorization Machines, Bayesian Networks, Artificial Neural Networks or decision trees). Finally, those approaches can be combined, in what is called hybrid collaborative filtering.

Content-Based Recommender Systems

Another group that is commonly studied in the literature is known as content-based recommender systems, which goes in the opposite direction to collaborative filtering. They assume that all the information that explains user preferences is contained on the descriptions of each product. Therefore, they define each product using a set of descriptors (e.g. price, name, categories, brand, color, latent spaces of neural networks, etc.), that can be used to extract the properties that are important for each user. They assume that if a user tends to like products with a particular property, they will like unseen products with that same property(Felfernig, Friedrich, Jannach, & Zanker, 2006; Lops, de Gemmis, & Semeraro, 2011; Martínez, Barranco, Pérez, & Espinilla, 2008). Content-based recommender systems are able to adapt dynamically to changes of the preferences of users and they are not as adversely affected by the cold start problem (Lam et al., 2008). Therefore, they are ideal for domains in which preferences change rapidly and there are not many users in the database that could be used to find patterns with. The success of those systems depends on the quality and quantity of the available descriptors, and how much the user interacts with the system. Despite their advantages, they show problems that can make them unsuitable for many domains. Most notably, they do not exploit inter-user similarity, the recommendations they provide their users with are typically very similar to what they have rated before (Isinkaye et al., 2015), each user must be modelled individually, which can be computationally costly, and, in general, the recommendations are not as accurate as what collaborative filtering is capable of.

Learning user preferences in content-based recommender systems can be modelled as a supervised learning problem, in which we are given a set of tuples (item descriptors, user rating), and we want to learn, from data, a function that maps the item descriptors to the user ratings, with the goal of generalizing to unseen products. As the domains in which content-based recommender systems are implemented are usually not populated with a great amount of data, learning in those systems is a typical few-shot supervised learning problem. Therefore, simpler learning algorithms, such as Naïve Bayes, Logistic Regression, Linear Discriminant Analysis or Support Vector Machines (Lops et al., 2011), are more popular in content-based recommender systems than more complex algorithms, such as neural networks or boosting methods. Moreover, simpler methods are faster to train and less memory-heavy, which is beneficial as one model is needed for each user in the system.

Hybrid Recommender Systems

The third group in our list is known as hybrid systems(Chen et al., 2010; Li et al., 2005; Su & Khoshgoftaar, 2009), which combine different sources of information to model user preferences. Usually, they combine collaboratively-sourced preferences with item descriptors, by weighting the predictions of collaborative filtering and content-based methods. They can also benefit from other data, such as user profiling (gender, age, nationality, etc.). A common way of implementing hybrid systems is having two independent models, a content-based system and a collaborative filtering system, and combine their predictions using a model on top on both. This model can be simple (averaging both predictions) or more complex (by training a learning model that learns to weight both predictions together).

Challenges and Future Trends

Despite the capabilities of the aforementioned models, which have shown success in different domains, there are challenges that neither approach have been able to fully address. Data sparsity and scalability concerns have been partially resolved by model-based recommender systems, which apply dimensionality reduction or machine learning methods to obtain a smaller representation of the preferences of the user without losing accuracy. The cold start problem in collaborative filtering systems has not been solved, which can create extremely inaccurate predictions. This is a problem for the user experience, and ultimately can be detrimental for obtaining new users or keeping current customers.

Hybrid recommender systems have the potential to solve the problems that content-based and collaborative filtering systems individually pose, but they come with a cost. One of the motivations behind using collaborative filtering is that defining the set of descriptors for each product is costly and can reduce the dynamism of the system because it can increase the time it takes to include a new product in the system. Nevertheless, for some domains, it is possible to automatically define this set of descriptors, by means of using natural language processing or by using a machine learning system to do this task (for example using an autoencoder to find a dense numeric representation of the product). In the future, we can expect that the use of new deep learning approaches can significantly increase the accuracy of the models, and better data storage systems and sources of information will enrich those systems.

Nonetheless, one of the challenges the recommender systems literature has not been able to fully solve is how to include dynamic, time-dependent, information that can influence the preferences of users. User preferences may change significantly in short periods of times, in different ways and time windows for each user. Failing to include those patterns in recommender systems will diminish their quality and will create less value for customer and revenue for companies. Context-aware recommender systems are a first approximation to tackling this problem.

Evaluating Recommender Systems

The way in which recommender systems are evaluated is typically related with the accuracy of the predictions they perform. Simply put, we compare the real ratings users give to products with the predicted ratings, using a similarity metric like the mean squared error, correlation or cross-entropy. This is advantageous in scientific terms, as learning can be done over those metrics via differentiation, and those metrics are widely used in many scientific domains. Nevertheless, there is some controversy on the use of those metrics, because they do not consider the value created for the user or the revenue created for the company that owns the recommender system (e.g. the system could be recommending products that the user likes but that do not provide a lot of revenue due to their price or financial or operating reasons).

Regardless of this controversy, there are empirical studies that provide insights onto which of the many available recommender systems is most beneficial for a particular domain (Baltrunas & Ricci, 2014; Hu, Koren, & Volinsky, n.d.; Isinkaye et al., 2015; J. Lee et al., 2012; Lombardi, Anand, & Gorgoglione, 2009; Pu, Chen, & Hu, 2012; Tamine-Lechani, Boughanem, & Daoud, 2010). From them, several interesting conclusions can be extracted. For instance, recommender systems that use matrix factorization or machine learning consistently obtain the best accuracies. Among them, singular value decomposition, probabilistic factorization machines and non-parametric principal component analysis stand out due to their balance of simplicity, lack of computational cost and accuracy. Other methods, such as memory-based collaborative filtering, provide less accurate predictions but their results are more easily interpretable.

As in many other problems in machine learning and data analysis, one of the deciding factors of the success of an automatic decision-making system is the amount of data that is available for learning patterns that can be used to make decisions. In the context of recommender systems, this is measured using the density of the ratings matrix (Panniello, Tuzhilin, Gorgoglione, Palmisano, & Pedone, 2009). For a fixed number of users and items in the database, this density increases when users provide more ratings, thus reducing the uncertainty of their preferences. The denser this matrix is, the more patterns can be learned, and the recommendations will be more accurate.

Context-Aware Recommender Systems

The widely-spread availability and popularity of portable electronic devices, such as smartphones or wearables, along with the development of algorithms capable of finding complex patterns on vast amounts of data has made it possible to estimate contextual information that can be used to feed recommender systems with additional data that they can use to improve their estimations.

Contextual information in recommender systems is information that can be used to understand the environment surrounding the user, which may influence the way they perceive the world, and therefore has an influence on their preferences (Dey, 2001). Contextual information is by nature dynamic and time-dependent. Therefore, the context in recommender systems is the set of items that can temporarily change the preferences of a user towards a set of items. Users may have different preferences depending on their location, the weather in that location, the time of the day, the activity there are doing, etc. Incorporating those variables in our predictive systems creates the opportunity of providing more value to the user, in unprecedented ways. Smartphones and wearables can be used to know the location of one user at any given time. This can be matched with external APIs to know the weather surrounding them, estimating the activity they are doing, knowing the amount of people in that same location, etc. Moreover, most smartphones provide activity recognition (the user is walking, running, in a bus, standing still, etc.) using data from the sensors they incorporate. It is likely, for instance, that users that are users that are running in the countryside have different preferences to users that are sitting on a restaurant in the city centre.

While in baseline recommender systems the basic database entry was <user, item, rating>, including contextual information adds another field to describe each rating, which becomes <user, **context**, item, rating>. This context is defined as a vector of smaller contextual variables. For example, weather, location, activity and time of the day. The more descriptive the representation of the context is, the bigger this vector will become, which can be problematic in terms of data sparsity. Simply put, if we are too granular when representing the context, we may not have enough observations for each possible <user, **context**, item, rating> tuples, which will make the recognition of patterns more difficult (Karatzoglou et al., 2010). Manually defining the granularity of the description of the contextual information can be cumbersome, which is why the typical approach is to store contextual information in the most granular way that is possible given the technology, and then reduce this granularity using a dimensionality reduction technique. For instance, the model will receive a contextual vector that represents 20 different contextual variables, and using principal component analysis or a wrapper method, the model will reduce those 20 variables to only 2 variables that represent the maximal amount of information. Nevertheless, the way in which contextual information is represented is an increasingly studied topic in the literature, so we may see changes to this approach in the future.

The goal of any context-aware recommender system is to find a function that maps the context, the user and the item to a numeric rating. The way in which context is included in the recommender system is not a fully solved problem and several approaches have been proposed in the literature. Three main approaches can be highlighted.

Pre-Filtering Context-Aware Recommender Systems

Pre-filtering context-aware recommender systems utilize a two-phased algorithm to predict ratings. As their name suggests, the first step when predicting new ratings is to filter the data that is relevant for the given context (G. Adomavicius & Tuzhilin, 2005; Gediminas Adomavicius, Sankaranarayanan, Sen, &

Tuzhilin, 2005; Gediminas Adomavicius & Tuzhilin, 2015). Then, that data is fed to a typical recommender system and the prediction is done without taking context into consideration anymore. In other terms, contextual information is used to take into account only the ratings that were done in a similar context. Then, those ratings are used by a typical collaborative filtering or content-based system for predicting the ratings over new items.

Pre-filtering systems have several advantages over other approaches. First, there is no need to predefine the granularity of the contextual information. When predicting a new rating, it is possible to provide the model with different levels of granularity(Lombardi et al., 2009; Zheng, Burke, & Mobasher, 2012), so that it takes into account more samples or, so the context is more similar to the input context. This creates the possibility of being adaptive to the number of samples for a given context and creates flexibility for both users and the designers of the recommender system. Additionally, this approach completely separates the recommender system from its context-awareness part, which is beneficial in terms of modularity. As such, you can optimize the recommender system by itself, without considering the context, and vice-versa.

Nevertheless, those advantages can be outweighed by its limitations. When filtering ratings, it is possible to filter too many samples in the database, thus limiting the number and complexity of patterns found by the recommender system. It is hard to balance the descriptiveness of the context and having a sufficient number of samples for the recommender system to work with. Moreover, as each new query to the system is made with different data, model-based recommender systems are harder to train, as you either need a big number of models per user and context, or you need to train a new model in every query, which can take time and the output of the query could be obtained after the users' context has changed and therefore the query is no longer useful.

Post-Filtering Context-Aware Recommender Systems

Oppositely, post-filtering systems revert the two phases described in the pre-filtering section of this chapter. Here, in the first phase, all ratings are considered, ignoring the context in which those ratings were created, as in any other recommender system. This allows the system to use the maximal amount of data as possible and alleviates some of the problems that were mentioned in the pre-filtering section.

Then, we obtain an estimated rating for all the items the user has never seen before. For this set of items, a filtering is done to discard those that do not make sense due to the context of the user. There are two ways in which this can be done. First, one can eliminate the items that the user may like but in a completely different context, or the system can learn to modify those predicted ratings so as to consider the contextual information.

As in pre-filtering, one disadvantage is that is hard to balance the filtering of the contextual information and the quality of the predictions. In this case, it can be difficult not to discard too many or too little items for recommendations, or to overfit or underfit the filtered estimations. It is computationally more costly than pre-filtering, as all ratings are taken into account by the learning system, but its predictions can be more accurate. There is no consensus on the literature onto which of those two approaches is better (Panniello et al., 2009; White, Bailey, & Chen, 2009), and it has been proven that both can be better than the other, depending on the goals of the system, its domain, the amount of data available or how much interpretability we want to impose on the predictions of the system.

Model-Based Context-Aware Recommender Systems

Despite the simplicity of pre and post-filtering systems in the domain of context-aware recommender systems, those approaches have been recently substituted by model-based systems (Gediminas Adomavicius et al., 2005; Gediminas Adomavicius & Tuzhilin, 2015; Gavalas, Konstantopoulos, Mastakas, & Pantziou, 2014; Karatzoglou et al., 2010; Kim et al., 2014; J. Lee et al., 2012; Lombardi et al., 2009; Millard, De Roure, & Shadbolt, 2005; Tamine-Lechani et al., 2010; White et al., 2009; Yao et al., 2015; Zheng et al., 2012), which can learn more complex relationships between user preferences and contextual information. In model-based systems, there is no separation between the phase of rating predictions and the phase of including contextual information in the model. As such, the context is considered as just another variable for the model to learn with.

Due to the data sparsity that is typical in these systems, the most popular approaches have used matrix factorization algorithms, which can dramatically reduce the dimensions of the ratings tensor, making the whole system computationally and memory efficient than filtering algorithms whilst returning more accurate predictions and making use of all the available data. We can expect the popularization of model-based systems in this domain, despite their lack of interpretability.

FUTURE RESEARCH DIRECTIONS

There are other techniques in artificial intelligence that have a potential applicability into retail and smart tourism applications. Recently, generative models and new types of autoencoders (most notably variational autoencoders) have been proven to be effective for different generative tasks and latent space interpolation. Those models could be used in different tasks for retail and smart tourism. For example, for generating *synthetic* customers that are plausible, which could be useful for simulations, or for improving datasets by generating more data that can be used to train machine learning models.

Additionally, recent advancements in natural language processing and computer vision create the opportunity of understanding more about customers and tourists. For example, by analysing the images posted in social media, or by reading the reviews of products written by them, it should be possible to better understand their context and their preferences.

Besides, it is likely that more sensors will be incorporated into handheld devices, which opens the opportunity of having richer contextual information. The way in which the data obtained by those sensors can be transformed into valuable information to be used by context-aware recommender systems is unknown and an interesting research question.

CONCLUSION

In this chapter, we have provided an introductory overview on the capabilities of machine learning in the smart tourism and retail domains. More precisely, we have explained the usage of supervised, unsupervised and recommender systems with a focus on the algorithms that we believe to be most useful for those domains. We have ordered the sections in the chapter with the purpose of providing a logical and coherent view over the capabilities of those fields into the retail and smart tourism domains. In particular, we believe that supervised learning can be of a great use towards building smart systems that can learn from data. The result of supervised learning can be applied as input to unsupervised learning methods in a more seamless way than in the inverse of this process. Conversely, by applying supervised and unsupervised learning to understand users or customers, it is possible to feed recommender systems with data that can be used to understand customers' preferences over items more precisely. In sum, this chapter provides a brief overview on the basic machine learning models that are the most useful for the domains we wanted to focus on.

In the future, when better algorithms, more data, better hardware and software is available, it is likely that we see a more widespread use of those techniques. We believe that the interplay between the three kinds of learning mentioned in this chapter will create a significant opportunity for creating value for customers, revenue for companies and other interests that public and private institutions have.

REFERENCES

Adomavicius, G. (2015). Context-Aware Recommender Systems. In Recommender Systems Handbook. Academic Press. doi:10.1007/978-1-4899-7637-6_6

Adomavicius, G., Sankaranarayanan, R., Sen, S., & Tuzhilin, A. (2005). Incorporating contextual information in recommender systems using a multidimensional approach. *ACM Transactions on Information Systems*, *23*(1), 103–145. doi:10.1145/1055709.1055714

Adomavicius, G., & Tuzhilin, A. (2005). Toward the next generation of recommender systems: A survey of the state-of-the-art and possible extensions. *IEEE Transactions on Knowledge and Data Engineering*, *17*(6), 734–749. doi:10.1109/TKDE.2005.99

Aksoy, S., & Haralick, R. M. (2001). Feature Normalization and Likelihood-based Similarity Measures for Image Retrieval. *Pattern Recognition Letters*, *22*(5), 563–582. doi:10.1016/S0167-8655(00)00112-4

Ankerst, M., Breunig, M. M., Kriegel, H.-P., & Sander, J. (1999). OPTICS: Ordering Points To Identify the Clustering Structure. *ACM SIGMOD'99 Int. Conf. on Management of Data.*

Arthur, D. (2007). *k-means++: The Advantages of Careful Seeding*. Academic Press.

Baltrunas, L., & Ricci, F. (2014). Experimental evaluation of context-dependent collaborative filtering using item splitting. *User Modeling and User-Adapted Interaction*, *24*(1–2), 7–34. doi:10.100711257-012-9137-9

Barber, D. (2010). *Bayesian Reasoning and Machine Learning*. Academic Press.

Ben Schafer, J., Frankowski, D., Herlocker, J., & Sen, S. (2007). Collaborative Filtering Recommender Systems. In The Adaptive Web (pp. 291–324). Academic Press. doi:10.1007/978-3-540-72079-9_9

Ben Schafer, J., Konstan, J., & Riedi, J. (1999). Recommender systems in e-commerce. *Proceedings of the 1st ACM Conference on Electronic Commerce - EC '99*, 158–166. 10.1145/336992.337035

Bilmes, A. J. (1998). A Gentle Tutorial of the EM Algorithm and its Application to Parameter Estimation for Gaussian Mixture and Hidden Markov Models. International Computer Science Institute, U.C. Berkeley.

Bin Mohamad, I., & Usman, D. (2013). Standarization and Its Effects on K-Means Clustering Algortihm. *Research Journal of Applied Sciences, Engineering and Technology*, *16*(7), 3033–3299.

Binwu Wang Danfeng Sun, H. L. (2014). Social-Ecological Patterns of Soil Heavy Metals Based on a Self-Organizing Map (SOM): A Case Study in Beijing, China. *International Journal of Environmental Research and Public Health*, 3618–3638. PMID:24690947

Bobadilla, J., Ortega, F., Hernando, A., & Gutiérrez, A. (2013). Recommender systems survey. *Knowledge-Based Systems*, *46*, 109–132. doi:10.1016/j.knosys.2013.03.012

Boe-Hansen, G., van den Berg, F. W. J., Amigo, J. M., & Babamoradi, H. (2015). Quality assessment of boar semen by multivariate analysis of flow cytometric data. *Chemometrics and Intelligent Laboratory Systems*, 142.

Breese, J. S., Heckerman, D., & Kadie, C. (1998). Empirical Analysis of Predictive Algorithms for Collaborative Filtering. *UAI'98 Proceedings of the Fourteenth Conference on Uncertainty in Artificial Intelligence*, 43–52.

Burguillo, J. C. (2013). Playing with complexity: From cellular evolutionary algorithms with coalitions to self-organizing maps. *Computers & Mathematics with Applications (Oxford, England)*, 66.

Chawla, N. V. (2005). Data Mining for Imbalanced Datasets: An Overview. *Data Mining and Knowledge Discovery Handbook*, 853–867.

Chawla, N. V., Bowyer, K. W., Hall, L. O., & Kegelmeyer, W. P. (2002). SMOTE: Synthetic minority over-sampling technique. *Journal of Artificial Intelligence Research*, *16*(1), 321–357. doi:10.1613/jair.953

Chen, X., Liu, X., Huang, Z., & Sun, H. (2010). RegionKNN: A Scalable Hybrid Collaborative Filtering Algorithm for Personalized Web Service Recommendation. *2010 IEEE International Conference on Web Services*, 9–16. 10.1109/ICWS.2010.27

Choung, B., & Do, S. B. (2008). What is the expectation maximization algorithm? *Computational Biology*, *26*(8), 897–899. PMID:18688245

Clevert, D.-A., Unterthiner, T., & Hochreiter, S. (2015). Fast and Accurate Deep Network Learning by Exponential Linear Units (ELUs). *ICLR*, *2016*, 1–14. doi:10.3233/978-1-61499-672-9-1760

Commons, A. (2016). *Clustering algorithms and distance measures*. Retrieved from http://commons.apache.org/proper/commons-math/userguide/ml.html

Cuadros, A. J., & Domínguez, V. E. (2014). Customer segmentation model based on value generation for marketing strategies formulation. *Estudios Gerenciales*, *30*(130), 25–30. doi:10.1016/j.estger.2014.02.005

Dey, A. K. (2001). Understanding and using context. *Personal and Ubiquitous Computing*, *5*(1), 4–7. doi:10.1007007790170019

Dougherty, J., Kohavi, R., & Mehran, S. (1995). Supervised and Unsupervised Discretization of Continuous Features. *Machine Learning: Proceedings of the Twelfth International Conference*, 194–202.

Dzobo, O., Alvehag, K., Gaunt, C. T., & Herman, R. (2014). Multi-dimensional customer segmentation model for power system reliability-worth analysis. *International Journal of Electrical Power & Energy Systems*, *62*, 532–539. doi:10.1016/j.ijepes.2014.04.066

Ekstrand, M. D., Riedl, J. T., & Konstan, J. A. (2011). Collaborative Filtering Recommender Systems. *Human-Computer Interaction*, *4*(2), 81–173. doi:10.1561/1100000009

Ester, Sander, & Xu. (1996). A Density-Based Algorithm for Discovering Clusters in Large Spatial Databases with Noise. *KDD: Proceedings / International Conference on Knowledge Discovery & Data Mining. International Conference on Knowledge Discovery & Data Mining*, (96), 227–231.

Felfernig, A., Friedrich, G., Jannach, D., & Zanker, M. (2006). An Integrated Environment for the Development of Knowledge-Based Recommender Applications. *International Journal of Electronic Commerce*, *11*(2), 11–34. doi:10.2753/JEC1086-4415110201

Freund, Y., & Schapire, R. E. (1997). A Decision-Theoretic Generalization of On-Line Learning and an Application to Boosting. *Journal of Computer and System Sciences*, *55*(1), 119–139. doi:10.1006/jcss.1997.1504

Friedman, J. H. (1999). *Greedy Function Aproximation: A Gradient Boosting Machine*. Academic Press.

Friston, K., Mattout, J., Trujillo-Barreto, N., Ashburner, J., & Penny, W. (2007). Variational free energy and the Laplace approximation. *NeuroImage*, *34*(1), 220–234. doi:10.1016/j.neuroimage.2006.08.035 PMID:17055746

Galili, T. (2015). dendextend: An R package for visualizing, adjusting and comparing trees of hierarchical clustering. *Bioinformatics (Oxford, England)*, *22*(31), 3718–3720. doi:10.1093/bioinformatics/btv428 PMID:26209431

Gavalas, D., Konstantopoulos, C., Mastakas, K., & Pantziou, G. (2014). Mobile recommender systems in tourism. *Journal of Network and Computer Applications*, *39*, 319–333. doi:10.1016/j.jnca.2013.04.006

Glorot, X., & Bengio, Y. (2010). Understanding the difficulty of training deep feedforward neural networks. In Y. W. Teh & M. Titterington (Eds.), *Proceedings of the Thirteenth International Conference on Artificial Intelligence and Statistics* (pp. 249–256). Retrieved from http://proceedings.mlr.press/v9/glorot10a.html

Goldberg, K., Roeder, T., Gupta, D., & Perkins, C. (2001). Eigentaste: A Constant Time Collaborative Filtering Algorithm. *Information Retrieval*, *4*(2), 133–151. doi:10.1023/A:1011419012209

Grubbs, F. E. (1950). Sample Criteria For Testing Outlying Observations. *Annals of Mathematical Statistics*, *21*(1), 27–58. doi:10.1214/aoms/1177729885

He, H., & Ma, Y. (2013). *Imbalanced Learning: Foundations, Algorithms and Applications*. Hoboken, NJ: IEEE Press. doi:10.1002/9781118646106

Hegenbart, S. (2015). *Deep Learning with Convolutional Neural Networks*. Academic Press.

Hennig, C. (2013). *Measurement of quality in cluster analysis*. Londres: University College, London.

Ho, T. K. (1998). The Random Subspace Method For Constructing Decision Forests. *IEEE Transactions on Pattern Analysis and Machine Intelligence*, 832–844.

Hu, Y., Koren, Y., & Volinsky, C. (n.d.). *Collaborative Filtering for Implicit Feedback Datasets*. Retrieved from http://yifanhu.net/PUB/cf.pdf

Isinkaye, F. O., Folajimi, Y. O., & Ojokoh, B. A. (2015). Recommendation systems: Principles, methods and evaluation. *Egyptian Informatics Journal, 16*(3), 261–273. doi:10.1016/j.eij.2015.06.005

Jaderberg, M., Dalibard, V., Osindero, S., Czarnecki, W. M., Donahue, J., & Razavi, A. (2017). Population Based Training of Neural Networks. Academic Press.

Karatzoglou, A., Amatriain, X., Baltrunas, L., & Oliver, N. (2010). Multiverse recommendation: n-dimensional tensor factorization for context-aware collaborative filtering. *Proceedings of the Fourth ACM Conference on Recommender Systems - RecSys '10*, 79. 10.1145/1864708.1864727

Kim, J., Lee, D., & Chung, K.-Y. (2014). Item recommendation based on context-aware model for personalized u-healthcare service. *Multimedia Tools and Applications, 71*(2), 855–872. doi:10.100711042-011-0920-0

Koren, Y., & Yehuda. (2008). Factorization meets the neighborhood. *Proceeding of the 14th ACM SIGKDD International Conference on Knowledge Discovery and Data Mining - KDD 08*, 426. 10.1145/1401890.1401944

Kotsiantis, S., & Kanellopoulos, D. (2006). Discretization Techniques: A recent survey. *GESTS International Transactions on Computer Science and Engineering, 32*, 47–58.

Lab, A. T. B. R. S. (2015). *Expectation Maximization On Old Faithful*. Retrieved from https://es.mathworks.com/matlabcentral/fileexchange/49869-expectation-maximization-on-old-faithful

Lam, X. N., Vu, T., Le, T. D., & Duong, A. D. (2008). Addressing cold-start problem in recommendation systems. *Proceedings of the 2nd International Conference on Ubiquitous Information Management and Communication - ICUIMC '08*, 208. 10.1145/1352793.1352837

Lee, J., Sun, M., & Lebanon, G. (2012). *A Comparative Study of Collaborative Filtering Algorithms*. Retrieved from https://arxiv.org/pdf/1205.3193.pdf

Lee, Y.-S., & Cho, S.-B. (2011). Activity Recognition Using Hierarchical Hidden Markov Models on a Smartphone with 3D Accelerometer. *Hybrid Artificial Intelligent Systems*, 460–467. doi:10.1007/978-3-642-21219-2_58

Li, Y., Lu, L., & Xuefeng, L. (2005). A hybrid collaborative filtering method for multiple-interests and multiple-content recommendation in E-Commerce. *Expert Systems with Applications, 28*(1), 67–77. doi:10.1016/j.eswa.2004.08.013

Liu, Y., Zhang, Y.-M., Zhang, X.-Y., & Liu, C.-L. (2016). Adaptive spatial pooling for image classification. *Pattern Recognition, 55*(C), 58–67. doi:10.1016/j.patcog.2016.01.030

Lombardi, S., Anand, S., & Gorgoglione, M. (2009). Context and Customer Behavior in Recommendation. *Work*. Retrieved from http://ids.csom.umn.edu/faculty/gedas/cars2009/LombardiEtAl-cars2009.pdf

Lops, P., de Gemmis, M., & Semeraro, G. (2011). Content-based Recommender Systems: State of the Art and Trends. In Recommender Systems Handbook (pp. 73–105). Academic Press. doi:10.1007/978-0-387-85820-3_3

Martínez, L., Barranco, M. J., Pérez, L. G., & Espinilla, M. (2008). A Knowledge Based Recommender System with Multigranular Linguistic Information. *International Journal of Computational Intelligence Systems*, *1*(3), 225–236. doi:10.1080/18756891.2008.9727620

MathWorks. (n.d.). *Cluster with Self-Organizing Map Neural Network*. Retrieved from https://es.mathworks.com/help/nnet/ug/cluster-with-self-organizing-map-neural-network.html

MathWorks. (2008). *Efficient K-Means Clustering using JIT*. Retrieved from https://es.mathworks.com/matlabcentral/fileexchange/19344-efficient-k-means-clustering-using-jit

Mathworks. (n.d.). *Dendrogram plot*. Retrieved from https://es.mathworks.com/help/stats/dendrogram.html

Millard, I., De Roure, D., & Shadbolt, N. (2005). *Contextually Aware Information Delivery in Pervasive Computing Environments*. doi:10.1007/11426646_18

Minh Phoung, T., Lin, Z., & Altman, R. B. (2005). Choosing SNPs using feature selection. *Bioinformatics (Oxford, England)*, *1*(1).

Minnesota, U. O. (n.d.). Ward's Method and Centroid methods. In Hierarchical Clustering (pp. 41–48). Academic Press.

MK, A. (2016). *Linear Discriminant Analysis (LDA)*. Retrieved from https://mlalgorithm.wordpress.com/tag/linear-discriminant-analysis/

Mojena, R. (2004). Ward's Clustering Algorithm. Encyclopedia of Statistical Sciences.

Mojena, R. (2006). Ward's Clustering Algorithm. Encyclopedia of Statistical Sciences. doi:10.1002/0471667196.ess2887.pub2

Nefedov, A. (2016). *Support Vector Machines: A Simple Tutorial*. Retrieved from http://svmtutorial.online/

Nielsen, M. (2017). *Deep learning*. Retrieved from http://neuralnetworksanddeeplearning.com/chap6.html

Orlov, A. I. (2011). Mahalanobis distance. *Encyclopedia Of Mathematics*. Retrieved from http://www.encyclopediaofmath.org/index.php?title=Mahalanobis_distance&oldid=17720

Panniello, U., Tuzhilin, A., Gorgoglione, M., Palmisano, C., & Pedone, A. (2009). Experimental comparison of pre- vs. post-filtering approaches in context-aware recommender systems. *Proceedings of the Third ACM Conference on Recommender Systems - RecSys '09*, 265. 10.1145/1639714.1639764

Penny, W. (2012). Bayesian model selection and averaging Bayes rule for models. *SPM for MEG/EEG*. Retrieved from http://www.fil.ion.ucl.ac.uk/spm/course/slides12-meeg/14_MEEG_BMS.pdf

Pu, P., Chen, L., & Hu, R. (2012). Evaluating recommender systems from the user's perspective: Survey of the state of the art. *User Modeling and User-Adapted Interaction*, *22*(4–5), 317–355. doi:10.100711257-011-9115-7

Quinlan, J. R. (1983). Learning Efficient Classification Procedures and Their Application to Chess End Games. In *Symbolic Computation: An Artificial Intelligence Approach* (pp. 463–482). Springer.

R. B., D., & W. J., D. (1951). Simplified Statistics for Small Numbers of Observations. *Analytical Chemistry*, 636–638.

Rendle, S. (n.d.). *Factorization Machines*. Retrieved from https://www.csie.ntu.edu.tw/~b97053/paper/Rendle2010FM.pdf

Rey-López, M., Barragáns-Martínez, A. B., Peleteiro, A., Mikic-Fonte, F. A., & Burguillo, J. C. (2011). moreTourism: Mobile recommendations for tourism. *Digest of Technical Papers - IEEE International Conference on Consumer Electronics*, 347–348. 10.1109/ICCE.2011.5722620

Ricci, F., Rokach, L., & Shapira, B. (2011). Introduction to Recommender Systems Handbook. In Recommender Systems Handbook (pp. 1–35). Academic Press. doi:10.1007/978-0-387-85820-3_1

Riddhiman. (2016). *Voronoi Diagrams in Plotly and R*. Retrieved from http://moderndata.plot.ly/voronoi-diagrams-in-plotly-and-r/

Rodriguez-Pardo, C., Patricio, M. A., Berlanga, A., & Molina, J. M. (2017). Market trends and customer segmentation for data of electronic retail store. Lecture Notes in Computer Science. doi:10.1007/978-3-319-59650-1_44

Roffo, G., & Ing-Inf05, S. S. D. (2017). *Ranking to Learn and Learning to Rank: On the Role of Ranking in Pattern Recognition Applications*. Retrieved from https://arxiv.org/pdf/1706.05933.pdf

Rohrer, B. (2015). Methods for handling missing values. *Cortana Intelligence Gallery*. Retrieved from https://gallery.cortanaintelligence.com/Experiment/Methods-for-handling-missing-values-1

Russell, S., & Norving, P. (2014). *Artificial Intelligence: A modern Approach*. Pearson.

Schonlau, M. (2002). The Clustergram: A graph for visualizing hierarchical and non-hierarchical cluster analysis. *The Stata Journal*, *3*, 316–327.

Su, X., & Khoshgoftaar, T. M. (2009). A Survey of Collaborative Filtering Techniques. *Advances in Artificial Intelligence*, *2009*, 1–19. doi:10.1155/2009/421425

Tamine-Lechani, L., Boughanem, M., & Daoud, M. (2010). Evaluation of contextual information retrieval effectiveness: Overview of issues and research. *Knowledge and Information Systems*, *24*(1), 1–34. doi:10.100710115-009-0231-1

Towers, S. (2013). *K-means clustering*. Retrieved from http://sherrytowers.com/2013/10/24/k-means-clustering/

University, P. S. (2016). *Principal Components Analysis (PCA)*. Retrieved from https://onlinecourses.science.psu.edu/stat857/node/35

Vandekerckhove, J., Tuerlinckx, F., & Lee, M. D. (2011). Hierarchical diffusion models for two-choice response times. *Psychological Methods*, *16*(1), 44–62. doi:10.1037/a0021765 PMID:21299302

Wang, C., & Blei, D. M. (2011). Collaborative topic modeling for recommending scientific articles. *Proceedings of the 17th ACM SIGKDD International Conference on Knowledge Discovery and Data Mining - KDD '11*, 448. 10.1145/2020408.2020480

Wang, H., Wang, N., & Yeung, D.-Y. (2015). Collaborative Deep Learning for Recommender Systems. *Proceedings of the 21th ACM SIGKDD International Conference on Knowledge Discovery and Data Mining - KDD '15*, 1235–1244. 10.1145/2783258.2783273

White, R. W., Bailey, P., & Chen, L. (2009). Predicting user interests from contextual information. *Proceedings of the 32nd International ACM SIGIR Conference on Research and Development in Information Retrieval - SIGIR '09*, 363. 10.1145/1571941.1572005

Yao, L., Sheng, Q. Z., Qin, Y., Wang, X., Shemshadi, A., & He, Q. (2015). Context-aware Point-of-Interest Recommendation Using Tensor Factorization with Social Regularization. *Proceedings of the 38th International ACM SIGIR Conference on Research and Development in Information Retrieval - SIGIR '15*, 1007–1010. 10.1145/2766462.2767794

Zheng, Y., Burke, R., & Mobasher, B. (2012). Differential context relaxation for context-aware travel recommendation. In *Lecture Notes in Business Information Processing* (Vol. 123, pp. 88–99). LNBIP. doi:10.1007/978-3-642-32273-0_8

KEY TERMS AND DEFINITIONS

Context-Aware System: Any system that can make use of contextual information to solve their tasks more efficiently or effectively.

Machine Learning: The field in computer science which is concerned on the development of algorithms that can make computers learn from data.

Recommender Systems: Informatics systems that aim to predict the ratings that users will give to an unseen product or item.

Retail: Economic sector that creates revenue by selling products or services to final customers.

Smart Tourism: The application of communication and computer science methods for the development of tools that are used in tourism.

Supervised Learning: The field in machine learning which is concerned on the development of algorithms that learn functions from labelled data.

Unsupervised Learning: The field in machine learning which is concerned on the development of algorithms that learn functions from unlabeled data.

This research was previously published in the Handbook of Research on Big Data Clustering and Machine Learning; pages 311-333, copyright year 2020 by Engineering Science Reference (an imprint of IGI Global).

Chapter 41
Comparative Study of Various Machine Learning Algorithms for Prediction of Insomnia

Ravinder Ahuja
https://orcid.org/0000-0002-7299-3131
Jaypee Institute of Information Technology Noida, India

Vishal Vivek
Jaypee Institute of Information Technology Noida, India

Manika Chandna
Jaypee Institute of Information Technology Noida, India

Shivani Virmani
Jaypee Institute of Information Technology Noida, India

Alisha Banga
Satyug Darshan Institute of Engineering and Technology Faridabad, India

ABSTRACT

An early diagnosis of insomnia can prevent further medical aids such as anger issues, heart diseases, anxiety, depression, and hypertension. Fifteen machine learning algorithms have been applied and 14 leading factors have been taken into consideration for predicting insomnia. Seven performance parameters (accuracy, kappa, the true positive rate, false positive rate, precision, f-measure, and AUC) are used and for implementation. The authors have used python language. The support vector machine is giving higher performance out of all algorithms giving accuracy 91.6%, f-measure is 92.13, and kappa is 0.83. Further, SVM is applied on another dataset of 100 patients and giving accuracy 92%. In addition, an analysis of the variable importance of CART, C5.0, decision tree, random forest, adaptive boost, and XG boost is calculated. The analysis shows that insomnia primarily depends on the factors, which are the vision problem, mobility problem, and sleep disorder. This chapter mainly finds the usages and effectiveness of machine learning algorithms in Insomnia diseases prediction.

DOI: 10.4018/978-1-6684-6291-1.ch041

INTRODUCTION

Insomnia is a subjective complaint of sleep disorder in which the patient has a difficulty to fall asleep or remain sleeping as long as desired. Insomniac usually have low energy, less concentrating power, less appetite, and mood swings, leading to low performance throughout the day at work (Mulaffer, Shahin, Glos, Penzel & Ahmed, 2017). Insomnia is mainly categorized into the following types on the basis of duration of disturbed sleep timings (Chouvarda et al., 2013): (i) Acute Insomnia: It prevails for a short duration of time (Maximum for a month). The main cause for its existence could be bizarre life events such as a stressful environment at work, jet lags due to traveling or existence of a certain problem at home. This does not require severe medical treatment and can be cured by general meditation (National Sleep Foundation, n.d; Saddichha, 2010) (ii) Chronic Insomnia: A person is said to be facing chronic insomnia if he/she suffers from a disturbed sleep more than 3 days a week and continuously for 3 or more months. The main causes are depression, anxiety, chronic stress, and pain or discomfort at night. Often it requires behavioral therapies; sleep restriction therapies, relaxation exercises and reconditioning for its cure (Zhang, Mo & Zhang, 2017) and, (iii) Comorbid Insomnia: It is also known as secondary insomnia. It is said to prevail when a person faces insomnia due to medical or psychiatric conditions or intake of drugs. Treatment of comorbid insomnia is done by separately treating insomnia and the co-morbid mental illness. Treatment and medication are suggested by the psychiatrist (Hu, 2017; Neikrug, 2010; Skaer, 2018).

According to Global health and an aging report presented by WHO in 2016, it was reported that the population of people with age group 65 or more was 524 million in 2010 which counts nearly 8.5% and is expected to increase up to 1.6 billion till 2050 that is 17% of the total population ("Global health aging", n.d). In America, it is projected that the population with age group 65 or above will nearly double over 3 decades that is 48 million to 88 million by 2050. The global population of elderly people (age 80 or above) is expected to be three times higher during 2015 and 2050 as estimated by the national institute of aging (United Nations, 2010). In India, the increase in decrepit patients rose from about 7% in 2000 to 9% in 2015.

Comparing the data of the previous 35 years, we find that each year the percentage of elderly people is increasing linearly around the globe, in India too we see a similar trend in the increase of the population of elderly patients. According to a survey of 1.1 million Individuals, people who sleep between 6.5 to 7.5 hours a day have been found to have the least mortality rate; whereas those who sleep under 6 hours or above 8 hours are found to have higher mortality rates (Kinsella, 2009; "Global health aging" n.d). Although till date it is not clear why sleeping more than 7.5 hours is associated with higher mortality (Banno & Kryger, 2006). According to research by the National Center for Biotechnology information, 50% of decrepit patients generally complain about deprived sleep, not just due to increased aging; but also due to factors like increased medication, stressful life, etc. These above-mentioned mortality factors can be responsible for insomnia, either is it acute, chronic or comorbid insomnia. Studies show that around 1 out of 3 people face either of the symptoms of insomnia. Owing to the seriousness of the situation, The American Academy of Sleep Medicine has declared Insomnia Awareness Day on March 12, 2018 (American Academy of Sleep Medicine, n.d).

The National Sleep Foundation, in 2005, carried a survey on American population and reported that 76% of the decrepit population thinks that they have a sleep problem. Surveys also reveal that nearly 70% of population experience at least one symptom of insomnia ("Sleep findings data" n.d)(Waking up too early, inconsistent sleep, Difficulty falling asleep, Tension, Headache, Unhealthy stomach and many more). In the 1991 National Sleep Foundation conducted a multicenter epidemiologic polling on a sample size of 1000 patients in which people of age group 18 years or older were taken and further divided into 6 age groups (15-19, 18-24, 25-34, 35-44, 45-54, 55-64, and ≥65). The result of which it was observed that approximately 9% of the patients reported chronic insomnia, and out of which 20% in the group ≥ 65 years reported chronic insomnia, the highest among all age groups (Morin, 2011).

According to the World Health Organization (WHO), being healthy does not merely mean the absence of a disease, but it means complete soundness of the physical and mental state of our body. Change in mental health and thought the process of a person with age is very common. With increasing age, generally, a person gets more mature, responsible and less carefree. The reasons can be many, it can be family issues, job-related issues, income issues or living spouse and it also depends on how much value does the person gives to address these issues (I. J. I. P. 2016). For example: if a person is working, he/she will be busy with work and have a big social circle thus will not focus much on small family-related issues; whereas if the person sits at home all day long with less interaction with people around, he/she will go through a continuous thought process over and over again for a small issue. All these thought processes cause deprived sleep leading to insomnia and hence leading to anxiety and depression and several heart-related issues. Although there is no as such exact treatment for insomnia, the only cure could be behavioral changes to maintain the quality of sleep and few drugs such as Zaleplon and Ramelteon (Li, 2011; Yang, 2011) would also help which can make a person stay asleep for a few hours and could help.

That is why detection of insomnia at a very first stage is necessary. In developing countries like India sleep disorder or insomnia is very highly prevalent due to the above-mentioned reasons. It contributes to approximately 12% of the global population and thus its urge of time to deal with issues like insomnia with the help of prediction tools using Machine Learning (ML) in order to avoid other serious health-related problems like anxiety, depression, hypertension, and heart-related problems. Considering the rapid increase in the world population of an insomniac and thus leading to increased patients with anxiety and depression World Sleep Society (WSS) announced world sleep day in March each year (sleep data, Chouvarda et al., 2012; de León, 2008). The major contribution of this study is, firstly we find out effectiveness and application of machine learning technique (15 classification algorithms) in Insomnia disease prediction. Secondly, by using the variable importance of each classifier, we can easily identify which factors out of 14 are playing an important role in Insomnia diseases. The main objective of this chapter to explore the machine learning algorithms in the prediction of Insomnia disease.

RELATED WORK

Despite the rapid increase in the number of an insomniac in decrepit population, a number of reports/papers discussed the prediction of insomnia with the help of socio-demographic factors and previous medical history. In the paper (Chaparro-Vargas, 2016) insomnia has been detected using the hypnogram generation of sleep onset patterns. Although we know the only sleep pattern is not enough to detect insomnia. Few researchers have also focused on detecting insomnia only by considering sleep to wake transition (Dissanyaka, 2016; Chouvarda, 2007). In some of the previous studies, Hjorth parameters extracted from the electroencephalogram (EEG) has been taken into account (Subhani, 2017), but we cannot justify our result based on one pattern only. Some studies have focused on distinguishing insomniac and healthy patients based on eye movements which are of two types: Non-Rapid Eye Movement (NREM) and Rapid Eye Movement (REM). Depending on these two eye movement states different measures are recorded in physiological signals: Electroencephalogram (EEG), Electrooculogram (EOG), Electrocardiogram (ECG) (Hamida, 2015) and based on these signals insomniac has been distinguished from healthy patients. But only eye movements are not responsible for insomnia. A lot of studies has been done only to predict insomnia with the mapping of EEG signals (Attaran, 2018). One of the researches include predicting insomnia but only SVM classifier had been used, also it lacks in attributes compared to our work (Dissanyaka, 2016). Respiratory signals have been used to classify different stages of sleep. Some studies have detected mental stress at multiple levels using the machine learning framework with the help of EEG signals (Thapliyal et al., 2017; Jáuregui, 2017). After having a glance to several types of research and papers we observed that almost all studies focus on predicting insomnia either by using only one or two features, or few algorithms have only been applied, whereas we have considered all fourteen major factors as well socio-demographic factors and the past medical history of patients. In the paper (Shahin, 2017), they have predicted anxiety and depression relating to deprived sleep. But we must consider the root causes of insomnia in order to build a relevant predictive model and hence we have considered almost all causes in the form of attributes and predicted insomnia by applying 15 classification algorithms. In the paper (Rashid & Abdullah, 2018), authors have proposed a hybrid model of Artificial Bee Colony, artificial neural network, and a genetic algorithm for classifying and diagnosing Diabetic Mellitus. They have considered two datasets i.e primary and secondary dataset. The primary data set consists of 31 features of 501 patients and the second dataset is Pima dataset. Three experiments were performed considering single artificial neural network, an artificial neural network trained with Artificial Bee Colony method, and artificial neural network with mutation-based Artificial Bee Colony. In a paper (Rashid, Abdullah & Abdullah, 2016), authors have explored the relationship between chronic diseases and blood sugar rate. The complete process is divided into two modules. In the first module, the artificial neural network is applied to predict the fasting sugar rate and in second module decision tree is used to describe the impact of fasting sugar rate and symptoms on the patient's health. In a paper (Rashid, Abdullah & Abdullah, 2016), the authors proposed an approach for doctors and physicians to provide good health treatment. They have applied four algorithms i.e artificial neural networks, C 4.5, regression tree and self-organizing map and found that artificial neural network is best out of all these.

MATERIALS AND METHODS

Data Collection

Data is collected from 500 OPD patients for their various medical problems with their consent at R.G. Kar Medical College and Hospital, Kolkata (A. Sau and I. Bhakta, 2017). The authors have applied a ten-fold cross-validation method, which is best suited for small datasets to increase the dataset and cross verify the result.

Also, we have selected attributed in dataset after consulting with the psychiatrists from different recognized hospitals on the basis of their knowledge of insomnia. Our dataset includes (i) Personal attributes(age, sex) (ii) Socio-Demographic Attributes (Literacy, Residence, Marital Status, Recent bereavement) (iii) Economic Conditions (Employment Status, Socio-Economic Status, PI) (iv) Past Medical History (The previous history of Anxiety and Depression) (v) Any kind of Addiction (vi) Current Medical Condition (Pain at multiple sites, Diabetes, HTN, Hearing Aid, Visual Impairment, Mobility impairment). These features represent different probable causative dimensions of insomnia among decrepit patients.

Attribute Selection

The attributes of our dataset have been selected in such way that it matches the seven questionnaires of insomnia severity index (ISI) so that the final result can be verified by matching the gold standards set by insomnia severity index scale. Insomnia severity index is a scale used to figure out the extent of insomnia disease in patients. Taking these attributes in our dataset will help to predict the outcome closer to the gold standards set by insomnia severity index, and finally, the result can be a match using an ISI scale for the reliability of the result. Overall, the authors have considered 14 leading factors in our dataset keeping in mind the symptoms of disease and questionnaires of ISI. Also, the authors have selected attributed in dataset after consulting with the psychiatrists from different recognized hospitals on the basis of their knowledge of insomnia.

Insomnia Severity Index

Insomnia severity index is a widely used scale used to measure the extent of insomnia disease in a patient. ISI contains seven different questionnaires (Begum, Chakraborty & Sarkar, 2015), on the basis of the answer of the question, a score (Zero to four) is assigned and finally, the score is summed up, and the final score ranges from zero to twenty-eight as shown in Table 1. If the score is zero to seven then it is No insomnia. If the score is eight to fourteen then it is sub-threshold insomnia. If the score is fifteen to twenty-one then it is clinical insomnia (moderate severity). If the score is twenty-two to twenty-eight then it is clinical insomnia (Severe) (Pandey, 2017). A research was organized in India in Jamia Millia Islamia, New Delhi, in which sample data were students of their university, which clearly suggests that ISI has excellent consistency and reliability. Hence, ISI can prove to be an outstanding tool for the prediction of insomnia.

Table 1. Insomnia severity index scale

ISI Score Intervals	Severity of Insomnia
0—7	Not Insomniac
8—14	Partially Insomniac
15—21	Moderately Insomniac (Need clinical treatment)
22—28	Severely Insomniac (Need clinical treatment)

The detailed methodology as shown in Table 2 has several steps (i) Data collection (ii) Attribute selection (iii) Apply classification algorithms and (iv) Result validation (v) Cross verification of the SVM model is done on data set of 100 new patients.

Table 2. Methodology in tabular form

Involved Steps	Explanation
Collection of Data	The data of 500 patients are collected
Attributes	The following features are used: Age, Sex, Living spouse, Family types, Literacy, Occupation, Substance abuse, Personal income, Diabetic Mellitus (DM), Hypertension (HTN), Hearing problem, Vision problem, Mobility problem, and Sleep problem.
Algorithms Applied	Classification Algorithms: K Nearest Neighbors(KNN), Support Vector Machine(SVM), Logistic Regression, Random Forest (RF), Naïve Bayes(Bernoulli), Bayesian Network, C 5.0, CART, AdaBoost, XGBoosting, Decision Tree, Multi-Layer Perceptron, Random Tree, Gradient Boosting, Gaussian Naïve Bayes
Result Validation	Confusion matrix corresponding to each algorithm was created after the ten-fold cross-validation method was applied, and finally, the respective accuracies were calculated.
Result Justification	A test data if 100 new patients Were given as test data to SVM classifier and results matched with ISI scale.
Variable importance is applied to Adaptive Boosting, XG Boosting, Decision Tree, Random Forest, C 5.0, and CART algorithms to find out important factors contributing to Insomnia	

Figure 1. Flowchart depicting methodology in a nutshell

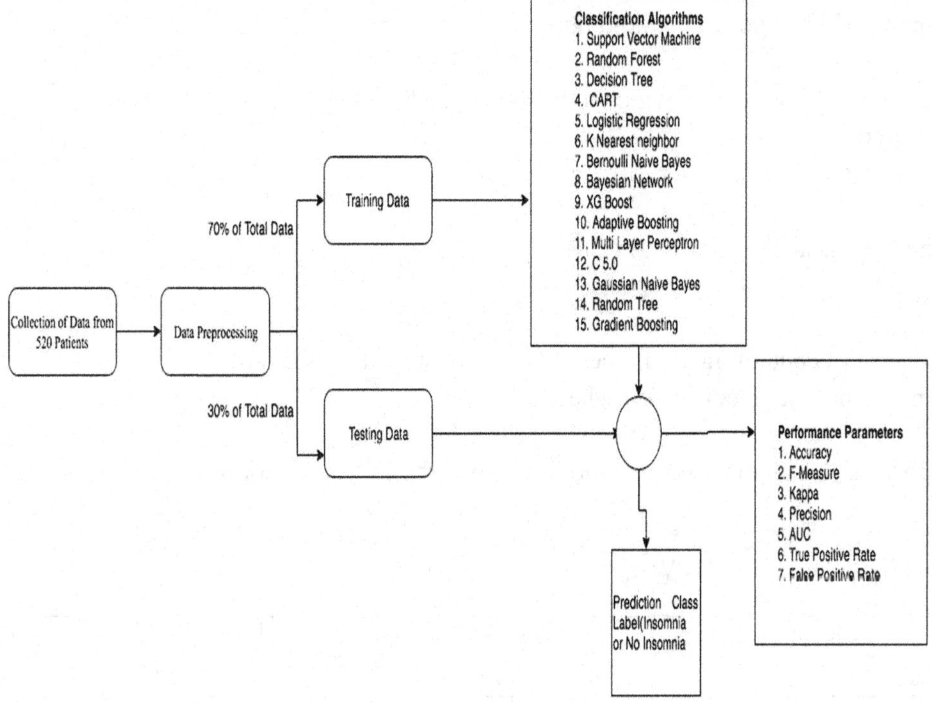

CLASSIFICATION MODELS

Classification is one of the promising domains used to solve trending problems in today's era. In classification usually, we assign a class label among the existing class values which are mapped to unseen instances comprising the set of variables. A learning algorithm is applied on a training set which consists of past instances and an equivalent variable set. In classification models, the authors already know the class level of each instance which is mentioned in the training set. After the model is trained, the prediction accuracy of the corresponding classifier is evaluated on an unknown testing set. In our case, the binary class classification algorithm is most suitable. In a binary class classification problem usually, the focus is on binary result i.e. either a person has insomnia (unhealthy) or no insomnia (healthy). We have applied the following 15 algorithms: **1.** K Nearest Neighbors (KNN) **2.** Support vector machine (SVM) **3.** Bernoulli Naïve Bayes (BNB) **4.** Logistic Regression (LR) 5. Decision tree (DT) **6.** Random Forest (RF) **7.** Multi-layer perceptron (MLP) **8.** Bayesian Network (BN) **9.** Adaptive Boost (AB) **10.** XG Boost (XGB) **11.** C5.0 **12.** CART **13.** Random Tree **14.** Gaussian Naïve Bayes **15.** Gradient Boosting

Algorithm 1: K Nearest Neighbors (KNN)

This algorithm is applied to N training vectors; it identifies the k nearest neighbors of test data by computing the Euclidean distance of test data from the training vectors. Then the authors predict the class value of test data by finding the maximum class represented in the k nearest neighbors. We have taken k=5. We find the 5 nearest neighbors of the test data. Among the 5 neighbors, if 3 of them belong to category 1 and 2 of them belong to category 2, then the test data belongs maximum numbers in both and hence goes to the category 1 (Nugrahaeni, 2016)

The Steps for KNN algorithm would be:-

1. Classify (A, B, c) // A: training data, B: the data label of A, c: testing sample
2. for i=1 to m
3. do

   Calculate Euclidean distance d (Ai, c)

4. end
5. Calculate set I containing all indices for k smallest distances d (Ai, c).
6. Return the majority label for (Bi where ε I)

After applying this algorithm the authors obtained the following confusion matrix.

Table 3. Confusion matrix of KNN

KNN	Predicted Insomnia (Yes)	Predicted Insomnia (No)
Actual Insomnia (Yes)	248	21
Actual Insomnia (No)	111	160

Algorithm 2: Support Vector Machine (SVM)

It is used in classification as well as regression problems (commonly used in classification). The main agenda is to plot the data in an n dimension plane wherein n is the number of features taken into consideration. Once this is done, the authors find the hyperplane with maximum margin by performing classification and ignoring the outliers (Liu, 2017)

The Steps for SVM would be:-

1. Initialize reduced data set by randomly choosing data from the training data.
2. Calculate the reduced kernel matrix
3. For each data point which is not in the reduced dataset, calculate their kernel vectors.
4. Calculate distance from these kernel vectors to the current reduced kernel matrix.
5. The authors form the reduced set by adding those points which have exceeded the threshold.
6. Repeat the above steps until the reduced set remains the same.

Table 4. Confusion matrix of SVM

SVM	Predicted Insomnia (Yes)	Predicted Insomnia (No)
Actual Insomnia (Yes)	246	20
Actual Insomnia (No)	22	249

Algorithm 3: Bernoulli Naïve Bayes (BNB)

It is a simple probabilistic classifier which is based on Bayes theorem (conditional probability) with strong independent assumptions made amongst the features. Gaussian NB is used when the features have continuous values, whereas Bernoulli NB is used when the features are independent (Bhargava, K., et. Al, 2017)

$$P\left(\frac{A}{B}\right) = \frac{P\left(\frac{B}{A}\right) * P(A)}{P(B)} \quad P(B) \neq 0 \tag{1}$$

Steps for BNB would be:-

1. A frequency table is made for all the features corresponding to the training data.
2. Calculate the probabilities and conditional probabilities of each element of the frequency table.

where, Conditional probability = No. of distinct feature values * No. of target values

Table 5. Confusion matrix of Bernoulli Naïve Bayes

Bernoulli Naïve Bayes	Predicted Insomnia (Yes)	Predicted Insomnia (No)
Actual Insomnia (Yes)	172	41
Actual Insomnia (No)	37	290

Algorithm 4: Logistic Regression (LR)

It is the appropriate regression analysis to conduct when there are more independent variables. The output is always measured in a dichotomous variable. The logistic function is used similarly to sigmoid function (Ying et al., 2015)

Steps for LR would be:-

Recursively:

{Calculate Gradient Average

1. Multiply by Average Learning Rate (α)
2. Subtract from Weights}

After applying this algorithm the authors obtained the following confusion matrix.

Table 6. Confusion matrix of logistic regression

Logistic Regression	Predicted Insomnia (Yes)	Predicted Insomnia (No)
Actual Insomnia (Yes)	215	49
Actual Insomnia (No)	101	175

Algorithm 5: Decision Tree (DT)

It is used for decision analysis. Decision trees where target values can take continuous values are known as the regression trees. Considering in the tree, input values are represented in a path from the root to the leaves, each leaf represents the target variable (Zhang, Y., et. al., 2018)

The Steps for DT would be:-

1. Form a tree with its nodes as features.
2. Select 1 feature to predict the output from the input, where the root node is that which contains the highest information gain.
3. Repeat the above steps to form subtrees based on features which are not used in the above nodes.

Table 7. Confusion matrix of decision tree

Decision Tree	Predicted Insomnia (Yes)	Predicted Insomnia (No)
Actual Insomnia (Yes)	235	22
Actual Insomnia (No)	40	243

Algorithm 6: Random Forest (RF)

It is a further approach to Decision Tree. In this classifier algorithm, rather than considering a single tree, the authors consider numerous decision trees, thus forming a forest, the denser the forest, i.e. the higher the number of trees, the higher will be the accuracy rate (El Majd, Y. A., El Ghazi, H., & Nahhal, T., 2017)

Steps for RF are as follows:

1. From a total of n features, randomly m features are selected. m<<n
2. A node d, which belongs to the set of m nodes, is calculated using the best split point.
3. Further, d is split into daughter nodes using the best split method.
4. Repeat steps 1-3 until a tree is formed with a root node and having the target as the leaf node.
5. Steps 1-4 represent the creation of a tree. Repeat them the number of times to create a forest.

Table 8. Confusion matrix of random forest

Random Forest	Predicted Insomnia (Yes)	Predicted Insomnia (No)
Actual Insomnia (Yes)	226	29
Actual Insomnia (No)	36	249

Algorithm 7: Multi-Layer Perceptron (MLP)

One hidden layer and three network layers used (Zhou, Q., 2017)

The Steps for MLP would be:-

1. Randomly initialize the weights of labels.
2. For each training example compute error
3. 3. Compute error

Error = Predicted value – Actual value

4. Compute change in weight for all the weights from the hidden layer to the output layer.
5. Compute change in weight for all the weights from the input layer to the hidden layer.
6. Update the weights of the network.
7. Return network

Table 9. Confusion matrix of multi-layer perceptron

MLP	Predicted Insomnia (Yes)	Predicted Insomnia (No)
Actual Insomnia (Yes)	220	26
Actual Insomnia (No)	64	230

Algorithm 8: Bayesian Network (BN)

It is a concept based on parameter learning. In this case, the authors are not very clear about the conditional probabilities but know the network very well. Formally, it is similar to the Directed Acyclic Graph (DAC). Human beings are not very comfortable with reasoning problems thus such a machine is designed. If Y= $\{A_1, A_2, A_{3...} A_n\}$ as the universe of variables in the Bayesian network and P (A_i) is a parent of A_i then probability function (joint) is given by P (X) as shown below (Fonseca-Delgado & Gomez-Gil, 2013; Dixit & Sahu, 2017)

Table 10. Confusion matrix of bayesian network

Bayesian Network	Predicted Insomnia (Yes)	Predicted Insomnia (No)
Actual Insomnia (Yes)	196	64
Actual Insomnia (No)	44	236

Algorithm 9: Adaptive Boosting (AdaBoost)

It is the first Boosting algorithm discovered. It is an ensemble classifier which is similar to Random Forest. It is most preferably used for binary classification. Its output converges to the logarithmic likelihood ratio. The idea is to use weak classifiers in succession repeatedly for more accurate predictions.

Table 11. Confusion matrix of adaptive boosting

AdaBoost	Predicted Insomnia (Yes)	Predicted Insomnia (No)
Actual Insomnia (Yes)	290	63
Actual Insomnia (No)	30	157

Algorithm 10: XGBoost

A self-contained derivation of Gradient Boosting. It is a software library and focuses on computational speed and model performance. Algorithm implementation includes Sparse Aware, Block Structure, and Continued Training. Trees are constructed individually in an organized manner which leads to decreased training time and high performance.

Table 12. Confusion matrix of XGBoost

XGBoost	Predicted Insomnia (Yes)	Predicted Insomnia (No)
Actual Insomnia (Yes)	236	26
Actual Insomnia (No)	29	249

Algorithm 11: C 5.0

It is a tree classifier algorithm, an extended version of a decision tree algorithm. It solves the problem of overfitting and error pruning. Using this algorithm relevant attributes can be identified. It acknowledges noise and missing data which helps improve performance.

Table 13. Confusion matrix of C 5.0

C 5.0	Predicted Insomnia (Yes)	Predicted Insomnia (No)
Actual Insomnia (Yes)	223	22
Actual Insomnia (No)	32	262

Algorithm 12: CART (Classification and Regression Trees)

A binary decision tree is constructed. Recursive binary splitting (greedy method) is used for the construction of the trees. Prediction for the new input after training is done by traversing the tree from root to leaf node where the predicted output is stored.

Table 14. Confusion matrix of the CART

CART	Predicted Insomnia (Yes)	Predicted Insomnia (No)
Actual Insomnia (Yes)	236	27
Actual Insomnia (No)	32	245

Algorithm 13: Random Tree (RT)

It is a classification algorithm where there are random trees i.e. a collection of tree predictors. The classifier classifies each feature with each tree and gives a result according to the maximum number of votes. The plus point in this algorithm is that accuracy estimation is not required to be done externally; it is done through the training process internally (Susanti, S. P., & Azizah, F. N., 2017)

Steps for RT would be:-

1. From a total of n features, randomly m features are selected. m<<n
2. A node d, which belongs to the set of m nodes, is calculated using the best split point.
3. Further, d is split into daughter nodes using the best split method.
4. Repeat steps 1-3 until a tree is formed with a root node and having the target as the leaf node.

Table 15. Confusion matrix of Random Tree

Random Tree	Predicted Insomnia (Yes)	Predicted Insomnia (No)
Actual Insomnia (Yes)	224	39
Actual Insomnia (No)	37	240

Algorithm 14: Gaussian Naïve Bayes (GNB)

It is a special Naïve Bayes classification algorithm, particularly used when features have continuous values and follow a normal distribution (Bhargava, K., & Katarya, R., 2017)

Steps for GNB would be:

1. A frequency table is made for all the features corresponding to each patient.
2. For each patient, the probability is calculated corresponding to each feature.
3. The conditional probability for all the patients is calculated using the given formula:

Table 16. Confusion matrix of Gaussian Naïve Bayes

Gaussian Naïve Bayes	Predicted Insomnia (Yes)	Predicted Insomnia (No)
Actual Insomnia (Yes)	219	27
Actual Insomnia (No)	38	256

Algorithm 15: Gradient Boosting

The idea is to use weak classifiers in succession repeatedly for more accurate predictions. It involves 3 steps: 1. Loss Function: It uses a logarithmic loss function. 2. Weak Learner: Decision Trees are constructed using the best split points in a greedy manner. 3. Additive Model: Trees are added one by one and the previous trees are not changed.

Table 17. Confusion matrix of gradient boosting

Gradient Boosting	Predicted Insomnia (Yes)	Predicted Insomnia (No)
Actual Insomnia (Yes)	250	46
Actual Insomnia (No)	44	200

10-Fold Cross-Validation of Classifiers

Ten-fold Cross-validation: In ten-fold cross-validation method our original data set of 500 patients is partitioned into ten equal-sized sub-segments (50 patients in each segment). Out of all 10 sub-segments, one partition as testing data and remaining nine as training data. This cross-validation technique is repeated 10 times, where each sub partition is taken as testing data at least once. These ten results obtained from the above repetitions are averaged or otherwise combined to produce a single estimation. The advantage of using this validation method is that every single data is used for training as well as testing the model which increases and each entry in the dataset is used for validation of the result at least once (Tong, Kan & Yang, 2018). After ten-fold cross-validation the authors calculated the performance metrics (accuracy, Kappa Coefficients, Sensitivity (TPR), Specificity, the False Positive rate (FPR), Recall, Precision) to measure the performance of each classifier for comparing different classification algorithms.

PERFORMANCE PARAMETERS

1. Accuracy corresponds to a fraction of the result that is predicted correctly by our model. It is a ratio of the number of correct predictions to total prediction.

$$\text{Accuracy}=\frac{\text{number of correct prediction}}{\text{total prediction}} \tag{2}$$

$$\text{Accuracy} = \frac{TP+TN}{TP+TN+FP+FN} \tag{3}$$

2. Cohen's Kappa coefficient gives a quantitative measure of agreement in any situation in which two or more observers are evaluating the same thing (Tong, W., 2018). It is the ratio of the difference of total accuracy and random accuracy divided by 1 - random accuracy.

$$\text{kappa}=\frac{\text{total accuracy-random accuracy}}{\text{1-random accuracy}} \tag{4}$$

$$\text{Random Accuracy}=\frac{\left(TN+FP\right)*\left(TN+FN\right)+\left(FN+TP\right)*\left(FP+TP\right)}{\left(TP+TN+FP+FN\right)^2} \tag{5}$$

3. Sensitivity is defined as a number of predicted true which are actually true. It is also known as the True positive rate (TPR). It estimates how many positives have been actually predicted as positive. It is also known as Recall.

$$\text{Sensitivity} = \frac{\text{predicted YES}\left(\text{TP}\right)}{\text{actual YES}\left(\text{P}\right)} \tag{6}$$

4. False positive rate means the expectancy of false positive ratio. It estimates how many negatives have been actually predicted as negative.

$$\text{FP rate} = \frac{\text{predicted NO}\left(\text{FP}\right)}{\text{actual NO}\left(\text{TN} + \text{FP}\right)} \tag{7}$$

5. Precision is a fraction of actually positive which have been predicted positive.

$$\text{Precision} = \frac{TP}{TP + FP} \tag{8}$$

6. Specificity is the ratio of predicted true negatives to actual negatives (TN+FP). It is a measure of how many negatives have been predicted correctly from actual negatives.

$$\text{Specificity} = \frac{TN}{TN + FP} \tag{9}$$

7. F-measure is the harmonic mean of precision and Recall (sensitivity). It is provided as a measurement tool for the test's accuracy.

$$\text{F} - \text{measure} = \frac{2^{*}\text{precision}^{*}\text{recall}}{\text{precision} + \text{recall}} \tag{10}$$

8. AUC (Area Under Cover): It relates the hit rate to the false alarm rate. It gives the probability that a randomly chosen positive instance gets the higher rank than a randomly chosen negative instance.

TP-True Positive TN-True Negative FP-False Positive FN-False Negative

RESULTS

As per research conducted by us for 500 decrepit patients among which 277(55.4%) were males and 223(44.3%) were females. The mean age of our data set is 66.5%. Among 540 decrepit patients, 45.6% of patients were suffering from at least one or the other symptom of insomnia. Personal information (PI) as a feature was not considered, the reason being people in India believe in certain cultural and social norms and thus are not comfortable to share such information. All these 14 attributes were applied on 15 classifiers. For each algorithm, a confusion matrix was created after applying ten-fold cross-validation. With the help of confusion matrix further true Positive (TP), False Positive (FP), the true positive rate (TPR), false positive rate (FPR), accuracy, precision, sensitivity, specificity (Recall), Cohen's kappa coefficient, F measure (F1 Score), and Area under the Curve (AUC) were calculated for each algorithm for comparison purpose as shown in table 19. The authors found that the support vector machine (SVM) is the best possible classifier with the highest Accuracy of 91.6% because the dataset is small and SVM works better in smaller dataset. Also, for SVM the TP rate is 91.3%, the FP rate is 8.06%, Precision is 93.05%, F-Measure is 91.72% and AUC is 92.85%. At last, the authors took a new data set of 100 decrepit patients and passed as testing data to the SVM classifier. A new confusion matrix was created and hence its performance matrix was also created, the final result was compared with the ISI scale for which accuracy came out to be 92%.

Table 18. Test data matched with ISI standard

SVM	Insomnia Severity Index(ISI)		Total
	Predicted Insomnia (Yes)	Predicted Insomnia (No)	
Actual Insomnia (Yes)	44	6	50
Actual Insomnia (No)	3	47	50
Total	47	53	100

Table 19. Performance of different measures

	Classification Algorithms	Percentage of Different Matrix						
		Accuracy	TPR	FPR	F-Measure	Precision	AUC	Kappa
1	Logistic Regression	72.22	81.43	36.59	74.13	68.03	85.71	0.45
2	KNN	75.55	92.19	40.95	78.97	69.08	75.71	0.52
3	SVM	91.6	92.48	8.11	92.13	91.79	92.85	0.83
4	Random Forest	87.9	88.6	12.63	87.4	86.25	75.71	0.75
5	Bernoulli Naïve Bayes	85.55	80.75	11.31	71.61	82.29	85.71	0.71
6	Decision Tree	88.5	91.4	14.13	88.32	85.45	65.71	0.59
7	MLP	83.33	89.43	21.76	79.3	77.46	83.34	0.77
8	Bayesian Network	80	75.38	15.71	75.3	81.67	72.43	0.71
9	Adaptive Boost	82.76	82.15	16.04	86.17	90.62	91.32	0.76
10	XG Boost	89.89	90.07	10.43	89.55	89.05	87.63	0.72
11	C 5.0	90.06	91.02	10.88	89.19	87.45	85.43	0.56
12	Gaussian Naïve Bayes	87.9	89.02	12.92	87.07	85.21	75.71	0.76
13	Gradient Boosting	83.33	84.46	18.03	83.33	83.33	82.86	0.68
14	Random Tree	85.9	85.17	13.35	85.49	85.82	88.09	0.71
15	CART	89	89.73	11.55	88.88	88.05	87.91	0.69

Variable importance represents the statistical significance of each feature in the data with respect to its effect on the calculated output. It is calculated by a sum of the decrease in error when split by a feature, the relative importance is the variable importance divided by the highest variable importance (0…1).

Figure 2. Performance measures of different classification algorithms

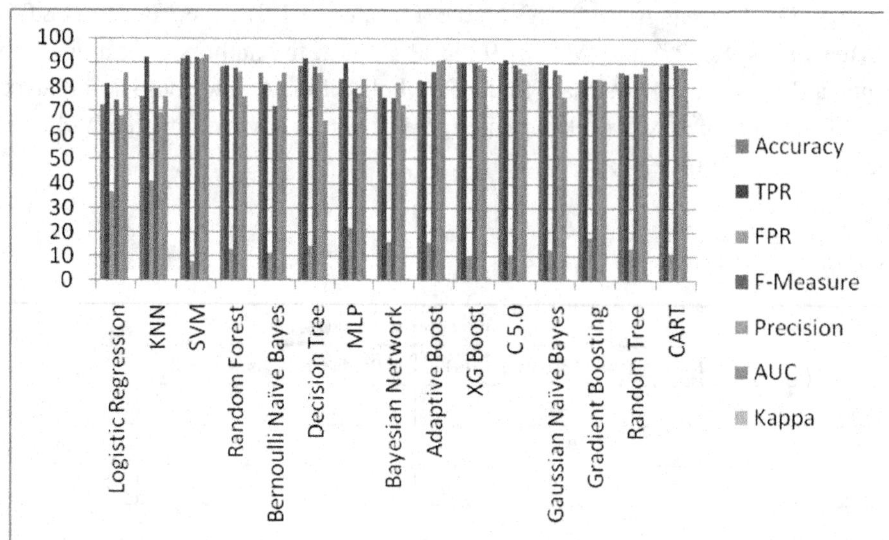

The Variable importance of Ad boost algorithm is given in Figure 3; the most important three factors are factor 8, 13, and 5. In XG boosting, the authors find out that the most important three factors are factor 12, factor 8, and factor 2 as shown in Figure 4. According to the decision tree algorithm, the three most important factors are 14, 12, and 9 as shown in Figure 5. As shown in Figure 6, according to the Random forest, the most important three factors are 14, 13, and 12. As shown in Figure 7, according to C 5.0 algorithm, the most important factors are 11, 14, and 12. According to CART, the three most important factors are 13, 12, and 14. Hence when the authors analyze the variable importance of all these algorithms, the authors find out that factor 14 i.e sleep disorder, factor 13 i.e mobility problems, and factor 12 i.e vision problems are the major factors contributing to Insomnia diseases that are common in all graphs of variable importance.

Figure 3. The importance of factors with adaptive boosting

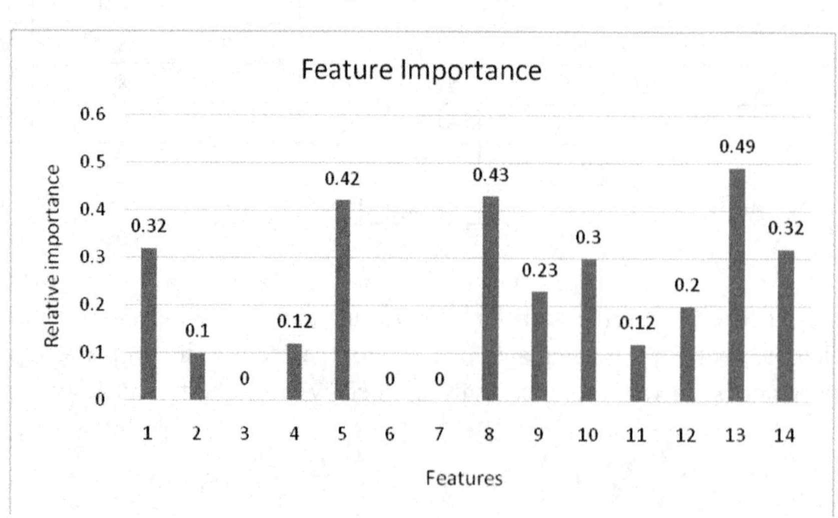

Figure 4. Importance of the factors with XG boosting

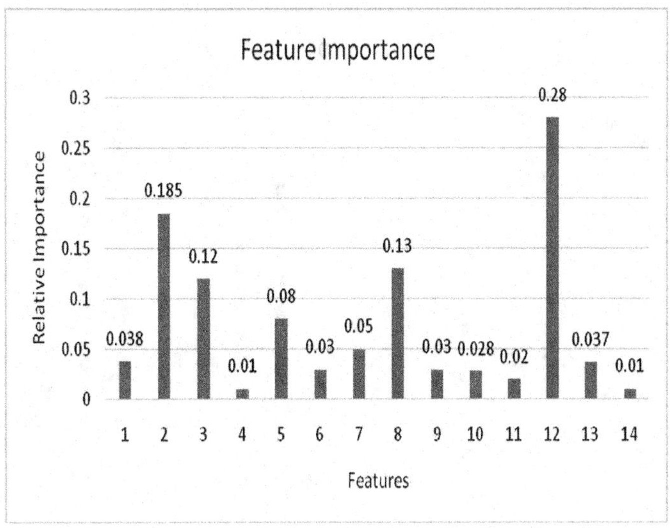

Figure 5. Importance of the factors with decision tree

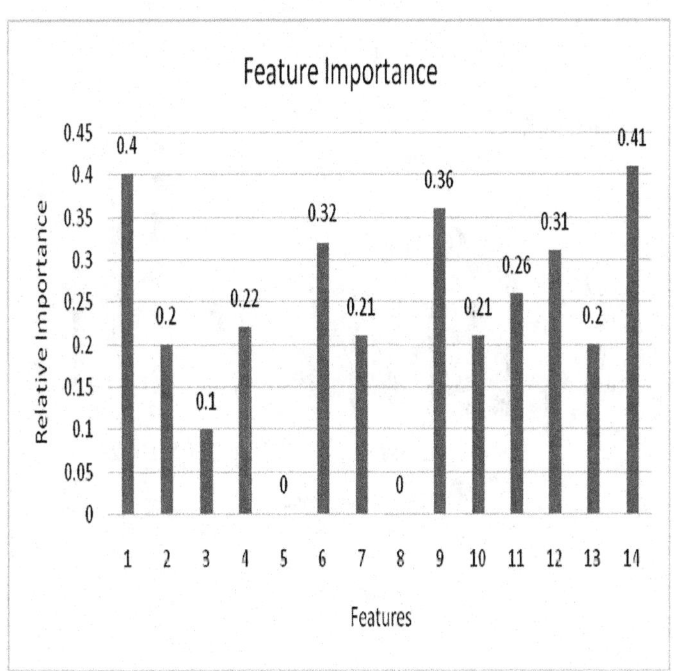

Figure 6. Importance of the factors in random forest

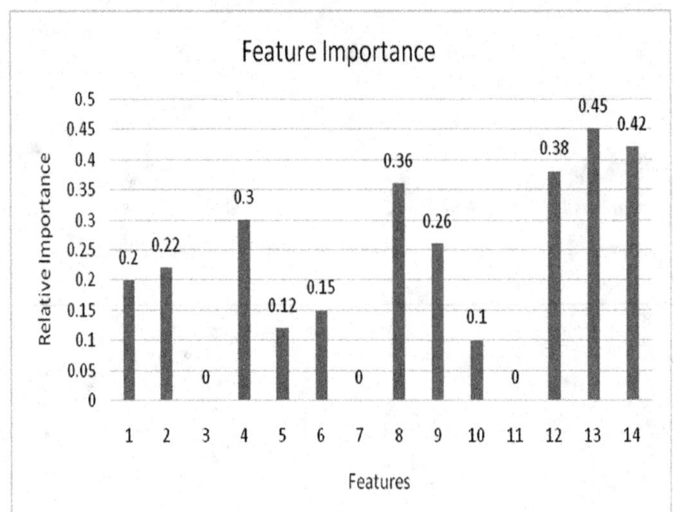

Figure 7. Importance of the factors in C 5.0

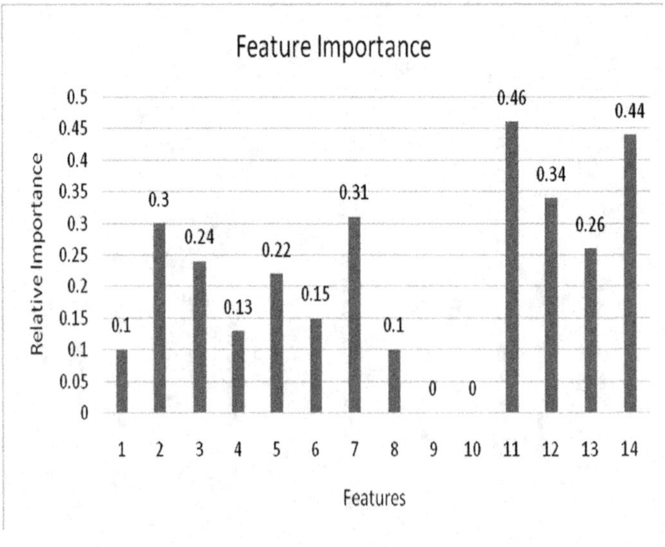

DISCUSSION

Machine Learning is considered to be one of the most promising tools for predicting a disease based on a given dataset. In this chapter, the authors have identified a new problem of predicting insomnia using existing machine learning algorithms. For the first time insomnia prediction is done using 14 leading factors and fifteen classification algorithms. After applying 15 classification algorithms we found the highest accuracy of 91.6% using SVM. The result was a cross verified in two layers; (i) Using the ten-fold cross-validation method, (ii) SVM model was tested on a new dataset of 100 decrepit patients. Evaluated results of these 100 patients matched with the Gold Standards set by Insomnia Severity Index (ISI) with

Figure 8. Importance of the factors in the CART

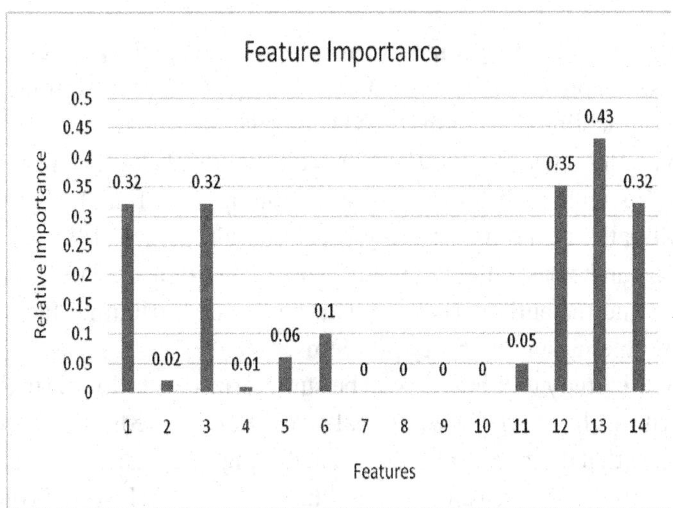

the accuracy of 92%. However, previous and ongoing researches have been in the realm of psychological signals associated with EEG and EOG signals. The comparison of our research with previous studies is as follows: Insomnia has been characterized using hypnogram to Graph spectral theory (Chaparro-Vargas, R, 2016) which differentiates between healthy and insomniac using only one classifier, i.e. logistic regression model. The above study comprises of overnight polysomnogram of 16 healthy and 16 insomniac samples. Wherein our research consists of 15 classifiers, also rather than focusing on a single overnight hypnogram collection, the authors have considered data set in which past medical history and 14 leading factors of insomnia have been considered for better results. Another study classifies insomnia based on the wake to sleep transition, according to this study they generated psychological signals based on rapid eye movements (REM) and non-rapid eye movements (NREM) (Dissanyaka et al., 2016). But the authors can't build a relevant predictive model based on only sleep to wake transition; therefore, the authors have considered hypertension, Diabetic Mellitus (DM) along with sleep which helps to build a better predictive model than existing. One more study involves Hjorth parameter extracted from EEG signals for identification of insomnia (Hamida, Ahmed & Penzel, 2015). We conclude from above researches that results of previous studies are dependent on a single overnight data of psychological signals (EEG and EOG), but insomnia is not an overnight issue, but it is a prolonged disease. So in order to detect insomnia properly, at least the authors should consider data of past six months along with the previous history. Also, insomnia is accompanied by behavioral changes in a person. So, there is a need to include the behavior of a person in our dataset. Insomnia also depends on the socio-demographic factors like living spouse, family type (nuclear or joint family), etc. Therefore sociodemographic factors have been included in the dataset. No researches have applied the standards of medical science (Scales for measuring insomnia) in their research. The authors have understood the importance of gold standards and therefore included the seven questionnaires of ISI scale in the prediction of insomnia. So after including all the above factors and fifteen classification algorithms the authors ended up with 91.6% accuracy using the SVM classifier. The result was also cross-validated using a ten-fold cross-validation method, and a new test data of 100 decrepit patients. None of the studies has matched their result with any standard scale, but we have matched our result with gold standards set by ISI scale.

CONCLUSION

Our Research provides the usages of machine learning algorithms in the prediction of Insomnia disease. The prediction of disease is applied to the dataset of 500 patients. Our dataset includes 14 essential features. Among all the classification algorithms SVM was found to have the maximum accuracy of 91.6%, precision of 93.05%, with the sensitivity of 91.3%, specificity of 91.2%, Kappa with 0.83. These results were also cross verified using the ten-fold cross-validation method. Finally, SVM was tested on a new data set of 100 decrepit patients and its accuracy was 92% with a 9.5% FP rate. Thus, the authors can say that SVM algorithm can be best suited to predict insomnia diseases. The variable importance of six algorithms is calculated and the authors find out that the most contributing factors to Insomnia are the sleep disorder, vision problems, and mobility problems.

The Contribution of this study to literature can be summarized as follows: firstly, the effectiveness of machine learning algorithms has been shown in real-world data to predict Insomnia. Secondly, variable importance analyses show that three major factors contributing to Insomnia are a sleep disorder, mobility problems, and vision problems. By focusing on these three parameters Insomnia diseases can be avoided.

REFERENCES

American Academy of Sleep Medicine. (n.d.). Dates of insomnia day. *American Academy of Sleep Medicine.* Retrieved on July 13, 2018 available at https://aasm.org/

Attaran, N., Puranik, A., Brooks, J., & Mohsenin, T. (2018). Embedded Low-Power Processor for Personalized Stress Detection. *IEEE Transactions on Circuits and Wystems. II, Express Briefs*, 1. doi:10.1109/TCSII.2018.2799821

Banno, K., & Kryger, M. H. (2006). Comorbid insomnia. *Sleep Medicine Clinics*, *1*(3), 367–374. doi:10.1016/j.jsmc.2006.06.003

Begum, S., Chakraborty, D., & Sarkar, R. (2015, December). Data classification using feature selection and kNN machine learning approach. In *Computational Intelligence and Communication Networks (CICN), 2015 International Conference on* (pp. 811-814). IEEE.

Bhargava, K., & Katarya, R. (2017, October). An improved lexicon using logistic regression for sentiment analysis. In *Computing and Communication Technologies for Smart Nation (IC3TSN), 2017 International Conference on* (pp. 332-337). IEEE.

Chaparro-Vargas, R., Ahmed, B., Wessel, N., Penzel, T., & Cvetkovic, D. (2016). Insomnia Characterization: From Hypnogram to Graph Spectral Theory. *IEEE Transactions on Biomedical Engineering*, *63*(10), 2211–2219. doi:10.1109/TBME.2016.2515261 PMID:26742123

Chouvarda, I., Grassi, A., Mendez, M. O., Bianchi, A. M., Parrino, L., Milioli, G., . . . Cerutti, S. (2013, July). Insomnia types and sleep microstructure dynamics. In *Engineering in Medicine and Biology Society (EMBC), 2013 35th Annual International Conference of the IEEE* (pp. 6167-6170). IEEE. 10.1109/EMBC.2013.6610961

Chouvarda, I., Mendez, M. O., Rosso, V., Bianchi, A. M., Parrino, L., Grassi, A., & Maglaveras, N. (2012). Cyclic alternating patterns in normal sleep and insomnia: Structure and content differences. *IEEE Transactions on Neural Systems and Rehabilitation Engineering*, *20*(5), 642–652. doi:10.1109/TNSRE.2012.2208984 PMID:22855235

Chouvarda, I., Papadelis, C., Domis, N., Staner, L., & Maglaveras, N. (2007, August). Insomnia treatment assessment based on physiological data analysis. In *Engineering in Medicine and Biology Society, 2007. EMBS 2007. 29th Annual International Conference of the IEEE* (pp. 6694-6696). IEEE.

de León, F. S., Nicklin, P., Rhodesf, C., & Kwankam, S. Y. (2008). *Promoting appropriate eHealth technologies in the developing world: The Sharing eHealth Intellectual Property for Development (SHIPD) initiative*. World Health Organization.

Dissanyaka, C., Cvetkovic, D., Abdullah, H., Ahmed, B., & Penzel, T. (2016, December). Classification of healthy and insomnia subjects based on wake-to-sleep transition. In *Biomedical Engineering and Sciences (IECBES), 2016 IEEE EMBS Conference on* (pp. 480-483). IEEE.

Dixit, D., & Sahu, P. R. (2017, September). Outage Probability of Cooperative Relay Networks in eta-μ, kappa-μ, and Mixed Fading Channels. In *Vehicular Technology Conference (VTC-Fall), 2017 IEEE 86th* (pp. 1-5). IEEE. 10.1109/VTCFall.2017.8288003

El Majd, Y. A., El Ghazi, H., & Nahhal, T. (2017, November). PaRRT: Parallel rapidly-exploring random tree (RRT) based on MapReduce. In *Electrical and Information Technologies (ICEIT), 2017 International Conference on* (pp. 1-5). IEEE.

Fonseca-Delgado, R., & Gomez-Gil, P. (2013, September). An assessment of ten-fold and Monte Carlo cross validations for time series forecasting. In *Electrical Engineering, Computing Science and Automatic Control (CCE), 2013 10th International Conference on* (pp. 215-220). IEEE.

Global health aging report of the total population. (n.d.). Available at http://www.who.int/ageing/publications/global_health.pdf

Hamida, S. T. B., Ahmed, B., & Penzel, T. (2015, December). A novel insomnia identification method based on Hjorth parameters. In *Signal Processing and Information Technology (ISSPIT), 2015 IEEE International Symposium on* (pp. 548-552). IEEE.

Hu, F., Qiao, Y., Xie, G., Zhu, Y., Jia, Y., & Huang, P. (2017, October). Symptom Distribution Regulation of Core Symptoms in Insomnia Based on Informap-SA Algorithm. In *Distributed Computing and Applications to Business, Engineering and Science (DCABES), 2017 16th International Symposium on* (pp. 229-232). IEEE.

Jáuregui, D. A. G., Castanier, C., Chang, B., Val, M., Cottin, F., Le Scanff, C., & Martin, J. C. (2017, October). Toward automatic detection of acute stress: Relevant nonverbal behaviors and impact of personality traits. In *Affective Computing and Intelligent Interaction (ACII), 2017 Seventh International Conference on* (pp. 354-361). IEEE.

Kinsella, K., & He, W. (2009). *An aging world: 2008: International population reports*. US Government Printing Office.

Li, Y., Xu, B., Chen, S., Liu, P., Ou, A., Xu, Y., . . . Zeng, L. (2011, November). A randomized, controlled study of efficacy and safety on mild to moderate insomnia intervened by Chinese medicine in the integrated program. In *Bioinformatics and Biomedicine Workshops (BIBMW), 2011 IEEE International Conference on* (pp. 732-739). IEEE.

Liu, P., Yu, H., Xu, T., & Lan, C. (2017, December). Research on archives text classification based on Naive Bayes. In *Technology, Networking, Electronic and Automation Control Conference (ITNEC), 2017 IEEE 2nd Information* (pp. 187-190). IEEE.

Morin, C. M., Belleville, G., Bélanger, L., & Ivers, H. (2011). The Insomnia Severity Index: Psychometric indicators to detect insomnia cases and evaluate treatment response. *Sleep, 34*(5), 601–608. doi:10.1093leep/34.5.601 PMID:21532953

Mulaffer, L., Shahin, M., Glos, M., Penzel, T., & Ahmed, B. (2017, July). Comparing two insomnia detection models of clinical diagnostic techniques. In *Engineering in Medicine and Biology Society (EMBC), 2017 39th Annual International Conference of the IEEE* (pp. 3749-3752). IEEE.

National Sleep Foundation. (n.d.). *Types of Insomnia*. National Sleep Foundation. Available at https://sleepfoundation.org/insomnia/content/what-are-different-types-insomnia

Neikrug, A. B., & Ancoli-Israel, S. (2010). Sleep disorders in the older adult–a mini-review. *Gerontology, 56*(2), 181–189. doi:10.1159/000236900 PMID:19738366

Nugrahaeni, R. A., & Mutijarsa, K. (2016, August). Comparative analysis of machine learning KNN, SVM, and random forests algorithm for facial expression classification. In *Technology of Information and Communication (semantic), International Seminar on Application for* (pp. 163-168). IEEE.

Pandey, P. S. (2017, July). Machine learning and iot for prediction and detection of stress. In *Computational Science and Its Applications (ICCSA), 2017 17th International Conference on* (pp. 1-5). IEEE.

Rashid, T. A., Abdulla, S. M., & Abdulla, R. M. (2016). Decision support system for diabetes mellitus through machine learning techniques. *Database, 7*.

Rashid, T. A., & Abdullah, S. M. (2018). A Hybrid of Artificial Bee Colony, Genetic Algorithm, and Neural Network for Diabetic Mellitus Diagnosing. *ARO-The Scientific Journal of Koya University, 6*(1), 55–64. doi:10.14500/aro.10368

Rashid, T. A., Abdullah, S. M., & Abdullah, R. M. (2016). An intelligent approach for diabetes classification, prediction, and description. In *Innovations in Bio-Inspired Computing and Applications* (pp. 323–335). Cham: Springer. doi:10.1007/978-3-319-28031-8_28

Saddichaa, S. (2010). Information about acute insomnia. *Annals of Indian Academy of Neurology, 13*(2). Available at https://www.ncbi.nlm.nih.gov/pmc/articles/PMC2924526/

Sau, A., & Bhakta, I. (2017) Predicting anxiety and depression in elderly patients using machine learning technology. Healthcare Technology Letters, 4(6), 238-243.

Shahin, M., Ahmed, B., Hamida, S. T. B., Mulaffer, F. L., Glos, M., & Penzel, T. (2017). Deep Learning and Insomnia: Assisting Clinicians With Their Diagnosis. *IEEE Journal of Biomedical and Health Informatics, 21*(6), 1546–1553. doi:10.1109/JBHI.2017.2650199 PMID:28092583

Skaer, T. L. (n.d.). *Treatment of Insomnia with Comorbid Mental Illness*. Retrieved from http://cdn.intechopen.com/pdfs/32274.pdf

Subhani, A. R., Mumtaz, W., Saad, M. N. B. M., Kamel, N., & Malik, A. S. (2017). Machine learning framework for the detection of mental stress at multiple levels. *IEEE Access: Practical Innovations, Open Solutions*, *5*, 13545–13556. doi:10.1109/ACCESS.2017.2723622

Susanti, S. P., & Azizah, F. N. (2017, November). Imputation of missing value using the dynamic Bayesian network for multivariate time series data. In *Data and Software Engineering (ICoDSE), 2017 International Conference on* (pp. 1-5). IEEE.

Thapliyal, H., Khalus, V., & Labrado, C. (2017). Stress detection and management: A survey of wearable smart health devices. *IEEE Consumer Electronics Magazine*, *6*(4), 64–69. doi:10.1109/MCE.2017.2715578

Tong, W., Kan, C., & Yang, H. (2018, March). Sensitivity analysis of wearable textiles for ECG sensing. In *Biomedical & Health Informatics (BHI), 2018 IEEE EMBS International Conference on* (pp. 157-160). IEEE.

United Nations. (2010). World population data available at United Nations. *World Population Prospects: The 2010*. Retrieved on July 13, 2018 available at http://esa.un.org/unpd/wpp

Yang, X. B., Yan, S. X., Zhou, Z. Y., Li, G. Z., Li, Y., & Guo, X. F. (2011, November). Balance-bagging-PRFS algorithm for feature optimization on insomnia data intervened by traditional Chinese Medicine. In *Bioinformatics and Biomedicine Workshops (BIBMW), 2011 IEEE International Conference on* (pp. 854-857). IEEE.

Ying, K., Ameri, A., Trivedi, A., Ravindra, D., Patel, D., & Mozumdar, M. (2015, November). Decision tree-based machine learning algorithm for in-node vehicle classification. In *Green Energy and Systems Conference (IGESC)* (pp. 71-76). IEEE. 10.1109/IGESC.2015.7359454

Zhang, J. A., Mo, G., & Zhang, K. (2017, October). The design and clinical application of sleep disorder treatment system. In *Image and Signal Processing, Biomedical Engineering and Informatics (CISP-BMEI), 2017 10th International Congress on* (pp. 1-5). IEEE.

Zhang, Y., Cao, G., Li, X., & Wang, B. (2018). Cascaded Random Forest for Hyperspectral Image Classification. *IEEE Journal of Selected Topics in Applied Earth Observations and Remote Sensing*, *11*(4), 1082–1094. doi:10.1109/JSTARS.2018.2809781

Zhou, Q., Zhao, M., & Bian, G. (2017, December). An HFC-based Bayesian Network Structure Learning Algorithm. In *2017 International Conference on Industrial Informatics-Computing Technology, Intelligent Technology, Industrial Information Integration (ICIICII)* (pp. 104-107). IEEE.

This research was previously published in Advanced Classification Techniques for Healthcare Analysis; pages 234-257, copyright year 2019 by Medical Information Science Reference (an imprint of IGI Global).

Chapter 42

Detection of Shotgun Surgery and Message Chain Code Smells using Machine Learning Techniques

Thirupathi Guggulothu
https://orcid.org/0000-0002-9081-2816
University of Hyderabad, Hyderabad, India

Salman Abdul Moiz
University of Hyderabad, Hyderabad, India

ABSTRACT

Code smell is an inherent property of software that results in design problems which makes the software hard to extend, understand, and maintain. In the literature, several tools are used to detect code smell that are informally defined or subjective in nature due to varying results of the code smell. To resolve this, machine leaning (ML) techniques are proposed and learn to distinguish the characteristics of smelly and non-smelly code elements (classes or methods). However, the dataset constructed by the ML techniques are based on the tools and manually validated code smell samples. In this article, instead of using tools and manual validation, the authors considered detection rules for identifying the smell then applied unsupervised learning for validation to construct two smell datasets. Then, applied classification algorithms are used on the datasets to detect the code smells. The researchers found that all algorithms have achieved high performance in terms of accuracy, F-measure and area under ROC, yet the tree-based classifiers are performing better than other classifiers.

INTRODUCTION

Code smells or bad code smells refers to an anomaly in the source code that may result in deeper problems which makes software difficult to understand, evolve, and maintain. According to (Booch, 2006) smell is a kind of structure in the code that shows a violation of basic design principles such as Abstraction, Hierarchy, Encapsulation, Modularity, and Modifiability. Even if the design principles are known to the developers due to inexperience, the competition that is in the market and deadline pressure are lead-

DOI: 10.4018/978-1-6684-6291-1.ch042

ing to violation of these principles. Fowler et al. (Fowler, 1999) have defined 22 informal code smells which are removed through refactoring techniques. These techniques are used to enhance the internal structure of the code without varying the external behaviour and to improve the quality of the software. The (Opdyke, 1992) authors have defined 72 refactoring techniques.

There are various methods and tools available in the literature to detect the code smells. Each technique and tool produces different (Fontana, 2012). Bowes et al. (Bowes, 2013), compared two code smell detection tools on message chaining and shown disparity of results between them. The three main reasons for varying results are: 1) The code smells can be subjectively interpreted by the developers, and hence detected in different ways. 2) Agreement between the detectors is low, i.e., different tools or rules detect a different type of smell for different code elements. 3) The threshold value for identifying the smell can vary for the detectors.

To address the above limitations, in particular the subjective nature, Fontana et al. (Fontana, 2016) proposed a machine learning (ML) technique to detect four code smells (Long Method, Data Class, Feature Envy, Large Class) with the help of 32 classification techniques. The authors have built 4 datasets, one for each smell. These datasets have been prepared based on the tools and manual labelling process. Tools are used to identify whether the code elements (instances) are smelly or not. But the tools may produce some false positive instances so, the authors manually validated the instances to avoid the biasness. In this paper, instead of using tools and manual validation, the authors have prepared two new method level code smell datasets of Fowler et al. (Fowler, 1999) from the literature; based on the detection rules and unsupervised learning i.e., clustering to validate the instances as smelly or not.

In the proposed work, an attempt is made to detect two code smells namely Shotgun surgery and Message chaining with supervised learning techniques. It is an application of machine learning (ML) classification approach used for code smell detection. It uses known data to determine how the new instances should be classified into binary classification i.e., based on the metrics used for a particular method, the ML approach helps in classifying a method to be prone to code smell or not. In this paper, the dataset instances are methods of 74 heterogeneous java systems. The metrics of object-oriented systems have been computed on method instances, which are the features or attributes of the dataset. For each smell, one dataset is prepared by using detection rules from the literature (Ferme, 2013). The researchers applied a random stratified sampling on the method instances to balance the datasets. Sample instances of the dataset are validated through unsupervised learning and added to the training dataset. Then applied some known classification algorithms on the trained datasets to detect the code smells, by using 10-fold cross validation method. To evaluate those algorithms, standard metric measures such as F-score, accuracy and the area under the ROC are used. The experimented algorithms have achieved high performance in both the smells.

The paper is been arranged as follows; The second section, introduces a work related to detection of code smells; The third section, defines two proposed approaches of code smell detections; The fourth section, detecting code smells using ML approach; The fifth section, presents experimental results; The sixth section, presents the code smell detection rules; and the final section, gives conclusion and future directions.

RELATED WORK

According to (Kessentini, 2014) approaches of code smell detection are classified into 7 categories (i.e., cooperative-based approaches, visualization-based approaches, search-based approaches, probabilistic approaches, metric-based approaches, symptoms based approaches, and manual approaches). In the manual approach developers and maintainers follow different reading guidelines to detect smells. As it requires human involvement, it consumes more time for large systems. In the metric-based approach, smell detection is based on source code metrics. Symptoms based approach uses different notations to detect smells. But the problem with this approach is, it requires analysis to convert symptoms or notations into detection algorithms. Probabilistic approach is based on applying fuzzy logic rules to detect smells. The visualization approach uses semi-automated processes to detect and visualize the smells with the integration of human capabilities. But the problem with this approach is that, it requires human effort, with increase in large systems. The search-based approach applies different algorithms to detect the smells. Most of the techniques use ML approaches. The success of this approach depends upon the training datasets. The cooperative approach performs different activities in a cooperative way.

Fontana et al. (2015) proposed a detection strategy for the code smells. The authors have derived metric thresholds to detect code smells, from a benchmark of 74 java software systems.

Fontana et al. (2016) experimented and compared the supervised ML algorithms to detect the code smells. The authors have used 74 java systems to prepare the training dataset which are manually validated instances. Then used 16 different classification algorithms and in addition to it, boosting techniques are applied on 4 code smells viz., Long Method, Data Class, Feature Envy, and Large Class.

In this proposed approach an attempt is made to detect two additional code smells called shotgun surgery and message chaining through ML classification techniques. In Fontana et al. (Fontana F. A., 2016) advisors (Tools) are used to identify whether the class is smelly or not, but the authors have considered the tools to be subjective to errors and not biased. So, they went for manual validation on the instances. But in the proposed approach, the researchers have used the code smell deterministic rules from literature (Fontana F. A., 2015) to identify whether the class is smelly or not and instead of manual validation unsupervised learning is used. In the proposed work, the training dataset size is larger than the previous work. A large dataset would generalize the instances effectively. In both proposed and previous work, the tree based classifiers are giving better performance than other classifiers.

CODE SMELL BASICS

In this work, the researchers have considered two code smells among 22 code smells identified by Fowler et al. (Fowler, 1999), to experiment on the smell detection approach. The reason for choosing these two code smells is to cover potential problems related to object-oriented quality dimension called coupling. Coupling is the relational strength between entities of the systems. High coupling may negatively impact the software quality dimension. In Table 1, the researchers have outlined the selected code smells and reported the smell definitions. There are usually two levels of affected entities in the code smell i.e., class level and method level and each code smell affect either an intra or inter class. Intra class means code smell affecting a single entity in the source code and inter class means code smell affecting more than one entity in the source code. In this paper, work is carried out on method level smells.

Table 1. Selected fowler code smell

Name of Code Smell	Affected Entities	Intra / Inter	Impacted on Object Oriented Quality Dimensions
Shotgun Surgery	Method	Inter class	Coupling
Message chaining	Method	Inter class	Coupling

Shotgun surgery says, to introduce a small new change, a developer has to change many classes and methods, and most of the time writes duplicated code, which violates the "Don't Repeat Yourself" principle.

The message chaining, code smell refer to a particular class or method which has high coupling with other classes or methods in chain-like delegations, i.e., methods that contain long sequences of method calls to get data from other classes.

CODE SMELL DETECTION USING MACHINE LEARNING APPROACH

The application of ML classification approach is to detect the code smell using known data to determine how the new data must be classified into a binary classification (code is smelly or not), Figure 1 describes the flow of activities in the proposed approach to detect code smells.

Figure 1. Flow of activities to detect the code smells

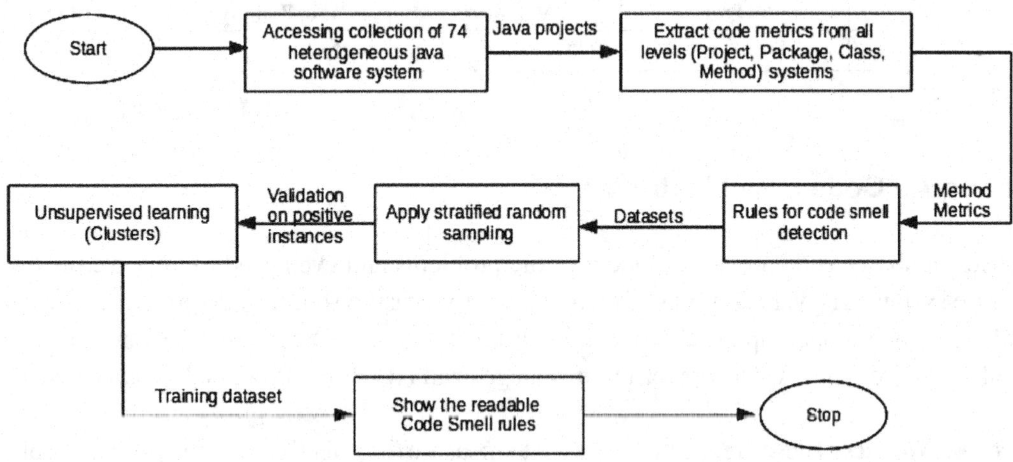

The summary of the flow chart will be described here. Following sections will give a detailed explanation of one each activities of the researchers approach during the code smell detection.

- A collection of 74 heterogeneous java systems are been collected and considered as input instances (methods) for creation of the dataset.
- From the given 74 systems, metrics extraction was done from all the levels such as Project, Package, Class and Method. These metrics become features to the dataset.

- For the binary classification of code smells, class variables are considered. To assign class variable (smelly or not) the researchers chosen code smell rules from the literature.
- The above steps result in a dataset which is imbalanced. The researchers applied a random stratified sampling on the method instances to balance the datasets.
- Sample instances of the dataset are validated through unsupervised learning and added to the training dataset.
- Known supervised classification algorithms are applied on the training dataset.
- Among the supervised classification algorithms, J48 and JRIP produces human readable code smell rules.

Collection of Java Software Systems

In order to prepare code smell classification dataset, java software systems are collected from (Fontana F. A., 2016). The author has provided a collection of 74 java systems with the compiled version, collected from (Tempero, Anslow, Dietrich et al., 2010). The 74 systems are having different sizes and various application domains. Table 2 reports, the characteristics of all 74 projects. The data selected are large enough to experiment on the ML algorithms. The large dataset would lead to more generalized ML algorithm results. The number of instances (methods) create the dataset.

Table 2. Summary of 74 projects

Number of Projects	Number of Lines in All Projects	Number of Packages in All projects	Number of Classes in All Projects	Number of Methods in All Projects
74	6,785,568	3420	56,225	4,15,995

Extracting All Code Level Metrics

The metrics of source code are used to identify the problems and even used to improve the quality of the software system. The various types of metrics used to measure source code properties are coupling, encapsulation, cohesion, complexity, size and inheritance. Software quality dimensions cover different aspects of the source code. Usually, metrics are categorized into three: Process, Resource, and Product.

1. **Process Metrics:** These are the metrics used to measure the effectiveness and efficiency of various process. Process metrics are related to function points, percentage of defective detection, defective density etc.
2. **Resource Metrics:** These are the metrics used to measure the quantity of cost, defects, productivity, schedule and estimation of various project deliverables and resources. Resource metrics are also related to schedule, cost, productivity and number of developers.
3. **Product Metrics:** These are the metrics used to measure the internal structure of software. Product metrics are related to software quality dimensions like coupling, encapsulation, cohesion, complexity, size and inheritance.

In this paper, the researchers particularly focused on product metrics because, software refactoring changes the internal structure of the software. As mentioned in the above definition, product metrics measures the internal structure of software. The six object oriented software quality dimensions are related to code-smell characteristics. In appendix section, Figure 7 listed the metrics which are categorized into quality dimensions and with their abbreviations. Each dimension is related to few metrics list which are mentioned below, that are independent variable of the dataset:

- **Size:** The size of the system depends upon number of packages, number of classes, number of methods, and number of lines of code and so on. Larger the system, the more difficult it is to manage. Size related metrics are LOC, LOCNAMM, NOM, NOPK, NOCS, NOA, and NOMNAMM.
- **Complexity:** It is measured based on the level of difficulty in understanding the structure of the class (Bansiya, Jagdish and Davis, Carl G., 2002). As the complexity of the class increases, it would be hard to understand it. Complexity related metrics are CYCLO, WMC, WMCNAMM, AMW, MAXNESTING, WOC, CLNAMM, NOP, NOAV, ATLD, NOLV, and AMWNAMM.
- **Cohesion:** It is used to measure the strength of relatedness among methods and attributes in a class (Balmas, Francoise and Bergel, Alexandre and Denier, Simon and Ducasse, Stephane and Laval, Jannik and Mordal-Manet, Karine and Abdeen, Hani and Bellingard, Fabrice, 2010). Cohesion metrics are LCOM5, TCC.
- **Coupling:** It is used to measure the strength of dependence among the objects in a design. Therefore, the stronger the coupling between the objects, the more difficult to change, understand, and correct. Coupling related metrics are FANOUT, ATFD, FDP, RFC, CBO, CFNAMM, CINT, CDISP, CC, and CM.
- **Encapsulation:** It is defined as binding of data and behavior within a single block called class. Without encapsulation in classes an unauthorized person can able to access it directly. The metrics related to encapsulation are LAA, NOAM, and NOPA.
- **Inheritance:** Is-a relationship between classes is measured by inheritance. That means acquiring the properties of one class to another class. The level of nested classes depends upon the relationship related to the inheritance hierarchy. As the complexity of the hierarchy increases understanding it become difficult, because of the inherited methods and attributes from the ancestor classes. Inheritance related metrics are DIT, NOI, NOC, NMO, NIM, and NOII.

The object oriented metrics (product) are grouped into four categories called class, method, package and project (LAB.(n.d)). Their corresponding few metrics are listed below, in the Table 3. These metric levels follow the containment relation, i.e., class is present in a package, method is present in a class etc. There are usually two levels of affected entities in the code smell i.e., class level and method level. In this paper, researchers are working on method level smells. The method level smells, not only includes method level metrics, but also includes class, package and project level metrics in the dataset as an independent variable.

Table 3.Object oriented metrics

Project Level Metrics	Package Level Metrics	Class Level Metrics	Method Level Metrics
NOPK, NOCS, NOI, NOMNAMM, LOC etc.	NOCS, NOMNAMM, NOI, LOC, NOM etc.	NOII, NOAM, NOCS NMO, ATFD etc.	CYCLO, NOP, NMCS LOC, LAA etc

Rules for Smell Detection

The supervised classification algorithm needs a training dataset which consists of instances (methods or classes), features (all level metrics) and class labels (code smells). In the dataset preparation, the class label should specify whether a method or a class instance is affected by the code smell or not. The data of 74 systems are large enough and heterogeneous. Hence, it is difficult to assign class labels for such large dataset and requires massive human intervention. This gave way to create a dataset, using sampling approach. The simplest method of sampling method is random sampling. Even, random sampling gives less code smells in this domain, i.e., the selected instances are less affected by the code smells in the training dataset. Here in this case, the researchers assigned class label instances with the help of detection rules proposed in the literature (Ferme, 2013). The researchers labelled 1 as an affected instance and 0 as an unaffected instance. The detection approach, composed of binary logical conditions (AND, OR). Figure 2 and Figure 3 shows, shotgun surgery and message chaining detection rules respectively. These rules will help to detect whether the method instances are smelly or not. The reason for choosing these detection rules is that, the threshold of the metrics are derived from a benchmark of selected 74 software system (Fontana F. A., 2015). The metrics CC, CM, and FANOUT are used to identify the characteristics of the shotgun surgery smell. Similarly, MaMCL, NMCS, and MeMCL are used to identify the characteristics of the message chaining smell. The computation of these metrics are defined in (Ferme, 2013). The outcome of this step results in a dataset.

Figure 2. Shotgun surgery detection strategy

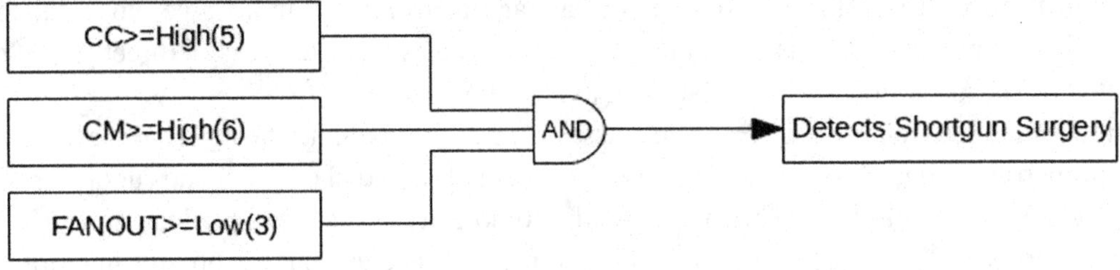

Figure 3. Message chain detection strategy

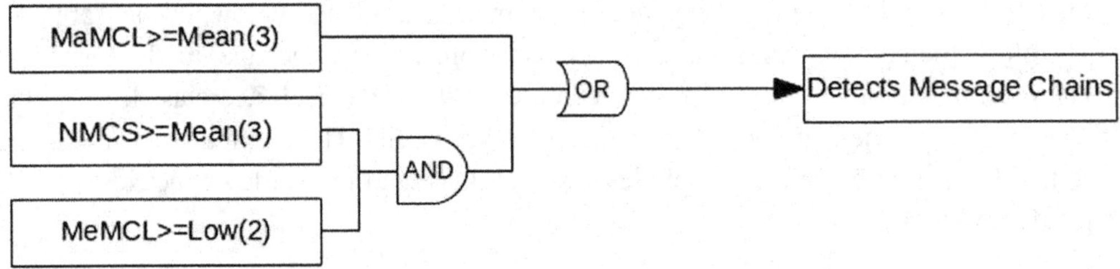

Unsupervised Learning

The researchers have applied unsupervised learning (clustering) on the entire method level dataset to know the number of clusters that can be formed. In this work, the method instances can be either smelly or not. So, the two clusters are considered to be binary classifiers. The algorithm used for clustering is k-means. The method instances which are affected (positive) by the above rules are compared with the formed clusters to validate the instances. If the instance produces same cluster as it's label then it is considered else discarded for training dataset.

Stratified Random Sampling on Datasets

Table 4 reports, the results after applying detection rules on the entire Qualitus Corpus dataset.

Table 4. Detection strategies of two smells on entire dataset

Code Smells	Method Instances	Positive Instances	Negative Instances
Shotgun surgery	415995	600	415395
Message chaining	415995	673	415321

It can be observed from Table 4 that the number of negatively affected instances are more when compared to positively affected instances. Using of open source system, resulted in increase of negative instances. Open source systems are used to produce the source code with poor quality (Stamelos, 2002). The recent study indicates that the open source systems and commercial systems are having almost the same code quality (Spinellis, 2008). From the observation it was found that when compared to commercial systems, pure open sources are giving better software structures (Spinellis, 2008; Capra, 2011). The Qualitas Corpus (Tempero, Anslow, Dietrich et al., 2010) has both "pure open source" and "open source" systems where there is a commercial participation. Thus, it is observed that affected smells (i.e., positive instances) detected using open source systems are less. This leads to highly imbalanced datasets (He, 2009). To balance the dataset, the researchers have used stratified random sampling approach which is organized as follows:

- For each project, group the negative instances for the dataset.
- Randomly, sample the negative instances of each group until approximately the double of the positive instances are obtained.
- For positive instances, unsupervised learning (clustering) is used for validation.
- The obtained positive and negative instances are placed in the training dataset.

An overview of the procedure is shown in Figure 4. This covers different domain instances having different characteristics.

Figure 4.

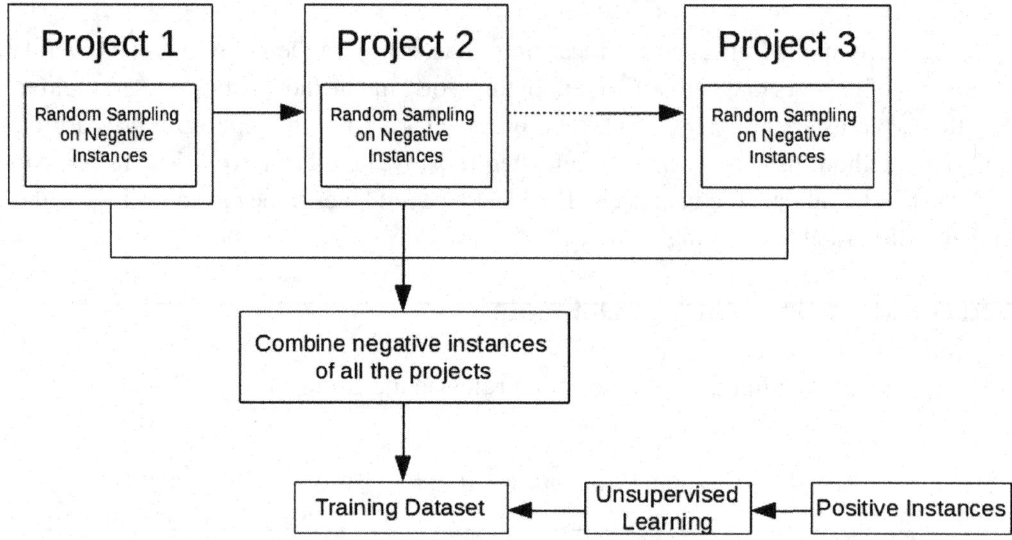

EXPERIMENTATION AND RESULTS

Experimental Setup

Researchers have used the application of supervised learning for the experiments and selected six known classification algorithms such as Bayesian networks, support vector machines, K-nearest neighbours, rule learner, decision trees, ensemble method (Random forest) and WEK (Hall, 2009) tool to provide the implementations of the selected algorithms. In general, tree based classifiers are performing better than the other classifiers in (Fontana F. A., 2016) detecting the code smells. Following steps gives a short description of the selected algorithms:

1. **J48 (C4.5) algorithm** (Quinlan, 1993)**:** Decision tree tries to recursively partition the dataset into subsets by evaluating the normalized information gain (difference in entropy) resulting from choosing an attribute for splitting the data. The attribute with the highest information gain is used for every step. The training process stops when the resulting nodes contain instances of single classes or no such attribute that can be found with information gain. The authors have used the default parameters supported by WEKA which are given below.
    1. **Criterion:** It defines the function to measure the quality of split. J48 support Entropy (measure the level of impurity) for information gain.
    2. **minNumObj:** Minimum number of instances required to split the internal nodes. By default, the value is 2.
    3. **Confidence vector:** The parameter altered to test the effectiveness of post-pruning was labelled by WEKA as the confidence factor. It builds a full tree and then work back from the leaves, applying a statistical test at each stage. By default, the value is 0.25.
2. **Random Forest** (Breiman, 2001): It generates different decision trees based on randomly selected attributes and instances. These trees become a forest called "random forest tree". It conducts voting

on all the instances to decide the class instance based on polling result. The default random forest tree parameters in WEKA are as follows:

  1. **maxDepth:** It indicates how deep the tree can be. The deeper the tree, the more splits it has, and captures more information about the data. By default, the value is 0 (unlimited) means the nodes are expanded until all leaves are pure or until all leaves contain less than minimum number of instances.
  2. **numTrees:** The number of trees to be generated. By default the value is set to 10.
  3. **minFeatues:** The number of attributes to be used in random selection is 7.

3. **JRip** (Cohen, 1995): It implements a propositional rule learner based on association rules. It is used to extract human understandable rules for code smells.
4. **Naive Bayes** (John, 1995)**:** It is a supervised classification algorithm based on the assumption that occurrence of certain attribute is independent of occurrence of other attribute.
5. **Sequential minimal optimization (SMO)** (Platt, 1998)**:** It is restricted to binary class. To apply support vector machine the researchers should implement the SMO algorithm in order to train the instances.
6. **K-nearest neighbours (k=2)** (Ah, 1991)**:** The learning is also known as "instance based" learning. It is based on similarity (distance) calculation between instances. In the classes – to - cluster evaluation, the researchers verified that the number of clusters are 2 in both the datasets. The error rate was minimal for 2 clusters, when compared to others.

Researchers used the cross validation (10-fold) technique to evaluate predictive models to find the best algorithms for the experimentation. They have applied three standard performance measures for ML algorithms.

- **Accuracy** is the percentage of correct prediction. It is insufficient to select a model when, the positive and negative instances are imbalanced, but this will never occur in this approach. As the researchers have balanced two datasets with stratified random sampling.
- **F-Measure** is the 2 * ((precision * recall) / (precision + recall)) i.e., harmonic mean of precision and recall.
- **Area under ROC** allows visualizing the performances of the classifier across all possible classification thresholds, thus helping to choose a threshold that approximately balances sensitivity and specificity.

Dataset Results

After applying stratified random sampling, the researchers have obtained two training datasets (one for each code smell) which are specified in Table 5. In Table 4, 600 positive instances are detected by the shotgun surgery rule. On applying unsupervised learning on the obtained instances, 141 instances belong to other cluster. So, researchers removed those instances and added remaining instances to the training dataset of shotgun surgery which are reported in Table 5. Similarly, among 673 positive instances detected by message chaining rule, 190 instances belong to other cluster are removed and remaining are added to the training dataset and reported in Table 5. From the table, it can be observed that the datasets are well balanced in terms of positive and negative instances. The supervised learning will take these datasets as input and trains the ML algorithms.

Table 5. Training datasets of two smells

Training Dataset	Method Instances	Positive Instances	Negative Instances
Shotgun surgery	1717	459	1258
Message chaining	1889	483	1406

Algorithms Results

The results of the proposed method of two code smell (Shotgun Surgery, Message Chaining) datasets with 10-fold cross validation and performance metrics are shown in Table 6 and Table 7, respectively.

Table 6. Shotgun surgery cross validation results

10-Fold Cross Validation							
Classifier	True Positive Rate	False Positive Rate	Precision	Recall	Accuracy	F-Measure	Area Under ROC
J48	100	0	100	100	100	100	1.00
JRip	100	0	100	100	100	100	1.00
Random Forest	99.9	0	99.9	99.9	99.8	99.9	1.00
SMO	94.5	0.074	94.6	94.5	94.4	94.5	0.93
KNN(k=2)	87.5	0.264	87.2	87.5	87.4	86.9	0.92
Naive Bayes	86.8	0.210	86.8	86.8	86.8	86.8	0.93

It can be observed from Table 6 report, J48 and JRip both gives 100 percentage accuracy. These two algorithms have given the best performance when compared to other algorithms, while the worst performance is shown by Naive Bayes based on F-measure and accuracy performance metrics. According to the area under the ROC metric, the best performance got from J48, JRip and Random Forest. The worst performance got from K-nearest neighbors (K = 1).

Table 7. Message chaining cross validation results

10-Fold Cross Validation							
Classifier	True Positive Rate	False Positive Rate	Precision	Recall	Accuracy	F-Measure	Area Under ROC
J48	99.6	0.005	99.6	99.6	99.6	99.6	0.99
JRip	99.6	0.001	99.6	99.6	99.5	99.6	0.99
Random Forest	99.5	0.002	99.5	99.5	99.5	99.5	0.99
SMO	99.4	0.002	99.4	99.4	99.4	99.4	0.99
KNN(k=2)	96.1	0.073	96.1	96.1	96.1	96.1	0.98
Naive Bayes	95.1	0.017	95.9	95.1	95.1	95.3	0.98

It can be observed from the Table 7 report that, JRip gives the best performance, while the worst performance is achieved by Naive Bayes based on F-measure and accuracy performance metrics. According to the area under the ROC metric, best performance is obtained by JRip, while the worst performance is seen in K-nearest neighbours (K=1).

Classifiers Comparison with ROC Curve

ROC curve is generally used to visualize the binary classifiers performance over all possible thresholds, and AUC (arguably) is used to show the advisable way of summarizing the performance into a single value. ROC curve is a 2D graph in which, specificity (false positive rate) is plotted on x-axis and sensitivity (true negative) is plotted on y-axis. The area under the ROC curve ranges between 0 and 1. The common rule to evaluate the classification algorithm performance is to find the area under the ROC (A-ROC) (Fawcett, 2006).

- If A-ROC < 0.5 means, something wrong;
- If A-ROC=0.5 means, it is not a good prediction;
- If 0.5 < A-ROC < 0.6 means, it is a poor prediction;
- If 0.6 < A-ROC < 0.7 means, it is a fair prediction;
- If 0.7 < A-ROC < 0.8 means, it is an acceptable prediction;
- If 0.8 < A-ROC < 0.9 means, it is an excellent prediction;
- If A-ROC >= 0.9 means, it is an outstanding prediction;
- If A-ROC = 1 means, it is a perfect prediction.

Table 6 and Table 7 reports that the result obtained for different classifiers can be compared with the help of area under ROC curve on two smells shown in Figure 5 and Figure 6, respectively.

Figure 5. Shotgun surgery area under ROC curve

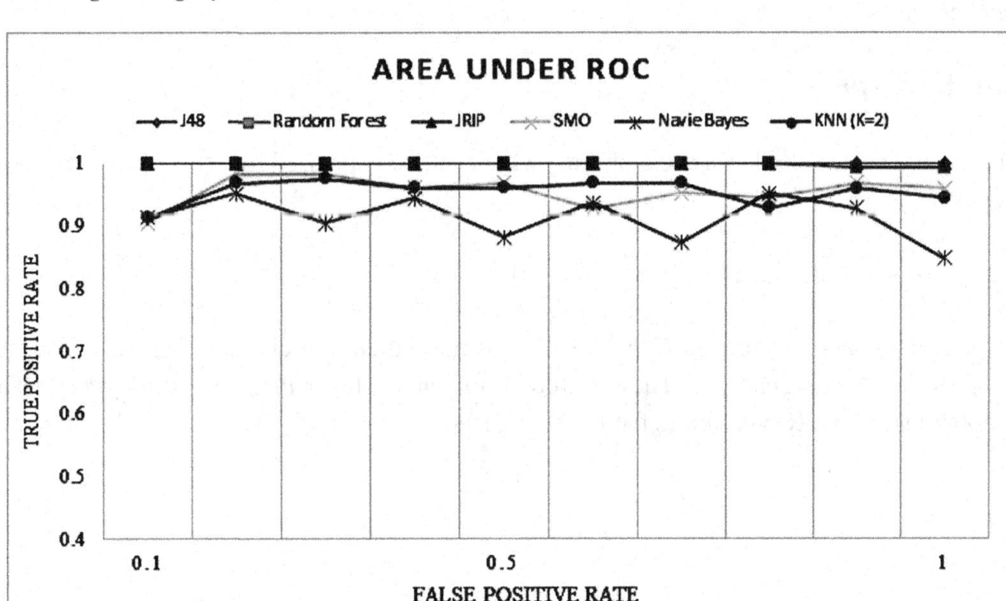

Figure 6. Message chaining area under ROC curve

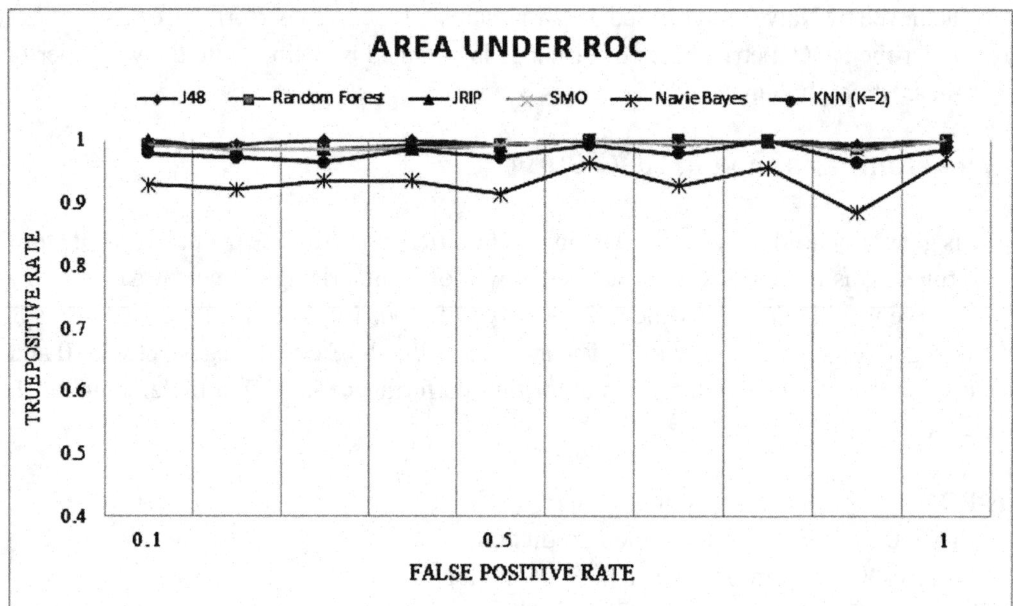

It can be observed from the Figure 5 and Figure 6 that, all the classifiers of the two smells in area under ROC curve are getting close to value 1 and from these observations, it can be said that the experimental results have achieved high performance under ROC metric.

CODE SMELL DETECTION RULES

The algorithms J48 and JRip gives the human readable detection rules for the shotgun surgery and the message chaining.

Shotgun Surgery

For shotgun surgery, J48 produces decision tree, which can be expressed in terms of logical conditions (AND, OR).

```
(CC_method > 4) AND  (FANOUT_method > 2)
```

The rule detects shotgun surgery, if the method has more than four classes, call the method and the method is subjected to being changed. These two conditions are included in the shotgun surgery definition.

For shotgun surgery, JRip produces the following rule.

```
(CC_method  >=  5) AND (FANOUT_method >= 3)
```

This gives the same rule as J48 algorithm, i.e., both J48 and JRips algorithm gives the same rule for shotgun surgery.

Message Chaining

For Message chaining, J48 produces decision tree, which can be expressed in terms of logical conditions (AND, OR).

(MeMCL_method > 0) AND (MaMCL_method >=3) OR (1)

(MeMCL_method > 0) AND (NMCS_method > 2) OR (2)

(MeMCL_method > 0) AND (NMCS_method <= 2) AND (CINT_method > 5) OR (3)

(MeMCL_method > 0) AND (NMCS_method <= 2) AND (MaMCL_method > 2) OR (4)

The rules detect message chaining occurances, when at least one of the above four conditions is verified. The first, second and fourth rules are partly in the message chaining definition and in the third rule, third condition is not linked with the code smell definition.

For the message chaining, JRip produces the following rule.

(NMCS_method >= 3) AND (MaMCL_method >= 3)

Some parts of the detection rules are placed in the message chaining definition.

In J48, and JRip algorithm, all rules of conditions produced are part of the conceptual definition of message chain, except one (*CINT_method > 5*) condition which is not a part of conceptual definition. This is because, there is a noise in the dataset.

CONCLUSION AND FUTURE DIRECTIONS

In this paper, the researchers have evaluated and compared both code smell detection (the shotgun surgery and the message chaining) datasets with the help of supervised ML techniques. This technique is used to evolve a new instance to check whether a particular code smell is correctly classified or not. This methodology can be utilized to detect other code smell also.

The researchers used two detection rules from the literature to identify the code smells. These rules produce imbalanced dataset. In order to balance the training dataset, researchers have used stratified random sampling. Then applied unsupervised learning on the positive instances to remove some of the false positive instances. Researchers have considered six known learning algorithms to detect the code smells in the dataset. To evaluate the performances of each algorithm 3 standard performance measures are used, i.e. F-measure, accuracy and area under the ROC. For shotgun surgery, the best performance is shown by J48, JRip algorithms and for the message chaining, the best performance is produced by JRip. Both the algorithms J48 and JRip provide the human understandable rules.

To improve the performance, attribute selection algorithm is used in ML. By default, an attribute selection is done by random forest algorithm and it is noted that it has performed better than KNN and naive bayes algorithm. In future, an attempt can be made to explore the performances of KNN and naive bayes with the help of feature selection.

REFERENCES

Ah, D. W. (1991). Instance-based learning algorithms. *Machine Learning*, *6*(1), 37–66. doi:10.1007/BF00153759

Balmas, Francoise and Bergel, Alexandre and Denier, Simon and Ducasse, Stephane and Laval, Jannik and Mordal-Manet, Karine and Abdeen, Hani and Bellingard, Fabrice. (2010). oftware metric for Java and C++ practices.

Bansiya, J., & Davis, C. G. (2002). A hierarchical model for object-oriented design quality assessment. *IEEE Transactions on Software Engineering*, *28*(1), 4–17. doi:10.1109/32.979986

Booch, G. (2006). *Object oriented analysis \& design*. Pearson Education India.

Bowes, D. a. (2013). The inconsistent measurement of message chains. In *Proceedings of the 2013 4th International Workshop on Emerging Trends in Software Metrics (WETSoM)* (pp. 62--68). IEEE.

Breiman, L. (2001). Random Forest. *Machine Learning*, *45*(1), 5–32. doi:10.1023/A:1010933404324

Capra, E. L., Francalanci, C., Merlo, F., & Rossi-Lamastra, C. (2011). Firms' involvement in Open Source projects: A trade-off between software structural quality and popularity. *Journal of Systems and Software*, *84*(1), 144–161. doi:10.1016/j.jss.2010.09.004

Cohen, W. W. (1995). Fast effective rule induction. In *Machine Learning Proceedings 1995* (pp. 115–123). Elsevier. doi:10.1016/B978-1-55860-377-6.50023-2

Fawcett, T. (2006). An introduction to ROC analysis. *Pattern Recognition Letters*, *27*(8), 861–874. doi:10.1016/j.patrec.2005.10.010

Ferme, V. (2013). JCodeOdor: A software quality advisor through design flaws detection [Master's thesis]. University of Milano-Bicocca, Milano, Italy.

Fontana, F. A. (2012). Automatic detection of bad smells in code: An experimental assessment. *Journal of Object Technology*, *11*, 5–1.

Fontana, F. A. (2015). Automatic metric thresholds derivation for code smell detection. In *Proceedings of the 2015 IEEE/ACM 6th International Workshop on Emerging Trends in Software Metrics (WETSoM)* (pp. 44-53). IEEE.

Fontana, F. A. (2016). Comparing and experimenting machine learning techniques for code smell detection. *Empirical Software Engineering*, *21*(3), 1143–1191. doi:10.100710664-015-9378-4

Fowler, M. a. (1999). *Refactoring: improving the design of existing code*. Addison-Wesley Professional.

Hall, M. a. (2009). The WEKA data mining software: an update. *ACM SIGKDD explorations newsletter, 11*, 10-18.

He, H. (2009). Learning from imbalanced data. *IEEE Transactions on Knowledge and Data Engineering, 21*(9), 1263–1284. doi:10.1109/TKDE.2008.239

John, G. H. (1995). *Estimating continuous distributions in Bayesian classifiers*. Morgan Kaufmann Publishers Inc.

Kessentini, W., Kessentini, M., Sahraoui, H., Bechikh, S., & Ouni, A. (2014). A cooperative parallel search-based software engineering approach for code-smells detection. *IEEE Transactions on Software Engineering, 40*(9), 841–861. doi:10.1109/TSE.2014.2331057

Machine learning for code smell detection. (n.d.). ESSeRE Lab. Retrieved from http://essere.disco.unimib.it/wiki/research/mlcsd

Opdyke, W. F. (1992). Refactoring object-oriented frameworks. University of Illinois at Urbana-Champaign, IL.

Platt, J. (1998). Sequential minimal optimization: A fast algorithm for training support vector machine.

Quinlan, J. R. (1993). *C4.5: Programs for machine leaning*. San Francisco, CA: Morgan Kaufmann Publisher Inc.

Spinellis, D. (2008). A tale of four kernels. In *Proceedings of the 30th international conference on Software engineering* (pp. 381--390). ACM.

Stamelos, I., Angelis, L., Oikonomou, A., & Bleris, G. L. (2002). Code quality analysis in open source software development. *Information Systems Journal, 12*(1), 43–60. doi:10.1046/j.1365-2575.2002.00117.x

Tempero, E., Anslow, C., Dietrich, J., Han, T., Li, J., Lumpe, M., ... & Noble, J. (2010). The Qualitas Corpus: A curated collection of Java code for empirical studies. In *Proceedings of the 2010 17th Asia Pacific Software Engineering Conference (APSEC)* (pp. 336-345). IEEE. 10.1109/APSEC.2010.46

This research was previously published in the International Journal of Rough Sets and Data Analysis (IJRSDA), 6(2); pages 34-50, copyright year 2019 by IGI Publishing (an imprint of IGI Global).

APPENDIX

Figure 7. Software metrics categorized into quality dimensions

Quality dimension	Metric Name	Metric Label	Level or Granularity
Coupling	FANOUT	-	Class, Method
	FANIN	-	Class
	ATFD	Access to foreign data	Method
	FDP	Foreign Data Providers	Method
	RFC	Response For Class	Class
	CBO	Coupling Between Objects Class	Class
	CFNAMM	Called Foreign Not Accessor or Mutator Methods	Class, Method
	CINT	Coupling Intensity	Method
	MaMCL	Maximum Message Chain Length	Method
	MeMCL	Mean Message Chain Length	Method
	NMCS	Number of Message Chain Statements	Method
	CC	Changing Classes	Method
	CM	Changing Methods	Method
Size	LOC	Lines of Code	Project, Package, Class, Method
	LOCNAMM	Lines of Code Without Accessor or Mutator Methods	Class
	NOPK	Number of Packages	Project
	NOCS	Number of Classes	Project, Package
	NOM	Number of Methods	Project, Package, Class
	NOMNAMM	Number of Not Accessor or Mutator Methods	Project, Package, Class
	NOA	Number of Attributes	Class
Inheritance	DIT	Depth of Inheritance Tree	Class
	NOI	Number of Interfaces	Project, Package
	NOC	Number of Children	Class
	NMO	Number of Methods Overridden	Class
	NIM	Number of Inherited Methods	Class
	NOII	Number of Implemented Interfaces	Class
Encapsulation	NOAM	Number of Accessor Methods	Class
	NOPA	Number of Public Attribute	Class
	LAA	Locality of Attribute Accesses	Method
Complexity	CYCLO	Cyclomatic Complexity	Method
	WMC	Weighted Methods Count	Class
	WMCNAMM	Weighted Methods Count of Not Accessor or Mutator Methods	Class
	AMW	Average Methods Weight	Class
	AMWNAMM	Average Methods Weight of Not Accessor or Mutator Methods	Class
	MAXNESTING	Maximum Nesting Level	Method
	CLNAMM	Called Local Not Accessor or Mutator Methods	Method
	NOP	Number of Parameters	Method
	NOAV	Number of Accessed Variables	Method
	ATLD	Access to Local Data	Method
	NOLV	Number of Local Variable	Method

Chapter 43
Identifying Patterns in Fresh Produce Purchases:
The Application of Machine Learning Techniques

Timofei Bogomolov
University of South Australia, Australia

Malgorzata W. Korolkiewicz
University of South Australia, Australia

Svetlana Bogomolova
https://orcid.org/0000-0003-4449-6514
Business School, Ehrenberg-Bass Institute, University of South Australia, Australia

ABSTRACT

In this chapter, machine learning techniques are applied to examine consumer food choices, specifically purchasing patterns in relation to fresh fruit and vegetables. This product category contributes some of the highest profit margins for supermarkets, making understanding consumer choices in that category important not just for health but also economic reasons. Several unsupervised and supervised machine learning techniques, including hierarchical clustering, latent class analysis, linear regression, artificial neural networks, and deep learning neural networks, are illustrated using Nielsen Consumer Panel Dataset, a large and high-quality source of information on consumer purchases in the United States. The main finding from the clustering analysis is that households who buy less fresh produce are those with children – an important insight with significant public health implications. The main outcome from predictive modelling of spending on fresh fruit and vegetables is that contrary to expectations, neural networks failed to outperform a linear regression model.

DOI: 10.4018/978-1-6684-6291-1.ch043

INTRODUCTION

Recent advances in technology have led to more data being available than ever before, from sources such as climate sensors, transaction records, scanners, cellphone GPS signals, social media posts, digital images, and videos, just to name a few. This phenomenon is referred to as Big Data, allowing researchers, governments, and organizations to know much more about their operations, thus leading to decisions that are increasingly based on data and analysis, rather than experience and intuition (McAfee & Brynjolfsson, 2012).

Big Data is typically defined in terms of its variety, velocity, and volume. Variety refers to expanding the concept of data to include unstructured sources such as text, audio, video, or click streams. Velocity is the speed at which data arrives and how frequently it changes. Volume is the size of the data, which for Big Data typically means large, given how easily terabytes to zettabytes of information are amassed in today's marketplace.

When it comes to consumer behavior and decisions, consumer data makes it possible to track individual purchases, to capture the exact time at which they occur, and to track purchase histories of individual customers. This data can be linked to demographics, advertising exposure, or credit history. Hence, researchers now have access to much more consumer data with greater coverage and scope, but also much less structure or much more complex structure than ever before. Traditional econometric modelling generally assumes that observations are independent, grouped (panel data), or linked by time. However, the Big Data we now have available may have more complex structure, and the goal of modern econometric modelling could be to uncover exactly what the key features of this dependence structure are (Einav & Levin, 2014). Developing methods that are well suited to that purpose is a challenge for researchers.

This chapter examines consumer food choices, in particular, purchasing patterns in relation to fresh fruit and vegetables. Consumption of fresh fruit and vegetables makes an important contribution to society in multiple ways. Increased consumption of fruit and vegetables can have a significant positive effect on population health (Mytton, Nnoahim, Eyles, Scarborough, & Mhurchu, 2014; World Health Organization 2015). Strong sales of fresh produce support primary production, contributing to rural and regional economies and farmers' livelihoods (Bianchi & Mortimer, 2015; Racine, Mumford, Laditka, & Lowe, 2013). Fruit and vegetable categories in supermarkets contribute some of the highest profit margins, compared to other product categories (e.g., packaged food), making these categories very important for supply-chain members. Therefore, better understanding and prediction of patterns of consumer purchases of fresh fruit and vegetables could have a substantial positive effect on a range of health, economic, commercial, and social outcomes.

Traditionally, consumer research into fresh fruit and vegetables has relied on consumer surveys, where consumers report their attitudes and intentions to buy fresh produce and barriers to doing so (Brown, Dury, & Holdsworth, 2009; Cox et al., 1996; Péneau, Hoehn, Roth, Escher, & Nuessli, 2006; Finzer, Ajay, & Ali, 2013; Erinosho, Moser, Oh, Nebeling, & Yaroch, 2012). The results were inherently biased by the indirect link between what consumers say in surveys and their actual behavior. When fresh produce purchases were examined, they were often based on self-reports, which typically are influenced by social desirability bias (Norwood & Lusk, 2011) and memory failures, resulting in over- or under-reporting of purchases (Ludwichowska, Romaniuk, & Nenycz-Thiel, 2017). Overcoming these limitations, this chapter draws on a more reliable Consumer Panel Dataset, which is one of the Nielsen datasets made available to marketing researchers around the world at the Kilts Center for Marketing, the University of Chicago Booth School of Business. Since participating households routinely scan all their purchases,

Nielsen Consumer Panel Dataset provides a complete and accurate account of their spending on fresh fruit and vegetables across all grocery outlets.

Leveraging off this unique and high-quality dataset, consumer purchasing decisions in relation to fresh fruit and vegetables are investigated using both unsupervised and supervised machine learning techniques, including clustering, artificial neural networks, and deep learning neural networks. By exploring the Nielsen Consumer Panel Dataset, the authors aim to illustrate the extent to which machine learning methods can lead to models that uncover previously unknown patterns of consumer behavior and that capture consumer purchasing decisions better. The specific objectives of this chapter are:

- To illustrate the application of unsupervised (clustering) and supervised (linear regression, artificial neural networks, and deep learning neural networks) machine learning techniques to household purchase data in fresh fruit and vegetables; and
- To highlight the advancement in knowledge and interpretation that could be obtained by the application of these machine learning techniques.

In economic terms, improved understanding of how consumers buy fresh produce could help growers and retailers to increase sales of fresh fruit and vegetables. This, in turn, would have a positive flow on effect on:

- Population health – fruit and vegetables are the healthiest of the foods, and research shows that people do not eat enough of them;
- Economic outcomes, especially for agrarian economies, including the United States and Australia;
- Social outcomes, by providing more jobs and income to food-growing communities and supply-chain members;
- The environment, by reducing consumption of meat products in favor of fruit and vegetables.

The structure of the chapter is as follows: the Nielsen Consumer Panel Dataset is introduced first, followed by an analysis of consumer purchasing decisions. The analysis begins with an exploration of consumer characteristics using clustering techniques. Groupings of households obtained from clustering are then compared in terms of their purchasing behavior, and observed differences are formally assessed using a non-parametric version of MANOVA. The second stage of the analysis incorporates household groupings resulting from clustering into supervised predictive modelling of consumer spending on fresh fruit and vegetables. The next section discusses main outcomes and contributions, followed by some suggestions for future research directions and a conclusion.

NIELSEN CONSUMER PANEL DATASET

In this chapter, patterns of customer purchases of fruit and vegetables are studied using the Nielsen Consumer Panel Dataset, which consists of a representative panel of households that continually provide information about their purchases using in-home scanners to record all their purchases intended for in-home use. Consumers provide information about their households and what products they buy, as well as when and where they make purchases. The dataset covers 13 years (2004 to 2016), with more than a billion purchases from up to 60,000 consumer households in any given year. It provides rich information about household purchasing patterns that allows researchers to study questions that cannot be addressed using other forms of data. For example, the dataset also includes purchases from retailers who traditionally do not cooperate with scanner data-collection companies. In addition, due to the national coverage (the entire United States divided into 52 major markets), there is wide variation in household location, seasonal patterns in availability of fresh produce, and demographics, adding to the richness of the captured consumer information. There are many examples of applications of this dataset in the economic and marketing literature, ranging from studies on tax effects, geography, price policies, in-store promotion and advertising to disaster relief sales, pharmaceutical products, liquor, etc. For a list of working papers that leverage Nielsen Consumer Panel Dataset, see additional reading. Yet, studies that use the Nielsen Consumer Panel Dataset and that focus on fresh fruit and vegetable purchases are relatively rare. A few exceptions are studies focused on organic purchases (e.g., Kim, Seok, & Mark, 2018; Kim, Seok, Mark, & Reed, 2018; Nelson, Fitzgerald, Tefft, & Anderson, 2017), and a study of retirement influence on fresh fruit and vegetable purchases (Hinnosaar, 2018).

The Nielsen Consumer Panel Dataset consists of the following files: Panelists, Trips, Purchases, Retailers, Products, Product Extra Attributes, and Brand Variations. Panelist files contain demographic, geographic, and product ownership information, which is updated annually. Demographic and product ownership variables are recorded for the entire household and the head of the household, as well as demographics for some other household members. Household describing variables (used in this analysis) include household size, income, presence and age of children in household, employment, education, marital status, occupation, type of residence, and race. There is also spatial information – ZIP code, state, county, region – as well as basic indicators of household assets – kitchen appliances, TV items, Internet connection.

Trips files provide summary information about each of the shopping trips made by panelists, such as the household ID, date, retail chain shopped, and the total amount spent for the trip. Since 2007, the number of shopping trips has varied between 10 and 11 million per year, and on average, there are about 180 shopping trips per household per year.

Purchases files provide information about the specific products a household bought on a shopping trip, including the product ID, the quantity, price paid, and any perceived deals. Specifically, there is a flag if a purchase was seen by the panelist as a deal, and the coupon value if the panelist used a coupon. For each year, there are more than 60 million transactions recorded.

Each Products file contains detailed product information for each unique product code, such as description, brand description, multipack and size. Products come from 10 Nielsen-defined food and non-food departments, approximately 4.2 million unique product codes in total for all years. The departments are dry grocery, frozen foods, dairy, deli, packaged meat, fresh produce, non-food grocery, alcohol, general merchandise, and health and beauty aids. Some products contain additional characteristics (e.g., flavor, variety, packaging, salt content, organic claim). These are recorded in Products Extra Attributes files for approximately one million products. Finally, the Retailers file contains an anonymized list of all retailers, each classified into one of 66 channel types (e.g., grocery, online shopping, discount store, hardware, drug store), from which products were purchased.

For the purposes of analyses presented in this chapter, only supermarket shopping is considered. That is, only shopping trips to retailers classified as "grocery" are analyzed, accounting for 66% of all shopping trips recorded. A single year (2013) was selected for the analysis, with data from other years (2014 and 2015) used for validation of outcomes. Given the authors' focus on fresh fruit and vegetables, products of interest belong to the "Fresh Produce" category.

ANALYSIS OF SUPERMARKET PURCHASING DECISIONS BY HOUSEHOLDS

The primary unit of analysis in this chapter is the household. In the field of shopper behavior, household level analysis is the most common, because many grocery purchases, especially from supermarkets, are made on behalf of the entire household. Purchases and trip information were therefore aggregated by household to produce the following variables to describe households' shopping behavior:

- Average number of shopping trips per month (num_trips).
- Average monthly number of items bought across all product categories (purchases).
- Average monthly spending on all product categories (spending).
- Average monthly number of purchases perceived as deals for all product categories (deals).
- Average monthly number of purchases labelled as organic for all product categories (organic).
- Average monthly number of items bought in the Fresh Produce category (fr_purchases).
- Average monthly spending on Fresh Produce (fr_spending).
- Average monthly number of Fresh Produce purchases labelled as organic (fr_organic).
- Average monthly number of perceived deals for Fresh Produce category (fr_deals).

Descriptive statistics for raw data from 2013 are reported in Table 1. On average, US households made 5.11 shopping trips to supermarket per month (median 4.25 trips). They bought 61.8 items (median 51.3) and spent on average $233.28 (median $189.14). That included 7.1 items (median 4.7) and $16.87 (median $11.63) on products from Fresh Produce category (fruit and/or vegetables). On average, households bought 0.8 (0.6) items labelled as organic, including 0.2 (0) items from Fresh Produce category. Also, households purchased on average 21.6 (10.5) items on a deal; only 1.6 (0.5) of them were from Fresh Produce category.

Table 1. Descriptive statistics for variables representing shopping behavior of households

Key	Mean	Std. Dev.	Median	IQR	Min	Max
num_trips	5.11	3.49	4.25	3.88	1.00	38.33
purchases	61.78	46.74	51.25	55.67	1.00	701.08
spending	$233.28	$183.65	$189.14	$211.15	$0.89	$3935.32
organic	0.84	2.68	0.17	0.58	0.00	91.91
deals	21.62	29.09	10.50	29.75	0.00	501.42
fr_purchases	7.08	7.27	4.73	6.67	0.00	132.58
fr_spending	$16.87	$17.60	$11.63	$15.30	$0.00	$712.52
fr_organic	0.19	0.71	0.00	0.13	0.00	43.73
fr_deals	1.61	2.90	0.50	2.00	0.00	84.17

Figure 1 shows average monthly spending on items from Fresh Produce category for different states. Spending pattern correlates with overall wealth of households – coastal states tend to have higher household incomes, and as a result, they might be spending more on all products, including fruit and vegetables.

Next, unsupervised and supervised learning techniques are employed to understand household shopping behavior further. More specifically, clustering is used to explore household demographic information and to create groupings based on similar household characteristics. The resulting household clusters are then compared in terms of their shopping behavior using variables defined in this section. This is followed by predictive modelling of household spending on fresh fruit and vegetables using selected supervised learning techniques. In the case of both unsupervised and supervised learning, multiple methods of varying complexity are employed and compared in relation to outcomes of interest. The purpose of employing multiple methods is to illustrate the impact (if any) of different approaches to the same task on results from that task, and to explore the extent to which more advanced machine learning techniques can be expected to produce better outcomes or predictions with panel data and in the context of studying consumer behavior.

Figure 1. Average monthly expenditure on fresh produce in 2013

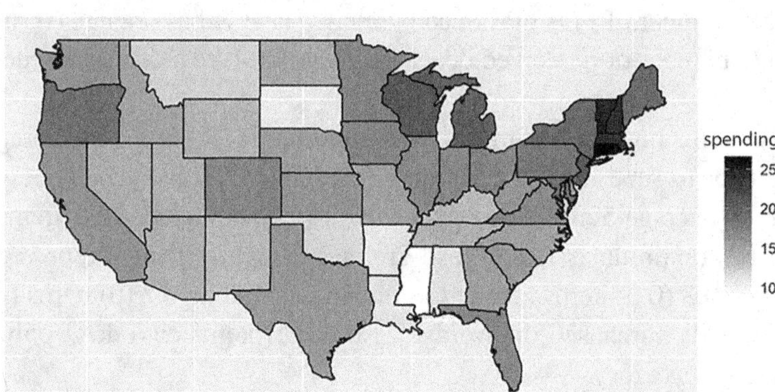

Exploratory Analysis of Nielsen Consumer Data Using Clustering Techniques

Unsupervised learning, more specifically, clustering techniques, are employed (a) to discover distinct clusters based on household characteristics, and (b) to determine how shopping patterns overall and in fresh fruit and vegetables differ between those clusters of households.

Clustering has been applied across many disciplines to place objects into groups or clusters suggested by available data so that objects in a given cluster are more similar (in some sense) than those placed in different clusters. The objective can be to find a hidden structure in the data or to reduce its dimensionality. Partitioning data into clusters may be an aim in itself or an input into further analysis.

Clustering is considered unsupervised learning, since there are no pre-defined classes into which to assign objects. In fact, the number of classes may need to be established as a part of the clustering process. Most commonly used clustering techniques are distance-based. As the name suggests, a distance metric of some kind (e.g., Euclidean distance) is used to separate observations into clusters with small within-cluster distances and large separation from other clusters. The algorithms involved are relatively simple to apply and interpret, but they suffer from a lack of well-defined rules on how to form clusters and how to assess the quality of clustering solutions. Despite numerous measures and criteria having been proposed in the literature, a decision what "similar enough" or "good enough" might mean in a particular application remains highly subjective. A comprehensive review of distance-based clustering methods and the underlying theory can be found in Hastie, Tibshirani, and Friedman (2009).

Distance-based clustering can be classified into two types: hierarchical clustering and partitional clustering. Hierarchical clustering comes in two forms, agglomerative and divisive. Agglomerative clustering starts with each observation in its own separate cluster; the algorithm then proceeds to find the most similar data points and to group them into larger clusters. In contrast, divisive clustering works in the other direction by first starting with a single cluster containing all observations and then dividing most dissimilar observations into separate, smaller clusters. Divisive clustering is more complex than agglomerative clustering, as it requires an additional clustering method as a sub-routine to divide existing clusters at each step. The divisive approach has not been studied in the literature as extensively as agglomerative methods, and it is rarely used in practice (Hastie et al., 2009; Jobson, 1992). Partitional clustering assumes there are central features around which the data can be clustered in non-overlapping partitions with the number of centers defined a priori, and it has the advantage of being relatively computationally inexpensive. One disadvantage of partitional clustering is that it requires the expected number of clusters to be known beforehand. In contrast, hierarchical clustering allows the researcher to decide the number of clusters in the data based on the analysis of a dendrogram, which is a tree-like graphical depiction of the structure produced by the algorithm. This makes hierarchical clustering a more flexible approach. Hierarchical clustering is also preferred when there is a perceived hierarchy in the data and for smaller datasets due to its computational complexity. In terms of distance-based clustering, this chapter focuses on hierarchical clustering, as it can be applied to categorical data.

However, clustering techniques are not limited to distance-based methods. There is also a range of model-based clustering techniques that rely on knowing the probability distribution of the data. Cases are assigned to clusters based on assessments of probability rather than a distance measure to find similarities between cases. Latent class analysis (LCA) is an example of a model-based clustering method, also referred to as a finite mixture model. As discussed in McCutcheon (1987) and elsewhere (e.g., Vermunt & Magidson, 2002), the method assumes that the population is composed of different unobserved groups, or latent classes, and the joint density of observed variables is a mixture of the class-specific density. The simplest form of a latent class model assumes that observed data come from a mixture of multivariate multinomial distributions. Cluster membership is decided based on probability calculated using the maximum likelihood method. As the method relies on distributional assumptions, it is possible to use formal tests or goodness-of-fit indices to decide the number of clusters. In that respect, the focus is on modelling the latent structure behind the data rather than looking for similarities, as is the case with distance-based cluster analysis. LCA is sometimes referred to as a "soft clustering" method, as it allows objects to belong to more than one class, and thus it offers more flexibility than a "hard clustering" method such as hierarchical clustering, where objects must be split into distinct clusters.

As argued in Anderlucci and Hennig (2014), cluster analysis is not a well-defined problem, in that differing meanings can be assigned to similar objects assigned to the same clusters. In distance-based clustering, the aim is to find well-separated clusters with low within-cluster distances whereas the model-based approach aims to uncover latent structure in the data. In both cases, "true" clustering of the data may be sought; however, there is not much literature to guide users as to which approach is most suitable for their particular application. In this chapter, both distance-based clustering (hierarchical) and model-based clustering (LCA) are applied to illustrate their use in the context of studying purchasing decisions by households. The authors' interest in LCA arises in part from its growing popularity facilitated by the availability of easily implemented LCA-based algorithms in statistical analysis software packages. Another reason for considering a model-based approach is the question of whether resulting partition represents true clustering of the data. It has been pointed out in the clustering literature (e.g., Ultsch & Lötsch, 2017) that by virtue of their design, commonly used algorithms including hierarchical clustering can impose structure on data even when there is actually none. Also, while a hierarchical cluster analysis always ensures that the most similar observations are in the same clusters, often there are situations where a cluster should be split and its members re-allocated to other clusters. However, no such step exists in the algorithm, and clusters created by hierarchical cluster analysis are commonly less homogeneous than clusters formed by other algorithms. This issue does not arise with LCA, and in addition, some researchers (Anderlucci & Henning, 2014; Vermunt & Magidson, 2002) have found the latent class approach relatively more successful at recovering the true cluster structure when such structure is known, albeit with artificial datasets. Other advantages of LCA clustering include being able to incorporate variables of different scale types, add covariates to the analysis, and overcome sparseness in the data (Vermunt & Magidson, 2002).

Both hierarchical clustering and LCA clustering are now applied to produce clusters of households based on their demographic characteristics. In both cases, the shopping behavior of the resulting clusters is compared. Similarities and differences between the two clustering solutions are also discussed.

Hierarchical Clustering

Figure 2. Cluster dendrogram for 2013 data

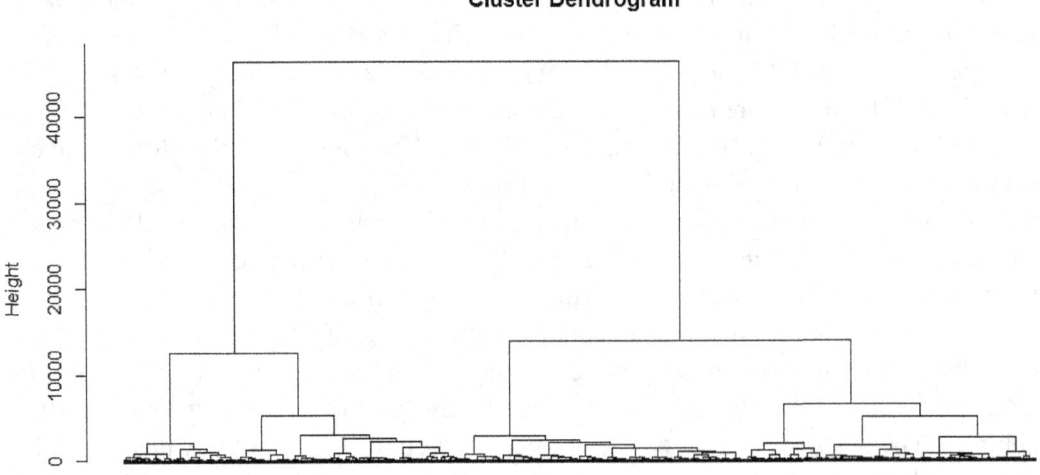

To investigate household purchasing behavior, clusters were first formed using agglomerative hierarchical clustering based on following household variables defined by Nielsen and stored in Panelist files: region_code, household_income, household_size, type_of_residence, household_composition, age_and_presence_of_children, race, and marital_status. As all these are categorical variables, they were converted into dichotomous dummy variables and then used to create a matrix of Manhattan distances. Ward's method of minimizing within-cluster variation was used to form clusters, as it produced the most interpretable clusters. The Manhattan distance metric is often chosen, as it is less sensitive to outliers

(Jobson, 1992). It is also preferred for high-dimensional and categorical data, and a mathematical justification for using it with Ward's linkage is given in Strauss and von Maltitz (2017).

As a first step, the algorithm was executed for a few small random samples to study the dendrograms and thus to determine the number of clusters to be produced. The dendrogram shown in Figure 2 suggested between 3 and 6 clusters. A 4-cluster solution was selected as the most optimal. Next, hierarchical clustering solutions for 4 clusters over different sub-samples of the dataset were investigated and shown to be very similar, and so the four-cluster solution was obtained. Household characteristics were then used to understand cluster composition better. Based on the distributions of proportions depicted in Figure 3, clusters can be characterized as follows:

- Cluster 1 predominantly consists of married couples with 2-3 children or other dependents. It appears that this cluster includes "traditional" families with children as well as so-called crowded nests (married couples living with adult children). It is the largest cluster, and it accounts for 31% of households. This cluster has the highest household size and the highest proportion of households with top income levels. It has a slightly lower proportion of White/Caucasian people and a slightly higher proportion of Asian people than other clusters. This cluster could be named *Families*.
- Cluster 2 has second highest proportion of households with top levels of income, and it consists mostly of White/Caucasian married couples without children or other dependents. This cluster is the same size as Cluster 1, and it accounts for 30-31% of households. It is comprised of DINKs (double income, no kids) including empty nesters (50+ couples whose adult children have left home). This cluster could be named *DINKs*.
- Cluster 3 is composed of single-member households, that is, males or females living alone, never married or widowed, divorced, or separated; predominantly with no kids. It accounts for 25% of households, and it consists mainly of females living alone (approximately 73%). This cluster has the lowest level of income and a somewhat higher proportion of multi-family housing than other clusters. Race distribution in Cluster 3 is similar to that in Clusters 1 and 4. This cluster could be named *SINKs* (single income no kids).
- Cluster 4 is the smallest cluster, accounting for 12% of households. It is the third in terms of incomes and the second in terms of household size (2-4 members). Most households in this cluster are headed by females. All marital status categories are represented, with the highest proportion in the separated/divorced category. This cluster includes single parents with one or more children plus other remaining family and relationship groups (e.g., unmarried couples). This cluster could be named *Single Parents Plus*.

All clusters have very few differences in terms of region, residence type, or race distribution (except Cluster 2 as mentioned above). Hence, the major driving characteristics are household composition and marital status.

Figure 4 shows the average values of variables characterizing shopping behavior for each cluster relative to the average for all households in the dataset. As the distributions of the shopper behavior variables are highly right-skewed, log transformation was applied in all cases. Transformed values were then standardized to produce z scores (mean = 0, standard deviation = 1). A bar near zero indicates a cluster average close to the overall average, while a bar with a positive or negative value indicates a deviation from the overall average in terms of higher or lower spending or the number of items purchased.

Figure 3. Household characteristics by cluster in the hierarchical solution

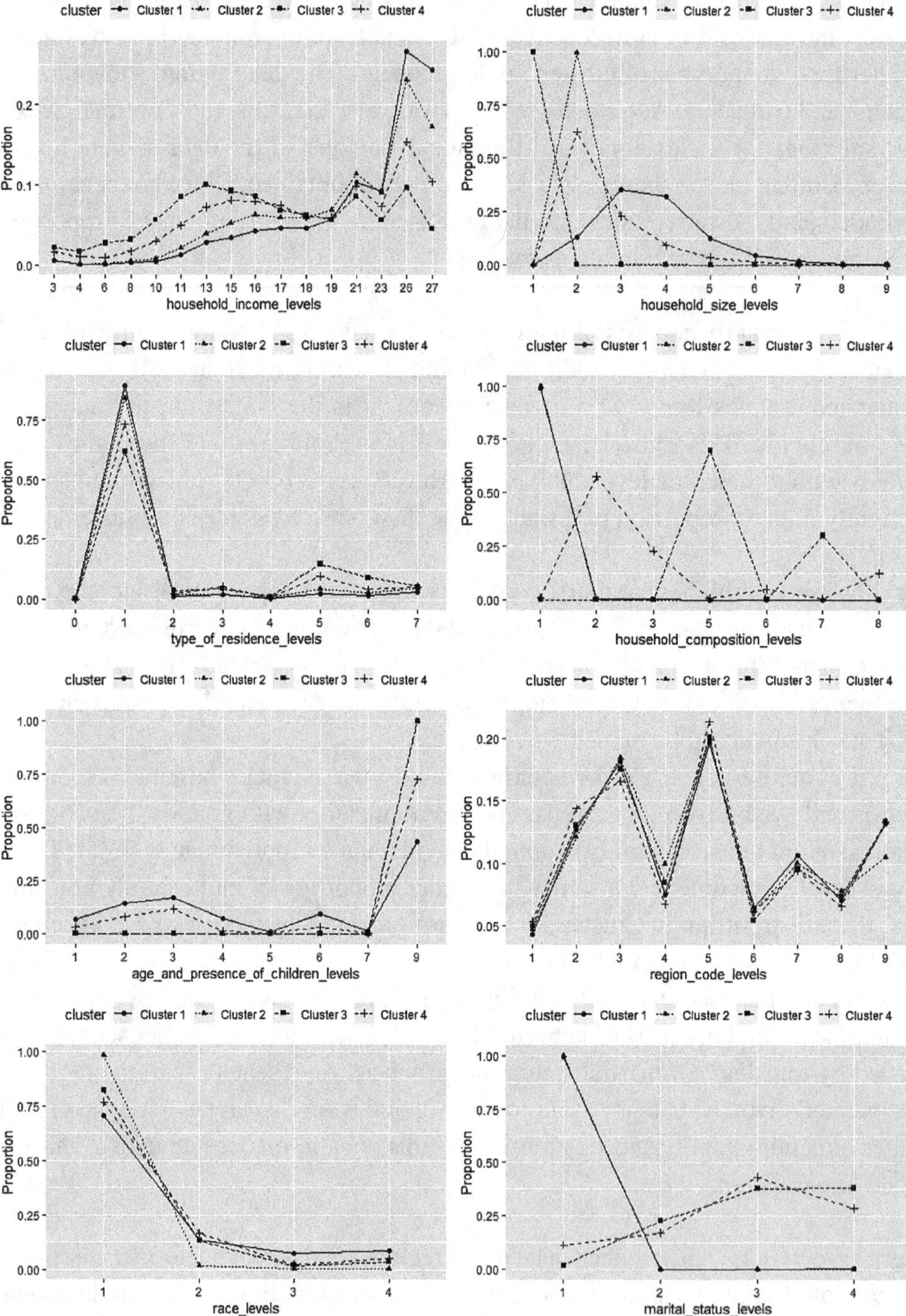

When interpreting, it is important to look at the relative size of the bars within each cluster; a disparity between spending patterns overall and on fresh produce could indicate useful patterns. Also, positive and negative deviations have different interpretations. For example, a high bar in the positive direction for total spending and a low positive bar in fresh produce spending means lower purchases of fruit and vegetables in relation to the total basket size. On the other hand, a high negative bar for the total spending and a low negative bar for the fresh produce spending means that the cluster has a higher proportion of fresh produce in the overall basket.

Many of the variables considered here are likely highly correlated, e.g., a high number of shopping trips in general is associated with a high number of items in all categories and high spending. Hence, the most important finding should come from observing disparities between these variables, e.g., if a household buys well below the average number of items overall but close to an average number of items with deals, it means frugal shopping and utilizing deals more frequently.

Based on Figure 4, the clusters can be described as follows:

- Cluster 1 – *Families* are *big spenders.* They shop with average or even slightly lower frequency, but they buy more than the average number of items and spend even more than the average amount across all product categories. That means they are prepared to pay higher prices for products. This is confirmed by a relatively low number of purchases of deals, compared to the overall shopping. They do the largest total shopping of all clusters, explained by their larger household size. At the same time, while their spending on Fresh Produce is above average, it is not as high as for the total grocery shopping, and it is below that for *DINKs*.
- Cluster 2 – *DINKs* are *shopaholics.* They are households that shop frequently, spend above the average overall, and buy more than the average number of items. They sometimes take advantage of deals, particularly on Fresh Produce, but they do not bother with organics. Their spending and number of items from the Fresh Produce category is the highest among all clusters and above their spending in all categories. *DINKs* really love their smashed avocado!
- Cluster 3 – *SINKs* are *economical shoppers.* They make less than the average number of trips to the supermarket, buy much less than the average number of items, and spend much less than average (explained by their small household size). They take advantage of deals. Their spending on Fresh Produce is relatively in line with the overall shopping and spending. They do not bother with buying organics.
- Cluster 4 – *Single Parents Plus* are the *least health-conscious shoppers.* They are the closest households to an elusive average. They make an average number of shopping trips, they buy close to an average number of items overall and from the Fresh Produce category, and they spend close to an average amount. At the same time, they show the highest disparity between overall shopping and shopping on Fresh Produce – they buy a smaller amount of fruit and vegetables compared to their overall shopping. In the same way, they buy fewer products with deals compared to their overall shopping; hence, they do not take an advantage of price promotions. They are also not particularly interested in buying organic.

In summary, *Families* and *Single Parents Plus* buy relatively lower proportions of fresh fruit and vegetables out of total grocery spend. That is, the proportion of Fresh Produce in their shopping baskets is lower than that in the baskets of *DINKs* or *SINKs*. This is extremely worrying, as both clusters represent household with children. From the public health perspective, these are the households that should be buying more fresh fruit and vegetables to support children's healthy development and to instill healthy dietary patterns in the next generation.

Figure 4. Normalized shopping behavior (means) by cluster in the hierarchical solution

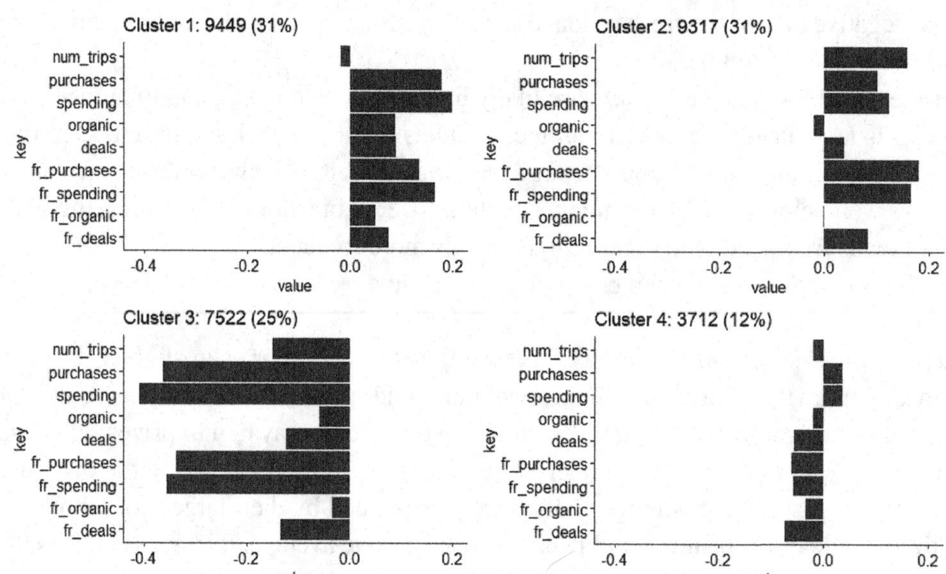

Table 2. Descriptive statistics for shopping behavior variables based on hierarchical clustering

	Mean (Std. Dev)	Median (IQR)	Mean (Std. Dev)	Median (IQR)	Mean (Std. Dev)	Median (IQR)	Mean (Std. Dev)	Median (IQR)
Cluster	**Families**		**DINKs**		**SINKs**		**Single Parents Plus**	
N	18,660 (31%)		18,726 (31%)		15,379 (25%)		7,586 (13%)	
num_trips	5.1 (3.6)	4.2 (3.9)	5.6 (3.6)	4.8 (4.2)	4.6 (3.1)	3.8 (3.4)	5 (3.5)	4.1 (3.7)
Purchases (item)	73.2 (55.1)	61 (67.7)	65.7 (44.3)	57.7 (56.7)	43 (30.6)	36.5 (36.8)	62 (45.8)	52.3 (54.4)
Spending ($)	277 (212)	228 (249)	252 (179)	216 (217)	157 (122)	129 (136)	233 (176)	194 (205)
Organic (item)	1.1 (3.3)	0.2 (0.8)	0.8 (2.6)	0.2 (0.6)	0.7 (2)	0.1 (0.5)	0.8 (2.2)	0.1 (0.6)
Deals (item)	26.2 (35.3)	12.3 (36.8)	22.4 (27.9)	11.8 (32.2)	15.5 (20.1)	8.1 (21.7)	20.7 (28.3)	9.9 (29.1)
fr_purchases (item)	8 (8.1)	5.4 (7.4)	8.1 (7.8)	5.6 (7.6)	5 (5.2)	3.4 (4.3)	6.5 (6.4)	4.4 (6)
fr_spending ($)	19.5 (20.4)	13.6 (17.5)	19 (18.3)	13.5 (17)	11.7 (12.2)	8.3 (10.4)	15.4 (15.1)	11 (13.8)
fr_organic (item)	0.2 (0.9)	0 (0.2)	0.2 (0.7)	0 (0.2)	0.2 (0.6)	0 (0.1)	0.2 (0.5)	0 (0.1)
fr_deals (item)	1.8 (3.2)	0.6 (2.3)	1.8 (3.2)	0.6 (2.3)	1.2 (2.1)	0.4 (1.6)	1.4 (2.5)	0.4 (1.8)

Managerially, it is also important to look at the absolute spending and the items bought, not just standardized figures, to ensure the differences between the clusters are substantial enough to develop actionable strategies for each cluster. Summary statistics in Table 2 are now discussed to gain further insights into the shopping behavior of households. Due to the right-skewness of the distributions for all variables of interest, median might be a better centrality measure. Hence, median is reported along mean values, and it is used to describe typical behavior. It should also be noted that reported standard deviations and interquartile range (IQR) values indicate that there is a lot of variability between individual households in each cluster.

The results in Table 2 reinforce the conclusions from the standardized values analysis in Figure 4. An average US household shops at a supermarket 4.25 times a month (Table 1). Households from clusters *Families* and *Others* undertake almost the same number of shopping trips, 4.2 and 4.1 respectively. At the same time, two-person households in the *DINKs* cluster undertake 13% more, and single-person households in the *SINKs* cluster undertake 10% fewer shopping trips per month than the average household, 4.8 and 3.8 trips respectively.

Shopping trip frequency does not always translate into purchasing activity. Despite a somewhat lower number of shopping trips, *Families* buy the highest number of items (median of 61) and spend the top dollar ($228), which is 20% above the national averages of 51.25 items and $189. Frequently shopping *DINKs* households buy 57.7 items and pay $216, which is about 13% above the national average. While *SINKs* households make just 10% fewer shopping trips, their spending is 30% below the national average, 36.5 items and $129 respectively. Households from the cluster *Other* are very close to the average household, with 52.3 items and $194.

In terms of Fresh Produce, a shopping trip typically results in between 3.4 (*SINKs*) and 5.6 (*DINKs*) Fresh Produce items being purchased, costing between $8.30 (*SINKs*) and $13.60 (*Families*). In terms of organic products, a typical household in clusters *Families* and *DINKs* buys one organic item for every five shopping trips. For clusters *SINKs* and *Single Parents Plus*, one organic product is typically purchased for every 10 shopping trips.

Looking at the ratio of Fresh Produce out of a total grocery basket items, it is clear that the two types of households with children (*Families* and *Single Parents Plus*) have lower proportions of fresh items (8.8% and 8.3% respectively) than the other two clusters (*DINKs* 9.8% and *SINKs* 9.4%). These results highlight a difference between clusters that is significant from the perspective of supply-chain managers and public health policy-makers. The overall picture also highlights that all households are buying relatively lower amounts of fresh produce, showing that less than 10% of their grocery baskets are fresh fruit and vegetables.

Real-life applications of clustering techniques suffer from non-replicability or instability of cluster solutions (see, for example, Ben-David, von Luxburg, & Pál, 2006; Leisch, 2015; Levine & Domany, 2001). To address this shortcoming in the present setting, the same clustering procedure was repeated independently for 30,000 panelists randomly sampled from the data for 2013, 2014 and 2015. Figure 5 shows the same nine shopping-related variables as in Figure 4, but for three different years. While there are some minor differences in cluster sizes and in the values of individual variables, the overall structure of clusters remains the same from year to year, which demonstrates the strong validity of the presented approach.

The differences in the shopping behavior of different groups of customers presented in Table 2 offer managerially significant insights. However, it is necessary to investigate whether there are statistically significant differences among the four clusters. The classical parametric MANOVA (multivariate analysis of variance) cannot be used for these data, as all nine shopping behavior variables are right skewed, and they do not follow a normal distribution. Hence, they do not meet the assumption of multivariate normality required for MANOVA. A nonparametric test for the comparison of multivariate data samples (Burchett, Ellis, Harrar, & Bathke, 2017) was employed to test statistical significance on the global level,

Figure 5. Spending behavior means by cluster for 2013, 2014, and 2015

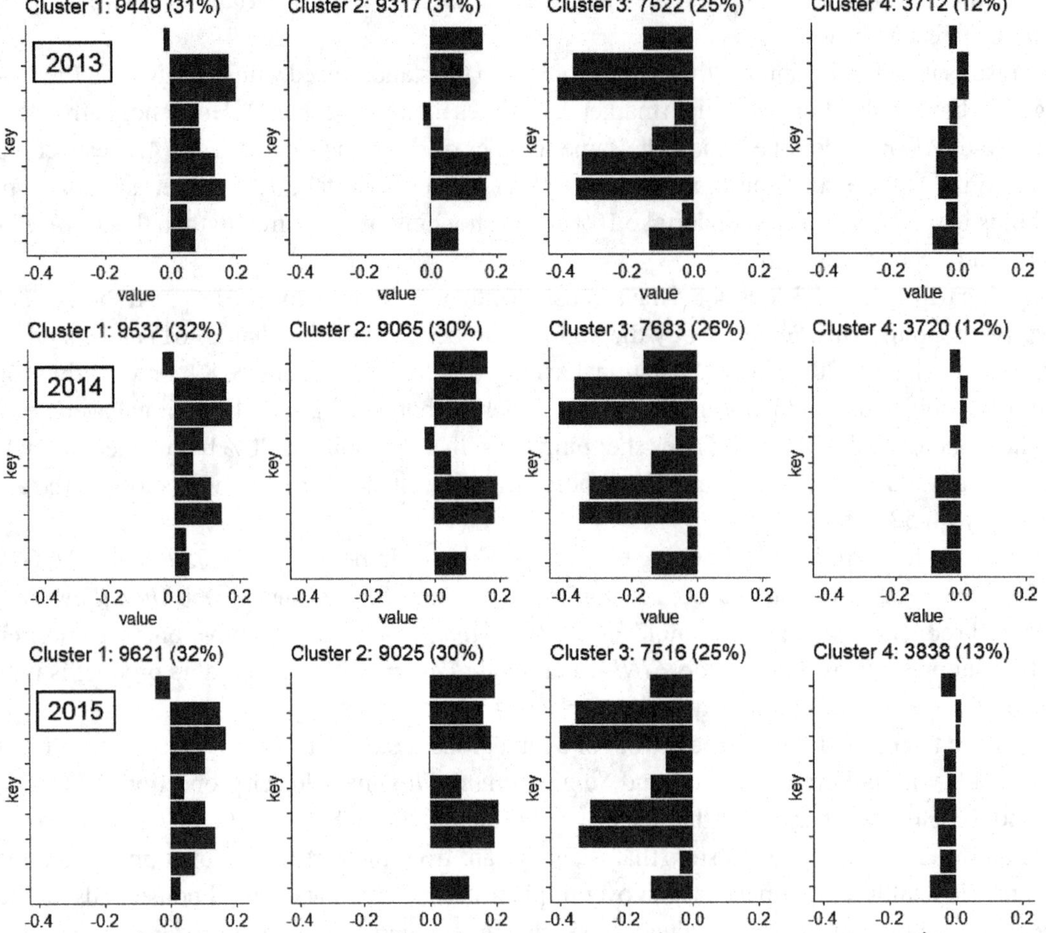

as well as to identify statistically significant response variables and factor levels, while controlling the familywise error rate.

Global test results were highly significant (p-value = 0), indicating that there is a statistically significant difference among the clusters in relation to the nine spending pattern variables, namely the number of shopping trips plus the number of purchases made, the total amount spent, the number of purchases perceived as deals, and the number of organic products bought, both overall and in the fresh produce category. As the global hypothesis of no difference among clusters was rejected, a detailed follow up analysis was carried out to test for differences for all possible permutations of clusters and shopping behavior variables. A null hypothesis of equality for all appropriate subsets of factor levels (clusters) and response variables (shopping behavior variables) was rejected, while maintaining the maximum overall Type I error rate at a significance level alpha of 0.05. It should, however, be noted that the large sample size may have been a deciding factor in producing statistical significance, and so not all the differences detected may be meaningful in practical terms.

Clustering Based on Latent Class Analysis

LCA is now performed to obtain another clustering solution based on the same demographic information about the households as before. As discussed above, LCA is a "soft clustering" method, where a probability of belonging to each cluster is calculated for each observation. This means that the same household could belong to more than one cluster, so the resulting clusters may overlap, and not be mutually exclusive. This characteristic of LCA, arguably, could be beneficial for the analysis of shopping behavior. Household needs could be changing over time, and/or the same households could display different characteristics in relation to their spending and consumption patterns, or preferences towards fresh produce could vary. With this flexibility in multiple cluster memberships, it is possible to see other clustering structures, which might offer different insights into shopping behavior.

Figure 6. Scree plot based on model fit measures for different numbers of clusters in LCA

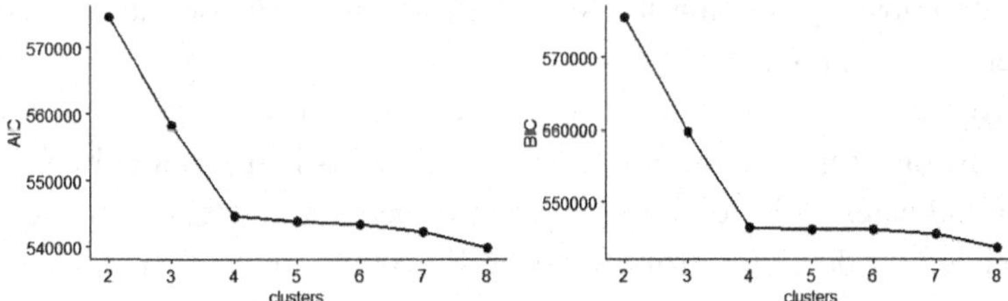

To investigate consumer purchasing behavior further, a range of LCA clustering solutions was considered and compared using the Bayesian information criterion (BIC; Schwartz, 1978) and the Akaike information criterion (AIC; Akaike, 1987). For further references regarding the choice of the number of latent classes see Nylund, Asparouhov, and Muthén (2007).

The results for solutions based on 2 to 8 clusters are shown in Figure 6. Both BIC and AIC statistics decrease as the number of clusters increases, indicating better model fit; however, the rate of decrease reduces significantly between 4 and 5 clusters. Therefore, a 4-cluster solution was selected for further analysis.

Household characteristics were again used to understand cluster composition better. Based on Figure 7, clusters produced by the LCA method can be characterized as follows:

- Cluster 1 predominantly consists of married couples with 2-3 children. It is a relatively small cluster, and it accounts for 19% of households. This cluster has the highest household size and the highest income level. It has a slightly lower proportion of White/Caucasian people and a slightly higher proportion of Asian people than other clusters. This cluster could be named *Families with Kids Under 18.*
- Cluster 2 predominantly consists of White/Caucasian married couples without children under 18. It is the largest cluster, and it accounts for 44% of households. This cluster has the second highest proportion of top income levels. In most cases, these are 2-person households but there is also a small proportion of households with one or two additional members. This suggests that this is a cluster of DINK households including the so-called empty nesters (parents whose grown up chil-

dren have left home) plus crowded nesters (parents living with adult children). This cluster could therefore be named *DINKs & Crowded Nesters*.

- Households in Cluster 3 are single-member households with a high proportion of females living alone, never married, widowed, divorced, or separated, hence SINKs. It accounts for 26% of households. This cluster has the lowest level of income and a somewhat higher proportion of households who live in multi-family housing (e.g., house sharing) compared to other clusters. This cluster could be named *SINKs*.
- Cluster 4 is the smallest cluster, accounting for 11% of households. It is third in terms of income and second in terms of household size. It is represented by single parents (predominantly female) with one or more children. Although predominantly White/Caucasian, relative to the other clusters it has higher proportion of African Americans. This cluster could be named *Single Parents*.

All clusters are again similar in composition in terms of region, residence type (single family house), and race (except Clusters 2 and 4, as mentioned above). The major drivers behind cluster membership are again household composition and marital status. Shopping behavior characteristics of households in LCA-based clusters are discussed next.

Figure 8 shows average values of variables characterizing shopping behavior for each LCA-based cluster relative to the average for all households in the dataset. As in the hierarchical clustering solution, a bar near zero again indicates a cluster average close to the overall average, while a bar with positive or negative value indicates a deviation from the overall average in terms of higher or lower spending or the number of items purchased. As before, shopping behavior patterns are inferred from observing disparities in how variables deviate from the average (the sign and size of the bar) within each cluster.

Based on Figure 8, clusters can be described as follows:

- Cluster 1 – *Families with Kids Under 18* are *big spenders*. They shop less than average, but they buy more than the average number of items, and they spend more than the average amount across all product categories. They spend the most on Fresh Produce of all four clusters, but they come second after *DINKs & Crowded Nesters* when it comes to the number of Fresh Produce items. They buy a lot of Fresh Produce, and they pay relatively higher prices than other clusters, which indicates a higher quality of fruit and vegetables. They take advantage of deals frequently, but they are also willing to spend more to buy organic products.
- Cluster 2 – *DINKs & Crowded Nesters* are *frequent shoppers*. They are households that shop more than average, spend above average overall, and buy more than the average number of items. They sometimes take advantage of deals, but they do not bother with organics. Their spending on items from the Fresh Produce category is second highest among all clusters, and they buy the largest number of Fresh Produce items. Also, they buy a higher proportion of fruit and vegetables than other clusters.
- Cluster 3 – *SINKs* are *economical shoppers*. They make fewer than the average number of trips to the supermarket, and they buy much fewer than average items and spend much less than average. Their spending on Fresh Produce is lower than the average, in line with their overall shopping and spending; however, the proportion of fruit and vegetables in their shopping is higher than the average household. They do not bother with deals or buying organics.
- Cluster 4 – *Single Parents* are the *least health-conscious shoppers*. They are households that are very close to the average. They do an average number of shopping trips, they buy close to an av-

erage number of items overall and from the Fresh Produce category, and they spend close to an average amount. At the same time, they show the highest disparity between overall shopping and shopping on Fresh Produce – they buy less fruit and vegetables compared to their overall shopping. They do not take advantage of price promotions overall, and even less so on Fresh Produce. They are also not interested in buying organic.

Figure 7. Household characteristics by cluster in the LCA solution

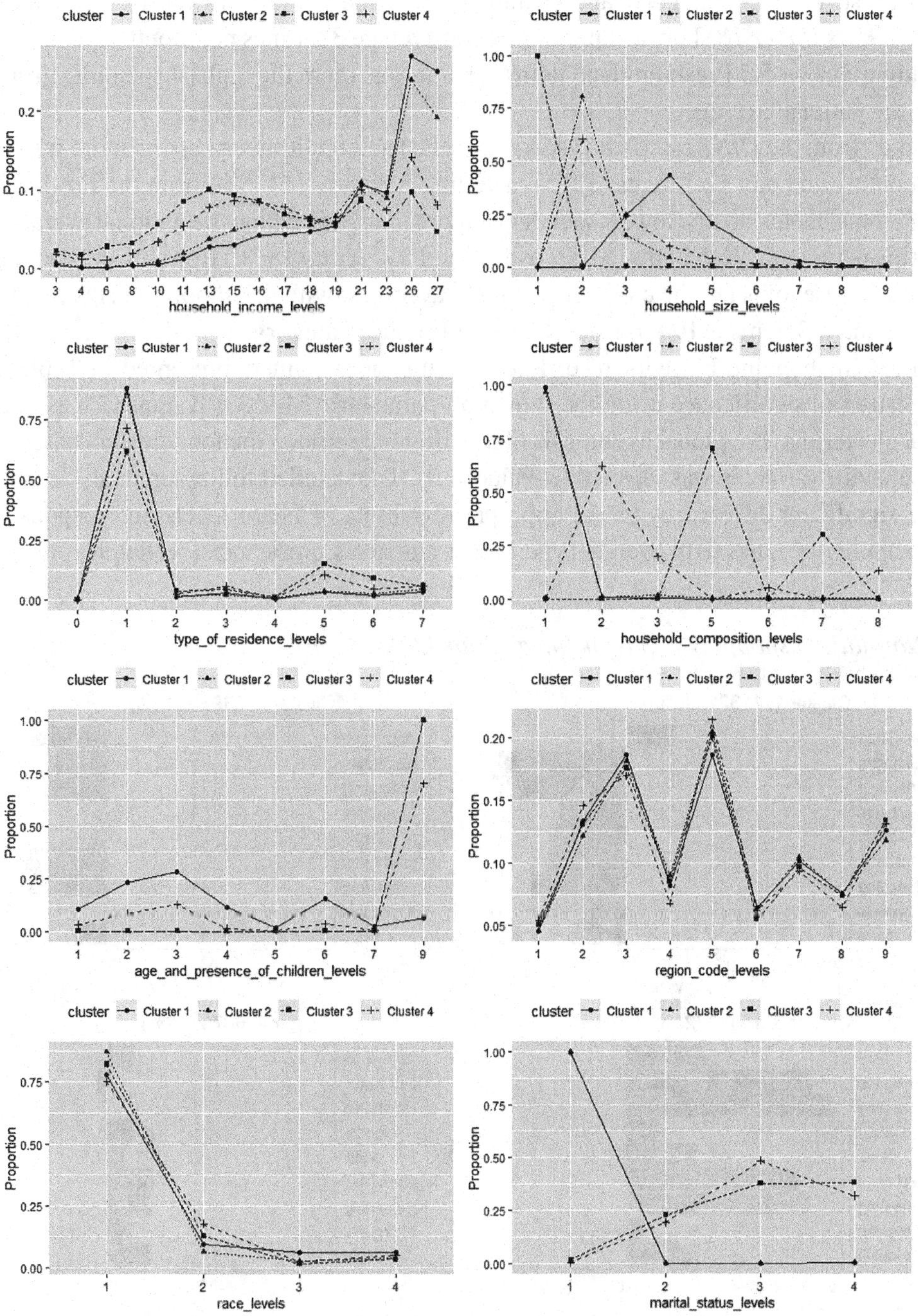

A comparison of the clusters shows the highest disparity between overall shopping and shopping for Fresh Produce category for *Families with Kids Under 18* and *Single Parents*. There is a much lower proportion of Fresh Produce items bought by these households compared to their counterparts from the *DINKs* and *SINKs* clusters and compared to the national average.

The summary statistics in Table 3 provide further insights into the shopping behavior of households in different clusters based on the LCA solution. Due to the lack of symmetry in the underlying distributions, median is again used to describe typical behavior in relation to the nine variables.

Compared to national averages of 4.25 shopping trips per month with 51.25 items, including 4.73 items from Fresh Produce category, and spending $189, including $11.63 on Fresh Produce items, *Families with Kids Under 18* shop at supermarkets on average 3.9 times per month, spend $242 for 64.9 items including $14 on 5.5 Fresh Produce items. That makes them the highest spending group – almost 30% above the national average.

Households from the *DINKs & Crowded Nesters* cluster shop in supermarkets more frequently – 4.7 times per month – and buy 57.1 items ($215) including 5.5 items ($13.40) from the Fresh Produce category. *SINKs* households are the lowest spenders – more than 30% below the national average – with 3.8 shopping trips per month, 36.5 items ($129) overall and 3.4 items ($8.30) from Fresh Produce category. *Single Parents* households are the closest to national averages, with 4.1 shopping trips per month, 51.8 items ($191), and 4.3 items ($10.80) from the Fresh Produce category.

Differences in shopping behavior of different groups of customers presented in Table 3 were assessed for statistical significance using the same non-parametric MANOVA approach as in the case of hierarchical clustering. The global hypothesis of no difference among the four clusters based on the nine shopping behavior variables was rejected (p-value = 0). The detailed follow-up analysis again showed statistically significant differences for all appropriate subsets of factor levels and response variables, while maintaining the maximum overall Type I error rate at a significance level alpha of 0.05.

Figure 8. Normalized shopping behavior (means) for LCA clusters

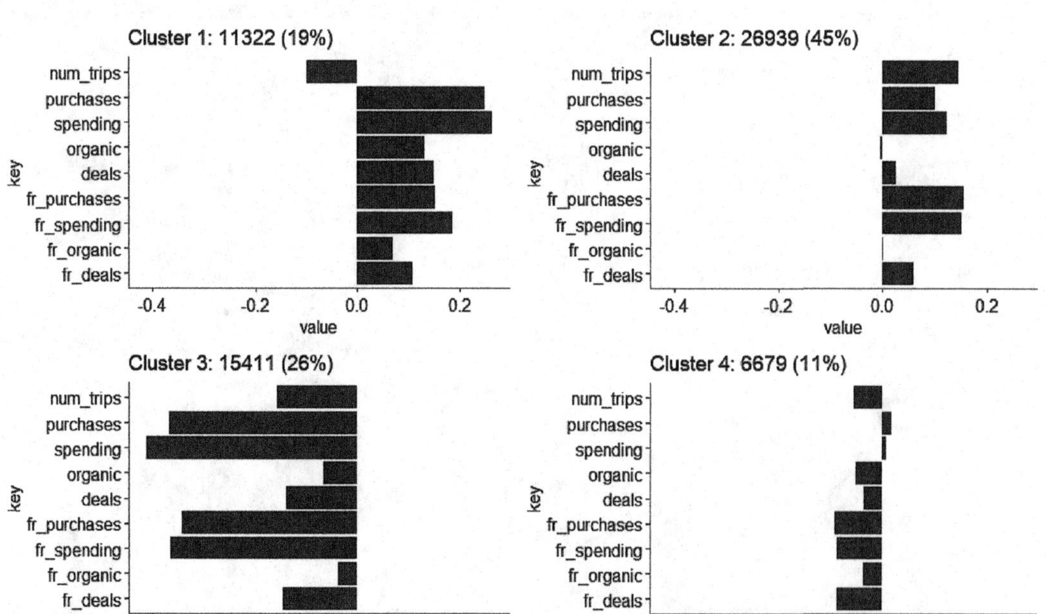

Table 3. Descriptive statistics for shopping behavior variables based on LCA clustering

	Mean (Std. Dev)	Median (IQR)	Mean (Std. Dev)	Median (IQR)	Mean (Std. Dev)	Median (IQR)	Mean (Std. Dev)	Median (IQR)
Cluster	**Families with Kids Under 18**		**DINKs & Crowded Nesters**		**SINKs**		**Single Parents**	
N	11,322 (19%)		26,939 (45%)		15,411 (26%)		6,679 (11%)	
num_trips	4.8 (3.4)	3.9 (3.6)	5.6 (3.7)	4.7 (4.2)	4.6 (3.1)	3.8 (3.4)	4.9 (3.5)	4.1 (3.7)
Purchases (item)	76.9 (56.3)	64.9 (70.8)	66.2 (46.8)	57.1 (58.2)	43 (30.7)	36.5 (36.8)	61.7 (45.8)	51.8 (54.1)
Spending ($)	289 (213)	242 (259)	254 (188)	215 (222)	157 (122)	129 (136)	230 (174)	191 (200)
Organic (item)	1.2 (3.7)	0.2 (0.8)	0.8 (2.6)	0.2 (0.6)	0.7 (2)	0.1 (0.5)	0.7 (2.2)	0.1 (0.5)
Deals (item)	28.2 (36.6)	14 (39.7)	22.6 (29.3)	11.2 (32)	15.5 (20.2)	8.1 (21.7)	20.8 (28.4)	10 (29)
fr_purchases (item)	8.1 (8)	5.5 (7.6)	8 (7.9)	5.5 (7.4)	5 (5.2)	3.4 (4.3)	6.3 (6.2)	4.3 (5.8)
fr_spending ($)	19.9 (19.9)	14 (17.9)	19 (19.1)	13.4 (17)	11.7 (12.2)	8.3 (10.4)	15 (14.6)	10.8 (13.3)
fr_organic (item)	0.3 (0.9)	0 (0.2)	0.2 (0.7)	0 (0.2)	0.2 (0.6)	0 (0.1)	0.2 (0.5)	0 (0.1)
fr_deals (item)	1.9 (3.3)	0.7 (2.4)	1.8 (3.2)	0.6 (2.3)	1.2 (2.1)	0.4 (1.6)	1.4 (2.5)	0.4 (1.8)

As mentioned previously, LCA is a soft clustering method, in that a probability of belonging to each cluster is calculated for each observation. This means that clusters may overlap, because certain observations can have relatively high probabilities of belonging to multiple clusters. In the case considered here, most households have probability 1 or close to 1 of being in some cluster, so there is no doubt over their cluster membership. However, for about 3% of households, the LCA model produced probabilities that could place them in two clusters. For example, a household with probabilities (0.33, 0, 0.67, 0) could belong to Cluster 1 or 3.

There are two possible strategies to deal with this situation and to get cluster summary statistics. One is to treat households with questionable membership as outliers and to exclude them from the analysis. The other is to overinflate sample size by adding questionable households to all possible clusters. Both approaches were tried and the resulting clustering solutions compared to the one described above, where each household was assigned to a single cluster indicated by the highest of the probabilities. There was no discernible difference between the resulting clusters, and hence no significant differences for cluster interpretability.

Comparing the Results of Hierarchical and LCA Clustering

The LCA solution thus described bears much similarity to the hierarchical clustering solution. The major difference in cluster membership between LCA and hierarchical clustering appears when it comes to households comprising married couples with children. As shown in Table 4, in the hierarchical clustering solution most two-parents-with-children households were placed in one separate cluster. In LCA clustering solution, they were split, and parents living with adult children were grouped together with married couples without children (DINKs) to form the largest cluster. The remaining married couples with children under 18 were assigned to a separate (smaller) cluster. Single parent and single person (SINKs) households appear to have been treated in the same way by the two methods, being placed into separate clusters of similar sizes.

Hence, the main source of disparity appears to be related to characteristics and consequently shopping behaviors of married couple households that include other adult relatives, most likely adult children. According to the LCA method, these households are more similar to DINK households than families with children.

In summary, managerially, it appears that both clustering methods – hierarchical and LCA, produce very similar four-cluster solutions, with largely similar shopping behaviors in respective clusters. Implications of these results are offered in the *Main Outcomes and Contributions* section.

Table 4. Crosstabulation for cluster membership based on hierarchical and LCA clustering solutions

		LCA Clusters			
		Families with KIDS Under18	**DINKs and Crowded Nesters**	**SINKs**	**Single Parents**
Hierarchical Clusters	Families	11,199	7436	3	22
	DINKs	34	18,680	0	12
	SINKs	0	11	15,368	0
	Single Parents Plus	89	812	40	6,645

Predictive Modelling of Household Spending on Fresh Fruit and Vegetables

This section describes an application of supervised machine learning techniques to the Nielsen Consumer Panel Dataset. Linear regression has been an important tool of data analysis since its introduction in the early 19th century. Traditionally it serves two purposes: (1) to make predictions for unobserved cases, e.g., out-of-sample or future observations; and (2) to identify the most important input variables (the strongest predictors in the model) through coefficient analysis. Linear regression remains one of the most popular types of data analysis today (Fox, Montgomery, & Lodish, 2004).

Artificial neural networks were introduced in the mid-1900s as an attempt to recreate human neural processing. A neural network is typically presented as three connected layers: an input nodes layer (independent variables or predictors), an output nodes layer (dependent variables or targets), and a hidden nodes layer between them. The number of nodes in the hidden layer can vary in a very wide range, and every node represents a multiple linear regression model with a possible addition of an activation function allowing it to control a process of results passing through. For more details, see Rojas (2013) or Hastie et al. (2009) and the references therein.

From the mathematical point of view, a neural network is a non-linear model resulting from a combination of many multiple linear regression models. Due to the very large number of coefficients in neural network models, their interpretations become much more problematic than linear regression models. However, their predictive ability seems to be superior to linear regression. Indeed, neural networks have been shown to be better predictive models than traditional predictive techniques for datasets where non-linear relationships might be expected or where relationships are simply unknown (Dasgupta, Dispensa, & Ghose, 1994; Sargent, 2001).

The most recent development in the area of machine learning is the introduction of so-called deep learning neural networks. These can be interpreted as neural networks with hierarchical architecture, created by adding multiple hidden layers of different sizes between input and output layers. Hence, a deep learning neural network becomes a non-linear model resulting from a combination of many neural networks. Deep learning techniques have demonstrated the ability to extract high-level, complex abstractions and data representations from large volumes of data in areas such as computer vision (Krizhevsky, Sutskever, & Hinton, 2012) and natural language processing (Mikolov, Sutskever, Chen, Corrado, & Dean, 2013), as well as customer behavior analysis (Shi, Xu, & Li, 2017).

In this chapter, all three types of supervised predictive models mentioned above (linear regression, neural network, and deep learning) are employed to predict household spending on products from the Fresh Produce category, that is, on fruit and vegetables, based on spending on other grocery product categories. For this purpose, transaction data was aggregated for individual trips in such a way that every observation is a vector of amounts spent in each of 119 product categories. The resulting dataset had 3.5 million observations (shopping trips) with the spending split across 119 product groups. Then, all observations were aggregated to calculate mean of monthly spending on each category for each household, and predictive models were run at the household level. The amount spent on fresh fruit and vegetables (variable Fresh Produce) was the target, and spending in all other product categories were predictors. Naturally, data were very sparse, as there were no purchases in many categories. All variables were log-transformed and normalized using min-max normalization, a typical process in machine learning that rescales all variables to take values between 0 and 1. This ensures that features measured on a larger scale do not exert undue influence on the overall results. One more variable had been added as a predictor – clustering membership to serve as a proxy for demographic information about each household.

Ordinary Least-Squares Regression

Ordinary least-squares regression was employed to predict the amount spent on Fresh Produce products by each household based on the information about the amount spent on products from other categories. More than 70% of the variables in the model were statistically significant due to the very large sample size. The model has an adjusted R-squared value of 0.57, which is considered a relatively good fit for consumer behavior data (Figure 9). There were no differences in prediction results from using different clustering solutions. Therefore, only results based on hierarchical clustering membership are reported below.

The model provides a few interesting insights into spending on Fresh Produce. The highest positive coefficient estimates, that is, product categories positively correlated with spending on Fresh Produce, were frozen unprepared meat, poultry, and seafood (0.2076), yogurt (0.1301), dried vegetables (0.1172), cheese (0.1135), salads and prepared food from the deli (0.0957), and canned vegetables (0.0875). Product categories with the highest negative coefficient estimates, that is, those negatively related to spending on Fresh Produce, were prepared food dry mixes (-0.0789), tobacco accessories (-0.0600), carbonated beverages (-0.0522), prepared frozen food (-0.0466), frozen pizza, snacks (-0.0437), and non-grocery types of products – shoe care, electronics, shaving. All these variables were highly statistically significant with p-values close to zero. These results seem logical: households that spend more on protein, dairy, and prepared vegetables – all healthful foods – also spend more on fresh fruit and vegetables.

Conversely, households that spend more on unhealthy foods (carbonated beverages, frozen pizza) and tobacco spend less on fresh produce.

While the directional effects of these coefficient estimates are easy to interpret, one needs to be cautious in trying to assign practical significance to these estimates' values. The predictive model operates with normalized log-transformed values of monthly spending in each category, including the target, the Fresh Produce category. Hence, this is a log-log model, and the coefficient estimate interpretation should be given as an expected percentage change in the target variable when predictor value increases by some percentage. For example, an interpretation for a coefficient 0.2076 for frozen unprepared meat, poultry, and seafood, which is the largest coefficient, is as following: a 10% spending increase in this category will result in the spending on Fresh Produce equal to exp(0.2076 log(1.1)) = 1.019983, that is, almost a 2% increase in spending on Fresh Produce. Another large (negative) coefficient for carbonated beverages (-0.0522) means that a 10% increase in spending for this category is expected to decrease Fresh Produce spending by 0.5% – spending equal to exp(-0.0522 log(1.1) = 0.9950. These conversions across the largest coefficients suggest that most of these associations are small in value, and they might have limited managerial significance.

Coefficients for clustering membership were statistically significant but relatively low in value at 0.008 for Clusters 1 and 3 and 0.017 for Cluster 2. This means that with all other variables held constant, compared to a household in Cluster 4, a household in Clusters 1 or 3 would spend 0.8% more, whereas for a household from Cluster 2 the difference would be 1.7%.

Figure 9. Actual vs predicted plot based on the OLS regression model to predict spending on fresh produce

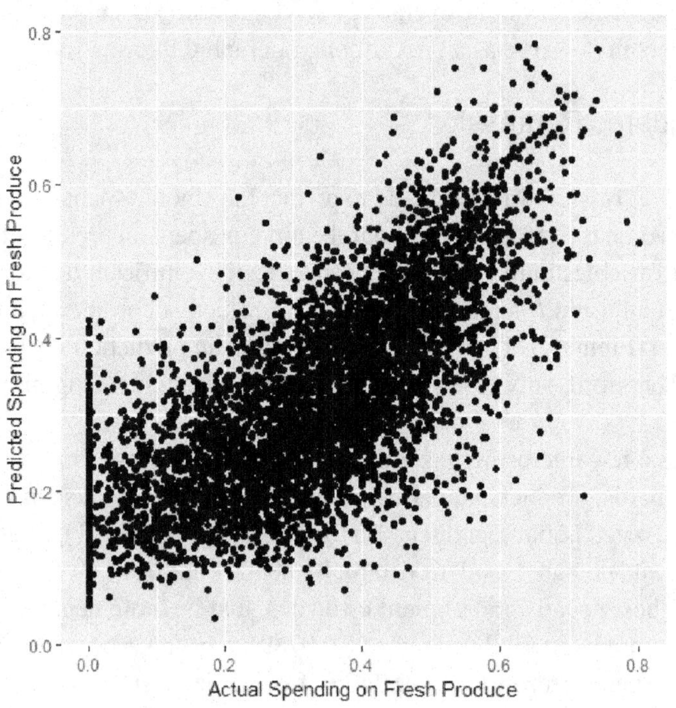

Artificial Neural Network

As the next step, the same prediction task was attempted using another form of supervised machine learning – artificial neural networks. A neural network with 122 input nodes (spending in 118 product categories and 4 cluster membership categories), 1 output node (spending in the Fresh Produce category) and one hidden layer of 180 nodes was created and trained over 40 epochs with a 20% validation split. The model used mean squared error as a loss function, and an RMSProp optimizer and a ReLU activation function for each layer. The model had 22,321 trainable parameters. The prediction result on the test sample was marginally worse than after the linear regression with R-squared = 0.54 (Figure 10).

Figure 11 shows the history of the loss function for training and validation datasets over 40 epoch training process. The maximal improvements in the model – the lowest values of the loss function – were achieved after 10-15 epochs. After that, the neural network was overfitting the training dataset without any real improvements in the predictions on the validation dataset. Therefore, despite the expectation, the artificial neural network model did not produce better predictions than a much simpler multiple linear regression model.

Figure 10. Actual vs predicted plot for the one-layer artificial neural network to predict spending on fresh produce

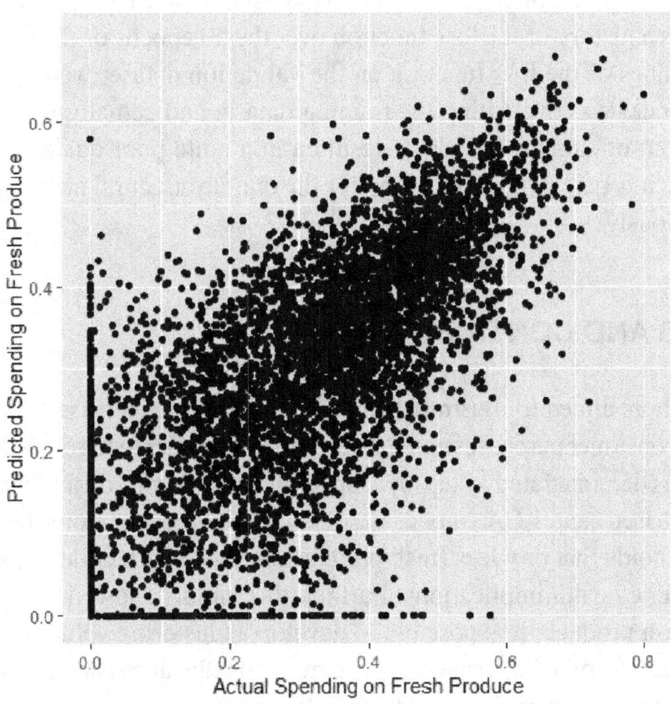

Figure 11. Loss function for training and validation datasets in the one-layer artificial neural network

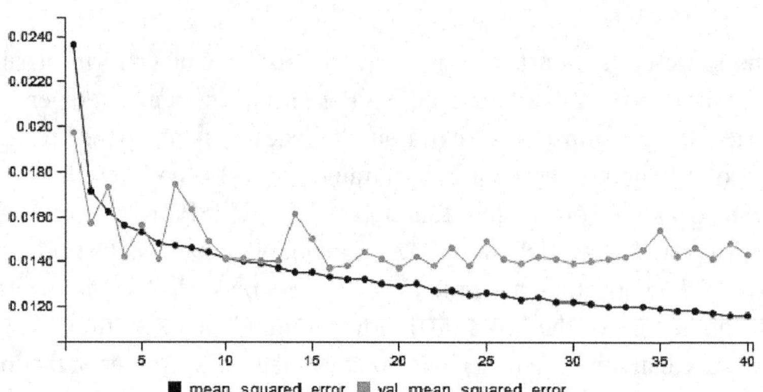

Deep Learning Neural Network

A deep learning modeling technique was also attempted for the same dataset. A new neural network had the same 122 input and 1 output nodes as before, plus 10 hidden layers of 180 nodes each. That resulted in 315,541 trainable parameters. The model was trained over 40 epochs with a 20% validation split. Figure 12 shows results of predicting spending on Fresh Produce for households from the test sample, while Figure 13 reports a history of the loss function over the 40 epochs of the neural networks training process. The lowest values of the loss function on the validation dataset were achieved after 4 epochs only. After that, the model was overfitting the training dataset and actually reducing the effectiveness of predictions on the out-of-sample data. That resulted in a quite poor quality of predictions with an R-squared of 0.46, which is below than R-squared for the one-layer neural network and the OLS regression model fitted previously.

MAIN OUTCOMES AND CONTRIBUTIONS

In this chapter, the authors aimed to illustrate the application of unsupervised and supervised machine learning techniques to consumer purchases panel data, with a particular focus on fresh fruit and vegetables.

First, the chapter has demonstrated a step-by-step application of two different clustering techniques: hierarchical (distance-based) and LCA (model-based). The key finding from the clustering analysis is that the types of households that buy less fresh produce are those with children – an important insight that carries serious public health implications. Further, the authors showed that in the context of consumer purchases in fresh produce, it is possible to develop a clustering solution that is replicable over time (three years) and across two different clustering methods (distance- and model-based). Such replication over years and across clustering methods, and the resulting robust clustering solution, makes an important contribution to the literature on clustering, where non-replicability of clusters is one of the major methodological challenges.

Second, the chapter has illustrated the application of three predictive modelling techniques – linear regression, artificial neural network, and deep learning, and it has compared the resulting models based on their predictive power. Despite common expectations, more advanced machine learning techniques (artificial neural network and deep learning neural network) were no more effective than a multiple regression model in predicting the amount spent on fresh fruit and vegetables based on household characteristics and spending in grocery categories other than fresh produce. This robust empirical evidence makes another valuable contribution to the field of machine learning, suggesting that in some circumstances (as presented here) more advanced techniques do not necessarily offer more insights or more predictive power. This finding is also useful for the field of marketing and econometrics to guide researchers' choices of analytical tools.

Figure 12. Actual vs predicted plot for the deep learning neural network

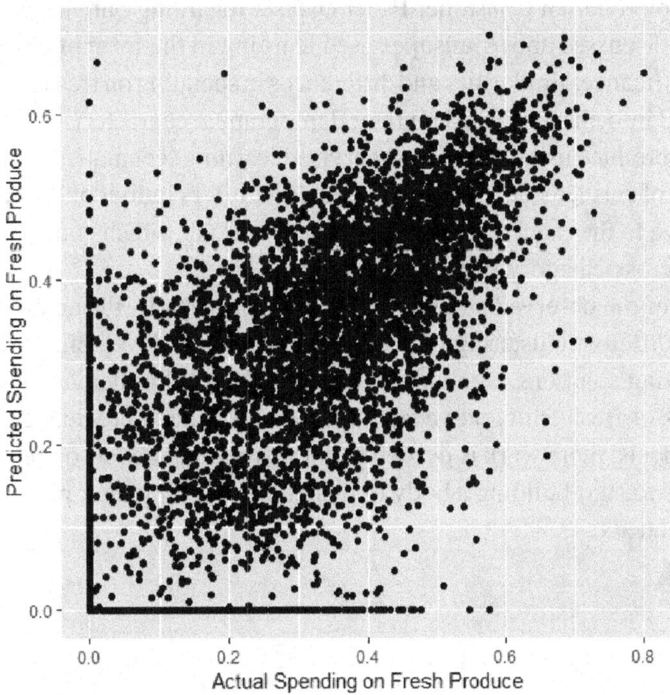

Figure 13. Loss function for training and validation datasets in deep learning neural network

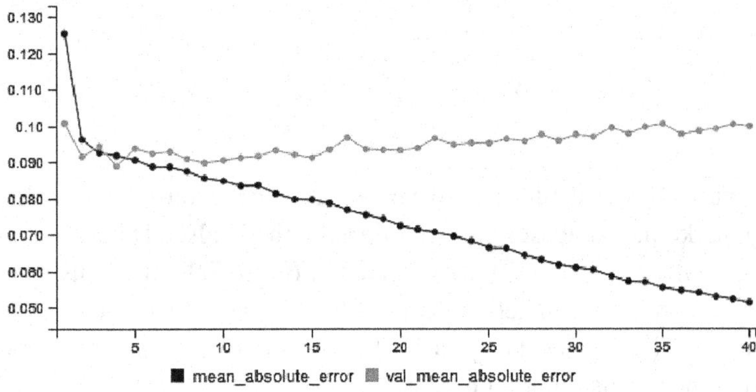

For the field of public health and agricultural economics, this chapter has offered a robust discovery of shopping patterns in fresh fruit and vegetables categories using scanner-based information, a major advancement on past studies dominated by survey-based information about consumer purchasing decisions. As such, this chapter has offered new insights into buying of fresh produce by US households, which is new knowledge that carries important implications for supply-chain and public health practitioners.

FUTURE RESEARCH DIRECTIONS

While promising, the analysis presented in this chapter offers only a glimpse into the wealth of insights that could be gained from Nielsen Consumer Panel Dataset regarding purchasing decisions made daily by US households. As discussed above, unsupervised learning in the form of clustering produced some results of practical significance; similarities and differences in spending on fresh produce were established for households grouped into clusters based on their demographic characteristics. Predicting the average amount spent on fresh produce using selected supervised learning techniques proved more challenging, and it could be subject of further study. The Nielsen dataset offers individual shopping trip information for all households, down to the exact contents of shopping baskets, which could be explored for patterns across time as well as cross-category purchase decisions.

Further replication of the observed patterns is needed. Specifically, the authors call for more studies that directly compare different clustering methods in a pursuit of developing procedures that provide more replicable clustering solutions. Similarly, while this chapter has demonstrated that in the context of consumer purchases of fresh fruit and vegetables, more advanced predictive models do not outperform the traditional models, more work is needed to compare these models on the same datasets to offer direct comparisons and to start building a body of evidence regarding their performance and predictive abilities in different contexts.

CONCLUSION

This chapter has illustrated the application of common machine learning techniques to a novel context of consumer purchases of fresh fruit and vegetables. The findings offer useful contributions to a number of academic disciplines: machine learning and statistics, marketing and econometrics, public health, and agricultural economics.

DISCLAIMER

1. Researcher(s) own analyses calculated (or derived) based in part on data from The Nielsen Company (US), LLC and marketing databases provided through the Nielsen Datasets at the Kilts Center for Marketing Data Center at The University of Chicago Booth School of Business.
2. The conclusions drawn from the Nielsen data are those of the researcher(s), and they do not reflect the views of Nielsen. Nielsen is not responsible for, had no role in, and was not involved in analyzing and preparing the results reported herein.

ACKNOWLEDGMENT

The authors acknowledge the support of the Ehrenberg-Bass Institute for Marketing Science, Business School, University of South Australia in gaining access to Nielsen Consumer Panel Dataset.

REFERENCES

Akaike, H. (1987). Factor analysis and AIC. *Psychometrika*, *52*(3), 317–332. doi:10.1007/BF02294359

Anderlucci, L., & Hennig, C. (2014). The clustering of categorical data: A comparison of a model-based and a distance-based approach. *Communications in Statistics. Theory and Methods*, *43*(4), 704–721. doi:10.1080/03610926.2013.806665

Ben-David, S., von Luxburg, U., & Pál, D. (2006). A sober look at clustering stability. In H. U. Simon, & G. Lugosi (Eds.), *Proceedings of the 19th Annual Conference on Learning Theory* (pp. 5-19). New York, NY: Springer. 10.1007/11776420_4

Bianchi, C., & Mortimer, G. (2015). Drivers of local food consumption: A comparative study. *British Food Journal*, *117*(9), 2282–2299. doi:10.1108/BFJ-03-2015-0111

Bodapati, A. V. (2008). Recommendation systems with purchase data. *JMR, Journal of Marketing Research*, *45*(1), 77–93. doi:10.1509/jmkr.45.1.77

Brown, E., Dury, S., & Holdsworth, M. (2009). Motivations of consumers that use local, organic fruit and vegetable box schemes in Central England and Southern France. *Appetite*, *53*(2), 183–188. doi:10.1016/j.appet.2009.06.006 PMID:19540288

Burchett, W., Ellis, A., Harrar, S., & Bathke, A. (2017). Nonparametric inference for multivariate data: The R package NPMV. *Journal of Statistical Software*, *76*(4), 1–18. doi:10.18637/jss.v076.i04 PMID:30220889

Cox, D. N., Reynolds, J., Mela, D. J., Anderson, A. S., McKellar, S., & Lean, M. E. J. (1996). Vegetables and fruit: Barriers and opportunities for greater consumption. *Nutrition & Food Science*, *96*(5), 44–47. doi:10.1108/00346659610129251

Dasgupta, C. G., Dispensa, G. S., & Ghose, S. (1994). Comparing the predictive performance of a neural network model with some traditional market response models. *International Journal of Forecasting*, *10*(2), 235–244. doi:10.1016/0169-2070(94)90004-3

Einav, L., & Levin, J. (2014). The data revolution and economic analysis. *Innovation Policy and the Economy*, *14*(1), 1–24. doi:10.1086/674019

Erinosho, T. O., Moser, R. P., Oh, A. Y., Nebeling, L. C., & Yaroch, A. L. (2012). Awareness of the Fruit and Veggies—More Matters campaign, knowledge of the fruit and vegetable recommendation, and fruit and vegetable intake of adults in the 2007 Food Attitudes and Behaviors (FAB) Survey. *Appetite*, *59*(1), 155–160. doi:10.1016/j.appet.2012.04.010 PMID:22524998

Finzer, L. E., Ajay, V. S., Ali, M. K., Shivashankar, R., Goenka, S., Pillai, D. S., ... Prabhakaran, D. (2013). Fruit and vegetable purchasing patterns and preferences in South Delhi. *Ecology of Food and Nutrition, 52*(1), 1–20. doi:10.1080/03670244.2012.705757 PMID:23282188

Fox, E. J., Montgomery, A. L., & Lodish, L. M. (2004). Consumer shopping and spending across retail formats. *The Journal of Business, 77*(S2), S25–S60. doi:10.1086/381518

Hastie, T., Tibshirani, R., & Friedman, J. H. (2009). *The elements of statistical learning: Data mining, inference, and prediction* (2nd ed.). New York, NY: Springer. doi:10.1007/978-0-387-84858-7

Hinnosaar, M. (2018, July 30). *The impact of retirement on the healthiness of food purchases*. doi:10.2139/ssrn.3235215

Jobson, J. D. (1992). Applied multivariate data analysis.: Vol. 2. *Categorical and multivariate methods*. New York, NY: Springer.

Kim, G., Seok, J. H., & Mark, T. (2018, February 13). *New market opportunities and consumer heterogeneity in the U.S. organic food market*. doi:10.2139/ssrn.2916250

Kim, G., Seok, J. H., Mark, T., & Reed, M. R. (2018, January 1). *The price relationship between organic and non-organic vegetables in the U.S.: Evidence from Nielsen scanner data*. doi:10.2139/ssrn.3176082

Krizhevsky, A., Sutskever, I., & Hinton, G. E. (2012). Imagenet classification with deep convolutional neural networks. In F. Pereira, C. J. C. Burges, L. Bottou, & K. Q. Weinberger (Eds.), Advances in neural information processing systems: Vol. 25. *NIPS 25* (pp. 1097–1105). Lake Tahoe, CA: Curran Associates.

Leisch, F. (2015). Resampling methods for exploring clustering stability. In C. Hennig, M. Meila, F. Murtagh, & R. Rocci (Eds.), *Handbook of cluster analysis* (pp. 637–652). Boca Raton, FL: Chapman and Hall/CRC.

Levine, E., & Domany, E. (2001). Resampling method for unsupervised estimation of cluster validity. *Neural Computation, 13*(11), 2573–2593. doi:10.1162/089976601753196030 PMID:11674852

Ludwichowska, G., Romaniuk, J., & Nenycz-Thiel, M. (2017). Systematic response errors in self-reported category buying frequencies. *European Journal of Marketing, 51*(7/8), 1440–1459. doi:10.1108/EJM-07-2016-0408

McAfee, A., & Brynjolfsson, E. (2012). Big data: The management revolution. *Harvard Business Review, 90*(10), 60–68. PMID:23074865

McCutcheon, L. A. (1987). *Latent class analysis*. Newbury Park, CA: Sage. doi:10.4135/9781412984713

Mikolov, T., Sutskever, I., Chen, K., Corrado, G. S., & Dean, J. (2013). Distributed representations of words and phrases and their compositionality. In C. J. C. Burges, L. Bottou, M. Welling, Z. Ghahramani, & K. Q. Weinberger (Eds.), Advances in neural information processing systems: Vol. 26. *NIPS 2013* (pp. 3111–3119). Lake Tahoe, CA: Curran Associates.

Mytton, O. T., Nnoaham, K., Eyles, H., Scarborough, P., & Mhurchu, C. N. (2014). Systematic review and meta-analysis of the effect of increased vegetable and fruit consumption on body weight and energy intake. *BMC Public Health, 14*(1), 1–11. doi:10.1186/1471-2458-14-886 PMID:25168465

Nelson, E., Fitzgerald, J. M., Tefft, N., & Anderson, J. (2017, September 1). *US household demand for organic fruit*. doi:10.2139/ssrn.3081997

Norwood, F. B., & Lusk, J. L. (2011). Social desirability bias in real, hypothetical, and inferred valuation experiments. *American Journal of Agricultural Economics*, *93*, 528–534.

Nylund, K. L., Asparouhov, T., & Muthén, B. O. (2007). Deciding on the number of classes in latent class analysis and growth mixture modeling: A Monte Carlo simulation study. *Structural Equation Modeling: An Interdisciplinary Journal*, *14*(4), 535–569. doi:10.1080/10705510701575396

Péneau, S., Hoehn, E., Roth, H. R., Escher, F., & Nuessli, J. (2006). Importance and consumer perception of freshness of apples. *Food Quality and Preference*, *17*(1-2), 9–19. doi:10.1016/j.foodqual.2005.05.002

Racine, E. F., Mumford, E. A., Laditka, S. B., & Lowe, A. (2013). Understanding characteristics of families who buy local produce. *Journal of Nutrition Education and Behavior*, *45*(1), 30–38. doi:10.1016/j.jneb.2012.04.011 PMID:23073176

Rojas, R. (2013). *Neural networks: A systematic introduction*. Berlin, Germany: Springer Science & Business Media.

Sargent, D. J. (2001). Comparison of artificial neural networks with other statistical approaches: Results from medical data sets. *Cancer: Interdisciplinary International Journal of the American Cancer Society*, *91*(S8), 1636–1642. doi:10.1002/1097-0142(20010415)91:8+<1636::AID-CNCR1176>3.0.CO;2-D PMID:11309761

Schwartz, G. E. (1978). Estimating the dimension of a model. *Annals of Statistics*, *6*(2), 461–464. doi:10.1214/aos/1176344136

Shi, H., Xu, M., & Li, R. (2017). Deep learning for household load forecasting—A novel pooling deep RNN. *IEEE Transactions on Smart Grid*, *9*(5), 5271–5280. doi:10.1109/TSG.2017.2686012

Strauss, T., & von Maltitz, M. J. (2017). Generalising Ward's method for use with Manhattan distances. *PLoS One*, *12*(1), 1–21. doi:10.1371/journal.pone.0168288 PMID:28085891

Ultsch, A., & Lötsch, J. (2017). Machine-learned cluster identification in high-dimensional data. *Journal of Biomedical Informatics*, *66*, 95–104. doi:10.1016/j.jbi.2016.12.011 PMID:28040499

Vermunt, J. K., & Magidson, J. (2002). Latent class cluster analysis. In J. A. Hagenaars & A. L. McCutcheon (Eds.), *Applied latent class models* (pp. 89–106). Cambridge, UK: Cambridge University Press. doi:10.1017/CBO9780511499531.004

World Health Organization. (2015). *Increasing fruit and vegetable consumption to reduce the risk of noncommunicable diseases*. Geneva, Switzerland: Author.

ADDITIONAL READING

Agresti, A. (2012). *Categorical data analysis*. New York, NY: Wiley.

Athey, S. (2018). The impact of machine learning on economics. In A. Agrawal, J. Gans, & A. Goldfarb (Eds.), *The Economics of Artificial Intelligence: An Agenda* (pp. 507–547). Cambridge, MA: National Bureau of Economic Research; Retrieved from https://EconPapers.repec.org/RePEc:nbr:nberch:14009

Hennig, C. (2015). Clustering strategy and method selection. In C. Hennig, M. Meila, F. Murtagh, & R. Rocci (Eds.), *Handbook of cluster analysis* (pp. 703–737). Boca Raton, FL: Chapman and Hall/CRC. doi:10.1201/b19706

Johnson, R. A., & Wichern, D. W. (2008). *Applied multivariate statistical analysis*. Englewood Cliffs, NJ: Prentice Hall.

Jordan, M. I., & Mitchell, T. M. (2015). Machine learning: Trends, perspectives and prospects. *Science*, *349*(6245), 255–260. doi:10.1126cience.aaa8415 PMID:26185243

Najafabadi, M. N., Villanustre, F., Khoshgoftaar, T. M., Seliya, N., Wald, R., & Muharemagic, E. (2015). Deep learning applications and challenges in big data analytics. *Journal of Big Data*, *2*(1), 1–21. doi:10.118640537-014-0007-7

Von Luxburg, U., Wiliamson, R. C., & Guyon, I. (2012). Clustering: Science or art? In I. Guyon, G. Dror, V. Lemaire, G. Taylor, & D. Silver (Eds.), JMLR Workshop and Conference Proceedings 27 (pp. 65–79). Washington, DC: MIT Press. Retrieved from https://www.chicagobooth.edu/research/kilts/datasets/nielsen/working-papers

KEY TERMS AND DEFINITIONS

Artificial Neural Network (ANN): A predictive computer algorithm inspired by the biology of the human brain that can learn linear and non-linear functions from data. Artificial neural networks are particularly useful when the complexity of the data or the modelling task makes the design of a function that maps inputs to outputs by hand impractical.

Cluster Analysis: A type of an unsupervised learning that aims to partition a set of objects in such a way that objects in the same group (called a cluster) are more similar, whereas characteristics of objects assigned into different clusters are quite distinct.

Deep Learning: A type of machine learning based on artificial neural networks. It can be supervised, unsupervised, or semi-supervised, and it uses an artificial neural network with multiple layers between the input and output layers.

Hierarchical Clustering: The most common approach to clustering. The method proceeds sequentially, producing a nested assignment of objects into clusters. It is typically agglomerative, with cluster sizes increasing as the number of clusters decreases. At each step of the process, a clustering criterion based on a measure of proximity between groups must be computed to decide which groups of objects are to be joined together.

Latent Class Analysis (LCA): A statistical technique used in factor, cluster, and regression modelling, where constructs or latent classes are identified from multivariate categorical data and used for further analysis. The probability that a case belongs to a particular latent class is calculated using the maximum likelihood method. The resulting models can also be described as finite mixture models.

Machine Learning: A branch of artificial intelligence that focuses on data analysis methods that allow for automation of the process of analytical model building.

Partitional Clustering: A commonly used approach to clustering that begins with a preselected number of groups or clusters. An initial allocation of objects to clusters is followed by reassignment to new groups based on a measure of proximity between each object and each group. The process continues until all objects have been assigned to their closest groups. A commonly used partitioning method is the k-means algorithm.

Predictive Modelling: A process of using data mining or machine learning techniques to predict outcomes of interest. Once variables that are likely to influence the outcomes are identified and the relevant data is collected, a model is formulated and tested.

Supervised Learning: A machine learning task designed to learn a function that maps an input onto an output based on a set of training examples (training data). Each training example is a pair consisting of a vector of inputs and an output value. A supervised learning algorithm analyzes the training data and infers a mapping function. A simple example of supervised learning is a regression model.

Unsupervised Learning: A class of machine learning techniques designed to identify features and patterns in data. There is no mapping function to be learned or output values to be achieved. Cluster analysis is an example of unsupervised learning.

This research was previously published in the Handbook of Research on Big Data Clustering and Machine Learning; pages 378-408, copyright year 2020 by Engineering Science Reference (an imprint of IGI Global).

Section 4
Utilization and Applications

Chapter 44
Machine Learning Algorithms

Namrata Dhanda
https://orcid.org/0000-0003-0395-0696
Amity University, India

Stuti Shukla Datta
Amity University, India

Mudrika Dhanda
Royal Holloway University, UK

ABSTRACT

Human intelligence is deeply involved in creating efficient and faster systems that can work independently. Creation of such smart systems requires efficient training algorithms. Thus, the aim of this chapter is to introduce the readers with the concept of machine learning and the commonly employed learning algorithm for developing efficient and intelligent systems. The chapter gives a clear distinction between supervised and unsupervised learning methods. Each algorithm is explained with the help of suitable example to give an insight to the learning process.

INTRODUCTION

Can a person with both his legs amputated still drive a car, or a man with impaired vision can cross a busy road without assistance. The answer to these questions, which once seemed impossible, is in affirmative now. This has become possible due to machine learning. So what is machine learning then? It is a field of science which provides systems the ability to learn and adapt from the environment conditions. Here, the objective is to develop programmed models that can access data and further use them for improving their performance without much human intervention. So straight away next question that comes into one's mind how these systems acquire intelligence? So the intelligence is acquired through learning. Learning is a very crucial component in developing an intelligent system. Learning may be supervised or unsupervised. Supervised learning refers to inferring a mapping function between input and output using a set of training data. Later the function can be employed for assessing testing data.

DOI: 10.4018/978-1-6684-6291-1.ch044

Unsupervised learning refers to developing hidden structure in the input data. These learning models can be employed in developing a classifier or a predictor. As an example let us consider a person with impaired vision and he is wearing intelligent goggles while moving on the roads. The intelligent gadget in the form of goggles is continuously monitoring the scenario on the road. Now if the person has to cross the road these goggles would take the input in the form of image and classify whether the road in front of the person is busy or not and would help him in making the decision of whether to cross the road or not. It is often observed that if one has browsed for the flight cost from Delhi to Mumbai two three times on the home page of an air services, and the next time when he logs on to the site, he gets a display of prices offered by various air service provider along with their routes for round trip between Delhi and Mumbai. This is an example of adaptive learning or more specifically, learning from the query. Thus objective is to create intelligent systems that could assist human in the areas where human intelligence has limitation. Lot of researches and investigations are going across the globe to evolve new and better learning methods.

Machine learning is a field of Computer Science which often uses statistical techniques to give computers the ability to learn. It is closely related to artificial intelligence which is enabling computers to perform human-like activities. Machine learning is giving computers the ability to learn without being explicitly getting programmed. Thus, this chapter introduces the reader with commonly employed supervised and unsupervised learning algorithms.

The chapter is organized mainly in four sections: first section deals with the introduction to Machine Learning and how intelligent systems can work for the betterment of life. Second section deals with parametric and nonparametric algorithms. Third section discusses in details the commonly employed supervised learning algorithm with example to assist readers gain an insight towards learning techniques. Fourth section deals with unsupervised learning algorithms example clustering and a priori methods.

BACKGROUND

Tom M. Mitchell provided a widely quoted, more formal definition of the algorithms studied in the machine learning field: “A computer program is said to learn from experience E with respect to some class of tasks T and performance measure P if its performance at tasks in T, as measured by P, improves with experience E” (Mitchell, 1997). This definition of the tasks in which machine learning is concerned offers a fundamentally operational definition rather than defining the field in cognitive terms. This follows Alan Turing’s proposal in his paper “Computing Machinery and Intelligence”, in which the question “Can machines think?” is replaced with the question “Can machines do what we (as thinking entities) can do?” (Turing, 2009). In Turing’s proposal the various characteristics that could be possessed by a thinking machine and the various implications in constructing one are exposed.

Machine learning is a technology that allows computers to learn directly from examples and experience in the form of data. Traditional approaches to programming rely on hardcoded rules, which set out how to solve a problem, step-by-step. In contrast, machine learning systems are set a task, and given a large amount of data to use as examples of how this task can be achieved or from which to detect patterns. The system then learns how best to achieve the desired output. It can be thought of as narrow AI: machine learning supports intelligent systems, which are able to learn a particular function, given a specific set of data to learn from. Machine learning has gained a significant importance in the recent years. A large number of applications have been developed using Machine Learning algorithms. Amongst several already existing applications, machine learning methods, in particular, help in coping up with large datasets (e.g., Clark & Niblett, 1989; Cohen, 1995; Dietterich, 1997; Mitchell, 1997; Michalski, Bratko, & Kubat, 1998).

PARAMETRIC AND NON PARAMETRIC ALGORITHMS

Before familiarizing readers with commonly employed learning algorithms, it is imperative to understand the terms parametric and non-parametric.

- **Parametric Algorithms**: Algorithms that simplify the function to a known form are called parametric machine learning algorithms. The algorithm involves two steps: first identification of the form of the function and second evaluating the coefficients of the function from the training data e.g is linear regression, logistic regression
- **Non Parametric Algorithms:** Algorithms that do not make any assumptions about the form of the mapping function are called nonparametric algorithms. Such algorithms have the flexibility to learn any functional form from the training data. However, such algorithms require large training dataset and take more time in learning e.g. support vector machine, kNN algorithm

SUPERVISED LEARNING ALGORITHMS

In supervised learning, idea is to learn a function that best maps input variable to the output variable. Here training data is in sets of input variables and their corresponding output. Thus the process of estimating a mapping function from the training dataset can be thought of as a teacher supervising the learning process. The algorithm iteratively makes predictions on the input training data (input data) and is corrected by the teacher (known output). Learning stops when the algorithm achieves an acceptable level of performance. Most commonly employed supervised algorithms are:

- Linear Regression
- Logistic Regression
- Linear Discriminant Analysis
- Linear Support Vector Machine
- K Nearest Neighbor Algorithm (KNN)

LINEAR REGRESSION

Linear regression is statistical approach to map input variable to their corresponding out. It is the a known and well understood algorithm in machine learning. Data can be modeled with simple linear equation as:

$$y= b_0+b_1x \quad (1)$$

This represent a line where *y* is the variable that we want to predict and *x* is the input attribute b_0 is the intercept and b_1 is called the slope. The coefficient b_0 and b1 are estimated using the labeled input and output variables. Once these coefficients values are estimated, the linear mapping function is ready to prediction for unknown input variables. If there were more input variable then this would become a multiple regression problem.

Example

For the given data develop a linear model of prediction

Table 1.

x	y
1	1
2	3
4	3
3	2
5	5

So, the aim to evaluate the linear coefficients $b_{0,}\ b_1$
We first evaluate the mean of x and y

Mean(x)= 3, Mean(y)=2.8

Error of each variable from the mean is then calculated as given in the table 2

Table 2.

x	e_x	y	e_y	$e_{x*}\ e_y$
1	1-3=-2	1	1-2.8=-1.8	3.6
2	3-3=-1	2	3-2.8=.2	-0.2
4	3-3=1	4	3-2.8=.2	0.2
3	2-3=0	3	2-2.8=-.8	0
5	5-3-2	5	5-2.8= 2.2	4.4

Sum of the multiplication = (3.6-0.2+0.2+0+4.4)=10
Slope can be then evaluated as $b_1=8/10=0.8$
Intercept can be calculated as

b_0=mean(y)-b_1*mean(x)=0.4

So the linear model is given by:

y=0.8x+0.4

LOGISTIC REGRESSION

Logistic regression can be employed for linearly as well as non-linearly separable problems. It is mostly employed for predicting the probability of an event. Application of logistic regression include: image segmentation, handwriting recognition etc.

So, Logistic regression is a statistical method for analyzing the given dataset in which more than one variable determine an outcome. The algorithm is mainly employed for classification purpose. The outcome is measured with a binary variable (either 0 or1). In Logistic regression a link is used to map the linear combination of independent variable onto Bernoulli distribution. This link is called 'logit' transformation. The equation is given as:

$$Logit(p)= b_0+b_1x_1+b_2x_2 \quad (2)$$

$$Logit(p) = ln(p/1-p) \quad (3)$$

$$ln(p/1-p) = b_0+b_1x_1+b_2x_2 \quad (4)$$

solving for p gives

$$p = e^{(b0+b1x1+b2x2)}/(1+ e^{(b0+b1x1+b2x2)}) \quad (5)$$

$$p=1/(1+e^{-(b0+b1x1+b2x2)}) \quad (6)$$

'*p*' refers to the probability of presence of the characteristics of interest.

So, modeling data in logistic regression refers to generating appropriate coefficients (b_0, b_1, b_2) of independent variables from the data set and estimate the probability of presence of new input data to a particular class.

Example

Develop a logistic regression model for the given data set (Table 3).

From the equation (6)

$$p=1/(1+e^{-(b0+b1x1+b2x2)})$$

we can employ stochastic gradient descent to the problem of finding coefficient for the logistic regression model as follows.

We start with initializing coefficient as:

b_0=0; b_1=0; b_2=0

with the first labeled input data we calculate the prediction as:

x1=2.78 x2=2.55 p=1/2=0.5

we now update the coefficients using the equation

b=b+alpha*(y-p)*p(1-p)*x

Here alpha is the acceleration factor and it is taken to be 0.3 for this problem
For calculating b_0 x=1is taken,
Similarly for calculating b_1 and b_2, x values of 2.78 and 2.55 respectively are substituted in the update equation

b_0=-0.037; b_1=-0.104, b_2=-0.09564

The entire process is repeated with next training data and coefficients are updated
After 10 iterations the values are b_0=-0.41; b_1=0.85, b_2=-1.10

Table 3.

x_1	x_2	y
2.78	2.55	0
1.46	2.36	0
3.39	4.40	0
1.38	1.85	0
3.06	3.00	0
7.62	2.75	1
5.33	2.08	1
6.92	1.77	1
8.67	-0.24	1
7.67	3.51	1

DISCRIMINANT ANALYSIS

Discriminant analysis is a classification technique based on the estimation of statistical distance of the raw input data and class centers under consideration. Statistical distance accounts for location size and shape of the class clouds. It is also called as Mahalanobis distance. On the assumptions that whenever the data come Gaussian distribution, the statistical distance employ a covariance matrix to evaluate the distance between new data and centroid of the class.

Consider two classes C_1 and C_2. Each data in these classes have three features and $\overline{F_{11}}$, $\overline{F_{12}}$, $\overline{F_{13}}$ represent average value of features for class C_1. The new input data has feature values as F_{1n}, F_{2n}, F_{3n}. The statistical distance between new data and class one can be evaluated as

$$F_1 = [\ \overline{F_{11}}\ \overline{F_{12}}\ \overline{F_{13}}\ ]^T \tag{7}$$

$$F_n = [\ F_{1n}\ F_{2n}\ F_{3n}]^T \tag{8}$$

$$D(F_n, F_1) = \sqrt{((F_n - F_1)^T S^{-1} (F_n - F_1))} \tag{9}$$

Here S represents covariance matrix between different predictors. Similarly the statistical distance between F_n and F_2 can be calculated. The lesser of the two values would identify the class for the new input. Similar procedure can be done for multiple class problems.

Example

As part of customer acquisition efforts, Bank A plans to run a campaign for current customers to purchase a loan. To improve target marketing, they want to identify the customers most likely to accept the loan offer. They use data from previous campaign on 5000 customers where 450 customers accepted.

So there are two classes: Acceptors and Non acceptors

For each of these class three attributes or features are employed (credit card average, age, income) and average of these features for both the classes are evaluated (using the database of customers).

Table 4.

	Non Acceptors	Acceptors
Average CCavg	1.73	3.91
Average Age	45.37	45.07
Average Income	66.24	144.75

So, if a new customer with feature as (CCavg=2.70, age=44, income=100) comes, the objective is to find which class he will fall into:

Now if the covariance matrix 'S' for acceptors is formulated (using the database) as:

Table 5.

	CCavg	Age	Income
CCavg	995.5	14.21	7.77
Age	14.21	4.39	-0.06
Income	7.77	-0.06	134.07

Then, statistical distance of the input class with acceptor class can be calculated as:

$D(x_0, x'_{acc}) = \sqrt{((x_0-x'_{acc})^T S^{-1}(x_0-x'_{acc}))}$

x' denote the average values of the features.

x-x'=[2.7 44 100]-[3.91 45.07 144.75]

inverse(S)=

Table 6.

0.0011	-0.0034	-0.0001
-0.0034	0.2388	0.0003
-0.0001	0.0003	0.0075

Substituting the values in equation ()

$D=\sqrt{15.22}=3.9$

LINEAR SUPPORT VECTOR MACHINES

Support Vector Machines (SVMs) are a good example of the way in which current machine learning research combines ideas from different research areas. SVMs were introduced in the early nineties by Boser and his co-authors (1992), bringing together ideas that had been around since the 1960s—and the topic has developed into a very active research area.

Suppose classification is to be made in two classes: class red and class blue and there are two features, then the objective is to find the hyper-plane that would classify the labeled data into two classes. Now, there may be many such planes that would classify the data correctly. So now the point is which hyper-plane would be suitable. The decision is made on the basis of support vectors. For each qualifying hyper-plane there are support vectors on either side. These vector are passing through the closest elements from the hyperplane on either side of the plane. We select the hyperplane which has the maximum margin with respect to its support vectors. Suppose the equation of the hyperplane is given as:

$$G(x) = w^t x + b \quad (10)$$

Here w is weight vector and x is vector of feature and b is constant. Refer Figure 1

Vector $w=[w1, w2...]$ is perpendicular to the hyper-plane (shown in blue). We choose x^- such that $g(x^-) = -1$ and $g(x^+) = 1$

$$\text{Also, } x^+ = x^- + r*w \quad (11)$$

Figure 1.

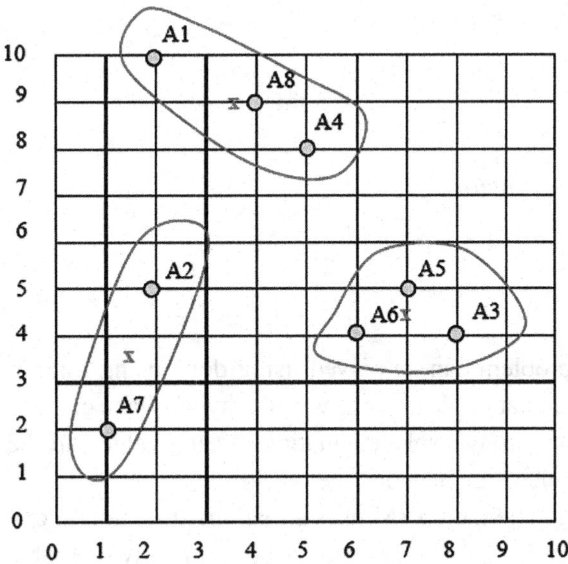

Now,

$$wx^{-} + b = -1 \text{ and} \tag{12}$$

$$wx^{+} + b = 1 \tag{13}$$

Substitution eq(11) in eq(13) we get

$$w(x^{-} + r^{*}w) + b = 1 \tag{14}$$

$$rw^{2} + wx^{-} + b = 1 \tag{15}$$

$$rw^{2} - 1 = 1 \tag{16}$$

$$r = 1 / w^{2} \tag{17}$$

$$M = x^{+} - x^{-} \tag{18}$$

$$= r^{*}w$$

$$r = 2 / w \tag{19}$$

Objective problem becomes

$$Max\left(\frac{2}{\sqrt{w^{T}w}}\right) \tag{20}$$

Such that all data lie on the correct side of the margin

We define $y^{(i)} = 1 \to wx^{i} + b \geq 1$

$$y^{(i)} = -1 \to wx^{i} + b \leq 1 \tag{21}$$

So the constraints can be written as

$$y^{(i)}\left(wx^{i} + b\right) \geq 1 \tag{22}$$

Now the optimization problem can be solved using done using Lagrangian function method and weights value (w) can be calculated. With these weights hyper-plane can be estimated. The variables of new input data are substituted in hyperplane equation to get a value and the sign of this value decides on which side of the hyper-plane the new data belongs to.

Now if the data is inseparable then SVM uses a mapping function to change the input data into another feature space in such a manner that the data becomes linearly separable. Such functions are called "Kernel' Functions.

K NEAREST NEIGHBOR ALGORITHM

K nearest Neighbor Algorithm (KNN) is a classification algorithm. Here the Euclidean distance between the raw input data and other labeled data is evaluated. K closest values are identified and ranked. The class which has majority of the closest values becomes the predicted class for the input data. The biggest advantage of the KNN is that it is robust to noisy training data. So, it can be said that KNN is an intuitive algorithm that identifies the class of unlabeled data based on its similarity with data in the training samples. So for classification purpose, KNN only requires: integer K, set of labeled example, and a metric to measure closeness (Euclidean Distance)

Example

We have data from the questionnaires survey and two attributes (acid durability and strength) to classify whether a special paper tissue is 'good' or 'bad'. Four training samples are given as:

Table 7.

X1	X2	y
7	7	BAD
7	4	BAD
3	4	GOOD
1	4	GOOD

Now a factory produces a new paper tissue with X1=3 and X2=7. The objective is to identify which class it belongs to but with exhaustive survey.

So, we start by taking k=3, then the distance between the query instance (new input) and all the training samples are evaluated

Table 8.

X1	X2	Distance
7	7	$(7\text{-}3)^2+(7\text{-}7)^2=16$
7	4	$(7\text{-}3)^2+(4\text{-}7)^2=25$
3	4	$(3\text{-}3)^2+(4\text{-}7)^2=9$
1	4	$(1\text{-}3)^2+(4\text{-}7)^2=13$

Distances evaluated are then ranked and 3 nearest neighbor are determined. We collect the classes of these nearest neighbors. So, since we have 2 'good' and '1 bad', we conclude that new tissue paper falls in 'good' class.

UNSUPERVISED MACHINE LEARNING

Unsupervised machine learning is the machine learning task of inferring a function that describes the structure of "unlabeled" data (i.e. data that has not been classified or categorized). Since the examples given to the learning algorithm are unlabeled, there is no straightforward way to evaluate the accuracy of the structure that is produced by the algorithm-one feature that distinguishes unsupervised learning from supervised learning and reinforcement learning. Unsupervised learning is where you only have input data (X) and no corresponding output variables.

The goal for unsupervised learning is to model the underlying structure or distribution in the data in order to learn more about the data.

These are called unsupervised learning because unlike supervised learning above there is no correct answer and there is no teacher. Algorithms are left to their own devises to discover and present the interesting structure in the data.

Unsupervised learning is the training of an artificial intelligence (AI) algorithm using information that is neither classified nor labeled and allowing the algorithm to act on that information without guidance.

In unsupervised learning, an AI system may group unsorted information according to similarities and differences even though there are no categories provided. AI systems capable of unsupervised learning are often associated with generative learning models, although they may also use a retrieval-based approach (which is most often associated with supervised learning). Chatbots, self-driving cars, facial recognition programs, expert systems and robots are among the systems that may use either supervised or unsupervised learning approaches.

In unsupervised learning, an AI system is presented with unlabeled, uncategorised data and the system's algorithms act on the data without prior training. The output is dependent upon the coded algorithms. Subjecting a system to unsupervised learning is one way of testing AI.

Unsupervised learning algorithms can perform more complex processing tasks than supervised learning systems. However, unsupervised learning can be more unpredictable than the alternate model. While an unsupervised learning AI system might, for example, figure out on its own how to sort cats from dogs, it might also add unforeseen and undesired categories to deal with unusual breeds, creating clutter instead of order.

Unsupervised learning methods are used in bioinformatics for sequence analysis and genetic clustering; in data mining for sequence and pattern mining; in medical imaging for image segmentation; and in computer vision for object recognition.

Unsupervised learning problems can be further grouped into clustering and association problems.

- **Clustering:** A clustering problem is where you want to discover the inherent groupings in the data, such as grouping customers by purchasing behavior.
- **Association:** An association rule learning problem is where you want to discover rules that describe large portions of your data, such as people that buy X also tend to buy Y.

Some popular examples of unsupervised learning algorithms are:

- k-means for clustering problems.
- Apriori algorithm for association rule learning problems.

CLUSTERING ALGORITHMS

The most common unsupervised learning method is cluster analysis, which is used for exploratory data analysis to find hidden patterns or grouping in data. The clusters are modeled using a measure of similarity which is defined upon metrics such as Euclidean or probabilistic distance. The most common clustering algorithms are:

- K-Means Clustering
- Hierarchical Clustering

K-Means Clustering

The k-means algorithm takes as input a parameter k and partitions a set of n objects into k clusters so that elements belonging to the same cluster possess similar properties. Or in other words we can say that the resulting intracluster similarity is high but the intercluster is low. We can measure the cluster similarity in terms of the mean value of the objects in the cluster. This mean can be viewed as the clusters center of gravity.

Method:

1. Randomly select k objects each of which initially represents a cluster mean or center.
2. For every other remaining object, find a cluster to which it is the most similar, based on the distance between the object and the cluster mean.
3. Compute the new mean of each cluster.

4. Continue Steps 1 to 3 until the criterion function converges. Typically the squared error criterion is used and it is defined as:

E= ∑i=1 to k ∑p€ Ci I p-mi I2

where E is the sum of square error for all objects in the database, p is the point in space representing a given object, and mi is the mean of cluster Ci (both p and mi are multidimensional).

The above mentioned criterion function E tries to make the resulting k clusters as compact and as separate as possible.

The method is relatively scalable and efficient in processing large data set because the computational complexity of the algorithm is O(nkt) where n is the total number of objects, k is the number of clusters and t is the number of iterations. Normally, k <<n and t<<n. The method terminates at local optimum.

This algorithm can be applied only when it is possible to define the mean of the objects. It is not always possible because in some applications categorical attributes are involved whose mean value cannot be determined. Another necessary condition is that the users must predefine the number of clusters k. The algorithm is sensitive to noise and outlier data points since the addition or deletion of small amount of data can substantially affect the mean value and hence the clusters obtained.

Example

Use the k-means algorithm and Euclidean distance to cluster the following 8 points into 3 clusters:

A1=(2,10), A2=(2,5), A3=(8,4), A4=(5,8), A5=(7,5), A6=(6,4), A7=(1,2), A8=(4,9).

Suppose that the initial seeds (centers of each cluster) are A1, A4 and A7. Run the k-means algorithm for 1 iteration only. At the end of this iteration show:

A. The new clusters (i.e. the examples belonging to each cluster)
B. The centers of the new clusters
C. Draw a 10 by 10 space with all the 8 points and show the clusters after the first iteration and the new centroids.
D. How many more iterations are needed to converge? Draw the result for each iteartion.

Solution: Part A

d(a,b) denotes the Eucledian distance between the points a=(x1,y1) and b=(x2,y2). It is obtained directly using the equation:

d(a,b)=√ (x2-x1)2+(y2-y1)2

The distance matrix based on the Euclidean distance is given in Table 9.

Let seed1=A1=(2,10), seed2=A4=(5,8), seed3=A7=(1,2)

Table 9.

	A1	A2	A3	A4	A5	A6	A7	A8
A1	0	$\sqrt{25}$	$\sqrt{36}$	$\sqrt{13}$	$\sqrt{50}$	$\sqrt{52}$	$\sqrt{65}$	$\sqrt{5}$
A2		0	$\sqrt{37}$	$\sqrt{18}$	$\sqrt{25}$	$\sqrt{17}$	$\sqrt{10}$	$\sqrt{20}$
A3			0	$\sqrt{25}$	$\sqrt{2}$	$\sqrt{2}$	$\sqrt{53}$	$\sqrt{41}$
A4				0	$\sqrt{13}$	$\sqrt{17}$	$\sqrt{52}$	$\sqrt{2}$
A5					0	$\sqrt{2}$	$\sqrt{45}$	$\sqrt{25}$
A6						0	$\sqrt{29}$	$\sqrt{29}$
A7							0	$\sqrt{58}$
A8								0

Iteration-1

See Table 10.

Table 10.

A1: d(A1, seed1)=0 as A1 is seed1 d(A1, seed2)= $\sqrt{13} > 0$ d(A1, seed3)= $\sqrt{65} > 0$ Hence, A1 $\in$ cluster1	A2: d(A2,seed1)= $\sqrt{25} = 5$ d(A2, seed2)= $\sqrt{18} = 4.24$ d(A2, seed3)= $\sqrt{10} = 3.16$ (smallest) Hence, A2 $\in$ cluster3
A3: d(A3, seed1)= $\sqrt{36} = 6$ d(A3, seed2)= $\sqrt{25} = 5$ (smallest) d(A3, seed3)= $\sqrt{53} = 7.28$ Hence, A3 $\in$ cluster2	A4: d(A4, seed1)= $\sqrt{13}$ d(A4, seed2)=0 as A4 is seed2 d(A4, seed3)= $\sqrt{52} > 0$ Hence, A4 $\in$ cluster2
A5: d(A5, seed1)= $\sqrt{50} = 7.07$ d(A5, seed2)= $\sqrt{13} = 3.60$ (smallest) d(A5, seed3)= $\sqrt{45} = 6.70$ Hence, A5 $\in$ cluster2	A6: d(A6, seed1)= $\sqrt{52} = 7.21$ d(A6, seed2)= $\sqrt{17} = 4.12$ (smallest) d(A6, seed3)= $\sqrt{29} = 5.38$ Hence, A6 $\in$ cluster2
A7: d(A7, seed1)= $\sqrt{65} > 0$ d(A7, seed2)= $\sqrt{52} > 0$ d(A7, seed3)=0 as A7 is seed3 Hence, A7 $\in$ cluster3	A8: d(A8, seed1)= $\sqrt{5}$ d(A8, seed2)= $\sqrt{2}$ (smallest) d(A8, seed3)= $\sqrt{58}$ Hence, A8 $\in$ cluster2

This ends iteration1.
New Clusters after iteration 1:

1: {A1}, 2: {A3, A4, A5, A6, A8}, 3: {A2, A7}

Part B

The centers of the new clusters can be determined as:

C1=(2,10)

C2=((8+5+7+6+4)/5, (4+8+5+4+9)/5)= (6,6)

C3=((2+1)/2, (5+2)/2)= (1.5, 3.5)

Part C

See Figure 2-5.

Figure 2.

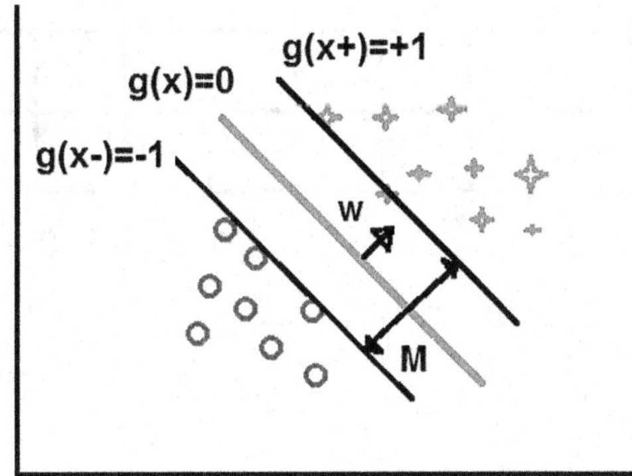

Figure 3.

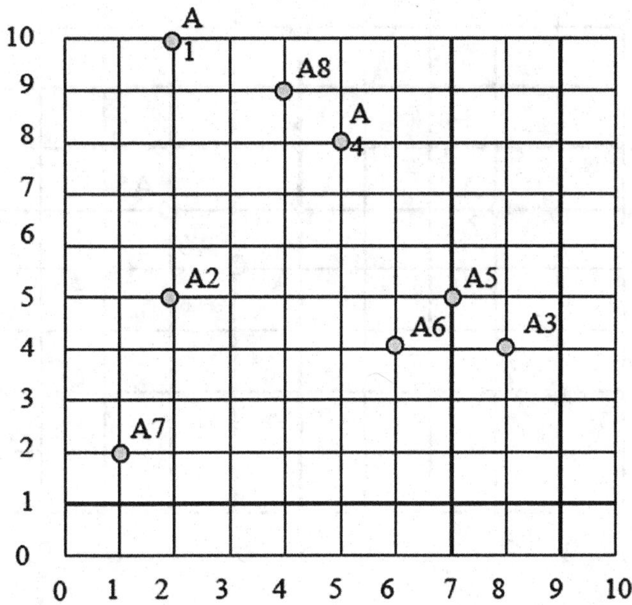

Figure 4.

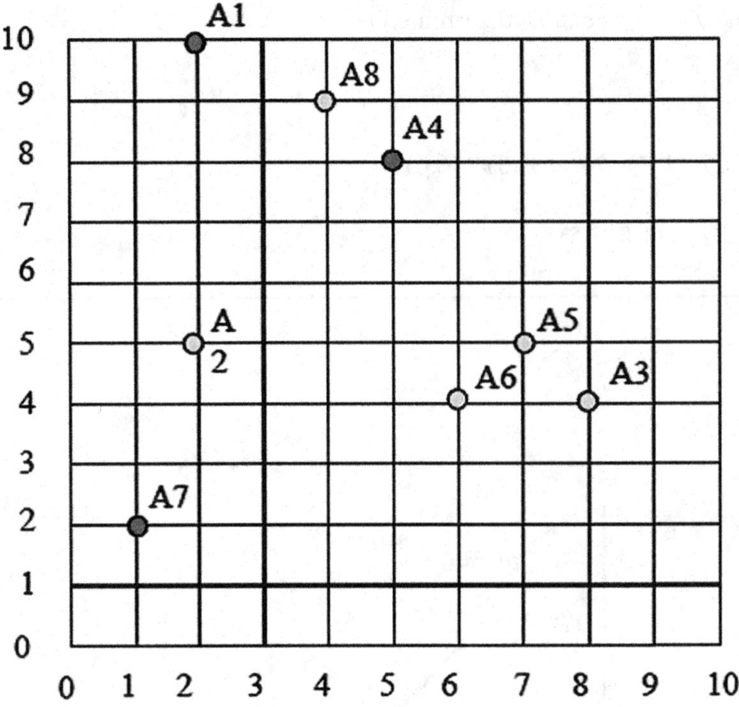

Figure 5.

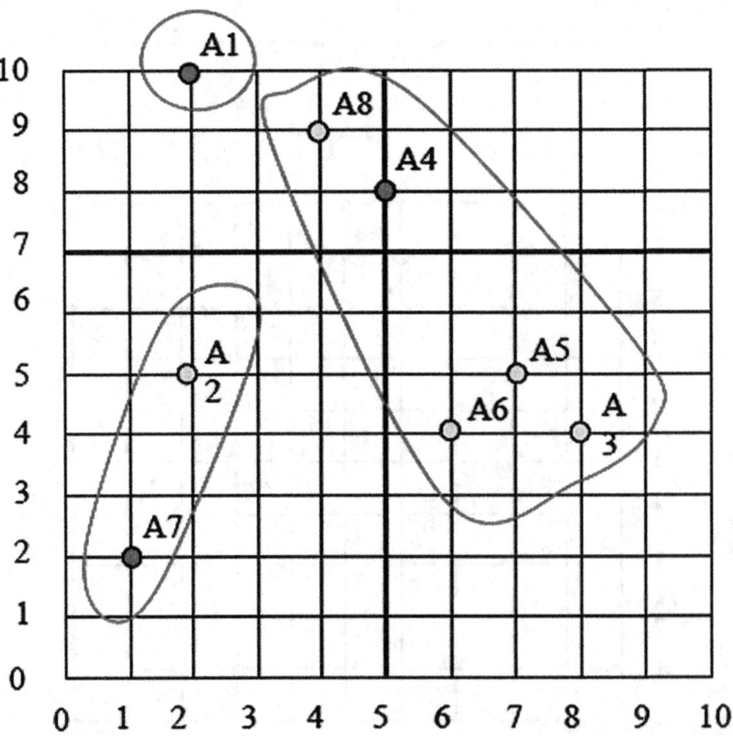

Part D

We need two more iterations.

After the second iteration the result would be:

1: {A1, A8}, 2: {A3, A4, A5, A6}, 3: {A2, A7} with centers C1=(3, 9.5), C2=(6.5, 5.25) and C3=(1.5, 3.5).

After the 3rd epoch, the results would be:

1: {A1, A4, A8}, 2: {A3, A5, A6}, 3: {A2, A7} with centers C1=(3.66, 9), C2=(7, 4.33) and C3=(1.5, 3.5).

Figure 6.

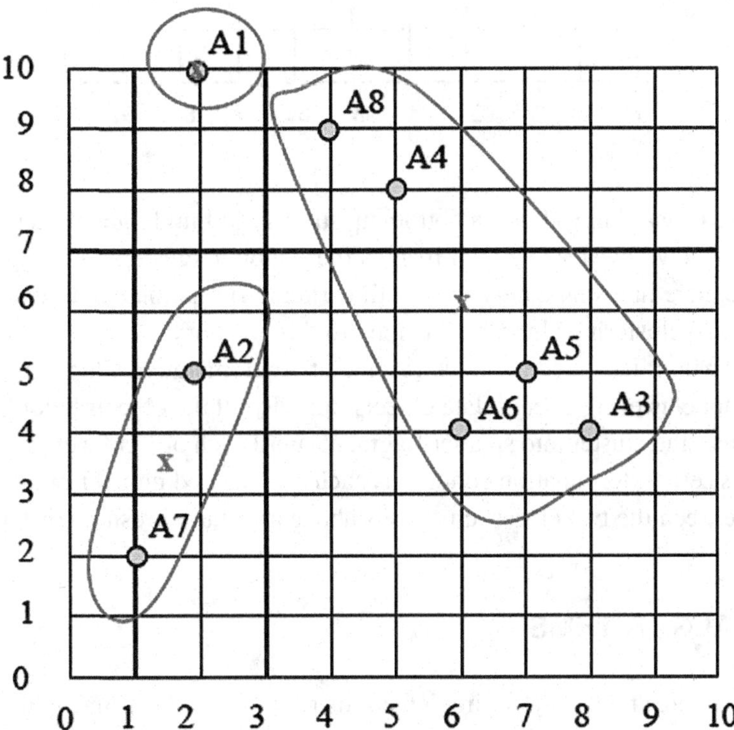

Hierarchical Clustering

The second commonly used clustering method is the hierarchical clustering method. In this method of clustering the data objects are grouped into a tree of clusters. Depending on whether the hierarchical decomposition is formed in a top down or bottom up manner, hierarchical clustering can be further divided into two types:

Figure 7.

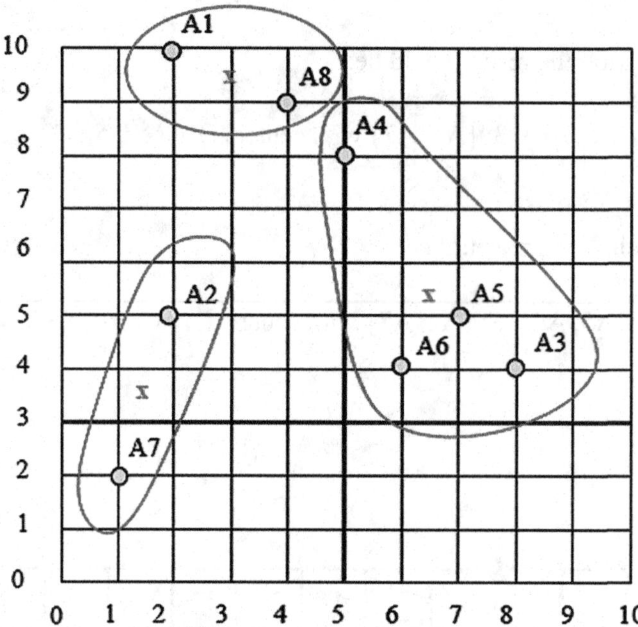

- **Agglomerative Clustering:** This is a bottom up strategy of building a cluster. It starts by placing each object in its own cluster and then merges these atomic clusters into larger clusters until all the objects are there in a single cluster or until certain termination conditions are satisfied. Most of the hierarchical clustering algorithms belong to this category.
- **Divisive Clustering:** This method is the reverse of Agglomerative Clustering. It follows the top down method for clustering a set of data objects. Initially all the objects belong to a single cluster. It then subdivides the cluster into smaller fragments until each object forms a cluster on its own or until it satisfies certain termination conditions such as a desired number of clusters is obtained or the distance between the two closest clusters is above a certain threshold distance.

ASSOCIATION ALGORITHMS

Association algorithms are another way of implementing unsupervised learning. Due to the rapid growth of data generation and its storage every day, there is an increasing interest among the companies to find the association rules in their databases. The discovery of association rules or the relationships among the various data items in the databases can help in many decision making processes as it will represent the dependencies among the data items. Association rules are represented by using if/then statements that will help to reveal the relationships between seemingly unrelated data in a relational database or other information repository. An example of an association rule would be "If a customer buys a computer system he is likely to purchase the antivirus software." In data mining, association rules are useful for analyzing and predicting the behavior of the customer. They play an important part in market basket data analysis, product clustering, catalog design and store layout.

An association rule is composed of two parts: an antecedent (if) and a consequent (then). An item that is found in the data is referred to as an antecedent whereas a consequent is an item that is found in combination with the antecedent or that has a high probability of occurrence with the antecedent.

Association rules are created by analyzing data for frequent if/then patterns and using the criteria support and confidence to identify the most important relationships. Support is an indication of how frequently the items appear in the database and Confidence indicates the number of times the if/then statements have been found to be true. Association rules are considered to be interesting if they satisfy a minimum support threshold and a minimum confidence threshold. These thresholds can be either defined by the user or the domain experts.

Apriori Algorithm

The Apriori principle can reduce the number of itemsets we need to examine. Put simply, the apriori principle states that if an itemset is infrequent, then all its subsets must also be infrequent. This means that if {beer} was found to be infrequent, we can expect {beer, pizza} to be equally or even more infrequent. So in consolidating the list of popular itemsets, we need not consider {beer, pizza}, nor any other itemset configuration that contains beer.

Step 1: Finding Itemsets With High Support

Using the Apriori principle, the number of itemsets that have to be examined can be pruned, and the list of popular itemsets can be obtained in these steps:

1. Start with itemsets containing just a single item, such as {apple} and {pear}.
2. Determine the support for itemsets. Keep the itemsets that meet your minimum support threshold, and remove itemsets that do not.
3. Using the itemsets you have kept from Step 1, generate all the possible itemset configurations.
4. Repeat Steps 1 & 2 until there are no more new itemsets.

Step 2: Finding Item Rules With High Confidence or Lift

We have seen how the Apriori algorithm can be used to identify itemsets with high support. The same principle can also be used to identify item associations with high confidence or lift. Finding rules with high confidence or lift is less computationally taxing once high-support itemsets have been identified, because confidence and lift values are calculated using support values.

Take for example the task of finding high-confidence rules. If the rule has low confidence, all other rules with the same constituent items and with apple on the right hand side would have low confidence too.

```
{beer, chips -> apple}
```

Specifically, the rules would have low confidence as well.

```
 {beer -> apple, chips}
{chips -> apple, beer}
```

As before, lower level candidate item rules can be pruned using the Apriori algorithm, so that fewer candidate rules need to be examined.

Limitations

- **Computationally Expensive**: Even though the Apriori algorithm reduces the number of candidate itemsets to consider, this number could still be huge when store inventories are large or when the support threshold is low. However, an alternative solution would be to reduce the number of comparisons by using advanced data structures, such as hash tables, to sort candidate itemsets more efficiently.
- **Spurious Associations**: Analysis of large inventories would involve more itemset configurations, and the support threshold might have to be lowered to detect certain associations. However, lowering the support threshold might also increase the number of spurious associations detected. To ensure that identified associations are generalizable, they could first be distilled from a training dataset, before having their support and confidence assessed in a separate test dataset.

CONCLUSION

Machine Learning is an evolving field of computer engineering where existing systems are given intelligence to assist humans in performing several tasks with increased efficiency and less computational time. Intelligence can be created through learning. Learning process can be classified as supervised and unsupervised. Thus this chapter aims to give readers an overview of the commonly used learning algorithms. These learning methods can be used to develop real time intelligent applications.

REFERENCES

Boser, B. E., Guyon, I. M., & Vapnik, V. N. (1992). A training algorithm for optimal margin classifiers. In *Proc. 5th Annual ACM Workshop on Computational Learning Theory*. Pittsburgh, PA: ACM Press. 10.1145/130385.130401

Clark, P., & Niblett, R. (1989). The CN2 induction algorithm. *Machine Learning*, 3.

Cohen, W. W. (1995). Fast effective rule induction. *Proceedings of the Twelfth International Conference on Machine Learning*.

Dietterich, T. G. (1997). Machine-learning research: Four current directions. *AI Magazine*, 18.

Han, J., Pei, J., & Kamber, M. (2011). *Data mining: concepts and techniques*. Elsevier.

Langley, P. (1996). *Elements of Machine Learning*. San Mateo, CA: Morgan Kaufmann.

Michalski, R. S., Bratko, I., & Kubat, M. (1988). *Machine learning and data mining: methods and applications*. John Wiley and Sons.

Mitchell, T. M. (1997). *Machine Learning*. New York: McGraw-Hill. Retrieved from http://www.cs.cmu.edu/~tom/mlbook.html

Mitchell, T. M. (1997). Does machine learning really work. *AI Magazine*, *18*(3).

Turing, A. M. (2009). Computing machinery and intelligence. In *Parsing the Turing Test* (pp. 23–65). Dordrecht: Springer. doi:10.1007/978-1-4020-6710-5_3

Witten, I. H., & Frank, E. (2000). *Data Mining: Practical Machine Learning Tools and Techniques with Java Implementations*. San Mateo, CA: Morgan Kaufmann. Retrieved from http://www.cs.waikato.ac.nz/ml/weka/

This research was previously published in Computational Intelligence in the Internet of Things; pages 210-233, copyright year 2019 by Engineering Science Reference (an imprint of IGI Global).

Chapter 45
Machine Learning for Web Proxy Analytics

Mark Maldonado
St. Mary's University, San Antonio, USA

Ayad Barsoum
St. Mary's University, San Antonio, USA

ABSTRACT

Proxy servers used around the globe are typically graded and built for small businesses to large enterprises. This does not dismiss any of the current efforts to keep the general consumer of an electronic device safe from malicious websites or denying youth of obscene content. With the emergence of machine learning, we can utilize the power to have smart security instantiated around the population's everyday life. In this work, we present a simple solution of providing a web proxy to each user of mobile devices or any networked computer powered by a neural network. The idea is to have a proxy server to handle the functionality to allow safe websites to be rendered per request. When a website request is made and not identified in the pre-determined website database, the proxy server will utilize a trained neural network to determine whether or not to render that website. The neural network will be trained on a vast collection of sampled websites by category. The neural network needs to be trained constantly to improve decision making as new websites are visited.

INTRODUCTION

Over the past couple of decades, the use of machine learning or artificial intelligence is a term that has been coined as the next goal of smart business or providing help to people in everyday life. While the term "Artificial Intelligence" is older than a few decades since John McCarthy coined the term in 1956 (Neapolitan & Jiang, 2012; Goranzon & Florin, 2012). The general concept of artificial intelligence is discovering ways to have machines reason and perform intelligently driven by software and algorithms. This effort is closely related to how the human brain works since we want these machines capable of learning and to think rationally. This is the overarching mindset we must use when moving forward

DOI: 10.4018/978-1-6684-6291-1.ch045

with a hardware or software-based design to implement a security product. Home network security is the number one issue any household is trying to overcome. With the sheer amount of malicious traffic generated, a general understanding of home network security must become mandatory. Ensuring security for a family has become a challenge due to the number of websites children and young teenagers can access. Without proper monitoring of network traffic, our youth can infect their devices, laptops, or other network components, which is just the tip of the iceberg. Now there are sufficient hardware devices and software products to help with these issues. Some issues with this approach are the cost of these hardware devices and the time or knowledge to implement. A software approach is feasible, but this will only protect the device it's installed on. Lastly, having someone understand the potential logs from a hardware device is overbearing or trying to fully understand what a piece of software is doing to protect is also a challenge. The general population needs something easy to use, install, and understand the information being generated from a product that can handle all these problem-sets. The idea is to have a proxy server (Luotonen & Altis, 1994; Weaver, Kreibich, & Paxson, 2014) to handle the functionality to allow the correct websites to be rendered per request. When a request is made and not identified in the pre-determined website database, the proxy server will utilize the neural network. This instance of the network will be tested against the already trained neural network to determine if the requested website is allowed or not.

MACHINE LEARNING

In the world of machine learning (Sebastiani, 2002; Michie, Spiegelhalter, & Taylor, 1994; Quinlan, 2014; Witten, Frank, Hal, & Pal, 2016; Pedregosa, et al., 2011) and/or artificial intelligence, one must find the perfect starting point and should have an idea where the project will go or possibly evolve into. There are several things we need to consider when picking a neural network design and what we want to achieve. A neural network (Kalchbrenner, Grefenstette, & Blunsom, 2014; Psaltis, Sideris, & Yamamura, 1988; Haykin, 1994; Hagan, Demuth, Beale, & De Jesús, 1996; Anthony & Bartlett, 2009) is generally comprised of 3 basic parts known as neurons, layers, and bias.

Neurons deal with numerous types of information to be processed. Each individual neuron must know how to handle these types of information: input values, weights and bias, net sum, and an activation function. Although a neuron is just a small portion, it is critical to have accurate processing of data.

Layers are important component in a neural network. There is a minimum of three layers: input, hidden, and output. Each layer must handle information being fed forward to create an expected answer. Starting with the input layer, it is critical to have information prepared accurate and normalized properly. This will lower the chance of unexpected results. The hidden layer is particularly unique, as there can be multiple depending on the complexity of processing. When more than one hidden is present, each layer will feed forward as normal and additional processing for back-propagation is acceptable. After information has traversed through the neural network layers, the output is equally important to have accurate results.

Bias has enough worth to the input during execution. Each layer provides a heavier weight to the neurons if preprocessed data is activated as such. The bias is known as a constant in the network with a predefined value to allow accuracy towards a specific answer. Not all inputs to the network will require a bias to be active.

Neural networks can take on multiple forms and complexity. With the flexibility implemented into this network, we are capable of quick changes for testing purposes. This feature will allow modifying the number of hidden layers, several neurons per layer and the number of cycles (epochs) the network will iterate through for learning. Before testing or even training a neural network, having an idea of what the overall goal of the network is required. For instance, dealing with web proxy logs and requested websites, having a neural network determine whether if a website is categorized as good or bad will be the overall question.

Figure 1. Neural network with 3 layers

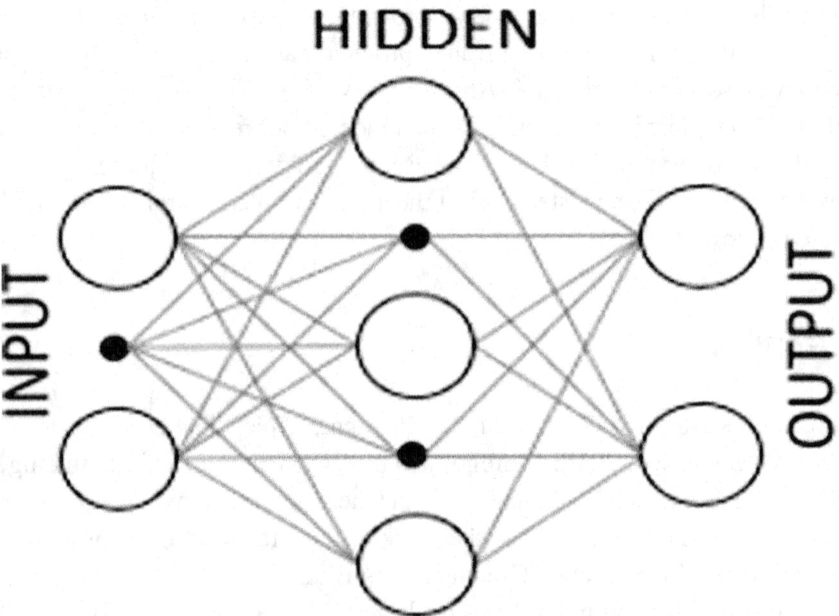

Figure 1 presents the layout design, which is the baseline for our analytics engine. The general scheme of the neural network used in our work has 3 layers: one input, one hidden, and one output. Each of these layers is handled differently as learning takes place. The input layer is predetermined with 32 neurons, a single hidden layer with 15 neurons and an output layer with two neurons or a calculated weight to determine if the suggested input was good or bad.

Analytics engines are a type of service which provides a complete picture of the information which is analyzed. With the amount of information collected and generated, we will utilize the analytical techniques known as search and knowledge discovery and stream analytics. These techniques will enable this system to define a robust information set to be displayed. On a broad scale, data analytics technologies and techniques provide a means of analyzing data sets and drawing conclusions about them to help organizations make informed business decisions. Business intelligence queries answer basic questions about business operations and performance. Big data analytics is a form of advanced analytics, which involves complex applications with elements such as predictive models, statistical algorithms and what-if analyses powered by high-performance analytics systems (Rouse, 2017; Zikopoulos, Eaton, DeRoos, Deutsch, & Lapis, 2012; LaValle, Lesser, Shockley, Hopkins, & Kruschwitz, 2011). The analytics engine is the main process running for the environment. After the initial start of a users' account, it will begin to create a baseline of general data and information flow. This baseline is determined by a default time-frame and will auto update after a user invokes an update or the main analytics engine does the periodic neural network training. This same information will be used to create a general-purpose database to store heuristics information. Any type of information outside the parameters of normal determined by both analytics engine and user input will create alerts for users.

NEURAL NETWORK LAYOUT AND DESIGN

The overall question needs to be answered if a website is determined good or bad with some automation. This process is only a small piece of the entire analytics engine. Although the input can be viewed as one of the most important components as it's the main basis for how the network will determine the outputs. Before any machine learning can take place, there must first be some pre-processing of text. A total of 36 websites collected, with half being dedicated to determining what is identified as either known good or bad content. As training takes place, we will use 32 websites to be utilized while the additional four are strictly for testing once completed. Python was the programming language used to create the text parser and proxy server. There are a number of modules provided in python to handle language processing. One is the module called natural language toolkit "nltk". Due to the nature of this work, natural language processing is a critical aspect. This module creates a starting point for training the network. The bag of words approach will be taken to help determine the bias for input neurons. The bag of words will be handled by taking every single unique word from all training data. This dictionary will be categorized by good or bad type content. Here is a sample bag of words model:

```
bow = {
      "good": [
            "word1",
            "word2",
            "word3"
      ],
      "bad": [
            "1word",
            "2word",
            "3word"
      ],
      "count": {
            "good": 1323,
            "bad": 234
      }
}
```

Each word category will contain the blueprints for determining the initial weight. Both the bag of words dictionary and each training document will have been normalized when processed through python's nltk module. Disregarding any word smaller than 3 and larger than 15 characters. After all training documents are parsed and the bag of words is created, the hidden layer will start to run through it's learning algorithms per neuron. A single neuron must have the functionality of knowing each connection to and from it, calculate weights, and the bias it's been presented. Weight calculation is also known as a summing function. Figure 2 shows the operations of a single neuron.

Figure 2. Operations of a single neuron

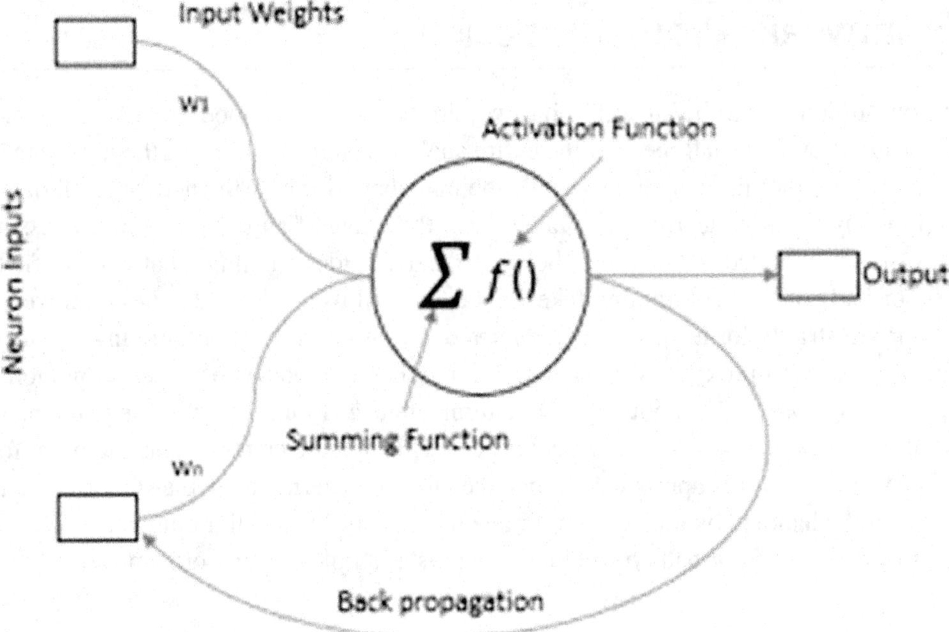

For each input connection, there is a weight associated with that specific connection. When a neuron is activated, the state is computed by adding the inputs multiplied by its corresponding connection's weight (Power Supply, raspberrypi.org). A detailed look at the summation function and adding bias before activation:

$$n = \sum_i w_i I_i + b \tag{1}$$

The values are as follows:

n = current neuron.
w = weight from previous neurons input
I = previous set of inputs
b = bias towards a specific category

Researchers have found out that a neural network using Rectified Linear Unit (ReLU) function, trains faster than other non-linear functions like sigmoid and tanh without a significant drop in accuracy. So, the ReLU function is one of the most important activation functions. A detailed look at the activation function which is ReLU:

$$f(x) = \max(0, x) \tag{2}$$

This function was selected to be the activation due to the speed and the lack of using negative numbers. After looking at the difference between ReLU and the sigmoid activation functions, it was determined ReLU to be faster in processing when the number of networks and neurons are increased.

During the training process there were many configurations used for the neural network. Finding the optimal number of neurons with epochs was a challenge. As defined earlier there was 1 input layer, 1 hidden layer and 1 output layer. This layer neural network had functionality to change the number of neurons in the hidden layer for testing purposes. The default output matrix will be 1 x 2. The output shows 1 neuron with two weights for each category. We have defined an error threshold of 0.2 which will drop any final output to 0 due to the low average. With the input matrix we have a 32 x 2246. This shows 32 neurons one per parsed document. Each neuron will have information regarding the binary sequence of values compared to the previously defined bag of words per category. After training we conducted testing against the set aside documents to check the accuracy of the neural network. Below are the results from tests:

```
TEST #1
Hidden layer neurons: 20
Epochs: 20000
Alpha (Error Threshold): 0.2
Processing Time: 29s
Testing Category Weights:
-         GOOD: 0%
-         BAD: 0%
```

This test group returned no value to the neural network and it was probably over trained with the number of epochs compared to the amount of hidden layer neurons.

```
TEST #2
Hidden layer neurons: 100
Epochs: 20000
Alpha (Error Threshold): 0.2
Processing Time: 148.45s
Testing Category Weights:
-         GOOD: 0%
-         BAD: 0%
```

This test group also returned no value. After picking up the number of hidden layer neurons, with the belief it might help during training, nothing valid from the test documents.

```
TEST #3
Hidden layer neurons: 10
Epochs: 5000
Processing Time: 11s
Testing Category Weights:
-       GOOD: 81%
-       BAD: 75%
```

This test group had a smaller number of neurons and epochs. This had better results during testing. After more research was conducted the conclusion to have a much larger training data set will provide a much better value during the testing phase.

SERVICE COMPONENTS

There are several services created to assist the machine learning and enable users to view their content or settings. These services are defined as a web server, application program interface "API", mobile application, and proxy server. Each of these services has a critical role to achieve full capabilities.

The proxy server is the first interface users will interact with when requesting websites. A proxy server sits in between clients and external servers, essentially pocketing the requests from the clients for server resources and making those requests itself. The client computers never touch the outside servers and thus stay protected from any unwanted activity. A proxy server usually *does something* to those requests as well [6]. This is a normal proxy with added features to help the general home user. Almost all proxies come with a logging capability and a way to track which user requested which websites. The proxy also has these capabilities, with the intent to create analytics out of recorded logs of user activity. Figure 3 shows the general flow of information for the proxy.

Figure 3. General flow of information for the proxy server

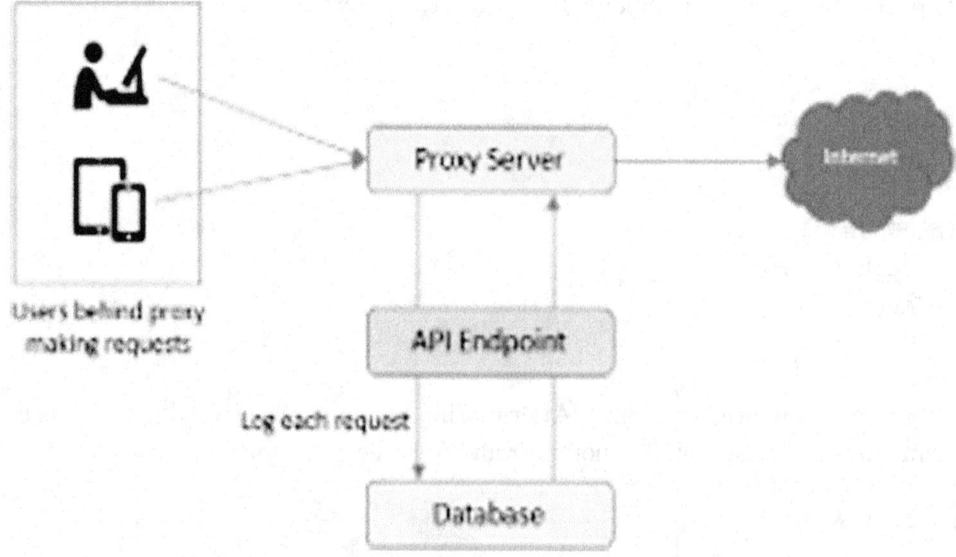

Along with the normal capabilities of a proxy, it will handle HTTP and HTTPS connections.

The user will have some initial setup and configuration settings to do. There will be a default configuration created upon the first run, which has the rules to help secure a home network for children and young teenagers. After the setup is completed the user will be able to use either the mobile application or website to further configure the proxy and enable rules they wish to use within their household.

The web server is integrated with a server-side API for mobile and remote web requests. Think of the World Wide Web (and of any other RESTful API) as a technology stack. URLs are on the bottom; they identify resources. The HTTP protocol sits on top of those resources, providing read access to their representations and write access to the underlying resource state. Hypermedia sits on top of HTTP, describing the protocol semantics of one particular website or API (Amundsen, Ruby, & Richardson, 2013). It is designed to present users informational pages, which are engineered to grasp the users' attention and provide meaningful content. This content is dynamic due to the constant change of information submitted by users. Figure 4 shows the general layout for the web server's architecture.

Figure 4. General layout for the web server's architecture

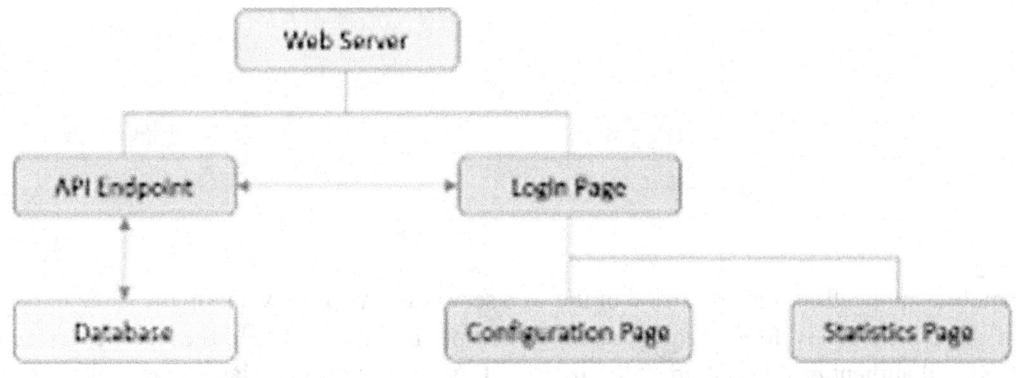

An initial login page will be provided before any user can configure the proxy settings. Once completed there will be an admirative account defined for a household. The server will display traffic traversing the proxy and analyzed by a heuristics engine. The web server will have direct access to a database server through an API. Database changes will be submitted through HTTP POSTs only. Any information requested will be through HTTP GET requests. The web server will provide charts regarding proxy usage. The charts are categorized by:

Websites visited
Access by hour of day
Access by day

Users will also be able to add, remove, or modify existing websites accessed. When machine learning is conducted on new websites and it has been determined as unknown or unable to categorize, the server will get a weighted sum of each category for users' viewing. A user can allow or deny suggested categories. These changes are taken into effect once updated. The API endpoint is an extension of the web server and will generate tokens to access user information. These tokens will be rotated out on a per-login basis. This endpoint is primarily used to provide information for any authenticated user browsing the website or on a mobile device.

Mobile applications are designed to provide the general population a way to view information while either at home or work. Some mobile applications are not elaborate by nature of the devices they are installed onto. Figure 5 is a basic layout and information flow.

Figure 5. General layout for the mobile architecture

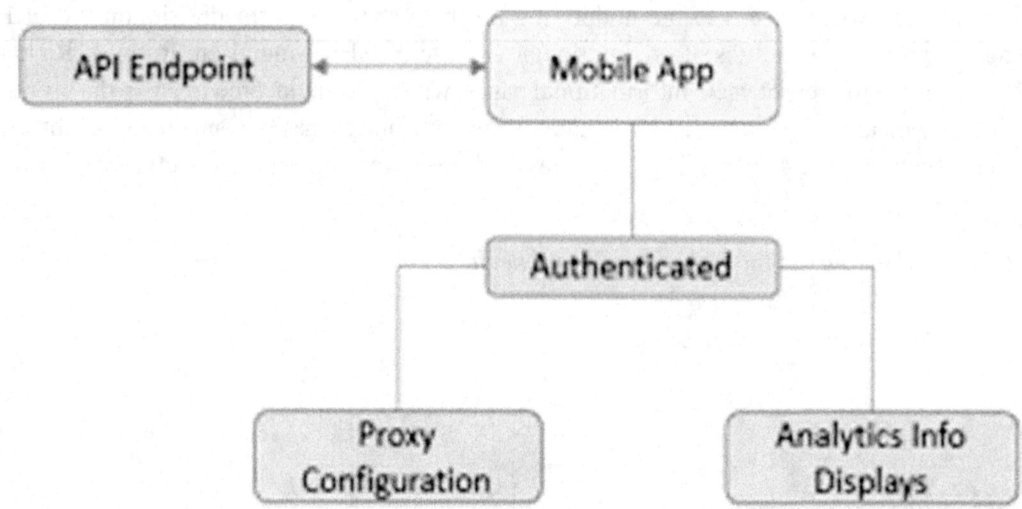

The mobile application is an extension of the web server as it will show nearly the same information. Some of these differences do not require as much computing power to help the mobile device render with speed. All authenticated users must log in using OAuth with google play services. The server will generate time-based tokens which are unique to each session. To reduce the amount of traffic delivered, the analytics will only show small amounts of data at any given time. Just like the web server, charts will be displayed to the mobile application. With the limiting processing capability charts will be tailored to show:

- Activity by hour of day
- Activity by day of week

The administration section of the mobile application has the same capability as the web server. The main account will be able to modify what configurations were setup initially from login. The ability to make changes wherever and whenever is provided by the mobile application. Tailoring the account to a specific user allows for each individual approved device to be monitored. Each device allowed will follow the rules from allowed, denied or suggested tables within the API database. Having the same API creates stability across the project and there will be a smaller room for error when programming.

The last component to enable the web server and mobile application is a backend database server. Database services are designed to hold large amounts of relational data sets. There are two types of databases to be utilized: Relational and Non-Relational. A relational database (RDB) is a collective set of multiple data sets organized by tables, records and columns. RDBs establish a well-defined relationship between database tables. Tables communicate and share information, which facilitates data searchability, organization and reporting. RDBs are Structured Query Language (SQL), which is a standard user application that provides an easy programming interface for database interaction (Techopedia). Non-Relational database provide information in a non-structured form for querying. Data-sets can be defined as a key, value pair. Figure 6 shows a general layout of the database services.

Figure 6. General layout for the database services

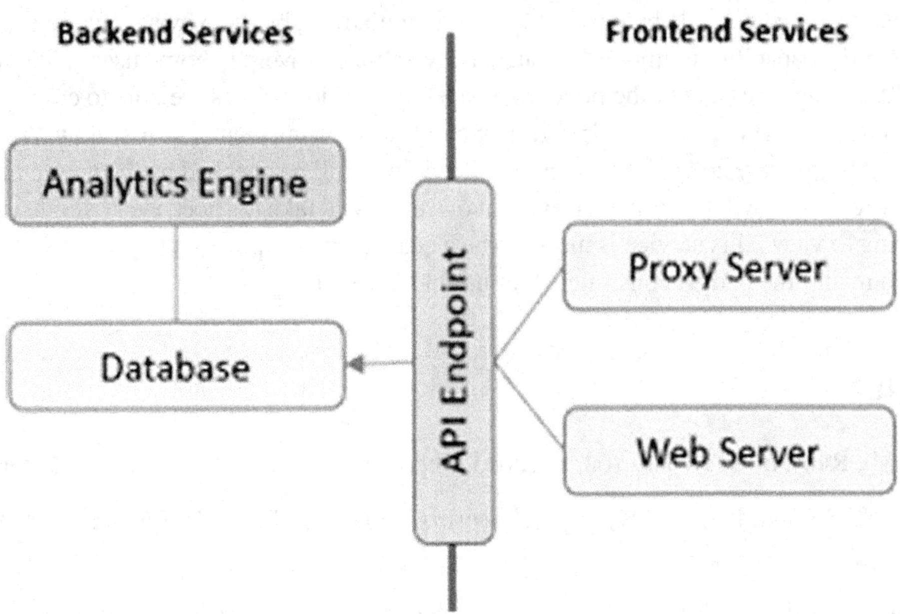

The database will be used to store and retrieve user specific data and supply an interface. This user specific data is tailored to help configuration settings are saved and queried when needed. There are also non-user specific tables and databases which are required for the machine learning synapses. This data and other backend services are required to save their configurations to a more secured portion of the database. Only database administrators can access these tables.

HARDWARE SPECIFICATIONS

Cost effectiveness is the model for consumers, a Raspberry Pi 3 "Pi3" has enough processing power to execute the proxy server as a multi-module software package. Typically, the model B uses between 700-1000mA depending on what peripherals are connected; the model A can use as little as 500mA with no peripherals attached. The maximum power the Raspberry Pi can use is 1Amp. If you need to connect a USB device that will take the power requirements above 1 Amp, then you must connect it to an externally powered USB hub (Power Supply, raspberrypi.org). The use of computers or mobile devices are available for each customer to utilize. This will allow to use the older versions of hardware. Updating the system to minimum requirements for desktop or laptop users might be needed to render or execute all aspects of the accessed services. Users are encouraged to upgrade systems as problems may arise. If minimum requirements are not met, then not all aspects of the server services might be function. Although a Pi3 might not be able to handle a large households worth of traffic, but it will handle a small amount until a larger device is discovered to handle the network throughput.

CONCLUSION

A proxy server powered not only by normal rules and regulations, but also by a machine learning neural network shows the capability to implement such a device for the average home user. With correct functionality built into each service of the proxy and back-end services, users are able to configure settings, save permissions, and provide a tailored profile for children or young teenagers to follow. With a machine learning aspect to this, any new or unknown website viewed will be checked by the neural network prior to allowing access. This will cut down the amount of time it will take to check every single website other users are trying to view. This service is meant to be a cost-effective approach to provide security for any household no matter the budget constraints that might be present.

REFERENCES

Amundsen, M., Ruby, S., & Richardson, L. (2013, September). *RESTful Web APIs*. Academic Press.

Anthony, M., & Bartlett, P. L. (2009). *Neural network learning: Theoretical foundations*. Cambridge, UK: Cambridge University Press.

Göranzon, B., & Florin, M. (Eds.). (2012). *Artifical Intelligence, Culture and Language: On Education and Work*. Springer Science & Business Media.

Hagan, M. T., Demuth, H. B., Beale, M. H., & De Jesús, O. (1996). *Neural network design* (Vol. 20). Boston: Pws Pub.

Haykin, S. (1994). *Neural networks* (Vol. 2). New York: Prentice Hall.

Kalchbrenner, N., Grefenstette, E., & Blunsom, P. (2014). *A convolutional neural network for modelling sentences*. Academic Press.

LaValle, S., Lesser, E., Shockley, R., Hopkins, M. S., & Kruschwitz, N. (2011). Big data, analytics and the path from insights to value. *MIT Sloan Management Review*, *52*(2), 21.

Luotonen, A., & Altis, K. (1994). World -wide web proxies. *Computer Networks and ISDN Systems*, *27*(2), 147–154. doi:10.1016/0169-7552(94)90128-7

Meyers, M., Weissman, J.S., & Meyers, M. (2018, July). *CompTIA Network+ Certification Passport* (6th ed.). Academic Press. (Exam N10-007)

Michie, D., Spiegelhalter, D. J., & Taylor, C. C. (1994). Machine learning. *Neural and Statistical Classification, 13.*

Neapolitan, R., & Jiang, X. (2012, August 4). Contemporary. *Artificial Intelligence.*

Pedregosa, F., Varoquaux, G., Gramfort, A., Michel, V., Thirion, B., Grisel, O., ... Vanderplas, J. (2011). Scikit-learn: Machine learning in Python. *Journal of Machine Learning Research, 12*(Oct), 2825–2830.

Power Supply. (n.d.). Retrieved from https://www.raspberrypi.org/documentation/hardware/raspberrypi/power/README.md

Psaltis, D., Sideris, A., & Yamamura, A. A. (1988). A multilayered neural network controller. *IEEE Control Systems Magazine*, *8*(2), 17–21. doi:10.1109/37.1868

Quinlan, J. R. (2014). C4. 5: programs for machine learning. Amsterdam: Elsevier.

Rouse, M. (2017). *Big Data Analytics – Definition "Whatis.com"*. Retrieved from http://searchbusinessanalytics.techtarget.com/definition/big-data-analytics

Sebastiani, F. (2002). Machine learning in automated text categorization. *ACM Computing Surveys, 34*(1), 1-47.

Techopedia. (n.d.). *What is a Relational Database (RDB)? Definition from Techopedia*. Retrieved from https://www.techopedia.com/definition/1234/relational-database-rdb

Weaver, N., Kreibich, C., Dam, M., & Paxson, V. (2014, March). Here be web proxies. In *International Conference on Passive and Active Network Measurement* (pp. 183-192). Cham, Switzerland: Springer. 10.1007/978-3-319-04918-2_18

Witten, I. H., Frank, E., Hall, M. A., & Pal, C. J. (2016). *Data Mining: Practical machine learning tools and techniques*. Burlington, MA: Morgan Kaufmann.

Zikopoulos, P. C., Eaton, C., DeRoos, D., Deutsch, T., & Lapis, G. (2012). *Understanding big data: Analytics for enterprise class hadoop and streaming data*. New York: Mcgraw-Hill.

This research was previously published in the International Journal of Cyber Research and Education (IJCRE), 1(2); pages 30-41, copyright year 2019 by IGI Publishing (an imprint of IGI Global).

Chapter 46

Machine Learning in Python:
Diabetes Prediction Using Machine Learning

Astha Baranwal
VIT University, India

Bhagyashree R. Bagwe
VIT University, India

Vanitha M
https://orcid.org/0000-0001-7726-2621
VIT University, India

ABSTRACT

Diabetes is a disease of the modern world. The modern lifestyle has led to unhealthy eating habits causing type 2 diabetes. Machine learning has gained a lot of popularity in the recent days. It has applications in various fields and has proven to be increasingly effective in the medical field. The purpose of this chapter is to predict the diabetes outcome of a person based on other factors or attributes. Various machine learning algorithms like logistic regression (LR), tuned and not tuned random forest (RF), and multilayer perceptron (MLP) have been used as classifiers for diabetes prediction. This chapter also presents a comparative study of these algorithms based on various performance metrics like accuracy, sensitivity, specificity, and F1 score.

INTRODUCTION

Diabetes is a disease which happens when the glucose level of the blood becomes high, which eventually leads to other health problems such as heart diseases, kidney disease etc. Several data mining projects have used algorithms to predict diabetes in a patient. Though, in most of these projects, nothing is mentioned about the dangers of diabetes in women post-pregnancies. While data mining has been successfully applied to various fields in human society, such as weather prognosis, market analysis, engineering

DOI: 10.4018/978-1-6684-6291-1.ch046

diagnosis, and customer relationship management, the application in disease prediction and medical data analysis still has room for improvement in accuracy.

Machine learning relates closely to Artificial Intelligence (AI) and makes software applications predict outcomes through statistical analysis. The algorithms used allow for reaching an optimal accuracy rate in predicting the output from the input data. Machine learning follows similar processes used in data mining and predictive modeling. They recognize patterns through the data entered and then adjust the actions of the program accordingly.

Machine learning algorithms are categorized as supervised learning and unsupervised learning. Supervised learning requires input data and the desired output data to build a training model. The training model is built by a data analyst or a data scientist. A feedback is then furnished concerning the accuracy of the model and other performance metrics during algorithm training. Revising is done as needed. Once the training phase is completed, the model can predict outcomes for new data. Classification is one of the many data mining tasks. Classification comes under supervised learning which implies that the machine learns through examples in Classification. In classification, every instance from the dataset is classified into a target value. Classification can either be binary or multi-label. Sometimes, one particular instance can also have multiple classes known as multi-class classification. Classification algorithms are majorly used for prediction and come under the category of predictive learning.

Unsupervised learning is used to draw inferences from the input data which do not have any labeled responses. This data is not categorized, labeled or classified into classes. Clustering analysis, one of the most common unsupervised learning method, is used to find hidden patterns in data or to form groups based on the input data.

While machine learning models have been around for decades, they have gained a new momentum with the rise of AI. Deep learning models are now used in most of the advanced AI applications. If these models are implemented for medical uses, they could be revolutionary for the society. Diagnosis of diseases like diabetes would be easier than ever. Machine learning in medical diagnosis applications fall under three classes: Pathology, Oncology and Chatbots. Pathology deals with the diagnosis of diseases with the help of machine learning models created with the data of diagnostic measurements of the patients. Oncology uses deep learning models to determine cancerous tissues in patients. Chatbots designed using AI and machine learning techniques can identify patterns in the symptoms of the patients and suggest a potential diagnosis or it can recommend further courses of action. This chapter falls under the pathological uses of machine learning as the model created will give diagnosis of whether a patient is diabetic or not.

This chapter focuses on implementing machine learning algorithms on the diabetes dataset in python. Python is a great language to support machine learning. It was created by Guido van Rossom. It is powerful, multipurpose, and simple and has an easy to use syntax. The length of a python code is generally relatively short. It is not overly strict. It is a fun language to work with because it lets us focus on the problem rather than the syntax. Python is a general purpose language with applications in a wide range of fields like web development, mathematical computing, graphical user interfaces, etc. These wide range of applications python most suitable for implementing machine learning algorithms. It is possible to implement some machine learning algorithms in python and later deploy the web service for it. Or it is also possible to create a graphical user interface for the deployed web service. This all becomes possible due to the diverse nature of the language. Various python libraries like, NumPy, SciPy, Matplotlib, Keras, Pandas, TensorFlow, and etc support machine learning in python. Scikit-learn library supports almost all the major machine learning classification, clustering and regression models. The Flask python web framework is used to create web apps from APIs created using the machine learning models. This web app can perform real-time predictions for individual and batch data inputs.

Background

About one in every seven U.S. adult citizen has diabetes currently, as per the Centers for Disease Control and Prevention. According to statistics, this rate could skyrocket to as many as one in three by the year 2050. Hence, it is of utmost importance that a proper diabetes prediction system should be built with high prediction accuracy. Several prior studies have proposed various models for the prediction of diabetes on the PIMA Indian Dataset. Accuracy up to 95.42% (proposed by Han Wu et al. 2018) has been obtained by first clustering the data using K-Means algorithm and removing the outliers and then creating the classification models. Patil et al. (2010) proposed a similar model with C4.5 algorithm as the final classifier model. They obtained an accuracy of 92.38%. Kandhasamy et al. (2015) applied machine learning classification techniques like Decision Tree J48, KNN Classifier, Random Forest and Support Vector Machine and obtained 86.46% accuracy. The paper proposed by the Sisodias (2018) applied three classification algorithms: Decision Tree, SVM and Naive Bayes and reported highest accuracy (76.30%) with the Naïve Bayes model.

Linear Discriminant Analysis (LDA) and Adaptive Network Based Fuzzy Inference System (ANFIS): LDA-ANFIS was proposed by Dogantekin et al. (2010) with an accuracy of 84.61%. R. Aishwarya et al. (2013) used Support Vector Machine to build the classification model. Temurtas et al. (2009) used a multilayer neural network structure which was trained by Levenberg–Marquardt (LM) algorithm. The accuracy stated was 82.37%.

Fatima and Pasha (2017) provided a comparative analysis of various machine learning algorithms and techniques for the diagnosis of serious diseases such as diabetes, heart diseases, liver diseases, dengue and hepatitis diseases. K Saravananathan and Velmurugan (2016) in the paper Analyzing Diabetic Data using Classification Algorithms in Data Mining use J48, support vector machine (SVM), classification and regression tree (CART) and K-Nearest Neighbor (KNN) to categorize the dataset that included 10 attributes from 545 patients in Weka. Kavakiotis et al. (2017) discovered that 85% of papers used supervised learning approaches and 15% by unsupervised ones, association rules, more specifically. Support vector machines (SVM) was stated as the most successful and popularly used algorithm. M. P. Gopinath and Murali (2017) provided a comparative study between various classification algorithms, namely Naive Bayes (NB), Support Vector Machine (SVM), Decision Tree (DT), Bayes net, etc, in their paper. Yasodha and Kannan (2011) used WEKA tool to classify the dataset and the 10-fold cross validation is used for evaluation and the results are compared. D. Nanthini and Thangaraju (2015) in their paper propose a method for building a hybrid on the diabetes dataset using three variations of the classification algorithm Decision Tree namely, C4.5, J48 and the FB tree.

Many other papers have reported a classification accuracy ranging from 50% to 80% on the PIMA Indians Diabetes dataset using various machine learning techniques. Research is underway for better accuracy rates using different advanced machine learning and deep learning algorithms and techniques.

MAIN FOCUS OF THE CHAPTER

Issues, Controversies, Problems

Medical diagnosis of Diabetes is possible only after the patient has acquired the disease and not before. This completely cuts down the possibility of prevention of the disease. This is an issue of the medical field. This problem can be sorted by aiding the medical field with the Information Technology sector.

Machine Learning algorithms are used in this chapter to predict if a person will have diabetes or not. This prediction is done based on some other lifestyle attributes of the person. The machine learning task used here is classification. Classification comes under supervised learning. Supervised learning is when the machine learns based on examples, like a human being, using the training dataset. In supervised leaning it is required that the data has a class label or a target value as an independent variable into which the instances will be classified. With respect to the PIMA diabetes dataset, the target variable is the outcome value which predicts whether the person will have diabetes or not. It is for this variable that the classification is carried out. If it is somehow possible to predict in advance if the person is going to contract diabetes or not, some preventive measures can be taken in order to avoid contraction of diabetes.

Thus, in this way, the use of machine learning in the medical field can help solve some critical issues and aid medical science in more ways than expected.

Section-Wise Description

1. **Platform Details:** This section provides a description about the platform used.
   a. Anaconda.
   b. Jupyter
   c. Python
   d. NumPy
   e. Pandas
   f. SciPy
   g. Matplotlib
   h. TensorFlow and Keras
2. **System Architecture:** This section briefly explains how the system works and how it is built using a flowchart and a textual description.
3. **Dataset Description:** This section gives a description about the selected PIMA diabetes dataset. It gives information about the datatype of the attributes along with their explanation.
4. **Data Cleaning:** This section shows how the data was preprocessed and cleaned using Weka. This included various processes like finding missing values and replacing them with suitable values.
5. **Data Visualization:** In this section the data was visualized using the Python Jupyter platform. Data visualization helps us in getting a better understanding of the data.
6. **Random Forest Model (Not Tuned):** This section explains how the basic random forest model is built on the PIMA diabetes dataset using machine learning in python. It also shows the results produced by this classifier.
7. **Random Forest Model (Tuned):** This section explains how the tuned random forest model is built on the PIMA diabetes dataset using machine learning in python. It also shows the results produced by this classifier.

8. **Checking with different Hyper parameter tuning:** This sections tests for random values of the three selected parameters namely, n_tree, max_features and max_depth for hyper parameter tuning.
9. **Logistic Regression (LR):** This section explains Logistic Regression classifier model is built on the PIMA diabetes datasetusing machine learning in python. It also shows the results produced by this classifier.
10. **Multilayer Perceptron:** This section explains how the multilayer perceptron (MLP), a type of Artificial Neural Network (ANN) is built on the PIMA diabetes dataset using machine learning in python. It also shows the results produced by this classifier.
11. **Performance Metrics**: This section gives a detailed information about the various performance metrics used for evaluating and comparing the various classifier models built on the PIMA diabetes dataset.
12. **Comparison between the models using various performance metrics**: This section provides a tabular comparison between the various classifier models built for predicting the outcome on the PIMA diabetes dataset.

SOLUTIONS AND RECOMMENDATIONS

Platform Details

Anaconda

Anaconda is a professional data science platform which we can use as a GUI as well as a console. Anaconda is a Python distribution which brings a lot of useful libraries with it, which are not included in Python standard library like Jupyter, NumPy, Pandas, SciPy, Matplotlib, etc. It can create different Python version environments.

Jupyter

The Jupyter Notebook is an open-source web app that allows the creation and sharing of documents that contain equations, live code, visualizations and narrative text in form of markdowns. It is included in the Anaconda distribution.

WEKA (Waikato Environment for Knowledge Analysis)

Weka is a software that is built in Java and can run on almost every platform. Weka gives provisions for various machine learning algorithms and can be used for data cleaning and data visualization.

Python

Python is a widely used high-level programming language which is interpreted, general-purpose, and dynamic.

The Python libraries used for data analysis, visualization and machine learning are:

NumPy

NumPy is a Python library that adds support for large and multi-dimensional arrays. It supports matrices.

Pandas

Pandas is a Python package designed to make the work with labeled and relational data be very simple and intuitive. It is designed for fast and easy data manipulation, visualization and aggregation.

SciPy

SciPy contains modules for statistics, linear algebra, optimization and integration. The principal functionality of SciPy library is based upon NumPy, and hence its arrays make considerable use of NumPy.

Matplotlib

Matplotlib is a Python library for 2D plotting which produces quality figures in a variety of hardcopy formats and interactive environments across platforms.

Tensorflow and Keras

Tensorflow is a Python Deep Learning library.

Keras is a simple neural networks library designed for high-level neural networks. It is written in Python and works as a wrapper to Tensorflow.

System Architecture

This chapter uses the PIMA Indians Diabetes Dataset for diabetes prediction by various machine learning models. The dataset is first explored. Data visualization helps to understand the data significance by identifying any useful patterns or abnormalities that are revealed in the data points of the dataset. Data visualization is done and correlation between each and every attribute is examined. The values of attributes are represented by binning for all the instances. The target variable 'Outcome' contains positive (1) and negative (0) values. The count of positive and negative instances can be identified.

The data cleaning involves removal of zero and missing (null) values from the dataset. This is done using the Weka Explorer software. Next, feature engineering is done. Feature engineering involves determination of useful attributes. The attributes which do not contribute much in predicting the outcome accurately are discarded. No attribute is discarded in making the models in this chapter. SkinThickness contributes the least in prediction of diabetes for the dataset but it is considered nonetheless. Logistic Regression (LR), Random Forest (RF) and Multilayer Perceptron (MLP) are selected for model building because they all are powerful machine learning algorithms which can be further hyper parameter tuned to obtain optimal accuracy. Multilayer perceptron classifier is a type of Artificial Neural Network (ANN). Confusion matrix and classification report for each model is generated. The results of the models are then compared based on various performance metrics.

Figure 1. The system architecture

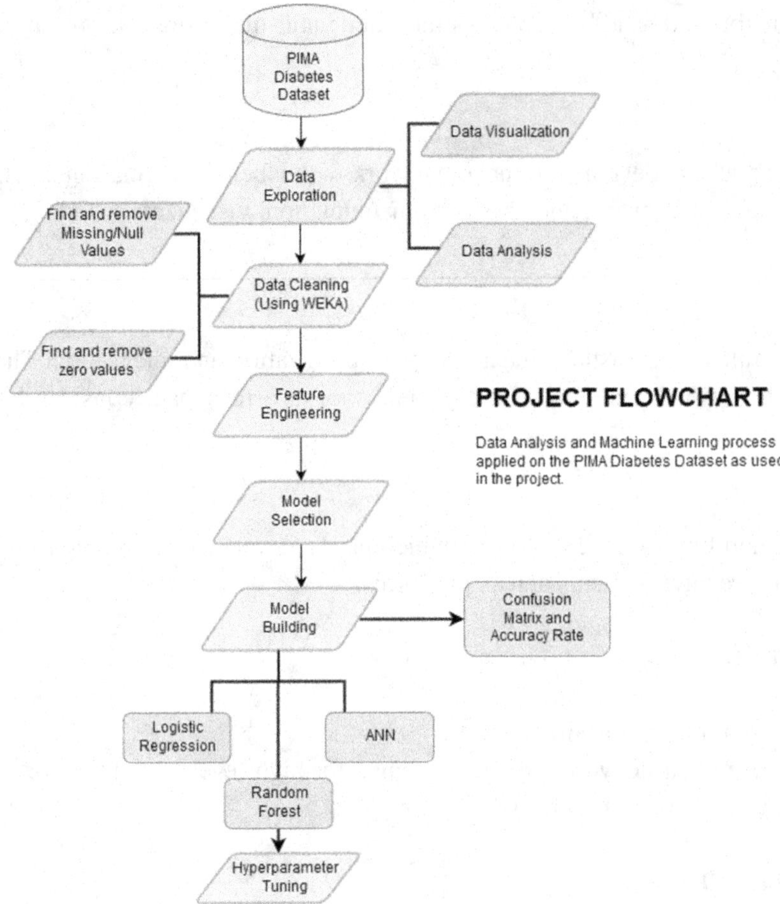

Dataset Description

The dataset used is originally contributed by the National Institute of Diabetes and Digestive and Kidney Diseases. It has 768 instances and 9 attributes. The goal is to predict whether a patient has diabetes based on diagnostic measurements. The datasets consist of several medical predictor (independent) variables and one target (dependent) variable, Outcome.

Several constraints were placed on the selection of these instances from a larger database. In particular, all patients here are females at least 21 years old of Pima Indian heritage.

Data Cleaning

The missing values and the null values are cleaned:

- There are instances with BloodPressure as 0. Blood pressure of a living person can never be 0.
- Plasma glucose levels, even after fasting, can never be 0.

- Skin Fold Thickness cannot be 0.
- BMI of a person can never be 0 as it is weight/height^2
- Insulin is never 0 in normal cases and there are about 374 instances with 0 insulin.

They are replaced by means of the values of the concerned attributes. The cleaned dataset has 768 instances and 9 attributes.

Table 1. Attribute description for the diabetes dataset

Sr. No.	Attribute	Description	Datatype
1	Pregnancies	Number of times pregnant	int64
2	Glucose	Plasma glucose concentration	int64
3	BloodPressure	Diastolic blood pressure (mm Hg)	int64
4	SkinThickness	Triceps skin fold thickness (mm)	int64
5	Insulin	2-Hour serum insulin (mu U/ml)	int64
6	BMI	Body mass index (weight in kg/(height in m)^2)	float64
7	DiabetesPedigreeFunction	Diabetes pedigree function	float64
8	Age	Age of patient (in years)	int64
9	Outcome	Class variable. 1 for diabetic and 0 for non-diabetic.	int64

Data Cleaning of the "Pima Indian Diabetes Dataset" by WEKA Explorer

Mark Missing Values

Attributes such as BloodPressure and BMI (Body Mass Index) have values of zero, which is impossible. These examples of corrupt or missing data must be marked manually. Since zero values are not considered as missing values by Weka, this needs to be fixed first.

Weka marks zero values as missing values by the NumericalCleaner filter. The steps below show how to use this filter to mark the missing values on the Pregnancies,BloodPressure, Glucose, SkinThickness, BMI and Insulin attributes:

The Pima Indians diabetes dataset is loaded in the Weka Explorer.

NumericalCleaner filter is selected. It is under unsupervized.attribute.NumericalCleaner. This filter is further configured.

TheattributeIndicies is set to 1-6. This is the indices of the attributes with 0 values. The minThreshold is set to 0.1E-8 (close to zero), which is the minimum value allowed for the attribute. The minDefault is set to NaN, which is unknown and will replace values below the threshold.

The filter configuration is applied on the dataset. The transformation for the BloodPressure attribute is shown for each step.

Notice that the attribute values that were formally set to zero are now marked as Missing.

Figure 2. The initial dataset

Relation: pima_diabetes

No.	1: Pregnancies Numeric	2: Glucose Numeric	3: BloodPressure Numeric	4: SkinThickness Numeric	5: Insulin Numeric	6: BMI Numeric	7: DiabetesPedigreeFunction Numeric	8: Age Numeric	9: Outcome Numeric
1	6.0	148.0	72.0	35.0	0.0	33.6	0.627	50.0	1.0
2	1.0	85.0	66.0	29.0	0.0	26.6	0.351	31.0	0.0
3	8.0	183.0	64.0	0.0	0.0	23.3	0.672	32.0	1.0
4	1.0	89.0	66.0	23.0	94.0	28.1	0.167	21.0	0.0
5	0.0	137.0	40.0	35.0	168.0	43.1	2.288	33.0	1.0
6	5.0	116.0	74.0	0.0	0.0	25.6	0.201	30.0	0.0
7	3.0	78.0	50.0	32.0	88.0	31.0	0.248	26.0	1.0
8	10.0	115.0	0.0	0.0	0.0	35.3	0.134	29.0	0.0
9	2.0	197.0	70.0	45.0	543.0	30.5	0.158	53.0	1.0
10	8.0	125.0	96.0	0.0	0.0	0.0	0.232	54.0	1.0
11	4.0	110.0	92.0	0.0	0.0	37.6	0.191	30.0	0.0
12	10.0	168.0	74.0	0.0	0.0	38.0	0.537	34.0	1.0
13	10.0	139.0	80.0	0.0	0.0	27.1	1.441	57.0	0.0
14	1.0	189.0	60.0	23.0	846.0	30.1	0.398	59.0	1.0
15	5.0	166.0	72.0	19.0	175.0	25.8	0.587	51.0	1.0
16	7.0	100.0	0.0	0.0	0.0	30.0	0.484	32.0	1.0
17	0.0	118.0	84.0	47.0	230.0	45.8	0.551	31.0	1.0
18	7.0	107.0	74.0	0.0	0.0	29.6	0.254	31.0	1.0
19	1.0	103.0	30.0	38.0	83.0	43.3	0.183	33.0	0.0
20	1.0	115.0	70.0	30.0	96.0	34.6	0.529	32.0	1.0
21	3.0	126.0	88.0	41.0	235.0	39.3	0.704	27.0	0.0
22	8.0	99.0	84.0	0.0	0.0	35.4	0.388	50.0	0.0
23	7.0	196.0	90.0	0.0	0.0	39.8	0.451	41.0	1.0
24	9.0	119.0	80.0	35.0	0.0	29.0	0.263	29.0	1.0
25	11.0	143.0	94.0	33.0	146.0	36.6	0.254	51.0	1.0
26	10.0	125.0	70.0	26.0	115.0	31.1	0.205	41.0	1.0
27	7.0	147.0	76.0	0.0	0.0	39.4	0.257	43.0	1.0
28	1.0	97.0	66.0	15.0	140.0	23.2	0.487	22.0	0.0
29	13.0	145.0	82.0	19.0	110.0	22.2	0.245	57.0	0.0
30	5.0	117.0	92.0	0.0	0.0	34.1	0.337	38.0	0.0
31	5.0	109.0	75.0	26.0	0.0	36.0	0.546	60.0	0.0
32	3.0	158.0	76.0	36.0	245.0	31.6	0.851	28.0	1.0
33	3.0	88.0	58.0	11.0	54.0	24.8	0.267	22.0	0.0
34	6.0	92.0	92.0	0.0	0.0	19.9	0.188	28.0	0.0
35	10.0	122.0	78.0	31.0	0.0	27.6	0.512	45.0	0.0
36	4.0	103.0	60.0	33.0	192.0	24.0	0.966	33.0	0.0
37	11.0	138.0	76.0	0.0	0.0	33.2	0.42	35.0	0.0
38	9.0	102.0	76.0	37.0	0.0	32.9	0.665	46.0	1.0

Figure 3. The BloodPresuure attribute before data cleaning

Name: BloodPressure   Type: Numeric
Missing: 0 (0%)   Distinct: 47   Unique: 8 (1%)

Statistic	Value
Minimum	0
Maximum	122
Mean	69.105
StdDev	19.356

Remove Missing Data

Now that missing values are marked in the data, they need to be handled. An easy way to deal with missing data in the dataset is to remove those data points that have one or more missing values.

This can be done in Weka using the RemoveWithValues filter.

However, this leads to loss in some data instances. It is advisable to impute the missing values instead of removing these instances altogether from the dataset.

Figure 4. Configuring the NumericalCleaner filter

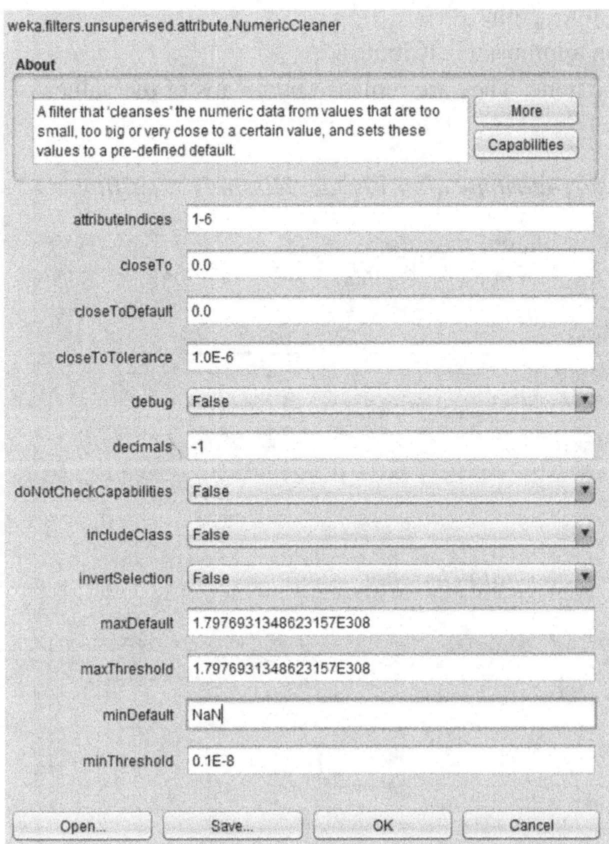

Figure 5. The BloodPressure attribute after applying NumericalCleaner

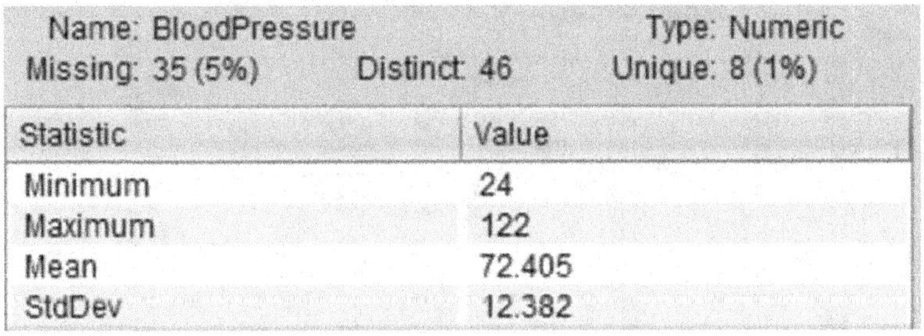

Name: BloodPressure Type: Numeric
Missing: 35 (5%) Distinct: 46 Unique: 8 (1%)

Statistic	Value
Minimum	24
Maximum	122
Mean	72.405
StdDev	12.382

Impute Missing Values

It is not necessary to remove the instances with missing values; the missing values can be replaced instead with some other value.

This is called imputing missing values.

It is not uncommon to impute missing values with the mean of the numerical distribution of an attribute. This can be done easily in Weka using the ReplaceMissingValues filter.

Missing values can be imputed by theReplaceMissingValues filter. It is under the unsupervized.attribute.ReplaceMissingValues path.

The filter is applied on appropriate attributes.

The missing values are gone. They are replaced by means of the values of concerned attributes.

Figure 6. The BloodPressure attribute after ReplaceMissingValues filter

Name: BloodPressure Type: Numeric
Missing: 0 (0%) Distinct: 47 Unique: 8 (1%)

Statistic	Value
Minimum	24
Maximum	122
Mean	72.405
StdDev	12.096

Figure 7. The final dataset after data cleaning

Relation: pima_diabetes-weka.filters.unsupervised.attribute.NumericCleaner-min1.0E-8-min-defaultNaN-max1.7976931348623157E308-r

No.	1: Pregnancies Numeric	2: Glucose Numeric	3: BloodPressure Numeric	4: SkinThickness Numeric	5: Insulin Numeric	6: BMI Numeric	7: DiabetesPedigreeFunction Numeric	8: Age Numeric	9: Outcome Numeric
1	6.0	148.0	72.0	35.0	155.5...	33.6	0.627	50.0	1.0
2	1.0	85.0	66.0	29.0	155.5...	26.6	0.351	31.0	0.0
3	8.0	183.0	64.0	29.153419593...	155.5...	23.3	0.672	32.0	1.0
4	1.0	89.0	66.0	23.0	94.0	28.1	0.167	21.0	0.0
5	4.49467275...	137.0	40.0	35.0	168.0	43.1	2.288	33.0	1.0
6	5.0	116.0	74.0	29.153419593...	155.5...	25.6	0.201	30.0	0.0
7	3.0	78.0	50.0	32.0	88.0	31.0	0.248	26.0	1.0
8	10.0	115.0	72.405184174...	29.153419593...	155.5...	35.3	0.134	29.0	0.0
9	2.0	197.0	70.0	45.0	543.0	30.5	0.158	53.0	1.0
10	8.0	125.0	96.0	29.153419593...	155.5...	32.4...	0.232	54.0	1.0
11	4.0	110.0	92.0	29.153419593...	155.5...	37.6	0.191	30.0	0.0
12	10.0	168.0	74.0	29.153419593...	155.5...	38.0	0.537	34.0	1.0
13	10.0	139.0	80.0	29.153419593...	155.5...	27.1	1.441	57.0	0.0
14	1.0	189.0	60.0	23.0	846.0	30.1	0.398	59.0	1.0
15	5.0	166.0	72.0	19.0	175.0	25.8	0.587	51.0	1.0
16	7.0	100.0	72.405184174...	29.153419593...	155.5...	30.0	0.484	32.0	1.0
17	4.49467275...	118.0	84.0	47.0	230.0	45.8	0.551	31.0	1.0
18	7.0	107.0	74.0	29.153419593...	155.5...	29.6	0.254	31.0	1.0
19	1.0	103.0	30.0	38.0	83.0	43.3	0.183	33.0	0.0
20	1.0	115.0	70.0	30.0	96.0	34.6	0.529	32.0	1.0
21	3.0	126.0	88.0	41.0	235.0	39.3	0.704	27.0	0.0
22	8.0	99.0	84.0	29.153419593...	155.5...	35.4	0.388	50.0	0.0
23	7.0	196.0	90.0	29.153419593...	155.5...	39.8	0.451	41.0	1.0
24	9.0	119.0	80.0	35.0	155.5...	29.0	0.263	29.0	1.0
25	11.0	143.0	94.0	33.0	146.0	36.6	0.254	51.0	1.0
26	10.0	125.0	70.0	26.0	115.0	31.1	0.205	41.0	1.0
27	7.0	147.0	76.0	29.153419593...	155.5...	39.4	0.257	43.0	1.0
28	1.0	97.0	66.0	15.0	140.0	23.2	0.487	22.0	0.0
29	13.0	145.0	82.0	19.0	110.0	22.2	0.245	57.0	0.0
30	5.0	117.0	92.0	29.153419593...	155.5...	34.1	0.337	38.0	0.0
31	5.0	109.0	75.0	26.0	155.5...	36.0	0.546	60.0	0.0
32	3.0	158.0	76.0	36.0	245.0	31.6	0.851	28.0	1.0
33	3.0	88.0	58.0	11.0	54.0	24.8	0.267	22.0	0.0
34	6.0	92.0	92.0	29.153419593...	155.5...	19.9	0.188	28.0	0.0
35	10.0	122.0	78.0	31.0	155.5...	27.6	0.512	45.0	0.0
36	4.0	103.0	60.0	33.0	192.0	24.0	0.966	33.0	0.0
37	11.0	138.0	76.0	29.153419593...	155.5...	33.2	0.42	35.0	0.0
38	9.0	102.0	76.0	37.0	155.5	32.9	0.665	46.0	1.0

Data Visualization

Importing the libraries and the dataset:

```
import numpy as np
import pandas as pd
import matplotlib.pyplot as plt
%matplotlib inline
import seaborn as sns
diabetes = pd.read_csv('pima_diabetes.csv')
```

Visualize the distribution of positive and negative instances for the Outcome attribute in the diabetes dataset:

```
diabetes.groupby('Outcome').size()
sns.countplot(diabetes['Outcome'],label="Count")
```

Figure 8. Positive and negative instances for the Outcome attribute in the diabetes dataset

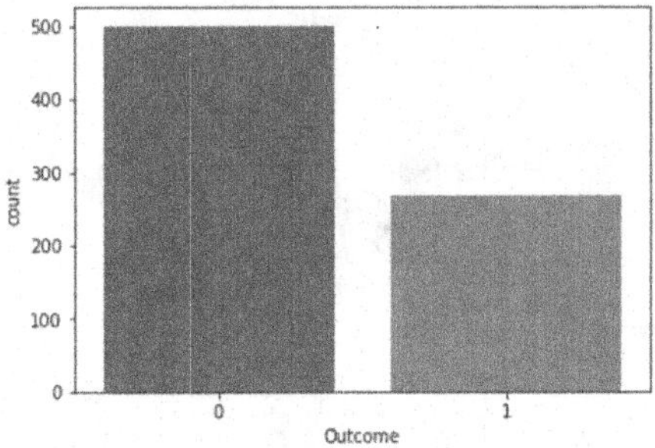

It can be identified that out of the 768 persons, 500 are labeled as 0 (Non-Diabetic) and 268 as 1 (Diabetic)

```
def plot_corr(df, size=11):
corr = df.corr()
    fig, ax = plt.subplots(figsize=(size, size))
ax.matshow(corr)
plt.xticks(range(len(corr.columns)), corr.columns)
plt.yticks(range(len(corr.columns)), corr.columns)
plot_corr(diabetes)
```

In the above visualization plot, lighter color represents maximum correlation and darker color represents minimum correlation. We can see none of the variable have proper correlation with any of the other variables.

Binning of the instances in dataset as per attributes:

```
diabetes.hist(figsize=(12,8),bins=20)
```

Figure 9. The correlation between various attributes of the diabetes dataset

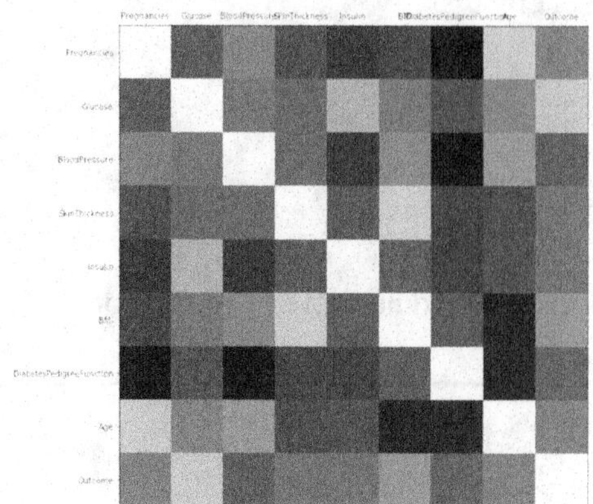

Figure 10. The values of attributes in the diabetes dataset represented by binning

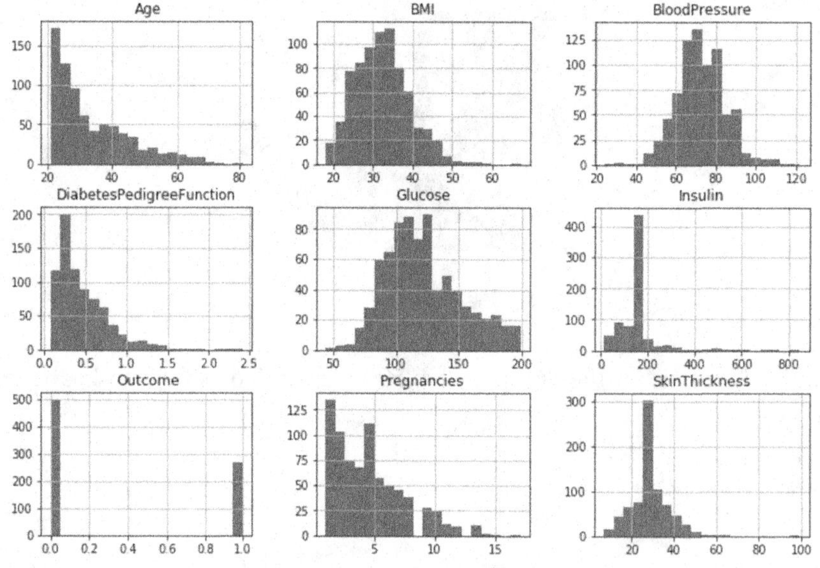

Model Selection: Comparison of Calibration of Classifiers

Model selection is the phase where the model with the best calibration and reliability estimate for the data set at hand is selected.

The "Classification Accuracy (Testing Accuracy)" of a given set of classification models is calculated with their default parameters to predict which model can perform better with the PIMA diabetes data set.

Seven classifiers namely K-Nearest Neighbors, Support Vector Classifier, Logistic Regression, Decision Tree, Gaussian Naive Bayes and Random Forest and Multilayer Perceptron are to be the contenders for the best classifier.

```
models = []

models.append(('KNN', KNeighborsClassifier()))
models.append(('SVC', SVC()))
models.append(('LR', LogisticRegression()))
models.append(('DT', DecisionTreeClassifier()))
models.append(('GNB', GaussianNB()))
models.append(('RF', RandomForestClassifier()))
models.append(('ANN', MLPClassifier()))

from sklearn.model_selection import train_test_split
from sklearn.metrics import accuracy_score
X_train, X_test, y_train, y_test = train_test_split(X, y, stratify = diabetes.
Outcome, random_state=0)

names = []
scores = []

for name, model in models:
model.fit(X_train, y_train)
y_pred = model.predict(X_test) #prediction of models
scores.append(accuracy_score(y_test, y_pred))
names.append(name)

tr_split = pd.DataFrame({'Name': names, 'Score': scores})
print(tr_split)

axis = sns.barplot(x = 'Name', y = 'Score', data = tr_split)
axis.set(xlabel='Classifier', ylabel='Predicted Accuracy')

for p in axis.patches:
    height = p.get_height()
axis.text(p.get_x() + p.get_width()/2, height + 0.005, '{:1.4f}'.
format(height), ha="center")

plt.show()
```

Logistic Regression is the best contender based on the plot obtained. Random forest gives a decent performance. ANN or the Multilayer Perceptron (MLP) classifier can use standard scalar to increase the accuracy.

Figure 11. Predicted Accuracy vs contender Classifiers

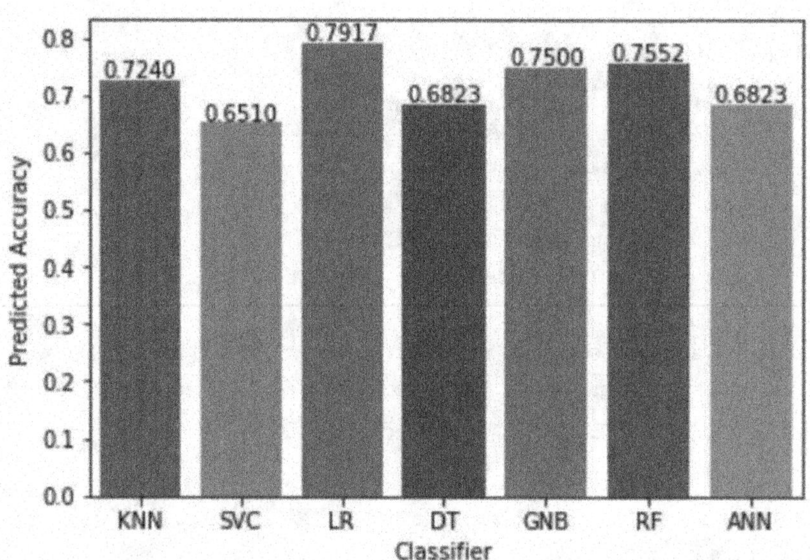

Random Forest Model (Not Tuned)

```
from sklearn import model_selection

# random forest model creation
rfc = RandomForestClassifier()
rfc.fit(X_train,y_train)

# predictions
rfc_predict = rfc.predict(X_test)

from sklearn.model_selection import cross_val_score
from sklearn.metrics import classification_report, confusion_matrix
rfc_cv_score = cross_val_score(rfc, X, y, cv=10, scoring='roc_auc')

print("Model Accuracy: {0:.4f}".format(metrics.accuracy_score(y_test, rfc_pre-
dict)))

print("Confusion Matrix")
print(confusion_matrix(y_test, rfc_predict))
print('\n')

print("Classification Report")
print(classification_report(y_test, rfc_predict))
print('\n')
```

Figure 12. Classification report for the Random Forest (not tuned) model

```
Model Accuracy: 0.7559
Confusion Matrix
[[146  30]
 [ 32  46]]

Classification Report
             precision    recall  f1-score   support

          0       0.82      0.83      0.82       176
          1       0.61      0.59      0.60        78

avg / total       0.75      0.76      0.76       254
```

Random Forest Model (Tuned): Hyper Parameter Tuning the Random Forest Model

```
from sklearn.model_selection import RandomizedSearchCV

# number of trees in random forest
n_estimators = [int(x) for x in np.linspace(start = 200, stop = 2000, num =
10)]

# number of features at every split
max_features = ['auto', 'sqrt']

# max depth
max_depth = [int(x) for x in np.linspace(100, 500, num = 11)]
max_depth.append(None)

# create random grid
random_grid = {
 'n_estimators': n_estimators,
 'max_features': max_features,
 'max_depth': max_depth
 }

# Random search of parameters
rfc_random = RandomizedSearchCV(estimator = rfc, param_distributions = random_
grid, n_iter = 100, cv = 3, verbose=2, random_state=42, n_jobs = -1)

# Fit the model
rfc_random.fit(X_train, y_train.ravel())

# print results
print(rfc_random.best_params_)
```

The results are: 'n_estimators' = 1200; 'max_features' = 'auto'; 'max_depth': 180. Now these parameters can be plugged back into the model to see whether it improved the performance.

Figure 13. Classification report for the random forest (tuned) model

```
Confusion Matrix
[[147  29]
 [ 30  48]]


Classification Report
             precision    recall  f1-score   support

          0       0.83      0.84      0.83       176
          1       0.62      0.62      0.62        78

avg / total       0.77      0.77      0.77       254
```

Checking With Different Hyper Parameter Tuning

```
import numpy
from matplotlib import pyplot
x = numpy.array([400,600,800,1000,1200,1400])
y = numpy.array([0.8299330484330485, 0.829940170940171, 0.8296937321937321,
0.8276780626780628, 0.8307606837606837, 0.8289601139601139])

fig = pyplot.figure()
ax = fig.add_subplot(111)
ax.set_ylim(0.80,0.85)
pyplot.plot(x,y)
pyplot.show()
```

Figure 14. Area Under the Curve (AUC) score versus the number of trees (n_tree) in the Random Forest

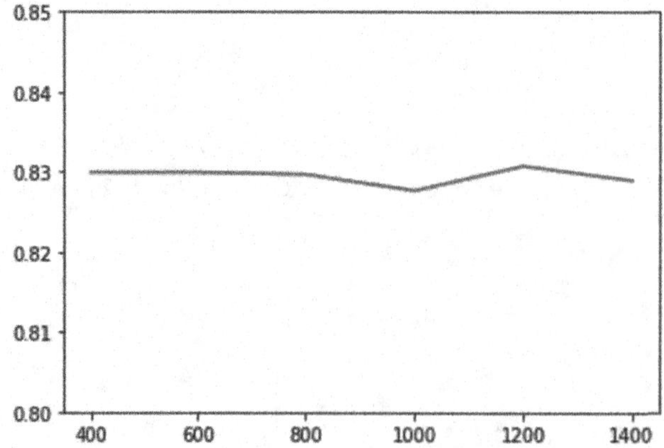

Clearly, at n_tree = 1200; max_features = 'auto'; max_depth: 180, the AUC score is highest and this, hence, will give the highest accuracy rate

Logistic Regression

```
from sklearn.linear_model import LogisticRegression

diab_lr_model = LogisticRegression(C=0.7, random_state=52)
diab_lr_model.fit(X_train, y_train.ravel())
lr_test_predict = diab_lr_model.predict(X_test)

print("Model Accuracy: {0:.2f}".format(metrics.accuracy_score(y_test, lr_test_
predict)))
print("")
print("Confusion Matrix")
print(metrics.confusion_matrix(y_test, lr_test_predict, labels=[1, 0]))
print("")
print("Classification Report")
print(metrics.classification_report(y_test, lr_test_predict, labels=[1, 0]))
```

Figure 15. Classification report for the Logistic Regression (LR) model

```
Model Accuracy: 0.77

Confusion Matrix
[[ 37  30]
 [ 14 111]]

Classification Report
             precision    recall  f1-score   support

          1       0.73      0.55      0.63        67
          0       0.79      0.89      0.83       125

avg / total       0.77      0.77      0.76       192
```

Multilayer Perceptron

```
from sklearn.neural_network import MLPClassifier
from sklearn.model_selection import train_test_split

X_train, X_test, y_train, y_test = train_test_split(diabetes.loc[:, diabetes.
columns != 'Outcome'], diabetes['Outcome'], stratify=diabetes['Outcome'], ran-
dom_state=66)
from sklearn.preprocessing import StandardScaler

scaler = StandardScaler()
X_train_scaled = scaler.fit_transform(X_train)
```

```
X_test_scaled = scaler.fit_transform(X_test)

mlp = MLPClassifier(random_state=0)
mlp.fit(X_train_scaled, y_train)

print("Accuracy on test set: {:.4f}".format(mlp.score(X_test_scaled, y_test)))
```

Figure 16. Classification report for the Multilayer Perceptron (MLP) classifier

```
Model Accuracy: 79.87012987012987%
Confusion Matrix
[[88 19]
 [11 36]]
Classification Report
             precision    recall  f1-score   support

          1       0.65      0.77      0.71        47
          0       0.89      0.82      0.85       107

avg / total       0.82      0.81      0.81       154
```

Performance Metrics

Performance metrics play an important role in the evaluation of the various machine learning models built. Choice of performance metrics determine how the machine learning models are compared and measured.This chapter compares the models based on the four performance metrics namely – Accuracy, Specificity, Sensitivity and the F1 score.

A confusion matrix is a performance metric table that is used to analyze the performance of a classification model (or "classifier") on a set of test data for which the true target attribute values are already known. It is also called as the error matrix.Python has confusion matrix and classification report functions under the sklearn.metrics library. Confusion matrix contains:

True Positive: The instances which are classified as positive and are actually positive.
True Negative: The instances which are classified as negative and are actually negative.
False Positive: The instances which are classified as positive but are actually negative.
False Negative: The instances which are classified as negative but are actually positive.

Sensitivity (True Positive Rate)

If a person has diabetes, how often will the classifier be able to predict it?

It is the ratio of true positives to the sum of the true positive and false negative. A highly sensitive test helps rule out diabetes. If the test is highly sensitive and the test result is test result is negative, it becomes nearly certain that the particular person doesn't have diabetes.

Sensitivity = True Positive / (True Positive + False Negative)

Specificity (True Negative Rate)

If a person doesn't have diabetes, how often will the classifier be able to predict it?

It is the ratio of true negatives to the sum of the true negatives and false positives. A highly sensitive test helps rule in diabetes. If the test is highly specific and the test result is test result is positive, it becomes nearly certain that the particular person has diabetes.

Specificity = True Negative / (True Negative + False Positive)

Accuracy

It is a metric used to predict the correctness of a machine learning model. The model is trained using the train data and a classifier is built. The test data is used to cross validate the classifier model. The percentage of correctly classified instances is termed as Accuracy.

F1 Score

F1 score is a combination function of precision and recall. It is used when we need to seek a balance between precision and recall.

Precision = True Positives / (True Positives + False Positives)

Here, the denominator (True Positives + False Positives) is the total predicted positives.

Recall = True Positives / (True Positives + False Negatives)

Here, the denominator (True Positives + False Negatives) is the total actual positives.

F1 Score = 2 * (Precision * Recall) / (Precision + Recall)

Accuracy vs F1 Score

In cases where there is an uneven class distribution i.e. there are large number of actual negatives, F1 Score might prove to be better than accuracy. Accuracy only checks the correctness of a model while F1 score strikes a balance between precision and recall.

Table 2. Comparison between various classifiers based on performance metrics

Algorithm	Accuracy	Specificity	Sensitivity	F1-Score
Random Forest (before hyper parameter tuning)	0.7559	0.8295	0.5897	0.5974
Random Forest (after hyper parameter tuning)	0.7677	0.8352	0.6153	0.6193
Logistic Regression	0.7789	0.7872	0.7255	0.6271
Artificial Neural Networks (ANN)	0.7987	0.8224	0.7659	0.7058

The model architecture is defined by several parameters. These parameters are referred to as hyper parameters. The process of searching for an ideal model architecture for optimal accuracy score is referred to as hyper parameter tuning. In this chapter, hyper parameter tuning of Random Forest model is done to give a better accuracy. At n_tree = 1200; max_features = 'auto'; max_depth: 180, the AUC (Area Under the Curve) score is highest and this, hence, gives the highest accuracy rate.

After building the models, Multilayer Perceptron (MLP) model gives the highest accuracy at 79.87%. Random Forest model was focused on to increase accuracy by Hyper-parameter Tuning. However, the highest accuracy obtained from it, i.e. 76.38%, could not exceed even the Logistic Regression model's accuracy (77.89%).

The neural network model built gives a better accuracy than LR and Random Forest classifier models. Diabetes is a huge threat to the modern world and devising an algorithm that tackles or even reduces its adversity can be a great help to diabetic patients.

Comparison Between the Models Using Various Performance Metrics

```
models = []
models.append(('LR', 0.7789))
models.append(('ANN (not tuned)', 0.7857))
models.append(('ANN (tuned)', 0.8052))
models.append(('Ensemble', 0.7512))
models.append(('Hybrid', 0.8377))
names = []
scores = []

for name, accuracy in models:
scores.append(accuracy)
names.append(name)
tb_split = pd.DataFrame({'Name': names, 'Score': scores})
print(tb_split)

axis = sns.barplot(x = 'Name', y = 'Score', data = tb_split, palette="GnBu_d")
axis.set(xlabel='CLASSIFIER', ylabel='ACCURACY SCORE')
sns.set(rc={'figure.figsize':(15,8)}, font_scale=1.5)
sns.set(font_scale=1.5)
for p in axis.patches:
    height = p.get_height()
axis.text(p.get_x() + p.get_width()/2, height + 0.005, '{:1.4f}'.
format(height), ha="center")
plt.show()
```

Clearly, accuracy of the Multilayer Perceptron (MLP) classifier is the highest at 79.87%, followed by the Logistic Regression model at 77.08%. Surprisingly, the Random forest did not perform better than the other two even after hyperparameter tuning the parameters. The accuracy of the Random Forest model increased only by 1.18% approximately after hyper parameter tuning.

Figure 17. Comparison between the accuracy score for each classifier

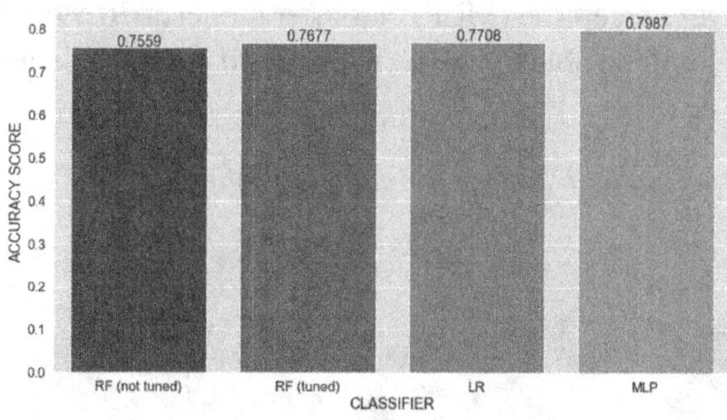

Figure 18. Comparison between the specificity for each classifier

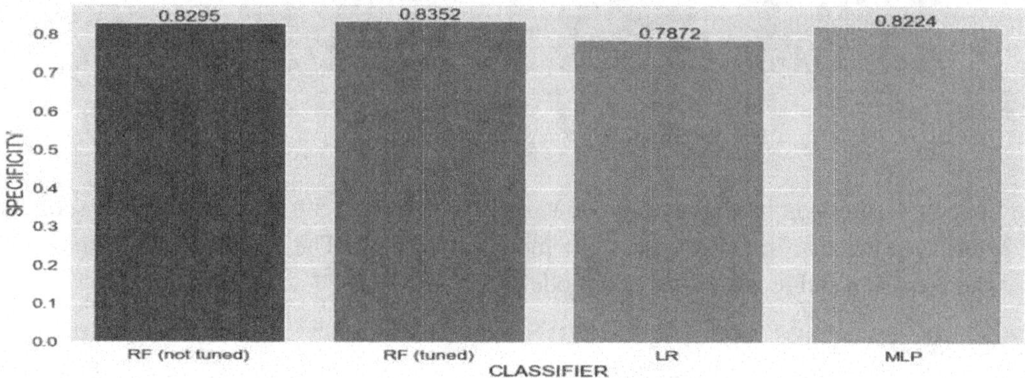

The Logistic Regression model gives the lowest specificity rate at 78.72%. The best specificity rate is given by the Random Forest (hyperparameter tuned) model at 83.52%. The specificity determines how often a given classifier will be able to correctly predict if a person does not actually have diabetes.

Figure 19. Comparison between the sensitivity for each classifier

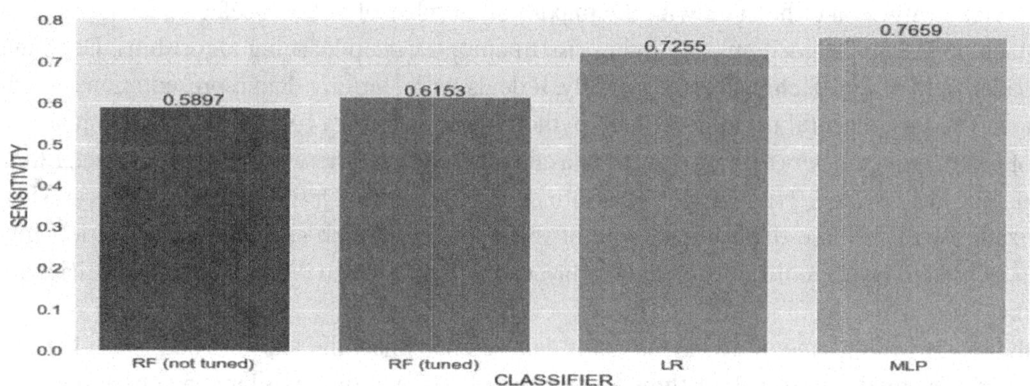

The Random Forest (not tuned) model gives the lowest sensitivity rate at 58.97%. The best sensitivity rate is given by the Multilayer Perceptron (MLP) classifier model at 76.59%. The sensitivity determines how often a given classifier will be able to correctly predict if a person actually has diabetes.

Figure 20. Comparison between the F1 score for each classifier

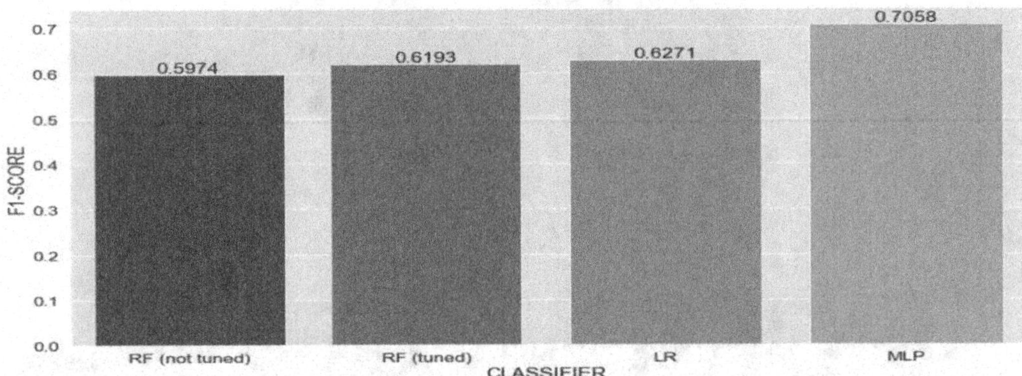

The Logistic Regression model gives the lowest F1 score rate at 59.74%. The best F1 score is given by the Multilayer Perceptron (MLP) classifier model at 70.58%. The F1 score establishes a balance between the precision and recall values of a model.

FUTURE RESEARCH DIRECTIONS

As a field of machine learning is progressing and improving day-by-day, researchers are diving into hybrid and ensemble modeling techniques. These complex hybrid and ensemble models are built by combining the traditional algorithms in a way that yields better performance metrics. Hybrid models are built in sequential blocks. The first block usually involves feature selection and is followed by blocks that contain various traditional classifiers. These classifiers can be further hyper parameter tuned. The ensemble model basically works on the concept of bagging. The prediction is made using multiple traditional algorithms and the class with the maximum number of votes is selected as the final prediction. Machine learning algorithms are giving rise to complex deep learning algorithms. Deep learning is a broader field of the machine learning family. It deals with learning data representations and pattern detection. The future neural network APIs in python libraries like PyTorch or Keras will just require a range of layers or parameters that are wanted in a customized neural network. Hyperparameter tuning by methods like Grid Search, Trial &Error, Random Search, Bayesian Optimization or Genetic Algorithm Optimization will increase the accuracy rate of these models. Batch size, epoch, activation function, number of hidden layers, units in each hidden layers, etc can result in distinct complex artificial neural networks.

Python is growing as the go-to language for data science, machine learning and is used even in big data. As the machine learning algorithms evolve, python is becoming the language of choice for most machine learning and data science professionals.

There are some limitations of the dataset taken in the chapter too which can be overcome to create an even more efficient and accurate diabetes prediction system/model. Considering the diabetes dataset taken is for women only, the complete scope of diabetes cannot be covered. Data for children, men, young and old people are not present in the PIMA diabetes dataset. There might be other risk factors that the dataset did not consider. Important factors like family history (i.e. if diabetes runs in the family), gestational diabetes, smoking; metabolic syndrome, inactive lifestyles, dietary patterns etc are not considered as attributes in the dataset. A proper model for prediction would need more data gathered from various sources to make the machine learning models more accurate. This can be attained by the collection of diabetes data from multiple sources, integrating these data and then generating a model from each dataset. The prediction model can be used as an API (Application Program Interface) for a Flask (python web framework) based web app which will give real-time prediction results of the entered data of a patient.

CONCLUSION

This chapter provides insights into various machine learning techniques used for classification. The code snippets demonstrate the use of python to build classifiers, hyper parameter tune them and visualize the data. It predicts the diabetes outcome based on other attributes. The classifiers like Logistic Regression (LR), Random Forest (RF) and Multilayer Perceptron (MLP) are used. It uses performance metrics like sensitivity, specificity, accuracy and F1 score to compare various classifiers and decide which gives the best results.

Python is one of the most suited languages to implement machine learning. It is easy and has a simple syntax to support diverse actions. Various python libraries make implementing machine learning a very easy process. The scikit-learn python library provides for almost all the major machine learning techniques and algorithms. Jupyter renders elegant graphical representations and code structures with results. Mark ups and headings provide further efficiency in presenting the work and code in a structured way. This chapter uses various python functions and libraries to implement the machine learning algorithms in order to build prediction models for the PIMA Indians Diabetes dataset.

The process of building a classifier starts with procuring data to train the model. The dataset selected for building classifiers in this chapter is the PIMA diabetes dataset. This dataset has attributes like number of pregnancies, glucose, blood pressure, skin thickness, insulin levels, the body mass index (BMI), the diabetes pedigree function and age. This dataset also has an independent or target variable namely outcome which predicts whether a person will have diabetes or not. Once the data is procured, the next step is data preprocessing. Data preprocessing includes, data cleaning, data reduction, data integration, data transformation, feature selection, dimensionality reduction, discretization and generating concept hierarchies. Data in the real world is dirty meaning it is incomplete, noisy and inconsistent. This makes data preprocessing inevitable. Low quality data is bound to produce low quality results. Thus, before building the classifier in this chapter, the data is preprocessed. It is made sure that all the attributes have the correct data types. Next, the missing values are found and replaced with some suitable values. Once the data is preprocessed, it is ready for the process of classification. Here, three classification algorithms are used, namely, Random Forest (RF), Logistic Regression (LR) and Multilayer Perceptron (MLP). Before the application of every algorithm, the dataset is divided into train and test dataset using percentage split technique for cross validation. Next, the algorithms are applied on the dataset and certain performance metrics like accuracy, F1 score, sensitivity and specificity are used to evaluate the performance of the algorithms.

The results show that the Multilayer Perceptron (MLP) performs the best with an accuracy of 79.87%, exceeding the second best performer – Logistic Regression (LR) by almost two percent. The Multilayer Perceptron (MLP) model gave the highest F1 score as well.

ACKNOWLEDGMENT

This work was supported by Vanitha M, Associate Professor, School of Information Technology and Engineering, Vellore Institute of Technology, Vellore. This research received no specific grant from any funding agency in the public, commercial, or not-for-profit sectors.

REFERENCES

Aishwarya, R., Gayathri, P., & Jaisankar, N. (2013). A Method for Classification Using Machine Learning Technique for Diabetes. *IACSIT International Journal of Engineering and Technology*, *5*(3), 2903–2908.

Dogantekin, E., Dogantekin, A., Avci, D., & Avci, L. (2010, July). An intelligent diagnosis system for diabetes on Linear Discriminant Analysis and Adaptive Network Based Fuzzy Inference System: LDA-ANFIS. *Digital Signal Processing*, *20*(4), 1248–1255. doi:10.1016/j.dsp.2009.10.021

Fatima, M., & Pasha, M. (2017). Survey of Machine Learning Algorithms for Disease Diagnostic. *Journal of Intelligent Learning Systems and Applications*, *9*(1), 1–16. doi:10.4236/jilsa.2017.91001

Gopinath, M. P., & Murali, S. (2017). Comparative study on Classification Algorithm for Diabetes Data set. *International Journal of Pure and Applied Mathematics*, *117*(7), 47–52.

Hayashi, Y., & Yukita, S. (2016). Rule extraction using Recursive-Rule extraction algorithm with J48graft combined with sampling selection techniques for the diagnosis of type 2 diabetes mellitus in the Pima Indian dataset. *Informatics in Medicine Unlocked*, *2*, 92–104. doi:10.1016/j.imu.2016.02.001

Kavakiotis, I., Tsave, O., Salifoglou, A., Maglaveras, N., Vlahavas, I., & Chouvarda, I. (2017). Machine Learning and Data Mining Methods in Diabetes Research. *Computational and Structural Biotechnology Journal*, *15*, 104–116. doi:10.1016/j.csbj.2016.12.005 PMID:28138367

Nanthini, D., & Thangaraju, P. (2015, August). A Hybrid Classification Model For Diabetes Dataset Using Decision Tree. *International Journal of Emerging Technologies and Innovative Research*, *2*(8), 3302–3308.

Patil, B. M., Joshi, R. C., & Toshniwal, D. (2010, December). Hybrid prediction model for Type-2 diabetic patients. *Expert Systems with Applications*, *37*(12), 8102–8108. doi:10.1016/j.eswa.2010.05.078

Pradeep Kandhasamy, J., & Balamurali, S. (2015). Performance Analysis of Classifier Models to Predict Diabetes Mellitus. *Procedia Computer Science*, *47*, 45–51. doi:10.1016/j.procs.2015.03.182

Ramezani, Maadi, & Khatami. (2018). Analysis of a Population of Diabetic Patients Databases in Weka Tool. *International Journal of Scientific and Engineering Research, 2*(5).

Saravananathan & Velmurugan. (2016). Analyzing Diabetic Data using Classification Algorithms in Data Mining. *Indian Journal of Science and Technology, 9*(43).

Sisodia, D., & Sisodia, D. S. (2018). Prediction of Diabetes using Classification Algorithms. *Procedia Computer Science, 132*, 1578–1585. doi:10.1016/j.procs.2018.05.122

Temurtas, H., Yumusak, N., & Temurtas, F. (2009, May). A comparative study on diabetes disease diagnosis using neural networks. *Systems with Applications, 36*(4), 8610–8615. doi:10.1016/j.eswa.2008.10.032

Wu, H., Yang, S., Huang, Z., He, J., & Wang, X. (2018). Type 2 diabetes mellitus prediction model based on data mining. *Informatics in Medicine Unlocked, 10*, 100–107. doi:10.1016/j.imu.2017.12.006

Yasodha & Kannan. (2011). A novel hybrid intelligent system with missing value imputation for diabetes diagnosis. *Alexandria Engineering Journal, 57*(3).

ADDITIONAL READING

Dey, A. (2016). Machine Learning Algorithms: A Review. *International Journal of Computer Science and Information Technologies, 7*(3), 1174–1179.

Pedregosa, F., Varoquaux, G., Gramfort, A., & Michel, V. (2011). Scikit-learn: Machine Learning in Python. *Journal of Machine Learning Research.*

Simon, A., Deo, M. S., Selvam, V., & Babu, R. (2015). An Overview of Machine Learning and its Applications. *International Journal of Electrical Sciences and Engineering, 1*(1), 22–24.

Van der Walt, S., Colbert, S. C., & Varoquaux, G. (2011). The NumPy array:a structure for efficient numerical computation. *Computing in Science & Engineering, 11*, 2011.

Zito, T., Wilbert, N., Wiskott, L., & Berkes, P. (2008). Modular toolkit for Data Processing (MDP*): A Python data processing framework. Frontiers in Neuroinformatics, 2*, 2008. doi:10.3389/neuro.11.008.2008 PMID:19169361

KEY TERMS AND DEFINITIONS

Accuracy: It is a metric used to predict the correctness of a machine learning model. The model is trained using the train data and a classifier is built. The test data is used to cross validate the classifier model. The percentage of correctly classified instances is termed as accuracy.

Area Under the Curve (AUC) Score: Area under the curve (AUC) is a binary classification metric. It considers all the possible thresholds. Different threshold values result in distinct true positive/false positive rates. As the threshold is decreased, more true positives (but also more false positives) instances are discovered.

F1 Score: F1 score is a combination function of precision and recall. It is used when we need to seek a balance between precision and recall.

Hyper-Parameter Tuning: The model architecture is defined by several parameters. These parameters are referred to as hyper parameters. The process of searching for an ideal model architecture for optimal accuracy score is referred to as hyper parameter tuning.

Logistic Regression: Logistic regression is a classification algorithm that comes under supervised learning and is used for predictive learning. Logistic regression is used to describe data. It works best for dichotomous (binary) classification.

Multilayer Perceptron: Multilayer perceptron falls under artificial neural networks (ANN). It is a feed forward network that consists of a minimum of three layers of nodes- an input layer, one or more hidden layers and an output layer. It uses a supervised learning technique, namely, back propagation for training. Its main advantage is that it has the ability to distinguish data that is not linearly separable.

Random Forest: Random forest is a supervised learning algorithm and is used for classification and regression. It is an ensemble learning method that operates by constructing multiple decision trees and merges them together to obtain an accurate and stable prediction. Generally, it produces great results even without hyper parameter tuning.

Recall: Recall is the ratio of true positives to the sum of true positives and false negatives.

Sensitivity/Precision: It is the ratio of true positives to the sum of the true positive and false negative.

Specificity: It is the ratio of true negatives to the sum of the true negatives and false positives.

Supervised Learning: Machine learning is broadly classified into two: supervised learning and unsupervised learning. In supervised learning, the machine learns from examples. Historical or train data is needed which is given as an input to the machine and a classifier model is formed. A supervised algorithm also needs a target value. On the contrary, unsupervised learning algorithms need neither the train data nor the target value.

This research was previously published in the Handbook of Research on Applications and Implementations of Machine Learning Techniques; pages 128-154, copyright year 2020 by Engineering Science Reference (an imprint of IGI Global).

Chapter 47
A Knowledge-Oriented Recommendation System for Machine Learning Algorithm Finding and Data Processing

Man Tianxing
https://orcid.org/0000-0003-2187-1641
Itmo University, St. Petersburg, Russia

Ildar Raisovich Baimuratov
Itmo University, St. Petersburg, Russia

Natalia Alexandrovna Zhukova
St. Petersburg Institute for Informatics and Automation of Russian Academy of Sciences (SPIIRAS), St. Petersburg, Russia

ABSTRACT

With the development of the Big Data, data analysis technology has been actively developed, and now it is used in various subject fields. More and more non-computer professional researchers use machine learning algorithms in their work. Unfortunately, datasets can be messy and knowledge cannot be directly extracted, which is why they need preprocessing. Because of the diversity of the algorithms, it is difficult for researchers to find the most suitable algorithm. Most of them choose algorithms through their intuition. The result is often unsatisfactory. Therefore, this article proposes a recommendation system for data processing. This system consists of an ontology subsystem and an estimation subsystem. Ontology technology is used to represent machine learning algorithm taxonomy, and information-theoretic based criteria are used to form recommendations. This system helps users to apply data processing algorithms without specific knowledge from the data science field.

DOI: 10.4018/978-1-6684-6291-1.ch047

INTRODUCTION

Due to the popularization of Internet people's lives are increasingly dependent on Internet technology. A lot of relevant data are generating from human daily activities. The information contained in these data is very valuable for Internet of Thing (IoT) developers and data analysts in various fields. Extracting useful information from huge data and applying it to life has become a hot topic in academia. Machine learning (ML) algorithms are the most effective tools to extract knowledge from data. Experts enhance and improve ML and data processing technologies, therefore, the number of different types of algorithms for ML increases, and the algorithms itself become more and more complicate. This situation causes the confusion about how to choose, when and how to apply the appropriate algorithm or technology for data processing for researchers.

Currently, the taxonomy of ML algorithms (Ayodele, 2010) is the main basis for researchers to make choices. But these taxonomies have some limitations. First, they usually do not cover all the information about data analysis, they represent only a single "has-a" relationship. Second, building a taxonomy is a complex, long-term process, while data processing technology rapidly advances, therefore, it is hard to keep an ontology up to date. Finally, a taxonomy cannot help the user to decide, which algorithm is more appropriate in one or another specific situation.

In opposition to this, authors propose a knowledge-oriented system to help data analysts build the process of data processing. It consists of two parts: ontology subsystem and estimation subsystem. The ontology subsystem uses the existing taxonomies of ML algorithms. Authors represent them with ontology techniques and create some new ontologies to describe the processes of ML algorithms (e.g. dataset features, output model features, mathematics, process). In these ontologies' authors define new properties to represent the performance of ML algorithms and the process of algorithms in more detailed way. To form recommendations about ML algorithms and evaluate the results of its implementation, authors propose the estimation subsystem. Several information-theory based measures were adopted and incorporated into a system of comprehensive estimation of data and results of ML algorithms implementation. It is worth mentioning that authors also create an ontology of preprocessing technology, which can provide solutions for the defects in dataset neatness.

The workflow of the knowledge-oriented system consists of the following steps. First, users need dataset feature estimation and task requirements as the basis for algorithm selection. After selecting the appropriate algorithm, the interpretation system will give the process of algorithm execution, related parameter settings and measure selection. Authors consider a clustering task as an example. After evaluating, the system suggests implementing clustering and propose a number of clusters for the output model.

The main advantages of this knowledge-oriented system are as follow: 1) This system describes the entire data processing including preprocessing and data analysis. 2) It is built based on ontology technology so that it is expandable and understandable. 3) This system provides a new information measure for estimate the output model.

BACKGROUND

Provide broad definitions and discussions of the topic and incorporate views of others (literature review) into the discussion to support, refute, or demonstrate your position on the topic.[1]

Data processing is a complex process. Kotsiantis (2007) provide a comprehensive review about Supervised machine learning. Satyanandam, N., & Satyanarayana, D. C. (2013) describe a taxonomy of ML and data mining for Healthcare Systems. Ayodele, T. O. (2010) represents main type of ML algorithms and their advantages and disadvantages are briefly introduced. But the main points in these reviews are the process of ML algorithms not the selection of algorithms. They are not friendly to non-experts.

The confusion of non-experts in data processing has also been considered in some researches (Dash & Liu, 1997; Reif, Shafait, Goldstein, Breuel, & Dengel, 2014). Even some advanced techniques are applied on this kind of problems (Zinnikus, Fraser, & Fischer, 2004; Bernstein, Provost, & Hill, 2005; Bechhofer, 2009; Anastácio, Martins, & Calado, 2011; Hilario, Nguyen, Do, Woznica, & Kalousis, 2011; Panov, Soldatova, & Džeroski, 2014). These systems build understandable conception models based on ontology technology. Users can achieve wanted information clearly. But these researches usually focus on specific tasks such as classification, clustering, measure etc. They have no universality for all kind of data processing problems.

Any recommendation system needs criteria to form recommendations. Different information-based characteristics can be used to evaluate data features and results of data processing. Therefore, several existing information characteristics are considered for applying in the estimation subsystem. There are the following characteristics in information theory at the moment (Gabidulin & Pilipchuk, 2007):

- *Self-information* for some value x_i of a discrete random variable X with probability distribution $P(x_i)$:

$$I(x_i) = -\log P(x_i)$$

- *Entropy* of a discrete random variable X:

$$\mathrm{H}(\mathrm{X}) = -\sum_{\mathrm{i}} \mathrm{P}(\mathrm{x_i}) \log \mathrm{P}(\mathrm{x_i})$$

- *Conditional entropy* of discrete random variables X and Y with probability distributions $P(x_i)$ and $P(y_j)$ and joint probability distribution $P(x_i|y_j)$:

$$\mathrm{H}(Y|X) = -\sum_{i}\sum_{j} P(x_i) P(y_j|x_i) \log P(y_j|x_i)$$

- *Relative entropy* (Kullback–Leibler divergence) of discrete random variables X and Y with n values:

$$\mathrm{D}(\mathrm{X}\,||\,\mathrm{Y}) = \sum_{\mathrm{i}} \mathrm{P}(\mathrm{x_i}) \log \frac{\mathrm{P}(\mathrm{x_i})}{\mathrm{P}(\mathrm{y_i})}$$

There is a group of information criteria amongst external criteria as well. These criteria are Mutual information I(X, Y) of two discrete random variables X and Y:

$$I(X, Y) = H(Y) - H(Y|X)$$

and adjusted mutual information (Vinh, N. X., Epps, J., & Bailey, J. (2010)). But external information criteria do not fit to the goals as they need some predefined ideal partitioning.

MOTIVATION

IoT technology is an important part of the new generation of information technology. Figure 1 shows the data processing process. Due to coming from real life, these IoT datasets have more uncertainty. They need to go through a complex preprocessing, and then be applied with the appropriate ML algorithms to extract useful information (Borodin, Zavyalova, & Meigal, 2017; Ulitin & Babkin, 2018). This problem is plaguing many non-computer professional data analysts.

Figure 1. Data processing process (preprocessing and classification/clustering are the main parts of data processing process)

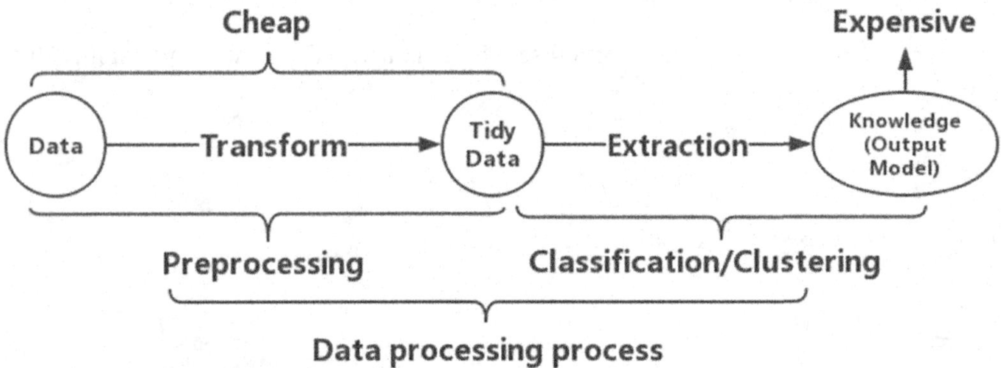

There are numerous algorithms and criteria present at the moment. According to tasks, different criteria can be used as ground for choosing one or another ML algorithm. But choosing of criteria is in turn not based on any formal approach and depends only on analysts' intuition. Besides, most of existing criteria are applicable only after an algorithm is executed.

Taxonomy is a traditional approach which is used to find suitable algorithms, metrics, models, etc. At present, a lot of taxonomies of ML algorithms have been proposed. Some researches on how to choose the right data analysis algorithm are developed. These taxonomies are mainly based on the type of algorithm. In practice such taxonomies do not provide users with valid choice suggestions. They are incomplete and too professional for some primary users. In particular ML technology is developing rapidly. These taxonomies are easy to become obsolete.

People need a way to intelligently choose the right algorithm for their data processing tasks to make the results more satisfying. When the user is not proficient in the ML algorithm, they want to get some information about the algorithm flow and parameter settings.

Authors propose a knowledge-oriented system for these requirements. They build an ontology of machine learning algorithms as the core of this recommendation system.

The Semantic Web is an emerging concept that is an intelligent network that can make judgments based on semantics to enable unobstructed communication between people and computers (McGuinness & Van Harmelen, 2004; Smirnov, Ponomarev, Levashova, & Shilov, 2017). Each computer connected to the Semantic Web not only understands words and concepts, but also understands the logical relationship between them. Ontology is such a conceptual modeling tool that describes information systems at the semantic and knowledge level. The goal is to capture knowledge in related fields, identify commonly recognized terms in this field, describe the semantics of concepts through the relationships between concepts, and provide a common understanding of the field knowledge (Van Rees, 2003).

The first part is a logical structure based on ontology, whose elements are the decomposed algorithm processes, and the second is an estimation system for evaluating data and choosing the most suitable algorithm. This system can provide users with suitable solutions.

To ground recommendations produced by this system authors develop the comprehensive evaluation subsystem. This system evaluates features of all elements of data processing: dataset, intermediate model and output model. In this article authors present only the part of the system which evaluates output models. Evaluating output model is the most relevant issue in clustering tusk, therefore, in the present work authors demonstrate the workflow of this system with respect to clustering.

SYSTEM STRUCTURE

As mentioned above, the existing recommendation systems for data processing have some limitations. The proposed system has the following advantages:

1. This system contains nearly 100 machine learning algorithms and data preprocessing methods and provides measurement and model selection for some of these algorithms;
2. This system is based on ontology technology so that it is easier to extend when a new ML algorithm is proposed, or a new data feature is considered;
3. This system can provide suggestions for selection algorithms for the entire process including preprocessing methods and data processing algorithms;
4. A new information criterion is applied to the evaluation of the output model in this system. The previous recommendation systems don't have this function.

This knowledge-oriented system consists of the ontology and the estimation subsystems.

Ontology Subsystem

The biggest difference between ontology and taxonomy is that ontology can define more complex relationships. The authors represent the knowledge related to data processing as a group of ontologies. The main idea is to enrich the existing taxonomies of ML algorithms, summarize the performance of the algorithm (Vorobeva, 2017) and express it into ontology and create the ontologies of the features of datasets and task requirements. Then the authors define new object properties to connect these ontologies to represent the logical relationships among them and new data properties to describe the value and range of algorithm parameters.

Figure 2. The basic structure of the recommendation subsystem

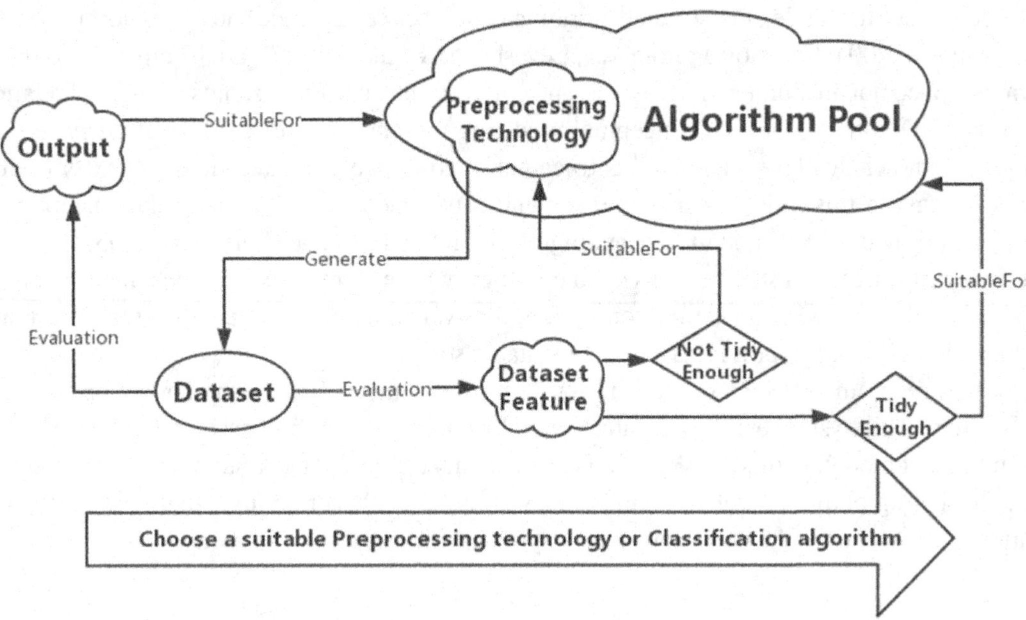

This ontology subsystem describes the performance and application of the ML algorithm by the recommendation subsystem which is shown in Figure 2. The user finds suitable pre-processing techniques and analysis algorithms according to dataset features and the requirements of task. So, the input is dataset features and the requirements of the task, and the output is the algorithm choice (and the process description of the algorithm by the interpretation subsystem which is shown in Figure 3, if necessary).

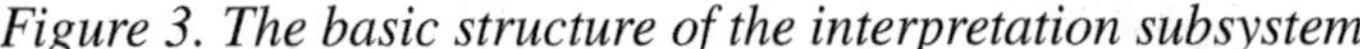

Figure 3. The basic structure of the interpretation subsystem

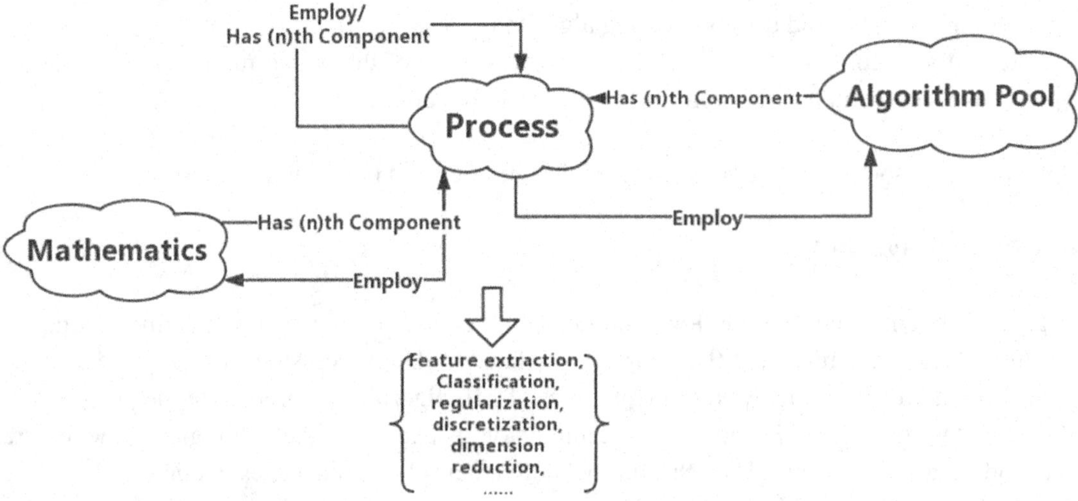

The ontology is written with OWL language and available at https://github.com/529492252/ontology. It is edited in Protégé-5.5.0 and was checked by HermiT 1.3.8.413 reasoner to make sure it is consistent. After inference there is no highlighted classes appeared. It means it is consistent. And in the inference process the defined individuals are classified into correct classed. It proves the sufficiency of this ontology.

To prove the completeness, the authors choose algorithms based on this ontology and compare with all the other available algorithms. In most cases the results are satisfactory. But the choice cannot be proven to always be the best. Actually, this is a characteristic of this system. When the system doesn't make good choice, it can be enriched with this new situation. So, it is not quite complete now, but it will be improved in use.

The main goal of this knowledge-oriented system is to provide effective data processing advice for any data processing tasks. So, except algorithm pool all the other ontologies that are integrated in this subsystem serve this purpose. Here are the main components (authors present some examples in Table 1).

Algorithm Pool

It is a set of ML algorithms and preprocessing technologies. It is based on the "Classification Algorithms" entry in DBpedia. Authors enriched it with some absent algorithms. The other part of the algorithm pool is data preprocessing technology. It includes almost 100 algorithms and technologies in this ontology.

Dataset Features

The basic characteristics of a dataset are the decisive factors for selecting the most suitable algorithm in data processing process (Dash & Liu, 1997):

1. Characteristics of data samples
2. Characteristics of data features

Mathematics

Another criterion for choosing a suitable algorithm is the mathematical model in the algorithm. There are mainly such theories:

1. Linear algebra
2. Probability and Statistics
3. Multivariate calculus
4. Algorithms and Complex Optimization
5. Other

Some other math topics are not covered in the four main areas above. These topics include real and complex analysis, information theory, function spaces and number sets.

Table 1. Some examples of the ontologies in system

Name	Subclass	Examples
Algorithm Pool	Preprocessing Technology	Clean Missing Data, Filter, Dimensionality Reduction
	Estimation Method	The information criterion proposed
	ML Algorithm	Bayesian, Decision Tree, Instance-Based Algorithm
Data Feature	Dataset Characteristics	Small/Normal/Big Size, Continuous/Discrete Attribute
	Dataset Defect	Missing/Noisy Value, Redundant/Irrelevant attribute
Mathematics		Measures Function, Probability model
Output Feature	Output Characteristics	No. of labels
	Intermediate Model	Tree, Regression, Bayesian
	Output Model Structure	Appropriate/poor /Redundant Structure
	Performance	Speed/Accuracy /Explanation Ability
Process		Discretization, Normalization, Regularization, Standardization

Output Features

The requirements for the output model are another important factor for selecting the ML algorithm.

Process

Process is an abstract ontology defined. Authors decompose each algorithm and technique into general steps like dimension reduction, regularization, discretization and so on and give them orders with special properties. These steps and the properties Authors define can describe the execution procedures of algorithm in detail. Then users will know what they should do in each step. And for every step it gives them the explainable description with same way. So, users can find all the operations from a general level to a detailed level.

In usual taxonomy only a "has-a" relationship is existing which can only express the algorithm belongs to a category. This kind of taxonomy does not give the user a suggestion about algorithm selection. In this regard, the authors also define some necessary Object properties which are shown in Table 2.

In addition to the above object properties, the authors also define a large number of data properties which provide some conditions about the values or ranges users need consider when they use some algorithms like "hasMean", "hasStandardDeviation" and so on. These data properties make the application of the algorithm more clear and easier to understand. These properties flexibly explain the knowledge of data analysis. Users can easily find useful information when they encounter some problems.

Estimation Subsystem

Authors expect the estimation system to be abstract enough to be independent from any particular machine learning algorithm and, therefore, being able to compare results of different types of algorithms. That is why authors suggest using information-based criteria. Though there is a group of information criteria present at the moment, author show that existing ones can't be used as criteria for choosing one or another model, because 1) they need some ideal structure to compare its informativeness with the informativeness of the resulting one or 2) optimal, according to these criteria, structures are trivial and, consequently, not intuitively informative nor practically applicable. Therefore, authors propose a new information criterion for the estimation subsystem.

Table 2. The major object properties in the ontology

Name	Relate From	Relate To	Description
employAlgorithm	Process	Algorithm Pool	specify the algorithm which is employed
employApproach	Process	Algorithm Pool	specify the approach which is employed
employMeasure	Algorithm Pool	Mathematics	specify the Measure which is employed by the algorithm
has(n)thComponent	Algorithm Pool / Process	Process	specify the steps and define an order
dealWellWith	Algorithm Pool / Mathematics	Data Feature /Output Feature	Connect the algorithm and the characteristics which they are suitable for
tolerantTo	Algorithm Pool / Mathematics	Data Feature /Output Feature	Connect the algorithm and the characteristics which they are suitable for
ownPerformance	Algorithm Pool / Mathematics	Data Feature /Output Feature	Connect the algorithm and the characteristics which they are suitable for
isAppliedOn	Mathematics	Algorithm Pool	It's used to choose the suitable algorithms based on a suitable mathematics theory which is applied on some algorithms
Other			Authors also define some other properties which present the relations in this system and explain this structure clearly

Existing Information Characteristics Analysis

First, authors show that conditional entropy $H(Y|X)$ in general case can't be used as information criterion for estimating data features, considered as partitions. Authors denote a number of elements of a partition C_k under condition x_i as n_{ik}:

$$n_{ik} = \left|X_i \cap C_k\right|$$

where X_i is a set of objects that satisfy the condition x_i. As for non-fuzzy case each $x_i \in X$ is assigned to only one partition C_k, for each i and k holds that $n_{ik} = 1$, therefore, for each C and X the conditional entropy $H(C|X)$ of non-fuzzy partition is zero:

$$H\left(C|X\right) = -\sum_{x_i \in X}\sum_{k}\frac{1}{N}\log_N 1 = 0$$

Second, authors the number of points N as base of logarithmic function of information criteria in order to get normalized values. Besides of other advantages of normalized variants, it will be easier to show with them that existing information criteria can't be used for choosing a partition. Authors can do so as base of the logarithmic function in the definitions of the criteria are not restricted.

Summing up, authors have following information characteristics, applicable to partitions:

- Partition informativeness *C*:

$$H(C) = -\sum_{k} \frac{n_k}{N} \log_N \frac{n_k}{N}$$

- Partition informativeness *C* relative to the original set *X*:

$$D(C \parallel X) = \sum_{k} \frac{n_k}{N} \log_N \frac{\frac{n_k}{N}}{\frac{1}{N}} = \sum_{k} \frac{n_k}{N} \log_N n_k$$

Now authors show that these information criteria can't be used for choosing a partition. To illustrate this fact, authors compare values of Calinski-Harabasz index (KH) with values of information characteristics *H*(*C*) and *D*(*C*||*X*) in the context of clustering task, with different numbers of clusters *n* from 1 to 10. Authors use Fisher's Iris flowers as dataset and *k*-means as clustering algorithm. The results of comparing are in the Table 3.

Table 3. The results of comparing the values of different criteria for 1-10 clusters

K	*CH*	*H(C)*	*D(C‖X)*
1	n/a	n/a	1
2	513	0,13	0,87
3	560	0,22	0,78
4	529	0,27	0,73
5	494	0,3	0,7
6	475	0,35	0,65
7	451	0,38	0,62
8	441	0,4	0,6
9	409	0,41	0,59
10	391	0,44	0,56

If authors use information criterion *H*(*C*) for choosing number of clusters *n*, authors should choose $n = 10$, or if *D(C||X), then* — $n = 1$ is used. Authors generalize this result as following:

$H(C) = 1 \Leftrightarrow \forall i |C_i| = 1$

$D(C||X) = 1 \Leftrightarrow C = X$

In other words, if information characteristic *H*(*C*) for choosing the number of subsets is used, then the optimal number of subsets equals to the number of objects, otherwise, if information characteristic *D*(*C*||*X*) is used, then the optimal partition is the set *X* itself. Both these options do not correspond to the objective structure of data nor values of practical criteria. In other words, basic information characteristics, such as entropy and relative entropy, considered as model selection criterion, are threatened by underfitting and overfitting.

There are several ways of preventing underfitting and overfitting, such as cross-validation, regularization or priors. Cross-validation and regularization are inappropriate in case of unsupervised learning, as they presuppose some loss function, which in turn presuppose some given target values. Therefore, for generality the authors propose to use a priors-based way of preventing underfitting/overfitting. Moreover, it is an uninformative prior, as it has such advantages as reparameterization invariance and objectiveness. The adjusted mutual information is indeed uninformative, or objective, prior-based, but it is inappropriate in case of unsupervised learning again, as it presupposes some "true" partition.

Information Criterion for Estimation Subsystem

Therefore, the authors propose a new information criterion for estimating data features, based on an objective prior. This criterion can be considered as conditional entropy *H*(*X*| *Part*(*X*)) of a set *X* with respect to the set of possible partitions *Part(X)* of *X,* where entropy *H(X)* is information estimation and the condition *Part(X)* is the objective prior. The objective prior distribution *P(Part(X))* is a probability distribution of all possible partitions *Part(X)* of the set *X* with respect to different combinations and permutations of elements in each subset. The partitions are considered as their entropy is invariant to those combinations and permutations of elements.

The description of the objective prior distribution *P(Part(X))* is following. The set χ=*XX* is a function space of the set X, i.e the set of all possible projections of the set X *to itself.* The power of χ, i.e. the number of all possible projections on X:

$$|\chi| = |X|^{|X|}$$

Given a partition $Part_i(X)$, such that $X = X_1 \cup \ldots \cup X_k$, $|X| = n$, $|X_i| = n_i$, $|Part_i(X)| = k$ and k_j is a number of all subsets X_i with the same number of elements n_i, the power $|Part_i(X)|$, i.e. the number of all possible projections on *X* with the same resulting partition $Part_i(X)$ is defined by the formula:

$$|\mathrm{Part}_i(\mathrm{X})| = \frac{n!}{n_1!\ldots n_k!}\frac{n!}{k!(n-k)!}\frac{k!}{k_1!\ldots k_m!}$$

therefore, the probability $P(Part_i(X))$ is:

$$P\left(\mathrm{Part}_i(X)\right) = \frac{\left|\mathrm{Part}_i(X)\right|}{|\mathcal{X}|}$$

Then the weighted entropy *P*(*Part*(*X*))*H*(*X*) and mean weighted entropy *H*(*X*|*Part*(*X*)) of the set *X* with respect to the set of all possible partitions *Part*(*X*) is:

$$H\left(X|\mathrm{Part}(X)\right) = \sum_i P\left(\mathrm{Part}_i(X)\right)H_i(X)$$

Beside of this numerical measure, it is useful to define a binary characteristic *H*+(X), which means the given partition of *X* is informative, i.e. its entropy *H*(*X*) is more than the mean value *H*(*X*|*Part*(*X*)) or equal:

$$H^{+}(X) = \begin{cases} 1, & \mathit{if}\ H(X) \geq H\left(X|\mathrm{Part}(X)\right) \\ 0, & \mathit{otherwise} \end{cases}$$

and a measure of difference *dH*(*X*) of entropy *H*(*X*) with some given partition of *X* from the mean value *H*(*X*|*Part*(*X*)):

$$dH(X) = |H(X) - H(X|\ \mathrm{Part}(X))|$$

Finally, the partition *Part**(*X*) is considered as optimal according to Bayes principal, i.e. its informativeness is the closest to the mean value:

$$Part^{*}(X) = \arg\min_i(dG(X))$$

This partition is useful when users need to get some expectations about the output values distribution.

Workflow

Many ML algorithms are currently existing. And nearly 100 technologies and algorithms are already included in the system. The dataset features (Reif, 2014) and the requirements of the output model are the basis for algorithm selection. This system provides users with reasonable advice based on information about the dataset and task.

This system works with a straight-back process and provides users all the procedures of data processing. Figure 4 presents the workflow of the system and Figure 5 presents the pseudocode of the workflow.

A user presents a pending dataset and the description of his demand. First, they need to pre-process the dataset. In this system, corresponding preprocessing solutions can be provided according to different characteristics of the dataset. These preprocessing techniques have a variety of processing methods including simple format conversion operations, common exception handling, and even feature extraction based on complex algorithms. In the algorithm pool this system provides as many available solutions as possible for different data defects.

Figure 4. The workflow of the knowledge-oriented system

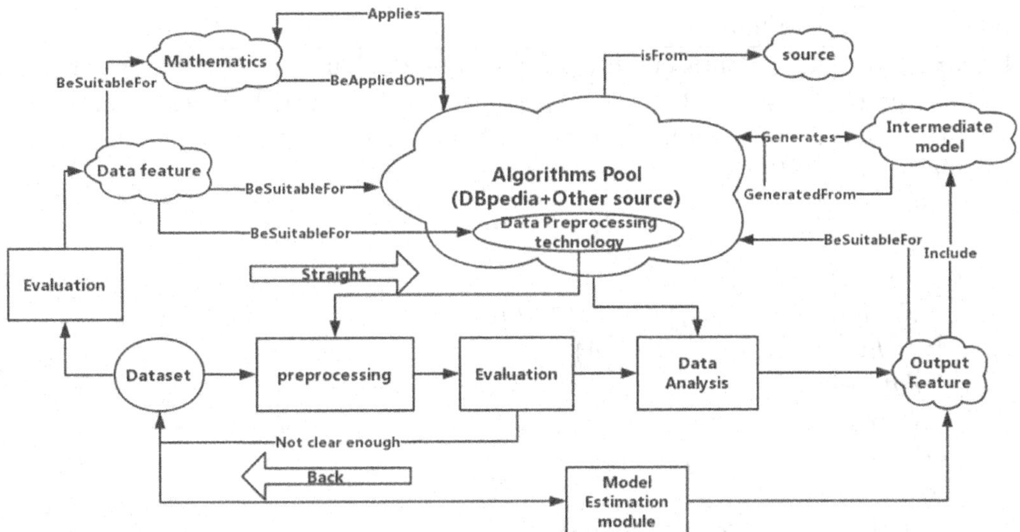

When the dataset is ready for analysis by classification or clustering algorithms, the estimation subsystem will evaluate the dataset to get the dataset characteristics and evaluate the user's needs to get the characteristics of the output. If it is a clustering task, the subsystem will estimate, is it reasonable to apply clustering or not, and if it is so, provide a reasonable number for clusters. If the user desires to perform a classification task which includes a determined output model structure, estimation result can still be used as an important reference solution since the existing labels in dataset may be not an optimal solution. The structure of the output model obtained at this stage is also an important basis for us to recommend the most suitable data analysis algorithm for users.

The information serves as the basis for finding the most appropriate algorithm in the system with the output model structure which obtained in last stage. In the system users can find the corresponding available algorithm set which the properties are specified to according to characteristics of dataset and output. The best result is that they have a common subset and users can combine the additional requirements to choose the most appropriate algorithm in it. But in many cases the results are not satisfactory. Then users need to sort the choices they consider and pick the most important feature to get a set of available algorithms. Based on other characteristics, users can remove the algorithms that do not meet the requirements until they get the only solution.

For many non-computer professional users, a suitable solution does not really help them get the job done. They need detailed guidance during the implementation process. The system provides such services. In the whole system authors use many property statements to connect all the ontologies and explain each algorithm. The system describes the procedures of all the algorithms includes the preprocessing techniques and the data analysis algorithms step by step. And this description is from the general level to the detailed level so that users can understand them easily.

Figure 5. The pseudocode of the workflow of this knowledge-oriented system

Algorithm 1 Workflow

Parameters: Input dataset *data*, Algorithm pool including ML algorithms and preprocessing technology $A\{a_1, a_2 \ldots a_n; t_1, t_2 \ldots t_n\}$, Evaluation module $eval()$, Estimation module $esti()$, Search technology or algorithm module $S\_tech(), S\_algo()$

```
eval(data)
//preprocessing
while (data! = tidy) do
    F_data{f1, f2 ... fi} ← eval(data)
    tech ← S_tech(F_data, A)
    data ← tech(data)
    F_output ← esti(data)
end while
//data analysis
F_task{t1, t2 ... tj} ← eval(task)
algo ← S_algo(F_data, F_task, F_output, A)
return algo(data)
```

This interpretation service is applied to the entire data processing process. Not only when users are doing ML algorithms, they can find the operational flow with its help. They also describe the implementation process of many data preprocessing techniques. At the same time, authors found that many other algorithms were called in the execution steps in many complex algorithms. And the interpretation subsystem makes such a complex execution structure very clear and easy to understand.

EXPERIMENT

Authors use Fisher's Iris dataset as the experimental dataset. It has 150 samples and 4 attributes (Sepallength, sepalwidth, petallength, petalwidth) and it is divided into three categories (setosa, versicolor, virginica) in the training set. Due to computational complexity and technical restrictions authors have to consider only the fragment of the dataset with the selected 70 samples (authors choose first 25 samples in label "setosa", first 25 samples in label "versicolor", first 20 samples in label "virginica" as a new dataset). In the experiment of the estimation subsystem they ignore the labels of this dataset and calculate the suitable range of the number of the output clusters. Then they choose a suitable classification algorithm based this estimation advice and other characteristics in the experiment of the ontology-based recommendation subsystem.

Since this is a common experimental dataset, it is already neat enough. Authors skip the stage of preprocessing. First, authors can use this estimation subsystem to evaluate existing labels. If existing labels are not informative enough, authors consider using the recommended structure as a new label structure.

To demonstrate the estimation method, they apply it to the Fisher's Iris dataset. The results are in the Table 4.

Table 4. The result of estimating 70 elements from iris dataset

Property	Value
X	[25, 25, 20]
I(X)	0.76, 0.76, 0.7
H(X)	0.74
H(X|Part(X))	0.13
dH(X)	0.61
|Part*(X)|	35

Summing up, the mean weighted entropy of the set with 70 elements is $H(X|Part(X)) = 0.13$, particular partition [25, 25, 20] is informative and on 0.63 more informative then the mean value, the partition $Part^*(X)$ has 35 elements. Therefore, the recommendation would be use clustering with no more than 35 clusters. It means 35 is the upper limit of the number of output clusters.

This dataset has existing labels whose number is 3. It fits the requirement of the estimation subsystem. Authors use the existing labels so that they can evaluate the accuracy of the experimental results. Suppose, they evaluated the other dataset features to get the dataset characteristics: small size (only 70 samples), interdependent attributes. Then authors evaluate the user's requirements: accuracy, speed, explainable ability (users want to know the rules of classifying these flowers). In this experiment both of accuracy and speed are necessary for us. And it is better to know the classification rules. Users can find a set of the suitable algorithms in the corresponding to each characteristic in this system, since the relations have been built based on a large number of performance experiments.

Users need to select some of the most important characteristics as the criteria for consideration. A reasonable rank of the conditions should be proposed which shown in Figure 6. For this dataset, speed, accuracy and explainable ability must be the most important. Because users must want to accurately classify these flowers and can find the difference between these flowers. Other characteristics can be used as a reference to find the most appropriate algorithm.

Based on this rank users should input the performance and characteristics one by one and get the suitable algorithms depending on the previous results. The inference process is shown in Figure 7.

In summary, J48 is the most suitable algorithm. Although it cannot deal well with the dataset whose size is small. But J48 is suitable for the other more important characteristics. Therefore, according to the recommendation of the system, authors selected J48 as the classification algorithm to do the classification task and compare with some common classification algorithms which is shown in Table 5.

According to the results, J48 has a good performance in terms of model building time and test time. There is no significant lower accuracy than other algorithms. At the same time, it is one of decision tree algorithms which can well explain the rules of classification. This is undoubtedly the most suitable algorithm for this task.

APPLICATION

Currently, this knowledge-oriented system includes nearly 100 machine learning algorithms and data preprocessing methods. Part of the algorithm pool is presented in Figure 8.

Figure 6. The rank of input conditions of dataset 'iris'

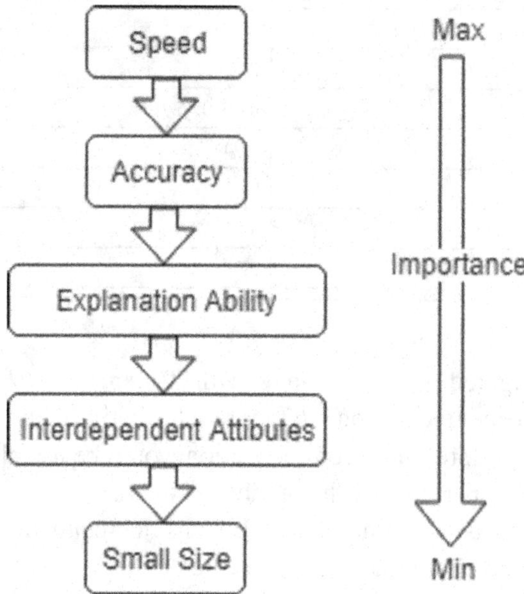

Figure 7. The inference process based on the rank of conditions (J48 is subclass of decision tree, so it inherits the performances of decision tree)

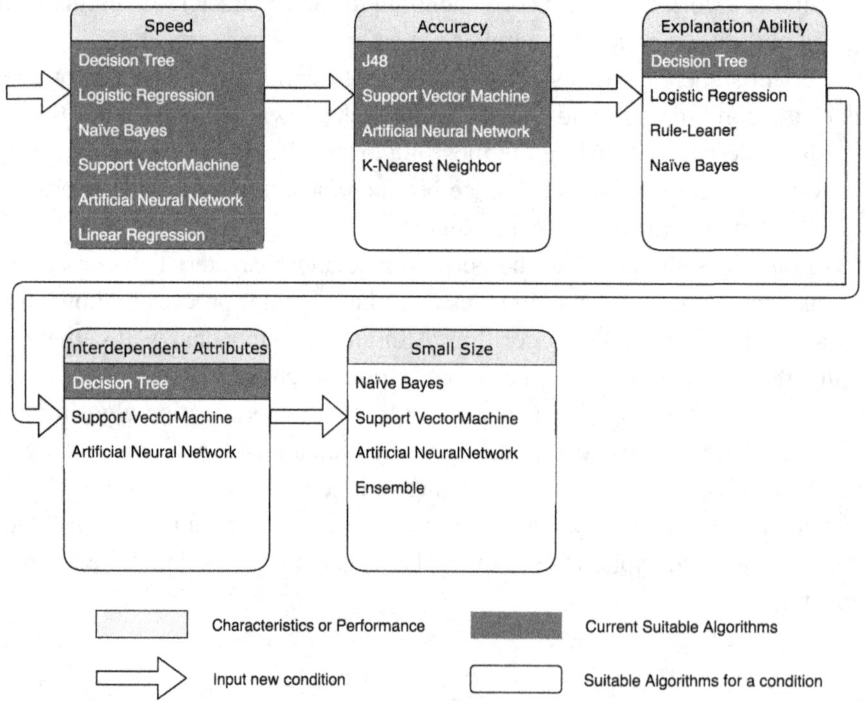

Table 5. The result of comparing the performance of different classification algorithms

Algorithm	IntermediateModel	Trainingtime(ms)	Accuracy (%)
Bagging	Ensemble	29	98.57
BayesNet	Bayesian	13	95.71
J48	Tree	14	98.57
Logistic	Regression	19	95.71
Multilayer Perception	Neural Network	213	95.71
Naive Bayes	Bayesian	11	95.71
PART	Tree	17	94.28
Random Forest	Forest	54	95.71
Support Vector Poly Kernel	Instance Based	24	95.71

Figure 8. Part of the algorithm pool

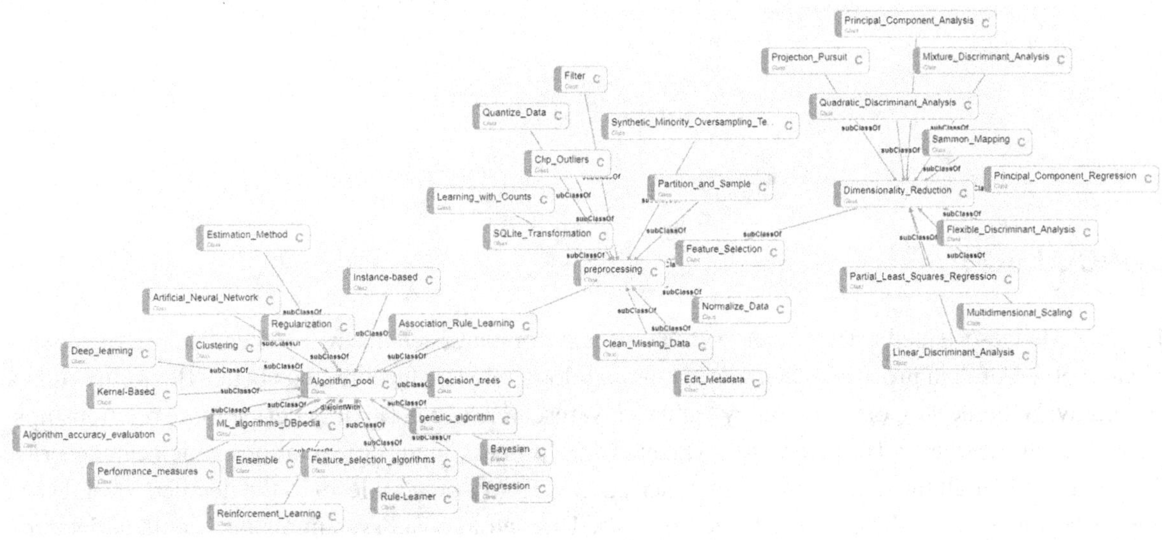

In addition to the already processed data sets, it also provides good advice for real world data processing tasks from many fields. Based on this system, the authors obtained good results for algorithms and model selection for the preprocessing and classification tasks of real medical data (Tianxing & Zhukova, 2018). In Figure 9 an example for searching suitable algorithms for a time series classification task is shown.

Often, real world data sets are always messy, so the preprocessing process is complex. Due to this situation, this system can provide useful information in more aspects.

Figure 9. An example for searching suitable algorithms based on this system

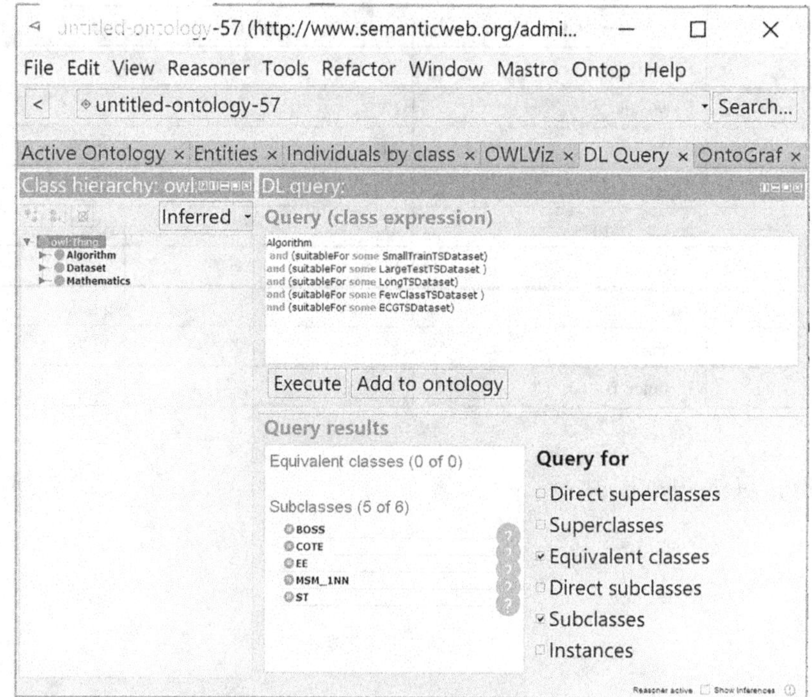

CONCLUSION

This knowledge-oriented system effectively helps non-computer science researchers choose the appropriate method of data processing. Obviously, an ontology of ML algorithm has better flexibility than a taxonomy. With the support of ontology technology, researchers can flexibly define more relationships. At the same time, they define a new abstract ontology "process" and some relations which can describe the procedures of all the algorithms. This description is from a general level to the detailed level. Users can be instructed what they should do step by step. The ontology subsystem makes people understand ML better. The authors also developed the estimation subsystem for the data processing. Based on this subsystem users can get reasonable recommendations about the most suitable algorithm.

This knowledge-oriented system is also constantly improving. The authors are currently focus on automatic comprehensive estimation of dataset features and classification of new algorithms based on experimental results.

REFERENCES

Amores, J. (2013). Multiple instance classification: Review, taxonomy and comparative study. *Artificial Intelligence*, *201*, 81–105. doi:10.1016/j.artint.2013.06.003

Anastácio, I., Martins, B., & Calado, P. (2011). Supervised Learning for Linking Named Entities to Knowledge Base Entries. In TAC 2011.

Antoniazzi, F., Paolini, G., Roffia, L., Masotti, D., Costanzo, A., & Cinotti, T. S. (2017, November). A web of things approach for indoor position monitoring of elderly and impaired people. In *Proceedings of the 2017 21st Conference of Open Innovations Association (FRUCT)* (pp. 51-56). IEEE. 10.23919/FRUCT.2017.8250164

Arthur, D., & Vassilvitskii, S. (2007, January). k-means++: The advantages of careful seeding. In *Proceedings of the eighteenth annual ACM-SIAM symposium on Discrete algorithms* (pp. 1027-1035). Society for Industrial and Applied Mathematics.

Ayodele, T. O. (2010). Types of machine learning algorithms. In *New advances in machine learning*. IntechOpen.

Baimuratov, I. R., & Zhukova, N. A. (2018, May). An Approach to Clustering Models Estimation. In *Proceedings of the 2018 22nd Conference of Open Innovations Association (FRUCT)* (pp. 19-24). IEEE. 10.23919/FRUCT.2018.8468286

Bechhofer, S. (2009). OWL: Web ontology language. Encyclopedia of database systems, 2008-2009.

Bernstein, A., Provost, F., & Hill, S. (2005). Toward intelligent assistance for a data mining process: An ontology-based approach for cost-sensitive classification. *IEEE Transactions on Knowledge and Data Engineering*, *17*(4), 503–518. doi:10.1109/TKDE.2005.67

Borodin, A. V., Zavyalova, Y. V., & Meigal, A. Y. (2017, November). Towards a mobile system for hypertensive outpatients' treatment adherence improvement. In *Proceedings of the 2017 21st Conference of Open Innovations Association (FRUCT)* (pp. 57-63). IEEE.

Caruana, R., & Niculescu-Mizil, A. (2006, June). An empirical comparison of supervised learning algorithms. In *Proceedings of the 23rd international conference on Machine learning* (pp. 161-168). ACM. 10.1145/1143844.1143865

Chuvak, A., & Surovtsova, T. (2018, May). Analysis of User Activity in Wireless Local Area Network of Petrozavodsk State University. In *Proceedings of the 2018 22nd Conference of Open Innovations Association (FRUCT)* (pp. 34-39). IEEE. 10.23919/FRUCT.2018.8468288

Dash, M., & Liu, H. (1997). Feature selection for classification. *Intelligent Data Analysis*, *1*(3), 131–156. doi:10.3233/IDA-1997-1302

Desgraupes, B. (2013). Clustering indices. *University of Paris Ouest-Lab Modal'X*, *1*, 34.

Gabidulin, E. M., & Pilipchuk, N. I. (2007). *Lectures on information theory*. MIPT.

Gupta, B., Agrawal, D. P., & Yamaguchi, S. (Eds.). (2016). Handbook of research on modern cryptographic solutions for computer and cyber security. Hershey, PA: IGI Global. doi:10.4018/978-1-5225-0105-3

Hilario, M., Nguyen, P., Do, H., Woznica, A., & Kalousis, A. (2011). Ontology-based meta-mining of knowledge discovery workflows. In *Meta-learning in computational intelligence* (pp. 273-315).

Huang, L., Milne, D., Frank, E., & Witten, I. H. (2012). Learning a concept-based document similarity measure. *Journal of the American Society for Information Science and Technology*, *63*(8), 1593–1608. doi:10.1002/asi.22689

Jain, A. K., & Dubes, R. C. (1988). Algorithms for clustering data.

Kanev, A., Nasteka, A., Bessonova, C., Nevmerzhitsky, D., Silaev, A., Efremov, A., & Nikiforova, K. (2017, April). Anomaly detection in wireless sensor network of the "smart home" system. In *Proceedings of the 2017 20th Conference of Open Innovations Association (FRUCT)* (pp. 118-124). IEEE.

Kaufman, L., & Rousseeuw, P. (1987). Clustering by means of medoids.

Kotsiantis, S. B., Zaharakis, I., & Pintelas, P. (2007). Supervised machine learning: A review of classification techniques. *Emerging artificial intelligence applications in computer engineering, 160*, 3-24.

Li, T., Gupta, B. B., & Metere, R. (2018). Socially-conforming cooperative computation in cloud networks. *Journal of Parallel and Distributed Computing, 117*, 274–280. doi:10.1016/j.jpdc.2017.06.006

McGuinness, D. L., & Van Harmelen, F. (2004). OWL web ontology language overview. *W3C recommendation, 10*(10).

Meigal, A., Reginva, S., Gerasimova-Meigal, L., Prokhorov, K., & Moschevikin, A. (2018, May). Analysis of Human Gait Based on Smartphone Inertial Measurement Unit: A Feasibility Study. In *Proceedings of the 2018 22nd Conference of Open Innovations Association (FRUCT)* (pp. 151-158). IEEE. 10.23919/FRUCT.2018.8468264

Panov, P., Soldatova, L., & Džeroski, S. (2014). Ontology of core data mining entities. *Data Mining and Knowledge Discovery, 28*(5-6), 1222–1265. doi:10.100710618-014-0363-0

Reif, M., Shafait, F., Goldstein, M., Breuel, T., & Dengel, A. (2014). Automatic classifier selection for non-experts. *Pattern Analysis & Applications, 17*(1), 83–96. doi:10.100710044-012-0280-z

Satyanandam, N., & Satyanarayana, D. C. (2013). Taxonomy of Data Mining and Machine Learning Approaches for Healthcare Systems. *International Journal of Innovative Research in Computer and Communication Engineering, 1*(2).

Shen, H., Chen, M., Bunescu, R., & Mihalcea, R. Wikipedia Taxonomic Relation Extraction using Wikipedia Distant Supervision. *Ann Arbor, 1001*, 48109.

Smirnov, A., Ponomarev, A., Levashova, T., & Shilov, N. (2017, November). Ontology-based cloud platform for human-driven applications. In *Proceedings of the 2017 21st Conference of Open Innovations Association (FRUCT)* (pp. 304-310). IEEE. 10.23919/FRUCT.2017.8250197

Smorodin, G., Kolesnichenko, O., Kolesnichenko, Y., Myakinkova, L., Prisyazhnaya, N., Yakovleva, D., . . . Litvak, N. (2017, November). Internet of Things: Modem paradigm of health care. In *Proceedings of the 2017 21st Conference of Open Innovations Association (FRUCT)* (pp. 311-320). IEEE.

Stergiou, C., Psannis, K. E., Kim, B. G., & Gupta, B. (2018). Secure integration of IoT and cloud computing. *Future Generation Computer Systems, 78*, 964–975. doi:10.1016/j.future.2016.11.031

Tianxing, M., & Zhukova, N. (2018). An Ontology of Machine Learning Algorithms for Human Activity Data Processing. *learning, 10*, 12.

Ulitin, B., & Babkin, E. (2018, May). An Object-Oriented Model for Smart Devices in Internet of Things. In *Proceedings of the 2018 22nd Conference of Open Innovations Association (FRUCT)* (pp. 263-271). IEEE. 10.23919/FRUCT.2018.8468302

Van Rees, R. (2003). Clarity in the usage of the terms ontology, taxonomy and classification. *CIB REPORT*, *284*(432), 1–8.

Viksnin, I. I., Gataullin, R., Muradov, A., Danilov, I., Tursukov, N., & Chechet, A. (2017, April). Modeling people behavior in emergency situations. In *Proceedings of the 2017 20th Conference of Open Innovations Association (FRUCT)* (pp. 478-483). IEEE. 10.23919/FRUCT.2017.8071351

Vinh, N. X., Epps, J., & Bailey, J. (2010). Information theoretic measures for clusterings comparison: Variants, properties, normalization and correction for chance. *Journal of Machine Learning Research*, *11*(Oct), 2837–2854.

Vorobeva, A. A. (2017, April). Influence of features discretization on accuracy of random forest classifier for web user identification. In *Proceedings of the 2017 20th Conference of Open Innovations Association (FRUCT)* (pp. 498-504). IEEE. 10.23919/FRUCT.2017.8071354

Yaseen, Q., Aldwairi, M., Jararweh, Y., Al-Ayyoub, M., & Gupta, B. (2018). Collusion attacks mitigation in internet of things: A fog based model. *Multimedia Tools and Applications*, *77*(14), 18249–18268. doi:10.100711042-017-5288-3

Yaseen, Q., Aldwairi, M., Jararweh, Y., Al-Ayyoub, M., & Gupta, B. (2018). Collusion attacks mitigation in internet of things: A fog based model. *Multimedia Tools and Applications*, *77*(14), 18249–18268. doi:10.100711042-017-5288-3

Zaki, M. J., Meira, W. Jr., & Meira, W. (2014). Data mining and analysis: fundamental concepts and algorithms.

Zinnikus, I., Fraser, C., & Fischer, K. (2004). An Ontology-Based Recommendation System. In Proceedings of Artificial Intelligence and Applications.

This research was previously published in the International Journal of Embedded and Real-Time Communication Systems (IJERTCS), 10(4); pages 20-38, copyright year 2019 by IGI Publishing (an imprint of IGI Global).

Chapter 48
Machine-Learning-Based Image Feature Selection

Vivek K. Verma
Manipal University Jaipur, India

Tarun Jain
Manipal University Jaipur, India

ABSTRACT

This is the age of big data where aggregating information is simple and keeping it economical. Tragically, as the measure of machine intelligible data builds, the capacity to comprehend and make utilization of it doesn't keep pace with its development. In content-based image retrieval (CBIR) applications, every database needs its comparing parameter setting for feature extraction. CBIR is the application of computer vision techniques to the image retrieval problem that is the problem of searching for digital images in large databases. In any case, the vast majority of the CBIR frameworks perform ordering by an arrangement of settled and pre-particular parameters. All the major machine-learning-based search algorithms have discussed in this chapter for better understanding related with the image retrieval accuracy. The efficiency of FS using machine learning compared with some other search algorithms and observed for the improvement of the CBIR system.

INTRODUCTION

In the last few decades, the dimensionality of the data associated with machine learning and information mining errands has hugely expanded. Information with high degree and dimensionality has becomes major challenge with classical learning techniques (Belarbi, Mahmoudi, & Belalem, 2017). With the expansive number of features, a learning model can be non-fitted, and it results poor accuracy. To address the information mining challenges and issue of the FS, a wide range of research reference are available. Image feature descriptors selection is the best way to eliminate noisy and redundant set from feature to be used in the classification. Major purpose of any FS method is to choose a subset of features that reduce the redundancy and maximize the significance to the target set. FS is used for refining learning

DOI: 10.4018/978-1-6684-6291-1.ch048

performance, reducing computation, and shrinking required space. To discriminate one class object from another for any pattern recognition algorithm features takes a major role. This chapter focuses on CBIR systems in which image features are extracted, and classified accordingly with one aspect of the relevancy of features with desired outcome. As a consequence FS plays a significant role CBIR and the improved selection process usually results in greater retrieval precision. Image classification is a generally contemplated issue in the analysis of images and also with, computer vision. Most of the classification frameworks can be separated into two major stages, include extraction of each image feature by a high-dimensional element vector. Next, these vectors are selected by help of classifier based on various search algorithms. Among feature extraction and the feature classification, an additional step can take place that is feature selection. This step, is about selection of a subset of features to improve the accuracy of information retrieval. Then again, include selection techniques have presently increased significant role to lessen semantic gap. Machine learning gives instruments by which vast amounts of information can be naturally examined. Feature Selection (FS) by distinguishing the most remarkable elements for learning, concentrates a learning computation on those parts of the information most helpful for investigation and future expectation. In such manner, this chapter is dedicated to show an idea of ways to deal with decrease the semantic gap using machine learning between low level visual components and irregular state semantics, through concurrent feature adjustment and highlight FS. To solve Feature Selection problem, a type of heuristic search algorithm can be used. Machine learning based search method is attractive intelligence optimization technique and many of the powerful method that has motivated and discussed in this chapter. Image feature subset selection is the way toward distinguishing and expelling however much immaterial and excess data as could reasonably be expected. This decreases the dimensionality of the information and may enable learning computations to work quicker and all the more adequately. Now and again, exactness on future characterization can be enhanced; in others, the outcome is a more reduced, effortlessly deciphered portrayal of the objective idea. On the basis of evaluation environments, FS procedures are divided into three major models as filter model, wrapper model and embedded model.

Importance of FS

Any machine learning based classification works on the simplest rule if set of features are waste (noisy data) it gives only waste as outcome. In case when size of feature set is large this becomes necessary for the relevant outcome. In most of the cases it is not necessary to include all the feature set for creating efficient algorithm. Only few set of features should be use for efficient and optimal result of the algorithms. Sometimes less is more accurate but accuracy depends on the optimal number of features i.e. not more or less but accurate. An optimal number of feature set generally reduces the time train as well as the performance time.

- **Faster Training:** One of the toughest difficulties in machine learning is getting the right data in the optimal size. An efficient CBIR system need machine learning algorithm and it commonly needs good size of training set for more accurate result but it upturns the complexity as well. If FS methods utilizes while constructing the training data set it improves the time complexity of algorithm.
- **Reduces Complexity:** Generally features selection procedures effort to discover the finest set of features that can isolate the classes but there is no open concern for problematic or informal samples and what should be used as training data. In enhancing, the algorithm picks out the fea-

tures that reduce the error. Therefore, the best set of feature reduces the processing time as well it gives accurate result.
- **Improves Accuracy:** As FS is a procedure to discover the best optimal subset of characteristics which well explains the association of independent data with target data. Based on field knowledge, this techniques select feature(s) and it may have higher effect on target data. This helps to visualize the relationship between data, which makes selection process easier and improves the accuracy.

Characteristics of FS Algorithms

FS algorithms with a few remarkable exceptions perform a search through the space of feature subsets and, as a result must address four elementary issues affecting the nature of the search:

- **Starting Point:** Direction of the search is affected by the starting point in the feature subset space from where one need to begin the search. First choice is to start with zero features and after that consecutively add more attributes. In this scenario, the search is said to proceed forward through the search space. On the contrary, the search can start by considering all features and consecutively remove them. In this scenario, the search proceeds backward through the search space. Another choice is to start somewhere in the middle and move outwards from this point.
- **Search Organization:** An exhaustive search of the feature subspace is prohibitive for all but a small initial number of features. For N features there exist 2^N possible subsets from N features. Heuristic search approaches are more feasible than exhaustive approaches and can provide better results, although they do not guarantee finding the optimal subset.
- **Evaluation Strategy:** How subsets of the features are evaluated is the only one main distinguishing factor among FS algorithms for machine learning. One model, dubbed the filter (Min, Hu, & Zhu, 2014) works independent of any learning algorithm—before learning begins undesirable features are filtered out of the data. These algorithms utilize heuristics based on common characteristics of the data to evaluate the merit of feature subsets. Another school of thought argues that the bias of a particular induction algorithm should be taken into consideration when selecting features. This approach, called the wrapper, utilizes an induction algorithm along with a statistical re-sampling method such as cross-validation to estimate the final accuracy of feature subsets.
- **Stopping Criterion:** When to stop searching through the space of feature subsets is the decision of feature selector. Depending on the evaluation approach, a feature selector might stop adding or removing features when none of the alternatives improves upon the merit of a current feature subset. Alternatively, the algorithm might continue to revise the feature subset as long as the merit does not degrade. A further option could be to continue generating feature subsets until reaching the opposite end of the search space and then select the best.

FEATURE SELECTION FOR CBIR

CBIR is the application of computer vision techniques to the image retrieval problem that is the problem of searching for digital images in large databases. In CBIR search don't considers the metadata such as keywords, tags, or descriptions associated with the image. It only considers contents of the image. The term "content" means here are colors, shapes, textures, or some other related information that can be directly derived from the image itself. CBIR is necessary because searches that based completely on metadata are dependent on annotation quality and completeness. The effectiveness of traditional keyword image search is subjective and it cannot be well-defined. CBIR systems also have similar challenges in defining success. Many of the FS method was utilized to choose the optimal set of features that take full advantage of the detection level and make simpler the computation of the image retrieval processing (Nikkam & Reddy, 2016). Most of the system selects the best suitable feature set from a large image features, generally includes shape, color, and textual features with some classification technique. Therefore, FS is takes a vital role for the greater accuracy of the retrieval system.

MACHINE LEARNING BASED TECHNIQUES

Many components influence the achievement of machine learning on a given undertaking. The portrayal and nature of the case information is most importantly. Hypothetically, having more elements should bring about all the more segregating power. Nonetheless, down to earth involvement with machine learning computations has demonstrated this is not generally the situation. Many learning computations can be seen as making a gauge of the likelihood of the class mark given an arrangement of components. This is an intricate, high dimensional conveyance. Acceptance is frequently performed on restricted information. This makes assessing the numerous probabilistic parameters troublesome. Keeping in mind the end goal to maintain a strategic distance from over fitting the preparation information, numerous computations utilize the predisposition to fabricate a basic model that still accomplishes some satisfactory level of execution on the preparation information. This inclination frequently drives a computation to favor few prescient properties over a substantial number of components that, if utilized as a part of the best possible mix, are completely prescient of the class mark. In the event that there is excessively superfluous and repetitive data exhibit or the information is boisterous and questionable, at that point getting the hang of amid the preparation stage is more troublesome. Image feature subset selection is the way toward distinguishing and expelling however much immaterial and excess data as could reasonably be expected. This decreases the dimensionality of the information and may enable learning computations to work quicker and all the more adequately. Now and again, exactness on future characterization can be enhanced; in others, the outcome is a more reduced, effortlessly deciphered portrayal of the objective idea.

Genetic Algorithms (GA)

The GA are productive techniques for variable minimization. In feature set choice setting, the expectation mistake of the model based upon an arrangement of highlights is streamlined. The hereditary computation imitates the characteristic development by displaying a dynamic populace of arrangements. The individuals from the populace, alluded to as chromosomes, encode the chose highlights. The encoding more often than not takes type of bit strings with bits relating to choose highlights set and others cleared. Every chromosome prompts a model manufactured utilizing the encoded highlights. By utilizing the preparation information, the blunder of the model is measured and fills in as a wellness work. Over the span of development, the chromosomes are subjected to hybrid and change. By permitting survival and proliferation of the fittest chromosomes, the computation viably limits the mistake work in ensuing ages. The achievement of GA relies upon a few variables. The parameters guiding the hybrid, change and survival of chromosomes ought to be deliberately enabled the populace to investigate the arrangement space and to forestall early meeting to homogeneous populace involving a neighborhood least. The decision of beginning populace is additionally imperative in hereditary element choice. To address this issue, e.g. a technique in view of Shannon's entropy joined with chart investigation can be utilized. Hereditary computation in light of the Darwinian survival of the fittest hypothesis, is a proficient and comprehensively material worldwide advancement computation. Rather than customary pursuit methods, hereditary computation begins from a gathering of focuses coded as limited length letters in order strings rather than one genuine parameter set. Moreover, hereditary computation isn't a slope climbing computation thus the subordinate data and step estimate count are not required. The three fundamental administrators of hereditary computations are: determination, hybrid and change. It chooses a few people with more grounded flexibility from populace as indicated by the wellness, and afterward chooses the duplicate number of individual as per the determination strategies, for example, Backer stochastic all-inclusive inspecting. It trades and recombines a couple of chromosome through hybrid. Transformation is done to change certain point state through likelihood. By and large, one needs to pick reasonable hybrid and change likelihood over and over through genuine issues.

Support Vector Machine (SVM)

SVM is based on the auxiliary hazard minimization guideline to look for a choice surface that can isolate the information focuses into two classes with a maximal edge between them. The decision of the correct piece work is the principle challenge when utilizing a SVM (Wei, Zhang, Yu, Hu, Tang, Gui, & Yuan, 2017). It could have distinctive structures, for example, Radial Function part and polynomial bit. The benefit of the SVM is its ability of learning in scanty, high dimensional spaces with not very many preparing cases by limiting a bound on the experimental mistake and the intricacy of the classifier in the meantime. Some of the mining tools utilizes the sequential minimal computation for SVM. The SVM frame a gathering of techniques coming from the basic hazard minimization standard, with the straight help vector classifier as its most fundamental part. The SVC goes for making a choice hyper plane that boosts the edge, i.e., the separation from the hyper plane to the closest cases from each of the classes. This takes into account defining the classifier preparing as an obliged streamlining issue. Essentially, the target work is unimodal, as opposed to e.g. neural systems, and in this manner can be enhanced successfully to worldwide ideal. In the easiest case, mixes from various classes can be isolated by straight hyper plane; such hyper plane is characterized exclusively by its closest mixes from the preparation set. Such mixes are alluded to as help vectors, giving the name to the entire strategy. Much of the time, in any case, no direct division is conceivable. To assess this issue, slack factors are presented. These factors are related with the misclassified mixes and, in conjunction with the edge, are liable to improvement. Along these lines, despite the fact that the mistaken grouping can't be stayed away from, it is punished. Since the misclassification of mixes firmly impacts the choice hyper plane, the misclassified mixes additionally move toward becoming help vectors.

Heuristic Search Base Algorithm (HSBA)

Searching the space of feature subsets within sensible time constraints is necessary if a FS algorithm is to operate on data with a large number of features. One simple search strategy is hill climbing using greedy approach, it considers local changes to the current feature subset. Often, a local change is simply the addition or deletion of a single feature from the subset which can give the optimal subset. When the algorithm considers only additions to the feature subset it is known as forward selection; considering only deletions is known as backward elimination (Vergara, & Estévez, 2014). Another approach, known as stepwise bi-directional search, uses both addition of features and deletion of features. Within each of these variations, the search algorithm may consider all possible local changes to the current subset and then select the best, or may simply choose the first change that improves the merit of the current feature subset. In either case, once a change of choice is accepted, it is never reconsidered in any step. If scanned from top to bottom, the diagram shows all local additions to each node; if scanned from bottom to top, the diagram shows all possible local deletions from each node.

MODELS OF FS

On the basis of evaluation conditions, FS algorithms are divided into three major models as filter model and wrapper model and embedded model.

Filter Model

The Filter Model for FS process is done as a pre-processing step with no induction algorithm. To select features the general characteristics of the training data are used i.e. distances between classes or statistical dependencies. This model performance is faster than the wrapper approach because filters methods usually involves less computation than wrappers and results in a better generalization because it works independently of the induction algorithm. Feature set produced by filter method is not tuned to a specific type of predictive model. It means feature set produced by this approach are more general as compare to wrapper and gives lower prediction performance. It is more valuable for showing the relationships between the features because the output feature set does not contain the assumptions of a prediction model. Many filter approaches provide output as feature ranking than an explicit best subset feature and cross validation is used to choose the cut-off point in the ranking.

Wrapper Model

This model features subset selection that can be done by utilizing the induction algorithm as a black box which means no knowledge of the algorithm is needed it just need the interface only. In this feature subset selection algorithm by utilizing the induction algorithm performs a search for a good subset itself as part of the evaluation function. In this accuracy of the induced classifiers is estimated using accuracy estimation techniques.

Embedded Model

The Embedded Model is a catch-all group of techniques which implement FS as part of the learning procedure i.e. model construction process. LASSO method is example of this approach which penalizes the regression coefficients with an L1 penalty, shrinking many of them to zero for constructing a linear model. LASSO algorithm select the any feature dataset which have non-zero regression coefficients. Bolasso is improvement over LASSO with bootstraps samples, and FeaLect which scores all the features based on combinatorial analysis of regression coefficients (Hansen, Reynaud-Bouret, & Rivoirard, 2015). Another approach is the Recursive Feature Elimination algorithm which is more popular and remove features with low weights and commonly used with Support Vector Machines (SVM) to repeatedly construct a model. Embedded approaches lie between filters and wrappers in terms of computational complexity.

Table 1. Pros and cons of FS techniques

S. No.	Modeling Used	Pros	Cons	Related Algorithms	Machine Learning Algorithm
1.	Filter Model (Wang, Zhang, Liu, Lv, & Wang, 2014; Javed, Maruf, & Babri, 2015; Roffo, Melzi, & Cristani, 2015; Roffo, & Melzi, 2016; Oreski & Oreski, 2014; Saeys, Inza, & Larrañaga, 2007)	Not dependent over classifier, Rapid, Accessible, Faster computation than wrapper method	Not domain feature based, Less Accessible	Classical FS Algorithm, Markov Algorithm, Welch's t-test, Infinite FS, Symmetrical Tau, Eigenvector Centrality	Decision Tree, Correlation-based Algorithms
2.	Wrapper Model (Diao & Shen, 2012; Zhang, Wang, Phillips, & Ji, 2014; Bermejo Gámez, J. A., & Puerta, 2014) Wrapper	Simple, Relates with classifier, feature related dependencies	Over fitting problem, Not guarantee for optimal solution as it uses greedy search	Harmony search, Binary PSO with Mutation, Iterated Local Search	Genetic algorithm, Ants colony
3.	Embedded Model(Tabakhi, Moradi, & Akhlaghian, 2014; Hansen, Reynaud-Bouret, & Rivoirard, 2015; Wei, Zhang, Yu, Hu, Tang, Gui, & Yuan, 2017)	Relates with classifier, Faster computation than wrapper methods, Models feature dependencies	FS only based on classifier	Lasso, Bo-Lasso	Naïve Bayes, SVM based Algorithm
4.	Hybrid Model (Chuang, Ke, & Yang, 2016; Jing, 2014)	Faster as Filter Model, Knowledge of learning algorithms as Wrapper Model	Not efficient for small feature set	Hill-Climbing	Hybrid Genetic Algorithm

CONCLUSION

This chapter concluded as conducted analysis of different methods of FS by using different search algorithm especially machine learning based techniques. The numerous FS techniques proposed by different authors has been discussed depend on very extraordinary standards. The major focus area of this work is to analyses the use of FS within image retrieval context. The efficiency of FS using machine learning compared with some other search algorithms and observed for the improvement of the CBIR system. A comparison has been included for various search algorithms with different models of FS in context of related pros and cons. It can be considered that machine learning based FS techniques gives better performance for image retrieval system. The result accuracy always depends on the desired outcome from image retrieval system with the nature of training data set.

REFERENCES

Belarbi, M. A., Mahmoudi, S., & Belalem, G. (2017). PCA as Dimensionality Reduction for Large-Scale Image Retrieval Systems. *International Journal of Ambient Computing and Intelligence*, *8*(4), 45–58. doi:10.4018/IJACI.2017100104

Bermejo, P., Gámez, J. A., & Puerta, J. M. (2014). Speeding up incremental wrapper feature subset selection with Naive Bayes classifier. *Knowledge-Based Systems*, *55*, 140–147. doi:10.1016/j.knosys.2013.10.016

Chuang, L. Y., Ke, C. H., & Yang, C. H. (2016). *A hybrid both filter and wrapper Feature Selection method for microarray classification*. Academic Press.

Diao, R., & Shen, Q. (2012). FS with harmony search. *IEEE Transactions on Systems, Man, and Cybernetics. Part B, Cybernetics*, *42*(6), 1509–1523. doi:10.1109/TSMCB.2012.2193613

Hansen, N. R., Reynaud-Bouret, P., & Rivoirard, V. (2015). Lasso and probabilistic inequalities for multivariate point processes. *Bernoulli*, *21*(1), 83–143. doi:10.3150/13-BEJ562

Javed, K., Maruf, S., & Babri, H. A. (2015). A two-stage Markov blanket based Feature Selection algorithm for text classification. *Neurocomputing*, *157*, 91–104. doi:10.1016/j.neucom.2015.01.031

Jing, S. Y. (2014). A hybrid genetic algorithm for feature subset selection in rough set theory. *Soft Computing*, *18*(7), 1373–1382. doi:10.100700500-013-1150-3

Min, F., Hu, Q., & Zhu, W. (2014). Feature selection with test cost constraint. *International Journal of Approximate Reasoning*, *55*(1), 167–179. doi:10.1016/j.ijar.2013.04.003

Nikkam, P. S., & Reddy, E. B. (2016). A Key Point Selection Shape Technique for Content based Image Retrieval System. *International Journal of Computer Vision and Image Processing*, *6*(2), 54–70. doi:10.4018/IJCVIP.2016070104

Oreski, S., & Oreski, G. (2014). Genetic algorithm-based heuristic for Feature Selection in credit risk assessment. *Expert Systems with Applications*, *41*(4), 2052–2064. doi:10.1016/j.eswa.2013.09.004

Roffo, G., & Melzi, S. (2016). Features selection via eigenvector centrality. Proceedings of New Frontiers in Mining Complex Patterns-NFMCP 2016, 1-12.

Roffo, G., Melzi, S., & Cristani, M. (2015). Infinite Feature Selection. *Proceedings of the IEEE International Conference on Computer Vision*, 4202-4210.

Saeys, Y., Inza, I., & Larrañaga, P. (2007). A review of Feature Selection techniques in bioinformatics. *Bioinformatics (Oxford, England)*, *23*(19), 2507–2517. doi:10.1093/bioinformatics/btm344 PMID:17720704

Tabakhi, S., Moradi, P., & Akhlaghian, F. (2014). An unsupervised Feature Selection algorithm based on ant colony optimization. *Engineering Applications of Artificial Intelligence*, *32*, 112–123. doi:10.1016/j.engappai.2014.03.007

Vergara, J. R., & Estévez, P. A. (2014). A review of Feature Selection methods based on mutual information. *Neural Computing & Applications*, *24*(1), 175–186. doi:10.100700521-013-1368-0

Wang, D., Zhang, H., Liu, R., Lv, W., & Wang, D. (2014). t-Test Feature Selection approach based on term frequency for text categorization. *Pattern Recognition Letters*, *45*, 1–10. doi:10.1016/j.patrec.2014.02.013

Wei, J., Zhang, R., Yu, Z., Hu, R., Tang, J., Gui, C., & Yuan, Y. (2017). A BPSO-SVM algorithm based on memory renewal and enhanced mutation mechanisms for Feature Selection. *Applied Soft Computing*, *58*, 176–192. doi:10.1016/j.asoc.2017.04.061

Zhang, Y., Wang, S., Phillips, P., & Ji, G. (2014). Binary PSO with mutation operator for Feature Selection using decision tree applied to spam detection. *Knowledge-Based Systems*, *64*, 22–31. doi:10.1016/j.knosys.2014.03.015

This research was previously published in Feature Dimension Reduction for Content-Based Image Identification; pages 65-73, copyright year 2018 by Information Science Reference (an imprint of IGI Global).

Chapter 49
Machine Learning Application With Avatar-Based Management Security to Reduce Cyber Threat

Vardan Mkrttchian
https://orcid.org/0000-0003-4871-5956
HHH University, Australia

Leyla Gamidullaeva
Penza State University, Russia & K. G. Razumovsky Moscow State University of Technologies and Management, Russia

Yulia Vertakova
https://orcid.org/0000-0002-1685-2625
Southwest State University, Russia

Svetlana Panasenko
Plekhanov Russian University of Economics, Russia

ABSTRACT

This chapter is devoted to studying the opportunities of machine learning with avatar-based management techniques aimed at optimizing threat for cyber security professionals. The authors of the chapter developed a triangular scheme of machine learning, which included at each vertex one participant: a trainee, training, and an expert. To realize the goal set by the authors, an intelligent agent is included in the triangular scheme. The authors developed the innovation tools using intelligent visualization techniques for big data analytic with avatar-based management in sliding mode introduced by V. Mkrttchian in his books and chapters published by IGI Global in 2017-18. The developed algorithm, in contrast to the well-known, uses a three-loop feedback system that regulates the current state of the program depending on the user's actions, virtual state, and the status of implementation of available hardware resources. The algorithm of automatic situational selection of interactive software component configuration in virtual machine learning environment in intelligent-analytic platforms was developed.

DOI: 10.4018/978-1-6684-6291-1.ch049

INTRODUCTION

Existing security systems offer a reasonable level of protection; however, they cannot cope with the growing complexity of computer networks and hacking techniques. Moreover, security systems suffer from low detection rates and high false alarm rates. In order to overcome such challenging problems, there has been a great number of research conducted to apply Machine Learning (ML) algorithms (Tran, et al., 2012). Machine learning techniques have been successfully applied to several real world problems in areas as diverse as image analysis, Semantic Web, bioinformatics, text processing, natural language processing, telecommunications, finance, medical diagnosis, and so forth (Gama, and Carvalho, 2012).

Recent definition of machine learning is developed by I. Cadez, P. Smyth, H. Mannila, A. Salah, E. Alpaydin (*Cadez, et al., 2001; Salah and Alpaydin, 2004).* The issues of the use of machine learning in cyber security are disclosed in many works *(Anagnostopoulos, 2018; Edgar and Manz, 2017; Yavanoglu and Aydos, 2017; Khan, et al., 2014; Khan, 2019; Dinur, 2018*). Using data mining and machine learning methods for cyber security intrusion detection is proposed by the authors. (Kumar, et al., 2017)

Object classification literature shows that computer software and hardware algorithms are increasingly showing signs of cognition and are necessarily evolving towards cognitive computing machines to meet the challenges of engineering problems (*Khan, et al, 2014).* For instance, in response to the continual mutating nature of cyber security threats, basic algorithms for intrusion detection are being forced to evolve and develop into autonomous and adaptive agents, in a manner that is emulative of human information processing mechanisms and processes *(Khan, et al., 2014; Khan, 2019).*

In connection with the widespread use of information technologies in the military and state fields, along with the classical requirements for the controlling system (stability, continuity, efficiency, secrecy, efficiency), today also introduces fundamentally new requirements, such as:

- adaptability to changing conditions and methods of using the Armed Forces and State;
- providing a single information space on the battlefield;
- openness in terms of building and capacity building;
- possibility of reducing the operational and maintenance staff;
- evolution in development;
- technological independence.

Thus, the maintenance of cyber security can significantly differ depending on the requirements for the control system, its purpose, the specificity of the managed object, the environmental conditions, the composition and state of the forces and controls, and the management order. Why do we need to distinguish between information and cyber security? What tasks can be achieved with this distinction? This need is conditioned by the transition to a new socio-economic formation, called the information society.

If earlier the problems of ensuring cyber security were relevant mainly for the military organization, in connection with the existence and development of the forces and means of information confrontation and electronic warfare, now such problems exist for the state as a whole.

Among the reasons for this situation can be called:

- The absence of an international legal basis prohibiting the use of information weapons and conducting information operations;

- Imperfection of the regulatory legal framework establishing liability for the commission of crimes in the field of information technology;
- Development by individual states of doctrines and strategies of offensive and subversive actions in the information space;
- Intensive development of military information technologies, including means of destruction of civil and military control systems;
- Leveling the role of international organizations and their bodies in the field of ensuring international information security;
- Creation and use of Special Forces and means of negative impact on critical information infrastructure;
- The existence of special samples of malicious software affecting the automated control systems of industrial and other objects of critical infrastructure;
- The emergence of forms of civil disobedience associated with encroachments on the information infrastructure in protest against the policy of the state and the activities of government bodies;
- Penetration of information technologies in all spheres of state and public life, building on their basis systems of state and military control;
- Development of state projects and programs in the field of information (electronic document management, interagency electronic interaction, universal electronic cards, provision of public services in electronic form) aimed at the formation of an information society;

Thus, the tasks of ensuring cyber security for today exist, both for the state as a whole, and for certain critical structures, systems and objects.

Let us examine in more detail some of these reasons that necessitate the isolation of cyber security as an independent type of security.

One of the new negative phenomena that pose a threat to the information sphere is the emergence of hacker groups taking an active social position and covering their activities in social networks and the media. Unlike classic hacker groups that seek not only to hide their activities, but also the fact of their existence, so-called hack activists position themselves as fighters against injustice and arbitrariness, and follow certain independently developed rules and principles. Moreover, the analysis of the activities of such groups allows us to conclude that they pursue non-commercial goals. In their work, ideological (political), rather than material motivation, prevails, which turns them into a more serious threat to the state and commercial companies, compared to ordinary criminals. The analytical study as one of the tendencies of information security in now indicated an increase in attacks on top management. Top executives are no longer visible on the web. Firms should be allowed the possibility that hackers already have complete information about their leadership, which can be used both to discredit and damage the reputation of the company, and for targeted attacks. These facts allow us to conclude that part of the hacker community has become interested in the political and economic situation and is trying to influence it by organizing and holding mass protests and large-scale hacker attacks on the resources of state, including military and commercial structures. The existence of such groups, their ideology and political motivation, negative attitude of their members to public authorities and disregard for the established law and order, present a real danger to the state, including military administration and its infrastructure.

Many experts on information security call hack activism one of the main negative trends of the past and the coming years. Given the fact that the activities of such groups are of a Tran's boundary nature and are expressed in the conduct of unlawful actions in the information space, it is also a threat to the information spheres around the world.

BACKGROUND

Another serious threat for cyber security professionals is the emergence and development of malicious software hitting automated control systems. By embracing social networking tools and creating standards, policies, procedures, and security measures, educational organizations can ensure that these tools are beneficial. At present, many world organizations and enterprises underwent a virus attack, information about which has not been disclosed for security reasons. These incidents attracted the closest attention of security experts around the world. As a result of numerous studies, vulnerabilities have been found in almost all cyber security systems. Much vulnerability allows attackers to remotely execute code in the most important systems responsible for monitoring equipment and receiving inbound information. At the same time, the authors of the chapter believe that the creation of such complex malicious programs are highly skilled personnel and large financial resources, and further appearance of new similar samples should be expected, therefore, modern cybernetic safety must be built as a multidisciplinary science at the highest level of professionalism. The authors of this chapter, as specialists in intellectual control and communications in sliding mode, offer their own, original approach to solving the problem based on the author's method - machine learning applications with avatar-based management techniques. Thus, the described facts make one look at the security of industrial facilities, including defense enterprises, in a new perspective. Along with classical security measures, now it is necessary to pay attention to the security of control systems, to identify and eliminate possible vulnerabilities in their components and infrastructure.

Another example, which makes it necessary to separate cyber security as a separate category, is the activity of foreign countries in the creation of special units and structures. The so-called centers of cyber defense (defense) have appeared in a number of countries lately. Such centers in one form or another already exist in the United States, UK, Australia, Israel, Iran, China, and Germany.

In general, the tasks of such units in all countries are approximately the same - together with special services and law enforcement bodies they protect government bodies, as well as civilian and military critical facilities from harmful effects (hacker attacks, malicious software, etc.). However, their very name, purpose, main tasks and affiliation, in most cases, to a military organization, testify to the priority of the goals of ensuring the security of state and military management. As our research has shown for information confrontation, special information and strike groups of forces and means are created, the objectives of which are as a rule: neutralization or destruction of the information and strategic resource of another (opposing) entity and its armed forces and ensuring the protection of its information and strategic resource from the similar impact of the enemy.

MAIN FOCUS OF THE CHAPTER

Issues, Controversies, Problems, Solutions and Recommendations

The main objects of impact for these forces and assets are:

- Software and information support;
- Software and hardware, telecommunications and other means of information and management;
- Communication channels that ensure the circulation of information flows and the integration of the management system;
- Human intellect and mass consciousness.

Emphasizing the special importance of the information sphere and related processes for the defense of the state, this author identifies military information security as one of the types of military security.

Recently, the attitude towards the information confrontation has changed significantly, it is no longer perceived only as an activity accompanying military operations. More and more factors are forced to treat him as an independent and most promising type of negative impact on the enemy.

In its new quality, such an impact is not only outside the framework of classical military operations, but also gets wider content.

It becomes a powerful, invisible and undeclared by international law means, allowing in the shortest possible time to paralyze the main forces and assets of a hostile state without causing fatal damage to its industrial facilities and territory.

That is why it is necessary to further develop the corresponding developments of military science and their application not only within the framework of the military organization, but also the entire information sphere of any state. The current situation and the specifics of new threats blur the boundaries between peaceful and war time and require the constant participation of all the forces and means of the state in ensuring its information security.

To achieve these goals, complete consolidation of efforts and a clear interaction of law enforcement agencies, special services, military units, research organizations, the media, public associations and commercial companies are necessary.

The Avatar-Based Management technique developed by V. Mkrtchian for the use in modern education process was introduced in journals and books published by IGI Global in 2014-2018 *(Mkrttchian, et al, 2014; Mkrttchian, 2015; Mkrttchian, et al, 2016; Mkrttchian and Aleshina, 2017; Mkrttchian and Belyanina, 2018).* For the purpose of breaking down language and cultural barriers in modern Russian corporations, V. Mkrttchian proposed to use the technology and methods of Avatar-Based Management for training and the improved RTI technology - Respond to Intervention, successfully used in the US in the special education system. Response to Intervention has been in existence for only a short period, yet it has had a powerful impact on the academic achievement of students across the United States. The National Center on Response to Intervention (2010) defined Response to Intervention as a delivery service model that integrates assessment and intervention within a multi-level prevention system to maximize student achievement and reduce behavior problems. With Response to Intervention, schools identify students at risk for poor learning outcomes, monitor student progress, provide evidence-based interventions and adjust the intensity and nature of those interventions depending on a student's responsiveness, and identify students with learning disabilities or other disabilities. To solve the problems with the Russian language, they propose using the previously obtained teaching technologies together with the RTI technology for a new field of application - training the Russian language for personnel of state corporations *(Vertakova and Plotnikov, 2014; Mkrttchian, 2017; Epler, 2013).* The authors of the chapter developed the innovation tools, based on the analysis results of the deliberations of citizens in social networks on topics related to online services, using Intelligent Visualization Techniques for Big Data Analytics with Avatar-Based Management Techniques *(Mkrttchian, et al, 2019).* Social networks and the blogosphere, which is a popular and active area of mass communication, may become the subject of study and data source for the demand for e-government services. Social networks enjoy great popularity among Russian citizens. According to com. Score, nearly every Russian Internet user (99.7% of the average domestic Internet users) has an account in social networks. Scale users of Russian social networks account for more than 52 million people. The average Russian social network user spends 12, 8 hours per month on social networks, which is the highest rate in the world (the world average is 5.9 hours per month) (source and compare). Over the past decade, the social network came on the audience of the Central Russian TV channels. These facts highlight the demand and popularity of social media in Russia, as well as the possibility of using the discussions in social networks to identify attitudes, opinions of citizens and their assessment of the activities of the state.

The problem of discrepancy between the legal basis, both international and domestic, of modern information relations deserves special attention; its inability to take into account the danger of new negative phenomena threatening the information sphere in general and its separate elements, but this problem is beyond the scope of this chapter and will be considered separately by the authors. World policy for cyber security advice in the World Economy requires a thorough understanding of the relevant economic mechanisms that are responsible for the (overall) effects of policy measures in the digital economy *(Mkrtchian, et al., 2019)*. As they do not see a model which reflects their perception of the world advice based on highly abstract vehicles of thinking is likely to be rejected. Avatar-based models may be less prone to be rejected by policymakers as they usually are characterized by a lot more economic structure. This is not to say that an avatar-based modeler would choose any other general approach of building his model than a more orthodox economist. It is rather the larger toolbox that avatar-based models offer which allows him to bring into the picture features of the system that policymakers may find more convincing. Avatars can for example be endowed with different behavioral rules which policy makers recognize from own experience. It is feasible to model an economy along its spatial dimension, and institutions can be incorporated in a much more fine-grained way as in more traditional approaches. As the policy-maker's part is usually about deciding on the institutional environment and possible changes of that, having a more accessible model in that respect may be of great value for a fruitful interaction between policy advisers and policymakers. While most of our discussion so far focused on how to write down an avatar-based model that brings into the picture a simultaneous analysis of various non-negligible institutional, spatial or economic features for a better policymaking, an underdeveloped branch of avatar-based modeling is certainly the positive analysis of economic policy making. It occurs to us that avatar-based models are far from being fully exploited as a means of positive policy analysis. More should be done to bring together a meaningful economic model with an equally meaningful political model that does justice to the intricate rules which characterize democratic societies and shape policy outcomes. Admittedly most of our selling points had the flavor of "we – the avatar-based modelers - can do more". This should not be misunderstood as an argument that in general bigger models are better. Quite on the contrary, it seems crucial to us, that, regardless whether analytical or simulation methods are employed, models are carefully built in a way that only those aspects of the economic environment which seem directly relevant for the policy question at hand are modeled in some detail. A closed macroeconomic avatar-based model has to contain all relevant market, but this does by no means imply that all these markets have to be modeled with identical granularity and institutional richness. Nevertheless, closed macroeconomic avatar-based models typically are quite large and building big models requires big computing power. But machines that potentially can do the job exist and are used by other professions like meteorologists or physicists. However, a lesson learned from our Triple H Avatar project was that running economic models on parallel machines brings up new and non-trivial problems. The reason behind these technical issues is quite intuitive: parallelization requires the slicing up of a big task into digestible smaller chunks. The question becomes how to cut through an economic system. This chapter goal is about machine learning with avatar-based management security; use to optimize threat for cyber security professionals. The chapter illustrates results developed new triangular scheme of machine learning, which included at each vertex one participant: a trainee, training and an expert. Realize the goal set by the authors of the chapter, an intelligent agent is included in the triangular scheme, developed the innovation tools, using Intelligent Visualization Techniques for Big Data Analytic with Avatar-Based Management Techniques. Developed algorithm, in contrast to the well-known, uses three-loop feedback system, that regulate the current state of the program, depending on the user's actions, virtual state and the status of implementation of available hardware resources. Algorithm of automatic situational selection of interactive software component configuration in virtual machine learning environment in intelligent-analytic platforms was developed see fig.1 and fig.2).

Figure 1. Triangular scheme of virtual machine learning environment

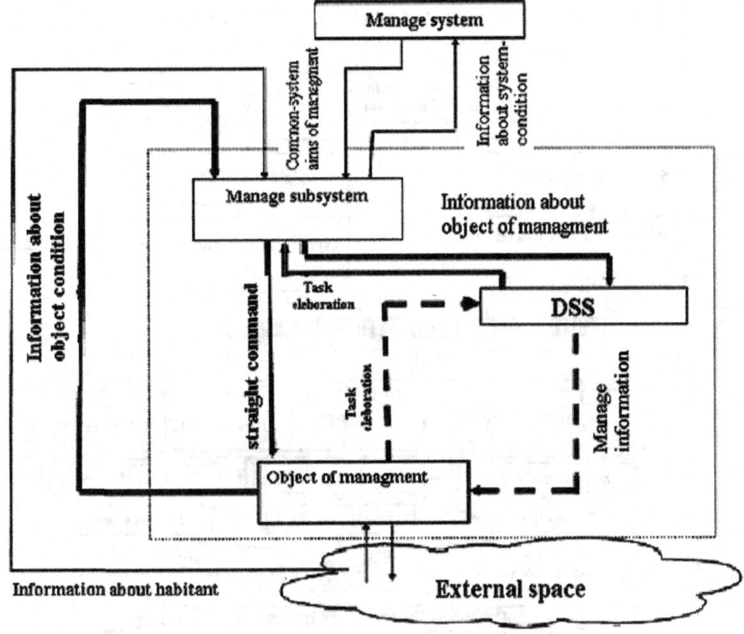

An obvious candidate is the spatial dimension of an economic model, i.e. to allocate the computing to be done for a particular region to a particular processor. However, as there is considerable interaction between regions as in economic models factor and product markets are typically highly interdependent across regions via the flows of worker, capital, intermediate or final goods, a lot of communication between processors has to be organized which can considerable slow down the computing. In order to be able to use avatar-based models for economic policy advice in a way we sketched it, problems of parallelizing code or in general computing issues need to be resolved. In addition and coming back to our argument of convincing policymakers of the appropriateness of the framework on which the policy advice is based, easy to use and intuitive graphical user interfaces (GUIs) need to be developed. Ideally, at some point these GUIs would be so user-friendly that any interested person would be able to run his own simulations. Another issue down the road, which we find important as we want to precede to using avatar-based models for economic policy advice, is the behavioral foundations of the (heterogeneous) avatars that populate our models. Once we deviate or even abandon the perfectly rational avatar model of High Technology there are many degrees of freedom on what to assume for the behavior of an avatar, may it be a worker, firms or a government agency. In the Triple H Avatar project we followed the modeling philosophy to apply management rules for modeling firm behavior. For most decision problems firms face the management literature offers standard procedures (which are often heuristic methods). Examples are specifications on how firms plan their production volume or replenish their stocks. Some of these suggestions are even implemented in standard software that is purchased by firms to automatize on these operational management decisions. As we want to base the policy advice on models where firm behavior is as close as possible to the performance of real world firms it seems natural and also for outsiders convincing to rely on such standard rules where available. For the modeling of the behavior of individuals a promising approach seems to be incorporate findings from experimental studies.

Figure 2. Algorithm of Self-organizing intelligent and analytics platforms

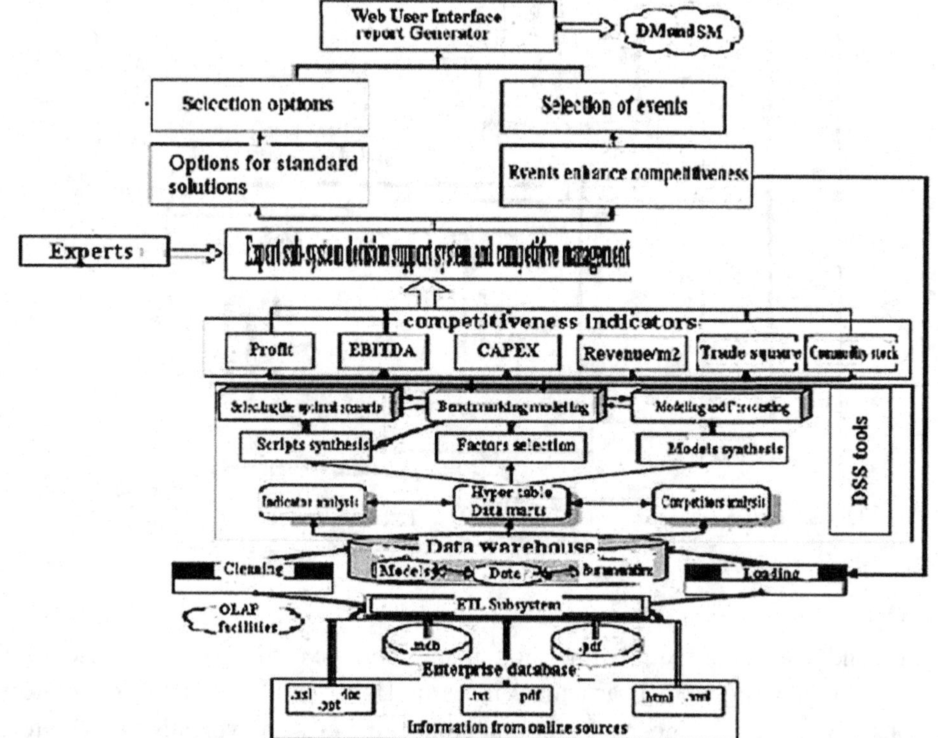

CONCLUSION

In the present conditions, cybernetic security, as a scientific and legal category, exists not only within the framework of information warfare and military security, but also the information sphere as a whole, and therefore should be viewed as an independent type of security. The maintenance of cyber security can significantly differ depending on the requirements for the control system, its purpose, the specificity of the managed object, the environmental conditions, the composition and state of the forces and controls, and the management order.

In conclusion, the authors came to the following research results:

- **Cyber Security:** The state of security management, in which its violation is impossible.
- **Ensuring Cyber Security:** Activities aimed at achieving a state of security management, in which its violation is impossible.
- **Cybernetic Threats:** Phenomena, acts, conditions, factors that pose a threat to management information, management infrastructure, governance entities and governance. The danger lies in the possibility of disrupting the properties of one or more of these elements, which can lead to disruption of control.
- **Cybernetic Attack:** Actions aimed at violation of management.
- The isolation of cyber security as an independent type of security is due to the current level of development of the information sphere, it is justified and allows to fully realize the potential of legal, organizational and technical protection measures, taking into account the specifics of the corresponding systems and management processes. In turn, this implies an increase in the requirements for the protection of systems and management processes, depending on their level, composition and purpose.
- In order to increase the legal protection of cybernetic systems of critical facilities, it seems necessary to expand the list of crimes in the field of computer information and to establish a more severe criminal liability for infringement of such objects.

ACKNOWLEDGMENT

The reported study was funded by RFBR according to the research project No. 18-010-00204_a.

REFERENCES

Anagnostopoulos, C. (2018). Weakly Supervised Learning: How to Engineer Labels for Machine Learning in Cyber-Security. *Data Science for Cyber-Security*, 195–226. doi:10.1142/9781786345646_010

Belyanina, L. A. (2018). Formation of an Effective Multi-Functional Model of the Research Competence of Students. In V. Mkrttchian & L. Belyanina (Eds.), *Handbook of Research on Students' Research Competence in Modern Educational Contexts* (pp. 17–39). Hershey, PA: IGI Global. doi:10.4018/978-1-5225-3485-3.ch002

Cadez, I. V., Smyth, P., & Mannila, H. (2001). Probabilistic modeling of transaction data with applications to profiling, visualization, and prediction. *Proceedings of the Seventh ACM SIGKDD International Conference on Knowledge Discovery and Data Mining - KDD '01*. doi:10.1145/502512.502523

Dinur, I., Dolev, S., & Lodha, S. (Eds.). (2018). Lecture Notes in Computer Science Cyber Security Cryptography and Machine Learning. Springer. doi:10.1007/978-3-319-94147-9

Edgar, T. W., & Manz, D. O. (2017). Machine Learning. *Research Methods for Cyber Security*, 153–173. doi:10.1016/b978-0-12-805349-2.00006-6

Epler, P. (2013). Using the Response to Intervention (RtI) Service Delivery Model in Middle and High Schools. *International Journal for Cross-Disciplinary Subjects in Education*, *4*(1), 1089–1098. doi:10.20533/ijcdse.2042.6364.2013.0154

Gama, J., & de Carvalho, A. C. (2012). Machine Learning. In I. Management Association (Ed.), Machine Learning: Concepts, Methodologies, Tools and Applications (pp. 13-22). Hershey, PA: IGI Global. doi:10.4018/978-1-60960-818-7.ch102

Khan, M. S. (Ed.). (2019). Machine Learning and Cognitive Science Applications in Cyber Security. Academic Press. doi:10.4018/978-1-5225-8100-0

Khan, M. S., Ferens, K., & Kinsner, W. (2014). A Chaotic Complexity Measure for Cognitive Machine Classification of Cyber-Attacks on Computer Networks. *International Journal of Cognitive Informatics and Natural Intelligence*, *8*(3), 45–69. doi:10.4018/IJCINI.2014070104

Kumar, R., & Rituraj, S. (2017). Using Data Mining and Machine Learning Methods for Cyber Security Intrusion Detection. *International Journal of Recent Trends in Engineering and Research*, *3*(4), 109–111. doi:10.23883/IJRTER.2017.3117.9NWQV

Mkrttchian, V. (2015). Use Online Multi-Cloud Platform Lab with Intellectual Agents: Avatars for Study of Knowledge Visualization & Probability Theory in Bioinformatics. International Journal of Knowledge Discovery in Bioinformatics, 5(1), 11-23. Doi:10.4018/IJKDB.2015010102

Mkrttchian, V. (2017). Project-Based Learning for Students with Intellectual Disabilities. In P. L. Epler (Ed.), *Instructional Strategies in General Education and Putting the Individuals With Disabilities Act (IDEA) Into Practice* (pp. 196–221). Hershey, PA: IGI Global. doi:10.4018/978-1-5225-3111-1.ch007

Mkrttchian, V., & Aleshina, E. (2017). *Sliding Mode in Intellectual Control and Communication: Emerging Research and Opportunities*. Hershey, PA: IGI Global. doi:10.4018/978-1-5225-2292-8

Mkrttchian, V., & Belyanina, L. (Eds.). (2018). *Handbook of Research on Students' Research Competence in Modern Educational Contexts*. Hershey, PA: IGI Global. doi:10.4018/978-1-5225-3485-3

Mkrttchian, V., Bershadsky, A., Bozhday, A., Kataev, M., & Kataev, S. (Eds.). (2016). *Handbook of Research on Estimation and Control Techniques in E-Learning systems*. Hershey, PA: IGI Global. doi:10.4018/978-1-4666-9489-7

Mkrttchian, V., Kataev, M., Shih, T., Kumar, M., & Fedotova, A. (2014). Avatars "HHH" Technology Education Cloud Platform on Sliding Mode Based Plug- Ontology as a Gateway to Improvement of Feedback Control Online Society. International Journal of Information Communication Technologies and Human Development, 6(3), 13-31. Doi:10.4018/ijicthd.2014070102

Mkrttchian, V., Palatkin, I., Gamidullaeva, L. A., & Panasenko, S. (2019). About Digital Avatars for Control Systems Using Big Data and Knowledge Sharing in Virtual Industries. In A. Gyamfi & I. Williams (Eds.), *Big Data and Knowledge Sharing in Virtual Organizations* (pp. 103–116). Hershey, PA: IGI Global. doi:10.4018/978-1-5225-7519-1.ch004

Salah, A. A., & Alpaydin, E. (2004). Incremental mixtures of factor analysers. *Proceedings of the 17th International Conference on Pattern Recognition.* 10.1109/ICPR.2004.1334106

Tran, T. P., Tsai, P., Jan, T., & He, X. (2012). Machine Learning Techniques for Network Intrusion Detection. In I. Management Association (Ed.), Machine Learning: Concepts, Methodologies, Tools and Applications (pp. 498-521). Hershey, PA: IGI Global. doi:10.4018/978-1-60960-818-7.ch310

Vertakova, J., & Plotnikov, V. (2014). Public-private partnerships and the specifics of their implementation in vocational education. *Proceeded Economics and Finance, 16*, 24–33. doi:10.1016/S2212-5671(14)00770-9

Yavanoglu, O., & Aydos, M. (2017). A review on cyber security datasets for machine learning algorithms. *2017 IEEE International Conference on Big Data (Big Data).* 10.1109/BigData.2017.8258167

ADDITIONAL READING

Mkrttchian, V. (2012). Avatar manager and student reflective conversations as the base for describing meta-communication model. In G. Kurubacak, T. Vokan Yuzer, & U. Demiray (Eds.), *Meta-communication for reflective online conversations: Models for distance education* (pp. 340–351). Hershey, PA, USA: IGI Global; doi:10.4018/978-1-61350-071-2.ch005

Mkrttchian, V. (2015). Modeling using of Triple H-Avatar Technology in online Multi-Cloud Platform Lab. In M. Khosrow-Pour (Ed.), Encyclopedia of Information Science and Technology (3rd Ed.). (pp. 4162-4170). IRMA, Hershey: PA, USA: IGI Global. Doi:10.4018/978-1-4666-5888-2.ch409

Mkrttchian, V., & Aleshina, E. (2017). The Sliding Mode Technique and Technology (SM T&T) According to Vardan Mkrttchian in Intellectual Control(IC). In *Sliding Mode in Intellectual Control and Communication: Emerging Research and Opportunities* (pp. 1–9). Hershey, PA: IGI Global; doi:10.4018/978-1-5225-2292-8.ch001

Mkrttchian, V., Amirov, D., & Belyanina, L. (2017). Optimizing an Online Learning Course Using Automatic Curating in Sliding Mode. In N. Ostashewski, J. Howell, & M. Cleveland-Innes (Eds.), *Optimizing K-12 Education through Online and Blended Learning* (pp. 213–224). Hershey, PA, USA: IGI Global; doi:10.4018/978-1-5225-0507-5.ch011

Mkrttchian, V., & Belyanina, L. (2016). The Pedagogical and Engineering Features of E- and Blended Learning of Aduits Using Triple H-Avatar in Russian Federation. In V. Mkrttchian, A. Bershadsky, A. Bozhday, M. Kataev, & S. Kataev (Eds.), *Handbook of Research on Estimation and Control Techniques in E-Learning Systems* (pp. 61–77). Hershey, PA, USA: IGI Global; doi:10.4018/978-1-4666-9489-7.ch006

Mkrttchian, V., Bershadsky, A., Bozhday, A., Noskova, T., & Miminova, S. (2016). Development of a Global Policy of All-Pervading E-Learning, Based on Transparency, Strategy, and Model of Cyber Triple H-Avatar. In G. Eby, T. V. Yuser, & S. Atay (Eds.), *Developing Successful Strategies for Global Policies and Cyber Transparency in E-Learning* (pp. 207–221). Hershey, PA, USA: IGI Global; doi:10.4018/978-1-4666-8844-5.ch013

Mkrttchian, V., Bershadsky, A., Finogeev, A., Berezin, A., & Potapova, I. (2017). Digital Model of Bench-Marking for Development of Competitive Advantage. In P. Isaias & L. Carvalho (Eds.), *User Innovation and the Entrepreneurship Phenomenon in the Digital Economy* (pp. 288–303). Hershey, PA, USA: IGI Global; doi:10.4018/978-1-5225-2826-5.ch014

Mkrttchian, V., Kataev, M., Hwang, W., Bedi, S., & Fedotova, A. (2014). Using Plug-Avatars "hhh" Technology Education as Service-Oriented Virtual Learning Environment in Sliding Mode. In G. Eby & T. Vokan Yuzer (Eds.), *Emerging Priorities and Trends in Distance Education: Communication, Pedagogy, and Technology*. Hershey, PA, USA: IGI Global; doi:10.4018/978-1-4666-5162-3.ch004

Mkrttchian, V., Kataev, M., Hwang, W., Bedi, S., & Fedotova, A. (2016), Using Plug-Avatars "hhh" Technology Education as Service-Oriented Virtual Learning Environment in Sliding Mode. Leadership and Personnel Management: Concepts, Methodologies, Tools, and Applications (4 Volumes), (pp.890-902), IRMA, Hershey: PA, USA: IGI Global. Doi:10.4018/978-1-4666-9624-2.ch039

Mkrttchian, V., & Stephanova, G. (2013). Training of Avatar Moderator in Sliding Mode Control. In G. Eby & T. Vokan Yuzer (Eds.), *Project Management Approaches for Online Learning Design* (pp. 175–203). Hershey, PA, USA: IGI Global; doi:10.4018/978-1-4666-2830-4.ch009

Tolstykh, T., Vasin, S., Gamidullaeva, L., & Mkrttchian, V. (2017). The Control of Continuing Education Based on the Digital Economy. In P. Isaias & L. Carvalho (Eds.), *User Innovation and the Entrepreneurship Phenomenon in the Digital Economy* (pp. 153–171). Hershey, PA, USA: IGI Global; doi:10.4018/978-1-5225-2826-5.ch008

KEY TERMS AND DEFINITIONS

Avatar-Based Management: Is a control method and technique introduced by Vardan Mkrttchian in 2018.

Cyber Security Professionals: Are professionals of information security, within the framework of which the processes of formation, functioning and evolution of cyber objects are studied, to identify sources of cyber-danger formed while determining their characteristics, as well as their classification and formation of regulatory documents, implementation of security systems in future.

Intelligent and Analytics Platforms: Is engineering section of avatar-based management.

Machine Learning: Is a class of methods of artificial/natural intelligence, the characteristic feature of which is not a direct solution of the problem, but training in the process of applying solutions to a set of similar problems.

Optimizing Threat: Is situations at cyber security.

Self-Organizing Algorithm: Is section of avatar-based management use for cyber security.

Triangular Scheme of Machine Learning: Is engineering section of Machine learning techniques.

Variability Model: Is section of avatar-based management use for cyber security.

This research was previously published in Machine Learning and Cognitive Science Applications in Cyber Security; pages 123-138, copyright year 2019 by Information Science Reference (an imprint of IGI Global).

Chapter 50
A Review of Machine Learning Methods Applied for Handling Zero-Day Attacks in the Cloud Environment

Swathy Akshaya M.
Avinashilingam Institute for Home Science and Higher Education for Women, India

Padmavathi Ganapathi
Avinashilingam Institute for Home Science and Higher Education for Women, India

ABSTRACT

Cloud computing is an emerging technological paradigm that provides a flexible, scalable, and reliable infrastructure and services for organizations. Services of cloud computing is based on sharing; thus, it is open for attacker to attack on its security. The main thing that grabs the organizations to adapt the cloud computing technology is cost reduction through optimized and efficient computing, but there are various vulnerabilities and threats in cloud computing that affect its security. Providing security in such a system is a major concern as it uses public network to transmit data to a remote server. Therefore, the biggest problem of cloud computing system is its security. The objective of the chapter is to review Machine learning methods that are applied to handle zero-day attacks in a cloud environment.

INTRODUCTION

Cloud Computing (CC) is an international collection of hardware and software from thousands of computer network. It permits digital information to be shared and distributed at very less cost and very fast to use. Cloud Computing has become popular in organizations and individual users. Cloud Computing is the foremost technology which has been emerging in all fields of network applications.

DOI: 10.4018/978-1-6684-6291-1.ch050

Cloud Computing and web services run on a network structure and they are open to network type attacks. Security issues such as data loss, phishing and botnet pose serious threats to organization's data and software. It has become a serious challenge to contain security threats and vulnerabilities. Of all the security threats Zero-Day attacks are the most vulnerable and complex one. Zero-Day Attack (ZDA) could not be easily detected. Zero-Day attack may be from outside or inside. Managing Zero-Day attack is a challenging task.

Cyber Security Ventures recently predicted that there will be one new zero-day exploit per day by 2021. Zero-day attacks are purposively created and developed by many companies and they are sold for profits. For instance, Trend Micro and Zerodium offer up to $500,000 for zero-day attacks.

The number of zero-day exploits detected keeps increasing at an alarming rate. The well-known WannaCry Ransomware attack that hit the majority of the world in May 2017 is an example of the worst-case scenario that could happen due to a Zero-day attack. Zero-Day attacks are difficult to detect as they are not known. Zero-Day attacks usually exploit vulnerabilities that unknown to public including network defenders.

Cloud Environment Attacks

Cloud Computing: A New Vector for Cyber Attacks - Cloud computing technology provides a shared pool of computing resources over the internet at any time for little to no cost. Using cloud computing, many individuals and businesses have already improved the efficiency of their operations while reducing IT costs (Ammar, Gupta, et.al, 2013). While cloud computing models are full of advantages compared to on-site models, they're still susceptible to both inside and outside attacks. Therefore, cloud developers need to take security measures to protect their users' sensitive data from cyber-attacks are shown in table. 1.

Table 1. Cloud Computing Overview

Cloud computing	
Definition	• Delivery method for providing data and computing resources over the network on demand
Core Attributes	• On-demand service • Broad network access • Resource pooling • Rapid elasticity • Measured service
Use cases	• Software as a Service • Platform as a Service • Infrastructure as a Service
Advantages	• Cost saving compared to maintaining physical infrastructure or on-premise solutions • Availability and ease of use • Performance and stability • All updates and patches are applied automatically by the vendor
Disadvantages	• Privacy considerations – your data in the hands of another company • Security considerations – security of your data depends on another company • Availability considerations – cloud computing depends on internet access, virtualization can work without it • Potentially high costs – in some cases, cloud computing can be more expensive than virtualization
Summary	• Used to save costs on computing resources and infrastructure • Convenient subscription-based model, where vendor handles all the issues and client just uses service as needed

Attack Vectors for Cloud Computing

The main goals of cyber-attacks against cloud computing are getting access to user data and preventing access to cloud services. Both can cause serious harm to cloud users and shatter confidence in the security of cloud services. When arranging attacks in the cloud, hackers usually intrude into communications between cloud users and services or applications by:

- Exploiting vulnerabilities in cloud computing.
- Stealing users' credentials somewhere outside the cloud.
- Using prior legitimate access to the cloud after cracking a user's passwords.
- Acting as a malicious insider.

ATTACKS ON CLOUD

There are many ways to attack cloud computing services, and hackers are constantly working on developing more sophisticated ones. However, becoming aware of at least the most common will help cloud developers design more secure solutions. Here's a list of most common types of cyber-attacks performed against cloud users which are shown in figure 1.

Figure 1 Cloud Attack Classifications

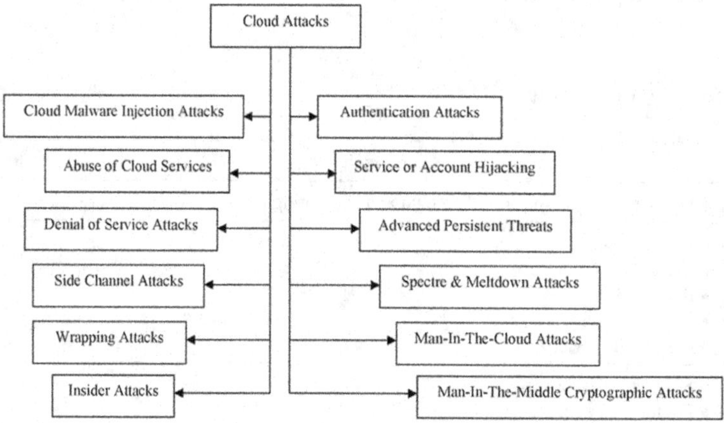

Cloud Malware Injection Attacks

Malware injection attacks are done to take control of a user's information in the cloud. For this purpose, hackers add an infected service implementation module to a SaaS or PaaS solution or a virtual machine instance to an IaaS solution. If the cloud system is successfully deceived, it will redirect the cloud user's requests to the hacker's module or instance, initiating the execution of malicious code. Then the attacker can begin their malicious activity such as manipulating or stealing data or eavesdropping. The most common forms of malware injection attacks are

Abuse of Cloud Services

Hackers can use cheap cloud services to arrange DoS and brute force attacks on target users, companies, and even other cloud providers. For instance, security experts Bryan and Anderson arranged a DoS attack by exploiting capacities of Amazon's EC2 cloud infrastructure in 2010. As a result, they managed to make their client unavailable on the internet by spending only $6 to rent virtual services.

Denial of Service Attacks

DoS attacks are designed to overload a system and make services unavailable to its users. These attacks are especially dangerous for cloud computing systems, as many users may suffer as the result of flooding even a single cloud server. In case of high workload, cloud systems begin to provide more computational power by involving more virtual machines and service instances. While trying to prevent a cyber-attack, the cloud system actually makes it more devastating. Finally, the cloud system slows down and legitimate users lose any availability to access their cloud services. In the cloud environment, DDoS attacks may be even more dangerous if hackers use more zombie machines to attack a large number of systems.

Side Channel Attacks

A side channel attack is arranged by hackers when they place a malicious virtual machine on the same host as the target virtual machine. During a side channel attack, hackers target system implementations of cryptographic algorithms. However, this type of threat can be avoided with a secure system design.

Wrapping Attacks

A wrapping attack is an example of a man-in-the-middle attack in the cloud environment. Cloud computing is vulnerable to wrapping attacks because cloud users typically connect to services via a web browser. An XML signature is used to protect users' credentials from unauthorized access, but this signature doesn't secure the positions in the document. Thus, XML signature element wrapping allows attackers to manipulate an XML document. For example, vulnerabilitywas found in the SOAP interface of Amazon Elastic Cloud Computing (EC2) in 2009. This weakness allowed attackers to modify an eavesdropped message as a result of a successful signature wrapping attack.

Man-In-The-Cloud Attacks

During this type of attack, hackers intercept and reconfigure cloud services by exploiting vulnerabilities in the synchronization token system so that during the next synchronization with the cloud, the synchronization token will be replaced with a new one that provides access to the attackers. Users may never know that their accounts have been hacked, as an attacker can put back the original synchronization tokens at any time. Moreover, there's a risk that compromised accounts will never be recovered.

Insider Attacks

An insider attack is initiated by a legitimate user who is purposefully violating the security policy. In a cloud environment, an attacker can be a cloud provider, administrator or an employee of a client company with extensive privileges. To prevent malicious activity of this type, cloud developers should design secure architectures with different levels of access to cloud services.

Account or Service Hijacking

Account or service hijacking is achieved after gaining access to a user's credentials. There are various techniques for achieving this, from fishing to spyware to cookie poisoning. Once a cloud account has been hacked, attackers can obtain a user's personal information or corporate data and compromise cloud computing services. For instance, an employee of Sales force, a SaaS vendor, became the victim of a phishing scam which led to the exposure of all of the company's client accounts in 2007.

Advanced Persistent Threats (APTs)

APTs are attacks that let hackers continuously steal sensitive data stored in the cloud or exploit cloud services without being noticed by legitimate users. The duration of these attacks allows hackers to adapt to security measures against them. Once unauthorized access is established, hackers can move through data center networks and use network traffic for their malicious activity.

Spectre and Meltdown Attacks

These two types of cyber-attacks have already become a new threat to cloud computing. With the help of malicious JavaScript code, adversaries can read encrypted data from memory by exploiting a design weakness in most modern processors. Both, Spectre and Meltdown break the isolation between applications and the operating system, letting attackers read information from the kernel. This is a real headache for cloud developers, as not all cloud users install the latest security patches.

Authentication Attacks

Authentication is a weak point in cloud computing services which is frequently targeted by an attacker. Today most of the services still use simple username and password type of knowledge based authentication, but some exception are financial institutions which are using various forms of secondary authentication (such as shared secret questions, site keys, virtual keyboards, etc.) that make it more difficult for popular phishing attacks. Some authentication attacks are:

- **Brute Force Attacks**: In this type of attack, all possible combinations of password apply to break the password. The brute force attack is generally applied to crack the encrypted passwords where the passwords are saved in the form of encrypted text.
- **Dictionary Attack:** This type of Attack is relatively faster than brute force attack. Unlike checking all possibilities using brute force attack, the dictionary attack tries to match the password with most occurring words or words of daily life usage.

- **Shoulder Surfing:** Shoulder Surfing is an alternative name of "spying" in which the attackers pies the user's movements to get the password. In this type of attack the attacker observes the user; how he enters the password i.e. what keys of keyboard the user has pressed.
- **Replay Attacks:** The replay attacks are also known as the reflection attacks. It is a way to attack challenge response user authentication mechanism.
- **Phishing Attacks**: It is a web based attack in which the attacker redirects the user to the fake website to get passwords/ Pin Codes of the user.
- **Key Loggers**: The key loggers are the software program which monitors the user activities by recording each and every key pressed by the user.

Man-In-The-Middle Cryptographic Attacks

A man in the middle attack is one in which the attacker intercepts messages in a public key exchange and then retransmits them, substituting his own public key for the requested one, so that the two original parties still appear to be communicating with each other. In the process, the two original parties appear to communicate normally. The message sender does not recognize that the receiver is an unknown attacker trying to access or modify the message before retransmitting to the receiver. Thus, the attacker controls the entire communication. Some type of MIM attacks are:

- **Address Resolution Protocol Communication (ARP)**: In the normal ARP communication, the host PC will send a packet which has the source and destination IP address inside the packet and will broadcast it to all the devices connected to the network. The device which has the target IP address will only send the ARP reply with its MAC address in it and then communication takes place. The ARP protocol is not a secured protocol and the ARP cache doesn't have a foolproof mechanism which results in a big problem.
- **ARP Cache Poisoning**: In ARP cache poisoning, the attacker would be sniffing onto the network by controlling the network switch to monitor the network traffic and spoof the ARP packets between the host and the destination PC and perform the MIM attack.
- **DNS Spoofing**: The target, in this case, will be provided with fake information which would lead to loss of credentials. This is a kind of online MIM attack where the attacker has created a fake bank website, so when the user visits the bank website it will be redirected to the website created by the attacker and then the attacker will gain all the credentials.
- **Session Hijacking**: In this once the session is established between the host PC and the web server the attacker can obtain certain parts of the session establishment which is done by capturing the cookies that were used for the session establishment.

Countermeasures for Cloud Attacks

- As customers lose control over their data as soon as they move that to cloud, Customers must make sure that the data stored in cloud is encrypted and if possible should retain the keys with them only.
- Detect the side-channel attack during the placement phase only. This can be done by collecting logs for new machines starting and stopping and feed them to a SIEM solution. High number of

new machines being spawned and shut down within a defined time interval could be an indicator of an attacker perform the co-residency check.

- Instead of simple username and password authentication check, multifactor authentication must be implemented.
- Hiring a CCSP (Certified Cloud Security Professional) to manage the cloud.
- Check for the integrity of data by implementing encryption /decryption for the data over wire.
- Implement Firewalls, IPS and other ACL filters at perimeter. Apply black holing and sink holing.
- Implement a combination of Virtual Firewall and Randomized Encryption/Decryption. Placement can be protected by enabling virtual firewalls at VM level which restricts traffic between VM and to protect against side-channel attack, implement randomized encryption and decryption thus making the process more complex to break.

Vulnerability - Key Cloud Computing Vulnerabilities

Cloud technology is still being actively developed, and thus it has much vulnerability that can be exploited by cybercriminals or malicious insiders (Sitalakshmi & Mamoun, 2018). The key cloud computing vulnerabilities that raise security concerns among cloud users are depicted in figure 2.

Figure 2 Cloud Vulnerabilities and Solutions

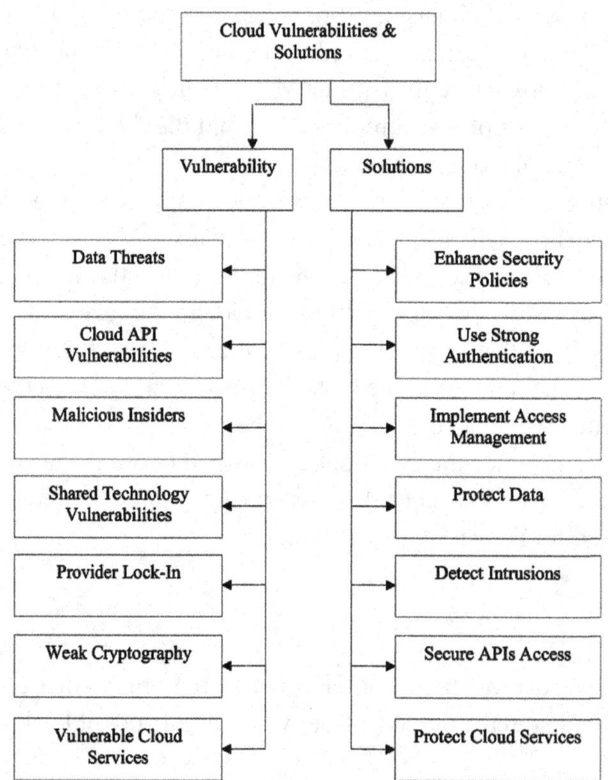

Cloud Vulnerabilities

Data Threats

Cloud users store various types of data in cloud environments, and a lot of that data contains sensitive information about users or business activities. However, this data is susceptible to loss, breach, or damage as the result of human actions, application vulnerabilities, and unforeseen emergencies. It's obvious that a cloud service provider can't prevent all data threats, but cloud developers should apply modern encryption algorithms to ensure the integrity of data in transit from the user to the cloud.

Cloud API vulnerabilities

Application programming interfaces (APIs) allow users to interact with cloud-based services. However, vulnerabilities in APIs may significantly impact the security of cloud orchestration, management, provisioning, and monitoring. Cloud developers need to implement strong controls over APIs.

Malicious Insiders

Legitimate cloud users who act maliciously have many ways to arrange attacks or leak data in cloud environments. This threat can be minimized by cloud developers, however, by implementing identity and access management (IAM) technologies.

Shared Technology Vulnerabilities

Cloud computing involves the use of shared technologies such as virtualization and cloud orchestration. Thus, by exploiting vulnerabilities in any part of these technologies, attackers can cause significant damage to many cloud users. Weaknesses in a hypervisor can allow hackers to gain control over virtual machines or even the host itself. In the case of a virtual machine escape, hackers can gain unrestricted access to the host through shared resources. So it's necessary to pay attention to the security of the cloud provider that entrust with cloud solution.

Provider Lock-In

Most modern cloud service providers make their clients dependent on their services with high switching costs. Many cloud users feel locked in when providers aren't able to provide all the services they need. Make sure that the solution has tools to help users easily migrate from other providers, such as the ability to import data in various formats.

Weak Cryptography

Though cloud providers use cryptographic algorithms to protect data in storage, they usually use limited sources of entropy (such as the time) to automatically generate random numbers for data encryption. For instance, Linux-based virtual machines generate random keys only from the exact millisecond. This may not be enough for strong data encryption; however, as attackers also use sophisticated decoding mechanisms to hack information. Cloud developers should think about how to secure data before it moves to the cloud.

Vulnerable Cloud Services

While cloud computing platforms are designed as distributed systems of cloud services, these services have little protection against each other. An attacker can exploit vulnerabilities in any one cloud service to gain unauthorized access to data of legitimate users. For instance, the OpenStack cloud platform had more than 150 known weaknesses in its cloud services in 2016. Creating a strong architecture can isolate a user's operations in the cloud.

To Ensure the Security of Cloud-Based Vulnerability Solutions

The dynamic nature of cloud services breaks the traditional security model used for on-site software. It's obvious that a cloud service provider is unable to ensure total security in the cloud. Part of the responsibility also lies with cloud users. While the best way to protect user data in the cloud is by providing a layered security approach, cloud service providers should implement industry best practices to ensure the utmost level of cloud security (Jordan & Mitchell, 2015). There are some seven key points on how cloud developers can ensure the security of their cloud-based vulnerability solutions.

Enhance Security Policies

By providing cloud services, software vendors should limit the scope of their responsibility for protecting user data and operations in the cloud in their security policies. Inform the clients about what to do to ensure cloud security as well as what security measures they need to take on their side.

Use Strong Authentication

Stealing passwords is the most common way to access users' data and services in the cloud. Thus, cloud developers should implement strong authentication and identity management. Establish multi-factor authentication. There are various tools that require both static passwords and dynamic passwords. The latter confirms a user's credentials by providing a one-time password on a mobile phone or using biometric schemes or hardware tokens.

Implement Access Management

To increase the security of services, cloud developers should let cloud users assign role-based permissions to different administrators so that users only have the capabilities assigned to them. Moreover, cloud orchestration should enable privileged users to establish the scope of other users' permissions according to their duties within the company.

Protect Data

Data in the cloud environment needs to be encrypted at all stages of its transfer and storage:

- At the source (on the user's side)
- In transit (during its transfer from the user to the cloud server)
- At rest (when stored in the cloud database)

Data needs to be encrypted even before it goes to the cloud. Modern data encryption and tokenization technologies are an effective defense against account hijacking. Moreover, it's important to prove end-to-end encryption for protecting data in transit against man-in-the-middle attacks. Using strong encryption algorithms that contain salt and hashes can effectively deflect cyber-attacks. Data stored in the cloud is also vulnerable to unintentional damage, so ensure its recovery by providing a data backup service.

Detect Intrusions

Provide cloud-based solution with a fully managed intrusion detection system that can detect and inform about the malicious use of cloud services by intruders. Use an intrusion detection system that provides network monitoring and notifies about the abnormal behavior of insiders.

Secure APIs Access

Cloud developers should be sure that clients can access the application only through secure APIs. This might require limiting the range of IP addresses or providing access only through corporate networks or VPNs. However, this approach can be difficult to implement for public-facing applications. Implement security protection via an API using special scripts, templates, and recipes.

Protect Cloud Services

Limiting access to cloud services is necessary to prevent attackers from gaining unauthorized access to a user's operations and data through weaknesses in cloud services. When designing cloud service architecture, minimize event handler permissions to only those necessary for executing specific operations. Moreover, restrict security decisions to only those cloud services that are trusted by users to manage their data security.

Zero-day Attack

Zero-day vulnerability is a computer-software vulnerability that is unknown to those who would be interested in mitigating the vulnerability. Until the vulnerability is mitigated, hackers can exploit it to adversely affect computer programs, data, additional computers or a network. The security infection in the software is susceptible to malware infection remains unknown and unfixed by the vendor which is further exploited by the malicious cyber criminals even before the vendor becomes aware of it (Louridas & Ebert, 2016). This type of exploit is called zero day attack which is further explained in figure 3.

Terminology of Zero-Day

Zero-day attacks require extra security safeguards to ensure the framework; the customary protections are feeble against them.

Figure 3 Zero-day Terms

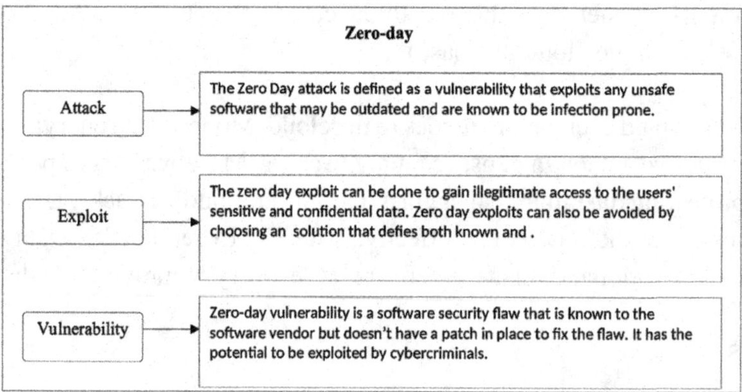

- **Zero-day Vulnerability:** Zero-day vulnerability is one for which no fix is promptly accessible and seller could conceivably know. The nonattendance of a fix for multi day helplessness introduces a zero-day risk to sellers and clients.
- **Zero-day Exploit:** A zero-day exploit is a type with bit of programming, piece of information or arrangement of directions that exploits zero-day weakness.
- **Zero-day Attack:** A zero-day attack is one that abuses zero-day helplessness.
- **Obfuscation:** Refers to procedures that safeguard the program's semantics and usefulness while, in the meantime, make it harder to comprehend or peruse the program's structure.
- **Packing:** In packing, malignant code is covered up by more than one layer of pressure or encryption.
- **Polymorphic worm:** A worm which changes its format with every contamination. The payload is scrambled and utilizes diverse key for every contamination.
- **Metamorphic worm:** A worm that makes semantically proportionate totally extraordinary variants of code at every instant.
- **Alarm:** An alarm created by finder proposing that a framework is or being assaulted.
- **True Positive**: Number of accurately distinguished noxious code.
- **False Positive:** Number of mistakenly distinguished amiable code as vindictive code. Finder creates caution when there is no real assault.
- **False Negative:** Number of inaccurately dismissed pernicious code. Finder neglects to recognize real assault and no caution are created while the framework is under assault.
- **Noise**: Data or impedance that can trigger a false positive.

Zero-Day Vulnerability Lifecycle

Amontip et. al. groups defenselessness life-cycle into five classifications and addresses different components, for example, accessibility of patches and endeavor code that add to the likelihood of Zero-day assault (Mamoun, Sitalakshmi, et. al, 2011). Figure 4 describes the lifecycle of zero-day.

- **Zero-Day Assault (ZDA)**: The defenselessness is found by a dark cap and isn't pitched. The dark cap works unobtrusively on an adventure code.

- **Pseudo Zero-Day Assault (PZDA)**: This is like ZDA, it results from mercy with respect to framework directors not having any significant bearing a specific fix despite the fact that the fix was discharged by merchant sometime prior.
- **Potential for Pseudo Zero-Day Assault (PPZDA)**: This is like PZDA. Notwithstanding, helplessness has not been assaulted, yet has a high probability of being misused in spite of the accessibility of a fix.
- **Potential for Assault (POA)**: Vulnerabilities and their subtleties are uncovered and computerized exploit code or projects are known. The merchants are not yet ready to create patches for wide conveyance and in this way, the defenselessness of this sort progress toward becoming ZDA after the flare-up of assault.
- **Latent**: In this, exploit codes have not yet been created or accessible.

Figure 4 Zero-Day Vulnerability Lifecycle

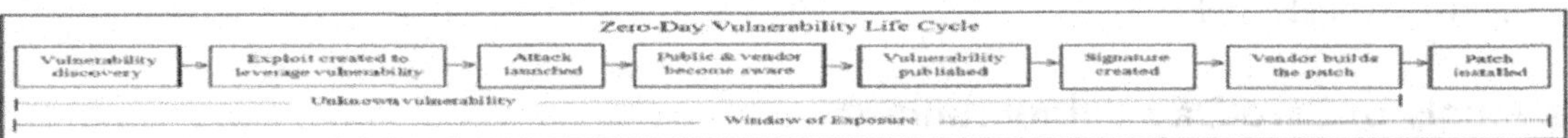

Examples of Zero-Day

The following are the some examples of zero-day exploits.

2017 Zero-Day Exploits

- CVE-2017-8759- SOAP WSDL Parser Code Injection Recently detected a malicious Microsoft Office RTF document leveraging CVE-2017-8759, SOAP WSDL parser code injection vulnerability. This vulnerability allows a malicious actor to inject arbitrary code during the parsing of SOAP WSDL definition contents.
- CVE-2017-0261- EPS “restore” Use-After-Free Detected a “restore” use-after-free vulnerability in Encapsulated PostScript (EPS) of Microsoft Office- CVE-2017-0261- being used to deliver SHRIME malware from a group known as Turla, and NETWIRE malware from an unknown financially motivated actor.
- CVE-2017-0262-Type Confusion in EPS Observed APT28 using a type confusion vulnerability in Encapsulated PostScript (EPS) of Microsoft Office-CVE-2017-0262- to deliver a GAMEFISH payload.

2016 Zero-Day Exploits

- CVE-2016-4117 Flash Zero-Day Exploited in the Wild Detected an attack exploiting a previously unknown vulnerability in Adobe Flash Player (CVE-2016-4117) and helped facilitate release of a patch just four days later.

- CVE-2016-0167 Microsoft Windows Zero-Day Local Privilege Escalation Identified more than 100 organizations in North America that fell victim to a campaign exploiting previously unknown elevation of privilege vulnerability (CVE-2016-0167) in Microsoft Windows.
- CVE-2016-1019 Security Advisory for Adobe Flash Player A critical vulnerability (CVE-2016-1019) exists in Adobe Flash Player 21.0.0.197 and earlier versions for Windows, Macintosh, Linux and Chrome OS. Successful exploitation could cause a crash and potentially allow an attacker to take control of the affected system.

2015 Zero-Day Exploits

- Adobe Flash Zero-Day: CVE-2015-3113 APT3 threat group sent spear-phishing emails with links to compromised web servers.
- CVE-2015-2424 Microsoft Office Zero-Day CVE-2015-2424 leveraged by Tsar Team.
- CVE-2015-1701 Adobe & Windows Zero-Day exploits likely leveraged by Russia's APT28 in highly targeted attack.

Essentials of Zero-Day Vulnerabilities

- Keep the software up-to-date to help protect against zero-day vulnerability.
- Check for a solution when zero-day vulnerability is announced. Most software vendors work quickly to patch security vulnerability.
- Don't underestimate the threat. Cybercriminals will seek to exploit security holes and gain access to devices and personal information. They can use information for a range of cybercrimes including identity theft, bank fraud, and ransomware.
- Always use reliable security software to keep devices safe and secure.

Different Zero-Day Attack handling Mechanisms

The following section deals with different handling mechanisms for zero-day attack shown in the figure 5.

Techniques

The startling idea of zero-day attacks is a genuine concern, particularly on the grounds that they might be utilized in focused assaults and in the proliferation of vindictive code (Payam, Timo, et.al, 2016). The figure 6 describes the steps involved in zero-day exploits.

Detection

Any association associated with the web has one regular danger of zero-day assaults. The reasons for these assaults are, detecting private data, observing target's activities, robbery of business data and framework interruption. This segment broke down the examination endeavors done in course of safeguard against zero-day abuse. The essential objective of safeguard systems is to recognize the endeavor as close as conceivable to the season of abuse, to dispense with or limit the harm caused by the assault.

The examination network has comprehensively ordered the guard procedures against zero-day misuses as measurable based, signature-based, conduct based, and half and half methods.

- **Statistical-based**: Statistical-based assault discovery procedures keep up the log of past adventures that are presently known. With this authentic log, assault profile is made to create new parameters for new assaults recognition. This strategy decides the ordinary exercises and distinguishes the exercises which are to be blocked. As the log is refreshed by verifiable exercises, the more drawn out any framework using this method, the more precise it is at learning or deciding typical exercises. Measurable based procedures manufacture assault profiles from authentic information, which are static in nature; in this manner they are not ready to receive the dynamic conduct of system condition. In this way, these systems can't be utilized for identification of malware progressively.

Figure 5 Zero-Day Handling Mechanisms

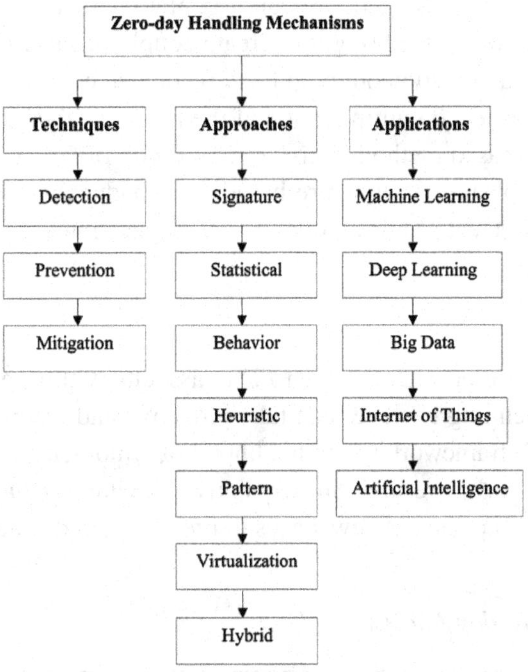

Figure 6 Steps for Zero-Day Exploit

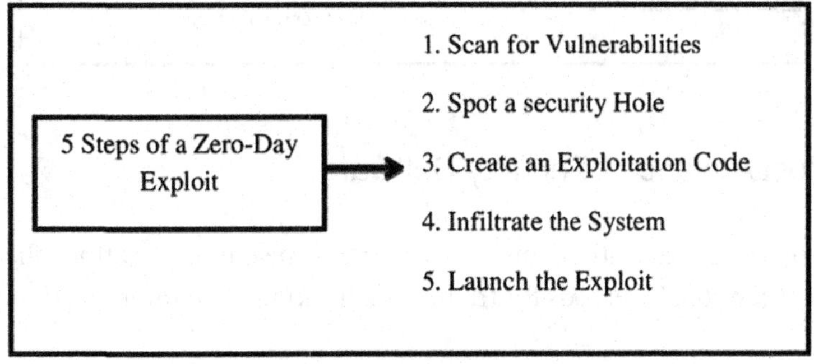

- **Signature-based**: For discovery of polymorphic worms, signature-based procedures are utilized to distinguish their new portrayals on each new contamination. There are essentially 3 classes of mark based location systems: content-based marks, semantic based marks and helplessness driven marks. These strategies are commonly utilized by infection programming merchants who will accumulate a library of various malware marks. These libraries are always being refreshed for recently distinguished marks of recently misused vulnerabilities. Mark based systems are frequently utilized in infection programming bundles to protect against malevolent payloads from malware to worms.
- **Behavior-based**: These systems depend on the capacity to foresee the stream of system traffic. They will likely foresee the future conduct of system framework so as to oppose the peculiar conduct. The expectation of future conduct is finished by machine learning approach through the present and past collaborations with the web server, server or injured individual machine. Conduct based strategies decide the basic attributes of worms which don't require the examination of payload byte designs Intrusion location and interruption counteractive action marks incorporate these safeguard systems. These marks need two fundamental characteristics first; they ought to have a high discovery rate. Second, they ought to create couple of false alarms. The objective of any strategies utilized by an association ought to be to recognize continuously the presence of a zero-day misuse and avoid harm and multiplication of the zero-day abuse.
- **Hybrid-based**: Hybrid-based methods join heuristics with different blends of the three past systems which are measurable based, signature-based, and conduct based procedures. Utilizing a half breed show system will defeat a shortcoming in any single strategy.

Prevention

Zero-Day vulnerabilities can be powerless to Zero-Day assaults with grievous outcomes to business. This sounds a bit of overwhelming however can take proactive and receptive safety efforts. Zero-day defenselessness will open the framework to the likelihood of a moment assault that could have lamentable outcomes and grave monetary results. Subsequently, it's vital to be aware of this probability and act if and when powerlessness appears. A few stages to prevent zero-day attacks are shown in figure 7.

Figure 7 Steps to prevent Zero-day Attacks

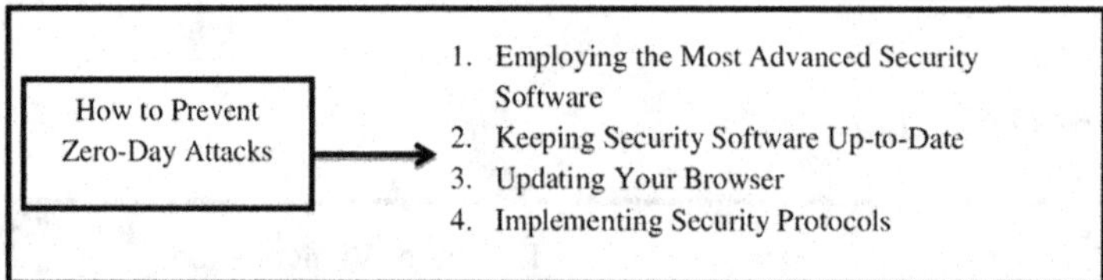

Employing the Most Advanced Security Software

Basic security programming is essentially insufficient in the present online atmosphere, where programmers utilize the most exceptional methods for framework hacking. Programming that just ensures against realized dangers is no counterpart for the programmer who grows better approaches to assault, since Zero-Day assaults are, by definition, assaults not yet known.

Keeping Security Software Up-to-Date

As new techniques for hacking wind up known, security programming is refreshed to forestall such hacks. Just with normal, convenient programming updates can adequately shield the system from a zero-day abuse.

Implementing Security Protocols

For a system to be completely prepared to follow up on zero-day helplessness, all organization work forces must be prepared on the accepted procedures for security. Create and actualize a succession of safety efforts and show your workforce when and how to sanction these measures.

Use refreshed programs

Programs are most loved focuses for Zero-Day assaults. Updates to programs are regularly programmed, yet ensure programs are altogether refreshed as they frequently contain patches to vulnerabilities. Check for explicit program refresh guidelines.

Establish security best practices

Ensure you set a case of individual online security best practices and have every one of your representatives do likewise.

Mitigation

Zero-day misuses are not kidding security escape clauses that are abused around the same time they are uncovered. They are relevantly named “multi day” in light of the fact that the system chairmen have zero days to fix the security blemish, which could have just been abused. Here are five of the prescribed procedures on the best way to alleviate zero-day assaults. The following figure 8 deals with defence against zero-day attacks.

Figure 8 Defend Against Zero-Day Attacks

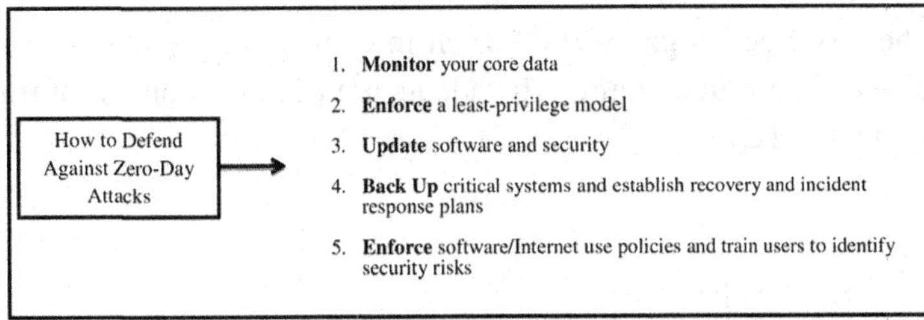

Limit the Use of Email Attachments

- Networks where clients are probably going to accidentally take part in sending or accepting vindictive email connections are frequently inclined to hacking.
- To guarantee they work in safe client situations, organizations should survey their arrangements and firmly limit email connections by sifting them through.
- Hackers will in general cover up malevolent code in connections, which can trade off the system's security when opened by a clueless client.
- Only connections with the concurred expansions should then be allowed in the system. This will wipe out any zero-day abuses, since connections that neglect to meet the concurred criteria are rejected on landing.
- Furthermore, deactivating HTML messages is likewise a vital system in barrier against zero-day assaults. To convey dangers and assaults on an organization's system, programmers can cover up vindictive code in HTML messages before sending them out.
- In this way expanding the dangers of zero-day abuses. It is prudent, hence, to inactivate HTML to relieve such dangers.

Pay special mind to Anomalous Activity

- Any unpredictable action on your processing foundation should raise a warning.
- For precedent, controlling how your framework interfaces or speaks with different frameworks inside the system can help in confining any harm that may happen on account of zero-day misuses.
- Based on the organization's necessities, there ought to be decides that expound on how and which frameworks can interface and the degree to which different parts of the framework can be gotten to.
- This keeps any contaminations from spreading inside the system in the event that it goes under assault.

Filter through Outbound Traffic

- Hackers and different aggressors will in general introduce bot projects and Trojans on active exchanges or associations with catch and change directions to a remote framework for various strategies.
- Installing firewalls and outbound intermediaries will help in distinguishing and blocking such associations.
- Companies should set up borders that permit explicit inbound traffic and deny and obstruct any outbound associations on the switch as a matter of course.
- For precedent, the movement sign on the switch in connection to inbound and outbound traffic over some undefined time frame ought to be adequate in figuring out what traffic ought to be allowed and what ought to be refused.

Set up Robust Preventive Security Procedures

- Limiting authoritative benefits to a solitary client can help in keeping remote programmers from completely picking up control of the framework. For instance, it is fitting to kill JavaScript to shield clients from the expansive outcomes of the web-established ANI misuses.
- In expansion to leading helplessness examines all the time, it is imperative to utilize boycotting programming to bolt out any pernicious exercises and whitelist destinations that represent no dangers.
- Furthermore, appropriate client training, content sifting of ANI documents, and utilizing refreshed antivirus programming are other preventive techniques that can help in relieving zero-day abuses.

Create Disaster Recovery Measures

- Since zero-day abuses happen quickly, it is important to build up thorough techniques that can be pursued to recuperate from harms at whatever point the assault happens or moderate the threats once they are detected.

Approaches

- **Signature:** This method matches the signatures of already known attacks that are stored into the database to detect the attacks in the computer system.
- **Statistical:** This approach detects the abnormal behavior or attacks in the computer networks by comparing the new traffic with the already created profiles.
- **Behavior:** This technique detects faulty behavior when malicious codes are executed, improved version of heuristic-based technique.Malicious behavior is revealed not only in executable files, but also in document files, such as PDF, DOC, and HWP. This technique determines characteristics of malicious behaviorbased on file, registry, network, process, etc.
- **Heuristic:** This technique determines specific behavior of malicious codes, so this can check new and variant codes by analyzing abnormal behavior not signatures.
- **Pattern:** After defining the specific pattern of existing malicious codes as their characteristics, malicious codes are detected and blocked by matching defined pattern with a pattern of incoming codes.
- **Virtualization:** This approach is closely related to dynamic heuristic-based technique. Malicious codes are analyzed in virtual system.
- **Hybrid:** Combines various methods mentioned above.

Applications

- **Machine Learning:** Machine Learning (ML) is a method of data analysis that automates analytical model building. ML is a category of algorithm that allows software applications to become more accurate in predicting outcomes without being explicitly programmed. The basic premise of machine learning is to build algorithms that can receive input data and use statistical analysis to predict an output while updating outputs as new data becomes available.

- **Deep Learning:** Deep learning is a collection of algorithms used in machine learning, used to model high-level abstractions in data through the use of model architectures, which are composed of multiple nonlinear transformations. It is part of a broad family of methods used for machine learning that are based on learning representations of data.
- **Artificial Intelligence**: A branch of computer science dealing with the simulation of intelligent behavior in computers and has the capability of a machine to imitate intelligent human behavior.
- **Big Data:** Big data is an evolving term that describes a large volume of structured, semi-structured and unstructured data that has the potential to be mined for information and used in machine learning projects and other advanced analytics applications.
- **Internet of Things:** The internet of things, or IoT, is a system of interrelated computing devices, mechanical and digital machines, objects, animals or people that are provided with unique identifiers (UIDs) and the ability to transfer data over a network without requiring human-to-human or human-to-computer interaction.

MACHINE LEARNING

Machine learning (ML) is an application of artificial intelligence (AI) that provides systems the ability to automatically learn and improve from experience without being explicitly programmed. The primary aim is to allow the computers learn automatically without human intervention or assistance and adjust actions accordingly (Pierre, Julio, et.al, 2018). The figure 9 accounts ML advantages and disadvantages.

Figure 9 ML Advantages & Disadvantages

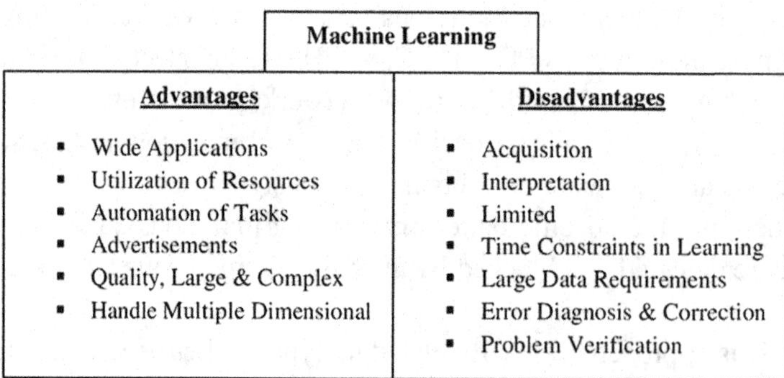

Requirements for ML

- Data preparation capabilities
- Algorithms – basic and advanced
- Automation and iterative processes
- Scalability
- Ensemble modeling

Process of ML

- Identifies relevant datasets and prepares them for analysis.
- Choose the type of machine learning algorithms to use.
- Builds an analytical model based on the chosen algorithm.
- Trains the model on test data sets, revising it as needed.
- Runs the model to generate scores and other findings.

Machine Learning Methods

- **Supervised Machine Learning** can apply what has been learned in the past to new data using labeled examples to predict future events (Prakash, Lei, et.al, 2013). Starting from the analysis of a known training dataset, the learning algorithm produces an inferred function to make predictions about the output values. The system is able to provide targets for any new input after sufficient training. The learning algorithm can also compare its output with the correct, intended output and find errors in order to modify the model accordingly.
- **Unsupervised Machine Learning** is used when the information used to train is neither classified nor labeled. Unsupervised learning studies how systems can infer a function to describe a hidden structure from unlabeled data. The system doesn't figure out the right output, but it explores the data and can draw inferences from datasets to describe hidden structures from unlabeled data.
- **Semi-Supervised Machine Learning** fall somewhere in between supervised and unsupervised learning, since they use both labeled and unlabeled data for training – typically a small amount of labeled data and a large amount of unlabeled data. The systems that use this method are able to considerably improve learning accuracy. Usually, semi-supervised learning is chosen when the acquired labeled data requires skilled and relevant resources in order to train it / learn from it. Otherwise, acquiring unlabeled data generally doesn't require additional resources.
- **Reinforcement Machine Learning** is a learning method that interacts with its environment by producing actions and discovers errors or rewards. Trial and error search and delayed reward are the most relevant characteristics of reinforcement learning. This method allows machines and software agents to automatically determine the ideal behavior within a specific context in order to maximize its performance. Simple reward feedback is required for the agent to learn which action is best; this is known as the reinforcement signal.

Machine learning enables analysis of massive quantities of data. While it generally delivers faster, more accurate results in order to identify profitable opportunities or dangerous risks, it may also require additional time and resources to train it properly (Sahoo, Liu & Hoi, 2017). Combining machine learning with AI and cognitive technologies can make it even more effective in processing large volumes of information.

Machine Learning Algorithms

Basically, there are two ways to categorize Machine Learning algorithms which are shown in figure 10 (Sharma, Kalita & Borah, 2016).

- The first is a grouping of ML algorithms by the learning style.

Figure 10 Machine Learning Algorithms

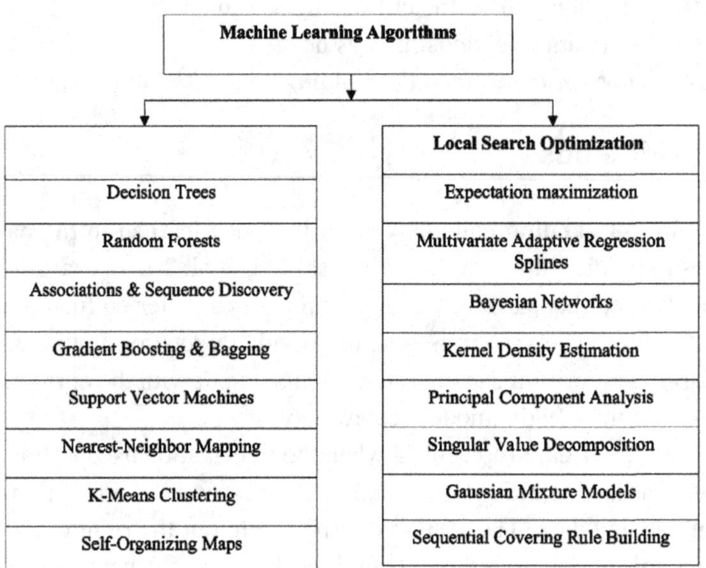

- The second is a grouping of ML algorithms by a similarity in form or function.

Risks in Machine Learning

Machine learning models come with risks which include large false positives due to bad learning algorithms that the hackers can exploit (Sitalakshmi & Mamoun, 2018). Another unwanted guest to the model is the contaminated or compromised data from a recently hacked host (Umesh, Chanchala & Suyash, 2016).

- Hacker can use fake biometric fingerprints, Iris and facial characteristics to impersonate a legitimate user.
- Hacker can fool a machine learning model into classifying malicious training samples as legitimate at test or execution time.
- This can cause the model to behave significantly and widely different than the expected outputs.
- **Perform Ethical Hacking:** An ethical hacker is a trusted security professional who breaks into a system to discover machine learning vulnerabilities overlooked by a firewall, an intrusion detection system or any other security tools. In a simple scenario of gaining access, the ethical hacker uses a fake finger reconstructed from the fingerprint left behind by a legitimate user on a dirty device. Once in the system, the ethical hacker sneaks into a fingerprint database, retrieves a biometric template belonging to another legitimate user and then reconstructs a fake finger. To combat these risks, the device reader must be free of dirt, grease and moisture after each use and the database should be encrypted.

- **Encrypt Security Logs:** A system administrator has super user privileges to analyze machine learning log files. The reasons for doing it include checking for compliance with security policies, troubleshooting the system and conducting forensics. Encrypting log files is one way of protecting log files from being hacked. Encryption keys needed to change log contents are not revealed to the malicious hacker. If this hacker tries to delete a log file on hacking activities, the administrator should get an immediate loud-sounding alert on the always-on desktop computer.
- **Clean Out Training Data:** A machine learning model behaves well when it is fed by good training data. The model developer must know where the data comes from. The data must be clean and free of biases, anomalies and poisoned data. It must be avoided if the source host has been attacked. Bad data can cause the model to behave differently and ultimately shut down the system. When using multiple learning tools to assess data for a particular task, the model developer should restructure all data into a common format.
- **Apply Devops To Model Lifecycle:** Hackers can take advantage of false positives from a machine learning platform. One way of combating this and other risks in machine learning is to apply DevOps to the learning model lifecycle. DevOps lets the development and training, quality assurance and production teams collaborate with one another.
- **Implement a Security Policy:** A security policy should be implemented on the course of actions to take for machine learning risk management. In a simple scenario, the policy should consist of five sections: purpose, scope, background, actions and constraints. The scope section puts a fence around what's to be covered: machine learning model type, training data and data mining algorithm -- regression, clustering or neural networks. The background section looks at the reasons behind the policy, the actions section covers how the risks can be combated using DevOps and the constraints section considers machine learning limitations, and availability of test data.

MLM Applied in Zero-Day Attack

There are wide varieties of machine learning applications available, the following table. 2 illustrates the machine learning models applied so far in zero-day attack Vishal, Kyungroul, et.al, 2017).

CONCLUSION

Cloud computing technology is extremely popular among users due to its many advantages. However, this technology also introduces vulnerabilities that can become new vectors for cyber-attacks. With the rapid increase in the adoption of cloud computing by many organizations, security issues arise. Overall, zero-day attack prevention and detection are extremely difficult problems, but there's no denying the high demand for solutions in these areas. As cloud computing is on the rise, and especially due to its enormous attraction to organized criminals. This chapter deals with various aspects of zero-day attack. It provides a detailed account of machine learning aspects related to zero-day attack.

Table 2. MLM Applied in Zero-Day Attack

Author Names	Title	ML Approach	Problem	Outcome
Pierre Parrend, Julio Navarro, Fabio Guigou, Aline Deruyverand Pierre Collet - 2018	Foundations and Applications of Artificial Intelligence for Zero-day and Multi-Step Attack Detection	Statistical approaches include rule-based and outlier-detection-based solutions. Machine learning includes the detection of behavioural anomalies and event sequence tracking	Zero-day attacks that are not publicly disclosed	Eases the characterisation of novel complex threats and matching Artificial Intelligence-based Counter-measures
Sitalakshmi Venkatraman and Mamoun Alazab - 2018	Use of Data Visualisation for Zero-Day Malware Detection	Hybrid method of feature based and image-based visualisation	Similarity mining to Identify and classify malware accurately	Efficient and accurate in identifying malware visually
Vishal Sharma, Kyungroul Lee, Soonhyun Kwon, Jiyoon Kim, Hyungjoon Park, Kangbin Yim, and Sun-Young Lee - 2017	A Consensus Framework for Reliability and Mitigation of Zero-Day Attacks in IoT	Context behavior- Reliability and consensus	Mitigation of zero-day attacks in IoT networks	Mitigate the zero-day attacks in IoT network without compromising its performance
Payam Vahdani Amoli, Timo Hamalainen, Gil David, Mikhail Zolotukhin, Mahsa Mirzamohammad - 2016	Unsupervised Network Intrusion Detection Systems for Zero-Day Fast-Spreading Attacks and Botnets	Unsupervised machine-learning algorithms	To detect fast spreading, known and zero-day intrusion	A-NIDS increases the detection rate of zero-day and complex attacks
Umesh Kumar Singh, Chanchala Joshi, Suyash Kumar Singh - 2016	ZDAR System: Defending Against the Unknown	Supervised classification & unsupervised classification -ZDAR (Zero-Day Attack Remedy) system	To sense network traffic that detects anomalous behavior of network in order to identify the presence of zero-day exploit	This method is effective and efficient in detecting zero day attacks than the typical statistical based anomaly detection techniques
Ammar Almomani, B. B. Gupta, Tat-Chee Wan, Altyeb Altaher, Selvakumar Manickam - 2013	Phishing Dynamic Evolving Neural Fuzzy Framework for Online Detection "Zero-day" Phishing Email	Phishing dynamic evolving neural fuzzy framework (PDENF), hybrid (supervised/ unsupervised) learning approach	To detect a new zero-day phishing emails	To increase the level of accuracy and increase the performance of classification and prediction of phishing email values
Prakash Mandayam Comar, Lei Liu, Sabyasachi Saha, Pang-Ning Tan, Antonio Nucci - 2013	Combining Supervised and Unsupervised Learning for Zero-Day Malware Detection	Tree-based Feature Transformation, SVM	To detect known and newly emerging malware at a high precision	Identify flows of existing and novel malwares with very high precision
Mamoun Alazab, Sitalakshmi Venkatraman, Paul Watters, and Moutaz Alazab - 2011	Zero-day Malware Detection based on Supervised Learning Algorithms of API call Signatures	Supervised Learning Algorithms, The Sequential Minimal Optimization (SMO) Algorithm, Artificial Neural Networks (ANN) Algorithm, J48 Algorithm, K-Nearest Neighbors (kNN) Algorithm	To detect and classify zero-day malware with high levels of accuracy and efficiency based on the frequency of Windows API calls	Data mining algorithm over the other for accurately detecting zero-day malware

REFERENCES

Alazab, M., Venkatraman, S., Watters, P., & Alazab, M. (2011). Zero-day Malware Detection based on Supervised Learning Algorithms of API call Signatures. In *Proceedings of the Ninth Australasian Data Mining Conference* (vol. 121, pp. 171-182). Australian Computer Society.

Almomani, A., Gupta, B. B., Wan, T., Altaher, A., & Manickam, S. (2013). *Phishing dynamic evolving neural fuzzy framework for online detection zero-day phishing email.* Academic Press.

Amoli, P. V., Hamalainen, T., David, G., Zolotukhin, M., & Mirzamohammad, M. (2016). Unsupervised Network Intrusion Detection Systems for Zero-Day Fast-Spreading Attacks and Botnets. JDCTA, 10(2), 1-13.

Buczak, A. L., & Guven, E. (2016). A survey of data mining and machine learning methods for cyber security intrusion detection. *IEEE Communications Surveys & Tutorials, 18*(2).

Comar, P. M., Liu, L., Saha, S., Tan, P., & Nucci, A. (2013). Combining Supervised and Unsupervised Learning for Zero-Day Malware Detection. In 2013 Proceedings IEEE INFOCOM (pp. 2022-2030). IEEE.

Jordan, M. I., & Mitchell, T. M. (2015). Machine learning: Trends, perspectives, and prospects. *Science, 349*(6245), 255-260.

Parrend, P., Navarro, J., Guigou, F., Deruyver, A., & Collet, P. (2018). Foundations and Applications of Artificial Intelligence for Zero-day and Multi-Step Attack Detection. EURASIP Journal on Information Security, 2018(1), 4.

Sahoo, D., Liu, C., & Hoi, S. C. H. (2017). Malicious URL detection using machine learning. *Survey (London, UK).*

Sharma, V., Lee, K., Kwon, S., Kim, J., Park, H., Yim, K., & Lee, S. Y. (2017). A Consensus Framework for Reliability and Mitigation of Zero-Day Attacks in IoT. *Security and Communication Networks.*

Sharma, R. K., Kalita, H. K., & Borah, P. (2016). Analysis of machine learning techniques based intrusion detection systems. In *Proceedings of 3rd International Conference on Advanced Computing, Networking and Informatics* (pp. 485-493). New Delhi, India: Springer.

Singh, U. K., Joshi, C., & Singh, S. K. (2016). ZDAR System: Defending against the Unknown. *International Journal of Computer Science and Mobile Computing, 5*(12), 143-149.

Venkatraman, S., & Alazab, M. (2018). Use of Data Visualisation for Zero-Day Malware Detection. *Security and Communication Networks.*

This research was previously published in the Handbook of Research on Machine and Deep Learning Applications for Cyber Security; pages 364-387, copyright year 2020 by Information Science Reference (an imprint of IGI Global).

Chapter 51
Cyber Secure Man-in-the-Middle Attack Intrusion Detection Using Machine Learning Algorithms

Jayapandian Natarajan
https://orcid.org/0000-0002-7054-0163
Christ University, India

ABSTRACT

The main objective of this chapter is to enhance security system in network communication by using machine learning algorithm. Cyber security network attack issues and possible machine learning solutions are also elaborated. The basic network communication component and working principle are also addressed. Cyber security and data analytics are two major pillars in modern technology. Data attackers try to attack network data in the name of man-in-the-middle attack. Machine learning algorithm is providing numerous solutions for this cyber-attack. Application of machine learning algorithm is also discussed in this chapter. The proposed method is to solve man-in-the-middle attack problem by using reinforcement machine learning algorithm. The reinforcement learning is to create virtual agent that should predict cyber-attack based on previous history. This proposed solution is to avoid future cyber middle man attack in network transmission.

INTRODUCTION

Data security and data analytics are a two major pillars of the modern business world. Cyber security is not only the association of data security and privacy, it also consists of a multiple of other components. Cyber security is a process that comprises data, network, storage and computing. The market growth of cyber security reached around 135 billion US dollar in the year 2017. The expected market growth during the period 2018 to 2022 is projected to be 200 billion US dollars (Steve Morgan, 2018). Almost all the utilization services are migrating to the cloud platform. These utilization services are storage,

DOI: 10.4018/978-1-6684-6291-1.ch051

network and infrastructure. The reason for this migration is easy accessibility and lower cost. The other positive aspect of this migration is reducing establishment and computational costs. Third party service providers are also facing serious data security problems. This security problem is termed cybersecurity and addresses data and network security. Cyber security issues and crimes are officially published in many documents in more than fifty countries (Gercke, 2012). The nature and scope of the problem is network security. Cyber security is similar to the banyan tree, where the leaf of this tree is to maintain security and risk management. This cybersecurity is a part of information security to manage various security tools (Kaufman, 2009). The Figure 1. illustrates different elements of cyber security (Schatz, Bashroush & Wall, 2017). The role of the roots is to provide higher security data.

Figure 1. Cyber Security Elements

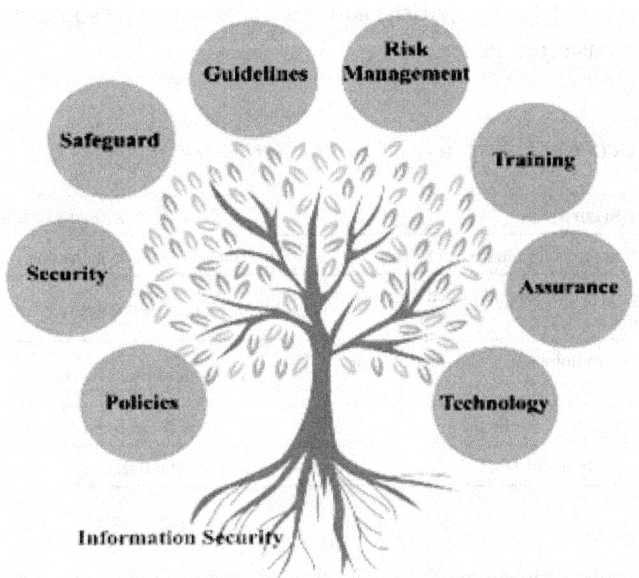

Cyber security is the attainment of data organization and device computation. This device computation relates to various computers and deals with many traditional and non-traditional data. The objective of information security is a circle of three elements that is termed availability, integrity and confidentiality (Jouini & Rabai, 2019). Data availability refers to accessing data from server machines. The second element is integrity which deals with data accuracy and quality (Luo, Hong & Fang, 2018). The most important element is confidentiality which concerns handling data security mechanisms. Both cybersecurity and information security are communication security protocols (Von Solms & Van Niekerk, 2013).

The Table 1 illustrates the fundamental differences between cyber and information security systems (Luiijf, Besseling, Spoelstra & De Graaf, 2011). The primary difference between these two securities mechanisms refers to dealing with physical and digital data. The second difference is dealing with its own organization and public data. Public data means handling internet digital information. Cybersecurity signifies operating at a level above boundary level, which means handling cyber and physical attacks. Physical attack implies the physically theft of information (Pasqualetti, Dörfler & Bullo, 2013). This physical data protection consists of handling the information security protocols. Recently, apart from this physical data, all data is managed in digital format with the help of the cloud computing platform which is a technology that provides different levels of servers. Customers who utilize this technology store their data and access it anywhere in the world. The backbone of this technology is internet communication. On the other hand, the main heart of cyber and information security is information and communication technology (ICT), where all data communication is interlinked. ICT is incorporated in cloud technology, which finds its importance even in the educational sector (Jayapandian, Pavithra & Revathi, 2017). ICT security also provides security protocol and mainly focuses on data accountability. It, in addition, provides reliability and data authenticity. Cyber security deals with different level of attackers. A cybercriminal is an indirect attacker where there is no direct-attack on the data (Lau, Xia & Ye, 2014). The control and the prevention of hacking server machines can be implemented by controlling the physical system by using software applications. Disgruntled employees are another major domain of cyber-attacks. The professional hacker is known to attempt hacking some confidential data from cloud servers whose data are misused during terrorist activities. These reflect some of the major cyber-attacks practiced in modern data base storage.

Table 1. A Comparison between Cyber Security and Information Security

Cyber Security	Information Security
Cyber security deals with data protection in digital format.	Information security providing physical and digital security.
Client to server communication protect unauthorized digital communication access.	Major focus on availability of data with data confidentiality.
It concerns handling advanced technology and it is named internet communication.	Information security is a basic security mechanism.
Data breach and data phishing is a primary goal.	Basic security protocols used for data security.
Third party security is needed.	Inter security mechanism is enough.

Machine learning is a sub-division of the artificial intelligence technique. Artificial intelligence is the process of automatically detecting the solution from prior experiences (Michalski, Carbonell & Mitchell, 2013). The major advantage of this methodology is that it permits making decisions without human intervention. The basic working mechanism of machine learning algorithms is working with existing history. General machine learning is an application program that is similar to data mining. It retrieves and subsequently extracts data from the database. The best working model of machine learning is the neural network whose working methodology is to connect nodes in a loosely coupled structure. This loosely coupled node operates in a similar manner to biological brain structure. Conceptually, the biological brain structure is preinstalled and used in network connection (Brugere, Gallagher & Berger-Wolf, 2018). In the 1990's, machine learning dealt with the neural network structure. This deep learning technology is the hottest topic in the machine learning field. The Bayesian network structure also deals with machine learning algorithms (Chaturvedi et al., 2018). The reason behind this is that normal databases evolved into the concept termed big data. Handling this data base is very critical in the modern world. Massive volumes of data are accessed in short period of time necessitating that machine learning algorithms also adopt deep learning concepts. Compared to normal programming, machine learning is a low-cost implementation. This gives rises to a feasible structure with more accuracy. The reinforcement method is one of the best approaches in machine learning, which provides a better solution to solve network security problems. The principal objective of this chapter is to compare and analyze traditional and reinforcement algorithms. Different parameters are relating to this comparison that is packet transmission time and delivery percentage. The other objective and hypothesis of the chapter is to solve network security issues by using machine learning algorithms.

MACHINE LEARNING METHODOLOGY

The basic working principle of machine learning is gathering results from the existing methods. As a rule, there are three major components used to analyze and gather results from machine learning. This concept is elaborated in Figure 2. The first component is a representation that means using formal programming language to classify the data-set. This classification set is named, hypothesis space, which is very useful for the learning component. The second component is evaluation; this component is utilized to find a worthy classifier in the regular data-set. The alternate name of this evaluation function is the objective function, which signifies finding good objectives from the bad data-sets. The major and final component of machine learning is optimization (Luo et al., 2019) whose goal is to increase efficiency from learners. This concept of self-optimization technique implies that there is no human intervention to automatically optimize the data from the data-set.

Figure 2. Machine Learning Process

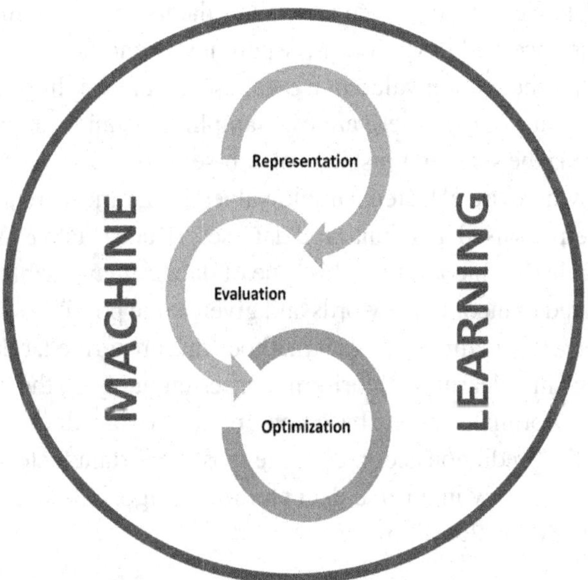

Machine learning representation is involved in several elements. Instance is a one of the important elements in the learning component. It – the instance - helps to find neighbor data elements and to support the vector machine. The extreme learning approach is one type of learning methodology utilized to predict data (Mahmoud, Dong & Ma, 2018). A decision tree is a reasonable application of the learning method essentially because the tree structure helps to take decisions in real-time applications (Park, Haghani, Samuel & Knodler, 2018). It creates a rule, whose task is to assist the logical program and finds the propositional solution. Neural networks and graphical models are used in network communication protocols; this structure is also incorporated in artificial intelligent mechanisms. The evaluation component is to provide accuracy and will also trace the error rate in the data-set. This component is used to obtain information at a lower cost. Optimization is a normal method; it has been previously used in basic data structure algorithms. Greed search is a search optimization method to find better solutions. There are two varieties of optimization employed, that is, assembled and continuous optimization. Greedy and beam search are example of assembled optimization methods (Fanjul-Peyro & Ruiz, 2010). In some cases, linear and quadratic programming is used during this optimization. Different types of machine learning algorithms are available and employed in a variety of applications. These algorithms are used in dynamic situations with a different types of predictive data-sets. This prediction instance is known as a label structure: also referred to as supervised method. Unlabeled structure implies an unsupervised algorithm (Fan, Su, Nien, Tsai, & Cheng, 2018). There are several problems faced while the implementing machine learning algorithm. The primary problem is data-set collection which is normally involved in field export structure. The most common method is the brute force technique implying a trial-and-error method; it finds the possible solution in a systematic way. This algorithm is used to find the best data-set in machine learning. Mining the data is also involved in the machine learning approach. This data mining is the process of data that is named data pre-processing, a technique that converts unreadable format data to normal raw data (Woo, Shin, Seo & Meilanitasari, 2018). There are a quantity of simulation tools available in data pre-processing methodology, among them are Weka, Rapid Miner and DataMelt (Rubab, Taqvi & Hassan, 2018). After data pre-processing, data cleaning is the toughest task. An example of this data cleaning of illegal values in a database. This family of problem is resolved by using mathematical variance and deviation. Misspellings is another commonly encountered issue which of sorting and finding the feature value in a database. Data sampling is a recent research option for data-set selection (Li, et. al., 2018). There are two sampling techniques normally used; the first one is random sampling, which is the selecting instance of sub-set values in a random structure. The second one is stratified sampling where are selected sample values in the most frequently accessed data-sets. Stratified sampling is sometimes used in imbalanced data-sets (Buda, Maki & Mazurowski, 2018). In the real-world data-set data values are incomplete; this type of data is unavoidable. In this situation existing data parameters are attributed to incomplete words and given some possible solution. The future sub-set selection process is categorized into three different methods that are termed, relevant data, irrelevant data and redundant data. The machine learning algorithm focuses uniquely on the method of future selection techniques which addresses optimal sub-sets based on previous data values. These are the general data prediction methods where the prediction accuracy is the most important factor (Ghahramani, 2015). It is not possible to archive this accuracy in normal data prediction algorithm necessitating the introduction of many special machine learning algorithms.

MACHINE LEARNING ALGORITHM

Machine learning is an algorithm that is categorized in many traditional structures. The methodology of this algorithm is gathering input from various sources and predicts the future based on experience. In general, the working structures of machine learning algorithms are based on predictive and mining approaches (Moeyersoms et al., 2015). The percentage of pattern matching is the most important factor. This model is compared with existing data patterns and provides the best result compared to existing structure.

Figure 3 elaborates the different machine learning algorithms.

Figure 3. Machine Learning Algorithm

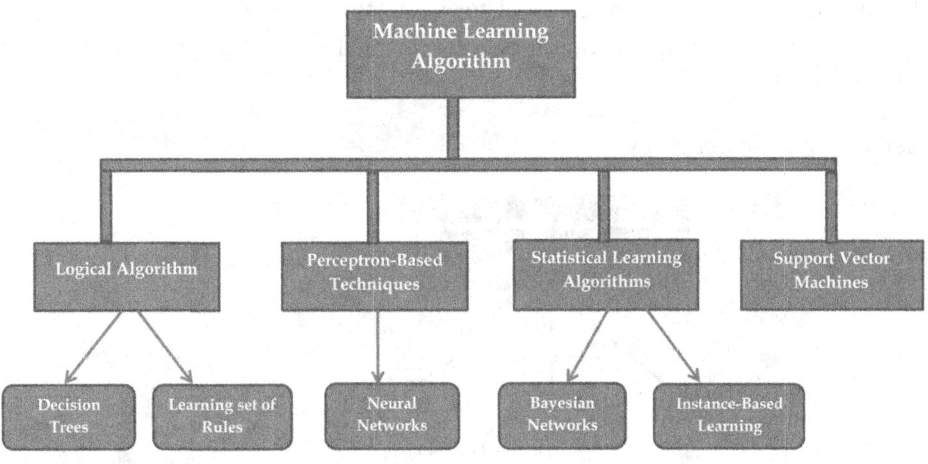

Logical Approach

The logical approach is the process of step-by-step procedure using logical conditions. This logical algorithm is used to solve logical problems in data processing systems (Wang & Pedrycz, 2017). It is the combination of conditional and mathematical operations. This approach solves the problem based on existing logical knowledge. Logical approaches are generally categorized into two major types, the first is a decision tree approach and another the rule or condition-based approach. The decision tree is the major part of a supervised machine learning algorithm. The primary aim of this decision tree method is to a create training data set that helps to predict the future result. This tree concept is used to predict the data elements by using nodes and leaves. Decision tree methods are implemented in different applications (Lino, Rocha, Macedo & Sizo, 2019). The working methodology of decision tree is a non-deterministic polynomial time (NP) complete problem, which is intended to find the best heuristic search to develop decision tree in the near-optimal structure (Boas, Santos & de Campos Merschmann, 2018). The best training data-set for this tree is root node and, based on this node decisions are subdivided and accessed. Finding the best data-set is to divide the tree structure from top to bottom. However, the true factor is never hundred percent correct. In order to find the best data-set value, individual data-set, together with group data-sets are compared with each other. This method works in a cyclic process until the best data set value in a database is detected. Thereafter, the training data-set is used to predict the target or class variable based on decision protocols. This protocol structure is to decide the result based on existing training set. Figure 4 is a working example of a decision tree structure; this diagram predicts the customer loan repayment history. Currently, most financial companies utilize this machine learning algorithm to analyze customer loan repayment history: based on this decision tree suggestion they decide to approve or disapprove the loan (Chen, Zhang & Ng, 2018). First step of the loan process is to check the customer credit score. If that score is above 800 it means that the customer loan application is automatically moved to the next approval process. Where the credit score is less than 700, indicating a poor credit history, the loan request is declined as suggested by the decision tree. For credit score between 700 and 800; the decision-making situation is critical. There is evidence of customer perfectly repaying their existing loan but due to some technical problems their loan history bears a negative remark. For example, sometimes electronic clearance system (ECS) or check clearance is activated due to the technical issue; this kind of problem indicates a negative score in the credit history. This type of problem is to be solved manually by the bank employee and the, loan application is checked manually based on previous repayment history.

Figure 4. Decision Tree Methodology

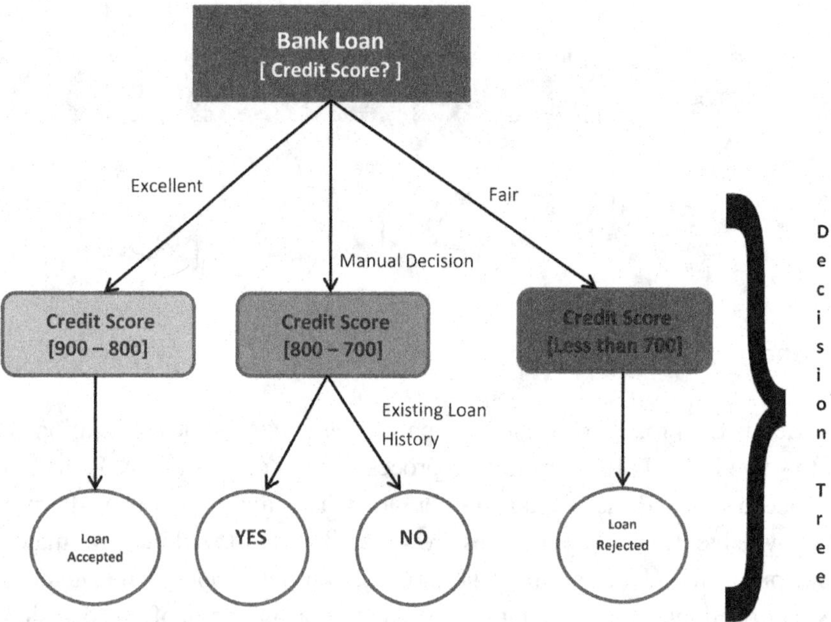

Figure 4 is a model diagram of a decision tree for loan approvals. The decision tree creates separate rules for each root node and leaf node. This rule is to apply individual data-sets and, that data-set assigns a variety of rules. These rules are divided into two categories. First, the smallest rule-based algorithm which maintains consistent levels in the training data-set. Second, is largest rule-based algorithm which maintains the level of the data-set. The concept of the data structure is used to find the best rule, either the divide or the conquer algorithm. Here the algorithm is separated by two different modules and it finds the optimal solution. This method is used to learn more on rule-based in dynamic situations. The rule is retrospectively implemented in-depth in the root and leaf node. There are many rule-based algorithms available in machine learning. One of the best rule-based algorithm is the Repeated Incremental Pruning to Produce Error Reduction (RIPPER) (Xuan, 2018). This is pure rule-based approach and, the working principle of these algorithms is two-process, that is, growing (incremental) and pruning. The incremental method is a higher restrictive phase during the training data-set process and is utilized to analyze very close structures. The growing method is generally a closed loop structure in the root-to-leaf node. The second method is pruning process; this is a normal restrictive structure. This method is to reduce over-fitting during rule analysis.

This is a multi-class structure to maintain lower to higher training data-sets. Like that of fuzzy rule-based algorithm, it is used in machine learning (Wang, Liu, Pedrycz & Zhang, 2015). It works with the principle of true value structure, which assigns the value of zero or one. The condition is set to true or false model, based on that condition rule is assigned and data is predicted from the data set. An alternative decision algorithm, PART (Hall et al., 2009) is used to minimize the post processing during rule association. Most of these decision tree algorithm function with similar type of rule-based decisions by using tree concepts. Inductive logic programming (ILP) is another decision analysis technique in machine learning. This method is to predict the future, based on previous positive or negative data for certain situations.

Perceptron Algorithm

Machine learning is the concept of predictions taken from various parameters. Binary classification is also one of the prediction mechanisms: it is termed the "Perceptron algorithm" and utilizes the concept of function (Min & Jeong, 2009). This prime mode of the algorithm is to decide the suitability of an input parameter. The function formation is created with sub-class vector numbers. In general, this is a sub-classification of linear classification mechanisms.

As both algorithms use restricted linear functions as their hypotheses, Winnow and Perceptron can be considered similar. The principal advantage of the Winnow algorithm is its utilization of multi-dimensional data. This method provides higher accuracy in comparison to other methods. Moreover the Perceptron algorithm is directly implemented in neural networks (Pérez-Sánchez, Fontenla-Romero & Guijarro-Berdiñas, 2018). It is acknowledged that biological nervous systems form the platform for artificial neural networks. The former collaborates with the functional part of brain and data processing. This information processing unit relates to the nervous structure. This nervous is generally connected to many interconnected structures. The interconnected structure is to solve various unison problems. Similarly, neural networks solve various complex problems in network communication. Machine learning neural network operate at three different levels (Camacho, 2018). The first layer is the input layer which deals with input parameters based on trained data-set. These input values are gathered from different network resources. The second layer is the output layer; this is an outcome that provides the final result. In between these two layers, is an important layer which deals with the prediction process, that is termed the hidden layer. These hidden layers are like those of a central processing unit (CPU) whose hidden layer predicts the result based on existing data. The major challenge of this structure is ingrained in the hidden layer node calculation where it is required to establish the best result. Both structures underestimate and overestimate creation of the hidden layer. The neural count, based on fact that a dynamic hidden layer creation is required, had proved to be unpredictable. An alternate name of this method is the feedforward neural network and the main advantage of this method is that data is transferred and moved uniquely in one direction.

Statistical Learning Algorithms

A statistical learning algorithm is a functional algorithm, used to predict the data from various statistics (Miller, Nagy, Schlueter, 2018). The combination of statistics and the functional model is implemented to predict the final result. This algorithm is mostly implemented in the field of computer virtual vision and bio-metric systems. In this algorithm, the primary goal is learning, and the secondary goal is prediction. The method is to implement both supervised and unsupervised learning methods (Chapelle, Scholkopf & Zien, 2009). Occasionally online learning is also used to predict the result. The online learning is utilized in online shopping, where, based on customers previous history system, it automatically predicts future customer needs and provides unique offers. This statistical model works with the probability structure. There are many network models implemented in this statistical algorithm. A Bayesian network is one of the important methods of this learning algorithm. It is categorized as a relational and probabilistic graphical structured model (Neal, 2012). The computational probabilistic condition is used to predict the data-set. Bayesian networks are implemented in the conception of directed acyclic graphs (DAG) (Li & Yang, 2018). The DAG method is used in different variables that are designated "S" and "X". S is a structure node in a graph and X is a feature prediction. This graph structure creates a table and maintains the parameter variable during dynamic situations. In networking there are two conditions used who possess respectively a structured network and an unstructured network. The structured network is a normal network structure and consequentially there is no complexity associated with this model. The network transmission variable is to maintain a separate table, the conditional probability table, whose function is to maintain all the network transmission and node connection details. This table is used to calculate the network connection estimation time. This table provides appropriate time for data in transit from one node to another node. Compared to other method major benefits of this Bayesian network is the inherent limitation (Wang et al., 2018). This limitation structure is used to analyze difficulties of the unknown network model. The model is to provide best available network based on previous table values. In many prediction systems they use greedy search optimization models to provide better prediction. Search optimization is implemented in the network node connection where this model is used to reduce the complexity of network connection. Local search optimization is also a familiar method network solution (Jayapandian, Rahman & Gayathri, 2015). This model updates the data at regular intervals in a local search on a particular data element.

Instance-based learning is one of the familiar methods in the machine learning algorithm (Zhang, 2019). The technical label of this technique is, memory-based learning algorithm. The previous network connection visited details, based on their memory structures, are updated in the table and, predict the future data connection. This method analyzes new problems with existing data elements. The prediction is only valid for working with instance-based mechanisms. Furthermore, the methodology works with the structure of hypotheses construction from the training data-set. The complexity level of prediction as well as growing hypotheses is reduced. If the training data-set of hypotheses is n, the complexity level is to solve is O(n), which is a new predicted instance based on previous learning. This notation provides advantage of not visiting previously failed data. The successful training data provides higher prediction mechanism in machine learning. The best example of this instance is the k-nearest neighbors search algorithm. This algorithm finds the nearest neighbors based on most visited data history. The previous data-set is stored and the training data-set value predicts the new instance data.

Support Vector Machine

The Support Vector Machine (SVM) is a category of supervised machine learning algorithm whose method is used to solve classification as well as time regression problems (Lorena et al., 2018). Classification problem segregate the training data-set during data prediction. The data-set is drawn into a separate plot in trained data elements. This plot creates a dimensional n-graph and creates a support line based on similarity index for data-sets. This method creates a hyper-plane and links the distance from one node to another. The support vector system is used to handle larger data-sets in a training instance. The data label is important because supervised learning algorithms are uniquely utilized in labeled data. At the same time unlabeled data-sets are used for unsupervised learning methods. Furthermore, support vector machine only use labeled data-sets and are thus unsuitable for the unlabeled.

MACHINE LEARNING APPLICATION

Recently machine learning had found its utility in many technological applications. Figure 5 demonstrates different real-time applications of the machine learning approach. Machine learning is also implemented in Internet of Things' (IoT) devices (Cui et al., 2018). IoT is known to encounter different security issues in the healthcare sector, which is a major research area in the machine learning approach (Bitra, Jayapandian & Balachandran, 2018). The technology applications of these kinds of machine learning algorithms are used in modern gadgets who are invariably associated with this internet technology. The virtual personal assistant is an example of a recent machine learning application (Karov et al., 2017). Currently, there are numerous products available related to this technology, for example, smart phones, smart speakers and mobile phone applications. The principal aim of this virtual assistant is to assist without human intervention. This happens based on our personal data and that of existing friends. If, for instance, an individual uploads a group photo, social media software automatically detects the associated face and traces the origin of the page. This happens thanks to machine learning face detection software (Sun, Wu & Hoi, 2018). In the technological domain, letter communication is facilitated by the email transmission. In many countries, email communication is one of the authorized communications for some government offices. The problem encountered in this type of communication is spam mail and malware viruses. Manual detection is not possible because of interminable email communication happening within short time intervals. It is essentially for this reason that machine learning algorithms detect viruses and hence protect user systems. An example of this type of machine learning virus filter (uni-variate or multi-variate predictors) is the C4.5 decision tree induction system (Mishra, Yadav, Kumar & Jain, 2019).

Online customer support is a natural supporting system on internet web pages utilized by most online based services to provide customer support. This technology works with a current customer requirement based on existing data. If any customer needs assistance for a product related query it is searched in the database and a predefined solution is provided for that customer. At the end stage if the customer needs additional assistance then manual customer support will be provided from the company side. That is the reason many online shopping companies use this machine learning algorithm to predict customer feature products and send recommendation for customers (Guan, Wei & Chen, 2019). Sometime based on user browser history they provide product suggestions. The Internet search engine is the heart of the internet technology where users utilize search engines to find information. This data searching is an arduous task because large quantities of data are available on the internet server. To solve this problem, machine learning algorithms provide the best solution for search engine optimization.

Figure 5. Machine Learning Application

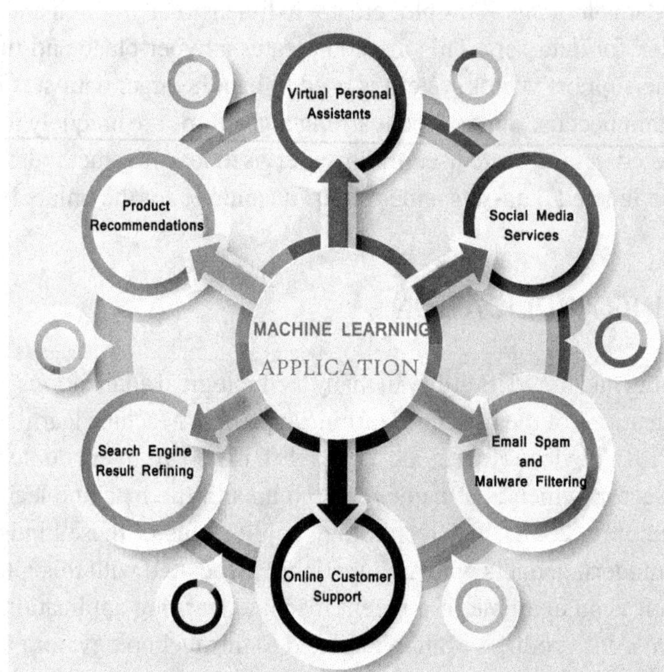

COMPONENTS OF MODERN NETWORKS

Networking is the heart of modern communication technology. Modern technology needs node-to-node data transmission with the help of this networking. Data is transferred from one terminal to another terminal. There are six major components involved in this network communication (Zhu & Choulli, 2018). By way of this networking structure, computer systems are connected from one remote terminal to another. These components are used to connect systems with with similar protocol structures thus permitting a collection of rules to maintain and establish reliable communications. Firstly, the component network interface card - a hardware component - is generally integrated with the computer motherboard. This end-to-end terminal concept is used to connect the network cable in this interface card (Huang, Zhao, Zhou, & Xing, 2018). Secondly, the component serves as a hub and connects more than one computer device to the common port (Cai et al., 2018). This is a central device connecting multiple devices to a single hub. The working methodology of this hub is to send signals from one computer device to all other computer devices on a common platform. The network interface card sends and receives signals from this hub port (Majumder & Nath, 2019). Thirdly the component switch is considered to be the most important one in networking. Switches transfer signals from one device to another. These transfers are actuated by precise signals from one terminal to another based on the device ID. In the hub a common transmitting structure transfers signals from one particular device to all other devices disregarding the device ID (Borky & Bradley, 2019). These three components function within the local area network (LAN) connection where for out of the LAN connection some smart devices are required such as a router. The router's task to connect one LAN network to another. This is important for a larger network connections. Routers are regarded as smart technology whose main advantage is to update the networking information in a dynamic manner. Communication media plays a major role in network connection where it helps to establish a physical connection from one computer terminal to another (Henry, Adamchuk, Stanhope, Buddle & Rindlaub, 2019). The technical name of this communication media is the ethernet cable where the concept is a twisted pair wire. Modern cables are used in the latest technology such as in optical fiber cables. This fiber optical cable is used to transfer signals more rapidly than traditional methods. The latter normal utilize electrical signals with the main drawbacks being data loss and less transmit power. A wireless router uses the same communication structure and procedure (Monteiro, Souto, Pazzi, & Nogueira, 2019). All of these components are hardware, but without the software component is not possible to establish computer communication. Transmission Control Protocol/ Internet Protocol (TCP/IP) is the most important software component in establishing network connections (Edwards & Bramante, 2015). Utilizing server layers, TCP/IP protocol has a set of rules which permit data communication. The application layer is normally an end-user layer used to create end-to-end connections; an examples of this layer being Domain Name System (DNS) and Hyper Text Transfer Protocol (HTTP). This layer creates a process and is utilized in some applications. The presentation layer is a data representation and data encryption process dealing with a Secure Sockets Layer (SSL) certificate and image encryption (Zhang, Yang, Castiglione, Chen, & Li, 2019). This layer is the most important in security situations. The session layer is to establish session connection from one port to another. The technical name of this layer is inter-host connection establishment; an example of this layer being socket connection and Application Programming Interface (API). The transport layer is an end-to-end connection to maintain protocol that is termed Transmission Control Protocol (TCP) and User Data-gram Protocol (UDP). The network layer transfers the packet from one device to another. All the data is converted into packages - normally computer communication is in packet structure. It determines the path and finds the logical address. The data link layer creates frames with physical addressing concepts to establish the physical connection using the Ethernet (Graveto, Rosa, Cruz & Simões, 2019). The physical layer then converts the signal into binary format which is in binary transmission structure. These are the basic hardware and software components of a network connection establishment. This cyber physical system handles the modern technologies that is named Internet of Things (IoT) and Smart City. This Internet of Things is involved in many modern applications like smart homes, smart schools, smart industries and smart world (Bitra, Jayapandian & Balachandran, 2018). These smart devices are handled and controlled with the id of IoT (Whitmore, Agarwal & Da Xu, 2015). During the next ten years without this internet none of the device will be operative, because speed with IoT technology is implemented in all of the applications. The major advantage of this IoT technology is that it can controlled anywhere in the world.

CYBER ATTACKS IN NETWORK

Data security deals with many encryption methods and algorithms which are intended to provide better security for the server or client machine. Encryption is specifically consists of two methods, symmetric and asymmetric (Jayapandian, Rahman, Radhikadevi & Koushikaa, 2016). The major challenge is network security, especially because data is transferred from one particular network terminal to another.

During this transmission some hackers attempt to get access to the data: whether data is encrypted or non-encrypted becomes a secondary secondary problem. This kind of network data attack is referred to as the Man-in-the-Middle (MITM) Attack. There are many cyber security attack problems faced in network data transmission. Denial of Service (DoS) is a common problem in data attack. In this attack, users try to access the information from the client machine to the server machine making data unavailable during that period. This type of attack - Distributed Denial of Service (DDoS) - is also directed at distributed network environments. The major difference between these two attacks is based on the character of the computer connectivity and data access. DoS deals with a single computer and internet connectivity while DDoS handles multiple computers connected to the internet network (Toklu & Şimşek, 2018). There are many methods to deal with this DDoS service; one of them being the User Datagram Protocol (UDP). Phishing attacks are presently considered as a normal events in internet world. In our contemporary world, a great deal of information is shared in email communication. This type of communication is not secure because of phishing attacks. This attack transfers the sensitive information like passwords and credit or debit card information (Krombholz, Hobel, Huber & Weippl, 2015). Spear phishing attacks are a sub-category of this attack. This attack only targets individual users or individual organizations. The attack is executed by installing malware which illegally accesses our personal data and transfers that data to hackers. Most of the time this type of attack happens via public network accessibility (Nithya & Gomathy, 2019). Drive-by overloads are a common method malware dispersal in some unauthorized websites. This kind of attack is executed by using HTTP or Hypertext Pre-processor (PHP) programs. Password hacking or cracking refers to the retrieved or to recover the password from the public computer system. There are two ways to retrieve the password, one is a stored password and another one is during transmission. This type of hacking happens because of less sensitive passwords. Sometimes users utilize their name or DoB in password combinations and is easily hacked. Stealing of data and interrupting the access control during data transmission is referred as an eavesdropping attack. This attack steals information from a server or network transmission. The Man-in-the-Middle attack (MITM) is the process of inserting or hijacking the information in the middle of data transmission from the client to server machine (Ahmad et. al., 2019). This type of attack is quite natural during the network data transmission. Sometimes session hijacking also happens during network communication. This session is the process of establishing a trusted connection between the clients to the server machine. IP spoofing is modifying IP header and unauthorized access to the server machine (Dayanandam, Rao, Babu & Durga, 2019). This is host-to-host communication to create a duplicate IP address and try to access the server machine. These are all the common attacks that occurred during network data transmission. Hybrid encryption also provides better data security in the cloud environment (Jayapandian & Rahman, 2017).

AVOIDING MAN-IN-THE-MIDDLE ATTACK USING REINFORCEMENT LEARNING

The previous section discussed various cyber security attacks in network communications. Network security is additionally a challenging task during online communication. This section examines another complex task; it concerns the Man-in-the-Middle attack. The operative mode of this type attack is some hacker tries to attack the data during network communications. Network communication happens both with internet and without internet. This attack mostly occurs with the internet connection. Operationally, the internet connects several computers and shares information from one remote location to another. The problem with this category of communication is the use of public networks where it very difficult to detect attackers. Furthermore, another challenge is that most of the users always depend on third-party servers. This is because maintaining individual servers is a burdensome task and that is expensive. This section will propose solution to solve this Man-in-the-Middle attack by using reinforcement learning. Before proceeding with to the proposed method, first discuss the reinforcement learning method.

The process of reinforcement learning is congruent with machine learning and is a sub-division of the artificial intelligence methodology. The main aim of reinforcement learning is to reduce the rewards in a perdition situation. It also provides special permission of finding the best prediction and behavior in computer machine and some third-party agents. This mechanism creates an additional component; the agent, which decides the next movement. In supervised learning, decisions are taken in the form of training data-sets. This reinforcement method is used to take decisions based on agent mechanisms based on previous experience. Supervised learning algorithms are used only for some test cases; it is not suitable for dynamic situations. The working principle of reinforcement methods is learning from experience. The user input level is maintained and starts the process. There is a different type of solution provided in a problem which is the unique advantage of this reinforcement method. Every individual solution is to provide some reward points where the points are based on the success ratio of that particular attempt. Machine learning is always keeping some training data-set; this training data-set is used to maintain all these solutions with reward points. The individual user will decide on the best solution; sometime the dynamic solution is also recommended for a problem. This is a sequential decision-making system where output is dependent on previous input in a problem. Each decision will have a unique label and based on that label, a decision is sequentially taken for a specific job. Reinforcement is categorized into two types, namely, positive and negative reinforcement. Positive reinforcement refers to the creation of higher strength in the behavior model frequency. It will create a positive approach in the behavior selection. The main advantage of positive reinforcement is to increase system performance. The long-term decision-making system is to sustain and provide a better solution. At the same time the drawback of this method is that the reinforcement state is damaged. The second type is negative reinforcement; this method is to provide a higher behavior model and avoid negative results. This structure is to increase model behavior during prediction. The proposed model uses the reinforcement learning concept during network data transmission to provide solutions for the Man-in-the-Middle attack. This architecture diagram in Figure 6. elaborates the functional components of Man-in-the-Middle attack with the reinforcement learning method.

Figure 6. Proposed Reinforcement Learning Approach

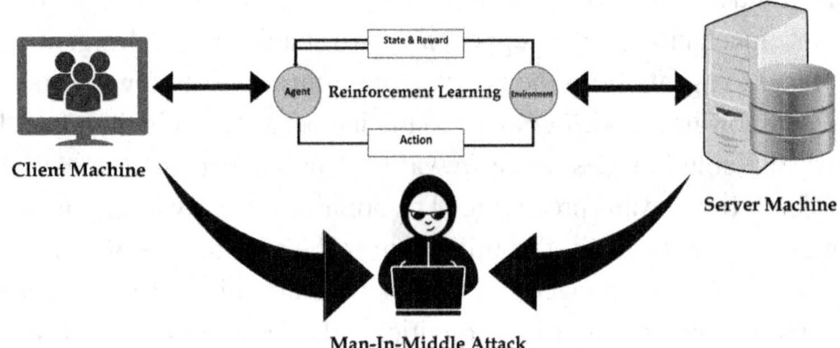

The client machine communicates data to the server machine through some network over the internet. This server works with the concept of cloud technology; most of the service providers are now moving to cloud platforms because of the cost effectiveness. The MITM attack is a network cyber attacker. This attacker is a professional who focuses on network protocol s and hacks the network data. The entire network data is transferred in the form of packets having two fields where one is header field and other one is the data field. The MITM attacker always focuses on this data field. There are two kinds of attacks that happen during network communication. The first one is data attack without modification which means the attacker does not modify any data during the data hack. This kind of hacking sometimes happens on social media by just hacking that data and disclosing it. This attack is faced by some government servers and terrorists that attack military information and disclose that information in public forums. Another kind of attack is data modification which means after the attack, the data hacker can try to modify that original data for a short duration of time. The major challenge of this task is to modify the data in some time interval, because networking protocol is working with time interval protocol. If the data is not reached within that time duration, that data is automatically disqualified and destroyed from the network terminal. This type of attack is also attempted in some banking and financial transactions. Most of the time this type of attack happens to individual server maintenance because individual server maintenance is more expensive so they do not concentrate on security. It is for this reason that many small industries depend on third party service providers which regrettably may not be trustworthy. The problem of third-party service providers is the lack of their privacy of their data. It also arrives that third party service providers misuse the client personal data for the purposes of marketing. So in either case, the security problem is permanently prevalent inciting the author to propose machine learning security protocol as a solution. The main objective of the network data transmission security is to deal with third eye or learning algorithm. In machine learning, there are many learning algorithms available, with reinforcement being the most successful. This proposed method is to create virtual agent during network transmission where the reinforcement decision is taken in the agent-based system. The purpose of this virtual agent is to avoid the middle man attack during data transmission. The MITM attack is involved at the mid-point between the client and server; similarly the agent mechanism is also installed in middle of the data communication. The working principle of this virtual agent system is to maintain a dynamic table and update all the network activity problems and solutions. Thus whenever a similar type of problem is encountered during network transmissions this virtual agent refers previous solutions and provide suggestions on how to avoid the current data attack. All this activity is happens in dynamic situations. The main advantage of this virtual method is that it is continuously attempting to find the best solution based on previous case histories. Reinforcement learning in two different terminals are referred to as an agent and environment. In this case environment is the network. There are three state conditions associated with the state mechanism. In the upper case, two states that are designated, state and reward; both states are connected to agents from the network environment. The reward state provides rewards for every individual solution in the virtual agent. This happens dynamically after the third or fourth cycle when that particular solution gets higher rewards. This virtual agent is automatically predicted the best solution based on this reward procedure. The solution give a warning to potential data attack activity to the client or service provider. The third state is the action state, which is the waiting signal from the agent component. This is engaged once the best solution is selected based on reward points. The network administrator always monitors the activities and subsequently provide higher security in the network terminal. The reinforcement learning algorithm functioning in dynamic situations thus provides situation-based solutions. Many other learning algorithms are also available under the machine learning concept, with the approach and uniqueness of this reinforcement algorithm being dynamism and its situational prediction mechanism.

RESULTS AND DISCUSSION

These result and discussion parts are focused on the analysis of security enhancement for network communication. This chapter uses reinforcement algorithm to solve network communication attacks. This proposed method is simulated with the help of Java Network Simulator (JNS). This JNS is used to create a network simulator (NS2) network environment by using Java. Network protocol is designed and establishes the connection between one computer system to another terminal. This proposed method concept is to store all the network activities in a separate table. That table is accessed in dynamic situations and is likewise updated in dynamic environments.

These network activities are updated in the memory table; system unique media access control (MAC) ID, IP address and type of network attacks. The purpose of this table is to compare the existing network attacks. The resulting type of attack is matched with that current table to existing table data. If that is matched, it means that a reinforcement agent provides a better solution based on the previous prediction match percentages. This simulation takes various parameters like the network attack ratio, Transmission time and Quality of Service (QoS). QoS parameter measures the following metrics that is named as throughput, packet delivery percentage and average packet delay ratio.

Figure 7. Packet Attack Ratio Analysis

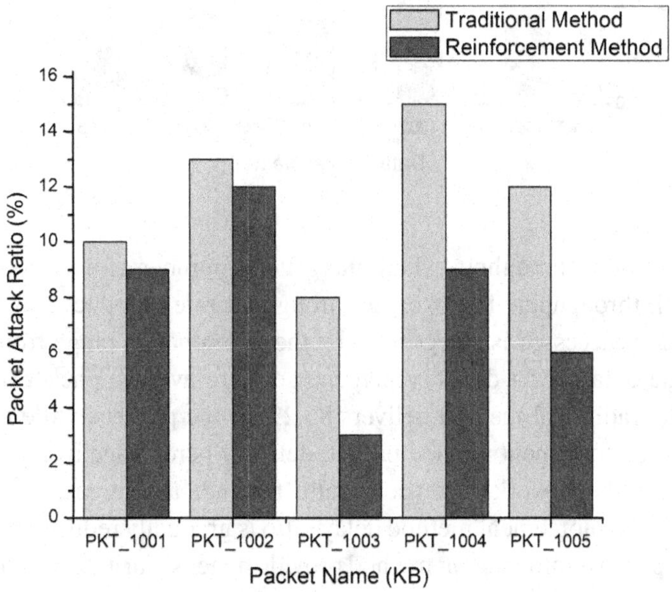

Figure 7 illustrates the network packet attacker ratio comparison between the stable methods, and proposed reinforcement method where the latter who provide better results. That means that the attacker ratio is reduced; in this case by 3.8%. The traditional method average attacker's ratio is 11.6% and at the same time, reinforcement algorithm method average attacker's ratio is 7.8%.

Figure 8 discusses network transmission time which is the overall transmission time used to calculate transmission of packets from one remote terminal to another. The average transmission time is almost 5.2% less in the proposed reinforcement method. Traditional method requires 0.5282 ms for five different data packet transmissions, while the reinforcement method takes only 0.4762 ms for the same data packets. It shows that the proposed method is taking less transmission time.

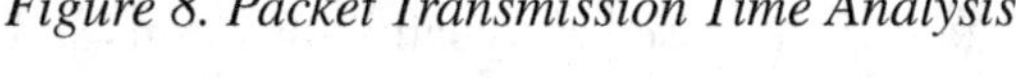

Figure 8. Packet Transmission Time Analysis

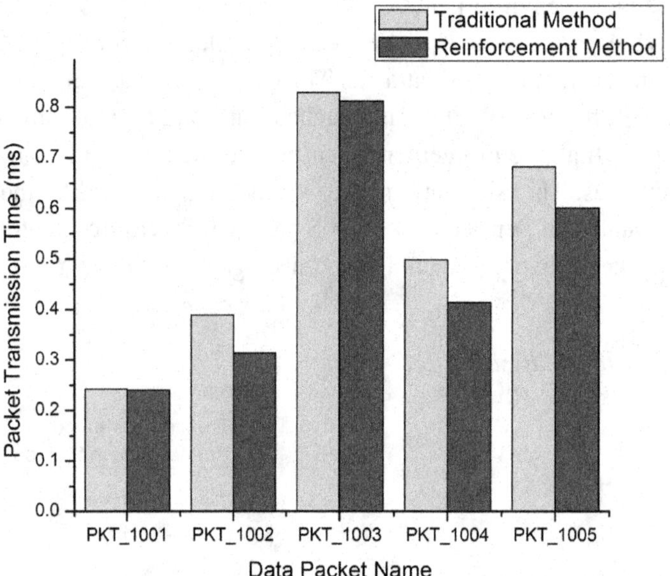

Figure 9 analyzes network throughput where the general number of user nodes increase implies a decrease in the network throughput. The average throughput rate is reduced by 0.01275%. The four-difference network node is accessed is categorized by the difference in range from node 25 to 100.

Figure 10 shows the data packet delivery percentage; here average packet delivery percentage is increased by 7.8%. The traditional method delivers 85.2% of the packets while for the same scenario, after implementing the reinforcement method packet, delivery percentage increases to 93%.

Figure 11 demonstrates the network packet delay ratio; this indicates direct network quality. Compared to the traditional method, reinforcement method delay ratio is gradually reduced by 13.265%. The above result indicates that proposed reinforcement method provide better security in network data transmission.

Based on the simulation result, the network attacker ratio, transmission time, throughput and packet delay ratio are decreased in the proposed method. The packet delivery percentage is increased which indicates that the proposed QoS is increased compared to the existing method.

Figure 9. Throughput Analysis

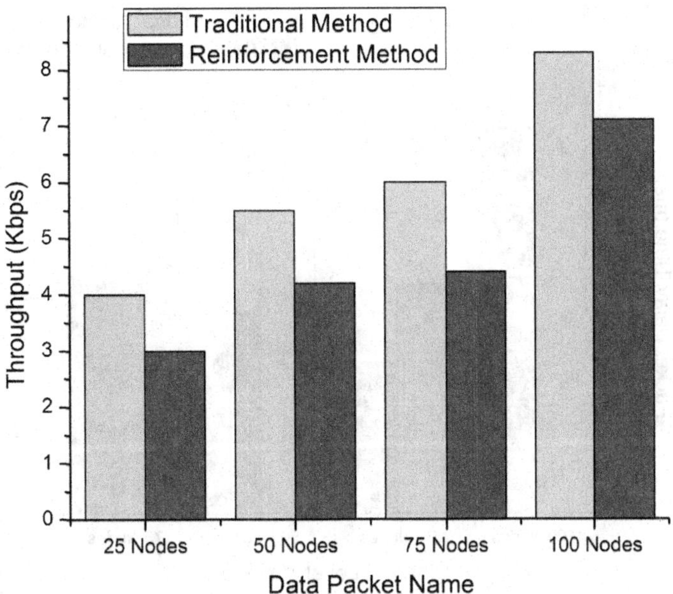

Figure 10. Packet Delivery Percentage Analysis

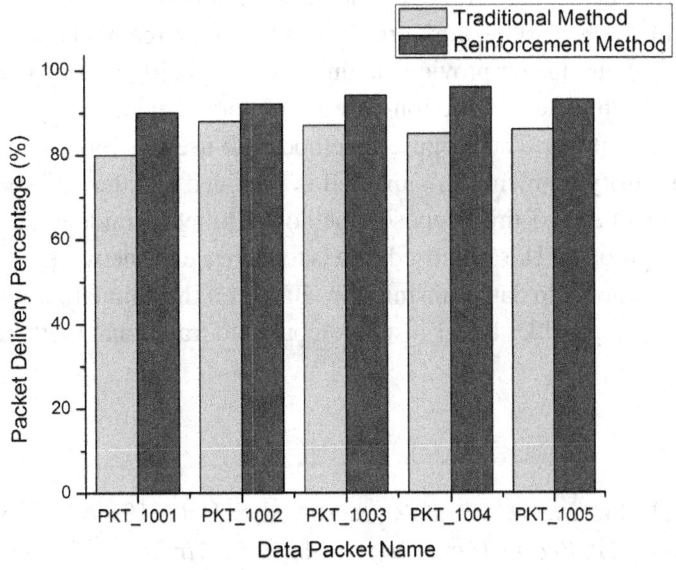

CONCLUSION

In our contemporary world modern technology is ineluctable. Network is a pillar of this modern and ever-expanding technology. Networking is not only utilized to connect computer devices, it is also used to connect modern gadgets. Machine learning and artificial intelligence algorithms are used in many traditional areas. These algorithms are used in the financial and banking sector to reduce the human

Figure 11. Packet Delay Time Analysis

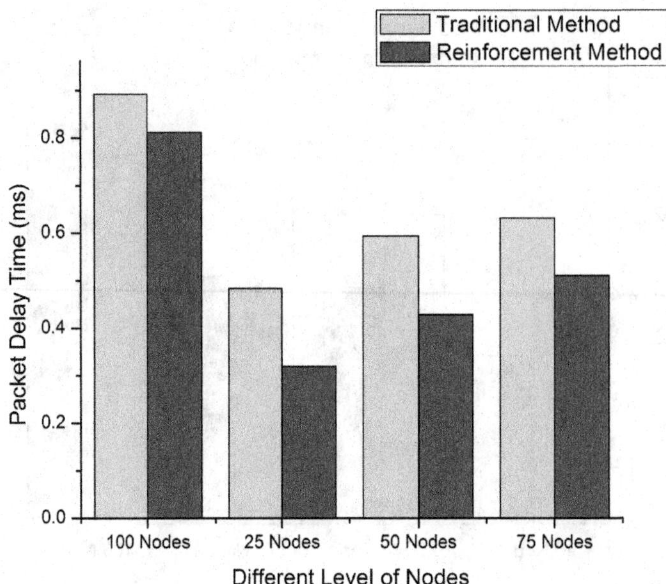

manpower. This chapter reviewed machine learning algorithms and networking components. At the present, nearly ninety-nine percentage of modern devices are employed in IoT technology and all these devices are working with the help of network protocols. One of the major challenges in this technology are network data attacks. This chapter provided an innovative solution for this network security attack. In machine learning, algorithm are a prediction-based. Reinforcement learning apparently is one of the best machine learning algorithms. The proposed method is to use this reinforcement learning method to solve this network security problem. This method is provided a better and more rapid solution for network hacking. The main aim of this proposed method is to avoid middle man attack by using this reinforcement learning approach. This proposed idea is to increase the network transmission quality and provide higher security protocol in data transmission. Based on the simulation result, it concludes that the reinforcement algorithm provides better result compared to traditional methods.

REFERENCES

Ahmad, M., Younis, T., Habib, M. A., Ashraf, R., & Ahmed, S. H. (2019). A Review of Current Security Issues in Internet of Things. In *Recent Trends and Advances in Wireless and IoT-enabled Networks* (pp. 11–23). Cham: Springer. doi:10.1007/978-3-319-99966-1_2

Bitra, V. S., Jayapandian, N., & Balachandran, K. (2018). Internet of Things Security and Privacy Issues in Healthcare Industry. In *International Conference on Intelligent Data Communication Technologies and Internet of Things* (pp. 967-973). Springer.

Boas, M. G. V., Santos, H. G., & de Campos Merschmann, L. H. (2018). Optimal Decision Trees for Feature Based Parameter Tuning: Integer Programming Model and VNS Heuristic. *Electronic Notes in Discrete Mathematics*, *66*, 223–230. doi:10.1016/j.endm.2018.03.029

Borky, J. M., & Bradley, T. H. (2019). Developing the Network Dimension. In *Effective Model-Based Systems Engineering* (pp. 327–344). Cham: Springer. doi:10.1007/978-3-319-95669-5_9

Brugere, I., Gallagher, B., & Berger-Wolf, T. Y. (2018). Network structure inference, a survey: Motivations, methods, and applications. *ACM Computing Surveys*, *51*(2), 24. doi:10.1145/3154524

Buda, M., Maki, A., & Mazurowski, M. A. (2018). A systematic study of the class imbalance problem in convolutional neural networks. *Neural Networks*, *106*, 249–259. doi:10.1016/j.neunet.2018.07.011 PMID:30092410

Cai, J., Wang, Y., Liu, Y., Luo, J. Z., Wei, W., & Xu, X. (2018). Enhancing network capacity by weakening community structure in scale-free network. *Future Generation Computer Systems*, *87*, 765–771. doi:10.1016/j.future.2017.08.014

Camacho, D. M., Collins, K. M., Powers, R. K., Costello, J. C., & Collins, J. J. (2018). Next-generation machine learning for biological networks. *Cell*, *173*(7), 1581–1592. doi:10.1016/j.cell.2018.05.015 PMID:29887378

Chapelle, O., Scholkopf, B., & Zien, A. (2009). Semi-supervised learning. *IEEE Transactions on Neural Networks*, *20*(3), 542–542. doi:10.1109/TNN.2009.2015974

Chaturvedi, I., Ragusa, E., Gastaldo, P., Zunino, R., & Cambria, E. (2018). Bayesian network based extreme learning machine for subjectivity detection. *Journal of the Franklin Institute*, *355*(4), 1780–1797. doi:10.1016/j.jfranklin.2017.06.007

Chen, Y. Q., Zhang, J., & Ng, W. W. (2018). Loan Default Prediction Using Diversified Sensitivity Undersampling. In *2018 International Conference on Machine Learning and Cybernetics (ICMLC)* (Vol. 1, pp. 240-245). IEEE. 10.1109/ICMLC.2018.8526936

Cui, L., Yang, S., Chen, F., Ming, Z., Lu, N., & Qin, J. (2018). A survey on application of machine learning for Internet of Things. *International Journal of Machine Learning and Cybernetics*, 1–19.

Dayanandam, G., Rao, T. V., Babu, D. B., & Durga, S. N. (2019). DDoS Attacks—Analysis and Prevention. In *Innovations in Computer Science and Engineering* (pp. 1–10). Singapore: Springer. doi:10.1007/978-981-10-8201-6_1

Edwards, J., & Bramante, R. (2015). *Networking self-teaching guide: OSI, TCP/IP, LANs, MANs, WANs, implementation, management, and maintenance*. John Wiley & Sons.

Fan, S. K. S., Su, C. J., Nien, H. T., Tsai, P. F., & Cheng, C. Y. (2018). Using machine learning and big data approaches to predict travel time based on historical and real-time data from Taiwan electronic toll collection. *Soft Computing*, *22*(17), 5707–5718. doi:10.100700500-017-2610-y

Fanjul-Peyro, L., & Ruiz, R. (2010). Iterated greedy local search methods for unrelated parallel machine scheduling. *European Journal of Operational Research*, *207*(1), 55–69. doi:10.1016/j.ejor.2010.03.030

Gercke, M. (2012). *Understanding cybercrime: phenomena, challenges and legal response*. Academic Press.

Ghahramani, Z. (2015). Probabilistic machine learning and artificial intelligence. *Nature*, *521*(7553), 452–459. doi:10.1038/nature14541 PMID:26017444

Graveto, V., Rosa, L., Cruz, T., & Simões, P. (2019). A stealth monitoring mechanism for cyber- physical systems. *International Journal of Critical Infrastructure Protection*, *24*, 126–143. doi:10.1016/j.ijcip.2018.10.006

Guan, Y., Wei, Q., & Chen, G. (2019). Deep learning based personalized recommendation with multi-view information integration. *Decision Support Systems*, *118*, 58–69. doi:10.1016/j.dss.2019.01.003

Hall, M., Frank, E., Holmes, G., Pfahringer, B., Reutemann, P., & Witten, I. (2009). *The Weka Data Mining Software*. Retrieved from https://dl.acm.org/citation.cfm?Id=1656278

Henry, E., Adamchuk, V., Stanhope, T., Buddle, C., & Rindlaub, N. (2019). Precision apiculture: Development of a wireless sensor network for honeybee hives. *Computers and Electronics in Agriculture*, *156*, 138–144. doi:10.1016/j.compag.2018.11.001

Huang, J., Zhao, M., Zhou, Y., & Xing, C. C. (2018). In-vehicle networking: Protocols, challenges, and solutions. *IEEE Network*, (99): 1–7.

Jayapandian, N., & Md Zubair Rahman, A. M. J. (2018). Secure Deduplication for Cloud Storage Using Interactive Message-Locked Encryption with Convergent Encryption, To Reduce Storage Space. *Brazilian Archives of Biology and Technology*, *61*(0), 1–13. doi:10.1590/1678-4324-2017160609

Jayapandian, N., Pavithra, S., & Revathi, B. (2017). Effective usage of online cloud computing in different scenario of education sector. In *Innovations in Information, Embedded and Communication Systems (ICIIECS), 2017 International Conference on* (pp. 1-4). IEEE. 10.1109/ICIIECS.2017.8275970

Jayapandian, N., & Rahman, A. M. Z. (2017). Secure and efficient online data storage and sharing over cloud environment using probabilistic with homomorphic encryption. *Cluster Computing*, *20*(2), 1561–1573. doi:10.100710586-017-0809-4

Jayapandian, N., Rahman, A. M. Z., & Gayathri, J. (2015). The online control framework on computational optimization of resource provisioning in cloud environment. *Indian Journal of Science and Technology*, *8*(23), 1–13. doi:10.17485/ijst/2015/v8i23/79313

Jayapandian, N., Rahman, A. M. Z., Radhikadevi, S., & Koushikaa, M. (2016). Enhanced cloud security framework to confirm data security on asymmetric and symmetric key encryption. In *Futuristic Trends in Research and Innovation for Social Welfare (Startup Conclave), World Conference on* (pp. 1-4). IEEE. 10.1109/STARTUP.2016.7583904

Jouini, M., & Rabai, L. B. A. (2019). A security framework for secure cloud computing environments. In Cloud Security: Concepts, Methodologies, Tools, and Applications (pp. 249-263). IGI Global. doi:10.4018/978-1-5225-8176-5.ch011

Karov, Y., Breakstone, M., Shilon, R., Keller, O., & Shellef, E. (2017). *U.S. Patent No. 9,772,994*. Washington, DC: U.S. Patent and Trademark Office.

Kaufman, L. M. (2009). Data security in the world of cloud computing. *IEEE Security and Privacy*, *7*(4), 61–64. doi:10.1109/MSP.2009.87

Kotsiantis, S. B., Zaharakis, I., & Pintelas, P. (2007). Supervised machine learning: A review of classification techniques. Emerging artificial intelligence applications in computer engineering, 160, 3-24.

Krombholz, K., Hobel, H., Huber, M., & Weippl, E. (2015). Advanced social engineering attacks. *Journal of Information Security and Applications*, *22*, 113-122.

Lau, R. Y., Xia, Y., & Ye, Y. (2014). A probabilistic generative model for mining cybercriminal networks from online social media. *IEEE Computational Intelligence Magazine*, *9*(1), 31–43. doi:10.1109/MCI.2013.2291689

Li, B., & Yang, Y. (2018). Complexity of concept classes induced by discrete Markov networks and Bayesian networks. *Pattern Recognition*, *82*, 31–37. doi:10.1016/j.patcog.2018.04.026

Li, J., Cheng, K., Wang, S., Morstatter, F., Trevino, R. P., Tang, J., & Liu, H. (2018). Feature selection: A data perspective. *ACM Computing Surveys*, *50*(6), 94.

Lino, A., Rocha, Á., Macedo, L., & Sizo, A. (2019). Application of clustering-based decision tree approach in SQL query error database. *Future Generation Computer Systems*, *93*, 392–406. doi:10.1016/j.future.2018.10.038

Lorena, A. C., Maciel, A. I., de Miranda, P. B., Costa, I. G., & Prudêncio, R. B. (2018). Data complexity meta-features for regression problems. *Machine Learning*, *107*(1), 209–246. doi:10.100710994-017-5681-1

Luiijf, H. A. M., Besseling, K., Spoelstra, M., & De Graaf, P. (2011). Ten national cyber security strategies: A comparison. In *International Workshop on Critical Information Infrastructures Security* (pp. 1-17). Springer.

Luo, J., Hong, T., & Fang, S. C. (2018). Benchmarking robustness of load forecasting models under data integrity attacks. *International Journal of Forecasting*, *34*(1), 89–104. doi:10.1016/j.ijforecast.2017.08.004

Luo, X., Jiang, C., Wang, W., Xu, Y., Wang, J. H., & Zhao, W. (2019). User behavior prediction in social networks using weighted extreme learning machine with distribution optimization. *Future Generation Computer Systems*, *93*, 1023–1035. doi:10.1016/j.future.2018.04.085

Mahmoud, T., Dong, Z. Y., & Ma, J. (2018). An advanced approach for optimal wind power generation prediction intervals by using self-adaptive evolutionary extreme learning machine. *Renewable Energy*, *126*, 254–269. doi:10.1016/j.renene.2018.03.035

Majumder, A., & Nath, S. (2019). Classification of Handoff Schemes in a Wi-Fi-Based Network. In *Enabling Technologies and Architectures for Next-Generation Networking Capabilities* (pp. 300–332). IGI Global. doi:10.4018/978-1-5225-6023-4.ch014

Michalski, R. S., Carbonell, J. G., & Mitchell, T. M. (Eds.). (2013). *Machine learning: An artificial intelligence approach. Springer Science* Business Media.

Min, J. H., & Jeong, C. (2009). A binary classification method for bankruptcy prediction. *Expert Systems with Applications*, *36*(3), 5256–5263. doi:10.1016/j.eswa.2008.06.073

Mishra, A. K., Yadav, D. K., Kumar, Y., & Jain, N. (2019). Improving reliability and reducing cost of task execution on preemptible VM instances using machine learning approach. *The Journal of Supercomputing*, *75*(4), 2149–2180. doi:10.100711227-018-2717-7

Moeyersoms, J., de Fortuny, E. J., Dejaeger, K., Baesens, B., & Martens, D. (2015). Comprehensible software fault and effort prediction: A data mining approach. *Journal of Systems and Software*, *100*, 80–90. doi:10.1016/j.jss.2014.10.032

Monteiro, A., Souto, E., Pazzi, R., & Nogueira, M. (2019). Context-aware network selection in heterogeneous wireless networks. *Computer Communications*, *135*, 1–15. doi:10.1016/j.comcom.2018.11.006

Neal, R. M. (2012). *Bayesian learning for neural networks* (Vol. 118). Springer Science & Business Media.

Nithya, S., & Gomathy, C. (2019). Smaclad: Secure Mobile Agent Based Cross Layer Attack Detection and Mitigation in Wireless Network. *Mobile Networks and Applications*, 1–12.

Park, H., Haghani, A., Samuel, S., & Knodler, M. A. (2018). Real-time prediction and avoidance of secondary crashes under unexpected traffic congestion. *Accident; Analysis and Prevention*, *112*, 39–49. doi:10.1016/j.aap.2017.11.025 PMID:29306687

Pasqualetti, F., Dörfler, F., & Bullo, F. (2013). Attack detection and identification in cyber-physical systems. *IEEE Transactions on Automatic Control*, *58*(11), 2715–2729. doi:10.1109/TAC.2013.2266831

Pérez-Sánchez, B., Fontenla-Romero, O., & Guijarro-Berdiñas, B. (2018). A review of adaptive online learning for artificial neural networks. *Artificial Intelligence Review*, *49*(2), 281–299. doi:10.100710462-016-9526-2

Quinlan, J. R. (2014). *C4. 5: programs for machine learning*. Elsevier.

Rubab, S., Taqvi, S. A., & Hassan, M. F. (2018). Realizing the Value of Big Data in Process Monitoring and Control. In *Current Issues and Opportunities. In International Conference of Reliable Information and Communication Technology* (pp. 128-138). Springer.

Schatz, D., Bashroush, R., & Wall, J. (2017). Towards a more representative definition of cyber security. *Journal of Digital Forensics. Security and Law*, *12*(2), 8.

Shon, T., & Moon, J. (2007). A hybrid machine learning approach to network anomaly detection. *Information Sciences*, *177*(18), 3799–3821. doi:10.1016/j.ins.2007.03.025

Steve Morgan. (2018). *2018 Cybersecurity Market Report*. Retrieved from https://cybersecurityventures.com/cybersecurity-market-report/

Sun, X., Wu, P., & Hoi, S. C. (2018). Face detection using deep learning: An improved faster RCNN approach. *Neurocomputing*, *299*, 42–50. doi:10.1016/j.neucom.2018.03.030

Toklu, S., & Şimşek, M. (2018). Two-Layer Approach for Mixed High-Rate and Low-Rate Distributed Denial of Service (DDoS) Attack Detection and Filtering. *Arabian Journal for Science and Engineering*, *43*(12), 7923–7931. doi:10.100713369-018-3236-9

Tsai, C. F., Hsu, Y. F., Lin, C. Y., & Lin, W. Y. (2009). Intrusion detection by machine learning: A review. *Expert Systems with Applications*, *36*(10), 11994–12000. doi:10.1016/j.eswa.2009.05.029

Von Solms, R., & Van Niekerk, J. (2013). From information security to cyber security. *Computers & Security*, *38*, 97-102.

Wang, H., Xu, Z., & Pedrycz, W. (2017). An overview on the roles of fuzzy set techniques in big data processing: Trends, challenges and opportunities. *Knowledge-Based Systems*, *118*, 15–30. doi:10.1016/j.knosys.2016.11.008

Wang, M., Cui, Y., Wang, X., Xiao, S., & Jiang, J. (2018). Machine learning for networking: Workflow, advances and opportunities. *IEEE Network*, *32*(2), 92–99. doi:10.1109/MNET.2017.1700200

Wang, X., Liu, X., Pedrycz, W., & Zhang, L. (2015). Fuzzy rule based decision trees. *Pattern Recognition*, *48*(1), 50–59. doi:10.1016/j.patcog.2014.08.001 PMID:25395692

Whitmore, A., Agarwal, A., & Da Xu, L. (2015). The Internet of Things-A survey of topics and trends. *Information Systems Frontiers*, *17*(2), 261–274. doi:10.100710796-014-9489-2

Witten, I. H., Frank, E., Hall, M. A., & Pal, C. J. (2016). *Data Mining: Practical machine learning tools and techniques*. Morgan Kaufmann.

Woo, J., Shin, S. J., Seo, W., & Meilanitasari, P. (2018). Developing a big data analytics platform for manufacturing systems: Architecture, method, and implementation. *International Journal of Advanced Manufacturing Technology*, *99*(9-12), 2193–2217. doi:10.100700170-018-2416-9

Xuan, S., Man, D., Yang, W., Wang, W., Zhao, J., & Yu, M. (2018). Identification of unknown operating system type of Internet of Things terminal device based on RIPPER. *International Journal of Distributed Sensor Networks*, *14*(10). doi:10.1177/1550147718806707

Zhang, Q., Yang, L. T., Castiglione, A., Chen, Z., & Li, P. (2019). Secure weighted possibilistic c-means algorithm on cloud for clustering big data. *Information Sciences*, *479*, 515–525. doi:10.1016/j.ins.2018.02.013

Zhang, X., Li, R., Zhang, B., Yang, Y., Guo, J., & Ji, X. (2019). An instance-based learning recommendation algorithm of imbalance handling methods. *Applied Mathematics and Computation*, *351*, 204–218. doi:10.1016/j.amc.2018.12.020

Zhu, X., & Choulli, E. (2018). Acquisition and communication system for condition data of transmission line of smart distribution network. *Journal of Intelligent & Fuzzy Systems*, 1-14.

KEY TERMS AND DEFINITIONS

Cyber Security: Cyber security is the category of information security system during internet communication data attack is happen avoiding this attack is named as cyber security.

Machine Learning: Machine learning is the process of predicting future result based on previous history.

Man-in-the-Middle Attack (MITM): Man-in-the-middle attack means hacking the data during network transmission in public network.

Network Security: Network security provides better security system during network data transmission.

Reinforcement Learning: Reinforcement learning method is to create virtual agent for the purpose of taking dynamic decision.

This research was previously published in AI and Big Data's Potential for Disruptive Innovation; pages 291-316, copyright year 2020 by Engineering Science Reference (an imprint of IGI Global).

APPENDIX: ACRONYMS

API: Application programming interface.
DAG: Directed acyclic graphs.
DDoS: Distributed denial of service.
DNS: Domain name system.
DoB: Date of birth.
DoS: Denial of service.
ECS: Electronic clearance system.
HTTP: Hypertext transfer protocol.
ILP: Inductive logic programming.
IoT: Internet of things.
IP: Internet protocol.
JNS: Java network simulator.
LAN: Local area network.
MAC: Media access control.
MITM: Man-in-the-middle attack.
NP: Non-deterministic polynomial.
PART: Partial decision tree (RWeka).
PHP: Hypertext pre-processor.
QoS: Quality of service.
RIPPER: Repeated incremental pruning to produce error reduction.
SSL: Secure sockets layer.
SVM: Support vector machine.
TCP: Transmission control protocol.
TCP/IP: Transmission control protocol/internet protocol.
UDP: User data-gram protocol.

Index

10-Fold Cross Validation 195, 254-255, 267, 269, 742, 776, 801, 810, 884

A

Adaboost 228, 239, 408, 418, 568-570, 572, 579, 581, 584-585, 786, 1236, 1287, 1291
Air pollutant prediction 1072
Anomaly Detection 107-109, 112-119, 121-123, 126, 128-133, 149, 168, 485, 597-598, 602, 604, 606, 627, 641, 928, 998, 1002-1003, 1102, 1144, 1156, 1160, 1188, 1209, 1214, 1327, 1446, 1448, 1451
antibacterial 292-293, 302-304, 306
Anxiety 776-779, 798, 1066, 1301, 1464
Apache Spark 1062, 1065, 1067, 1070, 1077, 1082-1083, 1381, 1387, 1392
Application in Engineering 26
Arduino 1488, 1491, 1493
Area Under the Curve (AUC) Score 898, 907
ART treatment 252, 254
Artificial Intelligence (AI) 1-2, 26, 28-29, 31, 36-39, 49, 68-70, 86-89, 103, 115, 119, 130, 138-140, 144-145, 148, 220, 308-309, 326, 344, 357-358, 379, 390, 395, 415, 418, 421-423, 426-431, 441-442, 444-447, 456, 458, 465, 468, 471-473, 477, 487, 527-528, 545, 604, 617, 622, 636-637, 640-641, 664, 677, 692, 697, 750, 753-754, 768, 770-771, 774, 846-847, 850, 859, 870-871, 881, 883, 926, 928-929, 937, 970, 975, 978, 989, 993, 996-998, 1038, 1056-1057, 1065-1066, 1070, 1073-1074, 1084, 1088-1090, 1103, 1106, 1129-1132, 1142, 1149, 1175, 1207, 1214, 1232, 1252-1253, 1271-1273, 1291-1292, 1294, 1301, 1303, 1307-1309, 1314, 1329, 1386, 1394, 1396, 1399, 1411, 1413, 1446-1448, 1460-1461, 1463, 1471, 1476-1482, 1490, 1492, 1512, 1514
Artificial Neural Network (ANN) 35, 37, 70, 86-89, 121, 242, 250, 260, 427, 432, 447, 471, 479, 620, 714-715, 733, 744, 750, 779, 839-841, 846, 886-887, 1017, 1072, 1077-1079, 1090, 1138, 1177, 1182-1183, 1185, 1210-1213, 1215-1216, 1233, 1235, 1241, 1252, 1262-1264, 1269, 1306, 1308, 1313, 1328, 1381, 1394, 1398, 1409, 1436, 1444, 1491
Association Rule 1, 4-5, 17, 20, 206, 230, 444, 624, 631, 668, 697, 860, 866-867, 1176, 1178, 1314, 1378, 1384
Attack Characterization 1165
Attack handling Mechanisms 952, 964
Automation 2, 27, 87-88, 139, 251, 325, 379, 384, 386, 392, 431, 442, 444, 637, 643, 798, 847, 873, 909, 970, 1036, 1162, 1216, 1253-1254, 1446, 1451-1452, 1460-1465, 1469, 1476-1481
autonomous driving 379-380, 382, 393
Avatar-Based Management 137-139, 141-142, 144, 148, 939, 942-943, 945, 950-951
AWS 228, 1488, 1493

B

Bagging 68, 70-73, 76, 85-87, 98, 194, 219, 222, 308-309, 316-317, 320-324, 326, 408, 484, 699-700, 904, 1011, 1086-1087, 1093, 1096, 1100, 1106, 1183, 1286-1287
Benign 149, 163, 170, 1351-1352, 1359, 1382-1383, 1403
Bias 10, 22, 43, 51, 75, 243, 295, 315, 335-336, 359, 492, 494, 572, 818, 845, 871, 873-874, 932, 1105, 1183, 1237, 1240-1241, 1243-1244, 1287-1288, 1290, 1332, 1411, 1464, 1467, 1470, 1473, 1480
Big Data 1-2, 25, 34, 40, 58, 66, 90, 103, 106, 119, 221, 223, 228-229, 238, 346, 413, 417, 421, 423, 426, 428, 431, 442-444, 446-448, 453, 455-457, 465, 468-474, 485, 526, 545, 594, 619, 621-623, 634, 640-641, 664, 676, 679, 712, 734-735, 737, 742, 749, 751, 753, 775, 818, 844, 846-847, 872, 880-881, 904, 909, 930, 939, 943, 945, 949, 970, 978, 995, 998-1000, 1037, 1057, 1062-1070,

1078-1079, 1083-1085, 1088, 1101-1102, 1104, 1130-1131, 1139, 1141-1142, 1152, 1164, 1255, 1257-1258, 1268-1269, 1303, 1308, 1311, 1326-1327, 1381-1382, 1386-1388, 1391-1394, 1429, 1447, 1453, 1458-1459, 1461-1463, 1472, 1482-1486, 1488-1493, 1513-1515
Big Data Analytics 66, 90, 229, 346, 469, 734-735, 749, 751, 846, 872, 881, 943, 999, 1063, 1070, 1078, 1083, 1130, 1141-1142, 1257-1258, 1382, 1386, 1391-1392, 1459, 1482-1484, 1486, 1492
Binary Classification 48, 93, 121, 235, 369, 482, 486, 495-496, 515-517, 519-521, 526, 577, 657, 698, 757, 786, 801, 803-804, 907, 983, 997, 1042, 1224, 1250, 1448-1449, 1487
Bioinformatics 57, 102, 105, 145, 225-230, 235, 237-240, 485, 771, 773, 798-799, 860, 937, 940, 948, 1141, 1182, 1348, 1378, 1386, 1392-1394, 1444
biopsy 1353, 1381, 1403-1404, 1411, 1413-1414
bond rating 734
brain tumor 1038, 1047, 1056-1057, 1059, 1061
Breast Cancer 234-235, 584, 1297, 1340, 1351-1353, 1358-1385, 1391-1395, 1397-1402, 1406, 1409, 1411-1413
business insight 447, 457

C

CAD System 1413, 1415, 1422
CBIR 930-933, 936
CD4 count 252-260, 262, 264-269, 271-272
Cellular Networks 129, 1494-1496, 1499-1501, 1504, 1506, 1510-1516
Cheminformatics 38
Civil Engineering 34, 37, 68-69, 88-89, 1089
Classification Algorithms 168-169, 172, 198, 212-213, 215, 217, 247, 250, 255, 333, 341-342, 355, 363, 408, 411, 534, 588, 606, 615, 683, 691, 755-758, 776, 778-780, 789, 792, 794-796, 800-802, 804, 808, 883-884, 905, 907, 915, 923, 925, 1036, 1105, 1314, 1317, 1331-1332
Classification Models 10, 13-14, 42, 255, 292-294, 302, 347, 349-351, 355, 625, 659, 758, 781-782, 884, 894, 1054, 1093, 1285, 1287, 1355-1356, 1491
Classifier 11, 14, 42-43, 49, 58, 72, 88, 98, 121-122, 130-131, 162-163, 175, 178, 193, 212-213, 216, 228, 232, 243-244, 255, 259, 267, 270-271, 275, 277-278, 280, 287, 316, 325, 329-330, 333-334, 337, 341-342, 367-368, 374, 378, 400-403, 406, 414, 418, 436, 438, 451, 463, 478-479, 496-504, 506-511, 515, 519-520, 523-524, 526, 533, 537-538, 540, 543, 568-570, 572-574, 578-579, 581, 583, 588, 603-605, 609, 614-615, 618-619, 626, 635, 654, 656, 659, 683, 685-686, 691, 693, 696, 698-699, 708-709, 737, 741, 744-745, 756-757, 778-779, 782-783, 785-787, 789, 791, 795, 809, 850, 884-887, 894-895, 900-908, 928-929, 931, 934, 937, 979, 1002, 1007-1017, 1061, 1064, 1077, 1093-1094, 1152-1153, 1157-1159, 1183, 1185, 1187, 1211-1212, 1226, 1235-1236, 1239, 1244, 1250, 1273, 1286-1287, 1290-1291, 1297, 1313-1314, 1317, 1325, 1330-1332, 1334-1338, 1346, 1348, 1356, 1358, 1377-1378, 1398-1399, 1409-1410, 1422, 1425, 1448, 1450, 1452
Cloud Computing 2, 38, 43, 59-61, 66, 130, 231, 469, 472-475, 484-485, 601, 618-619, 678, 928, 952-956, 958-960, 973, 978, 996, 1171, 1387, 1392, 1458, 1472, 1477, 1481, 1493, 1495
Cloud Figuring 454
Cloud Security Attacks 952
Cluster Analysis 17, 91, 96, 101-102, 104-105, 230, 294, 760, 771, 774, 823-824, 844-847, 860, 1355
Clustering 1, 4-5, 10-11, 17-22, 30, 34, 54-55, 57-58, 61, 98, 101-102, 106, 114, 119, 121, 129-130, 203, 206, 209, 211, 219, 221, 223, 230, 235, 238, 362-363, 365-367, 369-370, 372, 374-378, 381, 395, 422-425, 428, 432, 436, 439-440, 446, 470-471, 478, 480-481, 483-484, 533-536, 540, 542-543, 588, 605, 614, 619, 624, 627, 630-631, 634-636, 648, 668, 683, 697, 709, 753-754, 759-761, 769-771, 773-775, 801, 807, 817, 819, 822-825, 828-829, 831-832, 834-838, 840, 842-844, 846-847, 850, 860, 865-866, 883-884, 910-913, 918, 921, 923, 927-928, 973, 999, 1009, 1039, 1041, 1070, 1075, 1089, 1124, 1157, 1164, 1176, 1178-1179, 1182, 1188, 1228, 1313, 1359, 1378, 1384, 1386, 1389, 1421, 1424, 1448, 1498, 1507, 1512
CNN 381, 432, 463, 482, 484, 627, 1002, 1013-1014, 1182, 1406
code smells 800-804, 806, 808-809, 813
Coefficient of Variation 241, 243-245, 247, 250
Cognitive Science Applications 148, 680, 948, 951, 1232
computer aided diagnosis 1395-1396, 1398, 1412, 1419
Computer Vision 107-108, 175, 212, 220, 289, 387, 394, 421-423, 426, 429, 440, 443-444, 446, 458, 464, 488, 530, 641, 758, 768, 837, 860, 930-932, 937, 1020, 1058, 1129, 1142, 1300, 1396, 1398, 1407, 1464
Computer-Assisted Diagnosis 1414
concept link graph 339
concrete compressive strength 68, 70-71, 77, 82, 84-88, 325

Confidence Interval 265, 1038, 1047, 1050, 1053, 1394
Confusion Matrix 22, 60, 64-65, 262, 268-270, 444-445, 486, 495-497, 502, 504, 506-510, 520, 524, 538, 591-593, 609, 707, 756, 782-788, 790-791, 887, 896, 899-900, 1031-1032, 1118, 1227-1228
Context-Aware System 775
cost effectiveness 879, 990
CPS Intelligence 1188
CPS Security Objectives 1165, 1168
CPS Security Solutions 1165
Cross-Validation 9, 79, 88, 100, 247, 280-282, 288, 296-297, 357-358, 444, 537, 609, 617, 619, 719, 731, 742-744, 746-748, 756, 779, 788-790, 794-796, 919, 932, 1012, 1034, 1093-1094, 1237, 1241, 1250, 1252, 1332
Customers Behaviors Prediction 1210
Cyber Security 137-139, 141-142, 144-145, 148-149, 151, 170, 173, 175-176, 445, 474, 620-622, 627, 634, 636, 639-641, 653, 667, 677, 680, 927, 939-942, 944-945, 947-951, 953, 975-978, 988, 997-1000, 1143-1145, 1148-1149, 1155-1156, 1161, 1163-1165, 1172, 1175-1179, 1189, 1192, 1208, 1214, 1231-1232, 1478
cyber security professionals 939, 942, 945, 950
Cyber-Attacks 138, 149, 633, 667, 948, 953-954, 956, 961, 973, 978, 1143, 1148, 1155, 1165, 1173-1174, 1191
Cyber-Physical Systems 117, 131, 476, 998, 1165, 1191-1192, 1451

D

Data Analytics 37, 66, 87, 90-91, 103, 146, 198-199, 201, 203-205, 209, 229, 325, 346, 469, 474, 734-735, 749, 751, 846, 872, 881, 943, 976, 999, 1023, 1026, 1038, 1057, 1063, 1069-1070, 1078, 1083, 1102, 1130, 1141-1142, 1256-1258, 1261, 1310, 1352, 1381-1382, 1386-1387, 1391-1392, 1459, 1482-1484, 1486-1488, 1490-1492, 1512, 1515
Data Classification 239, 359, 417, 419, 568, 581, 585, 660, 796, 1110-1111, 1115, 1120-1121, 1271, 1332, 1349
Data Mining 16, 24-25, 36-38, 44, 87, 89, 114-116, 118, 128-130, 145, 175-176, 206-207, 219-221, 223-224, 229-232, 234, 238, 241, 243-244, 247-248, 251, 255, 272-273, 325-326, 346-347, 350, 357-359, 394, 413-414, 416, 418, 423-426, 435, 444-448, 457, 468, 470-471, 473, 526, 532, 536, 542, 546, 583, 604, 617-620, 624, 640, 662-663, 677, 691-692, 712, 770-772, 775, 815, 844, 847, 860, 866, 868-869, 881-884, 906-907, 911, 927-929, 940, 948, 973, 975, 978, 980, 996, 998-999, 1018, 1036, 1038-1041, 1045, 1055-1058, 1085, 1089, 1093, 1100-1101, 1103, 1105, 1125, 1130-1131, 1141, 1152, 1155, 1171, 1190, 1214, 1222, 1231, 1253, 1255, 1306, 1309, 1312-1314, 1316, 1326-1329, 1351-1353, 1358, 1378-1380, 1386, 1388, 1392-1393, 1443-1444, 1477, 1486, 1491, 1493, 1509, 1512-1513
Data Preprocessing 25, 327, 331, 338, 554, 556, 701-702, 905, 913, 915, 922-923, 1082, 1257, 1260-1261, 1274, 1302, 1316, 1318, 1428, 1438
data processing engines 1381, 1387-1388, 1390-1391
Data Science 106, 145, 624, 750, 753, 759, 886, 904, 909, 947, 1025, 1039-1040, 1077, 1211, 1214, 1226, 1231, 1331, 1394, 1475, 1480
Data Security 961, 976-977, 987-988, 996, 1142, 1210-1211, 1213, 1229, 1466, 1477
Dataset 5, 7-11, 14, 23, 30, 49, 60-63, 65, 77, 79, 115, 119, 122-126, 162, 164, 178, 190-191, 193-194, 213-216, 227-228, 230-233, 237, 241, 243-245, 247-248, 255, 257-258, 260, 264-265, 267, 271, 275, 277-278, 280-282, 284-288, 294, 300-302, 316, 319-320, 329, 334, 341-343, 349-351, 353-355, 366, 396-397, 400, 403, 405-406, 414, 422, 425, 427, 431, 440, 477, 484, 488, 490, 493, 498, 516, 535-538, 543, 572-574, 576, 579-580, 589-592, 596, 602, 605-609, 613-614, 616-617, 619, 625-626, 635, 654, 656-659, 681-684, 686-691, 693, 696-697, 700, 702, 704-705, 718, 755-759, 776, 779-780, 783, 789, 791, 794-796, 800-809, 813, 817-820, 825, 832, 836-837, 839-840, 842-843, 851, 853, 868, 883-890, 892-894, 905-906, 910, 913-915, 918, 920-924, 926, 935, 971, 1016, 1026, 1030-1033, 1035, 1039, 1046, 1055, 1059, 1061, 1068, 1074, 1078, 1080, 1082, 1136, 1144, 1150-1151, 1153, 1156-1157, 1159, 1163, 1212, 1216-1217, 1221-1224, 1230-1231, 1233, 1237, 1241-1242, 1244, 1247, 1250, 1255-1258, 1260-1263, 1265, 1305, 1313, 1317-1318, 1330-1337, 1339-1342, 1345, 1353, 1355-1361, 1371, 1377-1378, 1383-1384, 1386, 1398, 1403, 1449-1450, 1498
Decision Making 49, 61-63, 65, 206, 242, 344, 347, 413, 416, 431, 445, 457, 470, 480, 574, 584, 601, 866, 870, 1038, 1055, 1057, 1100, 1104, 1131, 1184, 1214, 1295-1296, 1298, 1308, 1311-1312, 1330, 1358, 1462
decision model 1427
Decision Tree 14-16, 58, 70-72, 115, 120, 130, 166, 242-243, 247-250, 255, 258, 267, 316, 325, 367, 370, 374, 376, 378, 401, 422, 432, 470, 479, 521,

532, 538, 546, 588-590, 595, 604, 657-658, 741, 757-758, 776, 779, 782, 784-785, 787, 792-793, 808, 812-813, 884, 894, 906, 923-924, 938, 979, 981-983, 985, 997, 1001, 1038, 1054-1057, 1060-1061, 1086, 1090-1091, 1093, 1101, 1104, 1183, 1185, 1226, 1232, 1256, 1286, 1306, 1309, 1312-1314, 1317, 1322-1323, 1332, 1334, 1356, 1358-1360, 1363-1364, 1372, 1377-1378, 1384, 1410, 1449, 1452, 1491
Deep Belief Network 432, 1143, 1157-1158, 1178, 1182
Deep Learning 2, 38, 65, 103, 149, 172-176, 220, 224-225, 234-240, 380, 384, 393-394, 421-422, 425-429, 431-432, 440-441, 443-447, 463, 469, 533, 538, 540, 620, 625, 627, 641, 655, 662, 667, 680, 757-758, 765, 771, 773, 775, 798, 817, 819, 837, 840-841, 845-846, 883-884, 887, 904, 970, 975, 978, 996, 998, 1013-1014, 1016, 1019, 1057, 1066, 1070-1071, 1077, 1079-1080, 1082, 1084, 1139, 1141-1145, 1152, 1155-1164, 1175, 1177-1178, 1182, 1190, 1192, 1212, 1225, 1231-1232, 1236, 1251, 1272, 1291-1292, 1296, 1299, 1305, 1308, 1326, 1331, 1334, 1348, 1386, 1389, 1393, 1395-1396, 1398, 1409, 1412, 1466, 1470, 1473, 1478, 1504, 1513-1514
Deep Learning Neural Network 837, 840-841, 1077
Deep Learning Techniques 65, 173, 175, 224, 421, 427, 431, 444, 655, 837, 1156, 1159-1160, 1236, 1291, 1296, 1305, 1409
Deep Neural Network 327, 329-330, 333, 335-336, 341-342, 345, 432, 450, 654, 1079, 1155, 1157, 1164, 1182, 1333, 1399
demand estimation 1086-1087, 1102
Dependent And Independent Variables 533, 1271, 1285
Depression 734, 776-779, 798, 1025, 1301
Descriptive Analytics 1493
Detection Rate 118-119, 128, 165, 596, 600, 602-605, 610, 615-616, 657, 666, 1002, 1015, 1151
Diabetes Prediction 241-243, 250, 882, 884, 887, 905
Diabetic Retinopathy 274-275, 289, 291, 344, 1419
Dimensionality Reduction 17, 21, 54, 162, 231, 238, 240, 440, 533, 624, 631-632, 737, 754, 759, 763-764, 766, 905, 930, 937, 1004, 1158, 1176, 1178-1179, 1239, 1389, 1450
Disease 3, 32, 48, 53, 105, 111, 199, 211, 217, 225-227, 230-231, 233-235, 237, 241-242, 250, 253, 272, 303, 396-398, 412, 414, 416-417, 488, 495, 515, 531, 778, 780, 794-796, 882-885, 906-907, 1038, 1045-1046, 1055-1056, 1058, 1062-1064, 1068-1069, 1072, 1076, 1101, 1148, 1295-1299, 1301, 1305-1308, 1314, 1332, 1334, 1348, 1352-1353, 1358, 1378, 1381-1382, 1386, 1391, 1394, 1399-1400, 1411-1417, 1421, 1424-1426, 1429, 1431, 1457, 1485, 1490, 1493
Dos 155-156, 450-451, 605-606, 608, 619, 642, 645, 649-652, 654, 656, 659, 662-663, 955, 988, 1001, 1127, 1145, 1150, 1208
drug design 292-293, 303
Drug Discovery 39, 292, 304, 530, 587, 719, 1062-1063, 1065-1066, 1070-1071, 1299
drug prediction 1062-1064, 1066-1069

E

EBusiness 1193
Ecommerce 425, 1193, 1197-1198, 1205-1207
Educational Data Mining 346-347
Electronic Health Record 544, 1302, 1331, 1348, 1350, 1482, 1493
emergency department 1311-1313, 1315, 1318, 1326-1329, 1430, 1443
Ensemble Model 321, 484, 568, 570, 747, 904
error analysis 362-363, 377-378
Evaluation Metrics 21, 81-83, 86, 255, 270, 283, 444, 577, 693, 1227, 1244, 1287
Extreme Learning Machine 71, 88-89, 274-276, 289, 291, 471, 568-569, 571, 581, 583-585, 605, 640, 677, 714-715, 731-732, 995, 997, 1313

F

F1 Score 22, 497-499, 790, 882, 900-901, 904-906, 908, 1342, 1348
FabI inhibitors 292-293, 300, 303-305
Fall Detection 198, 212-213, 215, 1300
False Alarm Rate 119, 128, 610, 615-616, 653, 790
Feature Engineering 8, 38, 42, 636, 887, 1262, 1275
Feature Extraction 8, 21, 34, 54, 162-164, 170, 173, 212, 214, 231, 274, 278, 285, 288, 330, 332, 340, 343, 425, 480, 540, 618, 660, 685, 702, 706, 709, 920, 930-931, 1007, 1014, 1019, 1082, 1214, 1262, 1398, 1404, 1407, 1409, 1419, 1421, 1423-1425
Feature Representation 1188, 1233
Feature Selection 5, 8-9, 16, 21, 68, 71, 76-77, 84-86, 88, 162, 165, 170, 212, 214, 241, 243-245, 247-251, 306, 346, 348-350, 352-353, 355, 359, 368, 593, 596, 602-605, 615-619, 625, 773, 796, 814, 904-905, 927, 930-932, 937-938, 997, 1015-1016, 1018, 1025, 1036, 1064, 1077, 1092, 1103, 1188, 1231, 1252, 1256-1258, 1262, 1315-1317, 1322-1323, 1327-1328, 1330, 1332-1335, 1337, 1342, 1347, 1349, 1358, 1379, 1393
financial health 734, 738

financial ratios 734, 738
flat clustering 362, 365-366, 370, 376
Flooding 203, 645, 651, 663, 955, 1108, 1145, 1157
Fog Computing 59-62, 65-67, 145, 202, 472-476, 480, 484-485, 667
FS algorithm 930, 934
Future of Humanity 1460, 1476
future solution 137

G

Gene Expression 33, 224-225, 228, 230, 233, 237-239, 1064, 1297, 1332, 1359, 1379, 1381-1382, 1386, 1391
Genetic Programming 71, 233, 358, 426, 459, 486, 488, 511, 515, 517, 521, 526-527, 1513
Genome 224-233, 235, 237-239, 254, 345, 1299, 1467
Geovisualization 1124, 1126
Gradient Boosted Machine 741, 747

H

Hadoop 460, 881, 1062, 1065, 1067-1068, 1077-1079, 1082-1084, 1152, 1386-1388, 1390, 1393, 1482, 1486, 1488, 1493
Haemotoxylin and Eosin 1414
HDFS 1062, 1068-1069, 1078-1079, 1486
Health Care 224, 253, 566-567, 679, 928, 1023, 1025, 1042, 1054, 1062-1065, 1067, 1069, 1101, 1295, 1298, 1301, 1303, 1307-1309, 1330-1331, 1334, 1352, 1386, 1393-1394, 1396, 1427-1430, 1441-1443, 1449, 1457, 1465, 1479, 1482-1487, 1489-1492
Health Policy 1427
heart disease 1038, 1045-1046, 1056, 1058, 1076, 1314, 1334, 1348, 1412
Heat Collection Rate (HCR) 733
Heat Loss Coefficient (HLC) 733
Herpes Simplex Virus (HSV) 1415, 1417
Hierarchical Clustering 19, 121, 130, 230, 362, 365, 367, 370, 374-377, 543, 627, 761, 771, 773, 817, 823-825, 828, 832, 834-835, 837, 846, 860, 865-866, 1384
High Dimensional Data 21, 90, 96, 103, 235, 349, 1299, 1331-1332, 1349
high performance concrete 68, 70, 87-88
High-Throughput Screening (HTS) 714, 716, 719, 731-733
histopathology 1395, 1397-1398, 1403-1406, 1411-1414
histopathology images 1395, 1397-1398, 1403-1406, 1411-1412
HIV/AIDS 252, 254-255, 272
Hybrid Models 68, 232, 904
hybrid prediction models 71, 308, 320
hyper parameter tuning 882, 886, 897-898, 902, 908
hyper-computation 137-138
Hypertension 258, 274-275, 776, 778, 795, 1488, 1493

I

ID3 Algorithm 14, 16, 587, 591-594, 604
Imbalanced Learning 415, 568, 584, 771
Information Retrieval 40, 58, 132, 328, 338, 443, 446, 710-711, 771, 774-775, 931
Intelligent and Analytics Platforms 946, 950
Internet Of Things 66-67, 132, 159, 198-199, 202, 219-223, 413, 421, 423, 442, 444, 446-447, 459-461, 464, 468, 470, 472-473, 475, 485, 583, 642-644, 661-663, 667, 676, 678-679, 869, 909, 928-929, 970, 985, 987, 994-995, 999, 1001, 1085, 1141, 1151-1152, 1155, 1157, 1164, 1167, 1214, 1295, 1308, 1411, 1446-1447, 1452-1453, 1455, 1457-1459, 1461, 1472, 1474-1476, 1482, 1484, 1492-1493, 1495
Intrusion Detection 107, 115, 117-119, 128-132, 145, 469, 596-606, 608, 615-620, 633-634, 640-641, 656, 658, 662-663, 666-667, 677, 712, 940, 948-949, 961, 972, 975-976, 998, 1093, 1100, 1103, 1144, 1149-1151, 1153, 1155-1156, 1160, 1163-1164, 1169, 1180, 1184-1185, 1189-1191, 1214, 1231, 1448
IP 162, 165, 183-185, 461, 606, 676, 957, 961, 987-988, 991, 995, 1001, 1146, 1150, 1160, 1415, 1452, 1496, 1500, 1502
ISI 677, 776, 780, 791, 794-795, 1208
iterative deepening search 1330, 1335-1336

J

jamming 663, 671
Jaya algorithm 309-312, 325

K

Kappa 295, 734, 742, 747-748, 752, 776, 789-790, 796, 1325
Kappa Statistic 734, 742, 747-748, 752, 1325
keratitis 1415, 1417
K-Nearest Neighbor 14, 41-42, 70, 122, 131, 133, 135, 212, 358, 415, 450, 543, 654, 663, 697, 884, 1024, 1184, 1290, 1314, 1317, 1322, 1342, 1384,

1422, 1448-1449
K-NN 122, 133, 212-213, 216, 229, 403-404, 416, 450-452, 605, 654, 656-657, 663, 1093, 1177, 1314, 1317, 1322-1323, 1357, 1399, 1410, 1448, 1504
KNN Algorithm 59-64, 162, 782, 851, 1449
Knowledge Discovery 2-3, 36, 129-130, 145, 219-222, 235, 325-326, 346-347, 414, 417, 425, 445, 470-471, 473, 583, 617-618, 692, 770-772, 775, 872, 927-928, 948, 1040, 1073, 1076, 1082, 1085, 1105, 1124, 1191, 1327, 1353, 1380, 1393, 1444

L

Latent Class Analysis (LCA) 533, 817, 823, 831, 844-846
Layer-specific Attacks 1165
length of stay 1311-1316, 1318, 1326, 1328, 1442-1444
Linear Regression 70, 91-93, 96, 99-101, 105, 177, 192-194, 196-197, 222-223, 233, 253, 347-348, 352-356, 358, 411, 433, 479, 489, 511, 533, 547, 588, 696, 718, 817, 819, 836-837, 839-840, 851, 1038, 1042, 1044-1045, 1047, 1057-1058, 1088, 1090-1091, 1273, 1286-1287, 1307, 1429, 1438, 1487, 1490, 1497
Logistic Models 91, 94-95, 103, 1326
Logistic Regression 91, 93-95, 104, 114, 132, 233-236, 254, 272, 367-368, 370, 374, 376, 411, 434, 479, 536, 583, 588, 626, 659, 737, 739, 742-743, 748, 750, 757, 764, 782, 784, 795-796, 851, 853, 882, 886-887, 894-895, 899, 902-906, 908, 1042, 1077, 1177, 1214, 1232, 1236, 1256, 1292, 1297, 1312, 1314, 1331-1332, 1334, 1342, 1348, 1384, 1448, 1487, 1490-1492, 1497

M

Machine Learning 1-8, 11-13, 21-23, 25-27, 29-41, 43-44, 47, 49-51, 53, 56-72, 76-77, 79, 84-85, 87-93, 99-100, 103-107, 109, 114-122, 127-129, 131-132, 137-142, 144-145, 148-149, 162-163, 166, 170-174, 176-180, 183-184, 190, 195-200, 203-206, 208-213, 217, 219, 222, 224-225, 227, 229-230, 232-235, 237-239, 241, 243-244, 250-255, 257, 259, 262, 267, 270-271, 273, 292-293, 303-305, 308-309, 314, 319-321, 324-327, 329-330, 333, 343-352, 354-355, 357-359, 362-363, 365, 367, 370, 376-377, 379-397, 404, 411-413, 416-418, 421-432, 441-442, 444-447, 449-451, 453-455, 458-459, 464, 468, 470-473, 475, 477-478, 480, 484-485, 486-488, 513-514, 526-531, 533-536, 538, 540-541, 543-552, 554-555, 557-558, 560-566, 569, 572, 583-584, 586-591, 594-596, 600-606, 616-625, 627-642, 645, 653-657, 659-670, 674-678, 680-687, 690-691, 693-699, 709-723, 726, 728-735, 737-738, 740, 743, 749, 753-756, 758-760, 763-765, 768-770, 775-776, 778-779, 794, 796, 798-801, 803, 814-815, 817, 819, 822, 836-837, 839-842, 846-847, 849-851, 856, 859, 868-871, 873, 876-877, 879-887, 900-901, 904-913, 916, 923, 927-933, 936, 939-940, 942, 945, 947-949, 951-952, 966, 969-973, 975-976, 978-986, 989-990, 993-1000, 1002-1008, 1010, 1013, 1015-1016, 1020, 1023-1026, 1031, 1035, 1037-1043, 1047, 1056-1058, 1062-1068, 1070-1077, 1083-1084, 1086-1089, 1094-1096, 1098, 1100-1107, 1109-1111, 1114-1116, 1119-1121, 1123-1126, 1129-1135, 1137-1145, 1148-1155, 1157, 1159-1165, 1175-1186, 1188-1194, 1205-1214, 1216-1217, 1222, 1225-1227, 1229-1237, 1239, 1251, 1253-1255, 1257-1258, 1262-1263, 1265-1266, 1268-1273, 1276, 1284-1285, 1288, 1291-1297, 1299, 1301-1315, 1317, 1322, 1326-1335, 1348-1356, 1358-1359, 1378-1386, 1388-1399, 1404, 1406-1407, 1409-1411, 1413-1415, 1417, 1421-1422, 1426-1431, 1436, 1438, 1442-1444, 1446, 1448, 1450, 1452-1453, 1456, 1458-1465, 1468, 1470-1471, 1476, 1478-1480, 1482-1483, 1486-1490, 1492-1495, 1497, 1499, 1501-1502, 1504, 1507, 1514-1516
Machine Learning Algorithms 1-2, 4, 7, 11-12, 38, 40, 43, 60-61, 63, 67-68, 70, 72, 90-91, 149, 171, 179, 196, 198, 203, 205-206, 208-212, 217, 225, 243-244, 252-255, 257, 259, 262, 267, 270-271, 319-320, 329, 348, 350, 383-384, 421, 425-426, 430-432, 442, 444, 472-473, 477-478, 480, 484, 528-529, 534, 536, 540, 546, 569, 588, 594-596, 600, 604, 616, 619, 621-622, 625, 630-632, 634, 636, 638, 641, 686-687, 697-699, 715, 728, 753, 756, 758, 763, 776, 778, 794, 796, 849-851, 882-887, 904-907, 909, 912-913, 923, 927 928, 949, 971-972, 976, 978-981, 985-986, 994, 1003, 1016, 1023-1026, 1042-1043, 1047, 1064, 1067-1068, 1074-1076, 1086-1087, 1102, 1105, 1110, 1123-1124, 1145, 1151-1152, 1154, 1163, 1185, 1188, 1191, 1210, 1213-1214, 1225-1226, 1255, 1257-1258, 1262, 1265, 1271-1273, 1285, 1288, 1294, 1299, 1301, 1303-1304, 1306, 1309, 1317, 1333-1334, 1349, 1351-1352, 1355, 1358-1359, 1378-1379, 1395-1397, 1406, 1422, 1446, 1448, 1470, 1480, 1483, 1487, 1516
Machine Learning Methods 31-33, 39, 68, 90, 107, 109, 115, 121, 145, 170, 174, 232, 238, 308, 314, 319,

324, 327, 348, 355, 363, 365, 396-397, 412, 451, 472, 526, 533, 569, 605, 640, 677-678, 682, 730, 732, 754, 759, 764, 819, 851, 940, 948, 952, 971, 975, 1038, 1040, 1086, 1088-1089, 1094-1096, 1098, 1105, 1141, 1176, 1188-1189, 1214, 1231, 1268, 1313, 1329, 1332-1333, 1335, 1351-1352, 1355, 1358, 1381, 1386, 1489-1490

Machine Learning Tasks 3, 21, 475, 629, 1177, 1180

Machine Learning Techniques 1-2, 13, 25, 31, 47, 61, 65, 68, 70-71, 128, 131, 163, 173, 200, 203-204, 222, 224, 229, 254, 292-293, 303, 305, 345-349, 357-358, 389, 404, 418, 422, 425-426, 431-432, 444-445, 547, 572, 586-587, 601, 622-623, 628-632, 637, 642, 645, 653-654, 656, 660-661, 674, 677, 681-683, 685-686, 690-691, 693, 695, 730, 734, 737-738, 743, 749, 798, 800, 814, 817, 819, 822, 836, 840, 842, 847, 883-884, 905, 908, 940, 949, 951, 975, 1039-1040, 1057, 1066, 1086, 1088-1089, 1101-1102, 1104, 1151, 1153, 1164, 1189, 1192, 1207, 1209, 1233, 1236, 1253-1255, 1266, 1268-1269, 1271, 1276, 1292-1297, 1302, 1304, 1307, 1309-1312, 1314-1315, 1317, 1322, 1326-1327, 1330-1332, 1334, 1350, 1356, 1358, 1378, 1381-1386, 1389, 1391, 1399, 1411, 1414, 1417, 1426-1431, 1436, 1438, 1442-1443, 1459, 1515

Machine Learning Toolkit 528, 540, 546, 1390

Malicious 108, 150, 152, 155, 157-160, 163-166, 170, 597, 600-601, 635-636, 645-648, 651, 655-656, 663, 667, 671, 674, 677, 696, 703, 711, 713, 870-871, 941-942, 954-956, 958-959, 961, 963, 969, 972-973, 975, 1144, 1146-1148, 1153-1156, 1158-1159, 1162, 1164, 1169-1171, 1186-1189, 1213, 1450-1451, 1468, 1470

Malware 145, 149-176, 449-451, 588, 594, 630, 634-636, 640, 654, 656-657, 660, 665-666, 668, 670, 674-675, 677-678, 954-955, 961, 963, 965-966, 975, 985, 988, 1016, 1144, 1146-1148, 1151, 1153-1160, 1163-1164, 1171, 1185, 1189, 1191-1192, 1451-1452

Malware Detection 149, 162-163, 165-167, 170, 175-176, 588, 594, 635, 656-657, 670, 975, 1016, 1156-1159, 1163-1164, 1185, 1189

Malware Techniques 149

Man-in-the-Middle Attack (MITM) 988, 1000

masquerade 636, 649, 663

Maximum Entropy 327, 329-330, 333-334, 341-342, 344-345, 368, 377-378, 681, 685, 691

mechatronic degree courses 379-380, 385-386, 395

mechatronics 379-381, 384-386, 389, 391-395

Mllib library 1062, 1067

Mobile Networks 131, 998, 1494-1495, 1497, 1500-1501, 1505-1508, 1510-1511, 1515-1516

Multi Class Classification 486, 488, 505

Multilayer Perceptron 70, 294, 314, 358, 402, 605, 656, 666, 882, 886-887, 894-895, 899-900, 902, 904-906, 908, 1079, 1090, 1312, 1358, 1384

Multiple Linear Regression 92, 96, 99-100, 718, 836, 839, 1038, 1044-1045, 1047, 1057-1058, 1088, 1429

N

Nagin 1415-1419, 1425

Nanomedicine 38-41, 43

Nanotechnology 40, 45

Network Attack 976, 991, 1157, 1171

Network Security 25, 107-109, 130, 444, 596, 600, 604, 619, 633, 641, 664-665, 675-677, 710, 871, 976-977, 979, 987-988, 994, 1000, 1020, 1089, 1156, 1173, 1180, 1208

Network Support data 586-587, 589

Neural Net 12, 1286, 1351, 1361, 1366-1367, 1373, 1377

Neural Network 12, 26, 30, 35-37, 51, 69-70, 86-89, 103, 121, 203, 220, 224, 233-234, 242-243, 247-250, 254, 260-261, 275, 277, 327, 329-330, 333, 335-336, 341-343, 345, 358, 388, 424-425, 427-428, 432, 443, 447, 450, 471, 479, 483-484, 533, 557, 568, 584, 605, 619-620, 640, 654, 656, 669, 714-715, 718, 732-733, 744, 750, 773, 779, 798, 836-837, 839-841, 843, 846, 870-875, 880-881, 884, 886-887, 902, 904, 978, 983, 1008, 1013-1014, 1017, 1019, 1021, 1066, 1070, 1072, 1077-1079, 1082, 1084, 1088, 1090, 1092, 1103-1105, 1138, 1142-1143, 1149, 1151, 1155, 1157-1160, 1163-1164, 1177, 1181-1185, 1210-1213, 1215-1216, 1223-1225, 1233, 1235-1236, 1241, 1252, 1255, 1262-1264, 1269, 1273, 1292, 1297, 1302, 1306-1308, 1313, 1328, 1333, 1342, 1357-1359, 1378-1379, 1381, 1384, 1394, 1396, 1398-1399, 1406, 1409, 1421, 1436, 1444, 1487, 1491

Nielsen Consumer Panel Dataset 817, 819-820, 836, 842-843

Non-Linear 70, 74, 87, 94, 118, 173, 178, 194, 242, 368, 479, 715, 718, 733-734, 737, 756-757, 836-837, 846, 874, 1073-1074, 1079, 1088, 1090, 1235, 1239, 1241, 1250, 1268, 1285, 1292, 1356, 1423, 1450

Non-Parametric 60, 76, 234, 655, 734, 737-738, 740-741, 749, 765, 819, 834, 851, 1234

Normalization 7, 17, 23, 245, 319, 769, 837, 929,

1014-1015, 1150, 1223, 1237, 1405, 1414

O

Objective Quality 177, 179-180, 189-190, 195, 197, 761
omics data 228
Oncology 883, 1294, 1296, 1304-1305, 1308-1309, 1400, 1412-1413
Online Social Network 693, 709
Ontology 146, 329, 345, 426, 909-917, 926-929, 949
Ophthalmologist 1415, 1417, 1419
Opinion Mining 444, 681, 692
Optimization 2, 34-36, 55, 66, 71-72, 92, 131, 178, 223, 231, 233-235, 239, 243, 303, 306, 308-313, 319, 321, 324, 326, 334, 357, 359, 382, 384-385, 395, 470, 482, 485, 528, 533, 548, 550-551, 554-556, 559, 562, 566-567, 571-572, 583-584, 595, 603-605, 610-611, 618-619, 656, 699, 714-716, 720, 726-730, 733, 757, 760, 799, 809, 815, 858, 887, 904, 915, 931, 937, 979-980, 984, 986, 996-997, 1013, 1015, 1018, 1074, 1102-1105, 1124, 1188, 1206, 1225, 1242, 1251, 1272, 1299, 1326, 1355, 1358-1359, 1379, 1396, 1480, 1483, 1495-1497, 1501, 1504-1507, 1511, 1513, 1515-1516
Optimizing Threat 939, 951
outbreak 1294-1295, 1305-1307, 1309-1310, 1417-1418
Outlier 7, 20, 24-25, 98, 107, 113-114, 126, 132-133, 135, 206, 212, 221, 223, 425, 589, 656, 741, 744, 761, 861, 1018, 1222
Outlier Detection 7, 24, 98, 107, 114, 132, 206, 221, 223, 656, 1018

P

Parametric Vs Nonparametric 849
Partitional Clustering 823, 847
passenger forecasting 1086-1087
Pathology 417, 883, 1294, 1296, 1411, 1457
Pattern Based Analysis 1255
Performance Evaluation 82, 255, 262, 268-270, 1257, 1317, 1324, 1326
personalized patient care 1485-1486
Petri Net 137, 1066
Platform Sleptsov Net-processor 137
Population Health 818-819, 1038, 1482-1490, 1492-1493
Predictive Analytics 2, 67, 220, 477, 586, 588, 1057, 1189, 1229, 1269, 1303, 1326, 1446, 1448, 1454, 1485, 1493
Predictive Modeling 66, 252, 526, 883, 1313, 1331, 1441-1442, 1484, 1486, 1493
Predictive Modelling 444, 477, 536, 817, 819, 822, 836, 840, 847, 1038, 1047, 1056-1057, 1302, 1331
Prescriptive Analytics 1493
Principal Component Analysis 21, 96-98, 104, 106, 115, 196, 219, 221, 350, 374, 378, 440, 543, 596, 605, 610, 613, 616, 755, 765-766, 1036, 1179, 1327, 1450
Problem-based learning 392, 394
progressive web application 1072
Project-Based Learning 392-393, 948
Proxy servers 553, 870
Public Policy 735, 1427
public transport 1086-1088, 1094, 1110-1112
public transportation 1086-1088, 1098, 1100
Python 58, 228, 351, 359, 384-385, 394, 528, 531-532, 535, 540-547, 591, 776, 873, 881-883, 885-887, 900, 904-905, 907, 1055-1056, 1059, 1061, 1112-1116, 1118-1120, 1211, 1216, 1222-1223, 1225-1226, 1253, 1259, 1261-1262, 1265, 1335, 1342, 1386

Q

QSAR 38-42, 44-45, 293, 300, 305-306
quality of experience (QoE) 177-179

R

R programming language 528, 532, 744
Radiology 394, 1057, 1294, 1297, 1302, 1305, 1308, 1413
Radiotherapy 1294-1295, 1304
Random Forest Algorithm 232, 654, 814, 1023-1025, 1036, 1287, 1349, 1392, 1446
Random Forests 96, 98-99, 104-105, 219, 222, 235, 237, 239, 294, 346, 348, 350, 352-357, 479, 484, 595, 630, 710, 734, 741, 749, 758-759, 798, 1061, 1092, 1101, 1177, 1235, 1258, 1349, 1428-1431, 1442
Random Tree 308, 316, 320-321, 323-324, 782, 787-788, 797, 1093, 1331
Raspberry Pi 879, 1488, 1491, 1493
Recommendation System 909, 911-912, 929, 1259
Recommender Systems 355, 357, 681, 753-754, 762-775
Regression Models 10, 41, 72, 91-92, 94, 96, 99, 101, 180, 192, 233, 411, 489, 511, 757, 836, 883, 1038, 1042, 1044, 1056, 1091, 1104, 1356
Reinforcement Learning 1-5, 10-11, 31, 56, 58, 121, 203, 208-209, 230, 381, 384-385, 388, 394-395, 431-432, 446, 451, 468, 470, 478-479, 487-488,

528-529, 588, 642, 654, 657, 660-661, 664, 668, 859, 971, 976, 988-990, 994, 1000, 1038, 1040, 1075, 1129, 1135-1137, 1149, 1180-1183, 1186-1187, 1355-1356, 1384, 1448, 1462, 1472-1473, 1476, 1497-1498, 1513-1516
Resource Utilization 24, 59-60, 65, 178, 646
retinal blood vessel 274, 289-291
RFID 199, 206, 220, 461, 644, 652-653, 663, 1455, 1457, 1490
Risk Assessment 665, 675-676, 750, 937, 1215, 1297, 1467
Robotics 32, 57, 379-384, 386-387, 389, 392-393, 395, 421, 430, 444, 540, 553, 566-567, 604, 1182, 1294, 1460-1461, 1463, 1465-1466, 1470-1471, 1473, 1475-1476, 1479-1480
Rule Based Induction 586-587, 589-593

S

Scaled Sigmoid 522-524, 526
Search Algorithm 426, 444, 604, 610, 614, 616, 618-619, 930-931, 935-936, 984
Self Organizing Networks 1494, 1496, 1500
self-configuration 1494, 1496, 1499-1504, 1510-1511, 1516
self-healing 1165, 1496, 1500-1501, 1507-1511, 1513, 1516
Self-Optimization 979, 1496, 1500-1501, 1504, 1507-1508, 1511, 1514, 1516
Self-Organizing Algorithm 951
Self-Organizing Cellular Networks 1494, 1515-1516
Semi-Supervised Learning 4, 7, 11, 115, 121, 424, 468-469, 477, 529, 640, 713, 971, 995, 1038, 1040-1041, 1075, 1077, 1149, 1180, 1182, 1394, 1487
Sensitivity/Precision 908
Sentiment Analysis 327-330, 333-334, 341, 344-345, 430, 433, 444, 677, 681-686, 690-692, 749, 796, 1208, 1253, 1272, 1291-1293, 1303-1304, 1380
Sentiment Classification 327-330, 336, 343-345, 682, 685-686, 691, 1332
Shareable Content Object Reference Model (SCORM) 148
Show Tech Support 586-587
SI calculation 182
Sigmoid Function 260, 315, 518-519, 522-524, 784, 1042
SINGLE-NUCLEOTIDE POLYMORPHISM 224, 230
sleep disorder 776-778, 792, 796, 799
Sleptsov Net (SN) 139, 148
Smart Card 221, 1193, 1204
Smart City 207, 987, 1084, 1208, 1446, 1452-1454
smart data 198, 206-209, 217
Smart Home 206, 222, 643, 928, 1452, 1485-1486
smart security 870
smart tourism 753-755, 759-760, 762, 768, 775
Smart World 421, 987, 1459
Soft Computing 344, 418, 582, 679, 692, 740, 937-938, 995, 1094, 1100, 1193, 1241, 1251, 1253, 1269, 1292, 1328
Softmax Function 336, 524-525
software refactoring 800, 805
Solar Water Heater (SWH) 714, 716, 732-733
spam posts 693, 695, 702-706, 708-709
spatial and temporal information 196
Statistical Analysis 98, 100, 102, 104, 332, 480, 532, 609, 711, 823, 846, 883, 969, 1025, 1257, 1272, 1315-1316, 1322, 1326
Statistical Modeling 90, 1022
steganalysis 1002-1010, 1013-1022
steganography 1002-1004, 1012, 1014, 1016-1021
Step function 516-518
Stock Forecasting 1271
Stock Market 25, 109, 1089, 1101, 1103-1105, 1233, 1235-1237, 1240-1241, 1250-1260, 1265, 1268-1270, 1272, 1291-1293
Stock Market Analysis 1251, 1255
stratified sampling 800-801, 804, 980
streaming data analytics 198, 201
subjective scores 177, 179-180, 183, 189, 196
Super-Turing Computation 148
Supervised Classification 53, 58, 291, 804, 806, 809, 1115
Supervised Learning 3, 7, 10-14, 52-53, 57, 92, 118, 120, 122, 128, 203, 208-209, 229, 233-234, 251, 254, 287, 333, 346-355, 357, 362, 365, 381, 395-397, 400, 404-406, 414, 432, 450-451, 477-480, 482, 529, 532, 588-590, 601, 603, 630, 642, 654-658, 668, 682, 697, 754-756, 759-761, 764, 768-769, 775, 800-801, 808-809, 822, 842, 847, 849-851, 859-860, 883-885, 908, 926-927, 947, 975, 985, 989, 1003, 1006, 1010, 1038, 1040-1042, 1074-1075, 1077, 1079, 1089, 1095, 1126, 1133-1134, 1136-1137, 1149, 1158, 1180-1182, 1285, 1288, 1331, 1337, 1355-1356, 1358, 1383-1384, 1410, 1422, 1449-1450, 1487, 1497-1498, 1504-1505, 1507, 1509, 1514, 1516
Supervised Learning Techniques 346, 400, 655-657, 801, 822, 842
Supervised Machine Learning 6, 67, 92, 162, 252, 255, 257, 262, 267, 354, 367, 376, 404, 413, 416, 486-487, 640, 659, 694, 709, 711, 740, 817, 819, 836, 839-840, 911, 928, 971, 981, 985, 997, 1005-

1006, 1089, 1262, 1285, 1315, 1443, 1450, 1514
supply chain management 1067, 1454-1455
Support Cyber Security 137, 142, 144
Support Vector Machines 70-71, 87, 96, 114, 118-119, 130, 166, 174, 196-197, 220, 223, 228-229, 233, 250, 252, 255, 257, 259, 267, 269, 271-272, 277, 288, 293-294, 346, 348-350, 353-355, 358, 377, 397, 401, 403, 405, 435, 533, 536, 543, 593, 641, 661, 681-682, 698, 734, 737, 740, 749, 757, 764, 773, 808, 856, 884, 936, 1008, 1088-1089, 1103-1105, 1149, 1164, 1185, 1191, 1252-1253, 1258, 1269, 1306, 1310, 1349, 1355-1356, 1422, 1429-1430, 1450, 1497
Support Vector Regression 71, 177, 192-194, 196, 220, 223, 411, 1089, 1103-1105, 1216, 1258
surgical risk 1330, 1333-1335, 1348
swarm intelligence 596, 600, 603-604, 617-618
symbiotic cycle 548-549, 551-552, 558-560, 562, 565
symbiotic simulation 548, 551-552, 560, 565-566
Synthetic Data 396-397, 406-407, 413, 558, 755
system identification 548-549, 566, 737

T

technical indicators 1233-1237, 1247, 1250-1253, 1256, 1271, 1273, 1275-1276, 1288
Text Mining 33, 38, 43, 47, 327-331, 338, 424, 587, 595, 1107, 1110-1112, 1114, 1116, 1120, 1123-1124
Training And Testing 79, 213, 216, 254, 487, 659, 684, 693, 704, 715, 718-721, 1010-1011, 1025-1026, 1214, 1237, 1273, 1283, 1290, 1335, 1407, 1421
translation error taxonomy 362-363, 369, 377
triangular scheme of machine learning 939, 945, 951

U

Unsupervised Learning 4, 7, 10-11, 17-18, 54, 101-102, 118, 121, 128, 178, 203, 208-210, 230, 365, 381, 395, 425, 432, 439, 450-451, 459, 477-478, 483, 487, 529, 535, 588, 601, 630, 635, 642, 654-655, 660, 668, 682, 697, 713, 753-754, 759, 761-762, 769, 775, 800-802, 804, 807, 809, 813, 822, 842, 846-847, 849-850, 859-860, 866, 883, 908, 919, 971, 975, 984-985, 1010, 1038, 1040-1043, 1075, 1089, 1133, 1135, 1149, 1158, 1180-1181, 1230, 1285, 1355, 1383-1384, 1497-1498, 1505, 1508, 1510, 1516
user generated content 1107, 1109

V

Variability Model 951
Volunteered Geographic Information 1107, 1109, 1125-1127

W

Wearable Devices 212, 223, 1023-1024, 1026, 1037
WSN 643, 648, 660, 663, 1142, 1457

Z

Zero-Day Attack 952-953, 961-962, 964, 973-974, 1159

Printed in the United States
by Baker & Taylor Publisher Services